SAMUEL JOHNSON

SAMUEL JOHNSON

A Biography

PETER MARTIN

THE BELKNAP PRESS OF
HARVARD UNIVERSITY PRESS
CAMBRIDGE, MASSACHUSETTS
2008

LIBRARY OF CONGRESS CATALOGING-IN-PUBLICATION DATA
Martin, Peter, 1940–
Samuel Johnson : a biography / Peter Martin.
p.   cm.
Includes bibliographical references.
ISBN-13: 978-0-674-03160-9 (alk. paper)
1. Johnson, Samuel, 1709–1784.   2. Authors, English–18th century–
Biography.   I. Title.
PR3533.M385
828'.609–dc22   [B] 2008 011327

For Maureen,

and in Memory of Cindy

To strive with difficulties, and to conquer them, is the highest human felicity; the next, is to strive and deserve to conquer. Ye who listen with credulity to the whispers of fancy, and pursue with eagerness the phantoms of hope; who expect that age will perform the promises of youth, and that the deficiencies of the present day will be supplied by the morrow; attend to the history of Rasselas, Prince of Abissinia.

SAMUEL JOHNSON

Contents

Part Six

BIOGRAPHY AND 'THE RACE

WITH DEATH'

List of Illustrations

SECTION ONE

Michael Johnson (*engraving by E. Finden; Hyde Collection, Houghton Library, Harvard University*)

Edial School (*watercolour by Maureen Pier, after an engraving by C.J. Smith; Private Collection*)

Elizabeth Porter Johnson (*artist unknown, eighteenth century; Hyde Collection, Houghton Library, Harvard University*)

Letter from Johnson to his wife (*Hyde Collection, Houghton Library, Harvard University*)

Johnson's tea service (*The Samuel Johnson Birthplace Museum, Lichfield*)

Molly Aston (*frontispiece to Aleyn Reade,* Johnsonian Gleanings, *part VI*)

St John's Gate (*by John Chessel Buckler, 1809; Museum of the Order of St John, St Johns Gate, London*)

Dr Johnson at Cave's the Publisher by Henry Wallis, 1854 (*Bridgeman Art Library*)

Elizabeth Carter by Joseph Highmore (*Dover Museum, Dover*)

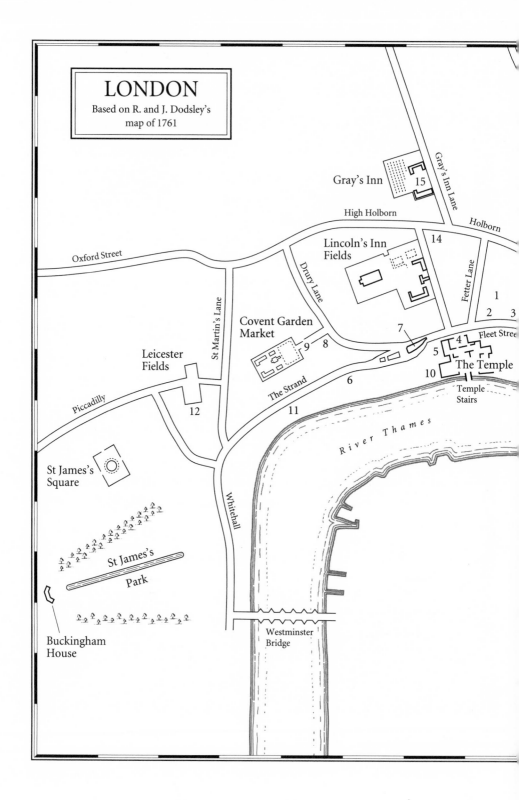

LONDON

Based on R. and J. Dodsley's
map of 1761

Gray's Inn
15

High Holborn

Holborn

Oxford Street

Lincoln's Inn
Fields

14

Fetter Lane

Drury Lane

1

2   3

St Martin's Lane

Covent Garden
Market

7

4   Fleet Stree

9 8

5

The Temple

Leicester
Fields

6

10

Piccadilly

The Strand

12

11

Temple
Stairs

St James's
Square

River Thames

Whitehall

St James's
Park

Buckingham
House

Westminster
Bridge

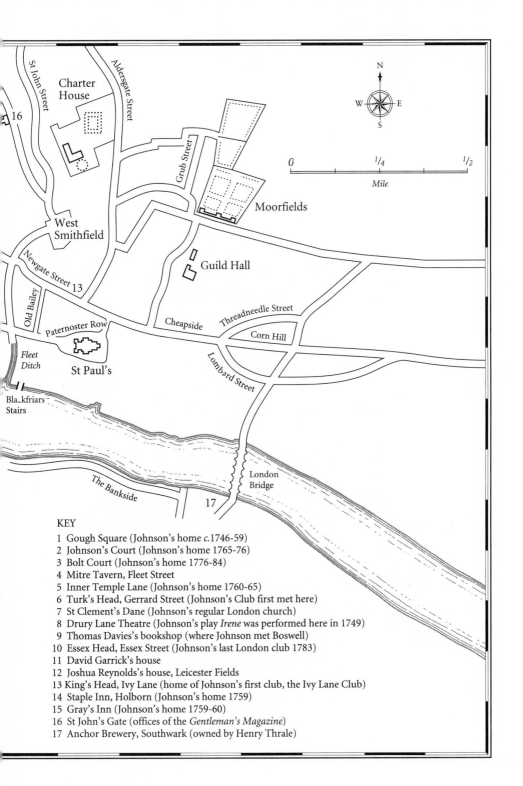

KEY

1 Gough Square (Johnson's home *c.*1746-59)
2 Johnson's Court (Johnson's home 1765-76)
3 Bolt Court (Johnson's home 1776-84)
4 Mitre Tavern, Fleet Street
5 Inner Temple Lane (Johnson's home 1760-65)
6 Turk's Head, Gerrard Street (Johnson's Club first met here)
7 St Clement's Dane (Johnson's regular London church)
8 Drury Lane Theatre (Johnson's play *Irene* was performed here in 1749)
9 Thomas Davies's bookshop (where Johnson met Boswell)
10 Essex Head, Essex Street (Johnson's last London club 1783)
11 David Garrick's house
12 Joshua Reynolds's house, Leicester Fields
13 King's Head, Ivy Lane (home of Johnson's first club, the Ivy Lane Club)
14 Staple Inn, Holborn (Johnson's home 1759)
15 Gray's Inn (Johnson's home 1759-60)
16 St John's Gate (offices of the *Gentleman's Magazine*)
17 Anchor Brewery, Southwark (owned by Henry Thrale)

Preface

I came to write a biography of Samuel Johnson for the tercentenary of his birth in 2009 through writing biographies of Edmond Malone and James Boswell, two good friends devoted to the great man who between them did the most to create a post-Johnson Johnsonian world. The leading Shakespearean of the eighteenth century, Malone quickly joined the Johnson circle after he moved to London from Ireland in the late 1770s to devote himself to literature. Boswell called him 'Johnsonianissimus'. By then Johnson had already been Boswell's dear friend and hero for fifteen years. When Boswell and Malone first met shortly before Johnson's death, Malone saw clearly that if Boswell was going to fulfil his longtime ambition of writing Johnson's life, he would need all the help and encouragement he could give him. He dedicated himself to that end, prodding and cajoling, lifting Boswell out of his wearying melancholia, and spending hundreds of hours with him reading out loud and correcting the manuscripts of both his *Tour to the Hebrides* and monumental *Life of Johnson* (1791), which has often been called the greatest biography in the English language. Without Malone's help, Boswell would probably never have published his *Life.*

But there are problems with Boswell's biography. Although it preserves the vast majority of Johnson's conversation that has come down to us – a huge artistic achievement of narrative skill, memory and persistence – and presents him dynamically in scenes among friends and in all sorts of social situations which make him come alive in ways that none of his other biographers have ever equalled, it perpetuates a popular perception of Johnson, which flourished in his own lifetime, chiefly as a personality and truculent conversationalist. This is only part of the picture.

After Johnson published his brilliant moral essays in the 1740s and his great *Dictionary* in 1755, he became the voice of the age, the rationalist epitome and sage of the Enlightenment. His reputation was enormous. Bewigged, muscular and, for his day, unusually tall at six feet, his massive frame famously dressed in crumpled and soiled clothes, beset by involuntary tics and erratic movements that startled many, opinionated, deferred to, feared for his strong rebuttals, powered in his inimitable and legendary conversation by a prodigious memory, Johnson became a literary and social icon such as no other man of letters in that age ever achieved. 'I believe there is hardly a day in which there is not something about me in the newspapers,' he remarked to Boswell a few years before he died. In his *Life*, Boswell celebrated these personality stereotypes and helped create a cult featuring Johnson as the Great Cham and the Great Clubman through a portrait so large and aggressive that for over a century and a half after Johnson's death the man dominated the writer. While in the nineteenth and early twentieth centuries Boswell's biography of Johnson became one of the best-known books in the English language, Johnson's own extensive and remarkable works became relatively unpopular. Johnson has been frozen in the minds of people who have never read him into a firm image of a man always in company talking and living up to the public's caricature of him: the great literary dictator and arbiter, the rigid neoclassical critic, the lexicographer and editor lacking poetic imagination, one who spent the better part of his waking hours acting out his role as the great 'club' man, the conservative spokesman for the Tory cause – indeed, the defender of tradition from language to politics to social behaviour. Virtually all of these tags are inaccurate and misleading. It was not until well into the twentieth century that, in a reaction against this lopsided view, critics and biographers began to direct attention to Johnson's writings, but the popular image refuses to fade away.

There are other problems with Boswell's *Life*. It presents a man essentially at peace in his own mind. Boswell did not want his portrait to be of a man wracked with self-doubt, guilt, fear and depression. He rarely cited from Johnson's writings, did not make sensational use of Johnson's diary extracts to which he had access, and was not privy to his friend's deepest secrets and worries as was Mrs Hester Thrale, Johnson's most intimate female friend who later after remarriage wrote his biography, with something of a bias against him, under her new name 'Piozzi', but whom for the sake of clarity I will always refer to as Mrs Thrale. She turned out to be, in Boswell's mind, his greatest rival as Johnson's biographer. Except for mentioning it, neither did he explore the manifestations of his subject's melancholia even though an assortment of fears connected to that 'vile melancholy' afflicted Johnson's entire life and deeply shaped much of his thought and behaviour. A horrible act about three weeks before he died throws a retrospective light on what he once called 'the general disease of my life'.

One cold day in late November or early December, dying and very likely in a depressed state of acute guilt for a life he felt had not lived up to God's and his own expectations, and accompanied by his faithful black servant Frank Barber, Johnson began rounding up his personal papers and taking them in arm-loads out into his garden at Bolt Court, just off Fleet Street. There for more than a week he did 'little else' than set fire to them in a conflagration or holocaust that has to be numbered as one of the greatest literary tragedies of all time. Letters and manuscripts of all kinds went up in flames. Hour after hour Johnson fed the fire, hoping it would help consume his guilt and prepare his soul for death. He burned his mother's letters with tears streaming from his eyes. Few letters written to him survived. We would have fewer still if Boswell earlier had not preserved many of his own to Johnson and if Johnson himself had not, as it appears, spared Hester Thrale's from the blaze. Even two of his large quarto diaries fed the flames. Only fragments of these have survived, again partly due to Boswell's enterprise. For a man who repeatedly urged Boswell and several others to keep journals, such an act seems recklessly contradictory. It surprised and horrified his friends.

How did such a literary calamity come to pass? Johnson's surviving prayers, meditations and diaries – most of which Boswell never saw – as well as his letters, abound with warning signs. Poised dangerously between control and madness, between doubt, fear and faith, tormented by the dread of loneliness and death and lacerated by physical as well as mental sickness, he often feared he would fall into madness. In his recent book, *Shakespeare: The Invention of the Human*, Harold Bloom wrote, 'I worship Johnson, particularly on Shakespeare, and suspect that his own perilous balance, the fear of madness, made him seek rational design where none exists.'[1] Shakespeare scholarship, the classics, lexicography, essay writing, biography, journalism, travel writing, sermons, allegorical fables, and a host of other forms of prose and poetry in which Johnson relentlessly probed himself and the world around him, not to mention his passion for conversation, all constituted rational triumphs against despair and depression. Ironically, his extraordinary religious faith deepened his fears. His growing certainty that he would not go to heaven, that he had let God down and not used his talents fully enough, and that he had wasted time through indolence and idle thoughts all conspired against him. The holocaust was a final, desperate effort to wipe the slate clean before death.

Who really was this man who his own and later ages have celebrated, even venerated, so thoroughly? There is a portrait by his friend Sir Joshua Reynolds painted in the 1760s, when Johnson was in his late fifties, which speaks volumes about the private Johnson. In it Johnson does not hide under the wig in which men were conventionally painted in the eighteenth century and which could blur the persona with an appearance of social respectability. He looks less cloaked and protected, vulnerable yet courageous, even defiantly introspective. The energy of the profile seems almost agonised, focused on troubled thoughts, wrestling with difficult ideas that lie deep within – a mind seemingly preying on itself. Instead of resting inert on a table or chair, Johnson's hands are held up prominently, gesticulating oddly, his fingers bent tensely, 'as if he had been seized with the cramp'.[2] The side view also accentuates Johnson's vitality and force, his physicality and great strength: a large, muscular frame with broad shoulders, large facial features and a massive neck. This is my favourite portrait

of the several Reynolds painted of him because it cuts through the clichés
about Johnson which prevailed during his lifetime and have persisted ever
since. It helps make him accessible to us not as a relic of the eighteenth
century but as a man beset by problems common to us all, with important
things to say about the human condition. The portrait invites us to confront tragic realities about Johnson's life and character which Boswell and
other early biographers more or less underplayed. His life was a journey
of agony and courage, a struggle to survive. It was never a level playing
field for him. When his wife died early in their marriage, he fell into a despondency and grief from which he really never recovered and which almost drowned him in recurring guilt for the rest of his life. And yet, the
portrait also projects Johnson's bravery and determination to overcome
such fearful odds.

The best way to get the measure of Johnson is to read him. I have often
thought that if I were stranded on a desert island, in addition to the
Bible and the complete works of Shakespeare I would wish to have with
me a complete run of Johnson's moral essays, especially those from the
Rambler – almost 450 of them in all. John Ruskin wrote that on their
foreign travels his father would carefully pack the *Rambler* and *Idler* in
their luggage because they contained 'more substantial literary nourish-
ment than could be, from any other author, packed into so portable compass . . . I at once and for ever recognised in him a man entirely sincere,
and infallibly wise in the view and estimate he gave of the common questions, business, and ways of the world . . . No other writer could have
secured me, as he did, against all chance of being misled by my own sanguine and metaphysical temperament. He taught me carefully to measure
life, and distrust fortune.'[3] Ruskin hit a nerve there. What makes Johnson
such a great character is that in all his writing he combines enormous
intelligence with frank personal weakness. He is able to unfold for us
endless shades of morality at the same time as guiding us into the labyrinths of human nature itself as an open book – making his own human
nature the greatest text. That was very empirical and English of him. That
was what the Argentinian writer Jorge Luis Borges, a rabid Anglophile
for whom Johnson was a literary hero, had in mind when, on a visit to

England, he surprised an audience by stating that Johnson was more English than Shakespeare.

Johnson was something of a hero of Jane Austen's, too. She showed a vigorous keenness for his moral essays especially and how they attacked social pretentiousness and prideful self-delusion. When one reads Johnson, one is struck by how modern he is. Far from being rigidly conservative, backward-looking and authoritarian, he was one of the most advanced liberals of his time. Author of some of the greatest critical writing ever written, his natural instinct was to prick bubbles of pretension and nonsense – what he called 'cant', 'a whining pretension to goodness' – under whatever labels or in whatever institutions they flourished. The anger and defiance in his writing often make one wince – a feature of his persona which has not been sufficiently stressed by biographers. He had a sharp tongue when he detected humbug, flimflam, smugness and insincerity, and sent many home licking their wounds. Interlopers, pompous hypocrites, people in power, the chattering aristocracy and irresponsible newspapers were certain to provoke his indignation and mockery. He was empirical, downright, willing to argue, brave, and deftly and sometimes severely humorous. He could be every bit as funny as modern humourists, savouring a comic thought like Oliver Goldsmith's vanity over his new purple coat for hours afterwards, his laughter filling a room and echoing along the streets. His directness and impatience with what today we call political correctness would have made him a popular guest for television interviews and talk shows. He was also unorthodox, which he felt was the only way to be a critic, judging not by conventional rules but according to his reading of human nature. On behalf of native populations, he hit hard against colonial expansion and imperialism, especially in the Americas. While the Government and people were strongly behind it, he was stridently opposed to the Seven Years' War. Far from being a spokesman for the Establishment and Tory cause, he was one of the strongest advocates for the abolition of slavery, treating his own black servant Frank Barber like a son, 'freeing' and educating him, and leaving most of his estate to him in his will.

Far in advance of his time, Johnson's encouragement of women writers and his respect for their works was legendary. 'Always fly at the eagle,' he implored his shy but witty young friend and admirer Fanny Burney. He treated women as intellectual equals and promoted their literary careers – a theme mostly untouched by Boswell. 'I dined yesterday at Mrs Garrick's with Mrs [Elizabeth] Carter, Miss Hannah More, and Miss Fanny Burney,' he wrote. 'Three such women are not to be found'.[4] His tireless charity and Christian benevolence towards the underprivileged, oppressed and poor were well known in his lifetime. All these themes I pursue in this book, benefiting hugely from the large body of recent critical scholarship that has explored new attitudes towards Johnson and his world.

How well known is Johnson today? He is a pervasive presence in the English-speaking world, the second most quoted literary figure in Britain (after Shakespeare). Sometimes it seems as if scarcely a day passes without his being cited in a travel guide, sports article, philosophical tract, sermon, newspaper report or advertisement (as recently for an Arab airline). The 2005 fifty-pence coin bears his name on it as the author of the *Dictionary*. And he was even the target of a hammer attack in August 2007 at the National Portrait Gallery when a man apparently furious over the plight of the English language and somehow blaming Johnson for it smashed through the glass and damaged the canvas of Reynolds's portrait of him, known as 'Dictionary Johnson' and valued at almost £2 million. A more positive event occurred in 2001 when I picked up the American biographer David McCullough at the St Louis airport for a talk he was delivering at the college where I was then teaching. He was nearing the final stages of his best-selling biography of John Adams and as we drove across the flat Illinois landscape he told me he had read Johnson's *Dictionary* to help him tune into the eighteenth-century English that Adams knew. Paradoxically, in spite of Johnson's iconic status and occasional programmes about him on television and on the radio, I have been surprised from spot interviews in the high streets of several English towns that only about a quarter of the people I spoke to could identify him. Some wondered whether he was a boxer, or a contemporary of Shakespeare's, or a Canadian sprinter convicted of drug-taking, or a leading Conservative MP.

One might have thought that the featuring of Johnson and his *Dictionary* in a hilarious episode of the British television sitcom *Blackadder* would have lodged his name somewhat more permanently in the general public's memory. With a little help several people did at last recall something about a dictionary. The problem is partly that few people read Johnson today. His works are rarely assigned in schools and scarcely ever appear in school examinations. As a great thinker and writer Johnson must be read, otherwise, even after decades of penetrating scholarship and biographical illumination, he will continue to take a back seat in the popular mind to his worshipper, Boswell.

My debts to Johnsonian research are obvious in my notes, but here I would like to express particular gratitude to a number of people who have made Johnson their life's work. The late Paul Korshin, a friend and founder and editor of *The Age of Johnson*, encouraged me in this enterprise and read several chapters before his tragic death. Robert Folkenflik has read the entire manuscript and provided minute and insightful criticism, drawing on his encyclopedic grasp of Johnson's life and writings; my debt to him is considerable. Jack Lynch has also read the manuscript and corrected a few errors, as has John Kulka. Thomas Kaminski also took time out from his busy schedule to carefully read several chapters and give me helpful suggestions on Johnson's early career in London. In an endless number of ways numerous other critics and Johnsonians have helped me find my way through this huge project.

No biography exists in a critical vacuum, and mine is no exception in being heavily indebted to the following biographical scholarship on Johnson over the past thirty years: Thomas Kaminski, *The Early Career of Samuel Johnson*; Robert DeMaria, *The Life of Samuel Johnson: A Critical Biography* and *Samuel Johnson and the Life of Reading*; John Wain's *Samuel Johnson*; Robert Folkenflik, *Samuel Johnson, Biographer*; Walter Jackson Bate, *Samuel Johnson*; and Lawrence Lipking, *Samuel Johnson: The Life of an Author*. Also extremely valuable and useful have been Bruce Redford's edition of Johnson's *Letters*, Roger Lonsdale's edition of *The Lives of the Poets*, Alvin Kernan's *Samuel Johnson and the Impact of Print*, Alien Reddick's *The Making of Johnson's Dictionary*, John Wiltshire's *Samuel*

Johnson in the Medical World, Pat Rogers's *The Samuel Johnson Encyclopedia*, several recent 'companion' volumes of Johnson criticism with a plethora of fresh insights into Johnson's life and works, and a host of essays that have appeared for almost twenty years now in Paul Korshin and Jack Lynch's splendid annual publication, *The Age of Johnson: A Scholarly Annual*. I should also mention Henry Hitchings's vivid and perceptive *Dr Johnson's Dictionary: The Extraordinary Story of the Book that Defined the World*.

The Johnsonian world of societies and clubs on both sides of the Atlantic still thrives, and it is a measure of Johnson's continuing strong influence that their members continue to maintain 'clubbability' and support each other in their efforts to make Johnson and his humanitarian contributions more widely known throughout the world. When I laid the wreath on Johnson's tomb in Westminster Abbey a few years ago as part of the annual Johnson Society of London's commemoration of his death, I palpably felt that I was one member of a world community expressing gratitude to this extraordinary man. It is hoped that the tercentenary events in 2009 commemorating Johnson's birth will do much to extend that world and especially make his writings more widely read.

I should also like to thank the Leverhulme Trust for granting me an Emeritus Fellowship in 2003 that enabled me to spend several months working at the Beinecke Rare Book and Manuscript Library at Yale University and with the Hyde Collection, now in the Houghton Library, Harvard University, but then at Four Oaks Farm, Princeton, New Jersey. My thanks, too, to Robinson College, University of Cambridge, for a Bye-Fellowship in the spring of 2003.

A word of remembrance for my former agent, the late Giles Gordon, whose friendship and help in the early stages of writing this book were critical. Thanks, too, to my agent David Godwin, my editor at Weidenfeld and Nicolson, Benjamin Buchan, who provided valuable detailed commentary on the manuscript and skilfully steered it through the press, and to Ion Trewin for his encouragement and many lunches at the Garrick. My late wife Cindy was at the heart of this project in its early days, a radiant support, while Andrew, Claire, Adele, and Iain have, as always, been as anchors in rough waters. Finally, Maureen Pier has been here to help me with editing, proofreading and collecting illustrations, as well as in a host of other ways that have smoothed the way and kept me, in Johnson's words, from being 'deranged through solitude and intense study'.

SAMUEL JOHNSON

Part One

STAFFORDSHIRE YOUTH

Anecdotes of Beggary

I

'I WAS BORN AT LICHFIELD.' These are the first words Johnson, in his mid-fifties, writes about himself in his *Diaries, Prayers, and Annals*. When he wrote the *Annals* he had somewhat resolved the uncomfortable ambivalence he had felt towards his birthplace ever since leaving it with David Garrick in 1737 at the age of twenty-seven for London, the vast scene of his eventual fame. He was to return three months later, then again two years later for several months. But after that he would not be back for twenty-two long years, three years after the death of his mother.

When he finally returned in the winter of 1761–2, a famous man and subsidised by a government pension, he wrote the following about his visit:

> I went down to my native town, where I found the streets much narrower and shorter than I thought I had left them . . . My playfellows were grown old, and forced me to suspect, that I was no longer young . . . I wandered about for five days, and took the first convenient opportunity of returning to a place, where, if there is not much happiness, there is at least such a diversity of good and evil, that slight vexations do not fix upon a heart.

It is understandable, though not for that reason less surprising, that Johnson should wipe so much about Lichfield, family and friends off his mental landscape for almost a quarter of a century. Relative poverty, health problems from infancy, depression, disappointments and family strife all conspired to deprive him of a happy Lichfield youth. It would not be until he was in his mid-fifties that the foundations of his affection for his Staffordshire roots would begin to surface and claim his attention and heart. When in 1767 he made his first lengthy visit 'home' since the winter of 1739–40, for about five months, the bookseller Thomas Davies, who famously first introduced Johnson to Boswell, thought it was significant enough to report it to Boswell: 'Dr Johnson is still at his beloved Lichfield, the place of his birth. I had a letter from him very lately . . . [he] is at last become sick of the place for want of proper amusement, and yet cannot assume resolution enough to break his fetters and come away to his friends.' 'Beloved' Lichfield certainly, but Davies touches on the fact that in later years Johnson tended to get bored there and long to return to the excitement of London. Not until his last fifteen years did he feel a pull strong enough to draw him to Lichfield almost every year until he died, which impelled him to think about and visit old friends and schoolmates, and even inspired him to come to the rescue of a few of them who were in dire personal and financial circumstances.[1]

Lichfield was no out-of-the-way place. By the middle of the eighteenth century England's notoriously miserable roads, largely unchanged since the Middle Ages and very dangerous, had begun to give way to comprehensive road improvements. As a result, the country developed a network of fast, convenient and relatively comfortable coaching routes far in advance of any other country in the world. Lichfield was helped prominently on to the map because it sat strategically at the crossroads of two major trunk routes: from London up to Liverpool, Manchester and the North-West, and from Bristol to Sheffield, Leeds and the North-East.[2] In spite of its energy as one of the most important coaching cities in the Midlands, however – and it was commonly referred to as a city – Lichfield looked and felt more like a close-knit market town. It had a village atmosphere to it, and people knew and gossiped about each other and luxuriated in the personal and beautiful character of the town's layout. Though Johnson remarked how altered it seemed to him, Lichfield had, in fact, changed relatively little for over a century, except for the establishment of several coaching inns. In Johnson's later years something stirred within him for the old place and for his vanished youth among the small lanes, leafy groves and watery ways. He lamented the deaths of old friends and his local attachment to particular scenes. Every time he returned, there were fewer old faces to see and therefore there was more boredom. 'This place grows more and more barren of entertainment,' he wrote in the summer of 1777. He also was vexed when Lichfield's Corporation clouded his evaporating memories with 'improvements' here and there, such as on the occasion he dined with the Corporation and 'talked against a workhouse which they have in *contemplation*'; or when one of his favourite haunts, Stowe Hill, lay 'much degenerated'; or when in the summer of 1769, after wandering by the streams and along the familiar lanes in a Virgilian fantasy, he discovered to his horror that 'they have cut down the trees in George Lane'. Lichfield's small-town atmosphere was valuable to him – in the last year of his life he returned to it in a tender Latin poem for his boyhood friend and classmate Edmund Hector – but he also found it disturbing because it revived memories of neighbours he had known in his boyhood who had died and been replaced by strangers. His roots were in these streets, but there seemed little there to afford him a feeling of stability or permanence.[3]

2

In his *Dictionary of the English Language*, Johnson defined 'lich' as 'a dead carcase', from which lichgate, a covered gateway to a churchyard through which the dead are carried to be buried, takes its name. He then elaborates: '*Lichfield*, the field of the dead, a city in Staffordshire, so named from martyred Christians.'[4] '*Salve magna parens*,' or 'Hail, great mother,' he added, saluting his place of birth. To have one's town described as 'the field of the dead' may not have entirely pleased Lichfield residents in the mid-eighteenth century, but there were grounds for believing that the 'lich' in Lichfield meant death instead of marsh, as had been more commonly believed at the time. Johnson was alluding to the massacre of early Christian Britons in the fourth century by Roman soldiers who, according to legend, massacred them all in an area where the town now sits. It was not until AD 669 that a Christian settlement was established there by St Chad, the Bishop of Mercia, who was a principal force in spreading Christianity in the Midlands. The story goes that he chose this spot for his see because St Augustine is supposed to have visited the site of the massacre and pronounced it hallowed ground. A primitive Christian church already existed there and St Chad quickly turned Lichfield into the ecclesiastical centre of Middle England. His cell was to the east of the centre of the modern town, at the east end of which was the hamlet of Stowe (Saxon for 'holy place'), now Stowe Pool, dear to Johnson's heart because it was where Molly Aston lived, one of the great loves of his life. The little twelfth-century church of St Chad, the oldest building in Staffordshire, sits peacefully there today next to Stowe Pool. The well where St Chad is thought to have baptised members of his flock is still known as St Chad's Well. According to 'The Venerable Bede' in his *Ecclesiastical History* (731), St Chad at his death in 672 was accompanied to heaven by a flight of angels, whereupon this religious settlement became known as a type of Fatima or Lourdes. For centuries until the Reformation pilgrims came to worship and be cured there.[5]

There was plenty of water on the site of the town from the start, a swampy or marshy valley cutting east-west through which streams glided peacefully and from which in the twelfth century two beautiful ponds were created, Minster Pool and Stowe Pool. It was on the north side of this valley, just above Minster Pool, that a Saxon church was first built in the seventh century, supplanted by a Norman church begun in 1085, which in turn was replaced by the present triumph of English cathedrals (built between 1195 and the 1330s), described by Daniel Defoe as 'one of the finest and most beautiful in England', with three spires known as 'The Ladies of the Vale'. To the south of the little valley and Minster Pool is where the modern town was laid out and where, a short walk across a little bridge from the cathedral and its close, Johnson was born and went to school next to the Market Place. By the time he was born, Lichfield had emerged as an important cultural centre in the Midlands, an increas-

ingly urbane semi-rural community of about three thousand inhabitants
for whom the vortex of ecclesiastical life and influence had diminished
considerably.[6]

3

When Defoe passed through Lichfield, mostly in the 1720s, he was
undoubtedly aware of a couple of the recent famous 'sons' of the town.
One was Elias Ashmole, the seventeenth-century antiquarian and astrolo-
ger, who was born in Breadmarket Street in 1617 and attended Lichfield
Grammar School. In 1682 he founded the Ashmolean Museum at Oxford
University by giving the university his large collection of curiosities, many
of them bequeathed to him by the famous naturalist and plant collector
John Tradescant. Joseph Addison, the most famous English essayist in
the century before Johnson, was also brought up in Lichfield. He was still
an infant when his father was appointed Dean of Lichfield and the family moved into the cathedral close. But Defoe (who died in 1731) would
have been impressed, even amazed, had he been told something of what
lay ahead for this little Midlands market town by way of intellectual, literary and scientific achievements during the rest of the century. 'We are
a city of philosophers,' Johnson once boasted. Apart from Johnson,
Lichfield's greatest gift to English culture in the eighteenth century was
David Garrick, whose meteoric career as an actor in London began soon
after he and Johnson arrived there together. Born in Hereford, brought
up in Lichfield, and also a pupil at the grammar school, Garrick was always a faithful friend to Johnson although his spectacular success and
considerable wealth provoked Johnson's jealousy.[7]

On the scientific side, Erasmus Darwin, the literary botanist, poet and
grandfather of Charles Darwin, was born in 1731, moved to Lichfield in
1756, and practised medicine there for many years. He established a famous botanical garden at his large house by the West Gate entrance to
the Close in Beacon Street, where he did much of the botanical research
leading to, among other things, ideas on the sexual behaviour of plants

and on evolution which influenced his grandson. After he left Lichfield in 1781, he turned literary and published his famous poem in heroic couplets, *The Botanic Garden* (1791), which left its mark on Shelley, Coleridge and other Romantic poets. As it happened, Darwin's radical and free-thinking religious and political views were such that he and Johnson took a dislike to one another, though that did not stop Johnson from taking Hester Thrale and her husband to visit him and his eight-acre botanical garden in 1774, where Mrs Thrale was particularly struck by Darwin's one hundred varieties of roses. Darwin contributed his radical and political views as well as his scientific insights to the proceedings of the famous Lunar Society in Birmingham which, with great entrepreneurs, inventors and industrialists such as Josiah Wedgwood, James Watt, Joseph Priestley and Matthew Boulton (whom Boswell called the 'iron chieftain') among its members, was one of the forces that kick-started the Industrial Revolution. The society, which took its name from its meetings at each full moon, occasionally convened in Lichfield. Johnson may have had no truck with the radical philosophies that permeated the proceedings of the society, nor with the newer generation of Lichfield personalities such as the educational moralist Thomas Day (who was inspired by Rousseau) or the socialist philosopher Richard Lovell Edgeworth (the father of the novelist Maria Edgeworth) who had links to it, but he had an instinctive sympathy with the remarkable industrial innovations its members were offering the country from that part of his world.

4

It was in the cathedral close that the best conversation and manners were to be found as Samuel was growing up. The town itself offered a few old Lichfield families and fine homes, but as the Johnsons had lived in the town for only two generations and were still regarded as newcomers, and as they were always stifled by lack of money, they did not move easily or naturally in those social orbits. His bookseller father and mother 'had not much happiness from each other,' Johnson wrote in his *Annals*. 'They seldom conversed; for my father could not bear to talk of his affairs; and my mother, being unacquainted with books, cared not to talk of any thing else. Had my mother been more literate, they had been better companions.' Apparently he confided in Mrs Thrale his unhappiness with his family in his youth, for later she wrote that he 'did not delight in talking much of his family – "one has (says he) *so* little pleasure in reciting the anecdotes of beggary".' Unable to leave the matter alone, a few pages later he added, 'My father considered tea as very expensive, and discouraged my mother from keeping company with the neighbours, and from paying visits or receiving them. She lived to say, many years after, that, if the time were to pass again, she would not comply with such unsocial injunctions.' It is unlikely, however, that if his mother had been more literate the marriage would have been significantly happier, for the seeds of its aridity lay in the starkly different backgrounds of Sarah Ford and Michael Johnson.[8]

Mrs Thrale remarked that he, clearly alluding to his mother's lack of learning, once told her, 'I did not respect my own mother, though I loved her.' In Johnson's autobiographical snatches there are precious few 'little memorials' of tender moments in his childhood home, but after recollecting a handful involving his mother he admitted that they 'soothe my mind'. By that he meant that they softened his memory of her and lessened his guilt about her. The guilt can be traced partly to his behaviour, perhaps an adolescent type of intellectual arrogance, which sprang from a lack of respect or regard for her knowledge of books, not from any lack of love or regard for her motherliness and practical wisdom, although he never once in later years referred to her as his *dearest* mother, as he did to several female friends. Johnson confided to Mrs Thrale one example of his arrogance towards his mother which is shocking in its disrespect. 'Poor people's children, dear Lady,' he told her, 'never respect them . . . one day, when in anger she called me a puppy, I asked her if she knew what they called a puppy's mother.' When she died in 1759, he wrote a heartfelt prayer for her petitioning God: 'Forgive me whatever I have done unkindly to my mother, and whatever I have omitted to do kindly. Make me to remember her good precepts, and good example.'[9]

Although Boswell maintained that Sarah Ford was 'a woman of distinguished understanding', there is no evidence to back this up, unless he meant simply that she was a sensible and practical homemaker. Indeed, Johnson stressed the opposite about his mother during his boyhood, 'My mother . . . lived in a narrow sphere . . . affected by little things . . . Her mind, I think, was afterwards much enlarged, or greater evils wore out the care of less.' Her great leverage in her marriage was that she came of a good yeoman family, even affluent, from the Birmingham area. Of this social status the Fords were fully conscious and naturally proud, as was Johnson who, in the epitaph he wrote for his mother, highlighted that she was 'of the ancient family of Ford'. In his *Annals* he also played up this assumed superiority and the ill-feeling it generated, urging it as a prevalent theme of contention between his mother and father: 'My mother had no value for his relations; those indeed whom we knew of were much lower than hers. This contempt began, I know not on which side, very early: but, as my father was little at home, it had not much effect.' It is a pretty dismal picture, one that Johnson painted for Mrs Thrale clearly and insistently enough to elicit this passage she wrote on the marriage in her *Anecdotes of the Late Samuel Johnson*, published a couple of years after Johnson's death:

> Mr Johnson's mother was daughter to a gentleman in the country, such as there were many of in those days, who possessing, perhaps, one or two hundred pounds a year in land, lived on the profits, and sought not to increase their income: she was therefore inclined to think higher of herself than of her husband, whose conduct in money matters being but indifferent, she had a trick of teasing him about it, and was, by her son's account, very importunate with regard to her fears of spending more than they could afford, though she never arrived at knowing how much that was; a fault common, as he said, to most women who pride themselves on their economy.

Johnson allowed that, as far as he could tell, his parents did not 'live ill together on the whole', but sadly that was because 'my father could always take his horse and ride away for orders when things went badly'.[10]

Johnson's great-grandfather Henry Ford was a substantial yeoman and miller at the start of the seventeenth century living in the parish of Aston, just west of Birmingham, and then later in West Bromwich, to the east of the city. After his death in 1648 his widow Mary Ford and their son Cornelius moved to the bucolic village of King's Norton, Worcestershire, five miles south of Birmingham, where they purchased a large property picturesquely called Haunch Hall for a substantial sum. Mary Ford's other son, Henry, became a highly successful London lawyer with a big house and lots of property also very near Birmingham. Cornelius married around 1661 and had eight children at Haunch Hall, which must have made it an energetic and lively place to grow up. But it was more than that, for Cornelius was far better educated than most of his village neighbours, appreciated books, and owned something of a library which uniquely nourished his children in their village setting and opened up opportunities and promising futures for them. The whole family had moved to another big house not far away in Curdworth, Warwickshire by 1688, and then to Packwood in the same county about thirteen years later. All of the boys either married well or became highly successful professionals in medicine, law and education. It was at Packwood that, after all her brothers and sisters had left, Johnson's mother stayed with her father in their new home following the death of her mother in 1701, entirely devoting herself (as she had previously) to the running of her father's household. This was her lot and as the years rolled by she was content with it.[11]

In 1706 she was thirty-seven. Unmarried at that advanced age and prepared for little except the routines of housekeeping, she was in a poor position to find a good husband except that she came from a good family. Her destiny seemed to be to live out her life as a spinster until her elder sister Phoebe came to her rescue. Phoebe had married a saddler named John Harrison of Lichfield whose father had been Sheriff of the city and claimed some murky aristocratic lineage. It was probably through the Harrisons, who lived in Lichfield, that Sarah was fatefully introduced to the 49-year-old Lichfield bookseller Michael Johnson and married him on 19 June 1706. Phoebe's marriage to Harrison, therefore, may be seen as a supreme gift to English literature and culture, but it was not an ideal mar-

riage for her. Harrison was a widower and had moved to Birmingham by
1719, when his nephew Samuel at the age of nine and his younger brother
stayed in his house for a few days during the Whitsuntide holidays. 'Why
such boys were sent to trouble other houses, I cannot tell,' Johnson wrote,
but 'my mother had some opinion that much improvement was to be had
by changing the mode of life', and also by exposing him to her side of the
family. His uncle disgusted him: 'My uncle Harrison did not much like
us, nor did we like him. He was a very mean and vulgar man, drunk every
night, but drunk with little drink, very peevish, very proud, very ostentatious, but, luckily, not rich.' Actually, his drunkenness may not have been
that unusual in Lichfield, Johnson told Boswell with some exaggeration,
because people of that generation drank mostly ale instead of wine, so that
'all the decent people in Lichfield got drunk every night, and were not the
worse thought of it.' However, Sarah had other more cultured relatives to
whom she could turn to broaden her children's horizons and who a few
years later would prove to be a distinctly positive, if risky, influence.[12]

Mrs Thrale described Michael Johnson as 'a man of still larger size and
greater strength than his son; who was reckoned very like him'. Boswell
added the word 'robust'. There is a sense about him that he was attractive
to women, for there are at least two stories, one true and the other probably not, of women who were ready and willing to marry him when he was
a young man. He was licensed to marry the daughter of a prominent
tradesman when he was twenty-nine but the wedding never came off. His
son may not have known this romantic fact about him, for it is the sort of
detail of family history that he surely would have mentioned in his *Annals*. Boswell tells another, certainly apocryphal, tale of a woman named
Elizabeth Blaney who conceived such a desire for the brawny Michael that
she in effect stalked him, taking lodgings across from his house in
Lichfield and indulging her 'hopeless flame' for months on end. As
Boswell tells it, Michael's 'generous humanity' eventually took pity on her
and he offered to marry her, but 'it was then too late: her vital power was
exhausted; and she actually exhibited one of the very rare instances of dying for love'. The details of the story were a fabrication, perpetuated prob-

ably by the poetess Anna Seward, known as 'the swan of Lichfield', who did not like Johnson, but it was one way to evoke a romantic early manhood for a man who, by the time he married and fathered his famous son, was an unromantic, late middle-aged, tired bookseller, financially burdened, desperate for someone like Sarah Ford to keep his house in order, and impressed by her family connections. For Sarah, eager to escape the fate of spinsterhood, marriage to Michael Johnson was nonetheless a good idea even if she felt she was marrying beneath her. A life full of books did nothing to make him more attractive to her, but at least he seemed to be selling them and coming up in the world.[13]

Samuel Johnson made the remarkable admission to Boswell that the Johnson family history was so obscure that 'I can hardly tell who was my grandfather'. He could squeeze out 'some pretensions to blood' from his mother's background, but for his father's family he mustered mostly bitterness and disdain because of the huge economic and social disadvantages in which its relative poverty placed him. Either he never had any interest in learning about his father's parentage and ancestors, or he was too ashamed of them to admit he knew very much. He did know that his grandfather William Johnson eked out a living of some sort, probably as a farm labourer, in Cubley, Derbyshire, on the road to Ashbourne about twenty miles north of Lichfield, where three sons and a daughter were born to him and his wife Catherine: Michael in 1657, Benjamin in 1659, Andrew in 1660 and Margaret in 1663. Soon after Margaret's birth the family made the dramatic and courageous move from sleepy Cubley to bustling Lichfield, hoping to enhance its economic prospects and the children's educational opportunities. What William did for a living in Lichfield is as much of a blank to us as, apparently, it was to his grandson, but we know he moved his home from street to street in the next few years and did not do well with whatever line of work he chose. The parish assessed his worth at almost the lowest in town. He died in 1672 and was buried at St Michael's Church in Lichfield, leaving behind an impoverished widow and four hungry young mouths.[14]

Various parish charities saved the widow and children from serious poverty and possibly even homelessness. The children very likely were also able to attend the superb Lichfield Grammar School. When Michael was five, he received a grant to defray school fees from the Lichfield Conduit Lands Trust, and then in 1673, when he was sixteen and just after his father died, the Trust paid his mother £4 (about £400 today),[15] including travel expenses, to have him apprenticed for eight years to a bookseller called Richard Simpson in London. This of course was a huge turning point in the boy's life, so off he went to London to be bound to Simpson in the bookshop the latter had just set up at the sign of The Harp in St Paul's Churchyard. Simpson turned out to be prominent in the London book trade and eventually Master of the Stationers' Company, so Michael was in good hands. Later his two brothers were also apprenticed to Simpson. Michael did not dally in London once his apprenticeship ended in 1681. He hastened back to Lichfield to set up a bookselling and bookbinding business at a prime commercial location in Sadler Street (later Market Street). So the families of both of Samuel's parents turned out to have books as an important part of their lives. The chief difference was that Cornelius Ford collected them while the Johnsons sold them.

Twenty-five years in the business would elapse before Michael Johnson married, but they were years which he appears to have put to good use if his reputation and civic role in the town are reliable clues. In three years he was elected Warden of the Conduit Lands Trust, which involved him, among other things, in a scheme for building a house for the headmaster of the grammar school – a headmaster, ironically, whom his son came to despise. Three years after that he became Overseer of the Poor and then a churchwarden of St Mary's Church, just around the corner from his shop. These were notable responsibilities, not likely to be given to someone who had not impressed the town's leaders as successful and reliable. Still, it remains a puzzle how a man who launched himself as a bookseller with no capital so quickly began to make a mark, and why he failed to translate this early success and his considerable industry and energy into sustainable prosperity in later years.

In the *Annals* Samuel Johnson gives us his take on this. He wrote impatiently of his parents that 'neither of them ever tried to calculate the profits of trade, or the expenses of living'. Presumably, this was Michael's problem before he was married as well. Johnson continues that his nagging mother 'concluded that we were poor, because we lost by some of our trades [business transactions]; but the truth was, that my father, having in the early part of his life contracted debts, never had trade sufficient to enable him to pay them, and maintain his family; he got something, but not enough.' Other diversifying enterprises for which he had to borrow included several costly forays into publishing, from which he made little profit, and in the late 1690s a bold move into the manufacture of vellum and parchment. He set up a little workshop or parchment factory on the marshy perimeter of Stowe Pool, in an area known as the Moggs halfway along the picturesque path to St Chad's Church. This 'factory' plodded along as a drain on his resources until 1717 when he was charged by the Lichfield Quarter Sessions for practising the trade without the required seven-year apprenticeship. Add to this his bad bookkeeping and the recipe for financial frustration is complete. As for his wife, she appears to have been no help with any aspect of the business and may even have demoralised her husband. 'Of business,' Johnson writes, 'she had no distinct conception; and therefore her discourse was composed only of complaint, fear, and suspicion.' Exasperated, Johnson adds that in about 1768 he picked up some family papers and computed his father's profits. 'This, I believe, my parents never did.' He does not tell us what he discovered, though in 1774 he still meant to but did not 'note down my father's stock, expenses, and profit'.[16]

There would be more borrowing. Michael Johnson was determined that as a newly married man he would have a book business and home befitting his new wife's social background. The costs of the effort conspired to render his family household perpetually poor in later years, although at first it must have felt prosperous enough owing to his wife's dowry of almost five hundred pounds and the carefully arranged marriage settlement by Sarah's father, who doubted Michael's ability to provide properly for his daughter and a future family.[17]

Michael started to spend heavily right away. In 1706, the year of his marriage, he threw himself off the deep end financially in an effort to advance to a higher league in the bookselling business. He borrowed to buy the entire library of no fewer than 2,900 volumes belonging to the Earl of Derby (who had died in 1702) at Knowsley, near Liverpool. This was supposed to expand his business dramatically, for which he must have thought he had encouragement from wealthy customers and the cathedral close's ecclesiastical population, but the unhappy reality was he had trouble selling the books. Many volumes from the collection hung around his shop unsold for decades. The next year he did something even more audacious. He purchased a seventeenth-century property on the corner of Market and Breadmarket streets, virtually across from St Mary's Church and commandingly facing Market Place with all its hustle and bustle of twice-weekly markets. He paid £80 for it and surely caused a stir in town by proceeding immediately to reduce the building to rubble. He leased extra land along the street from the Lichfield Corporation and in the place of the old building raised the tall, respectable residence where Samuel was born and which served as both home and shop. The imposing new home had a basement and four lovely storeys supported on outside pillars and cantilevered prettily on Breadmarket Street, the main entrance facing the market square. The house looked much as it does today, with the kitchen in the basement, a large bookshop on the ground floor, two parlours, and perhaps as many as ten or eleven bedrooms. The four bedrooms at the top were for servants and apprentices. All of this initially would have delighted Sarah Johnson, of course, but none of it was inexpensive and the reckoning would inevitably come, much of it to Samuel's conspicuous disadvantage.[18]

Given Sarah's age when they married, if the Johnsons were going to have a family they could not afford to wait. Childbearing was fraught with dangers. Yet more than two years elapsed before Sarah's first pregnancy, and it did not help that four months before she gave birth her father died, leaving them a meagre legacy. It also disturbed their domestic peace that a few weeks before the birth Michael was elected Sheriff of Lichfield, one of the town's highest offices. It was an honour (without financial benefits) but there was so much more to think about as a result, at a time when fewer distractions and demands on the family may have been desirable.

5

An important legacy of Michael Johnson's should be mentioned. It had nothing to do with money and it is unlikely that either Cornelius Ford or his daughter knew anything about it. He was born with a serious constitutional melancholy, 'a morbid disposition of both body and mind', which was aggravated by his family's money troubles and a wife who harped on them. Samuel was to inherit this disease in large measure. Referring to Michael's sturdy, large body, Boswell wrote in his *Life of Johnson*, 'as in the most solid rocks veins of unsound substance are often discovered, there was in him a mixture of that disease, the nature of which eludes the most minute enquiry, though the effects are well known to be a weariness of life, an unconcern about those things which agitate the greater part of mankind, and a general sensation of gloomy wretchedness'. This 'wrong-headed, positive . . . melancholy' was almost the first fact Mrs Thrale chose to mention in her *Anecdotes*, obviously convinced (as was Boswell) that Michael Johnson's morbidity was of enormous importance in understanding the character, attitudes and life of the son. The latter told her that his father, unlike him, was fortunate to be able to cope with the affliction through physical exercise and the demands of his job, 'leading him to be much on horseback [which] contributed to the preservation of his bodily health and sanity'. But there were periods of inertia at home oppressed with alarming danger signals of 'imagination' and 'madness':

> Mr Johnson said, that when his [parchment] workshop, a detached building, had fallen half down for want of money to repair it, his father was not less diligent to lock the door every night, though he saw that anybody might walk in at the back part and knew that there was no security obtained by barring the front

door. '*This* (says his son) was madness, you may see, and would have been discoverable in other instances of the prevalence of imagination, but that poverty prevented it from playing such tricks as riches and leisure encourage.'

It was such incidents and irrational habits that sank deep into the son's psyche as he grew up and terrified him that he would one day inherit his father's melancholy and lapse into an even worse kind of madness.[19]

CHAPTER 2

Stepping on the Duckling

I

MICHAEL AND SARAH JOHNSON'S eldest son, Samuel, was born
in the large bedroom over the bookshop in the new house on
Wednesday, 7 September 1709. It was an auspicious year in English literary history: the first Copyright Act was passed in Great Britain; Alexander Pope launched his poetic career with the publication of his *Pastorals*;
Nicholas Rowe published his famous edition of Shakespeare's plays, the
first important editorial instalment in a century of sometimes frenetic
Shakespeareana; and Joseph Addison and Sir Richard Steele published
the original issue of *The Tatler*, the first major British periodical. If Michael Johnson the bookseller was at all aware of these far off stirrings in
the nation's literature, he had little leisure to appreciate them.

The overwhelming theme of the first few pages of Johnson's *Annals* is
his terrible health in the first hours, months and years of his life. The appalling condition of his birth and the travails of his parents' efforts to keep
him alive made a profound impression on his self-identity for the rest of
his life, although growing up he had heard so many horror stories about
his first days that he admitted, 'confusions of memory I suspect to be common'. He did not exactly spring from the womb: 'My mother had a very
difficult and dangerous labour, and was assisted by George Hector, a man-
midwife of great reputation. I was born almost dead, and could not cry for
some time. When he had me in his arms, he said, "Here is a brave boy."'
Fearing he would die, the parents lost no time baptising him on the same

day. The baby's condition did not improve right away but it clung to life: 'In a few weeks an inflammation was discovered on my buttock, which was at first, I think, taken for a burn; but soon appeared to be a natural disorder. It swelled, broke, and healed.'[1]

Soon after the birth, Michael persuaded Sarah to have the baby sent out to a wet nurse and chose for the purpose Joan Marclew, whose brick-maker husband worked for him in some capacity or who herself had been one of his servants. They lived a few hundred metres away on George Lane. Johnson recollects with some pastoral nostalgia that when he was 'a bigger boy' he used to visit the Marclew orchard and 'eat fruit in the garden, which was full of trees'. It was common practice to use the services of a wet nurse, but that did not stop Sarah Johnson from missing her baby terribly. Johnson must have heard from her or his father that she contrived to visit him every day on George Lane, an unusual practice that neighbours could easily have read as a sign of maternal sentimentality or weakness. It was something she was embarrassed to admit and 'used to go different ways, that her assiduity might not expose her to ridicule; and often left her fan or glove behind her, that she might have a pretence to come back unexpected'. She 'never discovered any token of neglect' at the Marclews, however, in the way her baby was being cared for.

There were other, more serious problems: 'Here it was discovered that my eyes were bad; and an issue was cut in my left arm, of which I took no great notice, as I think my mother has told me, having my little hand in a custard. How long this issue was continued I do not remember. I believe it was suffered to dry when I was about six years old.' It turns the stomach to contemplate that for the first six years of his life in order to purge an infection that was thought to be affecting his eyesight the boy was burdened with an incision kept open with threads or horsehairs. It was the first in a lifetime of incisions and blood-letting to which Johnson, according to barbaric medical practices of that age, was subjected in efforts to relieve this or that malady.

Worse was to come: 'scrofulous sores' began to appear on the little body. The respected physician Samuel Swynfen, the baby's godfather, who had taken lodgings in the Johnsons' new spacious house as a convenient place to carry on his practice, remarked (according to Johnson), 'he never knew any child reared with so much difficulty'; the scrofula passed to the infant from the infected milk or 'bad humours of the nurse, whose son had the same distemper, and was likewise short-sighted, but both in a less degree'. Dr Swynfen was right, though Johnson added that his mother thought 'my diseases derived from her family'. The scrofula, a tubercular infection in the lymph glands, may have been the direct cause of the baby's damaged eyesight, leading to almost complete blindness in the left eye and partial vision in the right one. 'Now had I been an Indian, I must have died early', he confided to Boswell; 'my eyes would not have served me to get food'. Mrs Thrale noted, however, that one could not tell by looking at Johnson which eye was the blind one, and his friends in later years seemed unaware of this blindness, and aware only of his short-sightedness. His hearing also was affected by this tubercular disease. After ten weeks at the Marclews, he was brought home, 'a poor, diseased infant, almost blind'. Johnson recalls that his otherwise sweet-tempered aunt Jane told him harshly she 'would not have picked such a poor creature up in the street'. Mrs Thrale's take on his condition was that the 'scrofulous evil' so afflicted his childhood that it 'left such marks as greatly disfigured a countenance naturally harsh and rugged, besides doing irreparable damage to the auricular organs, which never could perform their functions since I knew him.'[2]

Even if he could not recall those ten weeks himself, Johnson knew from what others and his body told him that during that period the die was cast for much of his personal and emotional life. On his visit to Lichfield in 1767, he could not escape the psychological need to translate the imagined nightmare of those early months into the reality of an actual place. He wrote in the *Annals* that he 'went to look for my nurse's house; and, enquiring somewhat obscurely, was told "this is the house in which you were nursed"'. There was an unexpected shock waiting for him there, one that was nonetheless liberating in that it objectified for him the tragedy of his own physical history: 'I saw my nurse's son, to whose milk I succeeded, reading a large Bible, which my nurse had bought . . . some time before her death.' He was apparently unable to earn a living because of his eyesight, and was pitifully poring over a Bible in large print that his mother had bought him for solace and comfort.[3] Johnson's advantage over this man, and the reason the scrofula and its effects as well as other ailments did not debilitate him, was that in spite of suffering more severely he was endowed, like his father, with a strong, robust, large physical frame, not to mention a tenacity and a courage that showed themselves very early in his life and enabled him to overcome or minimise his handicaps.

Johnson was scarred by the enlarged lymph glands that scrofula causes, in his case chiefly around the neck, though whether or not the scars showed themselves dramatically in infancy is not clear. It is certain that his eyesight showed no improvement as the months passed. Increasingly desperate, Sarah Johnson decided to take things into her own hands. Johnson's impression was that one day in the second year of his thus far diseased existence on earth his mother gathered him up and rushed off to Trysul near Wolverhampton, the manor house of her wealthy first cousin Mrs Harriotts, where she could more conveniently consult the reputable oculist Dr Thomas Attwood of Worcester. Apparently there was no eye specialist in Lichfield. Nothing useful came of the visit except that Michael Johnson conceived from it a still greater dislike for his wife's relatives to whom she was wont to turn for help in emergencies and need. The visit rubbed salt into the tender wounds of his relative poverty. His injured pride, aggravated by his wife's lording her family over him, forced him over the years to retaliate by mischievously teasing and annoying Mrs Harriotts. His son wrote that he could do no more than that because his financial 'adversity' made him and his vanity powerless. Such behaviour, however, did not prevent Mrs Harriotts in 1728 from bequeathing to Sarah £40 along with 'a pair of her best flaxen sheets and pillow cases, as well as a large pewter dish and a dozen pewter plates'. She and Dr Attwood had been unable to help the infant in 1710, but this legacy at least, as we shall see, turned out to be hugely important in Samuel's education and unpromising young career.[4]

2

Desperate to find some other way of helping her baby overcome the plague of scrofula, Sarah made a dramatic decision. On the advice of the respected Lichfield physician Dr John Floyer, who must have felt as helpless as she did, she decided to take her baby to London to be 'touched' by Queen Anne. For centuries in England and France monarchs were believed to have the ability to heal scrofula by simply touching the sufferer in a healing ritual known as 'touching for the King's evil'. Thousands of people had been allegedly healed by this royal touch ever since the custom began during the reign of Edward the Confessor as the result of the legendary dream of a young woman. Evidence exists that this popular superstition still persisted in the Midlands itself. That year the Catholic King James II actually came to Lichfield and in the cathedral 'touched' a number of locals suffering from scrofula. Queen Anne went so far as to proclaim her own powers to heal in this way. In 1714 she 'touched' as many as two hundred people at one time who, like Sarah Johnson, were willing to try anything to conquer the disease. The practice died suddenly in the reign of George I, partly because of its Roman Catholic overtones. In March 1712 Sarah Ford cared little about ecclesiastical or monarchical niceties. She wanted her baby to be healed. In order to keep people from receiving the 'touch piece' unwarrantedly, applicants had to prove that the disease in question really was the King's Evil, so before leaving she had to obtain from a physician a statement that the child was in fact suffering from it, and that it had not had the royal 'touch' before. For her to take her ailing, probably noisy, thirty-month-old son on an uncomfortable, jolting two- or three-day journey via stagecoach all the way to London on such a blind mission of hope was a large undertaking and suggests, in addition to her desperation, a strongly religious and superstitious nature.

The family could ill afford the expense. Furthermore, Sarah was obliged to conceal that she was now two months pregnant with her second son Nathaniel, fearing she would not be allowed on the stagecoach if it became known. Johnson writes about this journey in his *Annals* from

his own faint, dreamlike recall of images, people, and events: 'I always retained some memory of this journey,' he wrote, 'though I was then but
thirty months old.' Such journeys, notwithstanding Christmas cards and
coaching prints showing gaily painted stagecoaches flying along rolling
green or snowy countryside with joy and expectation written across the
faces of coachman and passengers, were exercises in stamina, even without
a toddler like Samuel in tow. Inside, the passengers were squeezed together while the rest of the passengers braved the elements outside, hoping they would not freeze or be thrown off the coach by a sudden bump or
turn in the road. Half remembering, half reporting what he had been told,
Johnson wrote: 'We were troublesome to the passengers; but to suffer
such inconveniences in the stagecoach was common in those days to
persons in much higher rank. I was sick; one woman fondled me, the
other was disgusted.' From a shop at one of the stopping places along the
route, perhaps Coleshill, Coventry, Daventry or Stony Stratford, the kind
woman 'bought me a small silver cup and spoon, marked SAM. J. lest if
they had been marked S.J. which was her [his mother's] name, they
should, upon her death, have been taken from me'. She did not stop there
but also bought him a speckled linen frock which 'I knew afterwards
by the name of my London frock'. He kept the cup into his manhood until, sadly, the 'distress' of poverty early in his marriage forced his wife to
sell it – 'one of the last pieces of plate' – though he still had the spoon
when he wrote these lines.[5]

Johnson dimly recollected – 'I know not whether I remember the
thing, or the talk of it' – that in London he and his mother stayed near a
relative of hers in a bookseller's shop in Little Britain, a favourite haunt of
booksellers and prostitutes near St Paul's Cathedral where 'the booksellers
. . . were knowing and conversible men, with whom, for the sake of bookish knowledge, the greatest wits were pleased to converse'. It is probable
that Nicholson, the bookseller with whom mother and son stayed, was a
contact of Michael Johnson's from his days of apprenticeship. He remembered a jack weight at Nicholson's for turning a spit (into which he stum-
bled once), a string and bell given to him to play with by his cousin, the
shop counter, a cat with a white collar, and a dog called Chops 'that leaped

over a stick'. All this lingered in his mind as part of the ineradicable imagery of this desperate quest for a healing. He wrote nothing of seeing the Queen, only of hearing a boy cry at the palace, though he did tell Mrs Thrale 'he had a confused, but somehow a sort of solemn recollection of a lady in diamonds, and a long black hood'. The ceremony was quite religious, with the Queen flanked by chaplains who recited prayers. Nothing miraculous for Samuel immediately resulted from the royal touch, although the received wisdom was that the healing could occur anytime within the next six months and still be regarded as a miracle. It did not, however. Sarah and the baby then had to make their way back to Lichfield, taking with them a gold coin or 'touch piece' specially minted for such pilgrims and threaded on a white ribbon that the Queen hung around Samuel's neck. Johnson wore his under his shirt for the rest of his life.[6]

Their return journey was misery. To save 'a few shillings' Sarah booked passage this time on a stage-wagon, taking care also to sew two guineas into her petticoat 'lest she should be robbed'. These rumbling wagons, covered by canvas and pulled by a team of eight or more horses led by a waggoner on foot, were intended really for transporting goods but they also carried a handful of passengers. Travelling at three or four miles per hour, it took them about five days to get home, which would have seemed like an eternity even to someone without an infirm toddler in tow. Apart from some regular praying at St Chad's Well or at the shrine in the cathedral, as well as at home, the parents do not appear to have sought out any more miracle or superstitious cures.[7]

3

If Sarah and Michael concluded they could do no more to repair their son's damaged body, they could still address his spiritual needs. Michael apparently thought that a little religious preaching might do young Samuel some good. There is a story, probably spurious in some or possibly all of its details, that Boswell picked up from Mary Adey, Johnson's young Lichfield friend, describing how when the child was three his father took him to hear the famous preacher and author Dr Henry Sacheverell preach in Lichfield Cathedral. Boswell was sceptical of such stories 'which the credulous relate with eager satisfaction', but he included this anecdote in the *Life* because it suggested to him rather romantically Johnson's characteristic precociousness and fierce concentration even as a toddler. According to Mary Adey, her grandfather saw Johnson sitting on his father's shoulders during the sermon, 'listening and gaping at the much celebrated preacher'. The iconic story makes Johnson out to be a type of saintly visitant to the temple, eagerly taking in the scholarly and spiritual wisdom of the church elders. According to Boswell, Michael Johnson is supposed to have defended his bringing his infant son to church by explaining 'it was impossible to keep him at home; for, young as he was, he believed he had caught the public spirit and zeal for Sacheverell'. Like many fathers who have to drag their children to certain events because they cannot at the moment do anything else with them, Michael may well have listened while his son gaped in boredom from above. It is more plausible that the boy was gaping at other gaping children.[8]

It was Sarah, not Michael, however, who took in hand Samuel's spiritual education. She did what most mothers usually did to promote their children's religious education, although his physical problems gave her efforts a special urgency. Johnson described her earliest efforts to tell him about heaven and hell, what seems like, but was not, a Calvinist type of indoctrination about original sin and damnation, future reward and punishment. It was a normal, if to us severe, brand of Protestant fundamentalism to which most children were subjected. Johnson was only three and in bed at the time: 'I suppose that in this year I was first informed of a future state. I remember, that being in bed with my mother one morning, I was told by her of the two places to which the inhabitants of this world were received after death; one a fine place filled with happiness, called Heaven; the other a *sad* place, called Hell. That this account much affected my imagination, I do not remember.' Nevertheless, his mother's assiduous piety introduced a strong theme in his youth. She was so insistent that this lesson should sink in that she had him get out of bed immediately and repeat it to their servant Thomas Jackson, but his take on that, at least when

he talked to Mrs Thrale about it, had to do more with the general education of children than with religion: 'Little people should be encouraged
always to tell whatever they hear particularly striking, to some brother, sister, servant, immediately before the impression is erased by the intervention of newer occurrences.' In later years, when Johnson reminded his
mother of their talk, she was surprised she had waited until he was three
to lay out this scenario of hell and heaven for him.[9]

He did not say that his mother's religious instruction had any darker
effect on him than weariness, such as cultivating a fear of damnation, but
Boswell did think it damaged his 'tender imagination' and sowed the seeds
of what he called Johnson's 'diseased imagination'. All Johnson allowed
was that the whole business was hard going:

> Sunday [said he] was a heavy day to me when I was a boy. My
> mother confined me on that day, and made me read 'The Whole
> Duty of Man', from a great part of which I could derive no in-
> struction. When, for instance, I had read the chapter on theft,
> which from my infancy I had been taught was wrong, I was no
> more convinced that theft was wrong than before; so there was no
> accession of knowledge.

If his mother had possessed the ability and knowledge, he added, to
sweeten this religious teaching with observations on style and other 'excellencies of composition', so that his mind could have been uplifted by 'an
amusing variety of objects' and 'not grow weary', it might have benefited
him more.[10]

Sarah Johnson probably was no gloomier than the average mother in
the way she explained religion and committed no greater sin in her son's
eyes than that of being dull and unimaginative. She was disciplined in the
way she kept his attention on various forms of religion, especially on
learning passages by heart. One day in Lichfield in 1776, Johnson's step-
daughter Lucy Porter told Boswell, in Johnson's presence, that Sarah
Johnson once boasted about her son's precociousness: 'When he was a
child in petticoats,' Boswell writes, 'and had learned to read, Mrs Johnson

one morning put the common prayer-book [*The Book of Common Prayer*] into his hands, pointed to the collect for the day, and said, "Sam, you must get this by heart." She went upstairs, leaving him to study it: But by the time she had reached the second floor, she heard him following her. "What's the matter?" said she. "I can say it," he replied; and repeated it distinctly, though he could not have read it over more than twice.' While this sounds a bit like one of those stories that get embellished in the telling, the piety and discipline of the mother nonetheless ring true in it. *The Whole Duty of Man*, from which she required him to read regularly as soon as he was able to read, was the enormously popular Protestant manual by Richard Allestree, chaplain in ordinary to the King and Provost of Eton, published in 1658. For over a century in edition after edition it was obligatory fare for children. Written for even 'the meanest reader', it was little Samuel's earliest exposure to moral writing, divided into seventeen chapters which mostly addressed moral qualities such as temperance, obedience, and contentment and secular duties such as marriage. This stern regimen of reading and instruction laid the foundations of his lifelong piety and Christian discipline, the core of his morality.'

4

The religious recitations he was made to perform for family and friends both angered and saddened Johnson as he looked back on his childhood. In later years, he felt strongly that children should not be treated as exhibitions by their parents, remembering with acute displeasure how his parents would trot him out for performances. He told Mrs Thrale that a few days after his brother Nathaniel was born in October 1712, whose christening he remembered 'with all its circumstances', his mother made him learn how to spell and pronounce 'the words *little Natty*, syllable by syllable, making him say it over in the evening to her husband and his guests'. According to her, the 'trick which most parents play with their children, of showing off their newly-acquired accomplishments, disgusted Mr Johnson beyond expression'. His parents had treated him this way 'till he absolutely loathed his father's caresses, because he knew they were sure to precede some unpleasing display of his early abilities; and he used, when neighbours came visiting, to run up a tree that he might not be found and exhibited, such, as no doubt he was, a prodigy of early understanding'.[12]

In conversation with Boswell and Lucy Porter, Johnson also remembered another day when he and his father were out walking in Lichfield, perhaps along the green banks of Stowe Pool, and he accidentally stepped on a duckling, 'the eleventh of a brood', and killed it. His mother circulated the story many years later that on his father's urging him to write an epitaph for the duck's burial he quickly composed these verses and repeated them to her:

> Under this stone lyes Mr Duck
> Whom Samuel Johnson trode on
> He might have liv'd if he had luck;
> But then he'd been an odd one.

Mrs Thrale cites the poem in her *Anecdotes* as a sign of the boy's 'early expansion of mind, and knowledge of language'. Boswell, too, quotes it in his *Life*. Whether or not Michael Johnson wrote half of the verses, as Johnson maintained, or all of them, Johnson's exasperated complaint was that with them his father yet again proved himself 'a foolish old man – that is to say, foolish in talking of his children'. Johnson 'always seemed more mortified at the recollection of the bustle his parents made with his wit', Mrs Thrale added, 'than pleased with the thoughts of possessing it. "That (said he to me one day) is the great misery of late marriages, the unhappy produce of them becomes the plaything of dotage."' Sentimental about neither children, ducks, dogs, nor his own childhood, he often hurt or offended parents by going out of his way to avoid hearing their children recite verses or sing songs, particularly one father who asked him to listen to his two sons repeat separately Thomas Gray's 'Elegy Written in a Country Churchyard' so that he could judge which one had the 'happier cadence'. 'No, pray Sir', Johnson replied instantly, 'let the dears both speak it at once; more noise will by that means be made, and the noise will be sooner over.'[13]

5

With Nathaniel's birth in October 1712 life changed dramatically for young Samuel. He suddenly diminished as the anxious focus of his parents. There is virtually no record of the brothers' relationship as toddlers up through adolescence, but what there is reveals a mood of rivalry, if not a sad deficiency of brotherly love. Johnson spoke positively once to Mrs Thrale about Nathaniel's 'manly spirit' in later years with 'pride and pleasure', but this is almost the only surviving fond remark on the part of the elder brother. From him Mrs Thrale clearly received the impression that 'the two brothers did not . . . much delight in each other's company, being always rivals for the mother's fondness'. In fact, the severity of Johnson's observations on domestic life in his fable, *Rasselas*, she thinks, can be clearly traced to domestic friction in his childhood, much of it apparently between the two boys and much of it of his own making. Since he admitted to Mrs Thrale that as a boy he was of 'a sullen temper and reserved disposition', Nathaniel must have had a rough time of it. Whatever the causes, this domestic friction remained a soreness in Johnson's psyche for most of his life, likely to pain him whenever he witnessed family harmony, such as in his musical friend Dr Charles Burney's London home: 'Of this consanguineous unanimity I have had never much experience; but it appears to me one of the great lenitives of life.' He had almost nothing to say about his brother in any of his surviving writings, which in its own way is remarkable.[14]

6

Sarah Johnson did not have, in her son's eyes, knowledge enough to be able to 'sweeten' her religious teaching, but she began to teach him to read with the adventures of St George and the Dragon, which made a deep im-

pression: 'The recollection of such reading as had delighted him in his infancy, made him always persist in fancying that it was the only reading
which could please an infant.' What he relished most was robust romantic
adventure stories about 'giants and castles, and of somewhat which can
stretch and stimulate . . . little minds.' In 1780, at his dear friend Bennet
Langton's home in Rochester, Johnson once fell into conversation about
what children should and should not read. John Longley, the Recorder of
that city and eventual father of an archbishop of Canterbury, happened to
be there and noticed the vigour with which Johnson attacked their hostess's then fashionable notion that children benefited most from 'little
books published purposely for their instruction'. He rounded on her, 'asserting that at an early age it was better to gratify curiosity with wonders
than to attempt planting truth, before the mind was prepared to receive it
and that therefore, *Jack the Giant-Killer*, *Parisenus and Parismenus*, and
The Seven Champions of Christendom were fitter for them than Mrs [Anna
Letitia] Barbauld and Mrs [Sarah] Trimmer'. On another occasion he was
impatient with Mrs Thrale for giving her own children trifling and trendy
stories with moral agendas. 'Babies do not want to hear about babies,'
he told her bluntly, thinking of the diet of his publisher friend John
Newbery's instructional books such as *Goody Two Shoes* and *Tommy Prudent* to which she was subjecting them. He deplored this fad for spoiling
the innocence of children with stories that made them self-conscious
about morality, convinced that 'endeavouring to make children prema-
turely wise is useless labour'. 'One may write things to a child without being childish,' he urged in his *Life of Milton*. When Mrs Thrale defended
herself, he reminded her that 'the parents *buy* the books, and the children
never read them'.[15]

The great thing was to provoke the child's imagination. One adventure
story which he must certainly have heard of and grabbed quickly after it
came out in 1719 was Defoe's *Robinson Crusoe*. Along with Bunyan's *Pilgrim's Progress* and *Don Quixote*, it was one of the very few books he later
singled out as an exception to his notion that very few books were 'ever . . .
written by mere man that was wished longer by its readers'. As for the
imagination, a child could do no better than Shakespeare – 'he that pe-

ruses Shakespeare, looks round alarmed, and starts to find himself alone,' he once wrote. *Hamlet*, which he plucked off his father's shelves at the tender age of nine, certainly was not urged on him for instructional purposes. Reading it one day at home in the stillness of the basement kitchen and looking up, he was terrified to find himself in the company of the Ghost on the ramparts of Elsinore Castle. Throwing down the book, 'he suddenly hurried upstairs to the street door that he might see people about him'. He frequently told this story by way of celebrating Shakespeare's imaginative power but also because he liked to stress proudly that at a very young age he did not go in for 'small beer' and was already diving into Shakespeare and loved to read poetry. His strong imagination as a boy was repelled by little frivolous, tidy stories and had to be fed by more expansive adventures and romances set in strange lands with exotic characters. It was a taste that as he grew up merged into an unquenchable thirst for travel stories and accounts, especially ones informing readers about far-off lands, societies, cultures and manners.[16]

CHAPTER 3

Leaping over the Rail

I

JOHNSON ALWAYS HELD the profession of a teacher to be sacred, easily abused with tragic consequences. In his *Life of Joseph Addison* he remarked that in biography 'not to name the school or the masters of men illustrious for literature, is a kind of historical fraud, by which honest fame is injuriously diminished'.[1] Nonetheless, he thought his teachers were definitely a mixed bunch. He either revered or despised them for the rest of his life.

About one hundred metres from the Johnson house, along the Market Place and then left into Dam Street, lived Dame Ann Oliver, the sufficiently educated widow of a simple shoemaker who decided to open a school in her home when her husband died, leaving her with one or more children to bring up. Dame Oliver's home classroom was in the middle of Lichfield, and she seems to have had a confectionery business in her home as well by the time she began her school. It was most likely here when he was four or five, not at home, that Samuel first learned to read properly. Dame Oliver took a liking to this odd, disfigured little boy, which was reciprocated, for he remembered fondly how 'in the simplicity of her kindness' she proudly gave him one of her gingerbread biscuits as a going-away present when he went off to university and told him he was 'the best scholar she had ever had'.

Nothing more is known about his year or two with Dame Oliver except an account of an incident which Boswell picked up from Johnson in Bath in 1776. Johnson himself did not recollect what happened, having heard it only from his mother, but he thought it was important enough to mention to Boswell. One day after school when his mother was late coming to fetch him he started for home on his own, which was just around the corner, 'though he was then so near-sighted, that he was obliged to stoop down on his hands and knees to take a view of the kennel before he ventured to step over it'. Apprehensive, the schoolmistress followed him but did it 'slyly', hoping to stay out of sight apparently out of a healthy respect for his already evident independent and impetuous spirit. As he turned the corner, however, he caught sight of her and 'was so angry at being tended that he went back and beat her'. Dr Thomas Percy, the cranky literary historian and cleric, told Boswell that in a fury the boy actually kicked his teacher, 'an early proof of his irritable and violent temper'. Nobody knows where the priggish Percy got this kicking detail, but it is believable and conveys essentially the boy's defiant trigger-like challenge to anyone who was foolish enough to feel sorry for him on account of any of his physical handicaps.[2]

After a couple of years Dame Oliver, opting to dedicate her time to shaping gingerbread instead of children, passed Samuel on to Thomas Browne, a friend of hers a few doors down in Dam Street, another lapsed shoemaker of about sixty who decided to open a school. The boy's health probably was the reason he went there instead of directly on to Lichfield School at the age of five. A desk and chair it seems were the only furniture in the schoolroom, so the children spent most of the time sitting on the floor when they were not standing for recitation. The only thing Johnson thought memorable about his two years with this man was that he published a spelling book of which, although he dedicated it rather confidently to the universe, he feared, 'no copy of it can now be had'. Browne died within a year of Samuel's leaving the school.

2

At the age of seven, Samuel's education finally began in earnest at Lichfield Grammar School. Several months before, however, an accident at St Mary's Church upset his life and had a knock-on effect on his religious behaviour and outlook. This Gothic-style church (rebuilt in 1721) was where the Johnsons worshipped and rented a pew, and conceivably they were in it on Easter Sunday 1716 when parts of its stone spire fell away and landed on the roof and in one of the aisles, causing a panic that was reported as far away as London in the *Weekly Journal*: 'The people (being a numerous congregation) crowded so fast that they tumbled upon one another, and lay crawling in heaps . . . Hats, books, hoods, scarfs, cover-sluts or long riding-hoods, headdresses, spectacles, gloves, clogs, snuff-boxes, fans, etc. were left in abundance.' They had to break windows to get out. Johnson recalled the consequences of the calamity on him:

> I fell into an inattention to religion, or an indifference about it . . . The church at Lichfield, in which we had a seat, wanted repara-tion, so I was to go and find a seat in other churches; and hav-ing bad eyes, and being awkward about this, I used to go and read in the fields on Sunday. This habit continued till my four-teenth year; and still I find a great reluctance to go to church. I then became a lax *talker* against religion, for I did not much *think* against it.

It is a pleasant image he calls up: with books in hand, presumably includ-ing the Bible and *Book of Common Prayer*, taking to the fields around Lichfield as a substitute for public worship at St Michael's on the south side of town where his parents began to attend. In the fields he felt no awkwardness about his eyesight and other physical infirmities. There was a delicious sense of freedom.[3]

He became a 'lax talker' against religion but is careful to say he did not 'think' against it. On the contrary, he sought to know more about it. It was a pursuit he never abandoned, one that became the centre of his imagina-tive life, although he once admitted, 'I myself was for some years totally regardless of religion. It had dropped out of my mind. It was at an early part of my life.' What seems to have occurred was the first known crisis in his mental state at the early age of ten if we are to believe – Boswell did not – what after his death Mrs Thrale said he had told her:

At the age of ten years his mind was disturbed by scruples of
infidelity [doubts of Christian faith], which preyed upon his spirits, and made him very uneasy; the more so, as he revealed his uneasiness to no one, being naturally (as he said) 'of a sullen temper
and reserved disposition'. He searched, however, diligently but
fruitlessly, for evidences of the truth of revelation; and at length
recollecting a book he had once seen in his father's shop, intitled,
De Veritate Religionis, &c. he began to think himself highly culpa-
ble for neglecting such a means of information, and took himself
severely to task for this sin, adding many acts of voluntary, and to
others unknown, penance.

Once he found the book and realised he was too young to understand it
anyway, his guilt subsided, 'and not thinking to enquire whether there
were any English books written on the subject, followed his usual amusements'. Boswell indignantly described Thrale's reading of this early crisis
as a 'strange fantastical account', 'childish, irrational, and ridiculous' because of its superficiality and trivialisation. What is important is that
Johnson himself acknowledged the religious doubts and guilt he experienced at this early age.[4]

3

Lichfield Grammar School[5] was one of the major reasons Lichfield rose to
such eminence in the seventeenth and eighteenth centuries. Situated a
quarter of a mile south-west of the town centre, the school was established in 1495, by William Smith, the Bishop of Lichfield and co-founder
of Brasenose College, Oxford. Originally serving the church as an institution for the teaching of Latin grammar as part of St John's Hospital, it
was as a free school in St John's Street run by the town corporation that it
left its mark in the beginning of the seventeenth century. Under the forceful and fearful headmastership of the Revd John Hunter from 1704 to
1741, it became nationally famous. While grammar schools were established long before the Reformation, the teaching of Latin as the basis of

their system of education – 'the good old waie of teaching', 'clogged with much labour, wearinesse and difficulty' – clinging to the same textbooks and methods, and resistance to change and the introduction of more modern subjects (like English, for example) pushed them into decline in the seventeenth century. In the North, however, they thrived, where a good master could become famous and be a magnet for good pupils, most of whom boarded.

At the time Samuel was in the school, Hunter was responsible for and presided over a period of prosperity for the school. With over one hundred boarders, he cast a wide net that drew in the sons of gentlemen from Leicestershire and Derbyshire as well as Staffordshire. He educated a surprising number of nationally known and professionally distinguished men, including several judges who ended up sitting in the superior courts at Westminster, John Wyatt the inventor of the cotton spinning-machine, and David Garrick. With stern discipline and extensive learning, Hunter turned the school into a going enterprise, so that eventually he had to rent property nearby to house boarders in addition to local day pupils. The school still thrives today.

Samuel's career as a day scholar began well enough. He entered the lower school under the intelligent care of the usher or undermaster, Humphrey Hawkins, whom he described as 'very skillful in his little way'. Johnson recalled the almost two and a half years with Hawkins with unreserved pleasure, 'for I was indulged and caressed by my master, and, I think, really excelled the rest'. Hawkins's gentle encouragement was crucial because at the age of seven the boy's large frame, scrofula-scarred features, severely limited eyesight and increasingly odd gesticulations and movements, not to mention what Mrs Thrale described as his sullen and reserved disposition, were at first surely likely to make him the butt of his classmates' jokes. The two and a half years in the lower class flew by: 'The time, till I had computed it, appeared much longer by the multitude of novelties which it supplied, and of incidents, then in my thoughts important, it produced. Perhaps it is not possible that any other period can make the same impression on the memory.'[6]

The curriculum at grammar schools had remained virtually unchanged for two hundred years. Writing and arithmetic were no part of it, nor of course was science as we know it. There was some Greek grammar based on a study of Euripides, Sophocles, Xenophon and Homer, among others, but Latin grammar and translation were what it was mostly all about. The standard texts were Aesop's *Fables*, Cicero's letters, Ovid, Virgil, Horace, Pliny, Juvenal, Plautus and Livy. The books Johnson remembered reading in those first years of school were easy and mostly a pleasure for him. Most agreeable, of course, were the literary texts, Aesop's *Fables* in an edition by Charles Hoole (1687) with English and Latin on facing pages, and other classical fables and dialogues appealing to a boy's imagination and tending to make learning fun. Every Thursday there were examinations consisting mainly of recitation, but they posed no problems or challenges for anyone. According to Johnson, everybody looked forward to Thursday, in fact, because there was no need to prepare any lessons for that day and the questions were always ones the boys had been asked before and 'could regularly answer'. The boys learned Aesop by heart on Thursday nights and were examined lightly the next morning. The entertaining Latin dialogues or *Colloquies* of Mathurin Corderius, a friend of Calvin's, presented side by side with English translations in an edition also by Charles Hoole (1657), pleased the pupils because many of them involved the mischief of little boys their own age.

Johnson kept several of his schoolboy Latin grammar books on his shelves for the rest of his life, especially William Lily's *Short Introduction of Grammar*, used widely in schools all over the country since 1542 and (in a revised state) into the nineteenth century as the Eton Grammar. Lily, who became the first high master of St Paul's School in London, presented the parts of speech, conjugations, and other rules of Latin usage in little jingles to aid memorisation, calculated to appeal to children. Shakespeare based his hilarious Latin lesson in Act IV of *The Merry Wives of Windsor* on Lily's *Grammar*. The first section on 'accidence' or parts of speech, part of which at least he appears to have learned at home before he started school, appealed to him so much that he could repeat 141 lines of it 'without any effort of recollection'. Another more difficult section in Lily that deals with verb conjugations, however, he found 'disgusting'. With verbs, though, his mother was a great support in preparing for examinations, for which ever after he was tenderly grateful: 'This was very difficult to me; and I was once very anxious about the next day, when this exercise was to be performed, in which I had failed till I was discouraged. My mother encouraged me, and I proceeded better. When I told her of my good escape, "We often", said she, dear mother! "come off best, when we are most afraid."' 'I did not form them in ugly shapes,' he proudly announced to his mother on another occasion when she asked about his progress with verbs at school. She told him years later how she had delighted in having a boy who 'was forming verbs'. 'These little memorials sooth my mind', he recalled tenderly.[7]

During the Whitsun holidays of 1719 Sarah Johnson packed off her two boys to Birmingham sixteen miles away to be improved culturally and socially by spending a fortnight with her relatives there. At one uncle's house, possibly Samuel Ford's, he was 'much caressed' by his gossipy aunt, 'a good-natured, coarse woman, easy of converse'. His mother was appalled to hear, though, that at one sitting he devoured a huge portion of a boiled leg of mutton. She interpreted it as an early sign of her boy's coarse manners and warned that 'it would hardly ever be forgotten' – not by her, at any rate. Johnson's comment on this was simply that she lived in 'a narrow sphere' and that greater evils eventually replaced her worry over such small annoyances. When the boys moved on to stay with their alcoholic uncle John Harrison the widower, life was not as pleasant but at least there they were centrally located in Birmingham's High Street, next to the Castle Inn which Johnson briefly used as a forwarding address in the early 1730s. The best thing about the Harrison household, though, was his sweet-tempered cousin Sally Ford, his Uncle Cornelius Ford's eldest daughter, who was living there as a housekeeper. It sounds as if he contracted a puppy love for her – 'I used to say she had no fault.' Apparently, soon after the boys returned home, she visited them there and provided Samuel with the first illustration of how sustained concentration could defeat both her and time: 'I was writing at the kitchen windows, as I thought, alone, and turning my head saw Sally dancing. I went on without notice, and had finished almost without perceiving that any time had elapsed. This close attention I have seldom in my whole life obtained.' Sally may have been the reason why Samuel delayed his return home. He wrote to his mother (the letter is lost) with characteristic imperiousness asking for the horses that would fetch him to be delayed until Thursday of the first school week, 'and then, and not till then, they should be welcome to go'. He also mentioned his delight over a new 'rattle' for his whip. His father duly appeared with horses to fetch him and Nathaniel on that Thursday but the main thing he remembered about that was being offended by his father, who insulted his pride by casually telling the ostler within his earshot that he was burdened by having to travel with 'two boys under his care'. 'This offended me,' Johnson remembered. It was not the first or last time Michael Johnson underestimated his eldest son's kindling independence.[8]

More serious was what Samuel found waiting for him back at school. In his absence his comfortable world there had been turned upside down. In one fell swoop his class of eleven – all but one of whose names he remembered in later life – was moved up to the upper school and put under the tutelage of an assistant schoolmaster, the twenty-three-year-old Revd Edward Holbrooke, a recent graduate of Cambridge. Suddenly Samuel and his classmates found themselves in a less friendly, stricter, more demanding environment. Johnson remained sore about the move for the rest of his life, calling Holbrooke 'a peevish and ill-tempered man' when, in fact, others like Dr John Taylor, a classmate and one of Johnson's most intimate lifelong friends, called him 'one of the most ingenious men, best scholars, and best preachers of his age'. Johnson could not agree less, and for him the shift was tantamount to a loss of innocence – 'At this removal I cried.'[9]

Immediately he had to work harder. He found the new regimen of exercises with gerunds and syntax 'very troublesome', but promptly he began to excel. One typical day when his classmates completed the assigned sixteen exercises, he completed twenty-five. With a tact that his genius and drive for superiority had already told him were crucial if he was to remain liked by his classmates, he never showed Holbrooke all of his – 'five lay long after in a drawer in the shop,' he confessed. By then he had discovered his ability to read and work at a tremendous speed when he put his mind to it. His chief adversary, however, was not the exercises but dilatoriness, a lack of concentration, and an inability to sustain work for long. His mother understood this, saying to him once, 'though you could make an exercise in so short a time, I thought you would find it difficult to make them all as soon as you should'.[10]

Holbrooke right away 'raised' the boys from Aesop to Phaedrus (first century AD), who translated many of the Greek fables into Latin. The sheer volume of work Holbrooke set of translating, parsing and memorising from Phaedrus was onerous: 'It was the only book which we learned to the end. In the latter part thirty lines were expected for a lesson.' The resulting lessons in which the boys had to recite lengthily from this work surely were as painful to Holbrooke as to the boys, but still he piled on the work. 'What reconciles masters to long lessons is the pleasure of tasking,' Johnson observed dryly in his *Annals*. After hours of study they made 'little progress'. As Johnson saw it, one of the reasons for that may have been Holbrooke's incompetence, for he made the point of mentioning in his *Annals* that he and a few of the others noticed one day that their schoolmaster had no idea of the meaning of a particular passage in an exercise. The stakes were high because if the boys failed to master a passage they were sent up to the Revd Hunter to be punished. Samuel tolerated this the first time, but 'the second time we complained that we could not get the passage. Being told that we should ask, we informed him that we had asked, and that the assistant would not tell us.' Johnson says 'we' informed the headmaster, but there is a very good chance that he was the only one who defended himself in front of the menacing Hunter, with the very real possibility of a flogging as his reward.[11]

Samuel had little enough respect for his new schoolmaster, but worse was to come when he and others were promoted to Hunter's class at the top of the school either this or early in the next term. His recollections about this stage of his schooling turn deeply negative. In his *Annals* he is surprisingly silent about Hunter; elsewhere he is scathing. Nothing could be plainer about Johnson's Lichfield Grammar School years than that he and Hunter did not, to put it mildly, get on well together. It was a classic case of personality clash: the harsh disciplinarian pitted against a brilliant and ripening rebel of a boy. Hunter was not about to be deterred or defeated by a town boy of ten. On the other hand, he cannot have had anyone like Samuel in his class before: proud, defiant, sullen, reserved, physically handicapped, scarred by disease, prone to strange convulsive movements, and possessed of an amazing memory and quick intelligence. As the battle lines had already been drawn over Holbrooke's alleged incompetence, Hunter could not have been surprised by this boy's independent spirit. Samuel knew that in his new class he was involved in a steep learning curve, but his chief grievance was Hunter's brutality, as he protested to Boswell: 'He used to beat us unmercifully; and he did not distinguish between ignorance and negligence; for he would beat a boy equally for not knowing a thing, as for neglecting to know it.' Particularly galling was Hunter's savage tyranny in asking a boy a question, such as the Latin for a candlestick 'which the boy could not expect to be asked', and then beating him if he could not answer correctly. 'Now, Sir,' Johnson put it to Boswell, 'if a boy could answer every question, there would be no need of a master to teach him.'[12]

Still, the question of how severe a schoolmaster could reasonably and usefully be with his scholars was one that troubled Johnson in later years in a psychological confusion involving painful memories of Hunter and his own conviction that without the threat of corporal punishment of some sort a boy would learn much less. 'Severity must be continued until obstinacy be subdued, and negligence be cured,' he once said. Moreover, in the classroom Samuel knew he was learning more from Hunter than he had ever learned from anyone else. He rejected Boswell's notion that he was prejudiced against Hunter because he was a Scot. Hunter was not a Scot, Johnson shot back, and 'abating his brutality, he was a very good master'. 'My master whipped me very well,' he told a friend, but 'without that, Sir, I should have done nothing.' While Hunter was thrashing the boys 'unmercifully', he added, he would proclaim, 'and this I do to save you from the gallows'. But the flogging had to be just, not vindictive or cruel, and the boys must always understand the reasons for it, which in Hunter's class (according to Johnson) many did not.[13]

The force of Samuel's personality, his large uncouth presence in the classroom, and his academic brilliance made a lasting impression on his classmates as well as on Hunter: 'His favourites used to receive very liberal assistance from him.' His capacity to hear verses and recite them immediately had already become legendary at school. One of his classmates recalls how he once recited eighteen verses to his friend, 'which, after a little pause, he repeated verbatim, varying only one epithet, by which he improved the line'. Apart from academics, there was something of a magnetic influence that he exerted on classmates. Of the handful of schoolfellows cropping up in Johnson's letters years later were the two Congreve brothers, Charles and Richard, sons of the first cousin of the dramatist William Congreve, both of whom went up to Oxford from Lichfield. Charles became a clergyman but ruined his life with drink. In the oppressive and dirty London room where in 1774 Johnson found him 'a man much broken' and tried to revive him with questions of their past, he had 'the appearance of a man wholly sunk into that sordid self-indulgence which disease, real or imaginary, is apt to dictate'. Although Johnson was eager to see him after more than fifty years, he found it hard to believe that this man had no interest whatever in recollecting their precious school years together. Worse than that, in his reclusive 'sullen sensuality' he seemed to have forgotten everything about schooldays. Another visit a few days later to the same grubby room was again deeply disappointing for him. The younger Richard Congreve was another matter. In one of his earliest surviving letters when he was twenty-six, Johnson remembered their 'former familiarity' in school in which they were 'content to love without complimenting each other'. Their friendship's honest simplicity, he added, was exactly in tune with 'our rural retreats, shades unpolluted by flattery and falsehood, thickets where interest and artifice never lay concealed!'[14]

Another of the boys in the class whom Hunter flogged and who eventually rose to Lord Chief Justice, Sir John Wilmot, had a vivid image of Samuel, 'a long, lank, lounging boy' especially targeted by Hunter for idleness. It was his classmate and lifelong steadfast friend Edmund Hector, however, who provided Boswell with a windfall of information about his schooldays. Hector's sister Ann was his first love, for whom he said love 'imperceptibly' dropped out of his head although he saw her again in later years when she was living in Birmingham with her brother and always felt a 'kindness' towards her. Probably Samuel's best friend in school, Hector became a surgeon and lived most of his life in Birmingham, so they had the chance to see each other occasionally after Johnson began annual visits to Lichfield in the 1770s. 'Hector is . . . an old friend,' Johnson wrote just three years before his death, 'the only companion of my childhood that passed through the school with me. We have always loved one another.' In Hector's words, they took pleasure 'sauntering away the hours of vacation in the fields, during which Johnson was more engaged in talking to himself than to his companion.' In a stream of anecdotes for both Boswell and Sir John Hawkins, Johnson's early friend and other major biographer after he died, Hector stressed the effects of Samuel's prodigious academic ability on his classmates: 'As his uncommon abilities for learning far exceeded us, we endeavoured by every boyish piece of flattery to gain his assistance, and three of us, by turns, used to call on him in a morning, on one of whose backs, supported by the other two, he rode triumphantly to school.' There was only one rival for academic supremacy, Theophilus Lowe, eighteen months older and the son of a local plumber, who went on to win a fellowship at St John's College, Cambridge. But Samuel knew his superiority: 'They never thought to raise me by comparing me to any one; they never said, Johnson is as good a scholar as such a one; but such a one is as good a scholar as Johnson; and this was said but of one, but of Lowe; and I do not think he was as good a scholar'.[15]

Even the senior boys looked upon him as 'the head and leader' in the class, who 'acquiesced in whatever he proposed or did'. His only trouble was with Hunter who, according to Hector, took it out on him not only for his 'indolence and procrastination' but also for his 'talking and diverting other boys from their business, by which, perhaps he might hope to keep his ascendancy'. His difficulty in rousing himself to work steadily and systematically was already so acute that Hector remembered his friend's returning to school after long vacations an hour earlier than everyone else to 'begin one of his exercises, in which he purposely left some faults, in order to gain time to finish the rest'. Such dexterity and isolated power of concentration made him a classroom champion in the eyes of the boys but infuriated Hunter. Apart from flogging this Hercules among the boys with apparent regularity, Hunter, as we shall see, was biding his time for a serious slip from this impertinent boy that would enable him to take his revenge. What outraged him was the implied insult to the academic establishment and his own authority by this boy's treating the regimen of school studies in this way and getting away with it through the force of intellect. That the other boys celebrated Samuel could hardly have helped his relationship with the headmaster.[16]

Another classmate, John Taylor, deserves mention. He was second only to Mrs Thrale and Boswell as a correspondent, receiving one hundred known letters from Johnson and, over several decades, developing a unique intimacy with him. They turned out to be an odd couple, given Taylor's unintellectual, rural, inattentive clerical way of life and his fairly obtuse tactlessness at critical times – not to mention that as a strong Whig he was politically a polar opposite to Johnson although, as we shall see, Johnson was far from subscribing to the blind Toryism with which he has traditionally been identified – but Johnson did tell Mrs Thrale that Taylor was 'better acquainted with my *heart* than any man or woman now alive'. It was chiefly to Taylor that Johnson wrote about old classmates not seen for decades: 'How few does the man who has lived sixty years now know of the friends of his youth?' Yet Taylor maddeningly proved to be a relatively arid source for Boswell or any other biographer of Johnson. Another classmate who regrettably never provided any facts about Johnson's years in school (he died in 1776 before Boswell could get to him) but who figures in his life later on was Robert James. James practised medicine and became famous for his widely used fever-reducing James's Powder, a pharmacological compound of antimony and calcium phosphate. Oliver Goldsmith was said by some to have been poisoned by it.[17]

While Samuel was popular with his classmates, he found it difficult to take part in 'ordinary diversions' with them. Hector remembered, though, that 'he used to go upon Stowpool and make a boy pull off his stockings and shoes and put a garter round him and draw him on the ice'. This seems at least as likely, given his size, than the way Boswell told it: 'He took a pleasure in being drawn upon the ice by a boy barefooted, who pulled him along by a garter fixed round him.' During the summers he swam regularly in either Stowe Pool or in the leafy loneliness of the pure Curborough Brook not far from St Chad's Church and below Stowe Mill, where, with great insistence, his father taught him to swim. With a tenderness for these innocent boyhood days, in that nostalgic Latin poem that in the last year of his life he wrote for his old chum Hector, his mind floated back to the 'daytime darkness' of his favourite swimming haunt. Here they are in a translation from the Latin by the poet John Wain:

> Clear as glass the stream still wanders through green fields.
>   Here, as a boy, I bathed
> my tender limbs, unskilled, frustrated, while
> with gentle voice my father from the bank
> taught me to swim.
>   The branches made
> a hiding-place; the bending trees concealed
> the water in a daytime darkness.
>   Now
> hard axes have destroyed those ancient shades:
> the pool lies naked, even to distant eyes.
> But the water, never tiring, still runs on
> in the same channel: once hidden, now overt,
> always flowing.[18]

His father's swimming lessons provided him with one of the essential ways he got exercise and learned to coordinate his large and awkward limbs. He remained a strong and fearless swimmer for the rest of his life, whether in dangerous pools by Oxford or in the cold sea at Brighton (then called Brighthelmstone). Dancing lessons were also laid on to improve his coordination, but his eyesight was not up to them. What apparently his eyesight did not frustrate was a relish for running races and jumping over walls in reckless acts of bravado, especially to impress schoolmates. He remembered all this physical activity with undiluted joy, maintaining that 'a boy at school was the happiest of human beings'. A touching sign of this was his nostalgic return three years before his death to see Levett's Field behind the school. What happened was told by an anonymous writer:

> He had gone round Mr Levett's field (the place where the scholars play) in search of a rail that he used to jump over when a boy, 'and,' says the Doctor in a transport of joy, 'I have been so fortunate as to find it: I stood, said he, 'gazing upon it some time with a degree of rapture, for it brought to my mind all my juvenile sports and pastimes, and at length I determined to try my skill and dexterity; I laid aside my hat and wig, pulled off my coat, and leapt over it twice.' Thus the great Dr Johnson, only three years before his death, was, without hat, wig or coat, jumping over a rail that he had used to fly over when a school-boy.[19]

Only one schoolfellow seems to have become a poet and perhaps been good at making verses in school, Isaac Hawkins Browne the elder, about five years older than Samuel. On the basis of their friendship in school Johnson praised him as a person of great conversational powers, 'the most delightful with whom I ever was in company', with talk 'at once so elegant, so apparently artless, so pure, and so pleasing, it seemed a perpetual stream of sentiment, enlivened by gaiety, and sparkling with images'. Vast praise indeed. But Johnson remembered him also because of his odd behaviour. Late in life in a letter to Susanna Thrale, Mrs Thrale's thirteen-year-old daughter, he illustrated gluttony by describing how Browne, 'of great eminence in the learned and the witty world', disgustingly used to hang pots on his wall as nests in which to catch sparrows which he would then eat. 'I never heard any man speak of any future enjoyment with such contortions of delight as he exhibited when he talked of eating the young ones.' This eccentricity stuck in Johnson's mind perhaps because he thought it hinted at a streak of madness or at least some social maladjustment that typically fascinated him.[20]

In his solitary periods Samuel was certainly busying himself writing poetry by the time he was fifteen or sixteen. A few of his earliest poems and exercises in translation of Horace, Homer and Virgil (often for his own amusement) have come to light – the exercises appear to have been the first poems he attempted. On at least one occasion while he was at this school he won the prize of a guinea for a Latin poem he composed. Hector kept a number of these poems and sent them to Boswell the year after Johnson's death. The earliest were composed after Samuel was in his next school at the age of sixteen, but one, 'On a Daffodil', may well date from towards the end of his time at Lichfield Grammar School. It consists of six quatrains of alternating lilting rhymes conventionally full of allusions to stock pastoral forms celebrating the flower with such lines as 'May the morn's earliest tears on thee be shed,/And thou impearl'd with dew appear more gay.' The last eight lines about time's ravages and the fleeting joys of beauty in nature, woman and poetry are precociously philosophical for a boy of fifteen, three of which read: 'And ah! behold the shriveling blossoms die,/So late admir'd and prais'd, alas! In vain!' . . . Alike must fall the poet and his theme.' Apart from little Sally Ford back in Birmingham and Ann Hector in Lichfield, we know of no other girls in this stage of his life who may have inspired such verses.[21]

4

By the time Samuel was fifteen the seeds had been sown for many of his ideas about children and how they should be educated and treated. Several of them are angry and contentious, in which one may detect bitterness stirring, a distaste for the unquestioned authority of a parent. Often in his comments about education he took the side of children, urging that what adults and educational institutions think is best for them is not always in their best interests. 'Mr Johnson was himself exceedingly disposed to the general indulgence of children' without spoiling them, Mrs Thrale observed, 'and was even scrupulously and ceremoniously attentive not to offend them: he had strongly persuaded himself of the difficulty people always find to erase early impressions either of kindness or resentment, and said, "he should never have so loved his mother when a man, had she not given him coffee she could ill afford, to gratify his appetite as a boy".' The important thing, he felt, was to avoid the cold, negative, even neutral approach in bringing up children: "'My mother . . . was always telling me that I did not *behave* myself properly; that I should endeavour to learn *behaviour*, and such cant: but when I replied, that she ought to tell me what to do, and what to avoid, her admonitions were commonly . . . at an end."' Musing over what he would have done as a parent, he added, 'I would not have set their future friendship to hazard for the sake of thrusting into their heads knowledge of things for which they might not perhaps have either taste or necessity.' 'You teach your daughters the diameters of the planets,' he told Mrs Thrale, 'and wonder when you have done that they do not delight in your company.' With schooling more specifically in mind, he could easily shift into a strident tone. He was 'very solicitous to preserve the felicity of children' and once persuaded Dr Robert Sumner, Headmaster of Harrow, to ease up on the burden of study 'usually given to fill up boys' time during the holidays'.[22]

CHAPTER 4

Two Benefactors

I

IN THE AUTUMN OF 1725 Samuel's mother got it in her mind again to send him (this time apparently without Nathaniel) to spend some time with her flamboyant nephew Cornelius Ford, the son of her brother Joseph. She may simply have wanted to get him out of the house at a time when serious family financial problems had begun to surface. There were also signs of family strife, suggesting that Michael Johnson was undergoing some sort of emotional crisis, aggravated by attacks of melancholia, and that all was not well between him and his wife. In any case, if ever young Samuel had a watershed life-changing experience, this visit to Cornelius was it, the full effects of which his distracted mother could not have anticipated.

One sign that Sarah Johnson was finding things too much at home is that she hired a fifteen-year-old girl, Catherine Chambers, known as 'Kitty', to live with them as a household maid. Mrs Thrale got it wrong that Samuel had learned to read while sitting in Kitty's lap and hearing her tell the story of George and the Dragon, as he was sixteen by the time Kitty arrived. But he quickly conceived a great affection for her and spoke of her over the years with unfailing tenderness. She remained in the house long after his mother and father died, keeping the house and his father's bookshop running as well as taking in lodgers until her death in 1767.[1]

'Kitty' freed Sarah from some of the household drudgery so that she could spend more time in the bookshop organising her husband's affairs, but ultimately she could do little either about Michael's hypochondria or his chaotic way of running his business. This year he was in trouble again over the payment of taxes on his parchment business, an experience embittering his son enough to have fired his vicious definition of 'excise' in the *Dictionary* as 'a hateful tax levied upon commodities, and adjudged not by the common judges of property, but wretches hired by those to whom excise is paid'. Through thick and thin, Michael ended up keeping the business for a total of about thirty years in the course of which much of the moderate wealth he earned from books he lost in parchment. Parchment also distracted him from bookselling, printing, publishing, and selling prints, pocketbooks and other stationery-type items, which alone kept him extremely busy, especially as he had to sell his books at auctions at markets in the region. Scarred by the memories of his father's constant struggle as a country bookseller, Johnson wrote on one occasion that with meagre profits such a bookseller 'cannot live; for his receipts are small, and his debts sometimes bad'. As the years wore on the family finances steadily deteriorated and, according to what Johnson told Hawkins, his father eventually 'in the course of his trade of a bookseller, had become bankrupt', or at least insolvent, so that he had to be bailed out with money or credit by fellow bookseller William Innys, well known for his trade in St Paul's Churchyard in London. It was an act of charity that deeply and lastingly affected Samuel.[2]

2

Johnson's cousin Cornelius has become something of a legendary figure in the life of Samuel Johnson. The son of Sarah's brother Joseph from his first marriage, Cornelius was fifteen years older than his cousin, and was a Cambridge graduate and Fellow of Peterhouse in the early 1720s. He had a lot going for him as a first-class classical scholar, sparkling wit and conversationalist, and heir of a decent family estate when his father died in 1721. He inherited a house in Pedmore, close to Stourbridge, to which he moved from Cambridge, lured to exchange the stimulating but simple life of a Peterhouse don for a more genteel lifestyle in rural Worcestershire. Cornelius imprudently gave up his fellowship when he was thirty, married

the wealthy spinster Judith Crowley thirteen years older than he, and settled down to a reasonably prosperous life, a universe away from his privileged Cambridge existence.

Neither he nor his father by then knew the Lichfield Johnsons well.
It was a fresh breeze of energy and intelligence that blew through the
dull, troubled household of Michael Johnson when Cornelius travelled to
Lichfield one day to talk to Michael about certain financially unfulfilled
provisions of his 1706 marriage settlement – Cornelius's father was a
trustee of the settlement. Michael Johnson may have dreaded his visit as
he knew he owed the trustees £100, but Cornelius surprised them all with
a creative piece of financial management that ended up instead with his
giving Michael £100.

While he was there Cornelius was impressed with this strange, intellectual, curious, well-read, strong-minded prodigy of sixteen hidden within
the household and boundaries of Lichfield. Samuel had potential. Why
not invite him to Pedmore to learn a thing or two about a more worldly
life? It would be amusing. He could also help him with his classical studies. This may well have been arranged at the time of Cornelius's visit, to
Lichfield. Cornelius's polish and brilliance had thrilled Samuel during his
brief visit and the boy was eager to fly to him at Pedmore. Whether
Cornelius took him with him on the spot or he followed soon after, he felt
his luck had turned. In a matter of days he found himself delightfully settled in Cornelius's pleasant house in an entirely different environment
among his mother's prosperous relatives, removed for a while from the
financial worries and bickering of his own family. He arrived in September or October 1725.

Fairly wealthy, aged forty-three, and unexciting, Cornelius's wife had
succeeded in making her husband comfortable and prosperous. He found
amusement elsewhere, in reading and an intense social life of witty conversation and merriment. He cultivated an epicurean existence for which
there had been little scope at Cambridge. In the months just before Samuel's visit he was also awaiting preferment in the Church, which he eventually received at the hands of Philip Stanhope, the fourth Earl of Chesterfield, a friend from his Cambridge days whom almost thirty years later

Johnson would majestically snub on the eve of the publication of his *Dictionary*. Cornelius would soon enough become a prototype of the debauched parson, however, well known as 'Parson Ford', conscientious in many respects about his clerical calling but unable to control his profligacy in a turbulent London world of letters, wit, high society and dissipation. According to one unverifiable claim, made by both Hawkins (who rather blackened his name) and Mrs Thrale, among others, Cornelius even became the model for the presiding drunk parson in Hogarth's satiric painting, *Midnight Modern Conversation* (1731–2). He was also an acquaintance of Alexander Pope. Johnson's own view of his young mentor half a century later was that his abilities, 'instead of furnishing convivial merriment to the voluptuous and dissolute, might have enabled him to excel among the virtuous and the wise'. He told Boswell, 'I never saw him but in the country. I have been told he was a man of great parts; very profligate, but I never heard he was impious.' When the expectant Samuel walked into his house for what Sarah and Michael intended as a few days' visit, Cornelius was conscientious, discreet, lively and charming. There was no stain of profligacy about him.[3]

What happened to Samuel during his idyll with Cornelius and his wife? Nothing less than an expanded view of life's possibilities. Known as 'Neely', Cornelius instructed him in the classics, but that was only part of it. Whenever Johnson spoke of him to Mrs Thrale, she said it was 'always with tenderness, praising his acquaintance with life and manners'. The boy felt flattered, honoured by the flow of advice from a man fifteen years older who sketched out for him images of the way of the world and probably also the current far-off London literary scene. As Pope's translation of the first half of the *Odyssey* had just been published and was a general literary talking point, it is likely that Cornelius thrilled Samuel with first-hand accounts of Pope and his Homeric collaborators, William Broome and Elijah Fenton. Then there was Pope's new edition of Shakespeare, a hugely important publishing event of even more immediate interest to Samuel. Daniel Defoe was also continuing his success with novels, narratives and journals.

There was endless literary and social gossip, too, to which Cornelius was attentive. One thing he could not abide was pedantry, of which he had seen much at Cambridge. Mrs Thrale wrote in her diary: 'Neely Ford, his relation, the profligate parson immortalised by Hogarth, was he told me the man who advised him to study the principles of everything, that a general acquaintance with life might be the consequence of his enquiries. Learn said he the leading Precognita of all things – no need perhaps to turn over leaf by leaf; but grasp the trunk hard only, and you will shake all the branches.' A person who can talk about only one subject or perform in only one area 'is seldom wanted, and perhaps never wished for; while the man of general knowledge can often benefit, and always please'. This would become a code of social and scholastic conduct for Samuel. According to Mrs Thrale, Johnson also cited Cornelius's lecture to him about conversation: avoid questioning another man's excellence in conversation and your 'pretensions as a writer' will be more readily acknowledged. Whether he practised this remains to be seen.[4]

Neither of them left a record of their time together but before they knew it days had passed into seven or eight months. There were excursions to be taken, such as to the Lyttelton estate at Hagley Park where he may have met members of the family, especially the Whig first Baron (George Lyttelton) – a close friend of Pope and later an eminent political figure whose controversial biography Johnson wrote more than half a century later. Johnson's friend of later years, Thomas Percy, wrote of 'colloquial disputes' the boy is supposed to have had at Hagley with Lyttelton, his exact contemporary, from which he allegedly conceived a prejudice against him – a doubtful assertion considering the generally Whiggish Stourbridge-Pedmore-Hagley environment he was enjoying at the time with Cornelius. Contemplating a visit to Hagley in 1771, Johnson mused that the experience would give him 'the opportunity of recollecting past times' wandering through the cooling shades and sacred springs of Hagley Park and 'recalling the images of sixteen, and reviewing my conversations with poor Ford'. Here he would have been not the tradesman's son but the guest of a respected member of Worcestershire society. A native of the area, years later Percy wrote that Samuel was 'admitted into the best company of the place, and had no common attention paid to his conversation; of which remarkable instances were long remembered'. He stayed for the autumn and winter and through the spring, no fewer than nine months, not returning to Lichfield until Whitsuntide, an expectant and dramatically altered young man.[5]

Unknown to him and his parents, though, throughout all those months there was a ticking bomb in the person of the ominous Hunter. Hunter greeted Johnson on his return to Lichfield in early June 1726 with the news that after more than half a year of truancy he was not about to let him back into the school as if nothing had happened. Hunter apparently took his absence as an insult to his teaching and a flouting of the school's authority. It is tempting to read his defiance as a repayment for the irritation and frustration this precocious, stubborn day pupil had caused him. The end result was that the Johnsons had to scramble quickly to find another school. They failed to get him in at Newport Grammar School in Shropshire, but with Cornelius (who probably felt responsible for Samuel's dismissal from Lichfield Grammar School) and his half-brother Gregory Hickman's timely intervention – he was a former governor of the school – Samuel was quickly admitted as a boarder at the Stourbridge Grammar School. It was not a bad turn of events for the boy. Now he could be near Pedmore and his new mentor for months on end. After only a few days in Lichfield, he returned to Stourbridge to enroll in his new school. He began there after the Whitsuntide holidays in 1726.

The headmaster of Stourbridge Grammar School was the Revd John Wentworth, a bachelor, who had been in charge there since 1704. A good scholar, he was a far cry from the highly disciplined, organised taskmaster Samuel was used to in Hunter. The agreement, according to Thomas Percy, was that the sixteen-year-old would take on some teaching of the younger boys as a type of pupil-teacher. Wentworth was not kind to him, however. 'Mr Wentworth was a very able man, but an idle man, and to me very severe,' Johnson told Boswell, 'but I cannot blame him much. I was then a big boy; he saw I did not reverence him; and that he should get no honour by me. I had brought enough with me, to carry me through; and all I should get at his school would be ascribed to my own labour, or to my former master. Yet he taught me a great deal.' All in all, the educational

value of his months at the school was minimal, although he was surprised
to find there a good collection of folios of Greek and Latin classics, divinity, geography and history that occupied much of his time. He summed up
his education at Stourbridge and Lichfield schools by remarking to Percy
that at one he had learned much in the school but nothing from the master, at the other much from the master and nothing in the school.[6]

3

Whatever Johnson may have gained or wasted from his months at school
in Stourbridge, he made some good use of his time there to write verses.
Among the earliest of his attempts at poetry, they reveal that from the
start he showed a good ear for the music of verse, readiness to experiment
with English poetic forms, and sensitivity to rhythmic smoothness. Most
of the eleven poems that have survived from this period are school exercises in translating Homer, Horace and Virgil, written presumably more
under the watchful eye of Wentworth than in the privacy of his room, and
they must have been thought impressive enough to merit keeping by his
schoolmaster whose nephew sent them to Boswell after Johnson's death.
Most of the poetry being published at the time by Pope and others was in
heroic couplets, satirical or pastoral, focused on society, and was full of
classical allusions and elegant diction. Johnson's verses were conventional
enough in their elegance, rhythm and imagery, largely unaffected by private impulses, but on the whole unspectacular. Johnson himself did not
think well enough of them to merit revision and publication, but they offer a sprinkling of biographical glimpses.

While the poems are stocked with pastoral references, emotions and
other traditional devices of song, they also reveal his lyrical appreciation
for the lusciousness of nature and landscape – what one would expect
from a boy who has grown up walking solitarily through the shades and
meadows of Staffordshire and reading Virgil, Theocritus and Ovid amid
the cooling midsummer breezes. And Wentworth showed insight into his
character – as an impetuous boy in speech who had to slow down and
consider where his behaviour was leading him – by asking him to trans-

late a short poem, 'Festina Lente' with its ethical, moral impulse 'to make haste slowly': 'Observe your steps; be carefull to command/Your passions; guide the reins with steady hand/ . . . Rashness! thou spring from whence misfortunes flow!' It is not known how physically big he was at this time but his large frame must already have filled out with a heftiness resembling his father, and his awkwardness have been aggravated by gauche movements: 'Observe your steps . . . Nor down steep cliffs precipitately move.'[7]

One poem he wrote for himself was a love poem, an 'amorous lay', to an eighteen-year-old Quaker girl named Olivia Lloyd whom he met in Stourbridge, probably at Cornelius's house since she was his niece. She stirred Johnson's fancy with her own love of the classics. Alas, the poem has been lost. Nothing came of that young love and, in any case, after six months he was expelled from school. Hector recalled mysteriously that Samuel left precipitously, 'a difference arising between his Master and him about the purity of a phrase in his exercise'. Was the offending passage an overly erotic piece of translation? Whatever it was, it had to be a stiff, heated disagreement to conclude in Samuel being sent packing in November 1726. This was the second school to dismiss him in the space of six months. His independent spirit and contentiousness were bearing fruit in a way that were seriously beginning to threaten his education and life-prospects. He was now fed up with school and disinclined to think about it after he left Stourbridge – a disinclination that stayed with him for years. 'As we come forward into life,' he confessed to Hector in 1756, 'we naturally turn back now and then upon the past. I now think more upon my schooldays than I did when I had just broken loose from a Master. Happy is he that can look back upon the past with pleasure'.[8]

4

Samuel was suddenly trapped again in his dull family life in anticlimactic Lichfield, wrenched from the heady social environment Cornelius had opened up for him. Nothing much had changed at home except for the welcome presence of the young housekeeper Kitty Chambers. His father's finances continued to deteriorate. His brother was still at school, though even if he had not been the two had so little in common that it is doubtful they would have been good company for each other. John Taylor was finishing up at the Grammar School and soon to go off to university. Edmund Hector was purposefully studying and not as available as in former times. Samuel was now seventeen and too old to start at another school. He knew too much and was too argumentative for the average schoolmaster. Sending him to university was financially out of the question and he showed little urge to do anything in particular except read. It was time for him to earn some money and help with the family finances. Such an energetic, powerfully built young man even with defective eyesight could certainly pull his weight.

The obvious answer was to help his father in the book business, and perhaps even in the parchment factory. His father 'took him home, probably with a view to bring him up to his own trade,' Hawkins reasons, 'for I have heard Johnson say, that he himself was able to bind a book.'⁹ Many years later, when he was an old man, Johnson actually spotted a book on the bookshop shelves that he had bound during this period. This was a skill he seemed not to have forgotten when he bound a book or two for the Thrales fifty years later in their summer house. He also worked in the bookshop itself, but the problem was that he found selling books or anything else in the shop, from children's toys to sundry types of stationery, excruciatingly boring. He preferred reading the books to selling them, disinclined to have anything to do with the retail side of the business either in the shop or at any of the several markets in nearby towns where his father kept a stall on market days.

One of the more famous episodes in Johnson's life may have its source around this time. When his father asked him to assist him at his stall in Uttoxeter, twelve miles north of Lichfield, he refused. If this did not anger his exasperated father, it certainly increased tension in the household. Everyone was busy trying to make ends meet and here was the eldest son lying about day after day at home, not doing much of anything useful to anyone. As it turned out, not going to Uttoxeter was an adolescent decision and moment that rooted itself in his accumulating guilt. The year he died he told a young clergyman that while 'he could not in general accuse himself of having been an undutiful son', his pride on this occasion pained him so much that (according to one source) on the fiftieth anniversary of his disobedience he forced himself to perform an action of contrition: 'A few years ago, I desired to atone for this fault; I went to Uttoxeter in very bad weather, and stood for a considerable time bareheaded in the rain, on the spot where my father's stall used to stand. In contrition I stood, and I hope the penance was expiatory.'[10] The scene has been pictorially represented and cited so many times that it has become certified as one of the great images of Johnson's troubled soul.

Johnson admitted to Boswell that he was idle, scolded by his father for 'his want of steady application' and not having a 'settled plan of life', but later he backtracked, 'I would not have you think I was doing nothing then.' His father may have been happier if his reading had been more systematic, pragmatically leading to something, but he was reading omnivorously and impulsively. William Shaw, one of Johnson's best early biographers and a young clerical friend and scholar from the 1770s, tracked down boyhood friends and acquaintances who had seen Samuel reading either in school or his father's shop. He wrote this about young Samuel's eccentric tenacity as a reader which rendered him oblivious to everything around him, almost as if he had lapsed into a hypnotic or drug-induced state:

> Even in the act of devouring the sublimest passages of ancient literature . . . his perseverance was so singular and exemplary that all attempts to divert him from the task assigned, or which he assigned to himself, were uniformly without effect. [There was] a rapacity with which he commenced his primary pursuit [reading], and grasped at every object of classical intelligence . . .
>
> He is said, when a mere school-boy, to have read indefatigably, and probably picked up no despicable acquaintance with books, by occasionally attending his father's shop. Here he was, not infrequently, so absorbed by his predilection for the classical lore of antiquity, as entirely to neglect the business he had in trust. Being

often chid for disobliging some of his father's customers and friends, in this manner, he replied with great shrewdness, *that to supersede the pleasures of reading, by the attentions of traffic, was a task he never could master.*[11]

The bookshop was like a huge biblio-cabinet of curiosities, a bookish bower of bliss tempting him into divergent and crisscrossing intellectual, cultural, historical, literary, religious, scientific and geographic paths. His reading took him everywhere but at the same time (in his father's eyes) nowhere. 'Sir,' he said to Boswell, 'in my early years I read very hard. It is a sad reflection, but a true one, that I knew almost as much at eighteen as I do now. My judgement, to be sure, was not so good; but, I had all the facts.' From twelve to eighteen, he told his friend Bennet Langton, was his 'great period of *study*'. He read not merely entertaining works, 'not [only] voyages and travels, but all literature, Sir, all ancient writers, all manly: though but little Greek, only some Anacreon and Hesiod; but in this ir-regular manner . . . I had looked into a great many books, which were not commonly known at the universities, where they seldom read any books but what are put into their hands by their tutors.' His sweeping imagina-tion did not exclude books on metaphysics either. And if he hunted, as he did once, through the upper shelves of the shop for an apple his brother had hidden there, he might happen on a large folio of Petrarch or some other classic to pull down and devour pretty much on the spot. With a vivid imagination and mounting intellectual curiosity he went on turning the pages through the following year, 'roaming at large in the fields of lit-erature' to his father's irritation and doubtless to customers' occasional an-noyance.[12]

Thomas Percy's psychological take on what seemed to him (from John-son's description) an immoderate amount of isolation while he read 'ro-mances of chivalry' and 'extravagant fictions' was that it sowed the seeds of Johnson's restlessness and overactive imagination, bearing fruit shortly in severe melancholia. On top of this was the emptiness of Lichfield, at least compared to Stourbridge life, and the gnawing frustration of seeing school friends less able than he go on to Oxford and Cambridge. He was unhappy and standing still, a dangerous physical condition and state of mind for him. There was, however, a vital lifeline, the second in his life after Cornelius, at close hand over in the cathedral close, a bachelor almost thirty years older than he, Gilbert Walmesley.

A lawyer by training, Walmesley was one of the richest and most distinguished citizens of Lichfield, then Registrar (Judge) of the ecclesiastical court, whose father had been chancellor of the diocese. He lived in the most imposing house in town, the spacious Bishop's Palace, one of a series of beautiful ecclesiastic buildings on Dean's Walk next to the Deanery on the north side of the small cathedral close, which he had the opportunity to rent because up to 1868 the bishops of Coventry and Lichfield chose to live instead at Eccleshall in Staffordshire. Like Cornelius he was urbane and sophisticated, with access to the best society in the area. The palace allowed him graciously to entertain men and women of significance, people who could be counted on to generate sparkling conversation of a high order, much of it literary and political. He was also an enthusiastic book-collector and in the palace had the perfect place to house his fine library. Indeed, he bought many of his books at Michael Johnson's bookshop to which he could quickly walk, past Minster Pool, down Dam Street, and around a couple of corners to Market Place.

At the shop in the closing months of 1726, Walmesley noticed Samuel, really noticed him, for the first time. What particularly caught his attention is unknown – perhaps he caught the drift of his comments on certain books and simply liked the boy and became concerned that he was wasting time, going nowhere – but before long he invited him to the palace. It was a fateful act of social patronage. Johnson spoke for himself regarding Walmesley in an uncharacteristically celebrative passage from his *Life of Edmund Smith* more than fifty years later:

> Of Gilbert Walmesley, thus presented to my mind, let me indulge myself in the remembrance. I knew him very early; he was one of the first friends that literature procured me, and I hope that at least my gratitude made me worthy of his notice.
>
> He was of an advanced age, and I was only not a boy; yet he

never received my notions with contempt . . . His studies had
been so various that I am not able to name a man of equal knowledge. His acquaintance with books was great; and what he did not
immediately know he could at least tell where to find. Such was
his amplitude of learning and such his copiousness of communication that it may be doubted whether a day now passes in which
I have not some advantage from his friendship.[13]

This is dramatic praise, a gesture of gratitude deeply felt. For the seventeen-year-old the Bishop's Palace may as well have been the pot at the end
of a rainbow, so close yet so elusive; to be invited there was for him an unimaginable privilege. The fact that to some extent he made it into that society in town was especially sweet because for all his life it had been denied to him and his family.

What made Walmesley, in addition to his learning, encouragement,
and patience, so appealing and valuable to the young man was that in his
younger years he had 'mingled with the world without exemption from its
vices or its follies'. He differed from Cornelius, however, in that he 'had
never neglected the cultivation of his mind; his belief in Revelation was
unshaken; his learning preserved his principles: he grew first regular, and
then pious'. Walmesley was a perfect mentor for the young protégé: lively,
open, 'copious in communication', and worldly, yet his breadth of scholarship kept him open-minded and true to his Christian principles. It could
have been an irrecoverable problem, however, that politically and socially
Walmesley was also a Whig, which in his *Dictionary* Johnson briskly defined as a radical 'faction' and illustrated with passages suggesting that
Whigs were threats to Church, Crown, and the order of the state. Johnson acknowledged Walmesley was one, 'with all the virulence and malevolence of his party', but neither he nor Walmesley allowed it to get in the
way: 'Difference of opinion did not keep us apart. I honoured him, and he
endured me,' Johnson wrote.[14]

Samuel may have been disappointed that Walmesley was a Whig but
that would not have been a party-political disappointment. Walmesley
was part of a powerful social and intellectual Whig world that, in fact,

Samuel would have respected. All his life he admired this kind of company, people who were fashionable, well-informed, amicable, intelligent and forward-looking. The Whigs were the party of power and wealth, and had been since 1688, associated equally with innovative business as well as with inherited aristocratic privilege. The Whig and Tory parties were not then, as now, divided by the politics of right and left, of an industrial society that pitches labouring classes against the money-makers and affluent, but rather by attitudes to the past. The Whigs were linked with irreverence for the past while the Tories treasured it culturally, artistically, poetically and institutionally. That is why Johnson thought of himself as a Tory, not unhesitatingly sympathetic to the mighty and wealthy as much as attuned to the practices and sentiments of simpler townspeople and their worlds, to Christian virtues and associations, and to the beauties and solidity of a rural market town like Lichfield. The high and mighty Whigs were breathtaking to the teenager who, with Cornelius's help, had begun to shed his provinciality. Furthermore, Johnson as a boy and adolescent did not live in a closed and sheltered world of Tories. As Donald Greene, the historian of Johnson's politics, has urged, 'There was little of the starry-eyed about eighteenth-century politics in Staffordshire; Lichfield was far from being a Tory stronghold; and from his earliest days Johnson seems to have had at least as many and as opinionated Whig friends, acquaintances, and relations as Tory.'[15]

Johnson's father's Toryism was of little or no importance or influence on him. Greene frames Johnson's position in this society perfectly in these balanced words: 'Had he been a lesser person, he might have succumbed to their attraction and to the comfortable security of a ready-made intellectual pattern, accustoming himself to mouth their facile clichés . . . Something like this is, after all, what does happen to the majority of "bright young men". But as it was, Johnson could never stifle the acute awareness that he was not as they were, and never could be.' He knew poverty and deprivation as they had not, and he would give Walmesley's Bishop's Palace circle a run for their money just as he had the Stourbridge-Pedmore-Hagley circle. He drew the urgency and strength of his arguments, just as in the future he would his political ideas in general, from 'the world of small, ordinary, suffering, inarticulate people', from the disadvantaged to whom he was always drawn. He was not then, nor would be in maturity, a blind and retrogressive Tory. Walmesley became a model to Samuel of how an older man can nurture and assist a younger person struggling to develop self-respect and a clear persona. 'At this man's table,' Johnson remembered with pleasure, 'I enjoyed many cheerful and instructive hours, with companions such as are not often found.' Walmesley was a gracious, learned, worthy debating partner and friend. That was enough for him.[16]

One of the companions whom Walmesley welcomed to the palace was Samuel's schoolfellow Robert James, already mentioned as the inventor of the notorious James powder, but there was another, David Garrick, a boy eight years younger than Samuel who would become the most famous actor in eighteenth-century England and one of the greatest entertainers in all of Europe. 'Davy' had grown up in Lichfield, attended the Grammar School, and had already been 'taken on' by Walmesley when Samuel first made his appearance at the Bishop's Palace. The son of an army captain, his family was poor but genteel and, unlike Samuel's family, had social access to the finer citizens of Lichfield, including Walmesley. There is no evidence that he and Samuel knew each other before meeting at the palace because Davy began at the school two years after Samuel left. The contrast between them could scarcely have been greater. Davy was friendly, amazingly vivacious, and small for his age, with something of a tendency to be cheeky, while Samuel was 'long, lank, and lounging', awkward, melancholic and argumentative. Garrick endeared himself to just about everyone. Walmesley saw the promise in him even at the age of nine, delighting in his 'smart repartees and frolicsome actions'. At some point during this period when he had the run of the palace, Davy previewed his early thespian inclinations by precociously staging George Farquhar's rollicking *The Recruiting Officer*, most probably in the large drawing room of the palace. It is possible that Samuel was in the audience and near enough the action so that his poor eyesight and hearing did not prejudice him against the play, as it tended to do later towards the stage generally – there is no evidence of his ever wearing eyeglasses. What we do know is that the two young men became friends for life though it was an uneasy relationship, with Walmesley as a common, warm, secure point of reference in their youth to which they both looked back with gratitude and warmth.

Anna Seward, the spirited poetess who was more than thirty years younger than Johnson and turned against him partly because of what she felt was his rough rudeness, put a different spin on his tutelage under Walmesley. She came to live in the Bishop's Palace when her father Thomas Seward, Canon of Lichfield, had moved into the house with his family after Walmesley's death in 1751. Indeed, Johnson on several visits to Lichfield in later years made a point of visiting the Sewards in the palace, from which she gradually formed her opinion of him as liberal and compassionate but conversationally abusive. After a point, nothing she said about Johnson was ever likely to be offered without a dash of venom – a great shame since she was so well placed to learn about Johnson's youth and must have had a huge fund of anecdotes picked up through the years. Boswell's eventual hostility towards her and her prejudice for the most part ruled her out of his biography of Johnson as a credible witness. But it is interesting to place her reading of Samuel's introduction to the palace society alongside the dominant biographies that appeared shortly after his death. In spite of her bias against Johnson – which may also incidentally have had something to do with the fact that her mother was the daughter of Samuel's headmaster John Hunter and that she may have heard of her grandfather's irritation with this 'huge, over-grown, misshapen, probably dirty stripling' – she wrote:

> Within the walls which my father's family inhabits, in this very dining-room, the munificent Mr Walmesley, with the taste, the learning and the liberality of Maecenas, administered to rising genius the kind nutriment of attention and praise . . .
>
> Two or three evenings every week Mr Walmesley called the stupendous stripling and his livelier companion David Garrick, who was a few years younger, to his own plentiful board. There, in the hours of convivial gaiety, did he delight to wave every restraint of superiority formed by rank, affluence, polished manners and

the dignity of advanced life; and there, 'as man to man, as friend to friend', he drew forth the different powers of each expanding spirit, by the vivid interchange of sentiment and opinion, and by the cheering influence of generous applause.

This was magnanimous of Walmesley the Whig, she added, because Samuel came to the palace with a baggage of 'furious' pro-Jacobitism imbibed from 'his master's [Hunter's] absurd zeal for the forfeit rights of the house of Stuart'. This specific claim was not, so far as we know, made by anyone else who knew Samuel in Lichfield, including the communicative Hector, but she used it to construct her portrait of both his argumentative insolence and Walmesley's infinite patience within the palace walls. 'I am told [that] even at that early period of life,' she continued, Johnson 'maintained his opinions, on every subject, with the same sturdy, dogmatical and arrogant fierceness with which he now overbears all opposition to them in company'. How amazing therefore, she concluded, that Walmesley's love of genius 'induced him to suffer insolent sallies from the son of an indigent bookseller' concerning the risky topic of the legitimacy of the Hanoverian succession.[17]

Notwithstanding Johnson's apparent failure in his maturity to impress Anna Seward favourably on visits to the palace, Boswell makes the point that it was the company of women in particular at the palace which proved to be of huge importance to young Samuel. At Stourbridge he had recently been exposed to genteel women but at the palace he had a more sustained opportunity to talk to them and observe their grace and 'good breeding'. Boswell's point is that exposure to this class of women courtesy of Walmesley even as early as 1726 must be weighed against the contemporary reputation of Johnson as painfully awkward in society and of 'coarse and ferocious manners' and temper as well as appearance. Walmesley plucked him out of a relatively isolated existence in his father's bookshop and exposed him to the softening influences of happy female society, and for the rest of his life in all kinds of polite society he was both attracted to women and found attractive by them because of the flattering notice he took of them. Mrs Thrale noticed his keen interest in and awareness of what women wore. On entering a crowded room he invariably would make for the women first. The great Shakespearean editor George Steevens observed that he 'delighted in the company of women' and Boswell added, 'Some of the ladies have assured me, they recollected him well when a young man, as distinguished for his complaisance' or desire of pleasing. This urge sprang partly from a highly sexed nature, about which there will be more later, but more characteristically it was due to his capacity, learned early, to understand and enjoy female company. Frances Reynolds, sister of the painter Sir Joshua Reynolds, stated flatly that he placed 'a higher value upon female friendship than perhaps men'. There were several women in Lichfield alone who appreciated this in him and whom he made a point of visiting on his several trips there over the last twenty-five years of his life.[18]

Walmesley and the Bishop's Palace, debate, extensive reading, labour in his father's bookshop, and no small amount of frustration as he waited – for what he did not know – comprised the pattern of his days during these fallow years of 1726–8. Jonathan Swift published his caustic ironic romance satire *Gulliver's Travels* in 1726; in 1727 George I died (succeeded by his son George II), as did Sir Isaac Newton, and Spanish forces laid siege to the English garrison at Gibraltar; and in 1728 John Gay came out with his triumphant satiric-comic ballad opera *The Beggar's Opera* and Pope, already Samuel's great model of the professional author, published his scathing bombshell *The Dunciad*, a comprehensive mock-heroic satire of literary 'Dulness'. The world was moving ahead excitingly and England's great age of satire had dawned, but for Samuel the future did not look so bright.

Part Two

Despondency and Hope

CHAPTER 5

Oxford: Wielding a
Scholar's Weapon

I

SUDDENLY ANOTHER LIGHT APPEARED unexpectedly on Johnson's constricted horizon that had nothing to do with Walmesley. Sarah Johnson's rich cousin Elizabeth Harriotts, to whom in desperation she had taken Samuel for medical advice regarding his eyesight, died in February 1728 and left her a legacy. Mrs Harriotts specified that Michael Johnson was not to get his hands on any of it. In addition to sheets, pillow cases, and pewter dishes and plates, the joyful surprise was £40 (about £4000 today) she received 'for her own separate use'. The legacy was generous enough to make Michael in 'the humility of distress' change his mind about 'our good cousin Harriotts'. He could have plowed the money into the black hole of his faltering business, but since this was not possible they decided to use it to send their brilliant and restless son to university and hope that a scholarship or some other source of money would materialise in the course of his first year to enable him to remain there for the remaining two. With some prudence the money would surely pay for a year. They decided on Oxford partly because one of Samuel's school chums at Lichfield, Andrew Corbet, was already there and offered vaguely to help pay for his friend's expenses in order to have him there as a companion. As it happened, Corbet left Oxford only a few weeks after Johnson arrived, and with him disappeared his promise of help. Another likely reason for choosing Oxford was that Johnson's godfather, Dr Swynfen, who had recently moved his medical practice from Lichfield to Birmingham, was a Pembroke College graduate and possibly urged that college on the Johnsons. Pembroke it was to be.

The scene was set for the first great chapter in the life of the nineteen-year-old, one the family hoped would determine his career and unlock all the prosperity and distinction that promised to flow from it. On the morning in late October 1728 when he and his father mounted horses for the long ride to Oxford, there may well have been a small gathering to see him off: his two mentors Dr Swynfen and Walmesley cheering him on, his brother eager to have him out of the house again, his mother beaming with pride, interested neighbours struck by the uniqueness or novelty of having this unusual young man of limited means, who had not even completed his formal schooling, going off to study at a major centre of learning, and, not least, Dame Oliver with an offering of gingerbread in hand telling him he was the best pupil she ever had. He never forgot her remark at that memorable moment, as Boswell recalls: 'He delighted in mentioning this early compliment: adding, with a smile, that "this was as high a proof of his merit as he could conceive".'[1] With the clutch of books he had selected following later by wagon, he and his proud father set off for the academic Promised Land.

2

As a Catholic, Alexander Pope could not matriculate at Oxford, but in the autumn of 1717 at the age of twenty-five he caught the magic of the place as he rode up to it for a short visit with a friend. There is a romantic exultation about his description, in his case vicarious, which Johnson may well himself have felt as he and his father first caught sight of the approaching horizon of dreaming ancient spires:

> About a mile before I reached Oxford, all the bells toll'd, in different notes; the clocks of every college answered one another; and told me in a deeper, some in a softer voice, that it was eleven a

clock. All this was no ill preparation to the life I have led since; among these old walls, venerable galleries, stone porticos, studious walks and solitary scenes of the university, I wanted nothing but a black gown and a salary, to be as mere a bookworm as any there.[2]

The Gothic medieval beauty and mystery of Oxford that Pope was so acutely attuned to on this visit, especially in the evening or by moonlight, was something that Johnson would have plenty of time later to explore. Now the business at hand was to make for Pembroke College, take possession of his room, meet his tutor, and seek out one of the pro-Vice-Chancellors in order to matriculate and pay his fees. He entered the university on 31 October, though for some reason he did not formally matriculate until 16 December, apparently 'a delay unusual and against the University statutes'. He did have to hand over seven pounds immediately to the Bursar, John Radcliffe, as a 'caution' or deposit.

On their first night he and his father met both his appointed tutor Revd William Jorden and William Adams, then a young fellow at the college who became Johnson's intimate and lifelong friend and a fertile source of anecdotes about him. Adams, who was also educated at Pembroke and its Master from 1775, told Boswell about this first encounter. 'On that evening', Boswell wrote, Johnson's father 'who had anxiously accompanied him, found means to have him introduced to Mr Jorden, who was to be his tutor in Classics. His father seemed very full of the merits of his son, and told the company he was a good scholar, and a poet, and wrote Latin verses.' At first both Adams and Jorden were taken aback by the physical appearance of this large, muscular, scarred, short-sighted young man subject to odd, abrupt movements, but they recovered when they heard him speak: 'His figure and manner appeared strange to them; but he behaved modestly, and sat silent, till upon something which occurred in the course of conversation, he suddenly struck in and quoted the Roman grammarian Macrobius; and thus he gave the first impression of that more extensive reading in which he had indulged himself.' Over the past two lonely years he had foraged in the fields of literature and added to his mental storehouse; now was the time to reap the harvest. He felt his powers: 'When I came to Oxford, Dr Adams, now Master of Pembroke College, told me, I was the best qualified for the University that he had ever known come there.'[3]

3

There was never much chance that he would fit into Oxford academic and social life quietly. Right away he disturbed some of the equanimity and tempo of Pembroke. At his first morning tutorial he quickly discovered that his tutor Revd Jorden could not teach him much. He once remarked rudely that his tutor's lecture on logic was not worth half the twopence fine he incurred for missing it. 'He was a very worthy man, but a heavy man, and I did not profit much by his instructions. Indeed, I did not attend him much. The first day after I came to college, I waited upon him, and then stayed away four.' This was insolent enough in an undergraduate who had barely had time to unpack, especially as Jorden was a senior fellow, having been appointed Viceregent of the College just a few weeks before Johnson arrived. The Viceregent was nominated by the Master to act as his deputy and perform with all his authority when he was absent from college. When Jorden mildly confronted Johnson about his repeated absences after he finally reappeared, instead of backing off he rubbed it in with an arrogance of which he seemed unaware: 'I answered I had been sliding [skating] in Christ-Church meadow. And this I said with as much *nonchalance* as I am now talking to you. I had no notion that I was wrong or irreverent to my tutor.' Mrs Thrale noted that 'he laughed very heartily at the recollection of his own insolence'. Boswell was impressed. 'Fortitude of mind,' he called it. No, Johnson replied, it was 'stark insensibility', the words of a self-centred, arrogant youth.[4]

According to Thomas Warton, who heard it from Johnson himself twenty-six years later, Jorden summoned him ominously to his chambers. By then the truant had had time to reflect a little on his cheekiness. 'I expected a sharp rebuke for my idleness, and went with a beating heart,' but

he found Jorden offering only warmth and understanding, probably conscious of the limitations as a scholar that his new charge had spotted so
speedily: 'When we were seated, he told me he had sent for me to drink a
glass of wine with him, and to tell me, he was *not* angry with me for missing his lecture.' 'This was, in fact, a most severe reprimand,' Johnson recalled uncomfortably almost thirty years later. 'Some more of the boys
were then sent for, and we spent a very pleasant afternoon.' While that
evening salvaged Johnson's regard for Jorden's character, it appears not to
have had any effect on his attendance, although in a letter to Boswell on 12
July 1786, Adams denied Mrs Thrale's assertion that Johnson ignored
most of Jorden's lectures.[5]

Jorden stayed at Oxford until mid-December 1729 when he was in-
ducted to a clerical living about one hundred miles away. His students
then seem to have been passed on to the young Fellow William Adams
who humbly called himself his 'nominal' tutor and admitted to Boswell
that this wilful prodigy they had allowed into their midst 'was above my
mark' – a compliment which, when Johnson heard it, made his eyes flash
'with grateful satisfaction'.[6] 'That was liberal and noble,' he exclaimed. Adams explained that Johnson maintained a warm feeling the rest of his life
for Jorden's paternal care, whose death in 1739 he 'much regretted' and 'for
whom he seemed to retain the greatest regard'. 'Whenever a young man
becomes Jorden's pupil,' Johnson said, 'he becomes his son', though one
less charitable observer called him 'a noted pupil monger'. To Mrs Thrale
he expressed a similar affection for Jorden: 'That creature would defend
his pupils to the last: no young lad under his care should suffer for committing slight improprieties, while he had breath to defend, or power to
protect them. If I had sons to send to college, Jorden should have been
their tutor.' As we shall see, Adams never taught Johnson anything as a
tutor. Had he done so, Boswell wrote, 'his equal temper, mild disposition,
and politeness of manners, might have insensibly softened the harshness
of Johnson, and infused into him, those more delicate charities, those
petites morales, in which, it must be confessed, our great moralist was more
deficient than his best friends could fully justify'.[7]

4

Johnson soon realised he had not landed in the lap of a golden age of learning and scholarship. There were able, even brilliant, tutors but glaringly lacking were rules governing the degree of involvement of a tutor with a student, so students could easily go astray and tutors readily become lazy about their teaching and scholarship. Another flaw in the system was that many tutors were biding their time for clerical preferment, like Jorden himself, and could not generate much enthusiasm for the academic or even pastoral imperatives in their appointments. One historian has called the eighteenth century at Oxford 'The Great Depression', although others have maintained that the university was not as moribund as has often been maintained, with significant pieces of scholarship being published and a few colleges sustaining high standards of teaching. Certain scholars and dons like Thomas Warton were remarkably productive, but they were the exception, and even Warton had little taste for lecturing, sequestered as he was at either Trinity College or the Bodleian and preferring his 'ale and tobacco, and the riverside watermen and his cronies in the taverns'. He even wrote a poem, *Panegyric on Oxford Ale*, celebrating the libation as 'Sweet Helicon of logic'. On entering Warton's 'very elegant apartment' at Trinity College with Johnson in 1776, Boswell was surprised because he 'had heard that Tom kept low drunken company, and I expected to see a confused dusty room and a little, fat, laughing fellow. In place of which I found a good, sizable man, with most decent clothes and darkish periwig, one who might figure as a canon.' Richard West, a friend of the poet Thomas Gray who found himself at Christ Church in 1735, described Oxford as 'a country flowing with syllogisms and ale, where Horace and Virgil are equally unknown.'[8]

Students contracted their own peculiar brand of 'brisk intemperance' from the way the university ran itself. To begin with, they were admitted in a rigidly hierarchical manner that tended to foster its own breed of class consciousness and stifle creativity. Johnson entered Pembroke as a commoner, the largest group of students, ostensibly under the greatest supervision by assigned tutors and, led by the heads or scholars of their colleges who received special grants, likely to do the most serious academic work. They had to pay their own way and as sons of relatively poor families had severely limited budgets with which they had to cover their fees and expenses such as battels (college bills for food and other services), all of which were modest enough so that Johnson's forty pounds potentially could last him for a year. Commoners had to toe the line in all sorts of ways. They were required to attend lectures as well as chapel. If they were caught absenting themselves from academic duties with any kind of regularity they were punished with 'impositions' (written exercises). They had to eat dinner in hall, keep certain hours in college instead of whiling away the hours in ale or coffee houses where they were in danger of being hunted down by roving proctors, and dress appropriately for various occasions. Their compulsory daily dress in college and out in town was a simple ankle-length, sleeveless black gown of stuff decorated plainly with braided black streamers. Simple as it was and very soon looking grubby and worn, one wonders whether young Johnson fresh from Lichfield nevertheless became infected with 'the strong contagion of the gown', one of the destructive vanities he identifies in his poem *The Vanity of Human Wishes* twenty years later. It would appear he was mildly infected on a visit to Oxford in 1759 when he donned his Master's gown and was loath to take it off – 'It was at my first coming quite new and handsome' – but as a student it is more likely he was grateful for the gown as a way to conceal his increasingly threadbare clothes.

Finer, more embellished gowns were worn by the two socially more elevated ranks of students, the noblemen at the top and the gentlemen commoners next down. The noblemen were a small aristocratic group who enjoyed almost unlimited privileges with no need to have a tutor or take a degree. They often dined with the dons, could have pets, luxuriated in splendid private rooms, and generally indulged in a life of debauchery. Gentlemen commoners, the sons of wealthy families, were indulged almost as much and, with dangerously large amounts of money to spend, proved to be even more notorious in their idleness, drinking, eating and whoring – much of the latter in their rooms, an audacious breach of university rules. Gentlemen commoners considered commoners 'very *low* company (chiefly on account of the liquor they drank),' wrote the poet William Shenstone. With port and claret to oil the proceedings, 'they kept late hours, drank their favourite toasts on their knees; and, in short, were what we called "bucks of the first head".' Gentlemen commoners often left without taking a degree, and a few did not even bother to matriculate.[9]

Johnson was acutely conscious of his social inferiority and would never have attached himself as Shenstone did to an orgy of gentleman commoners. Nonetheless, in this rigid academic-social pecking order he was above the 'battelers', who had to feed and take care of themselves in return for a reduction of fees, and the lowest class of student, the servitor, whom he would describe in his *Dictionary* as 'one of the lowest order in the university'. The parents of servitors were so poor they could spare no money at all for their sons at the university. Servitors were assigned tutors and had free board and tuition, in exchange for which they had to perform certain duties in college, many of them quite menial and degrading, such as waiting on the gentlemen commoners and commoners in hall. One of the annoying tasks with which servitors were saddled, annoying to themselves as well as to others, was to knock periodically on their superiors' chamber doors to verify that they were in their rooms when they were supposed to be, reporting them if they were not. Fretting over this 'big brother' type of surveillance, which injured his pride and bred his resentment, Johnson contemptuously went out of his way to mislead the servitors and confound the system by deliberately ignoring the knocking at the door, scoffing at the regulations. He got himself reported and shrugged in indifference.[10]

Oxford's decline in the eighteenth century included a decline in student enrolment with the result that many colleges including Pembroke had rooms to spare. There was a good choice of rooms at Pembroke though chiefly for the more affluent students. Commoners and servitors had to put up with inexpensive small rooms high up near the roof line, reached through dark, bare, twisting stairways. Johnson had one of these for about £4 per year on the second floor above the Porters Lodge in the Gatehouse, a three-storey building in classical style and, as it turned out, rather prominently located next to the Master's House which extended out at right angles to the north or Gatehouse wing of the Old Quadrangle. The location of the room was potentially awkward for him since with his window open he could be, and at least once was, overheard mumbling to himself by the Master, Matthew Panting (Master from 1714 to 1738 and admired by Johnson as 'a fine Jacobite'). The stairway to his room today is not much different in its starkness and dinginess from what he was obliged to climb every day, except for the fire extinguisher halfway up. If he stuck his head out of his window and looked not left into the Master's rooms but to the right (east), he took in the high walls of Christ Church and a good view of Tom Tower a short distance away on the other side of Carfax. He also looked squarely out at St Aldgate's Church, a few feet away, where in the south aisle the college held its services and in the upper chamber accommodated its library.

Pembroke was a small and self-contained academic and social world but of course the town and countryside offered an abundance of both salubrious and nefarious amusements by day and night. Against rules enforced by roving proctors, Johnson seems to have known one or two of the no fewer than three hundred alehouses in town, many of them scenes of drunkenness and riot. If not at an alehouse, he could lose himself in conversation – even then his antidote to tedium – at one or other of the innumerable coffee houses, many of which catered to the members of particular colleges. With several intense conversations or 'bull-sessions' with Johnson in coffee houses, alehouses, or their rooms resonating in his memory, a fellow commoner at Pembroke, Oliver Edwards, told Johnson and Boswell half a century later, 'Sir, I remember you would not let us say *prodigious* at College.' Turning to Boswell, Edwards added, 'even then, Sir . . . he was delicate in language, and we all feared him'. Then with astonishing recall Johnson reminded Edwards of an Oxford alehouse conversation: 'O! Mr Edwards! I'll convince you that I recollect you. Do you remember our dining together at an alehouse near Pembroke gate?' At this old alehouse very near the college, probably late into the night, they had exchanged some Latin verses, and now all these years later he cited the lines and one of Edwards's anecdotes from memory.[11]

Ice-skating on the Isis or in Christ Church Meadow, as we have seen, was another popular pastime at Oxford which Johnson enjoyed, as was swimming in the Isis or some nearby pond, although the authorities were perpetually alarmed that the river had claimed by drowning many under-graduates neither as strong nor as good a swimmer as he was. There were many pleasant walks outside Oxford. A particularly convenient one for him just across the street from Pembroke was Christ Church Meadow, which one foreign traveller thought was a peaceful garden-paradise with its Broad Walk planted on each side with elm; another not far away was the sheltered walk beneath the south walls of Merton. There was also the Physic Garden (now known as the Botanic Garden), of course, opposite Magdalen, a bit messy, perhaps, early in the century but replete with topi-ary of yew reflecting the French and Dutch tastes of the day. But perhaps most appealing of all in town for Johnson, who in his boyhood was fond of rural walks, were the grounds behind Magdalen, including the extensive Deer Park. On his visit to Oxford in August 1754 – his first since leaving the university – Johnson took a walk with Warton such as he might well have taken as a student at a quicker pace than the one he now adopted. Warton described it: 'Johnson and I walked, three or four times, to Ellsfield, a village beautifully situated about three miles from Oxford, to see Mr [Revd Francis] Wise, Radclivian librarian . . . As we returned to Oxford in the evening, I out-walked Johnson, and he cried out *Sufflamina*, a Latin word which came from his mouth with peculiar grace, and was as much as to say, *Put on your drag chain* . . . In an evening, we frequently took long walks from Oxford into the country, returning to supper.'[12]

5

Poverty, defiant pride, academic arrogance, the declining fortunes of his family back home and resurgent melancholia were all responsible for Johnson's mental distress at Oxford. The keynote to much of it was bit-terness. He had been bitter for some time. When things for some reason went wrong at Stourbridge Grammar School and he was forced to return to Lichfield, his friend Hector, who knew him well, noticed something especially wrong: 'After a long absence from Lichfield, when he returned I was apprehensive of something wrong in his constitution, which might either impair his intellect or endanger his life . . .'[13] It was very likely a higher level than normal of despondency and bitterness. Johnson's robustness, strength of character, intellectual precociousness and detachment, and sense of humour for the most part enabled him to transcend the bitterness, but he co-existed with it. His good fortune in the small legacy that sent him to Oxford, one might suppose, could or should have dissolved or at least attenuated that bitterness, lifting him up to new ways of seeing himself. And possibly it would have, had it not been for the malevolent partnership of poverty and melancholia, and had he had more time.

William Adams told Boswell that Johnson could scarcely have been happier at Pembroke, that he 'was caressed and loved by all about him, was a gay and frolicsome fellow, and passed there the happiest part of his life'. 'Gay and frolicksome', however, is not the way Johnson remembered himself there. When Boswell shared Adams's remark with him, he instantly shot back, 'Ah, Sir, I was rude and violent. It was bitterness which they mistook for frolic.' Was it a mode of cynicism and irony, a 'violent' or reckless sort of satiric banter, that Adams mistook for an upbeat participation in college life? Percy added this: 'I have heard from some of his contemporaries that he was generally seen lounging at the College gate, with a circle of young students round him, whom he was entertaining with wit, and keeping from their studies, if not spiriting them up to rebellion against the College discipline, which in his maturer years he so much extolled.' 'How little any of us know of the real internal state even of those whom we see most frequently,' Boswell moralised, 'for the truth is, that he was then depressed by poverty, and irritated by disease.'[14]

The disease was melancholia. The poverty was his own meagre daily budget compounded by the regular spectacle in college of undergraduates with money to burn and his own stark realisation that his family was never going to help him economically. 'I was miserably poor, and I thought to fight my way by my literature and my wit; so I disregarded all power and all authority.' And if he were not successful there, he would go elsewhere to study, as the Master Matthew Panting once heard him through an open window declaiming to himself in a strong emphatic voice: 'Well, I have a mind to see what is done in other places of learning. I'll go and visit the universities abroad. I'll go to France and Italy. I'll go to Padua. And I'll mind my business.' Some day he would show these 'Athenian blockheads'.[15]

For his entire life Johnson's mind would dwell on the debilitating effects of poverty. 'He could not, at this early period of his life, divest himself of an opinion, that poverty was disgraceful,' Hawkins wrote, 'and was very severe in his censures of economy in both our universities, which exacted at meals the attendance of poor scholars, under the several denominations of servitors in the one, and sizers in the other [Cambridge]: he thought that the scholar's, like the Christian life, [should have] levelled all distinctions of rank and worldly pre-eminence.' But class discrimination was what made the Oxford world go round, Johnson understood, ugly as it was:

> What is it but opinion, by which we have a respect for authority, that prevents us, who are the rabble, from rising up and pulling down you who are gentlemen from your places, and saying 'We will be gentlemen in our turn'? Now, Sir, that respect for authority is much more easily granted to a man whose father has had it, than to an upstart, and so society is more easily supported.

The system was distasteful, even a scandal. Johnson's friend, Oliver Goldsmith, put the case starkly many years later in a way that Johnson the student-rebel would have applauded: 'It implies a contradiction, for men to be at once learning the *liberal* arts, and at the same time treated as *slaves*; at once studying freedom, and practising servitude.'[16]

How poor exactly was Johnson at Oxford? Did his bitterness, roused by the spectacle of students enacting the class system amid the ancient spires, make him think his poverty was worse than it really was? The Battels (or 'buttery') books which record individual items charged daily and weekly to everyone in residence reveal an average commons expense of eight and a half shillings per week charged to him, or a total of just over twenty-four pounds for forty-two weeks – a little below the average among commoners and two or three shillings more than the average servitor. Like others, he tended to spend three or four shillings more per week during the period of a feast or 'gaudy' such as Gunpowder Plot week, but that was neither unusual nor especially extravagant. The fact was, he had very little money to spend on entertainment such as at alehouses or coffee houses, a huge constraint for a young man who loved to hold forth in front of his peers. Instead he opted for draughts in the Pembroke common room. Visiting William Adams, then Master, at the College with Boswell in 1776, as they walked into the Common Room, Johnson suddenly was transported into 'a reverie of meditation' after which equally suddenly he exclaimed, 'Ay! Here I used to play at draughts with Phil. Jones and [John] Fludyer.' Both were Scholars so, presumably, he was in good intellectual as well as inexpensive company. Jones loved beer, said Johnson, but Fludyer 'turned out a scoundrel, a [violent] Whig, and said he was ashamed of having been bred at Oxford'. Was he a scoundrel in any other way than political, asked Boswell, cheating at draughts, for example? 'Sir, we never played for *money*,' Johnson replied quickly.[17]

There is other testimony of his financial extremity at Pembroke. Humphrey Hawkins, the undermaster at Lichfield Grammar School, gives a general picture of his wardrobe:

> The want of that assistance, which scholars in general derive from their parents, relations, and friends, soon became visible in the garb and appearance of Johnson, which, though in some degree concealed by a scholar's gown, and that we know is never deemed the less honourable for being old, was so apparent as to excite pity in some that saw and noticed him.

His deteriorating clothes and shoes were an acute embarrassment, especially outside the college, to which he responded with disdain and wounded pride.[18]

It was about this time that John Taylor 'was taken by his father . . . with the intention to enter him at Pembroke that he might be with Johnson as had been agreed between the two friends on account of their great intimacy which had been kept up by a constant correspondence by letters'. Taylor was dropped off at the Crown Inn, where Johnson met him. They walked to Pembroke together where Johnson closed his door and immediately announced: 'I cannot in conscience suffer you to enter here. For the tutor under whom you must be [Jorden] is such a blockhead that you will not be five minutes at his lectures till you find out what a fool he is and upbraid me with your looks for recommending you to him.' Taylor's friendship in college would have been an emotional lift, but he had done some scouting around the university and, discovering that the name of Revd Edmund Bateman of Christ Church was on everybody's lips as one of the most celebrated tutors, recommended that his friend matriculate there. Taylor did just that and Johnson in a sense followed him by crossing the street to Christ Church frequently after that to feast hungrily on Taylor's summaries of what Bateman had to say on the classics, logic and ethics, as well as on mathematics, which he taught as preparation for algebra. His threadbare clothes let him down, though. He began to notice the way people there looked at his dilapidated shoes. After that he came no more. Instead, Taylor came to Pembroke and repeated the lectures there for his friend. Johnson's shoes were noticed at Pembroke, too. Leaving his room one morning, he discovered a new pair on the landing outside his door. Hawkins relates that 'with all the indignation of an insulted man, he threw them away'. Whoever had made the gesture, a combination of generosity and bad judgement or taste, would have been amazed the next day to see the indigent student still shuffling around in his old shoes, still embarrassed but also angry. As is common with such anecdotes, we are never told by anyone what came next: how long he continued wearing those shoes, or if he ever discarded them while he remained at Oxford. Unless a pair were forthcoming from home, it is possible he stuck with them as a proud and sullen act of defiance.[19]

He appeared to be in debt when he left Oxford, as none of his caution money (seven pounds) was refunded afterwards. This suggests that without some supplement to the forty-pound legacy that brought him to Pembroke, he could not afford to stay. There was no other recourse in plain sight such as a scholarship – open scholarships were not available. He could not request a demotion to batteler or servitor because downgrading of students in that rigid social climate was for the most part out of the question. In any case, after a year as a commoner he would have looked upon life as a servitor as heinous and humiliating. His pride could not have borne it. As the weeks passed, he could only hope that somebody somewhere, perhaps Walmesley or his godfather Swynfen, would come forward with a loan or gift that would enable to him stay.

6

He pursued his studies in an unconventional manner partly because of his habit – to which he would adhere for the rest of his life – of devouring a book quickly without ever finishing it. 'He read by fits and starts,' Hawkins states, 'and, in the intervals, digested his reading by meditation, to which he was ever prone. Neither did he regard the hours of study, farther than the discipline of the college compelled him.' His melancholia also made his study habits erratic. It was while he and Boswell were talking in 1763 about his Oxford days that he brought it up: 'He mentioned to me now, for the first time, that he had been distressed by melancholy, and for that reason had been obliged to fly from study and meditation, to the dissipating variety of life.' Adams had taken over as his 'nominal' tutor after Jorden left, but Johnson was pretty much on his own and that was the way he needed and wanted it.[20]

Johnson would also have us believe that he was 'very idle and neglectful of his studies'. The remark seems disingenuous. Boswell insisted that 'idleness and reading hard were with him relative terms': 'I always thought that he did himself injustice in his account of what he had read, and that he must have been speaking with reference to the vast portion of study which is possible, and to which a few scholars in the whole history of literature have attained.' In fact, that he read hard at Oxford is the point of his comment in 1763 that while there an 'old gentleman' said to him, 'Young man, ply your book diligently now, and acquire a stock of knowledge; for when years come upon you, you will find that poring over books will be but an irksome task.' What he 'read *solidly* at Oxford was Greek, 'not the Grecian historians, but Homer and Euripides, and now and then a little Epigram'. He was especially fond of metaphysics and ethics since it helped him 'compose' his mind. What else he read at Oxford besides classical literature, theology and ethics is unknown but the close to one hundred volumes he left behind after leaving the university (hoping he would return), chiefly works of theology and classical literature as well as some modern literature by such as Shakespeare, Spenser, Milton, Waller, Dryden, Prior, Addison and Pope, provide some clues, although it is difficult to distinguish those he brought with him from Lichfield from ones acquired at Oxford.[21]

On his own terms, he nurtured an intense desire to compete and excel as a compensation for his poverty. Out of envy or a sense of superiority he could not bear a rival. John Meeke, a brilliant Scholar then at Pembroke who later become a Fellow of the College, was one whom he could not bring himself to hear when he 'declaimed or disputed in the hall', retreating 'to the farthest corner thereof, that he might be out of the reach of his voice'. 'I used to think Meeke had excellent parts, when we were boys together at the College,' he remarked to Warton just after they dropped in on him at Pembroke in the summer of 1754, 'but alas . . . I could not bear Meeke's superiority,' he added; 'about the same time of life, Meeke was left behind at Oxford to feed on a Fellowship, and I went to London to get my living: now, Sir, see the difference of our literary characters!'[22]

Still, it is clear that what he regarded as laziness was proving to be one of his personal devils. Under October 1729, after twelve months at Oxford, he wrote in his 1729–34 'Diary' a Latin line which Boswell translated as, 'I bid farewell to sloth, being resolved henceforth not to listen to her syren strains.' Hector confirmed that Johnson was drifting, listless and unable to do what was expected of him, much to the annoyance of the Master who 'seeing him frequently idling about had twice [fines] imposed him, without effect, and he called him up, and once more charged [that] if he did not comply with his request, he should take no farther notice of him. The Dr promised, and performed.' On 21 November 1729, in an effort to get down to study, he made a self-disciplining table of how much reading he could get done in a week, month and year if he read ten pages per day: 60, 240 and 2880 respectively. To begin with a meagre ten pages per day may suggest just how indolent he thought he had become. He soon realised that ten pages per day would get him nowhere, so he tabulated what he could achieve based on 30, 50, 60, 150, 300, 400 and 600 per day, though he did not take the last four as far as computing annual totals, realising the stark fantasy in such an exercise. Sixty would yield 17,280 for a year, and apparently he thought that was as much as he could realistically read. Such computations would become almost chronic with him as he struggled to impose order on a sense of disorder, 'as it fixed his attention steadily upon something without, and prevented his mind from preying upon itself'. He even counted the number of lines to be read in *The Aeneid* and other works by Virgil, as well as in works by Euripides, Horace, Ovid, Theocritus and Juvenal.[23]

This impulse to tabulate and count, incidentally, which later became compulsive, appears also to account for the appearance of a cryptic 'M' under 22 October in his 1729–34 'Diary'. If the Latin that follows is translated as 'Remember what I did on 9, 12, 17, 19, 22, 26 and 28 September', this would simply be an innocuous reference to what happened on those days that he either forgot to record in the diary or recorded elsewhere. Or it might mean something less savoury. One widely respected critic has urged that this 'M' refers to masturbation, others that it indicates sexual intercourse, and still others that it alludes to defecation. In the 1760s he used this 'M' more plausibly to chronicle his defecation because he was very ill then, suffering from insomnia and wishing to keep track of his bowel movements during the night. In 1729 the first two meanings may be more likely as it is certainly possible that, especially during periods of boredom in his room, he indulged in sexual fantasies. To keep a record of instances of masturbation by way of trying to control the practice, this same critic observes, is not uncommon, and it would have been a way of dealing with his guilt over it.[24]

Apart from what, how much, and how regularly he studied, Johnson made an impression at Pembroke as an intellectual prodigy, which it pleased him to perpetuate. A number of stories circulated by Boswell,

Mrs Thrale, Hawkins and other early biographers, some embellished, no doubt, and some perhaps spurious, celebrate him as a kind of academic wonderboy there. He told Mrs Thrale, for example, who liked stories of the unconventional Johnson, that 'when he made his first declamation, he wrote over but one copy, and that coarsely; and having given it into the hand of the tutor [Jorden] who stood to receive it as he passed, was obliged to begin by chance and continue on how he could, for he had got but little of it by heart; so fairly trusting to his present powers for immediate supply, he finished by adding astonishment to the applause of all who knew how little was owing to study.' Someone else who heard him say this exclaimed that he must have been taking a huge risk, to which Johnson replied, 'Not at all, no man I suppose leaps at once into deep water who does not know how to swim.' In Oxford, a few months before he died, he was in the full flow of boasting about this undergraduate intellectual bravado in the company of Dr Adams, his daughter and other guests when Miss Adams flattered him by supposing his exercises so brilliant that he could not have made them better. 'Yes, Madam, to be sure,' he replied, 'I could make them better. Thought is better than no thought.' The point is he chose not to make them better and unquestionably in this and other ways constructed a notoriety about himself inside and perhaps also outside Pembroke.[25]

For Johnson's first 5 November celebrations or 'gaudy' at the college Jorden asked his students to compose prose Latin exercises relating to the Gunpowder Plot. Johnson failed to produce his. Instead, he composed some Latin verses for Jorden entitled 'Somnium', a tongue-in-cheek literary prank relating a dream he said he had: 'that the Muse had come to him in his sleep, and whispered, that it did not become him to write on such subjects as politics; he should confine himself to humbler themes'. What those humbler themes may have been we do not know because the poem is lost, but Boswell saw it and judged its versification 'truly Virgilian'.[26]

Jorden's response to these unauthorised 'Virgilian' verses is unknown, but that he did not disapprove too strongly was borne out later by his asking Johnson to translate into Latin Pope's poem, the biblical-Virgilian pastoral The Messiah (1712), a poem imitating Virgil and drawn from the

Messianic visions of the prophet Isaiah. Johnson had the leisure to write it since he stayed at the emptied college right through the Christmas vacation with a handful of other students. Hector informed Boswell, '[Johnson] told me, that afternoon at the first [attempt] he finished more than one half and in the morning concluded the remainder of Pope's Messiah'. In later life Johnson claimed combatively that the poem gave him the chance 'to show the tutors what I could do, [not] what I was willing should be done. It convinced those who were well enough inclined to punish me, that I could wield a scholar's weapon as often as I was menaced with arbitrary inflictions. Before the frequency of personal satire had weakened its effect, the petty tyrants of colleges stood in awe of a pointed remark, or a vindictive epigram.' The poem's subject suited him because of its central meditative idea that Truth speaks inwardly without the clatter of words. It gave him a chance to reflect quietly on his feelings about religion and nature, both actual and Virgilian, as well as on the pomposity of the world (and of Oxford) that the light of Christ made look so dim. The result was an unqualified success. 'He performed it with uncommon rapidity,' Boswell reports, 'and in so masterly a manner, that he obtained great applause from it, which ever after kept him high in the estimation of his College, and, indeed, of all the university.' Hawkins and Boswell circulated the story that the poem was brought to the notice of Pope who, very impressed with it, was said to have remarked, 'The writer of this poem will leave it a question for posterity, whether his or mine be the original.' High praise indeed if the story were true. For Johnson the poem was the most memorable piece he wrote as an undergraduate. 'Here I translated Pope's Messiah,' he said reverentially as he and Warton paused at the gates of the College in 1754.[27]

7

'Where is religion to be learned but at an university,' Johnson once said, but at Oxford he was not doing very well in that vein in spite of Hawkins's assertion that his moral character was greatly 'fixed' by 'early calls to prayer, the frequent instruction from the pulpit, [and] with all the other means of religious and moral improvement'. He took his 'lax' talking against religion with him to university, though he had to rein it in because 'it would not be *suffered* there'. He was inclined to laugh at writers on religion, and it is unknown whether he attended chapel regularly. Oxford was not then an especially congenial environment for the growth of religiousness. George Whitefield, the Methodist, when he first received the sacraments at St Mary's in Oxford was immediately 'set up as a mark for all the polite students that knew me to shoot at'. Everyone was supposed to be present at the sacraments in church at the beginning of every term, he wrote, 'yet so dreadfully has that once faithful city played the harlot, that very few masters, and no undergraduates but the Methodists, attended upon it'. Whitefield complained that fellow students threw dirt at him for attending these services; others withheld payment to him for his services as a servitor.[28]

Deep religious feeling, though still submerged, still resonated in Johnson. He was not systematically reading religious works, searching for spiritual truth, but he rediscovered religion through a book he happened to pick up, William Law's *A Serious Call to a Devout and Holy Life* (1728), a treatise on practical morality. In his words this is what happened:

> When at Oxford, I took up Law's *Serious Call to a Holy Life*, expecting to find it a dull book (as such books generally are), and perhaps to laugh at it. But I found Law quite an overmatch for me; and this was the first occasion of my thinking in earnest of religion, after I became capable of rational enquiry.

While he confided in Hector in 1778, 'my health has been, from my twentieth year, such as has seldom afforded me a single day of ease', at least help now was at hand: 'It [religion] had dropped out of my mind. It was at an early part of my life. Sickness brought it back, and I hope I have never lost it since.' The effects of *A Serious Call* upon him were life-changing. He 'studied it hard' and its influence on his moral essays was fundamental. He also turned to it in his *Dictionary* for over two hundred citations.[29]

A *Serious Call* appealed to him profoundly because it addressed 'every part of our common life', everyday existence, not abstract religious dogma – he called it 'the finest piece of hortatory theology in any language'. Law's insistence, for example, that one should rise early so as to wrest control of one's life spoke powerfully and immediately to him. The book called the reader to private rather than public prayer, making religion a personal and individual affair between him and God. There was hope in that but it was also a double-edged sword. 'Every man knows something worse of himself than he is sure of in others' – in Johnson's words this was one of Law's recurring themes that deeply penetrated his psyche. The battle would be fought in his mind, not in church. Law was not 'a reasoner', Johnson once said. His strength instead was an ability to rouse the reader not with expostulations to stop sinning but with entertaining character portraits, many of them satiric, illustrating the human condition in its many aspects and providing individual cautionary tales. In the unhappiness of his closing months at Oxford, Law's book provided light with which to illuminate the gathering darkness.

8

As it turned out, Johnson's days at Oxford were numbered. Perhaps his depression, 'the flying vapours of incipient madness', brought matters to a head and sent him packing. The prospect of again remaining at college for the Christmas holidays with a handful of other students in the 'sullen solitude' of the lifeless and empty buildings, without his parents and missing Lichfield and the old haunts, was a bleak prospect. It may have been around this time that he heard his mother's voice calling him. He told Boswell 'that one day at Oxford, as he was turning the key of his chamber, he heard his mother distinctly call *Sam*. She was then at Lichfield; but nothing ensued.'[30]

On top of all this, the money was just not there. As Christmas 1729 approached the inescapable fact was that his finances would not allow him to remain even for the vacation. He had been at Pembroke about thirteen months and no further gift or loan had come his way. Nor did the college, so far as we know, offer him a scholarship – of which there were two. He would have been eligible for one of them, but as it was worth only £10 per year, however, it would not alone have enabled him to stay. He packed his very few personal belongings and left Oxford around 12 December. 'Johnson being miserably poor set out for Lichfield early in the morning having hid his toes in a pair of large boots,' said Taylor, who accompanied him as far as Banbury and returned at night. Johnson left his small library behind in the not so conscientious care of his old friend – Johnson's remark on Taylor's having 'never relished a book in his earlier days' might allude to his having neglected it. Since his name was left on the College books for almost two more years, it is possible someone decided he might return. Surely he must have left desperately hoping for the same thing. The fact that for years he did not request his books to be sent to him suggests as much.[31]

The anger, intellectual arrogance, depression and cramped finances that characterised his time at Pembroke, terminated ingloriously by his lonely departure, would appear to be overwhelming grounds for assuming that for the rest of his life he would nourish resentment towards Oxford University. Quite the contrary, however, was the case. Boswell quoted Adams saying that 'he contracted a love and regard for Pembroke College, which he retained to the last'. He frequently boasted about Pembroke's alumni, and he visited Oxford more than any other place in England, even more than Lichfield, at least twenty-seven times from 1754 until his death. Many of those visits were for several weeks at a time, mostly at New Inn Hall and University College, not Pembroke. Part of his affection for the place understandably resulted from the huge (though not universal) respect for him there once he became the famous moralist and scholar. He became almost an Oxford institution, toasted and bowed to by dons in one common room or another and entertained by his growing group of friends. On his visit in 1754 he was delighted still to find at Pembroke college servants he knew, especially 'a very old butler, and expressed great satisfaction at being recognised by them, and conversed with them familiarly', even if the Master of the College John Radcliffe conspicuously snubbed him.[32]

Close to the end of his life he took pleasure in showing Pembroke to his friend Hannah More, the evangelical moral reformer, author and emi-nent member of the Bluestocking circle. 'You cannot imagine with what delight he showed me every part of his own College,' she wrote. 'He would let no one show it me but himself – "this was my room; this Shenstone's". Then after pointing out all the rooms of the poets who had been of his college, "In short," said he, "we were a nest of singing birds".' Through the prism of succeeding years he increasingly viewed his thirteen months at Pembroke with gratification, but as he left in December 1729 mostly he felt the jarring pressures of failure, injured pride and wrecked nerves.[33]

CHAPTER 6

Horrible Imaginings

I

WHEN JOHNSON ARRIVED HOME shortly before Christmas, the inner gloom with which he had co-existed for months suddenly deepened and solidified. He was entering the bleakest, unhappiest period in his life as he fell into the tight grip of depression. Whether or not it was unremitting we do not know because for the next two years there are no diary entries, no letters, and only a little testimony from others about his existence. It is as if he went into hiding. The 'morbid melancholy' he inherited, aggravated by numerous experiences at different times during his short life, had finally triumphed at Oxford, and instead of returning to Lichfield like something of the conquering hero he rode into town and fell into a deep, dark emotional hole. He was at home again in the midst of his bickering parents, the understandable complaints of his 'noisy' brother Nathaniel – who appears to have inherited his father's melancholia and could not have been thrilled about having to share home space again with his brother – and the dullness of the bookseller's world in a provincial town which must have seemed like the end of the earth after Oxford. If his parents hoped he would now pull his weight in the bookshop, they were bound to be disappointed. There was also a disconcerting new feature of his behaviour which must have worried everyone. As a result of his physical illness he began to show signs of the 'tics and gesticulations' that stayed with him for the rest of his life.[1]

Boswell described Johnson's desperation:

> The 'morbid melancholy', which was lurking in his constitution, and to which we may ascribe those particularities, and that aversion to regular life, which, at a very early period, marked his character, gathered such strength in his twentieth year, as to afflict him in a dreadful manner . . . he felt himself overwhelmed with an horrible hypochondria, with perpetual irritation, fretfulness, and impatience; and with a dejection, gloom, and despair, which made existence misery. From this dismal malady he never afterwards was perfectly relieved; and all his labours, and all his enjoyments, were but temporary interruptions of its baleful influence.

Thinking possibly of this period, Johnson once told his friend John Paradise that he 'sometimes was so languid and inefficient, that he could not distinguish the hour upon the town-clock'. He admitted, 'I did not then know how to manage it.' Hector even feared he might commit suicide. He tried to exorcise these devils by describing them on paper. Whatever form it took, it is a huge loss that this piece of searching self-analysis has been lost. The only person to whom he showed it was his godfather, Dr Swynfen, who was so struck by 'the extraordinary acuteness, research and eloquence' in it that he circulated it among friends. Johnson was furious when he found out, 'so much offended that he [was] never afterwards fully reconciled to him'.[2]

Over the following months Johnson 'strove' to exorcise the black dog by other means, with 'forcible exertions' such as repeatedly walking in one day the thirty-two mile return trek between Lichfield and Birmingham. One can picture him shuffling his tall, ungainly form along swiftly, jaw set firm and fists clenched, his vacant eyes focused inward in a struggle to disentangle the turmoil inside. In a remark that Boswell chose to omit from his *Life*, Johnson said, 'I once walked a good deal. I left it off at two and twenty when I grew melancholy.' He must have meant specifically the intense, almost obsessive walking between Lichfield and Birmingham be-

cause movement of his body, either by walking, or riding in carriages, or
sailing through stormy Hebridean seas with Boswell, for the rest of his life
would remain a vital means of defeating stagnation and raising his spirits.
'Frequent and violent agitation of the body,' he would write later, was a
recipe for subduing depression. In Birmingham Hector helped him as
much as he could, such as getting his mind off his trouble by asking him
to write a love poem for a friend. 'I applied to Johnson,' Hector wrote to
Boswell, 'who was with me, and in about half an hour [he] dictated the
verses which I sent to my friend.' Forty years later Johnson recalled that
in fact he wrote the lines in five minutes when 'dear Mund' (his nickname for Hector) pressed him for 'the nonsense' people now 'keep such a
stir about'.[3]

2

Either at Oxford (as is commonly thought) or in this following dark
period, Johnson wrote his strongly autobiographical short poem, 'The
Young Author'. The earlier date obviously connects with Oxford because
the poem deals with the ambitions of a young writer and scholar who
has vain dreams of published glory. There are reasons to think, however, that he may have written it after he had removed himself from the
socially intense environment of Pembroke and could, on reflection and
with bleak detachment, view his own vanity as an aspiring author with
more poignant irony. From Lichfield, Oxford seemed like an oasis. While
he was there he could still imagine himself blossoming into authorship.
'The great advantage of a university,' he once told the politician William
Windham, 'is that a person lives in a place where his reputation depends
upon his learning.' There were people around him who encouraged such
hopes. After he left, he was on his own. Glancing back forty-five years
later he wrote simply and powerfully to Taylor, 'The transition from the
protection of others to our own conduct is a very awful point of human
existence'. This was the typically oppressive mental state of the melancholic – that he not only was unlikely to succeed at anything but also
could not even imagine succeeding.[4]

In 'The Young Author' he rationalised his defeat at the hands of circumstances and his own mind by depicting the saga of disappointments awaiting any youth who falls prey to delusion and casts his bread upon the precarious waters of literary fame. For such a victim of vanity and 'disorders of the intellect', as he was to put it in his moral fable and short psychological tale *Rasselas* (1759), 'fictions begin to operate as realities . . . and life passes in dreams of rapture or of anguish'. The lot of the aspiring poet is delusory, 'panting for a name,/And fir'd with pleasing hope of endless fame', because he trusts his fate to 'human kind,/more false, more cruel than seas and wind'. He sells his soul to the phantom of 'praise from nations yet unborn', scorning such 'transitory blessings' as wealth and title. What are the rewards for the self-deluding joys of his imagination? There are none except the 'hisses' of attacking pamphlets, from which the wounded young author flies, his vanity in tatters. There hidden in some refuge he is content to lick his wounds, merely 'Glad to be hid, and proud to be forgot'.[5]

Once he escaped from this particular dark night of mental illness, as he told Hector, he never really gained full control over the black dog. Neither did he ever outgrow his distrust of the imagination and how it can cheat with false hope, at every age and level. In *Rasselas* with a sombre eye turned inward, however, he has the philosopher Imlac say to young Rasselas:

> Disorders of intellect happen much more often than superficial observers will easily believe. Perhaps, if we speak with rigorous exactness, no human mind is in its right state. There is no man whose imagination does not sometimes predominate over this reason, who can regulate his attention wholly by his will, and whose ideas will come and go at his command. No man will be found in whose mind airy notions do not sometimes tyrannise, and force him to hope or fear beyond the limits of sober probability. All power of fancy over reason is a degree of insanity; but while this power is such as we can control and repress, it is not visible to others, nor considered as any depravation of the mental

faculties: it is not pronounced madness but when it comes ungovernable, and apparently influences speech or action.[6]

When fantasy prevails over reality there is a 'dangerous prevalence of imagination' – that is, a condition in which imagination overcomes rational balance, judgement and perspective. It ushers in depression and, as Macbeth put it, 'horrible imaginings' that are not just monsters of darkness but thrive as happily in full daylight. It could lead to 'insanity', an 'ungovernable' madness. That was the condition in which Johnson now found himself.

There is no surviving clue as to how much Johnson's family noticed his sickness. His moodiness and sullen loneliness would have been all too apparent within the walls of their house, and perhaps his father, who was a melancholic himself, picked up on certain signs that his son was going through something close to a breakdown. His brother Nathaniel had his own problems, as we shall see, and probably little patience with yet another of his brother's displays of antisocial behaviour. Perhaps Johnson spoke to his mother about his discovery of Law's *A Serious Call*. Religion was a type of bond between them. But this was not a close family in which the members freely shared with each other their worries and fears. Happy moments there must have been, but not lasting ones. Outside the family, Johnson could confide in Swynfen, though he was now in Birmingham. Hector, too, was in Birmingham. Cousin Cornelius was in London. In the way of patrons and mentors, that left Gilbert Walmesley. He was still in Lichfield, just around the corner, ready to welcome his protégé back to the Bishop's Palace and the society that had done so much good for him more than a year before.

3

Even if Johnson had been sufficiently in his right mind in 1730–31 and able to rouse himself enough to do something constructive, few obvious career options were open to him. The bookselling business was out. He had no appetite for it and his father was not a good advertisement for the kind of life one could lead as a bookseller. He was twenty and had no degree, no teaching credentials, no money, and no acumen for conducting a business. As Hawkins put it, 'His fortunes and circumstances had determined him to no particular course of study, and were such as seemed to exclude him from every one of the learned professions.'[7]

The months passed and then tragedy struck in the summer of 1731. On 22 August Cornelius died in London in Hummums, his favourite hotel in Covent Garden Piazza which served as a type of bagnio for its patrons. Virtually a resident of London by then, Cornelius had become known to Pope and a clutch of other poets and fashionable wits at various taverns and coffee houses. With lots of money to spend, he had surrendered completely to his taste for extravagance and fast living. He ran through his money, mortgaged his properties, and borrowed heavily, and only a few months before his death he landed in prison for debt. He died soon after his release. Had he lived, Cornelius could have made a monumental difference to Johnson's early literary career, though not necessarily an entirely positive one. His wayward literary life ended in prison and hastened on to impoverishment and an early death – an anticipation of the poet Richard Savage in whom Johnson took a consuming interest in his early London life.

The silence of these months in Lichfield suddenly came to an end on 30 October 1731, just over two months after Cornelius's death, when Johnson wrote his first surviving letter. Written to Cornelius's half-brother, Gregory Hickman, one of Stourbridge's prominent citizens, it reveals that the preceding summer with Hickman's help he had been making efforts to get a teaching job at the Stourbridge Grammar School.[8] Hickman's daughter Dorothy, in fact, had caught his eye when he was a pupil at the school. She was only twelve then. Now she was seventeen or eighteen and a rather more promising focus of amorousness – so much so that sometime during his summer visit to his relatives Johnson found himself falling in love and addressing an affectionate poem to her, 'To Miss Hickman Playing On the Spinet'. Disappointingly, the verses do not yield much autobiographically. In another love poem written about this time, 'To a Young Lady on Her Birthday', possibly also addressed to Miss Hickman, he dwells somewhat more personally on the conquering spell of the girl's beauty, imploring her to be fair and just and not squander her arts and powers on coquettishness. There is also an oblique allusion in this poem to feelings of inadequacy in courtship, an awareness of his physical uncouthness and roughness, not to mention the disfigurements of disease and birth defects: 'With his own form acquaint the forward fool,/Shewn in the faithful glass of ridicule'. A third poem, 'An Ode on a Lady Leaving Her Place of Abode; Almost Impromptu', written in the late autumn or early winter of 1731, laments his love's sudden departure, for London perhaps, depriving him of her 'wit, love and mirth', as well as her warming eyes. He pleads for her return north soon to bless him with 'continu'd day'. All this was a good sign. Love poetry and the pursuit of gainful employment, as well as breaking free of Lichfield and enjoying the company of a warm, healthy and loving family, gave him a momentary new lease on life.[9]

But winter was approaching and he had to return to the greyness of his own home and unhappy family, one temporarily even more crowded now that Cornelius's two maiden sisters began boarding there for about two months. Added to that was the bad news in September that he had failed to gain the teaching appointment, which went to a graduate of Trinity College, Oxford instead. As it turned out, Hickman's influence could not compensate for his lack of a degree. Oddly, on the heels of this disappointment – or was it his lack of success in Stourbridge with Gregory Hickman's seventeen-year-old daughter? – Hickman asked him to write a poem about his failure. The request angered him: 'Be pleased to consider that versifying against one's inclination is the most disagreeable thing in the world, and that one's own disappointment is no inviting subject.' The subject was so 'barren', he added, that it would be like trying 'to build without materials'. He concluded simply with, 'As I am yet unemploy'd, I hope you will if anything should offer, remember and recommend [me].'[10]

There was another even more personal shock to come. In early December, after an autumn of quickly deteriorating health owing to some respiratory ailment, Michael Johnson finally gave up the fight. He died from an 'inflammatory fever' at the age of seventy-five and was buried at St Michael's in Lichfield on 7 December. The family's much-loved servant

'Kitty' Chambers arranged the funeral, a sign of how intimately she had become involved in the life and affairs of the family. For the last two years the Johnsons had fallen on their hardest times yet, so Michael Johnson died thinking himself a defeated man without having provided adequately for his wife and sons. To his son he was a dispiriting example of how an able and strong man with such energy, well regarded in the community – the burial register describes him as 'a Magistrate of the City' – could fail as a result of comprehensive business incompetence. All that was left to Sarah was a few pounds, the home, and the shop with its ample stock of books, although without her eldest son's knowledge of books to help her she and her relatively uninterested second son Nathaniel were at a loss of how to acquire further good stock. The shop kept ticking over for many years, chiefly with Kitty's help, but it was never the same again, becoming merely the equivalent of a second-hand bookshop today instead of a well-known source in the region for antiquarian volumes and fine editions.

In his *Annales*, a separate diary he wrote in 1734 for the years 1725–34, Johnson mingles his sorrow over his father's death with a palpable fear. For the day of his father's death he merely scribbled the brief Latin phrase, '*Patre orbatus est*', but he also recorded that eight months later in Lichfield he collected what was due him from his father's effects, adding (as translated by Hawkins) a resolution never to let happen to him what happened to his father: 'June 15, I laid by eleven guineas; on which day I received all of my father's effects which I can hope for till the death of my mother (which I pray may be late), that is to say, nineteen pounds; so that I have my fortune to make, and care must be taken, that in the mean time, the powers of my mind may not grow languid through poverty, nor want drive me into wickedness.'[11]

Johnson collected his legacy – which today would be in the region of £2,000 – on his return to Lichfield in mid-June 1732 from Market Bosworth, Leicestershire, where he had been teaching. Back in March it suddenly looked as if his luck had turned when his application for the post of usher at the grammar school there, perhaps with Walmesley's intervention, was successful. The appointment was highly unusual because the school's statutes specified that the appointee had to have a Bachelor of

Arts degree.[12] On 9 March he made his way by foot to the pleasant town, about twenty-five miles east of Lichfield, to take up his post, hoping that this opportunity could prove to be the beginning of a successful teaching career.

The salary was meagre but the appointment also provided that Johnson would reside at Bosworth Hall, the late sixteenth-century country house of the local squire, Sir Wolstan Dixie, fourth baronet, whose ancestors founded the school and who tyrannically controlled its administration. In addition to teaching, his role was to officiate 'as a kind of domestic chaplain', as Boswell called it, to this boorish 'brutal rascal' of a squire, saying grace at meals and probably treated like something of a slave. Johnson's pride promptly revolted and he took to quarrelling with the baronet. Sir Wolstan merely responded with 'intolerable harshness'. That this went on for months suggests Johnson's desperation to have and keep the job. Sir Wolstan was bad enough, but even the teaching was 'painful drudgery', as he described it to Hector in complaining letters which Hector sadly seems either to have lost or kept from Boswell to prevent him from broadcasting the full extent of Johnson's fury at the time. 'He wrote me word [that] his business was to teach Lily's grammar to a few boys,' Hector told Boswell, but it 'was hard to say whose difficulty was greatest: he to explain nonsense, or they to understand it'. A poet had caught the essence of his wretchedness at the school, Johnson added, with the phrase '"*Vitam continet una dies*" [one day contains the whole of my life]; that it was unvaried as the note of the cuckow'. He stuck it out until the end of the term in July and then bid Sir Wolstan and his school good riddance, for the rest of his life preserving 'the strongest aversion, and even a degree of horrour' for both. His lifelong detestation of bullies and domestic tyrants, especially adults who take unfair advantage of young people, was born of experiences like this.[13]

He walked disconsolately and angrily back to Lichfield. Perhaps it was time to do something entirely different from teaching. He did not have much time to cool his heels at home thinking about career choices, however, because a few days after his return he received a letter from John Corbet, his schoolfriend Andrew's younger brother, telling him of a vacancy as usher at the grammar school in Ashbourne which had suddenly become vacant. Johnson was on John Corbet's mind because they had recently seen each other on 17 July at Sir Wolstan's home. 'On being called to dinner at . . . Dixie's,' Johnson wrote in his diary, 'I saw J. Corbet, a youth once very delightful to me, and not because if I am right, he then loved me very much.' Because a replacement was needed right away, the school might also be willing to hire someone without a degree. Best of all, Ashbourne was where Taylor lived, to whom he wrote off immediately, asking him to exert any influence he could. 'If there be any reason for my coming to Ashbourne, I shall readily do it,' he added; 'Mr Corbet has, I suppose, given you an account of my leaving Sir Wolstan. It was really *e Carcere exire* [leaving prison].' Taylor was not a school governor, however, and by the 1st of August the job had gone to another applicant who failed to take up the post but was quickly succeeded by a third candidate. It was especially galling to Johnson that these two men were preferred to him and yet, like him, neither had a degree. If he did walk the thirty miles to Ashbourne for an interview, it is perfectly possible his unusual appearance and involuntary movements, quite pronounced by then, put the governors off. 'To his dying day,' wrote William Shaw, 'he never thought, recollected, or studied, whether in his closet, or in the street, alone, or in company, without putting his huge unwieldy body in the same rolling, awkward posture.' Or his reputation for prickly independence and assertiveness may have preceded him.[14]

It may have been that autumn that he wrote 'An Epitaph on Claudy Phillips, a Musician', his first known of the many epitaphs he wrote in his life. Phillips was an accomplished Welsh touring violinist who died in poverty in 1732. It seems he played in Lichfield and was heard by both Johnson and Garrick. One day when the two of them were sitting together, perhaps in the Bishop's Palace, Garrick roused Johnson by quoting an epitaph on Phillips he had recently come across. As Boswell retells the anecdote told to him by Garrick, 'Johnson shook his head at these commonplace funereal lines, and said to Garrick, "I think, Davy, I can make a better." Then, stirring about his tea for a little while, in a state of meditation, he almost extempore produced the following verses.' What is interesting about Johnson's improvement in the following lines was his strong empathy for Phillips's poverty, an emotionalism that was easily aroused by the spectacle of a talented individual going to his grave unrewarded, unappreciated, and destitute:

> Phillips! whose touch harmonious could remove
> The pangs of guilty pow'r, and hapless love,
> Rest here, distrest by poverty no more,
> Find here that calm thou gav'st so oft before;
> Sleep undisturb'd within this peaceful shrine,
> Till angels wake thee with a note like thine.

From his own slough of disappointment, melancholia and indolence he could nonetheless animate himself and enter poetically and beautifully into another's distress. This was one of Johnson's most self-defining impulses in his early years and for the rest of his life, an identification with the poor and distressed that sprang from his own experience and began to trace a deeper, more meaningful Christianity within him than what his well-meaning mother had been able to impart to him.[15]

CHAPTER 7

Stirrings in Birmingham

I

CONCERNED OVER THE VACUUM and lack of direction in Johnson's life, towards the end of 1732, Hector invited him to Birmingham to live with him for an undetermined period in the apartment he was renting at the house of Thomas Warren, a bookseller across from the Swan tavern in the High Street. Johnson knew the area well. His unpleasant uncle John Harrison lived nearby, and his uncle Andrew who died three years earlier had kept a bookshop just down the road, where his aunt was still living.[1]

Hector's invitation was well-timed, and Birmingham was the perfect place for the idle melancholic to which to escape for a lengthy period. Change and excitement were in the air. Industrial forces then beginning to shape the emergent nation were all at work there as the city began its climb to keep up with Liverpool and Manchester in overtaking older cities like Bristol and Norwich as provincial centres. When Johnson joined Hector the city already possessed an intoxicating energy. Some thirty-five years later, Erasmus Darwin in a letter to Matthew Boulton, the great engineer and inventor of the steam engine, summed up where Birmingham was headed when he moaned he had to miss a meeting of the Lunar Society that Boulton had founded: 'Lord! what inventions, what wit, what rhetoric, metaphysical, mechanical, pyrotechnical, will be on the wing, bandied like a shuttlecock from one to another of your troupe of philosophers.' Johnson's remark in 1776 that Lichfield was a city of 'philosophers: we work with our heads, and make the boobies of Birmingham work for us with their hands', was merely a proud boast. He knew by then that the 'boobies' of Birmingham were at the head, not the tail, of England's future and that the Enlightenment had found its model in such groups as the Lunar Society. And on the arts side, thinking of Birmingham and Lichfield, he wrote in 1776: 'Staffordshire is the nursery of the arts, where they grow up till they are transplanted to London.'[2]

Johnson's companionship at first must have been heavy going for Hector, though from observation over preceding months Hector knew what to expect. He told Boswell he 'was afraid of Dr Johnson's head' during this period and that when, many years later, Johnson, who 'had been afraid to ask Hector for fear of an answer in the affirmative', asked him 'if he had observed in him a tendency to be disordered in his mind, Hector said he had'. In his *Life*, Boswell was sceptical of what Hector told him about Johnson's near 'madness' during these months, partly because tendencies towards insanity did not fit conveniently into the persona of his friend as the age's greatest rational moralist that he wished to perpetuate. Boswell thought Johnson 'fancied himself seized' by insanity, that 'his own diseased imagination' deceived him. It was stranger still, he added, 'that some of his friends should have given credit to his groundless opinion, when they had such undoubted proofs that it was totally fallacious'.[3]

Hector continued to do what he could to help Johnson through this prolonged depression. He tried to rescue him from his morbidity and his total lack of occupation in Lichfield by bringing him into regular contact with Warren whom he hoped would find Johnson and his knowledge of literature and bookselling useful. His generosity made a deep impression on Johnson, the memory of which he treasured more and more as the years passed. Writing to Hector in April 1755 after almost twenty years' separation and no communication, he recalled tenderly those 'evenings which we have passed together at Warren's and the Swan'. 'Gratifications and friendships of younger years operate very powerfully on the mind', he added. One month later he wrote again, grateful for the recovery of their intimate friendship in Birmingham, laced though it had been with suffering, 'Are you too come to the age in which *former days* begin to have an awful sound, and to impart an idea mixed of pain and pleasure?' Hector would have been sincerely saddened however to read this: 'From that kind of melancholy indisposition which I had when we lived together at Birmingham, I have never been free, but have always had it operating against my health and my life with more or less violence'.[4]

As it turned out, Warren proved to be very civil to him and welcomed him to his house and table with Hector, not least because he discovered Johnson could be useful to him in developing his new newspaper, *The Birmingham Journal*, by providing the occasional essay. In the after-glow of the publication of his majestic *Dictionary*, Johnson gratefully thought back to those difficult weeks and months of desperation and uncertainty, asking Hector, 'What comes of poor Warren? I have not lost all my kindness for him, for when I remember you I naturally remember all our connections, which are more pleasing to me for your sake.' We have only Hector's word for it that Johnson earned 'a little money' writing for Warren. All issues but one of the paper have been lost. Boswell looked high and low for copies and came up empty-handed: 'In what manner he employed his pen at this period, or whether he derived from it any pecuniary advantage, I have not been able to ascertain.'[5]

2

While he was living in Warren's house, Johnson mentioned having read at Pembroke College a French translation of Father Jerónimo Lobo's *Voyage to Abyssinia* and suggested that 'an abridgement and translation of it from the French into English might be a useful and profitable publication'.[6] Warren liked and encouraged the idea immediately. Travel literature was already popular on booksellers' publishing lists. During Johnson's life 'Britons conquered Canada and half of India, lost control of North America but won dominion over the Pacific, sent embassies into China and adventurers into Africa, colonised Australia and traded everywhere else, and bequeathed to Victorians one of the most extensive empires ever known to man.'[7]

The translation describes a seventeenth-century Jesuit missionary from Lisbon, Father Lobo, who embarked in the 1620s (at the age of twenty-

six) on a succession of hazardous journeys to the East Indies, first to Goa
and then across the Arabian Sea to the ancient Coptic Christian country
of Abyssinia where he finally arrived at the Jesuit house in Fremona, in-
land from the Red Sea. He laboured in that area of the world for many
years, teaching and perilously attempting the conversion of the locals to
the Church of Rome, eventually winding up in prison for several years before escaping from what had become a politically complex and dangerous
missionary environment. In his sixties he returned to Lisbon and wrote
up his remarkable adventures. His manuscripts in Portuguese remained
unpublished for the most part until he showed some of them, chiefly his
Itinerário, recounting his hair-raising voyages and cross-country expedi-
tions, to the British Ambassador to Portugal, Robert Southwell, who
asked him to write a series of short scientific essays on the Nile, the palm
tree and the Red Sea, among others, which the Royal Society published
anonymously in English in 1669. These proved to have an enormous appeal as many translations bearing Lobo's name followed in the next few
years. Then came along a Frenchman, Joachim Le Grand, who found
Lobo's manuscript of the *Itinerário* gathering dust in a library in Portugal
and published a translation in French in 1728, the edition Johnson saw at
Pembroke.[8]

Johnson suddenly had a substantial literary project with a clear line to
publication. For what would amount to a substantial piece of translation
Warren was to pay him a measly five pounds – although that was a quarter of his paltry annual salary teaching at Market Bosworth – but the
project was a light breaking in on his gloom. It was his first delicious taste
of writing for money. Le Grand's *Lobo* was nowhere to be had in Birmingham, so he quickly had a copy sent to him by someone at Pembroke. With
that in hand in early 1733 he set to work translating selected portions of it.
Warren's printer, a man named Osborn, was notified to expect copy flowing in and Johnson began giving it to him almost at once. It should have
been easy sailing on a project well within his literary abilities and knowledge of French. He had learned the language unsystematically on his own
along the way with the help of dictionaries – Boswell said he could under-

stand it perfectly but could not speak it 'readily'. But he had to overcome two old adversaries: persistent melancholia and indolence.

On 1 June, after having lived with Hector in Warren's house for no fewer than six months, he deposited himself in the home of an F. Jervis when Hector moved to his own lodgings on New Street. His work then stalled. He was 'very idle, lounged about with Hector, and had a few acquaintances'. Warren became impatient, Hector worried since he was familiar with his friend's dilatory ways, and Osborn was desperate because he badly needed the income from the work. What happened next was an early display of Johnson's instinctive sympathy for the needy. Hector knew his friend could not bear the thought of being the reason that 'the poor man and his family were suffering' and put it to him that if he did not apply himself Osborn could earn nothing. Alert to the recurring theme of a 'motive for humanity' in Johnson's life, Boswell embellished the story as Hector told it to him:

> Johnson upon this exerted the powers of his mind, though his body was relaxed. He lay in bed with the book, which was a quarto, before him, and dictated while Hector wrote. Mr Hector carried the sheets to the press, and corrected almost all the proof sheets, very few of which were even seen by Johnson. In this manner, with the aid of Mr Hector's active friendship, the book was completed.

As one critic has pointed out, there are people who do write in bed, but it would have taken no fewer than forty hours in bed to complete this 416-page translation. Nonetheless, with his back to the wall, Johnson was able even in his youth to turn near defeat into a sudden dramatic victory. What turned out to be an act of charity succeeded in getting the book done. In due course, with unaccountable delay, the book was published in 1735.[9]

Voyage to Abyssinia was his first effort in a long career of thinking and writing about travel. Exploration in the Western hemisphere was double-edged for him: it both fascinated and revolted him because of colonial atrocities committed there. Columbus 'gave a new world to European curiosity and European cruelty', he would write later. He had a similar distaste for European, especially Portuguese, imperialism along the African coastline, a subject about which he had read extensively and which would inspire his philosophical tale *Rasselas*, his play *Irene*, oriental tales in several moral essays, and general reflections on travel writing. A vogue for literary orientalism evident early in the eighteenth century in such works as Antoine Galland's *Arabian Nights* somewhat accounts for this fascination, but when he accepted the commission to translate Lobo he did so with an unusually deep knowledge of that exotic part of the world and with strongly negative views about how it was colonised.[10]

As for travel literature itself, the trick was to be the right kind of traveller. 'It may, I think, be justly observed, that few books disappoint their readers more than the narrations of travellers,' he wrote in 1760. Too frequently they are 'without incidents, without reflection' and 'tell nothing because nothing is to be told'.[11] The great object of any book of travel written for the entertainment of others should be to say something useful and revealing about 'human life' and examine the customs and laws of foreign nations. The genre was therefore extremely useful, he thought, to the health of the individual and a nation. Lobo was the type of traveller who brought back home something 'by which his country may be benefited; who procures some supply of want or mitigation of evil, which may enable his readers to compare their condition with that of others, to improve it whenever it is worse, and whenever it is better to enjoy it'. Johnson wrote in the Preface to the *Voyage* that Lobo did not indulge in 'romantic absurdities or incredible fictions' with trite and worn-out phrases as if he were writing a romance tale. Lobo's arduous journeys and long years of first-hand observation in India and Abyssinia qualified him as a realistic observer of human nature. Apart from its theme, the Preface is remarkable for its ring of authority. It points unmistakably to the argumentative persona he had been projecting as early as his pre-Oxford days.[12]

Johnson took aim at the social and political authority and abuse that

Father Lobo had brought to his attention. There is fury in the following passage, aimed here at the Jesuits:

> Let us suppose an inhabitant of some remote and superior region, yet unskilled in the ways of men, having read and considered the precepts of the Gospel, and the example of our Saviour, to come down in search of the *True Church*: if he would not enquire after it among the cruel, the insolent, and the oppressive; among those who are continually grasping at dominion over souls as well as bodies; among those who are employed in procuring to themselves impunity for the most enormous villainies, and studying methods of destroying their fellow-creatures, not for their crimes but their errors; if he would not expect to meet benevolence engaged in massacres, or to find mercy in a court of inquisition, he would not look for the *True Church* in the Church of Rome.

In spite of his definition of 'schismatick' in his *Dictionary* that suggests that the notion of the 'True Church' did exist for him, this barrage against the Jesuits, which underplays much that is positive in their mission, points to his fundamental hostility, even as a young man, towards any individual or religious group claiming to have a unique or exclusive pipeline to God, or claiming special miracles and insight denied to others. The Preface also anticipates Johnson's developing abhorrence of national and religious egotism on the part of power-hungry, imperialist, commercially predatory countries who think they know what is best for remote, less advanced nations.[13]

3

Johnson made only a few good acquaintances either at Warren's or Jervis's house, but among those whom he had it in mind to impress were Harry Porter, a dealer in textile fabrics and fine cloth who had a shop and house nearby on the High Street, and John Taylor, not his dear schoolmate but the clever Quaker inventor of the gild button and japanning of metals who amassed a fortune and, in 1765, with Sampson Lloyd III founded the first Birmingham banking-house that became known as Lloyds Bank. Lloyd, incidentally, was the nephew of Olivia Lloyd, the young Quaker in Stourbridge with whom Johnson had been 'much enamoured' and to whom he wrote love verses. Such people from the world of commerce and manufacturing seem to have been the extent of his contacts. Except for Warren we know of no literary friendships on his horizon, nor is anything known with any certainty of whom else he met or what he did or did not do for the next seven months while living in the Jervis house.[14]

He may have had a sexual interest, though. Hector told Boswell he did not believe certain anecdotes he had heard about Johnson's sexuality, but he did mention to him having heard from Peter Garrick, David's older brother, that on visits to Birmingham Johnson was one of three 'gallants' of the 'dissolute' wife of Lewis Paul, an inventor who later set up a cotton mill in Birmingham with the backing of several friends of Johnson's and whom Johnson also tried to help financially. One of the other gallants was 'fever powder' Robert James, his school friend six years older than he who also made appearances at Walmesley's table and whom Johnson regarded as one of the chief sources of information about his youth. The third member of this triumvirate and original source of the anecdotes was Benjamin Victor, eventually Poet Laureate of Ireland and theatre historian. Johnson met him in 1762 and described him as 'honest, indolent, conversable' with 'a great many anecdotes'. In this particular anecdote Victor told Garrick that 'the lady told him Johnson was the most seducing man she had ever known'. Boswell did not allow the anecdote into his biography, perhaps partly because it involved sexual flirtation with another man's wife and partly because he preferred to believe Hector when he said Johnson 'never was given to women' – in other words, that he was chaste and never partook of adultery: 'His juvenile attachments to the fair sex were . . . very transient; and it is certain, that he formed no criminal [i.e. carnal] connection whatsoever. Mr Hector, who lived with him in his younger days in the utmost intimacy and social freedom, has assured me, that even at that ardent season his conduct was strictly virtuous in that respect.'[15]

Hector also admitted that Johnson was not always an ideal companion. 'He drank freely, particularly Bishop with a roasted orange in it' – a kind of sangria containing wine, oranges and sugar, to which Johnson was especially partial. He might well have been drunk from time to time, though Boswell informed Hector that Johnson assured him 'there was no man alive who had seen him drunk'. To this Hector replied, 'Then he had forgot me', and proceeded to tell what happened one memorable night when one of Johnson's Ford relatives from Stourbridge, not Cornelius who had died the year before but probably one of his uncles, visited him in Birmingham. In Boswell's words:

> He [Ford] was it seems a hard drinker and he engaged Johnson and Hector to spend the evening with him at the Swan Inn. Johnson said to Hector, 'This fellow will make us both drunk. Let us take him by turns, and get rid of him.' It was settled that Hector should go first. He and Ford had drunk three bottles of port before Johnson came. When Johnson arrived, Hector found he had been drinking at Mr Porter's instead of saving himself. Hector went to bed at the Swan leaving Johnson to drink on with Ford. Next morning he perceived that Johnson who had been his bedfellow had been very drunk and he damned him. Johnson tried to deny the charge. *Literally* speaking Hector had not *seen* him drunk, though he was *sure* of the fact.

It is the sort of story that easily gets stretched into the realm of fiction in the telling and retelling. Boswell also left this anecdote out of his *Life*, but not necessarily because he did not believe it. It smacks of the truth, given Johnson's situation, companions and state of mind; moreover, Boswell himself acknowledged elsewhere that even in later life, although Johnson could be 'rigidly *abstemious*', he was not 'a *temperate* man either in eating or drinking'. He could keep himself from drinking, but once he

started it was hard for him to control it. Such roughness in Birmingham
included and probably aggravated a bad humour in his relations with others, a tendency that Hector identified during this period in Birmingham:
he would often be 'absent' – withdrawn, heedless, or neglectful – 'and talk
to himself and take peevish fits and abuse Hector who would then keep
aloof, upon which Johnson would come and coax him' into a reconciliation. Rough treatment like this of friends and acquaintances when he was
impatient or suddenly cross was not uncharacteristic of a harshness of
personality later on. The coaxing part also rings true. When Boswell describes an instance of it in his *Life*, he is quick to add that Johnson was essentially too good-natured not to attempt a reconciliation when he was
aware of having gone too far insulting or humiliating someone. With
Hector it would have been more a matter of jollying him along rather
than coaxing.[16]

4

Johnson wrote in his *Annales* that in February 1734 he finally returned to
Lichfield, having stretched his visit in Birmingham to just over one year.
Warren either had no more work for him or he had lost interest in writing for him. In the autumn, he had received a small legacy of five pounds
from his deceased godfather Richard Wakefield, but he was running out
of money and had to retreat to his home where his mother, Nathaniel and
Kitty Chambers awaited him. There he spent the next few months languishing without anything to do, though he could have done a bit of tu-
toring or teaching at his old school or helped a little in the bookshop, of
which his brother was now in charge.[17]

The main effect of Birmingham was that now he wanted to earn money
by writing. He was more certain than ever that he did not want to sell
books. He wanted to produce them. In the spring he asked an old
Pembroke College member, the Revd Robert Boyse, then living near Birmingham, to check out an edition of the fifteenth-century Italian Renaissance scholar Angelus Politian's Latin poems from the college library on
his next visit there. He remembered the book was there. Boyse checked

the book out on 15 June, noting it was for 'the use of Mr Johnson'. With it
in hand Johnson issued in August proposals for a subscription edition of
the poems. More than just an edition of the poems, this was to include a
history of Latin poetry from Petrarch to Politian as well as a life of
Politian. This is the first sign of his lifelong interest in writing biography
– the 'biographical part of literature,' he would say later, was 'what I love
most', especially the lives of 'great and learned persons'. It was the branch
of literature that 'comes near to ourselves, what we can turn to use'. People
were supposed to send in their subscriptions with a payment of half the
price to either him or his brother at the bookshop, 'N. Johnson, bookseller
of Lichfield', the rest to be paid on delivery. Subscriptions did not arrive in
any number, though, and he had to give up the project. The only thing
Johnson had to show for the project was the Pembroke copy of Politian,
which he seems never to have returned.[18]

   This stillborn project prolonged his dejection. There was no teaching
job within his sights and he had little sense of moving forward. A major
solace, as before, was Walmesley at the Bishop's Palace, where he again
saw Garrick and met the better sort of people of Lichfield, as well as an
expanding group of ladies, including the Aston girls who began to play a
part in his life the following year. The odd thing is that Johnson may now
have felt less at ease there. Older and more self-conscious about wearing
his continuing poverty among such people, he entered in Latin a passage
in his freshly revived diary about a poor man who has to devise a way of
disguising his tattered and torn clothes, as he did at Oxford, when he
moves among well-heeled company: 'For a poor man going among strangers, I have found useful things to be silk thread and pins of the same colour as one's clothes (silk thread, that is, of the kind used for knitting
stockings)'. At home now, his mother would have been of some use here,
though one of his friends in his later years spoke of his pride in being able
to do things for himself: 'He knew how to mend his own stockings, to
darn his linen or to sew on a button on his clothes. I am not (he would often say) a helpless man.' His confidence was boosted some time in the first
three months of 1735 when his *Voyage to Abyssinia* was finally published
by two London booksellers after the printed sheets had gathered dust in

Warren's shop for several months. It sold very poorly but at least now he had a book to his name.[19]

Given Johnson's lethargy, it may have been Walmesley who prodded him in November 1735 to act on the bold idea of writing to the editor, printer and publisher Edward Cave (1691–1754) in London, who in 1731 had the brilliant idea of founding *The Gentleman's Magazine.* As Cave had strong links with Birmingham, someone like Thomas Warren in the publishing business there could have suggested to Johnson that writing for Cave and his new monthly magazine might prove profitable. By 1734 the magazine was a going concern. Edited by Cave under the pseudonym Sylvanus Urban, it was the first ever significant London magazine of miscellaneous interest and history and became the most famous periodical in the eighteenth century. Cave read the market perfectly. He published monthly digests of news and articles from other papers and provided general information about the London entertainment world and public and private life, much of it gossipy or in the 'Talk of the Town' *New Yorker* mode. Cave also offered a section titled 'Poetical Essays' containing re-printed and original poetry. It was a convenient and pleasurable way for Londoners to keep up with what was going on across the spectrum of city life. Cave also hit on the clever and novel idea of circulating his magazine in the provinces so that they could easily keep abreast of what was happening in the capital and internationally.

From remote Lichfield Johnson sent a letter off to Cave with characteristic audacity, for some reason concealing his identity by cautiously giving his name as S. Smith. Not over modestly, he offered to overhaul the magazine's poetry section. Cave must surely be aware, he wrote, no less than his readers, of 'the defects of your poetical article'. He offered to put the section right 'on reasonable terms' by occasionally filling a column for him. The public would thank Cave, he urged, 'if beside the current wit of the month' the magazine added 'not only poems, inscriptions, etc. never printed before' which he would take it upon himself to supply, but also 'short literary dissertations in Latin or English, critical remarks on authors ancient or modern, forgotten poems that deserve revival, or loose pieces ... worth preserving'. This would make the poetry section worth the time of an intelligent reader much more than the present diet of 'low jests, awkward buffoonery, or the dull scurrilities of either [political] party'. If Cave agrees, he would like to know how much he would pay. If the publisher's offer in last month's issue of £50 for the best Latin or English poem on 'Life, Death, Judgement, Heaven and Hell' is any indication, he expects he will be 'generous'. While he was at it, he added he was willing to contribute to any other literary project of Cave's provided his ideas would not be stolen by others. Although Cave responded one week later – whether positively or negatively is unknown – nothing came of the effort. When Johnson wrote to him again in 1738 it was in his own name and as if for the first time.[20]

CHAPTER 8

Taking a Wife

I

IN SEPTEMBER 1734 something had happened that was to change the course of Johnson's life for ever and lift him for a time from his persisting melancholia. Harry Porter, the Birmingham dealer in textiles to whom he had been introduced by Hector, died insolvent at his shop on the High Street on 3 September at the young age of forty-three and after twenty years of marriage, leaving his widow Elizabeth and two sons and a daughter, Lucy, between the ages of ten and eighteen to survive him. Johnson had of course met Elizabeth Porter through Hector's circle of friends. Hector used to buy his clothes from Porter's shop. Anna Seward, whom several people, most vigorously Hector and Boswell, denounced for her gossipy and malicious tales about Johnson and the Porters, claimed that while Porter was ill Johnson actually 'passed all his leisure hours' at his house, 'attending his sick-bed', and that it was at this time that he secretly conceived a passion for his wife.

Elizabeth Porter was twenty years older than he. She was raised in a respectable propertied Leicestershire and Warwickshire family named Jervis, and although her father died when she was six she was accustomed to a more genteel existence than the one her husband gave her. She brought to him a dowry of at least £600, in spite of which he did not prosper. Anna Seward said that her mother 'perfectly remembered' Mrs Porter and that her beauty existed only in Johnson's imagination: 'She had a very red face, and very indifferent features.' There is a surviving portrait of her believed to have been painted in her forties, however, showing her as quite a beauty. The picture may be the same one her daughter Lucy once showed to Mrs Thrale long after her mother had died, in which Mrs Thrale thought she looked 'pretty'. 'Her hair was eminently beautiful,' Johnson told her, 'quite blond like that of a baby.'[1]

Soon after Porter's death Johnson began to court her. Her daughter Lucy saw it all begin to happen, able as the eldest daughter to respond to this astonishing development with more equanimity than her brother Jervis. At eighteen he was old enough to see the overtures of this strange-looking interloper only seven years older than he as a humiliation and grotesque absurdity. His ten-year-old brother was too young to feel such outrage. Probably all three of the children wondered why their mother could possibly want to enter into a relationship with a young man who was poor and had no prospects, was blotched with scrofula scars, had bad eyesight (though this may not have been immediately evident), and made disconcertingly odd movements with his head and upper body.

We tend to think of Johnson as he was when Boswell knew him, overweight and famous, when flesh had concealed the massive angularity of his large bone structure. He cut a different figure in 1734, as Lucy told Boswell in the only account anyone, even Hector and Taylor, has left of his youthful physique:

> Miss Porter told me, that when he was first introduced to her mother, his appearance was very forbidding: he was then lean and lank, so that his immense structure of bones was hideously striking to the eye, and the scars of the scrofula were deeply visible. He also wore his hair, which was straight and stiff, and separated behind; and he often had, seemingly, convulsive starts and odd gesticulations, which tended to excite at once surprise and ridicule.

This was disturbing enough, but after he died Mrs Thrale in her *Anecdotes* added detail about his eyes that would have characterised him in his youth as well: 'His eyes, though of a light grey colour were so wild, so piercing, and at times so fierce, that fear was I believe the first emotion in the hearts of all his beholders.' How, then, could Mrs Porter have been attracted to him? Part of the answer to that doubtless lies in his strength, height and robustness, also highlighted by Mrs Thrale:

> His stature was remarkably high [five feet eleven inches in his stockings], and his limbs exceedingly large: his strength was more than common, I believe, and his activity had been greater I have heard than such a form gave one reason to expect: his features were strongly marked, and his countenance particularly rugged; though the original complexion had certainly been fair, a circumstance somewhat unusual.

Sir Joshua Reynolds once was supposed to have been told that he should not paint Johnson in a full-length portrait because of the 'uncouth formation' of his limbs. On the contrary, Reynolds replied, far from thinking Johnson's limbs unsightly, he thought them well-formed.[2]

That was only the body that housed the soul, as Mrs Thrale put it, and for Mrs Porter it was by far the less important part of the picture. Lucy remembered that her mother seemed not to notice his body: 'Mrs Porter was so much engaged by his conversation that she overlooked all these external disadvantages [and advantages], and said to her daughter, "This is the most sensible man that I ever saw in my life."' That his conversation and mind, his down-to-earth common sense and insight, were enough for her to be able to see beneath the surface of his distorted physique and ignore his virtual poverty says a great deal about her own perspicacity. Except for him she was looking at a life of loneliness and deterioration. Her children would eventually be going their own way, so any hostility towards Johnson on their part counted for less than they thought. Lucy was not as upset with their mother as Jervis was. One of the early biographers claimed that her brother 'offered to settle a very handsome annuity on her [their mother] for life, provided she would break her engagements'. Her quick readiness to swim against such currents in this relationship and follow her own feelings with such abandon argues not only that she fell deeply in love with him but also that she had resources and emotions inside her that had not yet been tapped. Mrs Thrale judged that as a widow with children 'she must have been in most respects a woman quite like her neighbours', with nothing to distinguish her, but 'her second choice made her a person to enquire about'.[3]

What was there to appeal to him in a woman of her years, apart from her physical attractiveness? Although her husband had died insolvent, she had about £800 (about £80,000 today) to bring to the marriage. One wonders at what point he knew about the money. Did he think his chances of marrying someone else were very limited, that women were never likely to be attracted to him romantically? If we are to believe Hector and Boswell, his religious upbringing up to this point had kept him sexually innocent. Mrs Porter's interest in him, which she must have had to make quite plain to overcome his sexual shyness and inexperience, must therefore have seemed to him like an exciting, warm and luminous breeze of unfamiliar affection. She unlocked something in him: 'In a man whom religious education has secured from licentious indulgences, the passion of love, when once it has seized him, is exceedingly strong; being unimpaired by dissipation, and totally concentrated in one object.' That is the way Boswell read her initial effect upon him. Beyond that, he was impressed by her family background and could read in it something of 'the born gentlewoman'. And as he later said, he was taken with her ironic, satirical sense and slight signs of literary judgement – that she 'could read comedy better than anybody he had ever heard', though 'in tragedy she mouthed too much'.[4]

Their courtship continued for about nine months somewhere in Birmingham. It was not at her house on the High Street because since she was forced to give up the shop that was connected to the house, she had no choice but to vacate the house as well. Wherever she resided in Birmingham, probably without her disgusted eldest son who could not bear the sight of Johnson's wooing, it still meant that Johnson had to make frequent visits to the city to see her. Before long, they decided to marry and it was time for Johnson to explain his decision to his mother and, if possible, obtain her approval. Johnson hoped his mother would give them her blessing, but it would not deter him if she did not. He surely told her about Elizabeth's money and that if he were to be married, Mrs Porter's sons stood to be supported very well by their rich uncle, Joseph Porter. Sadly alienated, the eldest boy Jervis vowed never to see his mother again, as a result of which neither son ever saw his mother again after her re-marriage. Only Lucy would remain with her mother.

It was not only Mrs Porter's family who disliked Johnson and the idea of his marriage to her. Lucy Porter insisted to Boswell that 'The Birming-ham people could not bear Mr Johnson. She did not say why. I suppose from envy of his parts; though I do not see how traders could envy such qualities.' Envy, gossip, hostility: these undoubtedly were the reasons the couple decided to marry not in Birmingham but out of the way at St Werburgh's Church in Derby on 9 July 1735. Adding another layer of ec-centricity to the whole courtship, for some reason they decided to get there on horseback, not in a carriage, and a strange enough journey it was. 'His account of the wedding we used to think ludicrous enough,' Mrs Thrale wrote: 'I was riding to church (says Johnson), and she following on another single horse: she hung back however, and I turned about to see whether she could get her steed along, or what was the matter. I had how-ever soon occasion to see it was only coquetry, and *that I despised,* so quickening my pace a little, she mended hers; but I believe there was a tear or two – pretty dear creature!' For Boswell he added that her coquettish behaviour of riding too slow and then too fast, trying to keep him off bal-ance, came from reading too many frivolous 'old romances', which put into her head 'the fantastical notion that a woman of spirit should use her lover like a dog'. He was not about to become, he said, 'the slave of caprice', so he rode on out of her sight. Boswell judged that his behaviour showed 'manly firmness'.[5]

An objective witness may be more disposed to think it insensitive. A woman married for twenty years in dire need of companionship is not likely to have wanted to treat her new husband like a 'dog'. This little test of wills, coming early in a married life that turned out to have quite a few quarrels, was for her mingled with a good portion of grief. Within the space of less than a year she had lost her husband, married a highly eccen-tric man half her years disliked by her children and other relatives, and seen her family break up in ill will. And here was Johnson riding on ahead of her in her hour of need when he should have been next to her. That in later years he liked to tell his friends about this ride to Derby in a comical vein suggests he never grasped the full meaning of her tears. He married his 'Tetty' – his nickname for her, which Boswell called a provincial contraction for 'Elisabeth' and judged to be ridiculous enough 'when applied to a woman of her age and appearance' – feeling it was 'a love-marriage upon both sides'. His wife is supposed to have worn a portrait of him in miniature in a bracelet for the rest of her life. Boswell concluded that 'his regard and fondness for her never ceased, even after her death', a fact amply borne out by his searching prayers for her year after year. Still, there were quarrels and great pressures in their marriage. She brought him some money, which helped launch them as a married couple, but they were two very different people and soon enough they began to drift apart.[6]

2

Tetty's faith in him was such that with her money they decided boldly in the spring or summer to start a school, for which he took steps in May to recover the more than one hundred books and private papers he had left at Oxford with Taylor. In June and July they also placed advertisements in The Gentleman's Magazine in London for the school, where 'young gentlemen are boarded and taught the Latin and Greek languages, by SAMUEL JOHNSON'. 'I am now going to furnish a house in the country,' he wrote to his old Lichfield chum Richard Congreve, 'and keep a private boarding-school for young gentlemen whom I shall endeavour to instruct in a method somewhat more rational than those commonly practised, which you know there is no great vanity in presuming to attempt.' He wrote this from nearby Great Haywood, Staffordshire, where in May he had accepted a job for a few weeks preparing the nineteen-year-old son of Thomas Whitby for university. Whitby was former High Sheriff of Staffordshire, to whom Johnson had been recommended by the Revd John Addenbrooke, then the Vicar of St Chad's and eventually Dean of Lichfield – a 'kindness' Johnson recalled forty years later that included negotiating a salary.[7]

The prospect of being in charge of a school particularly excited him. No longer would he be enslaved by the whims and tyrannies of superiors who knew less about their subjects than he did, or stymied by curricula he did not think were in pupils' best interests. He was even restless to draw up a 'plan of education' for the school. He needed details of the 'different ways of teaching in use at the most celebrated schools' and asked Congreve to send him what he knew about Westminster and the methods at his own school Charterhouse – just 'under each class their exercises and authors'. He also had strong ideas of his own about teaching. Around about this time he advised his first cousin Samuel Ford about how best to prepare for university. 'Apply yourself wholly to the languages, till you go to the university' by focusing on Greek authors such as Xenophon, Homer, Theocritus and Euripides so as to be 'skilled in all the dialects'. As for Latin authors, 'it is proper not to read the later authors, till you are well versed in those of the purest ages', the likes of Terence, Tully, Caesar, Sallust, Virgil and Horace. But his main advice was rationalist and pragmatic, the earliest complete statement we have of what, above all else, as a boy and young man he had determined to master through relentless practice, and for which the world has come to know him: 'The greatest and most necessary task still remains, to attain a habit of expression, without which knowledge is of little use. This is necessary in Latin, and more necessary in English; and can only be acquired by a daily imitation of the best and correctest authors.'[8]

After only a few weeks at Great Haywood he was back in Lichfield and Birmingham, renting a farmhouse called Edial Hall for the school about two and a half miles west of Lichfield in a tiny rural crossroads in the middle of nowhere. Today it looks just as lonely as it must have seemed then. It was available and recommended by Walmesley. They moved into the house with his books and Tetty's daughter Lucy sometime late in the year or early in 1736. In the tiny group of three boarders he (with Walmesley's help) managed to net were Davy Garrick, who was then eighteen, and his younger brother George. Someone said that putting the Garricks in the school resembled the trick of country housewives of 'placing one egg in the nest of a hen to induce her to lay more'. Davy had interrupted his schooling at Lichfield Grammar School to be with his wine-merchant uncle in Lisbon, and on his return needed to be brought up to scratch in Latin before going on to university. While his father was in Granada as a captain in military service and his elder brother was away at sea, he more or less had become head of his debt-ridden family (mother and four other siblings) in Lichfield. By the time he entered the school, he had already shifted his attention from university towards a military career for himself, so his application to his studies was less earnest than it might have been. On top of which his distracting relish for theatre instead of the Romans and Greeks had already shown itself. When Johnson 'expected from him some exercise or composition upon a theme, he showed him several scenes of a new comedy, which had engrossed his time'. Forty years later Johnson was still complaining about Garrick's academic prowess: 'He has not Latin enough. He finds out the Latin by the meaning, rather than the meaning by the Latin.'[9]

Johnson's insurmountable problem with this school, apart from his lack of credentials, was that his frightening appearance and the same odd manner and assortment of tics and gesticulations that had put off potential employers also scared off potential parents and students. When he tried one last time in August perhaps under pressure from Tetty to secure a teaching post before going ahead with his own school, this time nothing less than as Master of Solihull Grammar School, he was rejected for this reason and because he was arrogant. One of the trustees or governors of the school wrote to Walmesley, who had spoken for him, explaining bluntly that everyone thought he was an excellent scholar but also disliked him for his insolence: 'he has the character of being a very haughty, ill-natured gentleman, and he has such a way of distorting his face (which though he cannot help) the gentlemen think it may affect some young lads'. They were looking instead for 'a soft tongue, a smooth face, or ceremonious carriage'. There was also the logistical problem at Edial Hall that with Lichfield Grammar School so close by there was no particularly good reason for parents to send their boys to Johnson. On this fragile basis of a little band of three students at their school, then, he and his wife began their married life, hoping that when word got out about his excellent teaching the students would flock to the school. They did not flock, however, even after he ran further advertisements in *The Gentleman's Magazine*. He trawled in a few from here and there but never had more than eight, several of whom were day boys. The enterprise was looking financially disastrous.[10]

Lack of interest in the school was only one strain on the marriage. Living in a remote spot like Edial was a huge change for Tetty from living on the high street in Birmingham. She would have had to fight boredom much of the time as Johnson got on with his teaching. There was also Lucy, confused and unhappy, muddying the waters. More seriously, Tetty soon discovered that her new husband's personal habits were a trial for her. A few of Mrs Thrale's allusions in 1777 to their quarrels, long after Tetty had died, could apply just as plausibly to this period as later: 'I asked him once whether he ever disputed with his wife (I knew he adored her). Oh yes, perpetually my dear says he; she was extremely neat in her disposition, and always fretful that I made the house so dirty – a clean floor is *so* comfortable she would say by way of twitting; till at last I told her, I thought we had had talk enough about the floor, we would now have a touch at the *ceiling*.' They had their disagreements about meals, too. The Johnson Mrs Thrale knew 'loved his dinner extremely', so one day she asked 'if he ever huffed his wife about his meat? Yes, Yes replied he, but then she huffed me worse; for she said one day as I was going to say grace – Nay hold says she, and do not make a farce of thanking God for a dinner which you will presently protest not eatable.'[11]

There was a larger problem. Her conversation may have struck him as too narrow to compensate for her querulousness. Could he have been thinking of his own marriage when he said, again after her death, 'a man of sense and education should meet a suitable companion in a wife. It was a miserable thing when the conversation could only be such as, whether the mutton should be boiled or roasted, and probably a dispute about that.' With his remarks Johnson in retrospect and inadvertently sends the message that he was not an easy man to live with, whatever her housewifery was like. Very telling in a more comprehensive way was Mrs Thrale's observation that in arguments between spouses that they both witnessed, he would always take the side of the husband:

> Women (says Dr Johnson) give great offence by a contemptuous spirit of non-compliance on petty occasions. The man calls his wife to walk with him in the shade, and she feels a strange desire just at that moment to sit in the sun: he offers to read her a play, or sing her a song, and she calls the children in to disturb them, or advises him to seize that opportunity of settling the family accounts. Twenty such tricks will the faithfulest wife in the world not refuse to play, and then look astonished when the fellow fetches in a mistress. And are the hours of pleasure so frequent in life, that when a man gets a couple of quiet ones to spend in familiar chat with his wife, they must be poisoned by petty mortifications?

Such tricks as Tetty played at are behind such sour views on marriage, but a man who thought the husband always right cannot have been easy to live with.[12]

Decades later Garrick loved to tell an anecdote about Tetty and Johnson's sex life at Edial, which with his unmatchable talent for mimicry and ridicule he caricatured to devastating effect. The anecdote highlights the additional stress on their married life of having Davy and the other boys at such close quarters in the house with them. Davy, moreover, unimpressed with Johnson as a teacher, was lively and mischievous enough to perplex them even more, and he probably was the ringleader in this nocturnal episode as told inimitably by Boswell:

> From Mr Garrick's account he did not appear to have been profoundly reverenced by his pupils. His oddities of manner, and uncouth gesticulations, could not but be the subject of merriment to them; and, in particular, the young rogues used to listen at the door of his bed-chamber, and peep through the keyhole, that they

might turn into ridicule his tumultuous and awkward fondness for Mrs Johnson.

Garrick, especially in his cups and in exclusively male company, when Johnson was nowhere to be seen, liked to amuse his friends by working up routines of what to him and doubtless the other boys was the easily burlesqued relationship between their highly sexed master and his older, decaying wife. Boswell reconstructs one of these from a conversation he and a friend had with the gossipy Mrs Desmoulins who was living in Johnson's house the year before Johnson died:

> BOSWELL: 'Do you know, Ma'am, that there really was a connection between him and his wife? You understand me.' MRS DESMOULINS: 'Yes, yes, Sir. Nay, Garrick knew it was consummated, for he peeped through the keyhole, and behaved like a rascal, for he made the Doctor ridiculous all over the country by describing him running round the bed after she had lain down, and crying, "I'm coming, my Tetsie, I'm coming, my Tetsie! Ph! Ph!" (blowing in his manner).'

In another version Johnson is so preoccupied working on a play in his bedroom that he is fairly oblivious to Tetty's calls to him to come to bed. When he absently mistakes the bedclothes for his shirt-tails and begins to stuff them hurriedly into his breeches, she finds herself suddenly exposed on the bed. Garrick did not entirely conjure up the pictures out of thin air, but he did invest them with images of Johnson and Tetty as they were ten or more years later in London. At Edial Hall she may already have begun to feel a pressure to look and act young in deference to her younger husband, taking to excessive cosmetics to create the desired effect. He resolutely objected to her dyeing her hair black.[13]

Whatever the causes, Johnson's eyes did turn elsewhere. 'Forty years ago, Sir,' he confessed to Boswell in 1776 on their visit to Lichfield, 'I was in love with an actress here, Mrs Emmet', though Garrick mistakenly did not think he was a careful observer of the female form. But if there really

Michael Johnson, Samuel's father. Johnson wrote impatiently of his parents that 'neither of them ever tried to calculate the profits of trade, or the expenses of living.'

Edial Hall, Lichfield, Johnson's failed school.

Elizabeth Porter, Johnson's wife and twenty years older than he, whom he called 'Tetty'. Thought to have been painted not long before they married on 9 July 1735.

Dearest Tetty

After hearing that you are in so much danger, as I apprehend from a hurt on a tendon, I shall be very uneasy till I know that you are recovered, And beg that you will . . . with nothing that can contribute to it, nor doing yourself any thing that may make confinement less melancholy. You have already suffered more than I can bear to reflect upon, and I hope more than either of us shall suffer again. One part at least I have often flattered myself we shall avoid for the future, our troubles will surely never separate us more. If N— does not easily succeed in his endeavours, let him not be . . . to call in another Surgeon to consult with him, . . . have two or three visits from Ranby or Shipton, who is . . . to be the best, for a Guinea, which you need not fear to part with on so pressing an occasion, for I can send you twenty pounds more on Monday, which I have received this night; I beg therefore that you will be more regard my happiness, than to expose yourself to any little hazards. I still promise myself many happy years from your tenderness and affection, which I sometimes hope our misfortunes have not yet deprived me of. . . . David wrote to me this

First page of the only surviving letter from Samuel Johnson to his wife Tetty, 31 January 1740. He writes with a sense of guilt for having been away from her for so long, especially while she had injured herself: 'You have already suffered more than I can bear to reflect upon, and I hope more than either of us shall suffer again.'

Tea service of Chinese design belonging to Samuel Johnson. Johnson often drank copiously, more than ten cups of tea at a sitting. Note the small teacups without handles.

Molly Aston, Johnson's great love, who lived in Lichfield.

St John's Gate, Edward Cave's *Gentleman's Magazine* offices, where he also resided. The doorway to the right of the arch led to Cave's office, a large room above the arch, where Johnson spent much time in the late 1730s and 1740s.

An imaginary scene, painted in the mid-nineteenth century, showing Johnson working intensely in Cave's offices at St John's Gate. The girl has brought him food.

Elizabeth Carter, poet, classicist, translator and early favourite of Johnson's in London.

The portrait of Samuel Johnson by Joshua Reynolds, *c*.1755,
included in the first edition of the *Dictionary*.

Self-portrait by Joshua Reynolds, 1753–4. Reynolds returned
to England from his Grand Tour in 1752 and soon became
immensely rich from his painting. After Johnson's death he
referred to 'thirty years' of intimacy with him.

was a woman with whom he fell in love during that year after his marriage and remained in love for the rest of her life, it was Molly Aston. Three years older than Johnson, she was one of eight daughters of Sir Thomas Aston of Cheshire, four of whom came to live in Lichfield. He had met her at the Bishop's Palace several years earlier when Walmesley began to cultivate the Aston girls – he married one of them, Magdalen, in 1736. When the Aston girls came on to the scene, the palace, which was always an enticing escape for him, sparkled as it never had before, and he shined as never before. Boswell described how Johnson could rise to the occasion in the company of women in Lichfield:

> In such families he passed much time in his early years. In most of them, he was in the company of ladies, particularly at Mr Walmesley's, whose wife and sisters-in-law, of the name of Aston, and daughters of a baronet, were remarkable for good breeding; so that the notion which has been industriously circulated and believed, that he never was in good company till late in life, and, consequently, had been confirmed in coarse and ferocious manners by long habits, is wholly without foundation. Some of the ladies have assured me, they recollected him well and when a young man, as distinguished for his complaisance.[14]

During the increasingly exasperating and grinding year at Edial Hall, this new feminine company at the palace would have had a magnetic effect upon him. He once described Molly as 'a beauty and a scholar, and a wit and a Whig'. She was bright and daunting to other women – Anna Seward described her as 'handsome but haughty'. That she was a Whig disturbed him no more than that Walmesley was one. What really must have turned his head was her beauty and intelligence, and her breeding, all of which is attested to in a ravishing portrait of her dating from this period showing her elegant face and figure, and an abundance of auburn hair. Eager to slip into her *Anecdotes* some titillating details from Johnson's past, Mrs Thrale wrote that when her first husband asked him what had been the happiest period or moment in his life, he did not hesitate to reply: 'It was that year in which [I] spent one whole evening with M—y As—n; but thoughts of it sweetened the whole year.' 'That indeed (said he) was not happiness, it was rapture.' In her journal Mrs Thrale stated plainly that they spent the evening tête-à-tête. 'She talked all in praise of liberty', he went on, so gallantly 'I made this [Latin] epigram upon her'. It was about her beauty, 'Pulchra Maria', to which he had become a slave – 'She was the loveliest creature I ever saw!!!!' Mrs Thrale translated the epigram immediately into, 'Persuasions to freedom fall oddly from you:/If freedom we seek – fair Maria, adieu!' Johnson added, 'The ladies never loved Molly Aston', alluding to her forthright intelligence. Mrs Thrale then pressed home by questioning him what his wife thought of this 'attachment'. His reply, which is an amazing and revealing piece of confidence to give to her, touched a nerve in his marriage:

> She was jealous to be sure (said he), and teased me sometimes when I would let her; and one day, as a fortune-telling gipsy passed us when we were walking out in company with two or three friends in the country, she made the wench look at my hand, but soon repented her curiosity; for (says the gipsy) your heart is divided, Sir, between a Betty and a Molly: Betty loves you best, but you take most delight in Molly's company: when I turned about to laugh, I saw my wife was crying.

He added quickly, 'Pretty charmer! she had no reason!'[15]

There are grounds for thinking she did have reason to cry and that in this disclaimer to Mrs Thrale he was shielding himself from the imputation that he was in love with someone else when he married. To begin with, Molly's letters to him over the next thirty years went missing so that none of his early biographers ever saw them, though he remarked that 'they should be the last papers he would destroy'. This may mean he finally burned them in his infamous bonfire.[16]

At about the same time as Johnson first met Molly, he became very friendly with the dashing Henry ('Harry') Hervey, captain in the 1st Dragoon Guards who was posted to Lichfield around 1730 and soon became

Molly's brother-in-law. As he had for others, Johnson wrote several love poems for Hervey, some included in the 'Stella' group that Hervey transcribed during their most intimate time in London between 1737 and 1743 and which Johnson published in *The Gentleman's Magazine* in 1747. Hervey undoubtedly wanted them for Molly's sister, his future wife Catherine, but it is not unlikely that Johnson got his inspiration for them from Molly herself. Two 'Stella poems', 'To Miss—on Her Playing Upon the Harpsicord in a Room Hung With Some Flower-Pieces of Her Own Painting' and 'To Miss—On Her Giving the Author a Gold and Silk Net-Work Purse of Her Own Weaving', flatter and please with pleasant though trite imagery and commonplace sentiments. 'The Winter's Walk', set in the Staffordshire countryside during the wicked winter of 1739–40, resonates more deeply, deploying winter as an emblem of life's miseries that, as it did then in Johnson's life, alternated with sunshine and joy: 'Tir'd with vain joys, and false alarms,/With mental and corporeal strife,/ Snatch me, my Stella, to thy arms,/And screen me from the ills of life.' The poem is full of longing and frustration, a fantasy that with his Stella he could some day find himself in a protecting, encouraging, intellectually satisfying love. That he never, so far as we know, satisfied his passion for Molly has to be regarded as one of his greatest personal sadnesses.[17]

3

As the months wore on, Johnson began to realise that his school was failing, that he was not cut out to be a teacher, and that the whole enterprise was wearing him out, deepening his frustration, and initiating what was to become a relentless process of romantic disenchantment between him and Tetty. The thought and accompanying guilt weighed on him, too, that he had got her to agree to spend much of her surviving fortune on this school. On 27 August he wrote in his diary, 'This day I have trifled away, except that I have attended the school in the morning.' It must have been a feeling he had many times a week. He was wasting his talents. He began to make resolutions and 'rules' for himself to do better and do more. On 7 September, his twenty-eighth birthday, as would become his habit on his birthday, he composed a little prayer asking God for help to make use of the year in a way that would bring him comfort 'in the hour of death, and in the day of judgement'. Then he added another resolution for good measure, 'I intend tomorrow to review the rules I have at any time laid down, in order to practise them.' If such 'rules' were anything like the many he made for himself for the rest of his life, they included going to bed and getting up at reasonable hours and not giving in to laziness, with all of which he was failing too often. Perhaps Robert Burton's *Anatomy of Melancholy* helped him, which he said 'was the only book that ever took him out of bed two hours sooner than he wished to rise'. It was hard to get up in the morning and face another day of systematic, patient teaching when his whole being and intellect ached to move swiftly, if unsystematically, 'by fits and starts, by violent eruptions into the regions of knowledge'. Having to force his 'gloomy and impetuous' mind into the harness of a schoolmaster made him irritable, and that only increased his guilt. He had the highest respect for a good teacher and knew that a good temper was a requisite for the job, but he also knew he lacked one.[18]

It was therefore strange that in 1736, probably late in the year, he applied for the assistant mastership of Brewood Grammar School in Staffordshire. It is likely Tetty put him up to it. As with most of his other teaching applications, this one came to nothing, which in this instance was especially regrettable because the Revd William Budworth, the headmaster of the school, was widely esteemed as a talented and benign instructor of youth. In the years to come, Budworth lamented more than once having to reject his application 'from an apprehension that the paralytic affliction' from which he suffered 'might become the object of imitation or of ridicule among his pupils'.[19]

There was nothing for it, then, but to hope that the school might suddenly catch the fancy of local parents. In the meantime, he needed to do something else as well, something literary that would help him preserve his sanity and self-respect and, who knows, perhaps earn him some money. He decided to write a poetic drama. He would call it *Irene* and base it on a piece of Turkish history. The story takes place between the fall of Constantinople in 1453 and the death of Irene in 1456. Constantinople was an appealing subject for him, for in his reading he had worked up a deep appreciation for it and the Mohammedan world generally. 'Sir, there are two objects of curiosity', he said to Boswell, 'the Christian world, and the Mahometan world. All the rest may be considered as barbarous.' For his source he used Richard Knolles's *A Generall Historie of the Turkes* (1603), which he much admired and used in his study of the Mohammedan Empire that had already borne fruit in the *Voyage to Abyssinia*.[20]

The plot is taken from an episode in the wars between the Greeks and Turks. It concerns the fate of Irene, a ravishingly beautiful Greek slave who after the fall of Constantinople is handed over to the Sultan Mahomet II and becomes his mistress. Her beauty holds too much of a sexual power over him, though she has abandoned her Christianity for him, and he is warned by his advisers to remove her from his life and court before his people turn against him. Her Greek friend Aspasia provides the Christian theme by striving to convince her to recover her moral sense. Irene, and to a lesser extent the unworldly Aspasia, provide the moral focus. Irene's weaknesses and tormentingly ambivalent values are the source of her own destruction – 'what Anguish racks the guilty Breast' – not politics or the Sultan's cruelty, and the play concludes with him lopping off her head when he suspects her of treachery. Since the whole play is poetry, it must have seemed to Johnson as he wrote page after page of verse in that isolated farmhouse-school outside Lichfield that here at last was the vehicle for the creative fulfilment of his poetic powers and a justification for all the reading he had done about the oriental world. The play looked to him like his ticket out of Lichfield, his first step to fame and fortune.

He began to write rather chaotically in a 'fragmentary eruption' of ideas, composing speeches without being sure who would actually speak them. The original manuscript, which tradition has it someone saved from the bonfire and someone else (much later) presented to the King, looks like the work of an inexperienced dramatist who was relying on his prodigious memory, propelled first by the impulse to get the speeches down on paper that in many instances he had already composed in his head. One critic has called the first draft more of a commonplace-book than a dramatic sketch, a sign of the 'radically untheatrical quality' of his imagination – a reason why the play, even after extensive revisions, 'lacked that dynamic of interlocking, opposing personalities and ideas in vivid and sinewy conflict that thrill us in the best drama'. One finds its characters remain wooden and its didactic morality laboured and cloying, unconnected to real human experience.[21]

Johnson turned Irene's dilemma into one between worldly or materialistic glory and Christianity, but her speeches trace the more rebellious theme of independence and individuality against the oppressiveness of society. At one point he has her defend herself from male arrogance and its autocratic suppression and disregard of women:

> Do not we share the comprehensive thought,
> Th' enlivening wit, the penetrating reason?
> Beats not the female breast with gen'rous passions,
> The thirst of empire, and the love of glory?

And there are other convincing speeches on female slavery and other types of suppression. Irene is in torment because of her socially and morally divided self. The fact that she is killed at the end expresses Johnson's indignation that social order is tyrannical, cutting down those who presume to violate it. Were Molly Aston's sentiments on liberty ringing in his ears? There is, to be sure, ambivalence in his attitudes towards Irene and Aspasia. Aspasia represents conventionality, Irene independence. It is better to act now and claim today before 'interposing death destroys the prospect!'; docility and deference always perpetrate a 'gen'ral fraud from day to day' and fill the world 'with wretches undetected'. Irene may be impure in her martyrdom for the Greek cause, but she is the tragic heroine and Johnson's sympathies were overwhelmingly with her.[22]

After writing three or more acts of the play, he took it to Walmesley at the palace for a mature judgement. Walmesley was so disturbed by the pathos of the heroine's emotional and moral plight that he asked Johnson,

'How can you possibly contrive to plunge her into deeper calamity?' Johnson's comeback was, 'Sir, I can put her into the Spiritual Court!' Pleased with 'this proof of Johnson's abilities as a dramatic writer', he advised him strongly to finish the tragedy and get it on the stage. What stage would that be? Where else but in London? It was time to leave Lichfield.[23]

Part Three

SLOW RISES WORTH

CHAPTER 9

Stranger in London

I

THE IDEA WAS TIMELY and caught hold. He and Tetty, partly under
Walmesley's influence, decided to close the school so he could travel
to London to acquire literary work. He left most of their money with
Tetty, who presumably continued to live with Lucy in Edial Hall, now
empty of boys. Notwithstanding the awkwardness over the marriage, they
could benefit from being close to his mother and could even have helped
her in the bookshop. Once he established himself in London, he would
send for them – a dangerously open-ended scheme. On the face of it, he
was eager to get away from both of them.

The plan was to travel to London with Davy, finish *Irene* there, try to
get it acted and published, and generally find his way in the professional
world of letters. Davy was to lodge as a paying guest with an old friend of
Walmesley's in Kent, the Revd John Colson, to be tutored by him on
mathematics, philosophy and 'humane learning' with a view to his entering the Temple and being educated to the Bar. Just after Johnson and his
former pupil disappeared down the road out of Lichfield on 2 March 1737,
Walmesley dutifully sat down to compose for Davy a letter of introduction to Colson, also mentioning that he would be in the company of a
Samuel Johnson:

> He, and another neighbour of mine, one Mr Samuel Johnson, set
> out this morning for London together. Davy Garrick is to be with
> you early the next week, and Mr Johnson to try his fate with a

tragedy, and to see to get himself employed in some translation, either from the Latin or the French. Johnson is a very good scholar and poet, and I have great hopes will turn out a fine trag-edy-writer.[1]

Walmesley may have hoped that Colson would take Johnson in for a few days, assist him in getting other lodgings in town, and generally help him on his way, but Colson surely would have had little idea of how to help him, short of setting him up somewhere in town closer to the hot-house atmosphere of writers and publishers.

Johnson now apparently had little money to spare for this experiment in London, and Davy may have had even less because his father was back from Spain and ill. They decided to ride to London but as the famous story goes had money enough only for one horse. Garrick used to say they adopted the proverbial 'ride and tie' method by which one of them would ride off on the horse, stopping and tethering it at some point and then walking on; when the other reached the horse he would mount it, trot past his companion, and in his turn tether it – and so on into London. The method was not conducive to sociability and one wonders whether the sudden change of their circumstances created some awkwardness be-tween them, especially as Davy had shown little taste for learning at the school. Johnson would never have a high regard for his companion's learn-ing. They left their master-pupil relationship behind them, however, and both knew that in a few days they would part company.[2]

The main coaching route from Lichfield to London had been remark-ably consistent for centuries, with eighteenth-century horsemen and coaches following much the same route as Roman soldiers marching along Watling Street. Just as Johnson the toddler had bumped along this route with his mother in 1712 on their way to be 'touched' by the Queen, he and Garrick now passed through Coleshill, Coventry, Dunchurch, Daventry, Towcester, Stony Stratford, Dunstable, St Albans, High Barnet, and on into London. Perhaps painful sensations coursed through him at Coventry where in October 1728 he and his father had turned their horses on to the Banbury

Road heading towards what they hoped would be a bright future at Oxford. The journey took Johnson and Garrick less than a week.

2

Whatever else happened in these first days, both suffered severe blows soon after arriving in London. Garrick heard the tragic news that his father had died while they were on the road. Grieving, he went on to Rochester, spent a few months there bored by mathematics, decided against his new plan of studying law at Lincoln's Inn, and then retreated back to Lichfield. He returned to London a few weeks or months later to set up the London end of a wine business he and his elder brother Peter had decided to go into together.

Johnson's blow was less expected: his brother Nathaniel had died at the age of twenty-five, apparently also when they were travelling to London. Nathaniel had fallen on hard times and seemed to have taken to drinking. He had plans to open a bookshop in Stourbridge, but there is a hint that while working in the family business at home he had committed some 'crime' that brought much trouble to his mother and prompted him to leave to work in some sort of extension of the business in Burton-on-Trent. It was from there perhaps that he wrote a most unhappy, dejected letter to his mother, lamenting his 'crime' but bitterly reproving her for not telling him he could have the use of certain (perhaps book-binding) tools that could have made a difference in his life. The melancholia that plagued his father and brother seemed also to have him in its grips. He lashed out particularly at his brother: 'As to my brother's assisting me I had but little reason to expect it when he would scarce ever use me with common civility and to whose advice was owing that unwillingness you showed to my going to Stourbridge ... If my brother did design doing anything for me, I am much obliged to him and thank him. Give my service to him and my sister. I wish them both well.' By his sister he meant Tetty. He planned in a couple of weeks to make a complete break by emigrating to General Oglethorpe's new North American colony of Georgia. He never got there.

The letter, in fact, sounds suicidal. When asked once if he thought people who committed suicide were 'mad', Johnson's reply could well have been gloomily tinged with a stabbing memory of his own brother's fate: 'Sir, they are often not universally disordered in their intellects, but one passion presses so upon them, that they yield to it, and commit suicide, as a passionate man will stab another . . . I have often thought, that after a man has taken the resolution to kill himself, it is not courage in him to do any thing, however desperate, because he has nothing to fear.'

It seems Johnson believed his brother felt things too deeply, that perhaps this had been at the root of the problem between them. In his copy of John Norris's *A Collection of Miscellanies* (1699), he wrote 'my brother' next to this passage: 'It is supposed by the Ancient Fathers, that the sufferings which our Blessed Saviour underwent in his body were more afflictive to him than the same would have been to another man, upon the account of his excellency and quickness of his sense of feeling.' Johnson almost never spoke about his brother afterwards. He did not return home for the funeral, nor noted anything about him in his diary except for 'a dream of my brother' he had many years later. He stayed in London, leaving his mother alone at home with Kitty Chambers to deal with her grief and bury Nathaniel next to his father in St Michael's Church in Lichfield.[3]

3

In dire need of money and on Garrick's suggestion, they both applied for it to a bookseller named J(ohn?) Wilcox, whom Garrick knew slightly. Johnson informed Wilcox that he intended to earn his living as an author, which was not a good opening. Wilcox took in Johnson's 'robust frame' and suggested instead that 'he had better buy a porter's knot'. He took pity on them, however, and lent them £5 (about £500 today). Wilcox, incidentally, kept a well-stocked bookshop in Little Britain. In an interesting coincidence, Benjamin Franklin had lodged next to this same Wilcox in 1725 and borrowed many of his books 'on reasonable terms'.[4]

Johnson's first lodging was an upstairs room or garret in the house of the staymaker Richard Norris in Exeter Street, a cul-de-sac just off the north side of the Strand, costing much less than the two shillings per week that an average poor family would have to expect to pay for a small furnished room in the house of a prosperous tradesman. He came to London hoping he could make it with the measly funds he had. He devised a system whereby he could make his coins go further and yet enjoy the society of a tavern or coffee house by day or night: 'I dined . . . very well for eight-pence, with very good company, at the Pine Apple in New-street just by . . . It used to cost the rest a shilling, for they drank wine; but I had a cut of meat for six-pence, and bread for a penny, and gave the waiter a penny; so that I was quite well served, nay, better than the rest, for they gave the waiter nothing.'[5]

From the beginning of his London career, it was more with tavern than coffee house life that Johnson was associated. The 'tavern chair' was for him 'the throne of human felicity'. Coffee houses were commonly the haunts of 'authors by profession' but they were more like debating societies, identified frequently by political affiliations and business interests. The coffee house has been described as the 'eighteenth-century business Internet', as well as a social centre. Taverns differed according to their clientele, but normally they were quieter and more intimate, more given to controlled and private conversation than to club-like banter or raucous contests of wit. This was the sort of environment in which Johnson luxuriated and where, whether drinking and eating or not, the solace of conversation could mitigate against the loneliness of his life in his lodgings. As for drinking, Boswell wrote, 'He at this time, I believe, abstained entirely from fermented liquors: a practice to which he rigidly conformed for many years together, at different periods of his life.' But Johnson once remarked, 'Early in life I drank wine: for many years I drank none. I then for some years drank a great deal.' 'I used to slink home, when I had drunk too much,' he admitted, but whether this early drinking refers to a period before he first came to London, this first period in London, or a year or two later when he was there with his wife, is unclear.[6]

It was a revelation to him to meet daily with these locals who rarely bothered to discover each other's names, whose practical and intellectual offerings had nothing to do with who they were or where they came from.

At the Pine Apple he found a rich and varied microcosm of London, patronised by a mix of high and low life, by men who were experts in a variety of fields, men who were failures and downtrodden on the edges of society, and the luckier ones who bathed in the sunshine of success and esteem. He was beginning a lasting love affair with London. 'A man is always *so near his burrow*' in London, he exulted. The city was his 'element', his 'heaven upon earth'. One of his most famous remarks was about London: 'When a man is tired of London, he is tired of life; for there is in London all that life can afford'.[7] And on a more personal note, he freely admitted that 'the spirits which I have in London make me do everything with more readiness and vigour. I can talk twice as much in London as anywhere else.' That was where, even in a garret, 'a man's own house is truly his *castle*, in which he can be in perfect safety from intrusion whenever he pleases'. He had embarked on the period of his first genuine independence, without obligations, without family and relatives, without old friends, and (dare he think it) without his wife.[8]

By choosing this area of London, Johnson landed himself in the centre of an urban vortex renowned throughout Europe. Exeter Street was in the middle of immense activity and liveliness, where he was bound to hear all the breaking news in the city and be up to date with the political ferment in which the Prime Minister Sir Robert Walpole featured so alarmingly to Tories like him, royal gossip, new publications and the latest reports about plays in the theatres. A riot in Drury Lane Theatre, in fact, on the very day he arrived in London would have been the sensational talking point of the moment. London was a violent city whose inhabitants were regarded by foreigners as dangerously and congenitally barbarous. Things had not improved by 1762 when, on his first visit to London, Boswell could not believe the dangers and enticements of violence all around him: 'The rudeness of the English vulgar is terrible,' he wrote in his journal. 'This is indeed the liberty which they have: the liberty of bullying and being abusive with their blackguard tongues.' To make matters worse, there was no professional police force in the city, and there would be none until Sir Robert Peel established one in 1829. Lawlessness was rife. Churches stood beside houses of pimps. Sports were violent, too: cock-fights, bear and bull-baiting, and dog fights were quite common entertainments for those who wanted a different sort of dramatic entertainment to what was offered in the theatres.[9]

London's violence and brutality existed in close proximity to unexpected tranquility and breathtaking architectural and garden beauties; where the ghastly misery of poverty watered by cheap gin often co-existed obscenely with unimaginable wealth just down a street or around a corner. It was a city of coffee houses, taverns and chocolate houses, clubs and societies, of beautiful Wren churches and innumerable chapels of nonconformist religions. In his classic study *England in the Eighteenth Century*, J. H. Plumb described this melting pot comprehensively as 'rough, coarse, brutal; a world for the muscular and the aggressive and the cunning. The thin veneer of elegance and classic form obscured but never hid either the crime and dissipation or the drab middle-class virtue and thrift.'[10]

After the Great Fire in 1666 the engines of wealth and power began to generate the renovation of London in a rebuilding and extension to the west, clearing away much of the old to make place for the commercially and fashionably new. The fire was in a way a blessing because its ancient centre had burned down, allowing the laying out of wider streets and more public spaces, the envy of cities like Paris. But it was not until around the mid-eighteenth century that the pace of growth really picked up. In 1757 the houses on London Bridge were demolished and foul Fleet Ditch was filled up. A few years later the City was opened up through the removal of its ancient gates, creating more fluid movement of trade and people. The city would not have lighting and paving throughout until the first Westminster Paving Act of 1762, the year Boswell first visited: gutters and underground drains, paving-stone replacing pebbles in the main streets, and a central system of street repair and cleaning making walking in London even safer and more pleasant. In the newer areas of London to the west lovely squares were created that became the addresses of the aristocracy and rich. As a modern historian of London has put it, 'From Covent Garden through St James's to Mayfair, the West End was wide and handsome, built to please those with money to burn and time to kill.' Indeed, Georgian London took shape as a 'well-mapped topography of pleasure', but Johnson's area, Fleet Street and the Strand connecting Westminster and the City, was the place to be to watch life pass by in all its variety. 'Fleet Street has a very animated appearance', Johnson wrote in later years, and he thought that at Charing Cross could be seen 'the full tide of human existence'.[11]

Most of all, London was the genuine city of the Enlightenment, the scene of ideas-in-action, pragmatic liberty and dashing, dazzling spirit. Eighteenth-century London was truly revolutionary long before the French Revolution, 'a revolution in mood, a blaze of slogans, delivering the shock of the new'. The French *philosophes* cast their eyes across the channel to England as the cradle of the modern, and anglophiles on the Continent 'celebrated Britain's constitutional monarchy and freedom under the law, its open society, its prosperity and religious toleration'. At just the time Johnson came to London, the city was embracing a print culture that proved to be the envy of the world, with periodicals and magazines of specialised and general interest – *The Gentleman's Magazine* was the most successful of the latter kind – cropping up out of nowhere, as well as novels, prints, and even pornography, all devoured by a hungry reading public. As Johnson put it, this was an 'age of authors' – of both sexes. There seemingly were no limits or boundaries. Travellers, 'knowledge-mongers', writers, musicians, artists, and scientists, they came in great numbers from distant regions and countries to see what it was all about, and many like Handel, Haydn, Benjamin Franklin, and Pasquale Paoli, the exiled Corsican patriot, lingered or stayed to create because their geniuses found the spirit of modernity and freedom congenial. Knowledge 'generally diffused' was the icon of the age – 'society is held together by communication and information', Johnson said. What intoxicatingly flooded into Johnson's life in those first heady days in London was uniquely English: 'England's modernisers had no stomach for indigestible scholastic husks; they were not ivory-towered academics but men (and women) of letters who made their pitch in the metropolitan market place.' Johnson very quickly came to subscribe to the notion of the uncloistered writer playing with social and market forces in order to get his message out to the public.[12]

4

He did not have Cornelius Ford to relieve what Boswell called 'the cold obscurity' of his first months in London by introducing him to the world of wits and letters, but Walmesley's patronage extended all the way to London. Henry Aston Hervey, husband to Walmesley's new sister-in-law Catherine Aston for whom Johnson had written poems, stepped in to help him. The younger son of the first Earl of Bristol, he kept a house in London to which he invited Johnson to meet some polite society. Hervey was a gambler and spendthrift, but he did not lack wit and Johnson took to him. Johnson had an 'avowed and scarcely limited partiality for all who bore the name or boasted the alliance of an Aston or a Hervey,' wrote Mrs Thrale. No less incongruously than when the worldly 'Parson' Cornelius Ford became ordained, the high-living Hervey left the army in 1742 and joined the Church soon after. On the principle that it was better to deliver good sermons than bad ones, Johnson wrote several of his. Late in life he told Boswell, 'He was a vicious man, but very kind to me. If you call a dog HERVEY, I shall love him.' The most interesting story about Hervey's charity towards his young Lichfield friend concerns an alleged act of gross ingratitude on Johnson's part with which Boswell confronted him. Boswell mentioned he had heard that at one point Hervey had 'shown him much kindness, and even relieved him from a spunging-house' – a place kept by a bailiff where debtors were taken before being committed to prison – but that one day at dinner with Johnson, after he had fallen on hard times, he was arrested for debt and taken off to prison. As this story went, when Johnson failed to spring to his friend's defence and just kept on eating and drinking, Hervey's sister rebuked him for ingratitude. Boswell asked Johnson if this were true. Absolutely not, came the answer: 'Sir, I was very intimate with that gentleman, and was once relieved by him from an arrest; but I never was present when he was arrested, never knew that he was arrested, and I believe he never was in difficulties after the time when he relieved me. I loved him much . . . Sir, I would have gone to the world's end to relieve him.' That Johnson in these earliest London years found himself in a 'spunging-house' is a measure of how uncertain, despite Hervey's help, his future was in London.[13]

A few disconnected reminiscences of this period in his diary for 1743, like glints of light passing through almost an opaque glass, touch on what his first 'home' in London was like. There was a cat with which his land-lord's wife 'fair Esther' liked to play, as well as children. On one occasion a palm reader seems to have been called in to amuse the children with an 'inspection of the hand'. For some reason he remembered a disgruntled customer on another day returning some stays. He also recalled having to pay one guinea in advance before being allowed by Norris, his landlord, or his fair wife to climb the stairs to his room. A guinea was about three months' rent. Norris's lodgings soon proved unsatisfactory, or the neigh-bourhood did, probably because of noise and interruption, and in a few months Johnson fled Fleet Street for Greenwich, next to the Golden Hart tavern in Church Street, where he hoped to have more peace and quiet and finish *Irene*. At Greenwich the tranquility pleased and bored him at the same time, especially the park where he was fond of walking while composing. He stayed there no more than a couple of months but carried away fond impressions of the place.[14]

In July, before leaving Greenwich with *Irene* still unfinished, he wrote again to Edward Cave. Describing himself now 'a stranger in London' and without mentioning his earlier letter from Lichfield, he proposed a specific project this time, a translation from the Italian of the seventeenth-century Catholic priest Paulo Sarpi's *History of the Council of Trent* (1619). Like the *Voyage to Abyssinia*, the project appealed to his fascination with history, in this case the convening of the Council of Trent by Pope Paul III in 1545 to decide if papal powers should be allowed to be curbed and Church doc-trine liberalised by secular states. As it turned out, Church reformers and interested Protestants were disappointed and outraged as papal authority had its own way of resisting reform. Johnson was well-equipped as a his-torian and linguist to take on the project and as we have seen instinctively was drawn to a translation of a book in which authority in the Church and tyranny of any kind was depicted as regressive and an obstacle to the free expression of ideas in man's relationship to God. Never mind that

Sarpi's book had already been translated into English back in 1619 – that did not deter him in the least. 'You cannot read three pages of the English History without discovering that the style is capable of great improvements,' he told Cave, adding that if he wanted to see a specimen demonstrating he could do it better, he should let him know. Johnson asked for a 'speedy answer' either way. But Cave, who at the time had another hefty translation project under contract that had not yet earned him any income, rejected the proposal.[15]

In spite of Johnson's economies, it was difficult to live in London with as little money as he had in his pockets. Moreover, he had made little progress with his *Irene*, which was beginning to seem like sowing seeds in arid ground, and it had been half a year since he had seen Tetty. It was time to return to her and talk about their next steps, reunite with his mother who by now had somewhat recovered from the loss of Nathaniel, and rejoin the Walmesley set with its feminine circle of Astons, especially Molly, the object of his secret longing. So at the end of the summer 1737 he made his way home for another homecoming tinged with failure. He had little to show for the last six months, though his love affair with London had been born.

CHAPTER 10

Sons of Misery:
Finding Richard Savage

I

JOHNSON STAYED IN LICHFIELD only three months. The homecoming was hardly triumphant. Returning was an appalling anticlimax to someone geared up for literary fame who for six months had tuned himself to the tempo of sprawling, disorderly London, discovering favourite haunts where he whiled away the hours talking with all manner of 'good fellows' and generally contracting an obsession with the atmosphere of taverns in late hours.

He finally completed the last two acts of *Irene* on this visit. Otherwise nothing is known of his Lichfield homecoming except for one exchange between him and his mother that had a little edge to it. When his mother lived briefly in London 'in the last age', he told Boswell thirty-six years later, there were two sets of people, 'those who gave the wall [were deferential], and those who took it; the peaceable and the quarrelsome'. When he was at home with his mother one day after his return, she somewhat contentiously, perhaps, or at least probingly, asked him whether he was 'one of those who gave the wall, or those who took it'. Whatever she was trying to stir up, he sidestepped it: 'Now, it is fixed that every man keeps to the right; or, if one is taking the wall, another yields it, and it is never a dispute' – as if to say, 'Now, mother, let us not quarrel.'[1]

He was reminded soon enough, as in all his homecomings, that nothing was going to happen in Lichfield to launch him into a career. One thing he was not going to do was take up the reins in the bookshop. It was decided that he and Tetty would return to London together – he could not very well leave her again – but what of Lucy? Boswell wrote vaguely that she 'was left with her relations in the country', but the warmer and more logical decision would have been to have her move in with his mother and Kitty Chambers and help them run the business.[2] If this did not happen immediately, the advanced age of Sarah Johnson soon made it not only convenient but imperative. Lucy's eventual residence in the house was a great relief to Johnson and a great boost to their growing intimacy. He mischievously told Mrs Thrale that he had 'the wit' to get Lucy 'on my side' before disputing with her mother.[3] She slipped naturally into life at the house on Market Square, helping Kitty with the running of the household, supporting his ageing mother, keeping the accounts, and generally taking charge. If Johnson and Tetty had not done so before, they gave up Edial Hall, which, if it involved the sale of household effects and furniture, would have provided additional funds. So, towards the end of 1737, off they went, this time not on horseback, for what Johnson hoped would be a happier marriage in a more stimulating and successful world than Lichfield.

The nervous couple had to find lodgings, which they did first in Woodstock Street near Hanover Square and then by April 1738 at a Mrs Crow's, No. 6 Castle Street, very near desirable Cavendish Square.[4] The address was not as good as it would become in the 1760s with the elegant development of the square and adjacent areas by the aristocracy, but it was good enough. Perhaps a mantle of peace and contentment would settle on them now and replace their quarrelling, but the Cavendish Square neighbourhood was not sustainable and over the next few years they would drift closer to the 'dungeons of the Strand' and Grub Street where his work would take him.

With *Irene* finished and burning a hole in his pocket, Johnson's first priority was to get it acted on stage. He had been dragging the tragedy around in its various stages of incompleteness for well over a year and was now sure it was fit for the stage and certain of its success. The play was ostensibly the reason he came to London in the first place, and on it rode his and Tetty's hopes for the future. There was more money in having it acted than in trying to get it published; moreover, the latter would follow easily if the play were a success on stage.

Davy was not in the picture during these early days of Johnson's Grub Street life. Ambitiously, Davy had chosen instead to cultivate the influential and affluent people he thought could help him get on stage instead of applying himself to his and his brother Peter's wine business. Peter therefore had to come to London to take over from his brother, and it was he, not Davy, who helped Johnson with *Irene*. One day they walked into the Fountain tavern and read it to each other, and with Peter's encouragement he made a move. He looked up Charles Fleetwood, a Staffordshire man who since 1734 had been the major patentee of Drury Lane Theatre, to persuade him to stage it there. Fleetwood looked at it – that is about all he did – and rejected it. In a few moments Johnson's fondest hopes for a year, a major reason for coming to London, seemed dashed. Peter thought Fleetwood rejected it 'probably because it was not patronised by some man of high rank'. Even this early, Johnson's prideful, stubborn and often arrogant insistence on getting ahead by his own merits ruled out his looking for a patron. Hawkins read this streak in Johnson well: 'Bred to no profession, without relations, friends, or interest, Johnson was an adventurer in the wide world, and had his fortunes to make: the arts of insinuation and address were, in his opinion, too slow in their operation to answer his purpose; and, he rather chose to display his parts to all the world, at the risk of being thought arrogant, than to wait for the assistance of such friends as he could make, or the patronage of some individual that had power or influence, and who might have the kindness to take him by the hand, and lift him into notice.' In an essay years later Johnson wrote on how he had learned that proud independence and aggressive intellectual self-assertion do not often win friends: 'I question whether some abatement of character is not necessary to general acceptance . . . the scholar whose knowledge allows no man to fancy that he instructs him, the critic who suffers no fallacy to pass undetected . . . are generally praised and feared, reverenced and avoided. He that would please must rarely aim at such excellence as depresses his hearers in their own opinion . . .'[5]

For the moment he had no choice but to shelve the play. There were pressing needs for income and he could not afford to waste any more time dallying with self-deluding dreams. Writing for Cave's monthly magazine still appealed to him. He told Boswell that when he first saw St John's Gate in Clerkenwell, where Cave ran his magazine, he 'beheld it with reverence'. For seven years Cave had continued to thrive with his magazine, going from strength to strength from a combination of his natural instinct for what would appeal to the public and a keen vigilance about keeping standards and sales high. Gathering himself up, Johnson took aim again at him in late winter, sending him his flattering twenty-four line Latin ode, 'Ad Urbanum', addressed to him in the pseudonym 'Sylvanus Urban' which he used in his magazine and which hinted at his targeting both urban and rural readership. Johnson referred to his speedily written Latin offering as a 'trifle' but it was a study in tact, if a little crudely sycophantic and definitely opportunistic, defending Cave against the 'rude treatment' he had suffered at the hands of rival magazines and journals such as the *London Magazine* and *Common Sense* and celebrating him, 'indefatigable man', as too great to take notice of such 'senseless sneerings of a haughty tongue'. This biographical theme would be repeated in the *Life of Cave* he wrote just after Cave died, in which he praised him for being a self-made man, one who had overcome social and economic disadvantages and 'risen to eminence' through diligence and ability. It was a quality he valued over almost all others in his biographical heroes. The poem was the work of an hour or two. Flattering as it was, how could it miss? Cave needed to raise the quality of his poetry section and this Latin poem – there was little Latin poetry in any of the magazines at that time – seemed a good way to start doing it, so he published it in March 1738 under 'S. J.' It was Johnson's first appearance in print as a London author. A parody of it appearing in the April issue of the *London Magazine* alludes to him as writing from 'Grubstreet garrets', bribed with 'ale and gin' but unable to rescue the 'mang'ling' *Gentleman's Magazine* – an allusion to Cave's successful method of taking essays from other periodicals and republishing them in digest form, severely abridged and edited.[6]

Encouraged by this success, a few days later Johnson was emboldened to write to Cave again, 'a pleasure I shall always think it to converse in any manner with an ingenious and candid man', enclosing another poem and appealing to Cave's generosity by passing it off as the work of some other needy soul in dire need of an advance: 'I do not doubt but you will look over this poem with another eye, and reward it in a different manner, from a mercenary bookseller, who counts the lines he is to purchase, and considers nothing but the bulk.' Desperate for some money, in his letter Johnson appealed to Cave's charity: as the author 'lies at present under very disadvantageous circumstances of fortune', a reply the next day is urgent, so that 'I may know what you can afford to allow him, that he may either part with it to you, or find out (which I do not expect) some other way more to his satisfaction'. By accepting this poem Cave would 'encourage learning, and relieve distress'.[7]

The offering was *London: A Poem*, an imitation of the third satire of the second-century Roman poet Juvenal. With such translations of (chiefly) Latin poetry he clearly felt his strengths as a poet, and these translations would comprise the most important and successful body of his lifelong poetic output. Recognising the energy and powerful animus in the poem, as well as its originality and currency in the present political situation, Cave immediately spotted it as a winner. Within a day or two Johnson received a small advance from him – a 'present' he called it – his first income as a London author, apparently with the seductive suggestion that the poem should be published separately by the bookseller Robert Dodsley (1703–64), who ran his business from Tully's Head, Pall Mall. It was a thrilling proposal. As a separate item, of course, the poem could command far more attention than if it were relatively hidden in the pages of *The Gentleman's Magazine*. Moreover, Dodsley was the young innovative bookseller-publisher of the hour, having set up his business by 1735 and boldly moved into the publishing world with a swift confidence, sponsoring poetry, publishing old plays, and writing plays himself. He has been described as a 'tough, neat, humorous, and determined soul'.[8]

Johnson asked Cave to send him back the poem promptly with a note for Dodsley so he could take it to him, 'read the lines to him', and see if he would consent 'to put his name in the title page'. He kept up the pretence that the poem was someone else's and that he was merely an interested intermediary and friend: 'As to the printing, if it can be set immediately about, I will be so much the author's friend as not to content myself with mere solicitations in his favour.' It is unlikely that Cave often dealt with any author, especially one totally unknown, who proposed with such exactness that five hundred copies of the poem be printed and that, in light of Cave's offer of letting all profits be kept by the author, he would repay any of the printer's costs. He even offered to repay the advance if the author reaped profits. The poem could be printed in five sheets, he added a day or two later, which would include at the bottom of each page the corresponding lines from Juvenal's poem, 'part of the beauty of the performance (if any beauty be allow'd it) consisting in adapting Juvenal's sentiments to modern facts and persons'. Johnson did take the poem to Dodsley, who paid him ten guineas outright for the copyright and published it in folio on 13 May 1738 for one shilling, just before the rising of Parliament in mid-May, without Johnson's name on the title page. Considering the poem's attacks on the Walpole ministry, Johnson may have felt it wise not to own himself the author at this point. Or if Dodsley had discovered Johnson was the author, perhaps it was he, against Johnson's wishes, who decided that anonymity might endow the poem with some mystery and curiosity and work more to his benefit than if it appeared as the work of an unknown Samuel Johnson. It was not long before a small group of people knew this man Samuel Johnson was the author, however. Regarding the ten guineas, Johnson told Boswell he 'might, perhaps, have accepted of less' except that another (inferior) poet recently had been paid that amount and he 'would not take less' than he. Within a week the poem sold out. Dodsley wasted no time getting a second edition out a week later, and when that sold out a third edition appeared in a couple of months. Cave was not about to be left out. By agreement with Dodsley he himself published sixty-six lines of the poem in the May issue of his magazine, so the success of the poem was like a dream come true for the young author. It was a promising step on the way out of obscurity.[9]

When Alexander Pope read the poem he declared it the work of a new, serious voice and took steps immediately to find out who the poet was.

His response to the information that it was a young man called Johnson was, 'He will soon be *déterré*.' So far as we know, they never met although, for seven years, they were in London at the same time – it was one of the greatest literary events that never happened: 'No, Sir, I never *saw* Pope,' Johnson once stated emphatically.[10]

He had written the poem rapidly, in three or four days. One of the sheets of the manuscript of the poem that was found in the 1920s among Boswell's manuscripts at Malahide Castle in Ireland, reveals that he composed much of the 263-line translation in his head rapidly before writing it down in a left-hand column, with revisions appearing in a column to the right. The manuscript shows all the signs of swift work: quick deletions and additions, tentative readings, discarded lines, and so on. As we shall see, his ability to compose verse on a still larger scale was a wonder even to himself – one he loved to boast about.

The urgency behind his furious speed of composition is only partly explained by the need for money. It was also the result of his anger and frustration over what he saw around him on the streets of London, in the political climate, and in his own personal, economic and professional predicament. Garrick once said the reason the poem was so successful, so 'lively and easy', was that Johnson wrote it when he was seeing much of the Herveys and 'saw a good deal of what was passing in life'. Hervey's orbit exposed him to the high life, where he could tune into the corruption, social and political, in the metropolis in a 'lively and easy' manner. But the power of the poem is far more personal and deep than that, far more internalised. It is an eruption: a crescendo of outrage, boosted perhaps by the facile, complacent conversation he heard in the Hervey circle but rooted mostly in dark thoughts that he had carried around with him and nourished from Lichfield boyhood and adolescence to Oxford, to various teaching disappointments, to Birmingham, to marriage, and now to London.

2

Before looking at *London* and what it tells us about Johnson's literary progress in the city, we need to get a further reading of his mental state and introduce a powerful new personality in his life who plays a major role in the poem.

On his twenty-ninth birthday in September 1738, not long after his poem came out, he composed a prayer – 'the first solemn prayer of which I have a copy,' he wrote; 'whether I composed any before this, I question.' In writing it he concocted a sort of hybrid consisting of a formal prayer following the wording of the *Book of Common Prayer* and a journal entry that satisfied his desire for communion with God and at the same time took him into private meditation and reflection on his own personal affairs and depressed mental state. 'In the days of childhood and youth, in the midst of weakness, blindness, and danger, thou hast protected me,' it begins, 'amidst afflictions of mind, body, and estate thou has supported me; and amidst vanity and wickedness thou hast spared me.' The next sentence raises themes present in virtually all his prayers for the rest of his life – guilt over squandering his talents (and thus dishonouring God) and what he calls unkindness towards others: 'enable me by thy Grace to use all diligence in redeeming the time which I have spent in sloth, vanity, and wickedness'. He prays 'to make use of thy gifts to the honour of thy Name; to lead a new life in thy Faith, Fear, and Love'. Whether the wickedness he twice mentions alludes to anything other than unkindness to others, such as sexual temptation, is open to question.[11]

A fresh boost to his disaffection and alienation, his sensations as an outsider, was also provided by someone he met in these early months in London. His name was Richard Savage. And thereby hangs a tale.

Savage (1697–1743) was one of Cave's poetry contributors, one of the few poets of ability whom he began to pay for verse in 1736 as part of his gradual move to obtain original contributions for his magazine. Johnson may have met him through their work for the magazine, at St John's Gate or perhaps at a tavern for supper with Cave. Or they may have met through the influential Thomas Birch, the biographer, historian, and adviser to *The Gentleman's Magazine*, through whom Savage made his work known to Cave. In his manuscript diary (now in the British Library) Birch never mentioned dining with both Savage and Johnson together, or even with Cave, but he did dine with them separately many times, the first time with Johnson on 22 August 1738 after the latter's emergence from the shadows with his *London*, which he knew Johnson wrote.[12]

Since Birch dined occasionally with Savage and perhaps Cave, and more often with the rising twenty-year-old poetess and classicist Elizabeth Carter (1717–1806), whose poems Cave published in his magazine and who had become a friend of Johnson's early in 1738, it is not unlikely that by early that year Johnson was also known to Savage. Savage deeply impressed him. In April Johnson seemed fascinated enough with Savage's poetry and notoriety, though it is unlikely he had yet met him, to supply Cave with an effusive Latin epigram on him as an appendage to a poem of his appearing in that month's issue of *The Gentleman's Magazine*. Translated, it reads:

> To Richard Savage, Esquire, Lover of Mankind.
> Devotion to your Fellow Man burns brightly in your Breast;
> O! that Fellow Man may cherish and protect Thee in return.

They probably got acquainted soon after Savage read this.[13]

Savage suffered from several overwhelming problems that both turned him into a national celebrity and ruined his life: continuing controversy about his birth, a persecution complex, an uncanny ability to bite the hand that fed him, reckless dissipation, and a murder in a coffee-house brawl in 1727 for which he was arrested and tried. Pope, his benefactor at the end of his life, called him 'a wrongheaded fool'.[14] He also possessed considerable charm and literary ability.

According to Savage, his bad luck began soon after his birth. He claimed he was the rejected illegitimate son of Anne, Countess of Macclesfield (wife of the second Earl of Macclesfield) through her liaison with the dissolute fourth Earl Rivers, although the evidence on balance seems to argue that he was an impostor. To his dying day he maintained he had been denied the rights of a rightful heir. The controversy was aired in the papers of the 1720s and Londoners were divided as to whether Savage was, as he claimed, the bastard repeatedly rejected and even persecuted by his mother or a bounder and brilliant impostor. Without hope of any legacy from his mother, he turned to literature. He wrote two plays, various odes and satires, and a poem titled *The Wanderer* (1729), inspired by his own wandering in endless searching and rejection, and dedicated to his patron Viscount Tyrconnel, Lady Macclesfield's nephew who half-heartedly supported his claim as her son. Two more notable poems followed in the 1730s, the scandalous *The Progress of a Divine* and *Of Public Spirit*, a scathing political satire. Johnson was especially pleased and roused by Savage's attack on the government's greedy exploitation of colonised countries in the name of progress: 'Savage has not forgotten . . . to expose the enormous wickedness of making war upon barbarous nations because they cannot resist, and of invading countries because they are fruitful; of extending navigation only to propagate vice, and of visiting distant lands only to lay them waste.' Although he did not feel that *Of Public Spirit* was well-written, these two poems, in fact, attracted him to Savage as a Grub Street companion, fellow struggling poet and kindred rebel.[15]

Savage's disarming charm and wit won him many friends and patrons along the way, including the Queen, Pope, the famous actress Anne Oldfield (who, unsolicited, gave him a generous allowance without any strings attached), the poets Aaron Hill, James Thomson and David Mallet, and Lord Tyrconnel. There seemed to be no end to his supporters, although his rebelliousness and querulousness made many of them wring their hands in exasperation. But in his sensational trial for murder presided over by a notoriously harsh judge, in which he undertook his own defence, he was convicted and sentenced to hang. Through the vigorous intervention of friends, he was pardoned in March 1728. Capitalising on the huge public interest in him and his relative success as an author, and presumably out of gratitude to his supporters and the general public, a couple of years later Savage thought well enough of himself to allow Lord Tyrconnel to propose him unsuccessfully for the poet laureateship that had recently become vacant. Angry when he failed, he cheekily started writing annual birthday poems of his own to Queen Caroline in 1732 under the sobriquet, 'Volunteer Laureate'. He kept up this audacity for five years and, quite extraordinarily, the Queen rewarded him for them with five annual allowances of fifty pounds (about £5,000 today). They stopped when she died, and at about that time a quarrel with Tyrconnel also brought an end to his patronage as well. Savage got back at him for not honouring a bill of his in a letter beginning with 'Right Honourable Brute, and Booby', that conveys the flavour of his ingratitude and forms part of a minor literary genre of the eighteenth century, the Letter to a Noble Lord, only in a different key from Johnson's famous snub and rejection of the Earl of Chesterfield over the *Dictionary* in 1756.[16]

Reduced to virtual pennilessness when Johnson knew him, Savage faced the sober reality that nobody would lend him any more money if he stayed in expensive London. Pope agreed to raise money for him and give him ten pounds himself every three months provided he left for Wales immediately. He agreed and left by stagecoach for Swansea in the summer of 1739, parting from Johnson 'with tears in his eyes'. But not long after getting there he began to complain of conspiracies against him and to criticise the 'inhumanity' of his benefactors, whom he took to calling his 'persecutors and oppressors'. In a letter to him in April 1742, Pope threatened to wash his hands of him, which he and other benefactors did soon after: 'It is with concern I find so much misconstruction joined with so much resentment, in your nature. You still injure some, whom you had known many years as friends . . . but I have no weight with you.' 'While he was thus spending the day in contriving a scheme for the morrow,' Johnson wrote, 'distress stole upon him by imperceptible degrees.' Bristol friends who had courted him began to desert him. Lodging 'in the garrett of an obscure inn', the White Lion, his money completely ran out. Pope expected him to return to London at this point, as probably did Johnson, who may have received the occasional letter from him, but he had no money for the journey. Finally, early in 1743, he was arrested with three pence halfpenny in his pocket and imprisoned in Newgate prison in Bristol for a debt of eight pounds. He died there after a sudden illness at the end of July.[17]

What particularly attracted Johnson to Savage, apart from his reputation as a poet, was his rebelliousness and readiness to challenge authority, as well as his poverty and hostility towards a society that he felt had deprived him of wealth and fame and condemned him first to eke out an existence in Grub Street cranking out hack work for Cave and others, and then, finally, to end his days in Wales. Savage was for him a damaged and spent genius. Hawkins saw him as Johnson's evil genius, equipped with 'the charms that wrought on Johnson, and hid from his view those baser qualities of Savage'. They were with each other in London less than two years before Savage was exiled to Wales.[18]

Hawkins seems not to have known Savage, but as he met Johnson in the 1740s when he himself was writing for *The Gentleman's Magazine* – Johnson gave him some help with a pamphlet titled 'Six Cantatas' (1742) – he must have known several people who did, and who had seen the two men together. Nonetheless, one must be wary of his censoriousness. In later years Hawkins became disaffected with most of Johnson's good friends and tended to censure, underplay, and misrepresent the importance of several of them, including Savage, in his biography.[19]

'They had both felt the pangs of poverty and the want of patronage,' Hawkins wrote: 'Savage had let loose his resentment against the possessors of wealth, in a collection of poems printed about the year 1727, and Johnson was ripe for an avowal of the same sentiments ... In speculations of this kind, and a mutual condolence of their fortunes, they passed many a melancholy hour.' He and Savage took to walking out at night together as night wanderers, prowling about on the fringes of society, not just in their own Grub Street territory but also in the West End where the panorama of wealth and privilege around every corner provoked their anger even more. Finding solace in each other's bitterness, once they began declaiming it was hard for them to stop: 'Johnson has told me', Hawkins wrote, that 'whole nights have been spent by him and Savage in conversations of this kind, not under the hospitable roof of a tavern, where warmth might have invigorated their spirits, and wine dispelled their care; but in a perambulation round the squares of Westminster, St James's in particular, when all the money they could both raise was less than sufficient to purchase for them the shelter and sordid comforts of a night cellar.'[20]

But Johnson himself was no pauper at this time, receiving regular pay from Cave and having his own lodgings with Tetty in Castle Street. Savage was profligate and expected others to pay for his expenses, but he too had free accommodation if he wished to take the trouble and risk the danger of walking several miles for it in the dark. As Thomas Kaminski has put it, 'Since there was no place of retirement open to both, and since Johnson was not likely to abandon his companion, the public squares had to furnish what comfort they could. Johnson and Savage wandered the streets not because they lacked the means to procure a room, but because they cherished one another's company more than sleep.' Johnson was enjoying himself, as he did all his life when he was in conversation in the deep of night. For him Savage was an intoxicating symbol of 'an exiled poetic conscience of the age'. He *wants* to go out into the cold night air with him: 'They both with the same eye saw, or believed they saw, that the then minister [Sir Robert Walpole] meditated the ruin of this country; that excise laws, standing armies, and penal statutes were the means by which he meant to effect it; and, at the risk of their liberty, they were bent to oppose his measures.' Johnson was thrilled with the excitement of discovery, which the night framed and dramatised into hours of heightened intellectual exchange.[21]

3

Johnson's *London*[22] was written in the middle of this prolonged 'night dream' with Savage, just before Savage's exile to Wales. The poem is set on the banks of the Thames at Greenwich, which Johnson knew well for its pleasant walks from a year earlier, where the poet and Thales – very likely his name for Savage in the poem although many contend that Johnson completed *London* before he knew Savage – wait with 'a sense of woe' for a wherry that will sail off for 'Cambria's solitary shore' with the 'injur'd Thales' and the meagre remains of his 'dissipated wealth'. Thales raises his contemptuous eyes towards the metropolis and launches into a dramatic monologue for the rest of the poem against all those forces he and the poet had radically and disruptively attacked on their nightly prowls in Westminster, St James's Square, Grosvenor Square, and even as far as Hyde Park, 'reforming the world, dethroning princes, establishing new forms of government, and giving laws to the several states of Europe, till, fatigued at length with their legislative office, they began to feel the want of refreshment, but could not muster up more than fourpence halfpenny'. The poem could be considered as Johnson's first version of Savage's biography. It is harsh in the manner of Juvenal, but (except that it is set in the city) also reminiscent of the eighteenth-century 'night school' of poetry in its nocturnal, reverie-like, meditative, psychologically complicated overtones. Johnson is portraying them both as frustrated, disillusioned poets, 'unacknowledged legislators' of society, buried by the night and their own personal distress. Thales's monologue can be seen also as Johnson's. His success was in adapting Juvenal's catalogue of urban evils in Rome to London, without allowing the poem to become too artificial, drawing on his own anger for the individual 'fire' of the poem.[23]

Thales depicts himself for the most part as an innocent victim, but in the lines, 'what, my friend, what hope remains for me,/Who start at theft, and blush at perjury', Johnson was thinking of himself, a newcomer, with plenty to learn and plenty more to suffer after the months of hardship he already had gone through. He had eyes and could see what reigned out there, from a generalised political evil to personal venality and aristocratic foppery. He laments the 'arts of insinuation', hypocrisy, effeminacy, pretentiousness, obsequiousness, that emaciate British manliness in a culture now that has taken to acting, playing 'a borrow'd part', that 'sap[s] the principles' of 'ancient British lineaments'.

The poem also reflects his compassion for the poor and persecuted members of society. In this he proved to be nobly different from Savage who lamented losing a fortune and feared for himself more than for the victims of wickedness and folly. All Johnson's life poverty and oppression remained a highly sensitive subject for him and roused his charity. The poem speaks ironically of 'starving merit' as if one had to be poor to be virtuous. 'When I was running about this town a very poor fellow,' he wrote many years later, 'I was a great arguer for the advantages of poverty; but I was, at the same time, very sorry to be poor. Sir, all the arguments which are brought to represent poverty as no evil, show it to be evidently a great evil. You never find people labouring to convince you that you may live very happily upon a plentiful fortune.' In the city, where vice was too often rewarded, not punished, 'All crimes are safe, but hated poverty./This, only this, the rigid law pursues,/This, only this, provokes the snarling muse'. He could have been much rougher with Mrs Thrale than he was when once she 'pertly' joked at the expense of the poor in a place in London called Porridge Island. 'Come, come (says he gravely), let's have no sneering at what is serious to so many: hundreds of your fellow-creatures, dear Lady, turn another way, that they may not be tempted by the luxuries of Porridge-Island to wish for gratifications they are not able to obtain.' Mrs Thrale wrote that when he was financially able he was not content with relieving poverty but 'wished to add also indulgence. He loved the poor as I never yet saw any one else do, with an earnest desire to make them happy.' He rounded on her severely once when she lamented the dusty roads during one summer drought and wished for rain to 'lay the dust': 'I cannot bear (replied he, with much asperity and an altered look), when I know how many poor families will perish next winter for want of that bread which the present drought will deny them, to hear ladies sighing for rain, only that their complexions may not suffer from the heat, or their clothes be incommoded by the dust; – for shame! leave off such foppish lamentations, and study to relieve those whose distresses are real.'[24]

In his opinion English poetry was fairly bankrupt of emotional representation of the poor: 'Whoever studies either the poets or philosophers, will find such an account of the condition expressed by that term as his experience or observation will not easily discover to be true . . . he will read of content, innocence, and cheerfulness, of health, and safety, tranquility, and freedom; of pleasures not known but to men unencumbered with possessions; and of sleep that sheds his balsamic anodynes only on the cottage.' Pope wrote about the charity of relieving the poor, he complained, but 'never saw the miseries' which he imagined 'easy to be borne'. It is not surprising, therefore, that he reserved for poverty several of the most emotional and sardonic lines in *London*, charged with autobiographical bitterness: 'Quick let us rise, the happy seats explore,/And bear oppression's insolence no more./SLOW RISES WORTH, BY POVERTY DEPRESS'D' (175–7). This is the only line in the poem completely capitalised. The poet

and Thales, or Johnson and Savage, are caught in a whirlpool of neglect
and poverty, struggling to avoid being sucked through the drain to igno-
miny and oblivion.[25]

These are private distresses, however. There are far more sinister public dangers lurking everywhere with which the poem dismally concludes:

> Prepare for death, if here at night you roam,
> And sign your will before you sup from home.
> Some fiery fop, with new commission vain,
> Who sleeps on brambles till he kills his man;
> Some frolick drunkard, reeling from a feast,
> Provokes a broil, and stabs you for a jest. (224–9)

These 'Lords of the street, and terrors of the way/ . . . Their prudent in-
sults to the poor confine', but there is no mistaking the pervasive malaise
and moral sickness infecting the whole of society. At the end, without any
redeeming vision of future hope, Johnson projects his own personal future
as a satirist – 'In angry numbers warn'st succeeding times; . . . Thy satire
point . . .'

It was as a moralist, not satirist, he would eventually decide to dedicate
himself as a writer, but at the centre of his own work would remain this
streak of anger and impatience, the rebel and radical, to which he would
add the rigorousness of an ironic commentator on vanities.

4

Although five years elapsed between *London* and Johnson's next literary
use of Savage, the logic of the connection dictates that we pass straight to
it. When Savage died, Cave possessed many of his papers, including recent correspondence from Wales and Bristol, and of course copies of all
his hack work for the magazine. Public interest in Savage's controversial
life had subsided somewhat, but his death in a debtors' prison revived it.
Johnson saw his opening and thought he had the inside track. Savage died
on 1 August and in that month's issue of the *Gentleman's Magazine* ap-

peared Johnson's letter to 'Mr Urban' (Cave) staking his claim to and advertising a project he and Cave had already plotted: a new biography of
'the unfortunate and ingenious Mr *Savage*' to be written by a person –
Johnson himself – 'who was favoured with his [Savage's] confidence and
received from himself an account of most of the transactions which he
proposes to mention to the time of his retirement to Swansea in Wales'.
'Others may have the same design', he informed the public, but 'as it is not
credible that they can obtain the same materials, it must be expected they
will supply from invention the want of intelligence, and that under the title of the *Life of Savage* they will publish only a novel filled with romantic
adventures and imaginary amours'.[26]

There is a note of urgency in his next letter to Cave. He had been ill
but now was ready to start writing: '*The Life of Savage* I am ready to go
upon and . . . reckon on sending in half a sheet a day.' But he was out of
money and needed candles and good pens – Cave's messenger boy had
found him 'writing this, almost in the dark, when I could not quite easily
read yours': 'If you could spare me another guinea . . . I should take it very
kindly tonight'. Once he began, he wrote briskly, staying up one entire
night to write forty-eight pages 'at a sitting' and then settling down to half
a sheet per day. He appears to have completed the first draft near the
end of the year, when on 14 December Cave paid him fifteen guineas
for the copyright of the work. On 11 February 1744, three months before
the death of Pope, Savage's last patron, and two months after he was paid
for finishing the job, the book came out with the title, *An Account of the
Life of Mr Richard Savage, Son of the Earl Rivers*. It was well received but
sold only moderately well and did not appear in a second edition until
1748.[27]

The book turned out to be one of the earliest psychological biographies
in Western literature. Instead of trying to uncover the complexity of behaviour that made up a person, biographical writing had largely been content with external historical events and well-known personal episodes, or
opted for panegyric, hagiographic celebrations in order to illustrate moral
lessons. Telling the truth about human nature, its shifting complex of
good and evil, remained a treacherous and neglected area because it neces-

sarily meant that the biographer had to include the good and the bad, the public and the private.

In his biography, however, Johnson at times was too ready to defend Savage. He was too inclined to accept Savage's story about parental rejection, have a high opinion of his poetry, and take his side against society. Take, for example, this misinformed and biased description of Lady Macclesfield:

> This mother is still alive, and may perhaps even yet, though her malice was so often defeated, enjoy the pleasure of reflecting that the life, which she often endeavoured to destroy, was at least shortened by maternal offices; that though she could not transport her son to the plantations, bury him in the shop of a mechanic, or hasten the hand of the public executioner, she has yet had the satisfaction of embittering all his hours, and forcing him into exigencies that hurried on his death.

The biography takes on its own life as a defiant protest. It did not matter to him that he had not properly researched Savage's claims, nor talked to enough people who had known him. It was enough that, as in *London*, he was ready to strike at the amorphous, quashing, nullifying spectre of authority. In the process, he made the work also into a kind of autobiography. He pictured himself a troubled, struggling, angry soul on the ragged edge of society, looking up with Savage at the well-lit windows of the powerful and great in the squares of Westminster and St James's from the cold streets below. If he portrayed Savage as 'the Poet as Outcast', some of that colouring spilled on him, too.[28]

Among the most interesting passages are those that tell us about Savage and himself at the same time. Although he only once drew attention to or mentioned himself as a character in the drama, he is there as the silent witness playing the part of a companion of the night. Much of the detail is so particular that he could not have learned of it except by actually being present. In the following famous passage, for example, read 'we' for 'he':

He lodged as much by accident as he dined, and passed the night
sometimes in mean houses, which are set open at night to any casual wanderers, sometimes in cellars, among the riot and filth of
the meanest and most profligate of the rabble; and sometimes,
when he had not money to support even the expenses of these re-
ceptacles, walked about the street till he was weary, and lay down
in the summer upon a bulk, or in the winter, with his associates in
poverty, among the ashes of a glass-house.

They must have spent enough nights like this for Johnson conceivably
to project it as, at times, a pattern of existence for them both: glass-houses
were small factories where glass of all kinds was melted and reprocessed in
ovens, leaving large amounts of warm grey ash in which tramps bedded
down for the night. Bulks were wooden stalls at the front of shops where
food could be laid during the day and on which by night tramps could find
relief from lying on cold stone. 'Mean houses' and cellars rounded off the
bedding accommodation for the two night prowlers: the former were vile-
smelling places of public lodging with wooden bunks for one penny per
night, the latter small basement doss-houses filled with filthy sacks and
people. In later years Johnson liked to tell people about these wild and
raw nights, as exhilarated by the memory as he had been by the actual experience. 'Elevated speculations, useful studies, or pleasing conversation',
Johnson wrote in the *Life*, were on the menu every night.[29]

Johnson gradually grew more critical of Savage as the biography prog-
ressed, and though remaining sympathetic moved away from his earlier
emotional identification with him by exposing his tragically flawed response to the brutal realities of poverty in Grub Street and later in
Wales.[30] This exposure also resonates with autobiographical echoes, such
as in his mention of Savage's ungrateful pride in the face of charity: 'he
never submitted to be treated otherwise than as an equal' and became
harshly indignant if he was not. There is a passage, in fact, based on first-
hand information, that brings to mind the humiliating Pembroke College
shoes episode:

His clothes were worn out, and he received notice that at a coffee-house some clothes and linen were left for him – the person who sent them did not, I believe, inform him to whom he was obliged, that he might spare the perplexity of acknowledging the benefit – but though the offer was so far generous it was made with some neglect of ceremonies, which Mr Savage so much resented that he refused the present, and declined to enter the house till the clothes that had been designed for him were taken away.

Johnson read in Savage's final months and years a cautionary moral tale, a Grub Street tragedy of poverty that sounded alarm bells for him in this early period of his own career.[31]

Johnson saw Savage's lack of realism as grotesque, epitomised by his flights of fancy that Wales would become his rural paradise. This sort of pastoral nonsense, 'flattering the imagination with Arcadian scenes', was already for Johnson – the country boy who understood the realities of rural life – a species of wanton wastefulness, allowing life to slide away without self-examination. The Welsh idyll that seduced Savage destroyed him, but so did insensitive and clumsy efforts to alleviate his poverty. Johnson was enraged by society's obtuse, clumsy, ill-conceived philanthropy that organised Savage's 'miseries of dependence' and coerced him to go west. Nobody comes off very well in this biography.[32]

At the end of the book Johnson returned once again to a personal theme that by 1743 had become his own permanent cross to bear – the fear of loneliness and melancholia:

> He was generally censured for not knowing when to retire, but that was not the defect of his judgement, but of his fortune; when he left his company he was frequently to spend the remaining part of the night in the street, or at least was abandoned to gloomy reflections, which it is not strange that he delayed as long as he could; and sometimes forgot that he gave others pain to avoid it himself.

'Those are not proper judges of his conduct', he added, 'who have slum-
bered away their time on the down of plenty, nor will any wise man presume to say, "Had I been in Savage's condition, I should have lived or written better than Savage."' One can either succumb, however, as Savage
ultimately did, or fight on. Johnson himself was a fighter and he felt he
had earned the right also to declare from his heart, without yet having
tasted the success for which he was battling in Grub Street, that prudence,
patience and courage were resources available to all in times of affliction:
'This relation will not be wholly without its use if those who languish under any part of his sufferings shall be enabled to fortify their patience by
reflecting that they feel only those afflictions from which the abilities of
Savage did not exempt him . . . Negligence and irregularity long continued
will make knowledge useless, wit ridiculous, and genius contemptible.'[33]

CHAPTER 11

'Slow Rises Worth by Poverty Depress'd'

I

A FTER THE ARTISTIC SUCCESS OF *London* and as he pushed Cave to agree to publish his translation of Sarpi's *History of the Council of Trent*, Johnson was certain he had the genius, courage and resilience to succeed in the uphill journey of establishing his literary reputation in London and earning a good income through it. At this point in Johnson's career, Cave was exactly what he needed in the way of a publisher. An honest if slow and methodical man, he was totally reliable and never kept his authors in doubt about what he thought of their writing. He also imposed strict deadlines and paid promptly. Hawkins, who began to write for the magazine in 1739, did not like him or his taciturn manner and claimed that Johnson 'saw very clearly those offensive particulars that made a part of Cave's character'. This might have been so, but Johnson also appreciated them. From his first meaningful contacts with Cave he had the highest regard for his practical literary instincts in sniffing out a good piece of prose and shaping it for his magazine. It was no accident that in eight years his magazine had become one of the most widely read in London. After Cave's death in 1754 Johnson wrote a memoir of him for *The Gentleman's Magazine* in which he admiringly remembered how Cave's taciturnity brought results: 'The same chillness of mind was observable in his conversation; he was watching the minutest accent of those whom he disgusted by seeming inattention; and his visitant was surprised when he came a second time, by preparations to execute the scheme which he [was] supposed never to have heard.' Although Johnson on his death-bed recalled Cave was a 'penurious paymaster', in these early years he was under no illusions about the going rates for hack-writing. Cave paid not significantly worse or better than other magazine editors.[1]

Until the late seventeenth century, the English press was not very free. Licensing acts enforced controls that protected the government from criticism and the Stationers' Company enjoyed a control of commercial publishing that effectively enabled it to monopolise the book trade. Near the end of the century there were only twenty master printers in London and fewer than two hundred people employed in the printing trade. It was a lucrative enough profession for those few but it was exclusive. In 1695 the Licensing Act lapsed, which removed censorship before publication, and although censorship of one kind or another persisted and taxes continued to cramp printers and publishers it was not long before this freedom bred a new and numerous generation of people in the trade. Presses sprang up in London and all over the country, making the English press the freest and most energetic in the world. By 1750 Samuel Richardson, the internationally successful author of *Pamela* and *Clarissa* and by profession a master printer, ran nine presses in his premises at Salisbury Court clattering away with about forty journeymen busy at work. Unlike Johnson, who in his youth had had enough of the bookseller's life and assiduously avoided anything to do with manufacturing and retailing books, he died rich.[2]

The new print culture into which Johnson launched himself without reservation in 1738 required some hard-headed realism. Print culture freed the author from the uncertain pursuit of patronage, but it also created its own uncertainties and pressures. For one thing, as we have already seen, it was chaotic, vulnerable to the constantly moveable feast of shifting commercial forces instead of the whims of a patron. For another, everyone seemed to be getting into the act, from all sorts of social classes and with uneven literary results. One historian of English print culture explains that print technology not only made 'simple fools into hack writers', but also turned 'honest mechanics into greedy printers and simple tradesmen into booksellers without scruples, taste, or morality, willing to steal and publish anything that will sell'. The worry was that England's literary culture would be corrupted by the growing and cheapening mass commercialism of print, contaminating the moral fabric of society, from politics to philosophy: 'A flood of printer's ink was a darkness that spread across the land, staining, as in [Pope's] memorable image of Fleet ditch running into the silver Thames, the white page, darkening the minds of the people and their rulers, obliterating polite letters.'[3]

Johnson himself wrote satirically of 'the itch of literary praise' in what had become 'the epidemical conspiracy for the destruction of paper': 'If we consider chiefly the state of our own country, [it] may be styled with great propriety The Age of Authors ... The province of writing was formerly left to those, who by study, or appearance of study, were supposed to have gained knowledge unattainable by the busy part of mankind; but in these enlightened days, every man is qualified to instruct every other man.' At the same time, he understood that print culture was now a way of life and that if he was to succeed as an author he had to plug into his age's version of 'on-line'.[4]

At the centre of this print whirlwind in London were the booksellers. A new Licensing Act in 1709 in theory threatened more explicitly than ever before their claim to own copyright, but in practice it was fairly ignored. When the bookseller commissioned or bought a work from an author, existing common law provided that he also bought the copyright and owned it in perpetuity – this in spite of the new Licensing Act granting him ownership of it for only twenty-one years in the case of existing works and fourteen for new works. It was not until 1774 that the House of Lords – in a legal case in which Boswell played a significant part – passed legislation outlawing perpetual copyright once and for always, which, in fact, had always been illegal. Booksellers were so powerful in the eighteenth-century publishing world that they had possession of copyright pretty much their own way in the intervening years.

Authors, printers, couriers – they were all dependent on the bookseller. He hired the printer and invested his money in producing the book. If he succeeded, he kept all the profits; if he failed, he absorbed all the losses.

Once the author sold the book and got paid, he was out of the picture completely, earning no royalties whatever. Moreover, the bookseller commanded virtually all the resources of distribution. It was not a level playing field for the other players. Those in the printing business who decided to go out on a limb to buy copyrights from authors and publish books themselves had to scramble to round up anything like a decent distribution. There were entrepreneurial trade publishers who would occasionally try to beat the system which booksellers tyrannised by publishing works, the copyrights of which were owned by others, under their own imprint, but such efforts were minimal. If a bookseller decided to challenge such a publication with bad publicity, he could usually succeed. Johnson's estimation of booksellers was that they looked on any author as 'criminal' who tried 'to enjoy more advantage from his own works than they are disposed to allow him', such as by getting a printer to print his work directly, leaving out the bookseller, and tasting some royalties.[5]

So as Johnson plunged into the universe of London publishing he had two broad choices. He could try cultivating booksellers and sell them his original work or take the more common, safer, anonymous route for aspiring authors via the periodical press. To put it another way, he was already writing literature in its broad eighteenth-century meaning – at times grumbling about his role as a translator for booksellers – and trying to be a poet. Thus far he had been unsuccessful with *Irene* but had managed to establish a promising relationship with Robert Dodsley by selling *London: A Poem* to him for ten guineas with Cave's help. This was the sort of writing he wished to do, but it was the more difficult route because he could not produce such works regularly enough to earn an income on which he and Tetty could live. As an unknown writer he would be paid little for such writing. Fifteen guineas for the 180 octavo pages of the *Life of Savage* was not much of an improvement on the ten guineas for *London*. He had no choice but to pursue the second alternative.

As the most successful entrepreneurial magazine publisher and editor in London, Cave was the obvious man with whom to link up, but Johnson understood the depressing dangers of becoming a Grub Street hack, which he articulated autobiographically years later in the *Rambler* with a retrospective shiver. These 'manufacturers of literature', he wrote, 'have set up for authors, either with or without regular initiation, and, like other artificers, have no other care than to deliver their tale of wares at the stated time':

> They have seldom any claim to the trade of writing but that they have tried some other without success. They perceive no particular summons to composition except the sound of the clock. They have no other rule than the law or the fashion of admitting their thoughts or rejecting them. And about the opinion of posterity they have little solicitude, for their productions are seldom intended to remain in the world for longer than a week.

He also had another potential problem, procrastination and idleness. 'I had books of every kind round me,' he recalled a decade later, 'among which I divided my time as caprice or accident directed. I often spent the first hours of the day, in considering to what study I should devote the rest; and at last snatched up any author that lay upon the table, or perhaps, fled to a coffee house for deliverance from the anxiety of irresolution, and the gloominess of solitude.' Like the poor soul who was driven out of his 'literary slumber' by a creditor, he had not proved to be one of those 'heroes of negligence' who could easily turn 'the dignity of imprudence' to his advantage.[6]

Nonetheless, he could always begin with Cave in a tentative sort of way as an interim measure. The variety of ways he could contribute to the magazine – criticism, poetry, essays, histories, translations, reviews, biographies, journalistic reporting, editorial work – might prove to be enlivening and a means of broadening his grasp of British and foreign contemporary affairs and literature. As a matter of fact, like many editors of the mushrooming magazines in the city Cave was in dire need of someone who could write distinguished prose and poetry, who knew Latin, Greek, French and Italian, who was widely read, and who possessed a journalist-editor's instinct for revision and public appeal. He needed Johnson, just as Johnson needed him.

2

Johnson had already shown Cave his poetic prowess and epigrammatic talents and was eager to show him more. Latin and Greek poetry such as he could write easily on demand, the work of a minute, was highly un- usual in a periodical magazine and had already given Cave's poetry section a sudden leg up on the *London Magazine* and other competitors. 'I have composed a Greek epigram to Eliza and think she ought to be celebrated in as many different languages as Lewis le Grand,' he wrote to Cave in April 1738 about the young authoress Elizabeth Carter. It delighted every- one, especially Carter, when Cave published it that month. In July ap- peared another Latin poem of his in praise of Eliza, followed by his trans- lation of it in August, 'To Eliza Plucking Laurel in Mr Pope's Garden'. He signed it 'Urbanus', a way of indicating that the piece was from the of- fice of Sylvanus Urban, Cave's *nom de plume*. The poem alludes to Pope's geniality and generosity in allowing Eliza to pluck her laurel from a branch as a tribute to her recognition as a poet. To reach the garden, inci- dentally, he would have needed first to pass through Pope's equally famous grotto, an inspiration, perhaps, for his later translation into Latin of Pope's verses on the grotto, published in *The Gentleman's Magazine* five years later.[7]

In the next few months Cave published others of his short poems. He took these pieces eagerly, together with excerpts from *London: A Poem* that he published in May. He was delighted, ranking *London: A Poem* that month as number one in his register of books while Pope's poem *One Thousand Seven Hundred and Thirty-Eight* came in at only number twenty-two. Here was a new poet better than Pope. All the signs were that Johnson would follow up *London: A Poem* with more verse sat- ire, modelled again on Juvenal or Horace. Nothing would have been more natural or expected.

But occasional verses, least of all epigrams, were not going to pay the bills. He needed more substantial, regular links to the magazine. In short, he needed to write prose for it – more words meant more printer's sheets filled, and more sheets meant more money. He said on his deathbed that Cave contracted 'for lines by the hundred'. Pressing him again regarding the translation of Paulo Sarpi's *Council of Trent*, he caught his interest this time and in July began working on it, receiving regular payments. These first payments made such an impression on him that he carefully recorded them on a slip of paper entitled, 'Account between Mr Edward Cave and Sam. Johnson, in relation to a version of Father Paul, &c. begun August the 2d, 1738'. Such a translation suited Cave. He badly wanted to rise in the publishing trade, like the fabulously successful Samuel Richardson, from printer and magazine publisher to the more lucrative and prestigious realm of book publishing. Authors were not about to offer him their manuscripts, however, unless he had achieved some reputation as a publisher of larger works. It was slow work but he was getting there and Johnson came along just at the right time.[8]

In less than three months after returning to London, Johnson had managed to win Cave's confidence by several means. One was personal testimony. Cave's office was a quiet, businesslike sort of place where only a few workers spent their time and where contributors were not often seen. Alehouses, coffee houses, and private dinners at homes were more likely meeting places. Birch and Savage, and also Moses Browne and Samuel Boyse, were among those few contributors with whom Cave seems to have developed personal relationships, although the snobbish Birch thought himself superior to Cave and his Grub Street world. All of them could be counted on to speak well to Cave of this young, energetic literary dynamo, his extensive reading, ideas, poetic sophistication, useful potential as a translator, and fascination with foreign (especially exotic) lands. Also impressive was his curiosity about the 'general principles of every science' which since boyhood he had dedicated himself to possess – to 'grasp the trunk' of knowledge and 'shake all the branches', as he once put it. He described his early years as so much 'running about the world with my wits ready to observe, and my tongue ready to talk'. It is revealing that with the exception of Pope and Dodsley, Johnson's earliest literary 'patronage' in

London was from word-mongers and peddlers of sentences in the print factories, not from established writers and people of note and influence.

The darling of this group, the one whose testimony may have penetrated Cave's taciturnity more than the others, was Elizabeth Carter. Carter's was the most impressive female intellect he would ever encounter. The daughter of the Revd Nicholas Carter in Kent, who was an accomplished classical scholar, she was taught by her father and worked assiduously throughout her Kentish youth in Deal to attain a command of Greek and modern languages, becoming at a young age one of the most distinguished female poets and scholars in Johnson's lifetime. She had been writing poetry for Cave's magazine since 1734. It was through Cave that she first met Johnson in April 1738 – 'Poor dear Cave,' he wrote to her years later after Cave's death, 'I owed him much, for to him I owe that I have known you.' Johnson loved her at once for her blend of modesty, confident piety, intellectual brilliance and poetical talents. He once said of her, 'My old friend Carter . . . could make a pudding as well as translate Epictetus from the Greek, and work a handkerchief as well as compose a poem'. He also admired her clear-headed moral understanding and independent spirit in believing that 'women had not their proper station in society, and that their mental powers were not rated sufficiently high'. Cave and his wife were very attentive to her, Birch seems to have fallen in love with her, and Johnson (eight years older) took her under his wing, becoming in a way her mentor. Occasionally, she wrote to her father back in Kent about him, apparently revelling in his attentions. Her father replied sceptically, 'You mention Johnson; but that is a name with which I am utterly unacquainted. Neither his scholastic, critical, or poetical character ever reached my ears. I a little suspect his judgement, if he is very fond of Martial.'[9]

One innovation of Cave's for the magazine especially caught Johnson's imagination. He hired William Guthrie to attend the House of Commons and Lords and report the debates there himself for the magazine instead of simply taking and digesting reports from rival periodicals, which he had been doing since 1732, much to the annoyance of his rivals. Guthrie had begun these in February 1738, but he wrote merely competently and

Cave needed someone to turn them into brisker and more imaginative prose. Johnson took them in hand in June and in the process slid gently into the role of Cave's fellow-editor and soon enough even his right-hand man.

Cave deployed a way of circumventing fresh parliamentary restrictions on the reporting of the debates in 1738. The Commons at that time did not want any reporting published in the papers even during the recess; nor did it want speakers identified by name. Either he or Johnson hit on the clever device, adapted from the *London Magazine*, of framing the debates as 'Debates in the Senate of Magna Lilliputia', taking advantage of the resonating irony of Swift's consummate satire in *Gulliver's Travels* a decade earlier. In June Cave duly published an introduction to the Lilliputian scheme, 'State of Affairs in Lilliput', that bears signs of Johnson's style, especially in the satiric attacks on the government.[10]

The elaborate artifice begins with Gulliver's grandson sailing to Lilliput to set the record straight about his grandfather. Lilliput, Blefescu, and other kingdoms in the region, he finds, exactly resemble Europe, and several institutions in Lilliput, mainly its parliament, correspond perfectly to England's. Parliamentarians in Lilliput are coyly given names resembling (but strategically not the same as) the main players in Britain's parliament, so nobody could be in any doubt about who was meant. This ironic camouflage created the freedom to report and embellish the debates without fear of prosecution. While Johnson was asked to look over Guthrie's prose, he also did a good bit of the writing of the debates himself. It was a brilliant idea that brought vigour and fresh esteem to the magazine, especially at a time when Sir Robert Walpole was in the final tumultuous phase of his rule and particularly vulnerable to such satire under the pretence of objective reporting.

There was also a flurry of harsh pieces which Cave gave Johnson the opportunity to write, including his first original paragraphs for the magazine, a 'letter' from 'Eubulus' on the arrogance of British colonialism in China. He also wrote current affairs articles on the moral question of condolences raised by the ill-timed and ill-conceived parliamentary panegyrics on the late Queen – his comments were also bitterly anti-Hanoverian

– and on epitaph-writing. The latter two especially roused his anger over effusive, facile and self-regarding expressions of sympathy which only make a sufferer feel more grief and show frivolous insensitivity to fearful death.[11]

A couple of months after Johnson began revising Guthrie, he became bored of sifting through his collaborator's prose. Cave apparently had a few stiff words with him about his letting too much of Guthrie's writing go unrevised, for in an August letter Johnson was defending himself:

> You seem to insinuate that I had promised more than I am ready to perform. If I have raised your expectations by any thing that may have escaped my memory I am sorry, and if you remind me of it shall thank you for the favour. If I made fewer alterations than usual in the debates it was only because there appeared, and still appears to me to be less need of alteration.

He was also unhappy about some new work for the poetry section. Cave asked him to judge poetry submitted on 'the Divine attributes' for one of the magazine's poetry prizes of £40 – a competition announced two years earlier and, given the subject, not eliciting much response from the readership. It meant a little more money so Johnson agreed, but he was constitutionally opposed to judging other people's verse in such an artificial exercise and tried to beg off, admitting 'a backwardness to determine degrees of merit, [which] is nothing peculiar to me'. He would do it if he had to, but 'I shall engage with little spirit in an affair, which I shall *hardly* end to my own satisfaction, and *certainly* not to the satisfaction of the parties concerned.' The competition eventually petered out the following year. The same ennui or depression, or perhaps problems with Tetty – all these could have been connected – struck at his translating of Sarpi: 'As to Father Paul, I have not yet been just to my proposal,' he informed Cave in August, 'but have met with impediments which I hope are now at an end, and if you find the progress hereafter not such as you have a right to expect, you can easily stimulate a negligent translator.' Cave probably did 'stimulate' him in some way – probably with a little money – because the work resumed and in October no fewer than six thousand copies of Johnson's proposal for the translation were published, with his name appearing attached to it.[12]

3

His first biographical offering, a 'Life of Sarpi', appeared in the November issue of *The Gentleman's Magazine* signed 'S. J.' and identifying him clearly as the translator of Sarpi. It was the magazine's means of advertising the translation Johnson had been at work on for almost half a year. Publicity was suddenly needed because soon after the proposals were published a rival translator reared his head who threatened to scuttle the whole Sarpi enterprise. Instead of backing off from the competition, Johnson and Cave decided to fight back by providing a sample biography, showing how well the translator could write and how fortunate the subscribers were to have him on the job. What it really illustrated was Johnson's powers not as a biographer but as a translator, since it is merely a severely abridged translation of an existing biography with a few of his own perspectives on Sarpi thrown in – at least to the extent that his single source could inspire any.

Cave then asked him to write a biographical piece on the famed William Boerhaave, the celebrated Dutch physician and Professor of Physick at Leiden who had just died on 23 September. Johnson was naturally interested in Boerhaave because his work was responsible for 'the most widespread assumptions of medical thought' just at the time he himself was studying medicine, especially 'the study of physic'. Again, he simply took a Latin eulogium on the physician published in Leiden and wrote another translation and abridgement. Unusually lengthy for the magazine, the 'Life of Boerhaave' was published anonymously over four issues beginning in January 1739. A measure of its importance in eighteenth-century medical thought at the time is that it was included slightly revised in Robert James's *Medicinal Dictionary* in 1742 and then again in the *Universal Maga-*

zine for 1743. James depended upon its systematised presentation of
Boerhaave's and other medical knowledge in several of his later writings,
including his *Modern Practice of Physic* (1746).[13]

In both these lives of Sarpi and Boerhaave he was using a single source
from which to translate, and although his tactical abridgement of each
shows his brilliance in taking a longer work and casting it into rhythmical
and balanced English prose, he did not see himself as what we think of as
a fully fledged biographer. Nor was he interested in doing any biographical research. He focused more on reflections on human nature than on researched facts. Boerhaave possessed two qualities which in Johnson's mind
were among the most important in his idea of a hero: usefulness to society
and, above all, self-confidence. The latter is a theme in all his biographies,
a quality he extolled for the rest of his life. Without it, no human excellence and achievement was possible. It was a quality he himself clearly
possessed, and knew he possessed, even if he was not sure at this point
where it was leading him and what good he would be able to do society
with it.[14]

Another idea for a translation that Cave and Johnson may have come
up with together was that of the Swiss theologian Jean-Pierre de
Crousaz's controversial attack on Pope's poem *An Essay on Man* (1733) in
1735–6. Crousaz had not liked Pope's deism in the poem, its fashionable
secular moralising about man and the universe and what he thought were
its logical contradictions. He condemned it in the name of both morality
and religion. Cave thought Crousaz's *Commentary*, if translated, could
pick up on the buzz Crousaz had caused in London. Perhaps Pope, who
was taken aback by the furore, would also appreciate it. Johnson did not
much like Pope's determinism either, but unlike Crousaz he was in a position to defend the brilliance of Pope's verse. The project almost collapsed
when the disreputable bookseller Edmund Curll beat Cave and Johnson
to it with his own translation of Crousaz. Although Cave was in no doubt
that Johnson could produce a far superior translation, he thought they
should consider abandoning ship, with which Johnson, stymied and disappointed, agreed: 'I am pretty much of your opinion, that the Commentary
cannot be prosecuted with any appearance of success, for as the names of

the authors concerned are of more weight in the performance than its own intrinsic merit, the public will be soon satisfied with it.' However, Cave then decided to push on since Curll had brought out only part of Crousaz's work and Cave thought that the whole of it might be marketable. Johnson took it up and wrote it at a furious pace, Boswell recording in his journal that he wrote six sheets of forty-eight quarto pages in one superhuman day. Cave had most of the 300-page book printed but did not publish it until November 1741, under his own imprint and without Johnson's name. It included notes by Johnson that are of particular interest because they are among his first published criticism. Cave was still sitting on unsold copies a couple of years later. Not for the first time, this publication was an unhappy literary exercise for Johnson, characterised by disappointments of money, time and lack of recognition.[15]

4

By April 1739, he had completed about fifty sheets of *Sarpi*, some four hundred quarto pages, a staggering amount in such a short time – four times as long as the *Crousaz*. Hence the shock when, only a quarter of the way through, Cave terminated his work. Formidable competition from a rival translator, however, turned out to be too much for them in spite of Johnson's having staked his claim with his 'Life of Sarpi'. It was too risky for Cave. Johnson's huge scholarly investment was suddenly all for nothing. Worse yet, his manuscript disappeared into the recesses of St John's Gate and was never seen again. At this point his publishing scorecard did not inspire confidence. *Irene* remained neglected, *Sarpi* had come to nothing, and *Crousaz* did little for his public reputation. He had done much to redefine and invigorate *The Gentleman's Magazine*, but hack work was hack work and he remained buried by it. He felt cheated. In his writing he had sublimated much of his anger and rebelliousness in nuanced moral reflections on a variety of subjects, but there was no mistaking the underlying acerbic tone of his thinking. Cave knew he had an angry genius on his hands who, among other things, was radicalising his magazine, prepared to lash out at many targets. The one element in Johnson's work, in fact, that sustained his morale was his satiric impulse, serving as a type of pressure valve, an original and creative release to vary the drudgery of editorial work. This was especially evident in the satirical muscles he flexed during a London periodical warfare fought for several months early in 1739, with Johnson leading the charge on behalf of the magazine and articulating various arguments against biased political writing in the public press. Cave put a stop to it in the spring fearing that his 'oracle', as someone called Johnson, was putting at risk his magazine's reputation for fairness and reliability.[16]

What were Johnson's mature views on Tories and Whigs? They certainly are not understandable in terms of neat modern oppositions between conservative and liberal, the right and left. 'A wise Tory and a wise Whig, I believe, will agree,' he insisted. 'Their principles are the same, though their modes of thinking are different.' The traditional myth of Tory Johnson that is part of the popular conception of him, and has been ever since the end of the eighteenth century, makes him into a stiff and backward-looking conservative, an unreserved defender of aristocratic hierarchy, sceptical of change, and intolerant of new ideas, especially if they threaten the established order.

A number of Johnson's Tory positions, however, were in fact strongly liberal. To be sure, he never equivocated his defence of the Church of England and its role in the lives of Englishmen. But notwithstanding his Tory-like isolationism, he was always hugely concerned, as we have seen, for the welfare of native peoples in distant and exotic lands threatened by the imperialistic policies of powerful nations; and he was always fascinated with, and frequently wrote about, their customs and manners. He was an economic isolationist, a Little Englander, stridently opposed to foreign military ventures on behalf of global British commercial interests. But in this he was, as has often been pointed out, in line with Walpole who strongly opposed such expensive and exploitative foreign policy and was frequently attacked for it by the country's powerful trading interests in the East India and South Sea companies. Johnson later despised the Whig William Pitt for ambitious foreign policies that took Britain into war – in America, for example – in greedy pursuit of economic expansionism. As Donald Greene has pointed out, this did not mean that John-son was opposed to trade and industry, for (not surprisingly, given his own bourgeois family background) he championed the middle classes and eco-nomic policy that would ameliorate the suffering and wants of the needy in his country – and in this, he supported Pitt against the growing wealth of the Whig aristocracy. Politically, he was horrified by the threat of civil conflict from any quarter, and the accompanying spectre of anarchy, but at the same time he was very critical of the abuses of monarchs. He also felt that if Britain had to fight a war to protect itself and its reasonable inter-ests, it should do so mightily. He did not wish America to be exploited commercially by Britain, but his anti-Americanism and vigorous desire to win the War of Independence sprang from what he regarded as the colo-nies' fraudulent arguments for independence and propagandistic and pop-ulist distortion of the history of their relationship to Britain.[17]

Johnson's political attitudes sprang from his embracing humanitarian heart, his distrust and scepticism where oppressive power raised its ugly head, his rooting for the underdog and all kinds of minority groups, his unwavering anti-slavery stance – all of this without creating dangers of anarchy, which he feared and hated. His charitable acts were legendary. He was highly sceptical of grandiose political plans and ingenious theories for social improvement. For his most social and political attitudes he drew simply on his own career as an ordinary citizen and human being, on 'the heart of man', not on the vagaries of political affiliations. That was where his power rested as a moralist, social and literary critic, and political sati-rist.

Little that he wrote was more venomous than a fifty-page pamphlet at-tacking Walpole in May which he titled *Marmor Norfolciense*. In this clever tour de force by a 'true Briton', as Boswell wrote rather simplisti-cally, 'he, in a feigned inscription, supposed to have been found in Norfolk, the county of Sir Robert Walpole, then the obnoxious prime minister of this country, inveighs against the Brunswick succession, and the measures of government consequent upon it.'[18]

The Brunswick succession needs some explaining as it was another complication in Johnson's political thinking. George I had been the Duke of Brunswick-Luneburg, a historical state within the Holy Roman Empire, when the English parliament passed the Act of Settlement in 1701 placing his mother Sophia, the electress of Hanover and granddaughter of James I, first in the line of succession to the Crown. When Queen Anne died in 1714, George I became the first Hanoverian king and the Whigs returned to power in force. After the succession, however, there lingered increasingly marginal and wistful Jacobite (from the Latin *Jacobus* or 'James') sympathies in Britain for the banished James II and his return to the throne. To what extent Johnson harboured such sympathies has been hotly debated, especially in the past twenty years or so, but it is probably fair to say his was only a lukewarm attachment to Jacobitism blended with a strong dislike of Georges I and II. He was never active in support of the cause and it is certain he never wished for another constitutional crisis connected with the monarchy.

In *Marmor Norfolciense*, with 'warm anti-Hanoverian zeal', Johnson lacerated Walpole's ministry and its venal hangers-on as well as George II and kings in general. His pamphlet, as Hawkins wrote in his painful prose, consists of 'an invective against a standing army, a ridicule of the balance of power, complaints of the inactivity [i.e. cowardice] of the British lion, and that the Hanover horse was suffered to suck his blood'. Johnson enjoyed writing the pamphlet as a way of releasing his political frustrations – Pope read it and thought it was 'very humorous' – but he was harsh and deadly serious, brimming with righteous indignation. It is also recklessly angry. He spitefully attacked not only foreign policy, especially as regards the overly pacific attitude towards Spain, but also the King's morals, frivolity and intelligence, adding the brazenly Jacobite line, 'Kings change their laws, and kingdoms change their kings'. With this kind of personal innuendo against the monarch, several pages long, Johnson stood apart from most Opposition writers. It was nearly treasonous. One story Hawkins told, suspicious because the authorities would have had no trouble finding him, is that the ministry identified him as the author and initiated proceedings, forcing him and Tetty both to go into hiding in a hideaway in Lambeth Marsh until the matter blew over.[19]

One of his targets in *Marmor Norfolciense* is censorship of anti-government publications, another subject that raised his temperature so much that in less than three weeks he wrote another biting pamphlet, *A Compleat Vindication of the Licensers of the Stage*, against the abuse of liberty as well as many of the corruptions of the Walpole government he had denounced in the earlier pamphlet. Adopting Swiftian satire again, he ironically portrayed Walpole's vindicator defending all that he hated about the secrecy and obscurantism of his government. Johnson's disgust here dated back to the Government's passing of a new Licensing Act in 1737 granting and publicising new measures for the examination and suppression of plays that attacked the Walpole government. Such powers had long existed but this Act's blatant and public declaration of them especially angered Johnson and many others. His revulsion over the obscene arrogance and arrogation of power at the expense of the individual in a flawed social system plays into this pamphlet.

The autobiographical content of these pamphlets is not found in whether Johnson was now, and later, a Whig in Tory clothing, or a Whiggish Tory, or a Toryish Whig, or just a Tory. As we have seen, he hated the excesses of party politics. Hawkins and Boswell both went so far as to maintain that he had 'a high opinion' of Walpole: 'He said of him, that he was a fine fellow, and that his very enemies deemed him so before his death: he honoured his memory for having kept this country in peace many years, as also for the goodness and placability of his temper.' Rather, the pamphlets speak volumes about his social and private persona. The Government's system of forcing people into 'subordination and dependence', and of keeping the public ignorant, that his vindicator in *Compleat Vindication* extols was ever anathema to him and a sure bet to provoke his fury.[20]

5

None of this government-bashing in *The Gentleman's Magazine* and pamphlets took him closer to his original literary goals. It earned him a little money, though barely enough to live on. Otherwise, it was largely a self-indulgent waste of time if his object was to make his name as a man of letters. Literary London seemed increasingly a wasteland for him where his efforts to succeed were shrivelling on Cave's vine. Moreover, London was not Tetty's favourite place, and later evidence suggests that out of boredom and neglect she may already have begun to resort to the pretence of happiness through drink and excessive make-up, with the danger of collapsing into an unattractive caricature of herself. So it is no surprise that when there was a vacancy for the headmastership in Appleby, Leicestershire, only twelve miles east of Lichfield, he decided to apply.[21] With not a little sense of failure or even despair, and leaving Tetty behind in their lodgings with the hope that she would join him soon when he got the job, he left London in August 1739. Whatever the reasons for her staying behind, it cannot have been good for her to remain in London alone.

There was a preferred candidate for the position but a division among the school's governors and trustees created a small breach that was Johnson's opportunity. The Bishop of Lincoln was to make the appointment in December, so there was time for jockeying of position and influence peddling. Johnson's lack of a degree was still his greatest handicap. His application therefore seemed pointless because the school's statutes specified that the headmaster had to have a degree from either Oxford or Cambridge. Friends came forward to support him, however, suggesting how he could get a degree.

His strong card was *London: A Poem*. First, William Adams at Pembroke was asked whether on the strength of the poem Oxford could be prevailed on to grant him a degree, but Oxford would not cooperate. Adams wrote to Boswell after Johnson's death: 'I was applied to by a common friend to know whether a Master of Arts degree could be granted him as a favour from the university, to qualify him for a school master's place which was then offered him. But this, tho' his character in the literary world began to rise [it] was thought too much to be asked.'[22]

Contacted possibly by Savage, Pope was also brought in to help. Lord Gower, Pope was told, had a friend who was an intimate of Swift, the

Dean of St Patrick's Cathedral in Dublin. Could Swift be reached through this friend with a view to using his influence at Trinity College, Dublin to obtain for Johnson a Master of Arts from that university? It was very much a long shot since the school statute specified a degree from an English university. Still, would Pope write to Gower about this? Pope did and the letter that Gower duly sent from Trentham, Staffordshire on 1 August contains some interesting facts. He identified Johnson as the author of *London: A Poem* and 'some other poetical pieces', a native of Staffordshire, and much respected in the region for his probity and learning. The headmastership, worth an annual salary of £60 (about £6,000 today) that 'would make him happy for life', is not likely to come his way unless Swift can persuade the university 'to send a diploma to me, constituting this poor man Master of Arts'. Johnson was willing, Gower added, to travel all the way to Dublin to submit to the 'strictest examination', 'choosing rather to die upon the road, *than be starved to death in translating for booksellers*; which has been his only subsistence for some time past'. Gower, however, was going through the motions only because Pope had asked him to on behalf of this 'poor man'. Gower thought the exercise was bound to be fruitless: 'If you see this matter in the same light that it appears to me, I hope you will burn this, and pardon me for giving you so much trouble about an impracticable thing.'[23]

If Swift ever did do anything for Johnson, we know nothing of it. Johnson did not receive his degree, but he decided to travel up to Lichfield and Appleby anyway to be interviewed by the governors, leaving London just a month after Savage fled to Wales. Presumably he was interviewed in August but no vote was taken and he had to wait until mid-December for the bishop's decision – based, of course, on the governors' recommendation. Without a degree and plagued by his 'infirmity of a convulsive kind', he failed to secure the position. Stourbridge, Market Bosworth, Ashbourne, Solihull, Edial, Brewood, and now Appleby – seven failed applications by the age of thirty. Neither Pope, nor Lord Gower, nor his network of friends in the area, nor several of the trustees who favoured his application, nor his extraordinary talents could overcome his physically grotesque and uncouth mannerisms and lack of credentials. If this, surely last, failure to secure a teaching position did anything it was to sharpen his bitterness and add to the sense of desolation with which he left London, the deepening feeling that, like Savage, he was an outsider, on the fringe, and unable to gain acceptance except in Grub Street.

CHAPTER 12

Wandering in the Midlands

JOHNSON COULD HAVE RETURNED to Tetty and London promptly in August or early September, after being reunited at home with his mother, Lucy and Kitty Chambers for a decent interval. But he did not. He waited until early spring 1740, seven or eight months later. The inevitable conclusion to be drawn from this neglect of Tetty is that he preferred to be with his family and even Lucy instead of with her, at least for the time being. Reluctant also to return to the harshly competitive literary fray in London, he found richly reassuring companionship in his native corner of England which he did not want to leave.

When he left for Appleby his parting from Tetty could not have been painful. For him the trip was partly an escape, and by then she was used to being on her own and was withdrawing into herself anyway. Hawkins thought Savage was at the root of the problems between them:

We are to remember that Johnson was, at this time, a husband: can it therefore be supposed that the society of such a man as Savage had any tendency to improve him in the exercise of the domestic virtues? Nay rather we must doubt it, and ascribe to an indifference in the discharge of them, arising from their nocturnal excursions, the incident of a temporary separation of Johnson from his wife, which soon took place, and that, while he was in a lodging in Fleet Street, she was harboured by a friend near the Tower. It is true that this separation continued but a short time, and that if indeed his affection, at that instant, was alienated from her, it soon returned.

Hawkins, however, did not take into account quarrels even before Johnson came to London and met Savage. That finances were one severe pressure on their marriage, worsening in London and continuing to be a source of friction, was highlighted by Shaw, though the following remark could apply to any period between 1739 and her death: 'She disliked the profusion, with which he constantly gave away all the money about him; and he found with astonishment and concern, that whatever he provided or laid up for family exigence, was always gone before he expected.' Another pressure may well have been Johnson's sexual fantasies. 'With all possible respect and delicacy', from what he had heard Boswell judged:

> his conduct, after he came to London, and had associated with Savage and others, was not so strictly virtuous, in one respect, as when he was a younger man . . . He owned to many of his friends, that he used to take women of the town to taverns, and hear them relate their history . . . Johnson was not free from propensities which were ever warring against the law of his mind . . . and that in his combats with them, he was sometimes overcome.[1]

In January, after more than five months in Lichfield without apparently writing to her except presumably immediately after he failed at Appleby, Johnson sent a letter to Tetty in Castle Street tinged with a sense of guilt. It is the best surviving letter he wrote to her. She was in a sorry state, having damaged a tendon in her leg to add to her loneliness and other woes. Whether it was she or someone else who wrote to him about this is unknown, but the injury may have resulted from a fall on ice. That winter everyone was talking about the big freeze, which would long be remembered as one of the most severe in memory – 'the dreadful winter of Forty', Johnson recalled years later. The Thames froze over completely

and an ice-fair was held on it; in north Staffordshire, people 'could gaze
upon the result of a rivulet dripping down a rock at Ipstones, in the shape
of a column of ice "10 yards 3 qrs. High, and 12 about"'. 'After hearing that
you are in so much danger,' he began urgently, 'as I apprehended from a
hurt on a tendon, I shall be very uneasy till I know that you are recovered, and beg that you will omit nothing that can contribute to it, nor
deny yourself anything that may make confinement less melancholy . . . I
beg therefore that you will not more regard my happiness, than to expose
yourself to any hazards.' He urged her to get the best medical help from,
among others, a couple of royal physicians who were said to be 'the
best' for a guinea. Never mind the expense, he added, because he and
his mother had just mortgaged the family home on Market Square to
Theophilus Levett, the Lichfield town clerk who befriended Johnson and
his family. He was keeping twenty pounds and would soon be sending
her the rest. It felt good to have some fresh cash in his pocket, and he
had promising news: 'David [Garrick] wrote to me this day on the affair
of *Irene*, who is at last become a kind of favourite among the players; Mr
Fleetwood promises to give a promise in writing that it shall be the first
next season, if it cannot be introduced now.' Not only that, the Drury
Lane prompter and stage historian William Rufus Chetwood 'is desirous
of bargaining for the copy, and offers fifty guineas for the right of printing
after it shall be played . . . I hope it will at length reward me for my per-
plexities.'[2]

It is possible to read the letter as an acknowledgement that all the suffering to which he said he subjected her is owing to his inability to earn
enough money to take care of her properly. Her injury had awakened his
remorse and made him curse his own failures: 'You have already suffered
more than I can bear to reflect upon, and I hope more than either of us
shall suffer again. One part at least I have often flattered myself we shall
avoid[;] for the future our troubles will surely never separate us more.' His
'esteem and affection' for her 'has only contributed to increase my unhappiness when I reflected that the most amiable woman in the world was exposed by my means to miseries which I could not relieve'.

But there is more going on here than mere remorse over his failure as the breadwinner. Phrases in it like 'most amiable woman in the world', and others like 'dear girl', and 'my charming love' all may be read as efforts to placate her for his prolonged absences, past and present, yet the letter does not acknowledge he was doing anything wrong in having already been away from her for more than five months. There is a deeper sense of self-blame at work in these sentences: 'I still promise myself many happy years from your tenderness and affection, which I sometimes hope our misfortunes have not yet deprived me of . . . Be assured, my dear girl, that I have seen nobody in these rambles upon which I have been forced, that has not contributed to confirm my esteem and affection for thee.' He added, 'Of the time which I have spent from thee, and of my dear Lucy and other affairs, my heart will be at ease on Monday to give a particular account, especially if a letter should inform me that thy leg is better, for I hope you do not think so unkindly of me as to imagine that I can be at rest while I believe my dear Tetty in pain.' In other words, he would feel less guilty telling her about these enjoyable visits and rambles over the past few months if he knew she was no longer in pain. Her injury had brought him back down to earth somewhat, but not enough to make him hasten back to her.

Johnson indeed appears to have enjoyed himself greatly during his absence, which is probably what lies behind his nervous assertion that he has not met anyone in his rambles who has made him forget her. If Mrs Thrale was right, he had had to reassure her like this before at Edial Hall after he met Molly Aston. The truth was he had discovered an entertaining new social world much to his liking, even more pleasing to him at the age of thirty than at the Bishop's Palace in his uncertain youth. He found most of these new delights of good society in Ashbourne and the countryside around it. His school chum John Taylor, who had recently given up law to become a clergyman, was at the top of his list of people to visit. It was about this time that Taylor took up residence in the comfortable manor of Ashbourne and began his existence as a type of eighteenth-century 'squarson', a parson who also played at being a farmer and squire, not budging too much from rural pursuits at home to see to his clerical duties in Market Bosworth. From this point on Taylor went from strength to strength. Over the years he became a local patron of Ashbourne, almost like a resident lord, and in the last fifteen years of his life Johnson made a habit of visiting Ashbourne almost annually, although his friends were mystified by what he found appealing enough in his boring and stuffy friend to detain him there that much. 'Sir, I love him,' he said to Boswell, 'but I do not love him more; my regard for him does not increase . . . His talk is of bullocks.' What he found there in 1739–40 was a comfortable and quiet self-enclosed world, a dramatic change of pace from London.[3]

Taylor was the centre but not boundary of Johnson's new Ashbourne social horizon. Three miles down the road he found more animated society at Bradley, the seat of the country squire Littleton Poyntz Meynell, as insular an Englishman as could be imagined who, forty years later, Johnson remembered as having said, 'For any thing I see, foreigners are fools.' His son Hugo became famous as the so-called 'father of fox hunting'.

It was the women at Bradley who impressed Johnson the most. One of them later wrote her impressions of him at Bradley. These found their way into Boswell's hands, and he quoted as follows from them: 'During his stay at Ashbourne, he made frequent visits to Mr Meynell, at Bradley, where his company was much desired by the ladies of the family, who were, perhaps, in point of elegance and accomplishments, inferior to few of those with whom he was afterwards acquainted'. Meynell's daughter, Mary Fitzherbert, was a particular delight – 'Of her, Dr Johnson said . . . that she had the best understanding he ever met with in any human being'. Mrs Thrale who thought Johnson's veneration for Mary was so highly pitched that it was 'very difficult to deserve', recorded his remark that she 'loved her husband as we hope and desire to be loved by our guardian angel . . . her first care was to preserve her husband's soul from corruption; her second to keep his estate entire for their children: and I owed my good reception in the family to the idea she had entertained, that I was fit company for Fitzherbert whom I loved extremely.' Was Mary attractive? Mrs Thrale asked him: 'She would have been handsome for a queen (replied the panegyrist); her beauty had more in it of majesty than of attraction, more of the dignity of virtue than the vivacity of wit.'[4]

Another feminine presence who sparkled for Johnson at Bradley and the Fitzherbert's seat at Tissington Hall was young Hill Boothby, daughter of Sir Brooke Boothby of Ashbourne Hall, a frequent guest and herself of an old Derbyshire family. After Mary Fitzherbert died in childbirth in 1753, 'in the flower of her age, distinguished for her piety and fine accomplishments', her six children were raised by Miss Boothby. Johnson's affection for her persisted and grew to the point that after Tetty died he may have entertained the idea of marrying her, if she would have him.

Before Johnson could marry Miss Boothby, however – if indeed that was ever likely to happen – she died in January 1756 from an illness during which Johnson wrote to her deeply affectionate letters. In a fascinating one written at midnight on 30 December 1755, he implored her, 'Continue, my dearest, your prayers for me, that no good resolution may be vain. You think, I believe, better of me than I deserve. I hope to be in time what I wish to be, and what I have hitherto satisfied myself too readily with only wishing ... You know Descartes' argument, "I think therefore I am." ... I might give another, "I am alive therefore I love Miss Boothby", but that I hope our friendship may be of far longer duration than life.' In his next letter he addresses her, 'My Sweet Angel'. Mrs Thrale, however, poured cold water on the relationship: 'he told me she pushed her piety to bigotry, her devotion to enthusiasm; that she somewhat disqualified herself for the duties of *this* life, by her perpetual aspirations after the *next*: such was however the purity of her mind, he said, and such the graces of her manner, that Lord Lyttelton [at nearby Hagley] and he used to strive for her preference with an emulation that occasioned hourly disgust, and ended in lasting animosity.' Mrs Thrale even went so far as to make the wild claim that a negative biography Johnson wrote of Lord Lyttelton forty years later was inspired by his jealousy of Lyttelton over Miss Boothby: 'She *would* delight in that fellow Lyttelton's company', she reported him saying, in spite of 'all that I could do; and I cannot forgive even his memory the preference [for] a mind like hers'. 'You may see', he allegedly said, 'that dear Boothby is at my heart still.'[5]

Such complications were not even imagined in the autumn, winter and spring of 1739–40, however, when the Derbyshire landscape was for him one of green innocence and delight in the company of these graces. These were scenes complete with a cast of characters worthy of Jane Austen, supplied even with the colourful and eccentric rector of Bradley, Dr John Kennedy, author of *A Complete System of Astronomical Chronology* and *A New Method of Scripture Chronology*, for which Johnson wrote a Dedication and Preface respectively, who also grew into a friend.[6] One can scarcely blame Johnson for not tearing himself away from all this and rushing back to Tetty. He discovered, really for the first time at the age of thirty, without a dragging sense of inferiority or weight of melancholia, that he could hold his own in a genteel setting with fine ladies and gentlemen, appreciated for his intelligence, wit, and honesty. His Grub Street existence seemed a lifetime away.

He had to get back to Tetty, though, and in late spring 1740, he finally forced himself away, leaving his mother, Lucy, friends, and any more thoughts of a schoolmaster's life, behind him. He would not return to Lichfield and Ashbourne for twenty-two long years.

Part Four

TRIUMPH:
THE DICTIONARY YEARS

CHAPTER 13

London Revived:
A Lion in Harness

I

BACK IN GRUB STREET in the spring of 1740, Johnson promptly re-paid Garrick's kindness for using his influence at Drury Lane on be-half of *Irene* by writing a prologue for his friend's new play *Lethe*.[1] Al-though in that poem he alludes to the recklessness and vanity of the dramatist like himself who 'dares to venture on the dangerous stage,/And weakly hopes to 'scape the critick's rage' even as he ducks 'the poignant or-ange' and tries to ignore the 'catcall's direful cry', he still had hopes that Fleetwood was serious about staging *Irene*. In the meantime, he slipped quickly again into the drudgery of revising Guthrie's debates, beginning in the May 1740 issue of *The Gentleman's Magazine*, and into some more hack work whipping into shape for the bookseller J(ohn?) Wilcox an abridged translation of an anonymous writer's *The History of Tahmas Kuli Khan, Shah, or Sophi of Persia*, a sensational French account of Nadir Shah of Persia's murderous military campaigns against Afghanistan and India. Wilcox, we recall, had lent Johnson and Garrick £5 soon after they arrived in London three years earlier. This is the only publishing ven-ture in which Johnson and Wilcox were ever connected, notwithstanding Johnson's calling the bookseller 'one of my best friends'.[2]

While Johnson was away the political landscape had altered. Britain had declared war on Spain and suddenly buzzed with nationalistic fer-vour. He returned to a city hungry for patriotic writing that would remind everyone of the country's (chiefly naval) greatness. Cave was only too happy to oblige and eager to call on Johnson to provide some of this with his rousing prose. The genre the two of them chose to capitalise on this market was biography – specifically, naval biography – which suited Johnson well. Biographies for the magazine encouraged him to think he was contributing something original. In fact, he did no research for them except for consulting earlier lives and reading some correspondence that had come Cave's way.

The first was the *Life of Admiral Blake*. As his source he simply used Thomas Birch's rather dry account of this colourful hero in the *General Dictionary, Historical and Critical*, condensing and restructuring it into seven pages in the magazine – a sizeable and successful contribution that Cave then reprinted in a fifteen-page pamphlet. In this biographical sketch Johnson often crudely and with the most obvious kind of patriotic cant exploited the public's impatience for the Government to fight the Spanish with force and dignity as Englishmen did in the past, not tentatively and anaemically as it was doing now. He wrote that, faced with a refusal to let his men draw water for his troops, Blake indignantly 'curled his whiskers, as was his custom when he was angry' and summarily captured Tunis.

Johnson followed this with more patriotic chest-beating in his next biographical assignment, the *Life of Drake*, details for which again he took mainly from four pamphlets comprising *Sir Francis Drake Revived*, an exciting tale of adventure and travel in South America and the Indies offering great opportunities for observations on human nature and customs in primitive lands. Drake's life in his hands became a national symbol of heroic adventure, a tribute to the dash and bravery of British explorers of the past, but it also turned out to be an excuse for Johnson to write about his greater and more lasting interest in the history of exploration and colonisation. He took a swipe especially at the nonsense of the noble savage archetype, that 'savages' like the Patagonians were more innocent and loving than an Englishman or any other European. Human nature was uniform throughout the globe, he contended, so to construct moral and social philosophies on the fanciful utopian idea that people untouched by 'civilisation' were superior to Europeans was idiocy. His old theme about the evils of colonial exploitation also appears strongly as he scourges the slaughter of the Patagonians by the cruel Spanish 'intruders'.

Another biography he wrote quickly was about the young German intellectual prodigy, Johann Philip Baratier, who in November 1740 had died at the age of nineteen. There was much about him in the press at the time. For this one Johnson did what he knew he did best, which had nothing to do with a chronological series of actions: on the basis of a few letters Cave let him see from the boy's father, he composed a moralist's biography, stressing the lonely self of a prodigy and how it coped in the world. It was the type of life-writing he liked most of all to do.[3]

2

This flurry of biographical activity creates the misleading impression that Johnson was as busy as ever working for Cave in 1740. In fact, the opposite was true: he was working much less for him than the year before. Even after Guthrie got fed up and stopped writing the debates in November, Johnson did not do the obvious and start writing them himself. He was deliberately resisting getting swallowed up by the magazine, holding out for alternatives that matched his notions of the kind of writer he wanted to be. *Irene*, however, continued to be a disappointment. By September 1741, when Cave wrote to Birch for ideas about helping with the play, Fleetwood had sneaked out of his promise to Garrick to stage it that season. Even if Fleetwood had been as good as his word, the income from the play would have been a one-off affair, and what Johnson sorely needed was steady income. Nothing else materialised, however, to save him from being sucked up by Cave's journalistic whirlpool, and from December onwards he increasingly was absorbed by the magazine – chiefly in writing the weekly essays – until in July 1741 he was completely in its grip. Notwithstanding a few acerbic lines he wrote about Cave in his biography of him, towards the end of his life Johnson had only grateful words for his employer and friend. Cave's road simply meant another road not taken, at least not for several years.

In the first six months of 1741, Cave called on his services more than ever before. Filling more than six pages per issue – eighteen in January – Johnson wrote for the magazine two short parliamentary debates that spared Cave the need to raid the *London Magazine* for its material; revised and 'abridged' into virtually an original work an old 112-page pamphlet (*Monarchy Asserted*, 1660) containing the famous debate between Cromwell and Parliament in 1657 concerning the petition to have him assume the title of King; translated and condensed a 350-page French history of the Amazons into his 'Dissertation on the Amazons'; and composed one of the magazine's so-called critical weekly essays entitled 'An Essay on Epitaphs' on the proper form and function of funerary epitaphs as an art.[4] That last essay expresses his growing conviction that the best biography is about the common man from whose life one can learn far more than from society's great heroes. He wrote all this with the gnawing awareness that it was relentlessly ephemeral prose, not adding up to anything very coherent or substantial. What he needed was a firm heart and steady resolution, a patient faith in his own abilities. Surely it was only a matter of time before his great break would come.[5]

Something did come up. Johnson had done wonders with Guthrie's parliamentary reporting but had mostly performed as a copy editor, shaping them into readable and interesting prose. In the summer, Cave offered him exclusive authorship of the debates. His task was to air issues and ideas that were being debated in Parliament in connection with particular legislation. Nobody reads his debates today because they are not easily accessible in modern editions, and they are rooted in mid-eighteenth-century issues and personalities, but they are far from dead in spirit and theme. Although their rhetoric makes a show of representing the politicians with dignity – given the magazine's political neutrality he had to do this – Johnson wrote his observations on the ambiguities and vanities of human nature in any sphere of activity, especially politics, through the lens of both the moralist and satirist.

It is surprising that in the last year of his life Johnson felt penitent about his debates; he felt that they were 'the mere coinage of his own imagination' and that they 'imposed' on the public because nobody in them really said exactly what he said they did, or in the way he had them say it. Fictionalised parliamentary speeches were commonplace at the time and had been part of the historical and biographical tradition of ancient Greek and Roman writers. Compelled to write them without attending Parliament or working from rough notes surreptitiously scribbled by someone who had, did not give him much of a choice in any case. Nonetheless, he regretted he became 'an author of fictions' in writing them.[6]

Still, this uneasiness did not preclude his vanity and pride over having pulled the deception off in the first place. His friend and biographer, Arthur Murphy, told of a dinner conversation one night at the home of the actor Samuel Foote during which a classical scholar present remarked that a speech by Pitt he recalled reading in the debates was better than anything Demosthenes had ever written. Johnson was there and allowed the conversation to proceed for a while without saying anything. Then he is supposed to have dropped his bombshell, 'That speech I wrote in a garret in Exeter street' – he must have meant Castle Street (if Murphy was not misremembering) since he had not lived in Exeter Street since 1737. There was general astonishment and when the scholar asked what he could possibly mean Johnson replied:

> Sir, I wrote it in Exeter Street. I never had been in the gallery of the House of Commons but once. Cave had interest with the door-keepers. He, and the persons employed under him, gained admittance: they brought away the subject of discussion, the names of the speakers, the side they took, and the order in which they rose, together with notes of the arguments advanced in the course of the debate. The whole was afterwards communicated to me, and I composed the speeches in the form which they now have in the Parliamentary debates.

Amazement turned to praise, especially for his alleged political impartiality, whereupon Johnson is supposed to have replied with this now iconic remark, 'That is not quite true. I saved appearances tolerably well; but I took care that the WHIG DOGS should not have the best of it.' On another occasion he stated that 'he always took care to put Sir Robert Walpole in the wrong, and to say every thing he could against the electorate of Hanover'. He would also have been proud (if a bit uncomfortable) had he heard that the debates had deceived Voltaire, who declared that 'the eloquence of ancient Greece and Rome was revived in the British senate'.[7]

Once the notes smuggled out of Parliament were put into his hands, he wrote at an astonishing speed. 'He never wrote any part of his works with equal velocity,' Boswell wrote; 'three columns of the magazine, in an hour, was no uncommon effort, which was faster than most persons could have transcribed that quantity.' Hawkins described how he did it: 'They were written at those seasons when he was able to raise his imagination to such a pitch of fervour as bordered upon enthusiasm, which, that he might the better do, his practice was to shut himself up in a room assigned him at St John's Gate to which he would not suffer any one to approach, except the compositor or Cave's boy for matter, which, as fast as he composed it, he tumbled out at the door.' Writing the debates as fast as he did, it is true he did not distinguish the speakers from each other by style and manner, identifying them chiefly by their positions on issues and their fictitious names. They all speak, whether vulgar or noble, pretty much in the same sustained oratorical style and without any regional accent or dialect. The dramatic give and take of debate, with sputterings, innuendo, and colloquialism, is not there. Johnson would have replied indignantly that he was interested in argument and reasoning, not characterisation.[8]

He has also been censured for deliberately putting speeches in the mouths of people who did not make them, or introducing arguments that were never uttered at all in the debates. As one of Johnson's commentators has urged, 'such a practice, abhorrent to the modern historian or journalist, was easily justifiable under the large demands of Johnson's rhetorical art. We must not forget that to value a speaker's real words, in all their paltriness, over a rhetorically perfected distillation of his meaning is a modern prejudice. It is to value the shell of a nut so greatly that it can never be cracked to get at the meat. It is to disdain the truth of art and to glorify the truth of "fact".'[9] Nonetheless, members of Parliament must surely have had some good gossip in their corridors of power about not having made the speeches with the oratorical brilliance that *The Gentleman's Magazine* published them.

As for his claim that he shaded the speeches to prevent the 'Whig dogs' from getting the best of it, a little political clarification is needed. To begin with, there were prominent Whigs in Opposition who were vicious in their clamour against Walpole, so which Whigs did he have in mind? Moreover, his constructions of Walpole's speeches are objective and characterised by his admiration of the man's expediency and pragmatic leadership. He endowed him with an understanding of the ambiguities and flaws of government and political power, and of human institutions generally, which he thought was no bad quality for a prime minister or any other leading political figure. He made Walpole sound convincing in denouncing the airy, insubstantial ranting of politicians who were not, like he is, held accountable for their fine speeches, and in defending himself with a wry, effortless loftiness. Less pleasing to Walpole would have been to read the speeches Johnson wrote for his enemies, including ones by Opposition Whigs, full of rancour and bitter reflections on his immorality and abuse of power. They have an energy and bite leaving no doubt that Johnson fundamentally thought he was a corruptive force in British life. All in all, however, it is the ambiguity of government, society and life in general that comes through. Life and human nature are complicated. Practice is more important than theory, and theory is easy to come by.[10]

In a positive and more universal vein, the debates have a life today in the libertarian vision they present. Many of the speeches are driven by Johnson's own, not the speaker's, passions regarding the individual's sanctity and freedom in the face of flawed, corrupt, and self-perpetuating institutions and government policy. Debates on Walpole's insistence on having a standing army, for example, produce arguments on whether compulsory military service is consistent with a free society. Is secrecy in government, even on behalf of national security, consistent with the individual's right to freedom of information? How much power should be vested in a leader like Walpole, who gets fat on it and uses it to tyrannise? Should the Government autocratically presume to define and legislate morality for the people – especially when it is itself corrupt? Slavery, taxation (called 'universal slavery') that especially punishes the poor, alliances and connivances that subvert freedom (not excluding those of the Hanoverian monarchy), war-mongering against Spain, and bribery and back-handing: these are all issues to which Johnson's imbedded hostility towards authority lends a fire and urgency, not unlike the virulence in *Marmor Norfolciense*. But a parallel theme is to what extent can the people be trusted? Facile, simplistic, idealistic, selfish, uninformed public resentment was useless. His scorn for impractical idealism was at times no less ferocious than his indictment of the abuses of power.

3

Johnson kept writing these debates until early 1744. In addition to them, he had his hand in the magazine in so many different editorial ways that, on average, he was pulling in a salary of about £100 per year (about £10,000 today). During this period he was cranking out copy at a rate of about twenty pages per issue, a significant increase over the previous year.[11]

His instincts to draw out the moral implications in issues and new publications during these months were never dormant, even in the rush to supply copy and earn his salary. It was biographies he turned to mostly to achieve this, urging its supreme importance, as distinct from history, in dwelling on common, personal details of subjects, 'in their private apartments, in their careless hours'. One such 'biography' that reflected his growing and lifelong interest in medicine was of the seventeenth-century English physician Dr Thomas Sydenham. It is the most autobiographical of his early lives. Cave wanted it because he needed the publicity for an edition of Sydenham's works he was publishing and knew that with his keen interest in medicine Johnson was the one to write it. In effect, he made something out of nothing because there was almost no factual material to go on and he made no effort to find any. Instead of writing a biography, Johnson turned the piece into a scornful denunciation of those who accused Sydenham of practising medicine purely on the basis of clinical experimentation. On top of this, Sydenham illustrates his common bio-graphical theme, even this early, that it is not so much a man's abilities and skills in rising to eminence but his Christian virtue which principally rec-ommends him, especially his charity and compassion.[12]

It was all anonymous work, however, and left Johnson hungrier than ever for reputation. One may wonder why he did not write new poetry for the magazine's poetry section during these months and years? After the excellent reception of London: A Poem, he had every reason to be con-fident of further success as a poet, especially with Cave and Dodsley's sup-port. Why not another imitation of Juvenal or perhaps Horace? Writing new verse could have helped alleviate the tediousness of this maze of edi-torial work in which he had become entangled. Cave asked him for some, but all he came up with, except for a new translation into Latin of Pope's verses on his famous grotto, was a handful of old unpublished poems he either pulled out of a drawer or dictated from memory. Published in the July 1743 issue, they included 'Friendship: An Ode' and 'The Young Au-thor'. Perhaps new poetry involved too great a shift of gears for him; or he may simply have felt he had no time for it. Or it may have been a matter of indolence.[13]

One critic has remarked that Johnson 'found the magazine amateur and left it professional', well on its way to a circulation of ten thousand and a readership much larger than that.[14] Instead of being run almost ex-clusively by Cave and occasional contributors of considerably varying abil-ities, by 1743 the magazine was staffed by talented professional writers like Johnson, Boyse, and an able newcomer, John Hawkesworth (1720–73), a protégé of Johnson's who would also become a friend and his closest liter-ary collaborator. Neither Boswell nor Hawkins acknowledged Hawkes-worth's importance in his life and work, Hawkins patronisingly calling him 'a man of fine parts, but no learning'; but Johnson once said that for details of his life 'after my coming to London to drive the world about a little, you must all go to Jack Hawkesworth for anecdotes'.[15] After Johnson weaned himself from deep involvement in the magazine by 1744, it was Hawkesworth who took over the debates and others of his functions and eventually became its literary editor. The magazine was Hawkesworth's making as a man of letters, which reminds us that Johnson's indefatigable work for Cave, while it delayed his full emergence as a bright literary star, also provided a great push towards fame. It established him in the world of printers and booksellers with a wide range of contacts.

4

Johnson's personal life during this long vigil at the magazine is sketchy. His reasonably good income from 1741–3 undoubtedly brought some peace of mind for Tetty, but otherwise things were not improving for her. Whether she had yet begun to lapse into alcoholism or not is unknown. It was generally understood she was headed in that direction, for as Shaw noted, 'It has been said that Mrs Johnson . . . had, especially in the latter part of her life, addicted herself to drinking'. In the autumn of 1742, she was ill in bed for several months. As Johnson told Taylor in the new year, 'Mrs Johnson was seized with such an illness, having not been well for some time before as will easily make you excuse my neglect at answering you. I believe it is now the twelfth week since she was taken with it, and last Thursday she walked about [her] chamber for the first time. I never saw any body do so much that did or did not recover.' She had become a 'difficult hypochondriac'. He added that otherwise 'nothing very ill has happened to me, which I know you will be pleased to hear'.[16]

In the spring of 1741 it seems he had taken lodgings again on his own 'at the Black Boy over against Durham Yard, the Strand', where Garrick had kept his wine stock during the brief time he was a wine merchant. Over the next five years it is difficult to keep track of where Tetty and he, or he on his own, lived – 'if I change my lodgings', he told Taylor, he would be sure to tell him – but almost forty years later he remembered his addresses during this period pretty much in this order: Boswell Court (Carey Street), the Strand again, Bow Street, Holborn, Fetter Lane, and Holborn again. Perhaps they were compelled to seek out less expensive lodgings, but the more serious possibility is that life was not working out between them, that Tetty was sliding steadily into the grotesque caricature Johnson's friends circulated years later and he had little sense of a home where he could work.[17]

He spent much of his time with Robert James, his old schoolfellow. Medicine kept them in touch. 'My knowledge of physic, I learned from Dr James,' Johnson told Boswell with overstatement. Musing at Mrs Thrale's house one day in 1777, on who would be his biographer, he remarked that except for Adams and Hector 'Doctor James can give a better account of my early days than most folks'. Receiving his B.A. in 1726 at Oxford and M.D. in 1728 at Cambridge and then practising in the Midlands for several years, James made his way to London where he traded in medicine, writing about it and realising he could make money by concocting marketable powders and potions. Two million doses of his fever powders, which acted as a diaphoretic and cathartic as well as emetic, were sold within twenty years of being patented in 1746. In spite of rumours about their violent after-effects, many testified to their positive results, including a number of Johnson's friends. In spite of any reservations he may have had about James's medical abilities, in the early 1740s, Johnson decided to help his old friend, this 'lewd fellow' whom he said 'for twenty years was not sober'.[18]

Part quack and part learned professional, James was an understandable medical phenomenon in the eighteenth century, as was Robert Levet, later a member of Johnson's household for many years, for medicine was something of a lottery in the mid-eighteenth century. There were no medical journals, for example, and no forum in which physicians could formally exchange information with each other. Neither was there any testing of cures, the compounds of many of which were guarded as money-making secrets: 'Testimonies and publicity, fashion and fruitless rivalry took the place of impartial assessment and made the advance of knowledge uncertain.' Johnson himself acknowledged this in his *Life of Akenside* thirty-five years later, 'A physician in a great city seems to be the mere play-thing of fortune; his degree of reputation is, for the most part, totally casual; they that employ him know not his excellence; they that reject him know not his deficience.'

In February 1742 James published the first part of his successful *Medicinal Dictionary*, a compilation of information from previous medical works with the purpose of distinguishing the useful from gossipy hand-me-down remedies. It appeared each fortnight and then was published in three volumes from 1743–5. Boswell said Johnson in 1743 'had written, or assisted in writing, the Proposals . . . and being very fond of the study of physic, in which James was his master, he furnished some of the articles'. There is a passage in them that encapsulates Johnson's no-nonsense denigration of inferior scholarship and points tantalisingly to the dawning of his ideas about writing a dictionary himself. There are other medical dictionaries, he wrote, 'by those to whom an impartial critic would have allowed neither the wages of labour, nor the laurels of science, who have transcribed truth and error without distinction, have been too ignorant to lop off the superfluities of their predecessors, and too lazy to supply their defects . . . the knowledge of words must necessarily precede the study of science'.[19]

After the emergence of James's powders in 1746, Johnson distanced himself from James and his medicine. He wrote to his friend, and a leading London physician, Dr Richard Brocklesby in the last year of his life, 'I never thought well of Dr James's compounded medicines. His ingredients appeared to me sometimes inefficacious and trifling, and sometimes heterogeneous, and destructive of each other.'[20]

5

In June 1742 Johnson's mind ran again along the lines of a huge project as the pathway to reputation. That month Edward Harley, the second Earl of Oxford, died. Harley, friend of Pope and son of Robert Harley the Tory Lord Treasurer in the reign of Queen Anne, was owner of the great estate of Wimpole Hall in Cambridgeshire. He owned a vast collection of books, manuscripts and tracts that he housed at Wimpole Hall, his house in Dover Street, and his magnificent mansion in Cavendish Square. The size of the collection included, some fifty thousand books and seven thousand volumes of manuscripts, not to mention coins, engravings, Greek and Roman antiquities, and more than five hundred paintings. His need to build elegant places to house them eventually brought on severe financial worries that may have hastened his death.

Keeping the manuscripts, which were eventually sold to the British Museum in 1753, his widow decided to sell the books as a whole instead of preserving them, as her husband had wished, as a public library. Three months after his death they were purchased (surprisingly) by the tasteless and ill-mannered bookseller Thomas Osborne for the huge sum of £13,000 but which was supposed to have been far less than what Harley had paid (£18,000) just for the bindings. Osborne is one of those eighteenth-century characters who attained a kind of immortality from the verbal and physical attacks he received from men of genius. Pope introduced him as one of the contenders for the prize of dullness among booksellers in the 1743 *Dunciad* as revenge for his outrageous violation of copyright in fraudulently selling copies of Pope's *Iliad* at half price. Building on his unsavoury reputation, biographers have used Osborne to add to the image of Johnson as the scourge of villainous bullies, a type of literary Hercules. Johnson is supposed to have knocked him down with a folio in his bookshop and then 'put his foot upon his neck'. 'Sir, he was impertinent to me,' he told Boswell, 'and I beat him. But it was not in his shop: it was in my own chamber.' 'Osborne was a man entirely destitute of shame, without sense of any disgrace but that of poverty,' Johnson later wrote in his *Life of Pope*. According to this anecdote, Osborne made a mistake not many others, given Johnson's size and strength, were foolhardy enough to make.[21]

Osborne beat the competition to buy the collection because of its sheer size and the difficulties of housing it. The Bodleian Library could not afford it and the Government was not yet into buying large libraries. He bought it in order to sell it piecemeal but it became a biblio-albatross and selling it turned out to be far from simple. He needed a convincing sales device and hit on the idea of drawing up a scrupulous, annotated catalogue of the entire collection that would appeal to scholars and men of learning, whose good will he needed if he was going to succeed. As he had met Johnson earlier through his involvement in publishing James's *Medici-*

nal Dictionary, and as Johnson came highly recommended in the trade, he offered him the job of compiling the catalogue. Johnson eagerly accepted. A few days later he sent Johnson's proposal, 'An Account of the Harleian Library', to Thomas Birch for his advice and with the request that he promote it among his fellow members of the Royal Society. On 9 October Johnson had dinner with Birch and two other Society members among the books in the Cavendish Square house. Osborne got more than just a money-spinning outline from Johnson's 'Account'. It amounts to a moral argument on the importance of literary culture to a nation: 'every man who considers learning as ornamental and advantageous to the community', he urged, must celebrate men like Harley as 'public benefactors who have introduced amongst us authors not hitherto well known, and added to the literary treasures of their native country'.[22]

Johnson's scheme was that 'the books shall be distributed into their distinct classes, and every class ranged with some regard to the age of the writers; that every book shall be accurately described; that the peculiarities of editions shall be remarked, and observations from the authors of literary history occasionally interspersed'. To sit down and do this for fifty thousand volumes was a thoroughly daunting task. So to help Johnson, Osborne also hired William Oldys, the able and indefatigable antiquarian and bibliographer and Harley's learned librarian who was later thrown into Fleet prison for debt and grew so fond of it that after he was released he liked to return to spend his evenings there. There is no record at all, unfortunately, of how they got on together week after week as they dived into the stacks. They set to work in Cavendish Square, but Osborne's impossible deadline of February 1743 for publication of the first two volumes covering more than fifteen thousand volumes meant many annoying compromises and shortcuts, and although the volumes with their Latin, French and English annotations turned out to be far more scholarly than the average book sales catalogue, the result fell far short of what Johnson's scheme outlined. Hawkins surmised that 'engaged in so servile an employment' Johnson 'resembled a lion in harness'. Osborne continued to frustrate Johnson's scheme and when the next two volumes duly appeared in January 1744 they were again a mediocre shadow of the original model. A fifth volume with which neither Johnson nor Oldys had anything to do came out more than a year later and consisted of not much more than routine transcriptions of titles. Osborne's sale of these books dragged on for at least twenty years.[23]

After the third and fourth volumes were published, Osborne handed over to Oldys the job of editing the *Harleian Miscellany*, a reprinting of pamphlets in the collection, and asked Johnson again to write proposals and an 'Introduction' to this venture. His 'Introduction' celebrates the 'boundless liberty' of the British Enlightenment, in which (as he wrote) the freedom to write and read pamphlets was unique, perpetuating 'new sentiments to the public without danger of suffering either ridicule or censure': 'It is observed that among the natives of England is to be found a greater variety of humour than in any other country . . . where every man has a full liberty to propagate his conceptions, variety of humour must produce variety of writers.' This short 'Introduction' can be taken as one of Johnson's earliest assertions that nowhere else in Europe was the Enlightenment so robust and practical.[24]

Not from any of these Harleian publications, unfortunately, did Johnson reap any reputation with the public, much less a good income. He needed money more urgently than ever. One day in December 1743 he had to take a break in Osborne's bookshop to write urgently to Theophilus Levett, Lichfield attorney and Town Clerk, about his failure to make a £12 mortgage payment on the Market Square house because of 'a great perplexity of affairs'. He would pay the interest owed in two months, he assured Theophilus Levett. Would he allow him this grace period? As it happened, he had to turn to Aston to make the payment. And he further pleaded with Levett: 'I look upon this and the future interest of that mortgage as my own debt, and beg that you will be pleased to give me directions how to pay it, and not mention it to my dear mother.' His relief was immense when Levett replied with 'humanity and generosity'. His and Tetty's poverty had reached such a pitch by then that they even tried to claim some £35 owed to them from her late husband's estate. He asked Levett to help him get it but appears not to have succeeded. That autumn he had to beg Cave to spare him a guinea as an advance on a new project, a history of the British parliament, 'but if you do not [I] shall not think it an injury'. He worked on the new history for several months, several sheets of which were printed off, but it came to a screeching halt when Parliament unexpectedly restricted access to its manuscripts. Another scheme, another defeat. He was already intensely at work on the *Life of Savage*, but he would not be paid the fifteen guineas for that until mid-December, and it would bring only temporary relief. An embarrassing hint of the discomfort of his poverty during these months was suggested by a possibly spurious anecdote that Boswell told: 'Soon after Savage's Life was published, Mr [Walter] Harte [the writer and tutor to Lord Chesterfield's son] dined with Edward Cave, and occasionally praised it. Soon after, meeting him, Cave said, "You made a man very happy t'other day." – "How could that be," says Harte; "nobody was there but ourselves." Cave answered, by reminding him that a plate of victuals was sent behind a screen, which was to Johnson, dressed so shabbily, that he did not choose to appear; but on hearing the conversation, was highly delighted with the encomiums on his book.'[25]

6

Johnson's life between the publication of the *Life of Savage* early in 1744 and the summer of 1746 is largely a blank. Money troubles, defeated hopes, a disintegrating marriage, little idea of how to gain fame and reputation beyond *London* and the *Life of Savage*, and a peripatetic life between London lodgings were calls to the black dog to dance into his imagination and spirit. His first known prayer to 'almighty and everlasting God' for New Year's day 1745, is a cry for help and repentance: 'Grant, O merciful Lord, that thy call may not be vain, that my life may not be continued to increase my guilt, and that thy gracious forbearance may not harden my heart in wickedness. Let me remember, O my God that as days and years pass over me, I approach nearer to the grave where there is no repentance . . .' Whether it was the paralysing effect of depression or some physical illness that lay at the root of his inactivity and despair, he wrote virtually nothing for most of 1744. It was Shakespeare who came to the rescue towards the end of the year.[26]

In the February 1745 issue of *The Gentleman's Magazine*, Cave announced that Johnson's pamphlet, *Miscellaneous Observations on the Tragedy of Macbeth* was 'speedily' to be published. It came out in April, and appended to it were 'Proposals for Printing a New Edition of the Plays of William Shakespeare, with Notes Critical and Explanatory'. Both items were anonymous, doubtless because Cave at this juncture did not want the prospects for the project diminished by a name that would not resonate at all with the public. Continuing his search for a project that would establish his reputation, Johnson had agreed with Cave that the best way to do this and at the same time provide Cave with a slice of the Shakespeare market was nothing less than a complete edition of the Bard in ten small volumes, selling at the knockdown price of one pound five shillings. It was a bold and, in theory, an inspired decision. Thomas Hanmer's edition, lavishly presented and short on critical insight, provided an easy target for Johnson's critical artillery. Moreover, more than ever before Shakespeare was fast becoming a patriotic winner in the literary marketplace. There was no better way for a critic to make a name for himself as a critic than by producing a complete edition, even though five editions had already preceded him in the eighteenth century. Johnson fell to the task probably in the summer or autumn of 1744 with characteristic intensity and energy, shutting everything else out, going through most of the plays and amassing a wealth of data and notes on Shakespeare's language and ideas in the individual plays.

Miscellaneous Observations is neither an edition of *Macbeth* nor a systematic critical analysis, but a display of the kind of commentary he could produce on selected passages. William Warburton, the friend of Pope, churchman and editor of Shakespeare, praised it as written by 'a man of parts and genius' – an endorsement Johnson remembered with gratitude for the rest of his life: 'He praised me at a time when praise was of value to me.' Much of the appeal in embarking on a Shakespeare edition was iconoclastically to rubbish the fanciful and pedantic nonsense that previous editors and commentators on the Bard had dished out to the public in edition after edition. In *Miscellaneous Observations* his caustic criticism of Hanmer previewed what he hoped to do in his own edition: attack the encrusted Shakespeare establishment not only by exposing errors of judgement and textual editing but also by revealing how consistently critics have wasted their efforts by not measuring Shakespeare against what they know about life from their own experiences. People like Hanmer, whose 'harmless industry may, surely, be forgiven, if it cannot be praised', should avoid the whole subject: 'No man should attempt to teach others what he has never learned himself.' Critics should 'disdain to labour in trifles'. The whole enterprise pointed to his determination to storm the exclusive club of Shakespeare scholarship through the breach that Hanmer's incompetence had opened up.[27]

It was good and promising while it lasted, but this magnificent project was doomed to the same fate that had killed earlier projects. Jacob Tonson, the publisher of an edition of Shakespeare in 1725 by Pope – who would die only two or three months after Johnson began working on his own edition without ever meeting the young poet he so much admired – claimed the copyright of Shakespeare's plays and within a week of the announcement of the edition threatened an injunction against Cave if he went ahead with it. Had Cave decided to fight back, he might well have won because Tonson's claim was a bluff. Booksellers illegitimately claimed copyright of all sorts of titles and authors as part of their unofficial membership in the inner circle of the publishing world. They were difficult and expensive to oppose, even by the most successful magazine editor of the day. Perhaps Tonson also offered Cave a sweetener to drop the project. As Warburton's own edition would appear in 1747, Cave must also have been frightened off by him. The upshot was that he capitulated and Johnson again was left high and dry, though several months of work on Shakespeare ultimately would not go to waste. He continued to sift through the plays, as if his massive collection of notes on Shakespeare's language had developed a life of its own, regardless of how it might be used. One critic has judged that his collection on index slips of thousands of passages illustrating Shakespeare's vocabulary turned him in a matter of months into the 'greatest living authority on Shakespeare's diction'. It was linguistic ammunition waiting to be deployed in as yet an undetermined way.[28]

The gap or silence that ensued in the last half of 1745 suggests that depression at some level must have set in again, compounded by his worsening finances. He was so disillusioned over not having been able to break into the money as an author that around this time he even asked Adams at Pembroke College to discover whether he could practise as an advocate in the Doctors' Commons 'without a doctor's degree in Civil Law'. It is extraordinary that he thought he might be able to. The answer, of course, was 'no'. Nor did he have any money to study law, telling Boswell twenty-five years later that if he had had the money he might as easily (and happily) have studied law as tragic poetry. It was also at about this time that in distress Tetty was forced to sell the silver cup the generous woman in the stagecoach had bought for him when his mother took him to London to be touched by the Queen: 'The cup was one of the last pieces of plate which dear Tetty sold in our distress.' In his *Annals* he poignantly remarked that he still clung to the silver spoon the woman also bought for him at the same time. According to Boswell, Aston saved him from being arrested for debt, which if true would have happened before Aston died in 1748 and before Johnson finally emerged from obscurity in 1746 with a boldness and courage greater than he had ever shown before.[29]

CHAPTER 14

A Lifeline:

The Dictionary

I

AFTER THE WRETCHED DISAPPOINTMENT OF the Shakespeare edition, through to the end of 1745 and into the spring of 1746, Johnson at the age of thirty-seven looked at his life and saw a wife who was deteriorating and unhappy and whose welfare he blamed himself for neglecting; a mother in Lichfield who thanks to his failures had been forced to mortgage the family house; a lifestyle in Grub Street still rewarding him very little for huge amounts of work; poverty; and a career almost mysterious with false starts and cruel disappointments yielding him almost no public notice. The Shakespeare fiasco seemed like the last straw. Even Gilbert Walmesley seemed dejected about his protégé in a letter to Garrick in November 1746: 'When you see Mr Johnson pray [give] my compliments, and tell him I esteem him as a great genius – quite lost to both himself and the world.'[1]

Johnson published virtually nothing in 1746 although Dr Adams told Boswell he was playing with the idea of a life of King Alfred, a potential patriotic bestseller if ever there was one: on which, given the 'warmth with which he spoke about it, he would, I believe, had he been master of his own will, have engaged himself, rather than on any other subject'.[2] We hear no more of it. Suddenly that spring his world and existence changed, however, and light poured into his darkening consciousness in the shape of a book proposal by his friend the successful bookseller Robert Dodsley, whom he called 'Doddy'. The book was nothing less than a dictionary of the English language, a monumental project that great authors such as Pope and Joseph Addison had contemplated and given up almost before they really got going and lesser men had trembled to think of compiling even as they grumbled and protested about the dire need Britain had for a dictionary.

Through his friendship with Cave and others in the trade, Dodsley had kept track of Johnson's mostly anonymous work. He was struck by the way Johnson raised Grub Street writing to unprecedented levels, able to take the writing of other contributors to *The Gentleman's Magazine* and transform it into witty, learned, colourful and rhythmically pleasing prose. He also knew that with his 'encyclopedic' cast of mind Johnson had shown himself ready to take on large projects requiring a good deal of stamina, organisation, and classification. Johnson's high writing standards by now were well known to others in the book trade as well. Dodsley's brother James, who joined him in the business several years later, told Boswell what happened. In Boswell's words: 'When Johnson was one day sitting in his [James's] brother Robert's shop, he heard his brother suggest to him, that a Dictionary of the English Language would be a work that would be well received by the public.' Having planted the seed, he stood back and waited as Johnson mulled over the idea: 'Johnson seemed at first to catch at the proposition, but, after a pause, said, in his abrupt decisive manner, "I believe I shall not undertake it."' Thirty years later Johnson confided to Boswell, 'Dodsley first mentioned to me the scheme of an English Dictionary; but I had long thought of it.'[3]

This was a brave, even reckless idea of Dodsley's. Johnson was still unknown with no clout to his name, and this dictionary would be a far larger project than Dodsley or almost any other publisher had ever undertaken. A dictionary was financially too risky for him or any other bookseller to take on alone, so he arranged for an impressive syndicate of them to become partners in the project. In addition to Dodsley, they were at the front of the profession and all knew the quality of Johnson's writing: the brothers John and Paul Knapton, Andrew Millar, Charles Hitch and Thomas Longman. Though not a bookseller, Cave might well have been included in the enterprise if he had been willing to put up some money for it. Together these men asked Johnson to come up with a proposal, which he did briskly with his nineteen-page 'Short Scheme for compiling a new Dictionary of the English Language'. It impressed them as the work of a man who had already thought long about what such a dictionary should achieve, as well as about the massive problems lying in wait for any brave soul embarking on such a journey. He made it clear that his dictionary would be innovative, especially with his extensive use of quotations drawn from the best English literary sources in order to illustrate the meanings of words. Realising they were on to a good thing, the proprietors gave him the green light. On 18 June 1746 he met with several of them at the Golden Anchor near Holborn Bar and over breakfast signed the fateful contract, promising to finish the job in the incredibly short period of three years. They agreed to pay him 1,500 guineas (£1,575) in installments, the equivalent today of close to £150,000. It was his first substantial payment for literary labour of any kind, a large contract for any author, especially for one who was virtually unknown to the general public.[4]

The contract instantly launched him into another orbit in his professional career and must have been the source of some jubilation at home for the longsuffering Tetty. Immediately, they were able to move to new lodgings at 17 Gough Square, just north of Fleet Street, which today still stands as a memorial to Johnson in the form of a museum of Johnson's domestic life – one of the very few museums of eighteenth-century literary figures in England. Seriously damaged during the Blitz but restored faithfully, it is one of the few houses of that period to survive in the City of London. It has three main storeys in addition to a basement, garret and five bays positioned amid a tangle of narrow lanes and dark alleys in a quiet square that when Johnson moved in was not as respectable as it had been when it was created at the end of the seventeenth century. The Fleet Street neighbourhoods, the Strand, Covent Garden and Charing Cross, had been invaded by coffee houses, taverns, chop houses, and a general culture of hedonism: wig-makers, condom shops, glovers, mercers, specialists in lace, snuff dealers, and gin shops. Prostitutes walked the streets everywhere. Fleet Prison lay close by, reminding one of the dismal consequences of excess and debt. Hygiene and sanitation were deplorable. Completing the scene were foul smells from open drainage, small local industries polluting the air and an atmosphere clogged with smoke from coal transported in collier ships from Newcastle. For the Johnsons, however, the house was perfect, with even a tiny garden described by Thomas Carlyle when he saw it in the 1830s as 'somewhat larger than a bed-quilt'[5] but large enough at least for Tetty to enjoy some private space outside. Most critical of all, the top floor of the house consisted of a large attic room ideal as a workshop for the small lexicographical industry that he needed to set in motion without delay if he was to have any chance of completing this massive book in three years. The house was close to the throbbing pulse of the book trade and, most importantly, the office of the highly successful printer William Strahan at 10 Little New Street whom the booksellers had chosen to print the enormous work and who would become one of Johnson's steadfast and most useful friends.

Even with one floor devoted exclusively to the *Dictionary*, it is surprising that Johnson decided to lease such a large house for just the two of them. Perhaps signs of Tetty's decline made him realise they needed a servant or two to live in the house; or he may also have been anticipating a need in the future for more companionship to live in the house with him. The house brought a change in lifestyle. 'I am always at home,' he wrote soon after moving there. Among his visitors was almost certainly the uncouth, sullen, 'obscure practiser in physic amongst the lower people' Robert Levet, an unlicensed doctor whom he met at a coffee house and who in 1762 came to live with him permanently. Around this time he also met Richard Bathurst, a Jamaican-born physician, educated at Peterhouse, Cambridge, for whom he developed a deep affection – after his death he 'hardly ever spoke' of him 'without tears in his eyes'. In 1750 Bathurst's father brought a slave boy to England from Jamaica who would play a major part in the rest of Johnson's life. Johnson saw in Bathurst a kindred spirit: 'Dear Bathurst . . . was a man to my very heart's content: he hated a fool, and he hated a rogue, and he hated a *whig*; he was a very good *hater*.'[6] Another probable visitor to Gough Square was George Psalmanazar, also a coffee-house friend, a reformed and penitent French literary impostor in

his mid-sixties for whom Johnson conceived an exaggerated respect because of his later piety and penitence. He once said Psalmanazar was one
of only three people he knew who lived a 'regular' or 'uniform' life 'planned
by choice', able to keep resolutions.[7]

2

Contrary to myths that have attached themselves to Johnson's *Dictionary*, his was by no means the first English dictionary. Dozens had already
appeared in the 150 years before Johnson became a lexicographer. The
Short Title Catalogue in the British Library lists 663 dictionaries of one
kind or another before Johnson's, though most of these were variations on
encyclopedias, reference works on particular professions and trades, word
lists for certain disciplines, and the like. Nor would his be the newest or
most trendy, the most comprehensive, or the most accurate. The first English dictionaries, going back centuries, were bilingual, mostly Latin-En-
glish and English-Latin, but they had very little to do with daily life. By
1582 when the famous headmaster of Merchant Taylors' school, Richard
Mulcaster, drew up a list of some eight thousand commonly used words
and called for a monolingual dictionary of English, it had already become
a national scandal that there was not one for Englishmen to turn to conveniently in their daily lives. The seventeenth century did not improve notably on Mulcaster, however, for the dictionaries that did appear were devoted to foreign and specialised 'hard words' and inkhorn terms, ignoring
the general plea for works defining common English words. It was more
useful to read Shakespeare's plays where dramatic contexts involving very
real people doing real things communicated what most words meant.[8]

It was not until 1721 that a dictionary recognisable as such today was
published in England by Nathan Bailey, *An Universal Etymological Dictionary*, which he followed up with his folio *Dictionarium Britannicum* in
1730 containing 48,000 head words (expanded to 60,000 in a second edition). His *Etymological Dictionary* became the most useful English dictionary in Britain before Johnson's and at a good price was even more commercially successful than his, appearing in twenty-eight editions over the

rest of the century and still going strong in the next. Its etymologies were good but its definitions were often paltry – a strawberry was 'a well known fruit', for example, and 'to wash' meant 'to cleanse by washing' – so that while it made life easier for a lot of people it did not define the language in a manner consistent with the greatness of the nation and its literary, cultural and scientific history. Then finally in 1748, while Johnson was hard at work on his dictionary, came Benjamin Martin's *Lingua Britannica Formata*. This one gave Johnson many sleepless nights, not least because Martin was the first lexicographer ever to give the multiple meanings of words. Although these dictionaries were competitive in the lexicographical market, by the mid-eighteenth century Britain still lagged behind both France and Italy in lacking a full dictionary of its language that with careful and multiple definitions, etymology, orthography and illustrative quotations could reflect the pride the British had in their tongue.[9]

Both the Italians and French could boast of dictionaries that honoured their national tongues, but both had been created by national academies, not by one struggling individual. In France, for example, Cardinal Richelieu founded the Académie Française in Paris in 1635, which assembled leading linguistic scholars to establish fixed rules for the French language and produce a dictionary that dictatorially would 'fix' it – that is, prevent or at least retard its changing. Some forty or so academicians began work in 1639 and no fewer than fifty-five years later the Académie published the *Dictionnaire de l'Académie* (1694). As one historian has put it, the *Dictionnaire* set the language in stone.[10]

The English had no Academy to produce a dictionary. The closest they came to one was the Royal Society of London for the Improvement of Natural Knowledge, founded in 1662. Its brief was science, not language, however, and although the Society set up a committee in 1664 to look into organising a grammar, normalising spelling and compiling a list of words, it met only four times and then disbanded. Over the next half century a succession of great writers called vigorously for a national dictionary: John Evelyn, John Dryden, Daniel Defoe, Addison, Pope and Swift. Swift complained bitterly that the language was a mess, a riot of chaos, inconsistency, foreign imports, abuses, and absurdities. More than anything else, he and others wanted a dictionary that, like the French and Italian, would put a stop to mindless, corrupting 'innovations', the province of dunces. His was like a voice crying in the wilderness. The English temper did not, it seems, travel well in the mode of committees and academies. Johnson himself was against creating an Academy. If ever an academy were to be formed, he later wrote, 'English liberty will hinder or destroy' it. His entrance into the dictionary arena, alone and well-armed from a lifetime of reading, was a patriotic, courageous, quintessentially English entrepreneurial publishing venture.

3

Dodsley and the other proprietors read the national mood well. Britain's extremity was their opportunity. They gambled that there was a marvellous publishing opportunity awaiting them. Boswell wrote that Johnson knew exactly what he was getting into and 'had a noble consciousness of his own abilities, which enabled him to go on with undaunted spirit'. One day the inquisitive Dr Adams, with whom he continued to stay in touch, dropped in at Gough Square to visit him in the early stages of the work. Seeing books, slips of paper, notebooks, and boxes strewn all over the attic room, and a handful of assistants scurrying about, Adams exclaimed, 'But, Sir, how can you do this in three years?' Johnson replied, 'Sir, I have no doubt that I can do it in three years.' But 'The French Academy, which consists of forty members, took forty years to compile their Dictionary,' Adams persisted. 'Sir, thus it is,' Johnson answered playfully; 'this is the proportion. Let me see; forty times forty is sixteen hundred. As three to sixteen hundred, so is the proportion of an Englishman to a Frenchman.' It remained to be seen whether such bravado held up.[11]

It took him more than a year to come up with a comprehensive statement of what kind of dictionary he was going to write and how he was going to go about it. *The Plan of a Dictionary of the English Language*[12] a thirty-four page pamphlet recasting his 'Scheme' and published in August 1747 under his own name, was both a declaration of intent and a publicity move to present himself and stake out his territory. It immediately made him a focus of public attention and scepticism such as he had never experienced before. To begin with, he and the proprietors decided they had to aim very high and dedicate it to Philip Dormer Stanhope, the fourth Earl of Chesterfield, generally thought of as 'the Maecenas of the age', one of the most respected arbiters of taste and high culture, and a highly regarded diplomat-politician and Member of Parliament who had just been appointed Secretary of State. He was also a prominent literary patron. Johnson explained to Boswell in 1777 how the Dedication came about: 'I had neglected to write it by the time appointed. Dodsley suggested a desire to have it addressed to Lord Chesterfield. I laid hold of this as a pretext for delay, that it might be better done, and let Dodsley have his desire. I said to my friend, Dr Bathurst, "Now if any good comes of my addressing to Lord Chesterfield, it will be ascribed to deep policy, when, in fact, it was only a casual excuse for laziness."'[13]

Encouraging the view that he was something of an authority on language, Chesterfield declared an interest in becoming the project's aristocratic champion. At about this time he and Johnson even appear to have met and talked about language: 'in the conversation which I had with him,' Johnson remarked, 'I had the best right to superiority, for it was upon philology and literature.' Whatever Johnson thought privately about Chesterfield's grasp of the subject, Dodsley and the others were desperate to have his Lordship's name attached to their enterprise. Thus Chesterfield became Johnson's patron. He gave him £10 as a token of the arrangement. It was all he would ever give. In the *Plan* Johnson insinuated Chesterfield's linguistic credentials and made it seem as if he was his spokesman: 'I may hope, my Lord, that since you, whose authority in our language is so generally acknowledged, have commissioned me to declare my own opinion, I shall be considered as exercising a kind of vicarious jurisdiction, and that the power which might have been denied to my own claim, will be readily allowed me as the delegate of your Lordship.' It looked like a good move. Who could argue with Chesterfield's 'delegate'?[14]

Chesterfield's umbrella of patronage therefore enabled Johnson to deflect criticism and shield himself from the general astonishment that one man, an unknown man at that, had the presumption to write the dictionary. Another method of deflecting criticism was self-deprecation: 'I knew, that the work in which I engaged is generally considered as drudgery for the blind, as the proper toil of artless industry,' he wrote, 'a task that requires neither the light of learning, nor the activity of genius, but may be successfully performed without any higher quality than that of bearing burdens with dull patience, and beating the track of the alphabet with sluggish resolution.' 'The unhappy lexicographer holds the lowest place,' so he has 'enter'd with the pleasing hope, that as it was low, it likewise would be safe'. Then at the conclusion he gave this show of diffidence a patriotic spin. He would be the new benign, trembling invader of Britain's sacred shores: he was 'frighted' at the extent of his own ambition as stated in the *Plan*, but 'like the soldiers of Cæsar' he looked on Britain's language as a 'new world, which it is almost madness to invade'. If he could not hope to 'complete the conquest' at least he could 'discover the coast, civilise part of the inhabitants, and make it easy for some other adventurer to proceed farther, to reduce them wholly to subjection, and settle them under laws'. He could not be faulted for trying should his achievement prove to be 'below the excellence of other dictionaries', for at least he will have fought the good fight and 'retired without a triumph from a contest with united academies and long successions of learned compilers'. It was a clever exercise in artful humility, for the benefit of both patron and public.[15]

Sandwiched in between this opening and concluding dissimulation, Johnson laid out his scheme and method with striking authority. He went so far as to claim that 'were he still alive, solicitous as he was for the success of this work', Pope 'would not be displeased that I have undertaken it'. He rolled up his sleeves and sent out this ringing challenge to the 'arrogant stupidity' of some would-be critics: 'I shall not be solicitous what is thought of my work, by such as know not the difficulty or importance of philological studies, nor shall think those that have done nothing qualified to condemn me for doing little.'[16]

4

As he began to plow through the lexicographical terrain in the *Plan*, he discovered a minefield of issues that threatened to blow up in his face if he did not tackle them head-on. The crucial thing was to sound confident about his tactics. He sounded so confident, in fact, that some commentators have judged the *Plan* to have even an overt moral cast about it, that he aspired to tame the language's licentiousness, dress up as a social and linguistic reformer, a champion of stability. The argument is that like many others in the past he wanted to 'fix' or freeze the language in a backward-looking, conservative sort of way, keeping it pure from several aggressive modes of corruption.[17] What comes across, however, in such sentences as the following in which he castigated the profligate spawning of words is the voice of the satirist at least as much as of the moralist: 'By tracing . . . every word to its original, and not admitting, but with great caution, any of which no original can be found, we shall secure our language from being over-run with *cant*, from being crowded with low terms, the spawn or folly or affectation, which arise from no just principles of speech, and of which therefore no legitimate derivation can be shown.'[18]

He recognised that the imposition of embalming strictures of usage on language flew in the face of what language is all about although in the course of writing the *Dictionary* his ideas about the nature of language changed and remain complex. In the *Plan* such glimpses as there are of a desire to fix the language, which to a large extent are utterances meant to accommodate and please Chesterfield and reassure his readership, are countered by his care and statements about linguistic realities: 'Language is the work of man, of a being from whom permanence and stability cannot be derived. Like humans, words do not remain in a time warp, a linguistic limbo: 'Like their author, when they are not gaining strength, they are generally losing it. Though art may sometimes prolong their duration, it will rarely give them perpetuity.' The 'decrees of custom' are not those of the most recent, sloppy instances of the 'licentious' but of broadly determined precedents by the 'correctest writers', and he saw it as his job to

examine the evidence 'on both sides'. He honoured popular language as
robustly as any lexicographer had ever done: 'words of general use; words
employed chiefly in poetry; words obsolete; words which are admitted
only by particular writers, yet not in themselves improper; words used
only in burlesque writing; and words impure and barbarous'. Certainly
not backward, that forcefully progressive position may well have made
Chesterfield more than just a little uncomfortable. One wonders, in fact, if
his feeble £10 gift and subsequent lack of interest in the project may be
traced to it. One influential Johnson critic has written, 'The habit of talking about Johnson's lexicography as "normative" or "dictatorial" or "authoritarian" is completely wrong'; his rationalism 'is prior to his tradition-
alism; and if a recognition of the priority of rationality is to be taken (as
some insist) as the distinguishing mark of the liberal or radical political
temperament, then Johnson must be classed as such a liberal or radical.' In
the published Preface to the *Dictionary* Johnson stated his position unre-
servedly, in spite of (with an eye on Chesterfield) having 'flattered' himself
momentarily in the tradition of prescriptiveness:

> When we see men grow old and die at a certain time one after an-
> other, from century to century, we laugh at the elixir that promises
> to prolong life to a thousand years; and with equal justice may the
> lexicographer be derided, who being able to produce no example
> of a nation that has preserved their words and phrases from mu-
> tability, shall imagine that his dictionary can embalm his language,
> and secure it from corruption and decay, that it is in his power to
> change sublunary nature, and clear the world at once from folly,
> vanity, and affectation.

The shifting meanings of words can no more be frozen 'than a grove, in
the agitation of a storm, can be accurately delineated from its picture in
the water'.[19]

Johnson's practical and liberal lexicography was evident from the start
as he considered which words to include: 'The value of a work must be es-
timated by its use'; 'It is to little purpose, that an engine amuses the phi-

losopher by the subtlety of its mechanism, if it requires so much knowledge in its application as to be of no advantage to the common workman.' However, if they have been sufficiently 'naturalised' by usage and familiarity, certain foreign words and terminology of science, the arts, common law, 'controversial divinity', medicine, professions, and war and navigation (for readers of travel books and history) would be included.[20]

His liberal view extended also to orthography and etymology. His 'chief rule' here would be compliance with 'general custom' and 'to make no innovation'. An imposition of rules, technically logical though they may appear as laid down by experts and etymologists, would inflict the language with yet another layer of chaos: 'The present usage of spelling, where the present usage can be distinguished, will therefore in this work be generally followed.' As for etymology, his strategy might often seem 'capricious' in its empiricism, he warned, but that is the nature of the beast: 'Our language is well known not to be primitive or self-originated, but to have adopted words of every generation, and either for the supply of its necessities, or the increase of its copiousness, to have received additions from very distant regions.' Neither can syntax be reduced to rules. It can be learned only by examples from the best writers.[21]

Finally, he acknowledged that the most challenging task, as others before him had discovered, was to define the words. The most common words were the most difficult because there is often only one word for one idea, and certain words like 'bright' and 'sweet' are often explainable in another language more easily, or because like certain verbs they have dozens of meanings. But he would not be content until he exhausted the following nuances and senses: the 'natural' or 'primitive' meaning, the metaphorical, the consequential or accidental, the poetical, the familiar, the burlesque, and the 'peculiar' as found in individual authors. And the definitions will be crowned by quotations that he intended as one of the glories of the *Dictionary*, quotations that he had already spent a year or more laboriously collecting from thousands of books, 'preferring writers of the first reputation to those of an inferior rank; of noting the quotations with accuracy; and of selecting, when it can be conveniently done, such sentences, as, besides their immediate use, may give pleasure or instruction by conveying some elegance of language, or some precept of prudence, or piety'.[22]

The *Plan* was well received. While Thomas Birch grudgingly approved, 'it is an ingenious performance, but the style too flatulent', Pope's learned friend John Boyle, the Earl of Orrery, was less equivocal, 'I think the specimen is one of the best that I have ever read . . . the language of Mr Johnson's is good, and the arguments are properly and modestly expressed . . . I have great expectations from the performance.' Notices in the press were also very positive, the upshot of which was that the *Plan* suddenly made Johnson known and encouraged the public to imagine he was smoothly and well into the book and would complete it promptly.[23]

5

In the attic room at the top of his house – frequently compared to Sir James Murray's famous Scriptorium at Oxford, for decades the engine room of the *Oxford English Dictionary* in the late nineteenth century – Johnson assembled the materials and people he needed, turning it into something resembling a 'counting house'. Hundreds of books (many of them large folios) had to be brought in to supplement his own collection, shelves were constructed, tables had to be set up to accommodate the various stages of research and the physical process of transcribing and cutting and pasting slips, boxes for filing had to be organised, and the odd chair and stool brought in for him and his assistants. Joshua Reynolds mentioned 'his books, all covered with dust' and 'a crazy deal table, and a still worse and older elbow chair, having only three legs'. That three-legged stool became legendary in his lifetime, following him from this study to others he would have in London.

As for books, he treated them, then and later, with a roughness for which modern librarians would have regarded him as a public nuisance. The problem, as Hawkins wrote, was that Johnson did not care about the external condition of books, 'tearing the heart' (as the poet Mary Knowles said) out of them and as likely as not leaving them on a table or on the floor after he was done with them. Hawkins described Johnson's library as 'a copious but miserably ragged one'. Nor were the books he borrowed for the *Dictionary* exempt from abuse. He treated them as tools, not as precious items in collections. He marked them up with black lead pencils and although he maintained that all the marks could be removed with breadcrumbs, they could not; nor did he try very hard to remove them, if at all. So notorious did he become for this treatment of books that people eventually were reluctant to lend him what he needed. Hawkins wrote that he often returned them 'so defaced as to be scarce worth owning, and yet, some of his friends were glad to receive and entertain them as curiosities'.[24]

By any reckoning, to finish the *Dictionary* in three years – even in six, or nine for that matter – would require herculean efforts and demand more of him by far than had any other previous task, especially since much of this was on the face of it dull work. '*To make dictionaries is dull work*,' he would write in his entry for 'dull', in the same self-deprecatory vein as his definition of 'grubstreet' as a place 'inhabited by writers of small histories, dictionaries, and temporary poems, whence any mean production is called 'Grubstreet', and of 'lexicographer' as 'a writer of dictionaries; a harmless drudge, that busies himself in tracing the original, and detailing the signification of words'. But he had a heroic sense of mission about the job. A recent writer on the *Dictionary* has summed up what the task required: 'It called for all the skills of the writer, but also for those of the editor, the explicator, the anthologist and the hod-carrier, the book-muncher, the pagemaker and the cultural steeplejack, and was as many as a dozen labours rolled into one.'[25] If he were ever to finish at all, never mind on time, he needed steady help.

Oddly, considering his legendary sniping at Scotland, of which there will be more later, he chose five Scots to help him – six amanuenses in all, five of whom had poverty in common. Boswell could not resist the comment, 'Let it be remembered by the natives of North-Britain, to whom he is supposed to have been so hostile, that five of them were of that country.' Never would all six work at one time in the attic – generally only four or fewer according to the stage of the work and whether there was anything at the time useful for them to do.[26]

Francis Stewart was the first to come on board. Johnson paid him, like the others, out of the advance from the booksellers, in spite of their poor salaries an expense that turned out to be a significant drain on his resources and made the advance quickly look much smaller than at first. Stewart's task was chiefly to copy illustrative quotations from hundreds of books that Johnson had already marked up in the early spring. He also helped Johnson define 'low cant phrases; all words relating to gambling and card-playing'. The others were hired in the weeks and months to follow and seem to have been paid equally poorly. Two of them, the brothers Alexander and William Macbean, entered the fray around 1748 and stayed until about 1754. They brought with them some practical experience with reference works. The eldest, Alexander, 'a very learned Highlander', appears to have provided Johnson with some sort of moral or even spiritual encouragement, perhaps having something to do with his melancholia. Not long before he died, Johnson remembered fondly that Alexander 'was one of those who, as Swift says, *stood as a screen between me and death* . . . He was very pious. He was very innocent . . . He was very highly esteemed in the house.' He was more than a copyist for Johnson, actually writing a few of the definitions for him and mischievously slipping into the text both his own name and a little of his own poetry. Robert Shiels was a fourth, a hack writer and sometimes biographer. He died of consumption two years before the *Dictionary* was published, lamented by Johnson as 'a man of very acute understanding, though with little scholastic education'. The fifth Scot was a 'Mr Maitland', about whom we know nothing, and the sixth an Englishman, V. J. Peyton, a linguist who later published a French grammar and was described by Johnson's friend Giuseppe Baretti, probably incorrectly given Baretti's strong prejudices, as 'a fool and a drunkard'. Peyton and Alexander Macbean were the ones still working for Johnson when the *Dictionary* was published. Johnson later would not be entirely pleased with the work of either of them.[27]

These 'laborious brethren' were among his first set of household guests in what would be forty years of having odd collections of indigent or otherwise needy souls living with him for varying periods of time. He not only gave them work but also allowed them occasionally to sleep at Gough

Square or visit him during unsocial hours. Long after the *Dictionary* was published, he continued to help them. 'Peyton and Macbean are both starving, and I cannot keep them,' he wrote in 1775, but he did, raising money for them, finding them lodgings, and paying for Peyton's funeral expenses. He wrote poignantly to Mrs Thrale about Peyton's death in 1776, how for many years 'he sat starving by the bed of a wife not only useless, but almost motionless, condemned by poverty to personal attendance, and by the necessity of such attendance chained down to poverty.' Stewart died before the *Dictionary* was published, but as late as 1780 Johnson was imploring Boswell not to forget his sister in Edinburgh, for 'the memory of her brother is yet fresh in my mind'.[28]

6

From the very beginning, the progress on the *Dictionary* was difficult. He was beset with doubts, plagued with persistent melancholia, and not entirely certain how to proceed. He was working in a vacuum, without a useful model. Nobody had done before what he wanted to do, not at any rate the way he wanted to do it. His work with the Harleian Library had familiarised him with specimens of dictionaries in the past, but mostly they provided lessons on what to avoid. His courage cannot be overstated. In the *Rambler* (essay number 122, written on 18 May 1751 when he was still a long way from reaching the summit of the lexicographical mountain he was trying to scale), he reflected with some agony on the chronic human dilemma of biting off more than one may be able to chew: 'Nothing is more subject to mistake and disappointment than anticipated judgement concerning the easiness or difficulty of any undertaking, whether we form our opinion from the performances of others, or from abstracted contemplation of the thing to be attempted.'[29]

He started by making a word list, then looked for the quotations to illustrate definitions. Obviously he had never tried to find quotations for less common words, otherwise he would have realised quickly enough that he would not have been able to complete his work in thirty years, much less three.[30] Instead, he built his word list of some 43,000 words from the quotations he took from what he considered the best authors, augmenting it by raiding earlier dictionaries, chiefly Bailey's. His governing principle was that the books of great writers determine the language. The method he used was to plunge into a volume, underline a word he decided to include, write it in the margin, and mark with vertical lines the beginning and end of the passage that contained it. He decided to choose his English authors from the period between Sir Philip Sidney and the Restoration, which he described as 'the wells of English undefiled' – before the language was heavily influenced by French and after the 'rudeness' of earlier eras – though in practice he ended up going further back for a few, such as to Chaucer and Sir Thomas More. The quotations turned out to be a map of his intellect and astonishingly vast range of reading. His favourite authors included Sidney, Spenser, Bacon, Milton, Thomas Browne, Richard Hooker and Dryden. He also drew on John Locke, Isaac Watts, Addison, Pope, Swift and William Law, among other post-Restoration writers, as well as on several 'living authors' such as his friend Samuel Richardson, in spite of having declared that he would ignore them lest he 'be misled by partiality, and that none of my contemporaries might have reason to complain'. Indeed, he even included himself and friends, several women among them including Charlotte Lennox, 'when my heart, in the tenderness of friendship, solicited admission for a favourite name'. After the *Dictionary* came out, Garrick told him people were grumbling that he had lowered the dignity of his work by including living authors. He replied famously, 'Nay, I have done worse than that: I have cited *thee*, David [under 'giggler'].'[31]

He amassed many more than the 116,000 quotations he included in the *Dictionary*, finding that because of the incredible bulk to which the volumes would swell and 'fright away the student' he was reduced to 'the vexation of expunging' thousands of them, or reducing them to 'clusters of words', or even rewriting them. Many he could not bear to purge or 'mutilate' because they 'intersperse with verdure and flowers the dusty deserts of barren philology'. As it was, the formidable fatness of the published volumes would be due chiefly to the quotations, which embrace encyclopedically virtually all knowledge in literature, religion, philosophy, science, law, manufacturing technology, crafts, and so on, making it 'part dictionary, part encyclopedia, part textbook'.[32]

Mitigating against the reputation of the *Dictionary*, however, as a universal and progressive display of knowledge, has been the controversial contention that Johnson's quotations reveal a moral, religious, philosophical and political bias. This is partly because he admitted he wanted quotations to do more than just illustrate a word: 'I therefore extracted from philosophers principles of science; from historians remarkable facts; from chemists complete processes; from divines striking exhortations; and from poets beautiful descriptions.' But which philosophers, divines and poets? There is no doubt that he chose or rejected many authors for their beliefs. It is clear at least that neither the quotations nor the definitions reflect a 'primary commitment' to these biases. Johnson is primarily illustrating words, not principles, but as a human being with strong feelings and ideas his choices do frequently reflect his attitudes and points of view. As Robert Folkenflik notes, 'dictionaries are ideological. They cannot be otherwise.' Johnson's *Dictionary* 'has a mind of its own. We can safely say what the *Dictionary* thinks; it is more difficult to make the claim about what Johnson thinks on the basis of *Dictionary* illustrations or even definitions. Controversial terms do not always call for a tendentious response.' Johnson's decisions 'come out of a head, not out of a hat'. As religion was central to Johnson's life and thought, for example, Christian writers such as Law, Richard Hooker, Robert South and John Tillotson are extremely well represented, as is the Bible (4,617 quotations) and the *Book of Common Prayer*. Other religious writers he omitted on account of their theological views. His exclusion of Thomas Hobbes and Bernard Mandeville and other 'wicked' writers – although he thought highly of Mandeville in other respects – was impelled by his intense dislike of both their 'principles' or unorthodox religions and social views and the damage he feared they could do to impressionable readers. 'I scorned, sir, to quote him at all', Johnson said of Hobbes.[33]

Readers have also censured the way Johnson allowed his personality to intrude: that he used the work to promote his own views, standing in the way of progress by misrepresenting the contemporary intellectual milieu.

He has also been accused of reinforcing the contemporary status quo, religious, political, and cultural. He was involved in suppressing insubordination and dissent, some of the argument goes. Given Johnson's vast range and catholicity of sources, these judgements sound extreme, for any points of view introduced by his illustrative quotations keep company with thousands of others that undercut them. It is unreasonable to claim that the *Dictionary* embodies any coherent political, social or personal orientation. Another way of looking at this issue is that the *Dictionary* was 'public', as Robert DeMaria has pointed out, and that for some of the same reasons accounting for his tact in the *Plan* he was wary of alienating potential purchasers, aiming at 'a broad but economically stable, politically conservative stratum of British society'.[34]

7

The booksellers were eager to see manuscript copy and have the printing begin, and Johnson himself, whose hunting through books for quotations was done in a void, needed to see how his method of collecting them first and then adding definitions, etymologies and other lexicographical material later would work. He therefore began to compose the text very early in the project. In order to contain the manuscript he and his assistants created as many as eighty notebooks by folding and cutting paper into quarto format and creating with it gatherings or sections of pages, slipped within each other. If, as Boswell said, each notebook contained two quires of paper, or about twenty-four quarto sheets, and each sheet eight pages, then each of these cumbersome notebooks numbered close to four hundred pages. Each page was divided into two columns. Johnson and his amanuenses then wrote the words to be defined in the columns; he had them copy the quotes from transcribed slips or (to save work) directly from the books into the spaces allotted for the particular word being defined. He judged the space he needed between words on the basis of how many quotations for a word he had already collected, how many senses of the word he had come up with, and what other lexicographical information he knew or anticipated he would include. Obviously he would have to add leaves and gatherings as he introduced new words, so he tied the notebooks loosely rather than stitched them together.[35]

Everyone had something to do and they made rapid progress in the first two or three years. As this was noticed, there was a buzz in the air that the *Dictionary* would soon be finished. But all was not well in the garret, and it is hard not to believe that Johnson had not for some time realised the huge problem that was rearing its nightmarish head.

If he had had a word processor, his sleepless nights would have been less troubled. With all the additions, expansions and revisions that inevitably continued, he constantly ran out of space under the entries and the text often became a confusing jumble. To begin with, he attempted to insert quotations before he had collected all of them. Many (with some difficulty) could continue to be slipped or written in wherever possible, though many could not. If the order in which he wished them to appear had to be changed, he was often out of luck. There was no room to do that. The fragile and chaotic state of the manuscript resulting from this alone would have been horrendous for the printer. Glued slips could fall out, as the manuscript notebooks were moved around the printing house. A bigger problem was the definitions. He continually underestimated the number of senses and variety of usage of words. His quotations were revealing by the hour how richly diverse and infinitely alive the language was in meaning, throwing up all kinds of meaning from usage that his earlier etymological scheme or straitjacket of tracing words down from their primitive meanings could not accommodate.[36] Extended definitions drawing on his reading had to be squeezed in where possible and the text rearranged. There were other problems. The amanuenses often entered the wrong headword, or entered it in the wrong place, if they reasoned incorrectly as to how to read a phrase Johnson had marked. His amanuenses gave him vital help and companionship, but inadvertently they interfered with his authorial control. Also, since quotations had been written into the manuscript from early in the process, Johnson's hands were tied if he wished to alter their wording, as he often did.[37]

The whole thing became a mess. The deeply depressing day finally arrived in 1749 or early 1750 when his worst dreams came true and he had to abandon both his method and manuscript, realising that instead of using confining notebooks he would have to adopt a more flexible method of using loose sheets that could be added as needed. This catastrophic decision brought a crisis both of mind and career. He understood the new method he had to use, and this gave him some hope, but, although he had not exactly wasted three years, the booksellers who hoped to publish at the end of that time thought he had and were not at all happy. He had used up all the advance and Tetty was in a more parlous state than ever, making more demands on the little money they now had left. Was he back where he had started three years earlier? Was this just another failure? For a time his work appears to have come to a screeching halt.

CHAPTER 15

Poetic Interludes

SOON AFTER ARRIVING IN LONDON with Johnson in 1737, Garrick had given up the wine business and begun to prosper on the stage. With his innovative emotional, naturalistic acting style, by 1747 he had made himself one of the leading actors in the country, in both comedy and tragedy. He would soon be swept up by Garrick fever in a theatrical world already ornamented with stars such as James Quin, Peg Woffington, Kitty Clive, Charles Macklin, Samuel Foote, Hannah Pritchard, and Susannah Cibber. His drawing power at the box office became enormous, mainly at the Theatre Royal in Drury Lane, which he had made his theatrical home since debuting there in 1742. In the spring of 1747 he decided to purchase a half-interest in Drury Lane for £12,000 as one its two patentees, thereby catapulting himself into the world of theatrical management to augment his powers on the stage. After a summer of structural improvements at the theatre and working out the repertory for the coming season and new contracts for his battalion of more than fifty actors, he opened his first season as manager on 15 September with a performance of *The Merchant of Venice*. What he did there for more than thirty years transformed the British stage and became legendary.

That opening night was the occasion of a minor collaboration between Garrick and Johnson. They had not seen much of each other for years while Garrick was rising to stardom, in the course of which their relationship became complex. While publicly acknowledging Garrick's acting genius, Johnson clearly envied his meteoric success and was repelled by his vanity, chronic name-dropping and artful social climbing. 'His being outstripped by his pupil in the race of immediate fame,' wrote Boswell, 'as well as of fortune, probably made him feel some indignation, as thinking that whatever might be Garrick's merits in his art, the reward was too great when compared with what the most successful efforts of literary labour could attain.' Neither did Johnson like what he regarded as Garrick's and others' 'artificial tone and measured cadence in the declamation of the theatre', especially in the acting of Shakespeare. One night in a tavern, after seeing Garrick act, Johnson remarked, 'the players . . . have got a kind of rant, with which they run on, without any regard either to accent or emphasis'. Arthur Murphy told of 'being in conversation with Dr Johnson near the side of the scenes during the tragedy of *King Lear*; when Garrick came off the stage, he said, "You two talk so loud you destroy all my feelings". "Prithee", replied Johnson, "do not talk of feelings, Punch has no feelings." Admirable as Garrick's imitation of nature always was, Johnson thought it no better than mere mimicry.'[1]

Indeed, Johnson seems to have been irritated especially by Garrick's role in transforming the nation's consciousness about Shakespeare, in turning him into a national icon, the Bard, a patriotic literary champion of Englishness. And yet, 'Dr Johnson considered Garrick his property,' said Reynolds, and 'would never suffer any one to praise or abuse him but himself'. 'It is certain', wrote Murphy, 'that he esteemed and loved Garrick; that he dwelt with pleasure on his praise; and used to declare, that he deserved his great success, because on all applications for charity he gave more than was asked. After Garrick's death he never talked of him without a tear in his eyes.'[2]

From isolated remarks by his contemporaries, the prevailing (and overstated) opinion seems to have been that Johnson did not have much use for the theatre. Boswell thought he was lukewarm about the theatre because he could not see or hear well enough and felt bitter about his failure to get *Irene* acted, as well as because of his envy of Garrick. Johnson's friend the Shakespearean critic George Steevens said he had it from Johnson himself that his eyesight was his great handicap at the theatre: 'To speak the truth, there is small encouragement there for a man whose sight

and hearing are become so imperfect as mine'. There was perhaps a more
fundamental reason for his ambiguities about the stage – the face rather
than the page, as the saying goes: he was not about to 'chase the new-
blown bubbles of the day' which the 'wild vicissitudes of taste' on stage every day held up as a mirror to the 'publick voice', a mockery of the great
national theatrical tradition.[3]

Nonetheless, he did attend plays at Drury Lane, Covent Garden and
elsewhere and, as we shall see, for a time even enjoyed lingering backstage
at Drury Lane. And he was pleased to accept Garrick's invitation to write
a prologue for that opening night of his management at Drury Lane.
Writing the sixty-two lines of the prologue for the big night gave him a
chance, with Garrick's encouragement and perhaps even at his request, to
describe the moral degeneration of contemporary English drama, which
he thought was a national disgrace, a plague threatening to infect the
other arts – 'the licentiousness and dissolute manners on stage', as Boswell
put it. It was a timely message: the new era Garrick was launching at
Drury Lane promised change and the prologue provided a manifesto for
it. He claimed that after composing the entire poem in his head, 'I did not
afterwards change more than a word in it, and that was done at the re-
monstrance of Garrick. I did not think his criticism just, but it was necessary he should be satisfied with what he was to utter.'[4]

The poem begins with an appropriate celebration of the former glories
of the stage in which Shakespeare's 'flame' and Ben Jonson's 'art' thrived.
The trouble began in the Restoration, when thespian 'wits' opted for 'easier ways to fame'. Johnson's harsh language leaves no doubt as to where he
stood on the moral vacuum that had ensued: 'Intrigue was plot, obscenity
was wit./Vice always found a sympathetick friend;/They pleas'd their age,
and did not aim to mend' (lines 20–22). The theatre became nothing less
than a 'pimp' for future generations. On top of that, its art declined,
'crush'd by rules' and 'refin'd' into effeminate weakness. Tragedy declined
through 'frigid caution' and 'declamation roar'd, while passion slept'. Virtue and 'Nature' fled, leaving the stage open for productions of vapid pan-
tomime and song. But the audience that night was lucky and privileged:

Garrick's new reign at Drury Lane was about to rescue the London stage. 'The pomp of show' was about to be chased off the stage by 'useful mirth and salutary woe', the moral radiance of truth and virtue.[5]

How much Johnson believed all this is open to question, but he was paid for the poem and surely it had already occurred to him that one favour deserved another and that Garrick now was in a position to help him with *Irene*. He was right. Garrick encouraged him to put some finishing touches to the play and promised to stage it at Drury Lane. To Johnson it must have seemed like a dream come true, a fulfilment or closure of those struggling years before and after moving to London. The play's resurrection also meant some badly needed income since it was customary for the playwright to receive the profits from every third performance.

First, there was work to be done on the play. More than a decade had elapsed since he wrote most of it, and the pseudo-classical pomposity of many of its lines struck Garrick as virtually unactable, even by the great actors and actresses he had in his stable under contract. Even after revisions, Hawkins judged, 'The diction of the piece was cold and philosophical; it came from the head of the writer, and reached not the hearts of the hearers.' One might have expected Johnson to respond gratefully to Garrick's recommendations based on years of acting and knowledge of the mechanics of the theatre, especially since he knew the play was an example of his writing when he was only in his twenties. But not so. He seems to have resisted Garrick's suggestions at every turn and was still resentful of what he saw as his friend's pushiness many years later. Enlisting Taylor to intervene after a 'violent dispute' between them, Garrick got an earful for his efforts: 'Sir, the fellow wants me to make Mahomet run mad, that he may have an opportunity of tossing his hands and kicking his heels.' (Garrick did not play Mahomet, perhaps as a result of their disagreements.) Nonetheless, Garrick had his way on many passages and on 29 November 1748 this note appeared in the *General Advertiser*: 'We hear a new tragedy called *Mahomet and Irene* will be acted at the Theatre Royal in Drury Lane after Christmas.'[6]

The play opened seven weeks later on 6 February. On the opening night Johnson paced anxiously up and down the theatre dressed totally out of character in what he thought was appropriate for a playwright, a scarlet waistcoat braided with gold and a gold-laced hat. Recognising quickly the absurdity of the figure he was cutting backstage in the Green Room as well as out in the side boxes, 'I soon laid aside my gold-laced hat, lest it should make me proud.' 'At that period all the wenches knew me', he remarked, 'and dropped me a curtsey as they passed on to the stage.' According to one unreliable story Boswell tells in his journal (and in an early draft of the *Life* that he later somewhat bowdlerised to make less racy), Garrick informed David Hume that Johnson, during these performances or later, 'out of considerations of rigid virtue', decided that he had to put an end to his backstage visits: 'No, David said he[,] I will never come back. For the white bubbies and the silk stockings of your actresses excite my genitals.' For publication, Boswell replaced 'genitals' with 'amorous propensities'. Johnson's nervousness on the opening night was not helped by the hissing and catcalls that issued from the audience before the play began. Once Johnson's combative Prologue began to be spoken, though, the audience grew silent, surprised by its strident note of defiance and indifference towards criticism. He was not about to get on his knees to the audience: 'Ye fops be silent, and ye wits be just!'[7]

In spite of a wonderful set and lavish costumes, and the best actors, Garrick's efforts proved insufficient. The play in several respects was beyond repair for the stage, though one of Garrick's revisions created its own problems. Against Johnson's wishes, he insisted that Irene (acted by the popular Mrs Pritchard) was to be strangled onstage in the fifth act, not out of view as Johnson wrote it, speaking her last two lines 'with a bowstring round her neck'. The melodrama proved too much for the audience, which cried '*Murder! Murder!*', and from that moment the scene crumbled in a chaos of jeers and taunts: Mrs Pritchard 'several times attempted to speak; but in vain. At last she was obliged to go off the stage alive.' The next night Irene expired safely offstage, but the hissing lingered on in subsequent performances. The play was not a flop, but its reception was only lukewarm. Garrick kept it going for nine nights, a good run for the eighteenth century, so that his friend could reap almost £200 in profits from a benefit every third performance, but he never liked it. He told Murphy decades later, 'When Johnson writes *tragedy, declamation roars, and passion sleeps:* when Shakespeare wrote, he dipped his pen in his own heart.' When asked how he had felt about the lukewarm reception of his play, Johnson replied, 'Like the Monument', unmoved and stoic. The income softened the blow, but he was far from unmoved. He stewed somewhat with mixed feelings about the actresses. Alluding to a typical attitude of actors in the eighteenth century, he complained of the superb Mrs Pritchard, whom Mrs Thrale said he blamed for the failure of the play and whom once he described as a 'vulgar idiot' in common life: 'She no more thought of the play out of which her part was taken, than a shoemaker thinks of the skin, out of which the piece of leather, of which he is making a pair of shoes, is cut.' As for Susannah Cibber in the role of Aspasia, he said he would rather 'sit up to the chin in water for an hour than be obliged to listen to the whining, daggle tailed Cibber'. The pain of not having a smash hit on his hands was eased by his selling the copyright to Robert Dodsley for £100, who published it on 16 February. In just over a week he made more money than previously in any entire year.[8]

Poetry and fable were safer. Several months earlier he had published a piece of visionary prose fiction on the theme of the futility of human happiness, *The Vision of Theodore: The Hermit of Teneriffe*, which Dodsley published in his *Preceptor: Containing a General Course of Education*. He also wrote the Preface for the *Preceptor*, which gave him a chance to draw on his strong feelings about his own education and the social imbalances in the education system.[9] *The Vision*, which he wrote in one night, fit nicely into Dodsley's publication because it is an allegory about how to acquire wisdom and morally constructive 'habits, sentiments, and passions'. Like other allegories of his, it turned out to be one of his more popular pieces with the reading public. A 'preceptor' or teacher, in a manner anticipating Johnson's great work *Rasselas* a decade later, instructs his 'dear pupil' in morality and tells him of a fable he heard related by a friend in the form of a 'a vision' illustrating how moral choices determine the happiness and fate of the individual. Theodore, a hermit, begins the ascent of a high peak in Teneriffe, the largest of the Canary Islands, but on the way up he has a dream in which a 'protector' appears to him and directs him to look down upon multitudes struggling up the mountain slopes. Some are making it up to a 'Temple of Happiness', others beset by 'a troop of pygmies' (human habits) are being waylaid by vices such as indolence, ambition, despair, intemperance and avarice. The whole allegory is draped in the archetypal tradition of a mountain gloom, mountain glory journey of discovery so popular in sixteenth- and seventeenth-century English literature, the most famous example of which was *A Pilgrim's Progress*.[10]

What is disturbingly evident in this 'dream' is Johnson's preoccupation with the temptations of his own bad habits and how they continually threatened his own happiness. 'Remember, Theodore,' concludes the preceptor, 'and be wise, and let not Habit prevail against thee.' Also at the core of unhappiness is the failure to check Admiration or Wonder, Fear, Pride, Anger and Love with 'prudent Sentiments and Opinions'. In his New Year's Day prayer in 1748, he had struck just that theme, as he would in prayer after prayer, year after year: 'Almighty and most merciful Father . . . grant that I may so remember my past Life, as to repent of the days and years which I have spent in forgetfulness of thy mercy and neglect of my own Salvation, and so use the time which thou shalt yet allow me, as that I may become every day more diligent in the duties which in the Providence shall be assigned me.' Diligence is a rational faculty, and, as in this petition to God, he recognised that prayer or obedience in his own life must be expressed through a capacity to be disciplined. Theodore himself is told by a sweet nymph who calls herself 'Reason' that his only protection is obedience, and that 'Reason' is the way to Religion. This was a weighty moral problem for Johnson, knowing as he did that his own obedience had always been a huge struggle, and explained the emotional force behind his dread of entangling, seducing vices – 'inchained by Habits, and ingulfed by Despair'. Indolence, especially when it teamed up with melancholia, terrified him:

The captives of Indolence had neither superiority nor merriment. Discontent lowered in their looks, and Sadness hovered round their shades; yet they crawled on reluctant and gloomy, till they arrived at the depth of the recess, varied only with poppies and

nightshade, where the dominion of Indolence terminates, and
the hopeless wanderer is delivered up to Melancholy: the chains
of Habit are riveted for ever, and Melancholy having tortured
her prisoner for a time, consigns him at last to the cruelty of
Despair.[11]

All of this was very close to the bone and may have impelled him to tell
Percy it was 'the best thing he ever wrote' – 'best' in the sense of being
morally self-defining.

Just before *Irene* was staged, he took up the theme of human happiness
again in a new poem in heroic couplets, *The Vanity of Human Wishes*, an
imitation of the tenth satire of Juvenal. It was his greatest achievement in
poetry and the first time his name ever appeared on the title page of one of
his works, but as he was still unknown to the public as a poet, Dodsley
paid him only fifteen guineas for it. He wrote *Vanity* probably in the early
autumn 1748, very rapidly for some quick money, as he stated in a characteristic boast: 'I wrote the first seventy lines . . . in the course of one morning, in that small house beyond the church at Hampstead. The whole number was composed before I committed a single couplet to writing.' He told
Boswell the same thing when describing his customary and eccentrically
precocious way of composing verses: 'The great difficulty is to know when
you have made good ones. I have generally had them in my mind, perhaps
fifty at a time, walking up and down in my room; and then I have written
them down, and often, from laziness, have written only half-lines. I remember I wrote a hundred lines of *The Vanity of Human Wishes* in a day.'[12]

The poem is, as the title suggests, essentially a Christian sermon rooted
deeply in human nature. Its great Christian theme is that it is idle and
dangerous for humans to seek to hold on 'permanently to human happiness, or even to try to find it, for that matter, for life is slippery and on the
whole unhappy, mainly a preparation for the afterlife. The great sin or human folly is to imagine that through either self-deception or prideful ego
one can escape that profound fact.'

Johnson's deteriorating progress with the *Dictionary* and the gloom that stole over him as a result possibly prompted him to write the *Vision of Theodore* and *Vanity of Human Wishes*[13] both of which are about the inability to make the right choices frequently enough and therefore the vanity of aspiring to lasting happiness. Emulating Juvenal, the Stoic, and adapting his satire to modern conditions, *Vanity* savagely chronicles how misguided hopes cruelly, ridiculously and pridefully have disappointed generation after generation. 'All times their scenes of pompous woes afford,' he writes. In a cavalcade of historical characters he drives the point home, from English political figures like Cardinal Wolsey who 'lost the pride of aweful state', the first duke of Buckingham who was murdered in 1628, and Robert Harley who suddenly fell from power when Queen Anne died in 1714, to continental legends like Charles XII of Sweden, Xerxes and the Holy Roman Emperor Charles VII.

In this poem he is still the angry young man who now is almost forty. The poem opens with a general, bleak assessment of mankind's parlous state in a dark and dangerous world:

> How hope and fear, desire and hate,
> O'erspread with snares the clouded maze of fate,
> Where wav'ring man, betray'd by vent'rous pride,
> To tread the dreary paths without a guide,
> . . . Shuns fancied ills, or chases airy good.

Everywhere 'Fate wings with ev'ry wish th'afflictive dart', and there is no end in sight of those who are betrayed by their restless ambition:

> Unnumber'd suppliants croud Preferment's gate,
> A thirst for wealth, and burning to be great;
> Delusive Fortune hears th'incessant call,
> They mount, they shine, evaporate, and fall.

Inviting the laughing philosopher Democritus to mock the folly and ghastly farce of human existence, he tells the reader he is going to 'Survey mankind, from China to Peru' – the great and powerful as well as the weak, foolish and vulnerable, like mothers and scholars – to determine how justified the mockery is. He finds that nobody is spared, but (unlike Juvenal) he pities mankind, as in his sketch of Cardinal Wolsey's fall from royal grace, 'With age, with cares, with maladies oppress'd' while 'Grief aids disease' as he hastens towards death.[14]

One of the most moving sections is on old age, the keynote to which Johnson sums up in the line, 'That life protracted is protracted woe.' Time has shut up 'all the passages of joy' and rendered 'the dotard' who has prayed for long life incapable of any sensuous enjoyment. All that is left to him is senile bullying and demands, 'perversely grave, or positively wrong'. He becomes a target of gathering sneers by bored, avaricious would-be heirs. His end is far more bleak than Jacques's portrait of old age in Shakespeare's *As You Like It*: 'Unnumber'd maladies his joints invade' as his avarice still flourishes and he turns his 'anxious heart and crippled hands' to his gold, which he counts up to the minute of his death. This appalling picture Johnson counters with a portrait of an ageing but wise and gracious woman who Mrs Thrale maintained was modelled after his own mother, 'The gen'ral fav'rite as the gen'ral friend.' But even she is afflicted with sorrows in old age. She decays until her 'with'ring life' is at last released by 'pitying Nature'.

There is also another sketch of a girl whose parents vainly pray that she will grow up to be pretty. The passage sympathetically concentrates on the vanity that inevitably germinates within such a girl and the moral pressures that women in general have to suffer in a society that stridently and cruelly programs them into conventional private and domestic roles:

> Ye nymphs of rosy lips and radiant eyes,
> Whom Pleasure keeps too busy to be wise,
> Whom Joys with soft varieties invite,
> By day the frolick, and the dance by night,
> Who frown with vanity, who smile with art,

And ask the latest fashion of the heart,

What care, what rules your heedless charms shall save,

Each nymph your rival, and each youth your slave?

The poor girl does not realise in the fullness of blooming youth and beauty that she is already on a slippery slope to rivalry, age, neglect and obscurity: 'Now beauty falls betray'd, despis'd, distress'd,/And hissing Infamy proclaims the rest.'

Where then, Johnson asks, 'shall Hope and Fear their objects find? Must man in ignorant solace' unaided 'Roll darkling down the torrent of his fate?' God is a very present help in trouble, he urges, to whom we must leave 'the measure and the choice,/Safe in his pow'r, whose eyes discern afar/The secret ambush of a specious pray'r'. Love, patience, and faith are the 'goods' for which we should all aspire, ordained by heaven. This is a spiritual happiness which has nothing to do with vain human wishes and provides the ultimate mockery of vanity. It may strike the reader that this conclusion is too easy and abrupt in terms of the profound complexity and tragedy of human sorrow that the poem has richly and emotively portrayed. But there is no alternative except terrible oblivion, Johnson thought, and oblivion is not the fate of those who call honestly upon God.

The poem was received tepidly, and no other separate edition of it appeared in his lifetime. Many thought it was too bleak in the abstract, though Garrick paradoxically judged that Johnson wrote the poem after 'he became more retired' – more comfortable and settled at Gough Square – than when his poverty and sense of alienation produced the more realistic pictures of 'common life' in *London*. It is 'as hard as Greek', Garrick complained: 'Had he gone on to imitate another satire, it would have been as hard as Hebrew.' The Romantics disagreed. Lord Byron found it a 'grand poem' of great truth: 'The lapse of ages *changes* all things – time – language – the earth – the bounds of the sea – the stars of the sky, and every thing . . . *except man himself* . . . The infinite variety of lives conduct but to death, and the infinity of wishes lead but to disappointment.' And

Sir Walter Scott remarked that he 'had more pleasure in reading *London* and *The Vanity of Human Wishes*, than any other poetical composition he could mention'. In the mid-twentieth century, T. S. Eliot declared that Johnson's claim as a major poet rested chiefly with *Vanity*; and in our own time, the poem has been judged as the first in a series of writings that has established him as a moral genius, or almost secular prophet, in modern thought.[15]

CHAPTER 16

Tetty and 'Amorous Propensities'

I

HAWKINS KNEW JOHNSON FAIRLY WELL during the late 1740s and had a bleak view of his mental state at the end of 1748. He stated flatly that his indolence and melancholia were chronic and mostly unrelated to his professional work and domestic life. This misconception undoubtedly was due to Johnson's scrupulousness in not speaking of himself and his anxieties. Even if he did not stress the isolating pressures of the *Dictionary* and demoralising effects of his life with Tetty, however, Hawkins did judge that Johnson's loneliness impelled him to found the Ivy Lane Club in the winter of 1748–9. Chance meetings in coffee houses were not enough; left largely to himself by Tetty at Gough Square, he needed to meet regularly for lively debates with people he enjoyed being with. As one of the founding members, Hawkins confirmed it was:

> a great relief to Johnson after the fatigue of study, and he generally came to it with both a corporal and mental appetite; for our conversation seldom began till after a supper, so very solid and substantial, as led us to think, that with him it was a dinner. By the help of this reflection, and no other incentive to hilarity than lemonade, Johnson was, in a short time after our assembling, transformed into a new creature: his habitual melancholy and lassitude of spirit gave way; his countenance brightened; his mind was

made to expand, and his wit to sparkle: he told excellent stories; and in his didactic style of conversation, both instructed and delighted us.[1]

The birth of the Ivy Lane Club marked the emergence of Johnson as the 'great Cham' or monarch of literature, an expression first used by the novelist Tobias Smollett in 1759 to describe him; or (in Hawkins's words) as a 'symposiarch, to preside in all conversations'. The club met every Tuesday evening at the King's Head, a beefsteak house in Ivy Lane between Newgate and St Paul's Cathedral. Every Tuesday Johnson would make his way to the King's Head with a spring in his step and 'a disposition to please and be pleased', for a few hours losing himself in humour and vigorous debate, forgetting 'painful reflections'. The club's members, in addition to Hawkins, included John Hawkesworth, his friend and associate at *The Gentleman's Magazine* since 1740; Dr Richard Bathurst, whom Johnson kept mentioning in his prayers for many years afterwards, the only person outside his family to be singled out in this way; and Samuel Dyer, the highly regarded dissenting scholar and linguist who thought Hawkins 'a man of the most mischievous, uncharitable, and malignant disposition' and, in later years, with too much money on his hands, became something of a 'sober sensualist', a tendency that Johnson tried to counter by attempting unsuccessfully to persuade him to write a life of Erasmus. Johnson occupied his tavern throne of human felicity, as he thought of it, during club sessions, from which he sometimes vexed other members by dominating the conversation intellectually. Hawkins noted he was able to 'reason and discuss, dictate and control' by his exactness of expression and also deploying his rich fund of humour, 'in which there hardly ever was his equal'.[2]

2

By 1748, Johnson was living mostly on his own at Gough Square in 'my recluse kind of life', oppressed by melancholic loneliness to a degree he had not felt since before his marriage. That year the deterioration of Tetty and their estrangement at last became well known when she moved out of the house and took simple lodgings in Hampstead.[3]

Whether or not Peter Garrick's remark to Boswell that Johnson once seduced 'a very fine woman' is true is something we may never know, but there is no doubt about his amorous propensities (in Boswell's phrase) and his drive to be gallant to women such as Hill Boothby. Neither are we ever likely to know if Johnson on occasion visited a prostitute. It is unlikely he did while Tetty was alive, but who knows what has remained secret in a pocket-book diary he began the year after she died – he was desperately worried when it went missing while he was on his deathbed. Hawkins had taken it to keep others (so he said) from reading it and never revealed what was in it, although at Johnson's house in 1776 Boswell secretly made a copy and used parts of it in his *Life*. The diary was destroyed shortly before Johnson's death. The fact that Johnson made a point of noting in this diary that during Tetty's funeral he was 'never once distracted by any thoughts of any other woman' suggests perhaps that before she died he frequently had been. Boswell did not use such passages in the *Life*, most likely because he did not wish to diminish Johnson's devotion to Tetty.[4]

After the contract for the *Dictionary*, Johnson was at home almost all the time, but up in the garret and totally preoccupied with the extraordinary demands the project placed on him – demands which worried him and themselves aggravated the tension between him and Tetty. She lost sexual interest in him and one day decided to deny him any more sexual favours for the rest of their married life, which for someone with such strong sexual appetites as his must have been a dismal development. Finally, she persuaded him (we may presume) to let her have her own lodgings in Hampstead, surely another source of strife and an expense they could ill afford but a place where at least she could enjoy healthier rural air in the higher ground of the village. Johnson's account of this move was that she was advised to sleep out of town and that she 'complained the staircase was in very bad condition, for the plaster was beaten off the walls in many places'. Not to worry, said the owner, 'that's nothing but by the knocks against it of the coffins of the poor souls that have died in the lodgings!'. If this remark was actually made, very likely it felt ominous to them both. Johnson visited this 'small house beyond the church' regularly while Tetty was in residence, composing the first seventy lines of *The Vanity of Human Wishes* there.[5]

It is pertinent at this point to bring in a conversation Boswell started with Johnson in October 1779 in London on the subject of conjugal infidelity. Johnson's personal revelations in the exchange strike the modern reader as outlandishly chauvinistic, even in Johnson's society of double standards regarding secular morality where female chastity was central to the marriage market of a hierarchical and propertied society, as well as to the need for absolute clarity regarding the inheritance of property and title. The 'friend' in the following passage is almost certainly Boswell himself:

> I mentioned to him a dispute between a friend of mine and his lady concerning conjugal infidelity, which my friend maintained was by no means so bad in the husband as in the wife. JOHNSON: 'Your friend is right, Sir. Between a man and his Maker it is a different question; but between a man and his wife a husband's infidelity is nothing. They are connected by children, by fortune, by serious considerations of community. Wise married women don't mind it. They detest a mistress but don't mind a whore.'

Then came the bombshell:

> 'My wife told me I might lie with as many women as I pleased provided I loved her alone.' BOSWELL: 'She was not in earnest.' JOHNSON: 'But she was. Consider, Sir, how gross it is in a wife to complain of her husband's going to other women. It is that she has not enough of—'

This dash at the end suggests that even in his journal Boswell could not bring himself to include what Johnson, perhaps crudely, said Tetty lacked, if indeed she said it. He later scribbled 'tail' above the dash, though in his final version he wrote, 'what she would be ashamed to avow'. He persisted:

> BOSWELL: 'And was Mrs Johnson then so liberal? To be sure, there is a great difference between the offence of infidelity in a man and his wife.' JOHNSON: 'The difference is boundless.' BOSWELL: 'Yes, boundless as property and honours.' JOHNSON: 'The man imposes no bastards upon his wife.' BOSWELL: 'But Sir, my friend's lady argued that a wife might take care that her infidelity should not be worse than that of her husband, which, said she, it would not be if she never went astray but when she was with child by her husband.' JOHNSON: 'Sir, from what you tell me of this lady, I think she is very fit for a bawdy-house.' BOSWELL: 'Suppose a woman to be of such a constitution that she does not like it. She has no right to complain that her husband goes elsewhere'. JOHNSON: 'If she refuses it, she has no right to complain.' BOSWELL: 'Then as oft as a man's wife refuses, he may mark it down in his pocket-book and do as he pleases with a safe conscience.'

Boswell had gone too far, however, and Johnson reined him in, 'Nay, Sir, you must consider: to whore is wrong in a single man, and one cannot have more liberty by being married.' Nonetheless, as far as Boswell was concerned, he had elicited Johnson's real sentiments about Tetty, though when he came to write the *Life* he could not bring himself to publish all of this conversation. The last passage cited above was actually printed for the first edition in a revised state but he withdrew even that at the last moment. As he wrote in 1791, he could not believe he had almost 'admitted this to the public eye'. At least one friend, the MP William Windham whom Johnson 'highly valued', was struck by the 'indelicacy' of it. 'It is however mighty good stuff,' Boswell added, but in spite of this he did not want to run the risk in the *Life* of either tainting Johnson's moral authority or of having the indelicacy of the passage 'hurt the book'.[6]

According to what he heard from Mrs Desmoulins, who, before she was married, lived with Tetty at Hampstead – probably at Johnson's request – Tetty mistreated Johnson: 'She indulged herself in country air and nice living, at an unsuitable expence, while her husband was drudging in the smoke of London, and that she by no means treated him with that complacency which is the most engaging quality in a wife.' Why did Johnson tolerate this? Putting the best spin on it he could, Boswell had an answer: 'This is perfectly compatible with his fondness for her, especially when it is remembered that he had a high opinion of her understanding, and that the impression which her beauty, real or imaginary, had originally made upon his fancy, being continued by habit, had not been effaced, though she herself was doubtless much altered for the worse.'[7]

Johnson's strong sexual appetite appeared to cause him mildly to sublimate his frustrated feelings by petting Mrs Desmoulins when he visited her in Hampstead. Or so at least Mrs Desmoulins herself told Boswell in an exchange that Boswell again decided to keep out of the *Life*.[8] It fills five pages of his journal under the heading of 'Tacenda' and begins when he and the painter Mauritius Lowe cornered Mrs Desmoulins one day at Johnson's house in April 1783, while he was taking a nap, to extract as much as they could from her about Johnson's sex life. Making allowances for Mrs Desmoulins's vanity and gossipy disposition, the account nonetheless rings true. Lowe first primed the pump: 'Now, Ma'am, let us be free. We are all married people. Pray tell us, do you really think Dr Johnson ever offended in point of chastity? For my own part I do not believe he ever did. I believe he was chaste even with his wife, and that it was quite a Platonic connection.' Mrs Desmoulins would have none of it: 'Ah, Sir, you are much mistaken. There never was a man who had stronger amorous inclinations than Dr Johnson. But he conquered them.' Baiting her, Boswell interjected, 'I have heard people . . . talk of Dr Johnson's seraglio [in his household], which included you as well as her, Madam. But nobody had a serious belief of anything for a moment.' And Lowe chimed in, 'I do still think the Doctor never has had any inclination for women.' 'But he has,' she replied. Lowe demurred, 'I do not believe his marriage was consummated.' She insisted that it was most certainly consummated back at Edial Hall, according to Garrick, at least, but adds:

> They did not sleep together for many years. But that was her fault. She drank shockingly and said she was not well and could not bear a bedfellow. And I remember once when at Hampstead a young woman came on a visit. I lay in the room with Mrs Johnson in a small bed. She said, 'It will not hold you both. So if you promise not to tell Mr Johnson, you shall sleep with me. But if he should know this, he'd say, "If you can bear a bedfellow, why not me as well as another?"' LOWE (waggishly): 'He has been so bad a bedfellow she could not bear him, and this has made her take drinking. He has had no passion.' MRS DESMOULINS: 'Nay, Sir, I tell you no man had stronger, and nobody had an opportunity to know more about that than I had.'

At this both Boswell and Lowe bolted upright in their chairs, craving more revelations. 'You'll forgive me, Madam', Boswell continued, 'but from what you have said, I beg leave to ask you if the Doctor ever made any attempt upon you?' 'No, Sir, I have told you he commanded his passion. But when I was a young woman and lived with Mrs Johnson at Hampstead, he used to come out two or three days in a week . . . The maid went to bed, as she could not be kept up, and I used to sit up for him; and I have warmed his bed with a pan of coals and sat with him in his room many an hour in the night and had my head upon his pillow.' Amazed, Boswell could not leave it alone, 'What, when he was in bed, Madam?' 'Yes, Sir', she replied, 'He'd desire me to go out of the room, and he'd go to bed; but to come back in a little while and talk to him – and I have come and sat on his bedside and laid my head on his pillow.' Then Boswell tried to bring these revelations to a climax:

> BOSWELL: 'And he showed strong signs of that passion?' MRS DESMOULINS: 'Yes, Sir. But I always respected him as a father.'

BOSWELL: 'What would he do? Come now, would he fondle you? Would he kiss you?' MRS DESMOULINS: 'Yes, Sir.' BOSWELL: 'And it was something different from a father's kiss?' MRS DESMOULINS: 'Yes, indeed.' LOWE (approaching his hand to her bosom): 'But would he, eh?' MRS DESMOULINS: 'Sir, he never did anything that was beyond the limits of decency.' LOWE: 'And could you say, Madam, upon your oath, that you were certain he was capable?' MRS DESMOULINS: 'Y-yes, Sir.' BOSWELL: 'But he conquered his violent inclination?' MRS DESMOULINS: 'Yes, Sir. He'd push me from him and cry, "Get you gone." Oh, one can see.'

The upshot of the interview was that as an unhappily married man of forty Johnson had strong urges which, according to Mrs Desmoulins, he was able to control. Edmund Burke, to whom Boswell confidentially related this conversation, thought it was 'just common human nature' for Johnson to act this way, but Boswell got Mrs Desmoulins to admit that if the lexicographer had indeed 'proceeded to extremities', 'such was my high respect for him, that I could not have had resolution to have resisted him', even though she had never been sexually attracted to him. When Boswell remarked that he could not imagine any woman being attracted to him this way, as 'his figure [was] so terribly disgusting', she offered the considered view that there was nonetheless something sexually appealing enough about him at the age of forty to attract a woman – 'his mind is such'. She was convinced that if a woman like the beautiful and engaging Duchess of Devonshire tried to seduce him, he might succumb if he momentarily allowed himself 'to deliberate'. Otherwise, he would 'spurn' her with ease in 'contempt and indignation'.

While Boswell packaged his portrait of Johnson's marriage with delicacy and restraint, others did not. Mrs Thrale, for example, was happy to transmit Garrick's brutal remark that Tetty was 'a little painted puppet [or 'poppet'], of no value at all, and quite disguised with affectation, full of odd airs of rural elegance'. Garrick, in fact, was especially unkind about her, perhaps still disgusted with recollections of the absurd incongruity of the figure she and Johnson cut together at their Edial school. Boswell did allow into the *Life* Garrick's harsh depiction of her looks: 'very fat, with a bosom of more than ordinary protuberance, with swelled cheeks, of a florid red, produced by thick painting, and increased by the liberal use of cordials; flaring and fantastic in her dress, and affected both in her speech and her general behaviour'.[9]

William Shaw maintained that although Johnson had no children to interfere with his work on the *Dictionary*, he did have his wife whose addiction to drinking and opium may have driven him to other women. He also reminded his readers, however, that Johnson's peevishness induced by study and disease did not make him easy to live with at home. Robert Levet, one of Johnson's long-term household guests, rounded it off by recalling that 'she was always drunk and reading romances in her bed'. Hawkins thought that Johnson's widely proclaimed love for her was embarrassing and did not ring true, and that her indifference to his personal appearance and habits in the 1740s bespoke a comprehensive indifference to him: his 'negligence of dress seemed never to have received the least correction from her, and who, in the sordidness of his apparel, and the complexion of his linen, even shamed her. For these reasons I have often been inclined to think, that if this fondness of Johnson for his wife was not dissembled, it was a lesson that he had learned by rote, and that, when he practised it, he knew not where to stop till he became ridiculous.' It was almost as if they were acting out an absurd, grotesque charade: 'As, during her lifetime, he invited but few of his friends to his house, I never saw her, but I have been told by Mr Garrick, Dr Hawkesworth, and others, that there was somewhat crazy in the behaviour of them both; profound respect on his part, and the airs of an antiquated beauty on hers.'[10]

3

Tetty was on a rapid downward curve even in the more salubrious air of Hampstead or with visits to hotels in Covent Garden known as 'hummums' where there were hot water and vapour baths – 'my wife went to the Hummums,' Johnson once recalled, 'it is a place where people get themselves cupped' – i.e. bled with a little 'glass-bell . . . upon the skin'. She was very ill when she was back again at Gough Square for a few days in July 1749. 'Your poor Mamma is come home but very weak,' he informed Tetty's daughter Lucy in Lichfield, 'yet I hope she will grow better', otherwise she would have to return to Hampstead. 'She is now upstairs and knows not of my writing.'[11]

He was nervous also about his own mother's health and, as he thought, imminent death. Death was on his mind: 'I was afraid your letter had brought me ill news of my mother, whose death is one of the few calamities on which I think with horrour. I long to know how she does and, how you all do.' He appeared to be preparing himself to deal with grief. When the mother of his friend James Elphinston, the Scottish schoolmaster and Strahan's brother-in-law, died in September 1750, he wrote to him a remarkable letter of consolation worth quoting in full for its capacious understanding:

> I hope you will not think me incapable of partaking of your grief. I have a mother now eighty-two years of age, whom therefore I must soon lose, unless it please God that she rather should mourn for me. I read the letters in which you relate your mother's death to Mrs Strahan and think I do myself honour when I tell you that I read them with tears but tears are neither to me nor to you of any further use, when once the tribute of nature has been paid. The business of life summons us away from useless grief, and calls us to the exercise of those virtues of which we are lamenting our deprivation. The greatest benefit which one friend can confer upon another, is to guard, and excite and elevate his virtues. This your mother will still perform, if you diligently preserve the memory of her life.

The best way to increase his wife's happiness, he added, was to be true to her values and virtue: 'Surely there is something pleasing in the belief, that our separation from those whom we love is merely corporeal; and it may be a great incitement to virtuous friendship, if it can be made probable that union which has received the divine approbation shall continue to eternity.' It felt to him as if the death of either Tetty or his mother might soon reveal to what extent the melancholic torment of grief would turn on him and how effectively he could fight it.[12]

CHAPTER 17

The Triumph of
the Moralist

I

IN SPITE OF ALL HE HAD DONE by 1750, Johnson still was relatively unknown to the public. *The Vanity of Human Wishes* put his name before the public for the first time with a published work, as distinct from the advertised and distant promise of the *Dictionary*, but it brought neither financial rewards nor wide recognition as a promising new literary personality. All that changed with his *Rambler* essays, which once they began to be published made people begin to talk and write about him and seek him out. He quickly became known as 'the Rambler'.

His distresses as a struggling author, scholar, and melancholic, his loneliness and anger over an oppressive society, and the shock of temporary defeat at the hands of the *Dictionary* shaped his philosophic and moral 'voice' for the *Rambler*. The 208 essays, which he began publishing on 20 March 1750 and which endowed him with a public identity, were crucial to his own mental health as well as to thousands of readers who were looking for essays with a hard moral realism blended with Christian benediction. As a modern editor of the *Rambler* has put it, with these essays Johnson established himself as 'one of the great moralists of modern times – as one of a handful of men, during the last three centuries, whose writing on human life and destiny has become a permanent part of the conscience of mankind'. As a distillation of his experience of life, they comprise his most representative single body of writing. And yet, for one of the great works of English literature, it is not often read today.[1]

With the *Dictionary* stalling, one might not think it was a propitious time for him to embark on a major new writing and publishing venture. But he needed the two guineas (about £200 today) per essay that Edward Cave and two other publishers were ready to pay him. Also, he had not written much prose for several years except for *Dictionary* entries and was hungry to express himself again fully and roundly in some literary way. The following remark in his penultimate essay (207) on 10 March 1752, on the complex psychology of writing for publication, is plainly autobiographical if we imagine Johnson at the end of the *Rambler* road reflecting on why he started writing these essays in the first place: 'if by the necessity of solitary application he is secluded from the world', an author 'listens with beating heart to distant noises, longs to mingle with living beings, and resolves to take hereafter his fill of diversions, or display his abilities on the universal theatre, and enjoy the pleasure of distinction and applause'. The *Rambler* satisfied this longing, providing him with a platform from which to interact with the reading public, not as a scholar but as a fully engaged guide to the human mind. It enabled him to escape from his study for immediate and regular discourse with the public, although it meant relentless deadlines twice per week for two years. In the last issue on 14 March 1752, he confessed to the pressures this had placed on him: 'He that condemns himself to compose on a stated day, will often bring to his task an attention dissipated, a memory embarrassed, an imagination overwhelmed, a mind distracted with anxieties, a body languishing with disease: he will labour on a barren topic, till it is too late to change it; or in the ardour of invention, diffuse his thoughts into wild exuberance, which the pressing hour of publication cannot suffer judgement to examine or reduce.'[2]

As a literary periodical, the *Rambler* was not modelled slavishly on the tradition of the periodical essay established by Addison and Richard Steele. It is not as topical and rooted in the eighteenth century as is the *Spectator*, for example, to which it has always been compared, though it does take up current talking points such as education, marriage, wealth, the pride of Londoners, the legal profession and criminality, the arts and theatre, fops, drinking and gambling, prostitution and poverty. In his last essay, in fact, Johnson made a point of distancing the *Rambler* from the topical periodical essay: 'I have never complied with temporary curiosity, nor enabled my readers to discuss the topic of the day.'³ Indeed, the essays were often criticised for being too sombre. He rejected criticism with relish, feeling he was on a superior trajectory. Nevertheless, only half of Johnson's *Rambler* essays are strictly speaking what we can call 'moral essays'. And there are obvious resemblances in style and form to the contemporary popular periodical with a 'letters to the editor' format, literary criticism (including a few essays on Milton's versification), and most of all contributions written to a deadline with a roughly consistent average of 1,500 words.

If the individual issues were going to sell in any number approaching the *Spectator*'s circulation of 10,000, they had to have some 'hot off the press' immediacy of appeal for the general reader and look like a pamphlet or magazine that could be plucked casually off bookshop counters by people passing by. This feel to the essays was achieved partly by their pages being joined by a pin instead of being sewn together. (Complete sets of the original issues are extremely rare today.) For posting to readers in the provinces, they were folded lengthways. Even the name of the periodical conveys the idea of a casual, wandering sort of table talk. Johnson remarked he had been going around in circles deciding what to call it until one night 'I sat down at night upon my bedside, and resolved that I would not go to sleep till I had fixed its title. *The Rambler* seemed the best that occurred, and I took it.' Boswell did not think the name 'suited to a series of grave and moral discourses', noting in 1773 that the Italians had translated the periodical under the name '*Il Vagabondo*'. It was true that 'ramble' to Johnson's contemporaries had a somewhat racy connotation, he himself defining 'ramble' in his *Dictionary* as 'to rove loosely in lust'. Otherwise, it has a sense of casualness and impermanence, even idleness, about it. But in *Rambler* 106, on the vanity of authors who hope for the 'bubbles' of fame, he made it clear that he was hoping for the largest possible audience by comparing his essays to those of the great Bacon, who first popularised the English essay, whose essays 'come home to men's business and bosoms'. So he was in a sense trying to have it both ways: appeal to casual readers wanting entertainment and also write what he hoped would amount to a lasting compendium of his breadth and depth as a practical moralist.[4]

He composed these essays 'hastily', often because he procrastinated until almost the last moment and then found himself 'every moment more irresolute' while his ideas 'wandered from the first intention, and I rather wished to think, than thought, upon any settled subject'. Mrs Thrale told of how people spoke of his composing number 134 on procrastination, of all subjects, at Reynolds's while a messenger boy from the press waited 'to carry it to press'. 'There was however some pleasure in reflecting', he noted, 'that I, who had only trifled till diligence was necessary, might still congratulate myself upon my superiority to multitudes, who have trifled till diligence is vain.'[5]

Hastily written or not, he took the essays very seriously, composing a short 'Prayer on the Rambler' just before the first number appeared, petitioning God 'that in this my undertaking thy Holy Spirit may not be withheld from me, but that I may promote thy glory, and the Salvation both of myself and others'. The *Rambler* became the most personal and psychologically sensitive body of prose he ever wrote. He never kept a private journal with the scope and consistency of a Pepys or Boswell, but the essays, with their reflections on the human predicament, go some way towards supplying us a commentary on his own life. He was immensely proud of them, once describing his other writings as 'wine and water' whereas 'my Rambler is pure wine', and in his last essay summing up his sense of triumph over what he had achieved in them: 'I . . . look back on this part of my work with pleasure which no blame or praise of man shall diminish or augment. I shall never envy the honours which wit and learning obtain in any other cause, if I can be numbered among the writers who have given ardour to virtue, and confidence to truth.'[6]

Precisely because they were so personal, initially he published these essays anonymously, not wishing to have himself measured against his own intricate moral reasoning and the sharp satire which characterise many of the essays. He was proposing to dive deep into human egotism and the complex texture of morality where he thought any man (especially he) was bound to feel naked and be found wanting. As he wrote in the autobiographically charged number 14, 'a man writes much better than he lives . . . We are, therefore, not to wonder that most fail, amidst tumult, and snares, and danger, in the observance of those precepts, which they laid down in solitude, safety, and tranquillity, with a mind unbiased, and with liberty unobstructed.' His rich sympathy with the fallibility of human nature made him angry at those who with knee-jerk, accusative stuffiness 'charge with hypocrisy him that expresses zeal for those virtues, which he neglects to practise'.[7] For the time being, it was best to remain relatively anonymous. A more mundane reason for anonymity may also have been that he did not want to be censured for playing truant from the *Dictionary*.

Very soon after the early numbers appeared, Garrick and others 'who knew the author's powers and style from the first' – the sonorous rhythms and elegant, balanced syntax transmitting an air of authority and dignity[8] – 'unadvisedly asserting their suspicions, overturned the scheme of secrecy'. It was not long before his name was on everyone's lips. After reading the first thirteen, Samuel Richardson told Cave he was 'inexpressibly pleased' with them, unable to remember anything in the *Spectator* 'that half so much struck me'. He added sincerely, 'for its own sake, I hope the world tastes them! There is but one man, I think, that could write them; I desire not to know his name, but I should rejoice to hear that they succeed, for I would not, for any consideration, [hear] that they should be laid down through discouragement.' 'I am vexed that I have not taken larger draughts of them before,' he added, 'that my zeal for their merit might have been as glowing as now I find it.' Cave replied, admitting that 'Mr Johnson is the *Great Rambler*, being, as you observe, the only man who can furnish two such papers in a week, besides his other great business.'[9]

The *Rambler* provided Johnson with a large canvas on which to protest aggressively against the Establishment and power-elites – the egotism, venality, selfishness, stupidity, discrimination, alienation and cruelty in society. He expressed his indignation in the last number: 'I have never been much of a favourite of the public, nor can boast that, in the progress of my undertaking, I have been animated by the rewards of the liberal, the caresses of the great, or the praises of the eminent . . . If I have not been distinguished by the distributors of literary honours, I have seldom descended to the arts by which favour is obtained. I have seen the meteors of fashion rise and fall, without any attempt to add a moment to their duration . . . I did not feel much dejection from the want of popularity.' There were festering wounds not far beneath the surface of these disclaimers.[10]

As for the essays themselves, they are brimming with reductive, ironic, biting wit; with character sketches of ludicrous people who dig deeper and deeper holes for themselves in the pursuit of their pitiful illusions and self-delusions; and with disdainful accounts of certain social institutions, customs and attitudes. Take, for example, the portrait of Gelidus in number 24, a prototype of cold and absurd 'men of learning', 'uninterrupted by their passions', who care not a fig for the welfare of mankind, nor even for their own families, so long as nobody disturbs them and they are left alone 'to study anything rather than themselves'. In this essay he vented his hostility towards the imposition of such people and the sometimes irreparable harm they do. It is one of the reasons he reprehended pedants in teachers' clothing who had no business meddling with young minds and hearts.[11]

Another signpost of Johnson's stridency is the abundance of 'tart, fidgety'[12] phrases, such as in this passage in number 183 on envy: 'The cold malignity of envy may be exerted in a torpid and quiescent state, amidst the gloom of stupidity, in the coverts of cowardice.' Or in number 144: 'Those that cannot make a thrust at life are content to keep themselves in play with petty malevolence, to tease with feeble blows and impotent disturbance.' He reserved special venom in number 136 for patrons, one of his favourite targets, who expect 'indecent and promiscuous dedication' and thus degrade literature: 'For what credit can he expect who professes himself the hireling of vanity, however profligate, and without shame or scruple celebrates the worthless, dignifies the mean, and gives to the corrupt, licentious, and oppressive, the ornament which ought only to add grace to truth, and loveliness to innocence?' Elsewhere he described patrons as proper company for 'cheats, and robbers, and public nuisances'.[13]

But he did not embrace the persona of a railing Juvenalian or Swiftian satirist.[14] 'Though no man perhaps made such rough replies as Dr Johnson,' wrote Mrs Thrale, 'yet nobody had a more just aversion to general satire . . . and for the most part professed himself to feel directly contrary to Dr Swift.' He was more interested in moral direction and Christian devotion. The *Rambler* essays configure moral landscapes of reconciliation and community, in which humans need to participate in each other's lives and try to understand each other. Commitment to community is all. Johnson does not cast himself as the detached preacher or teacher holding forth from a lofty perch. He is one of us, saying that we all have the same temptations and weaknesses, the same hopes and fears; he describes pitfalls all of us may fall into. Readers have always found it reassuring to have him analyse relentlessly this shared humanity from so many points of view and in such detail.[15]

2

Even in her distress, Tetty was touched by his having launched himself into this new orbit of literary vitality. 'Johnson told me, with an amiable fondness', Boswell noted, 'a little pleasing circumstance relative to this work. Mrs Johnson, in whose judgement and taste he had great confidence, said to him, after a few numbers of the *Rambler* had come out, "I thought very well of you before; but I did not imagine you could have written any thing equal to this."' That Johnson thirty-four years later still remembered this remark so vividly as to be able to quote it suggests that it was far more than just 'a little pleasing circumstance' for him.[16]

Tetty was not alone among women readers in praising the *Rambler*, but there were problems with the public response in general, and with women's response in particular. Keeping to his publishing track record thus far, in terms of sales Johnson did not succeed with the *Rambler*. Fewer than five hundred copies of any one number were sold. The essays proved to be insufficiently light or topical to crack the mass market of literate London. To achieve this it was felt by many that he needed to have come across as less 'solemn' and 'dictatorial' and more sprightly. Ironically, one of a handful not written by him, Samuel Richardson's *Rambler* 97 on courtship advice to unmarried ladies, was the bestseller. Richardson was particularly disappointed, in fact, that Johnson's papers were not selling: 'The encouragement, as to sale, is not in proportion to the high character given to the work by the judicious, not to say the raptures expressed by the few that do read it.' As Murphy noted, although Johnson had his four guineas per week for them, the bookseller lost money from the enterprise.[17]

Richardson provided clues, in his letters as well as in his essay, as to why the essays did not sell well. Much had to do with women. His essay consists of a letter from a correspondent urging the Rambler to write more for women, about the manners of women, 'the better half of the human species', and the foibles thereof. Women are plagued today, he moaned, with 'modern time-killers' and need instruction: 'Set, dear Sir, before the youthful, the gay, the inconsiderate, the contempt as well as the danger to which they are exposed. At one time or other, women, not utterly thoughtless, will be convinced of the justice of your censure, and the charity of your instruction', especially as they negotiate their way through the marriage market. Johnson recognised Richardson's sensitive understanding of women and referred approvingly to his famous novels *Pamela* and *Clarissa* as 'lectures of conduct and introductions to life'. On the other hand, he also felt that Richardson was too precious in his sensibilities and limited in his society: 'His love of continual superiority was such, that he took care to be always surrounded by women, who listened to him implicitly, and did not venture to controvert his opinions.' Richardson was stifled by an unquenchable thirst for applause: 'He could not be content to sail gently down the stream of fame unless the foam was continually dashing in his face, that he might taste it at every stroke of the oar . . . that fellow died merely for want of change among his flatterers: he perished for want of *more*, like a man obliged to breathe the same air till it is exhausted.' Richardson, however, was unapologetic, 'My acquaintance lies chiefly among the ladies; I care not who knows it.' The eminent editor and children's author, Anna Letitia Barbauld (1743–1824), put her finger on why Richardson's single essay in the *Rambler* had sold well and Johnson's essays had not, fastening on what she saw as Johnson's obtuseness, his assumption that everyone had to be as 'grave' as he was in his *Rambler* or as serious as in the *Dictionary*: 'The ladies he [Richardson] associated with were well able to appreciate his works. They were both his critics and his models, and from their sprightly conversation, and the disquisitions on love and sentiment, which took place, he gathered what was more to his purpose than graver topics would have produced. He was not writing a dictionary, like Johnson, or a history like Gibbon. He was a novel writer; his business was not only with the human heart, but [also] with the female heart.'[18]

Elizabeth Carter and her friend Catherine Talbot, both of whom contributed essays to the *Rambler*, were two other women who were certain they knew what Johnson needed to do in the *Rambler* to sell more copies. Their chatty letters are especially interesting because they highlight a unique mode of critical idolatry Johnson suddenly found was focused on him by intelligent women after his essays began to appear. One moment he was a 'harmless drudge' secreted in his garret at work on his *Dictionary*, the next a celebrated moralist and essayist who could nonetheless do with a bit of female advice. Talbot felt he needed to include more letters from correspondents and be more deferential towards them, use fewer 'hard' words (a common complaint) such as 'equiponderant' and 'adscititious' (number 20), and attempt 'papers of humour' for which London provided an endless swarm of 'amusing' material: 'odd clubs, advertisements, societies, meetings, and devices of various kinds, which this age produces'. In effect, she wanted the *Rambler* to be more like the *Spectator*. 'Any hint that is known to come from you', she urged Carter, 'will have great weight with the Rambler, if I guess him right, particularly given in that delicate manner you so well understand.'[19]

Perhaps because Elizabeth Carter spoke to him, Mrs Talbot became hopeful that Johnson might surprise them all by introducing 'humorous descriptions of, and reflections on, the London follies and diversions', and reign in his exaggerations: 'Mr Johnson would, I fear, be mortified to hear that people know a paper of his own by the sure mark of somewhat a little excessive, a little exaggerated in the expression.' A case in point was number 59 on Suspirus the 'human screech-owl', a perpetually complaining cynic and malcontent – 'so *many* merchants discouraged, so *many* ladies killed, matches broke, poets dismayed! The numbers are too large, five or six is enough.' If only Elizabeth Carter could have a word with him again: 'I have set my whole heart upon the success of the Rambler (what a noble paper his last [no. 78] upon death)'. She wrote on 17 December 1750, 'You could talk more persuasively to the author than anybody.' He must write more on 'the living manners of the times'. 'I say all this with fear and trembling,' she admitted, for 'humour and manners of the world are not his fort.' What he does excel in are 'the serious papers, that seem to flow from his heart, and from a heart amiable and delicate to a great degree'. When the *Rambler* ended, all was regret and exasperation that the periodical had not matched the *Spectator's* commercial success. Carter was appalled, 'a good deal out of humour with the world, and more particularly with the great and powerful part of it'.[20]

In spite of poor initial sales, the *Rambler* had a considerably wider exposure from the common practice of hundreds of pirated issues of the periodical published in a multitude of journals, magazines and London and provincial newspapers. There were over three hundred reprintings in magazines and over three hundred in provincial newspapers. Editors thought that individual issues made good feature articles. This was not all. Even before Johnson finished writing the essays, the publishers Bouquet and Payne – and Cave also got into the act, for Johnson assigned the copyright over to him in April 1751 and he printed the volumes – began to put together a collected 'correct and beautiful edition' of them in four volumes at twelve shillings, for which Johnson heavily revised the essays. Johnson said he stopped writing them because this edition had mushroomed to six volumes. He revised them for other editors as well in the next four years. Boswell was incredulous when, years later, Johnson told him he still could improve the *Ramblers*, 'But I will, Sir, if I choose. I shall make the best of them you shall pick out, better.' Most readers became familiar with the *Rambler* through these printed editions. Ten in all appeared in Johnson's lifetime, more than twenty by 1800, helping to establish his reputation as the greatest essayist of the age. By the end of the century and throughout the nineteenth century the *Rambler* was more popular even than the *Spectator*.[21]

3

Obviously it is not possible to represent accurately enough the wide range of the *Rambler*'s moral subjects and themes in a few paragraphs. One needs to read all the essays to obtain a sense of their uncanny coherence. A good way to appreciate their weight, moreover, is to connect them to certain stages, conditions and themes in his life, when often what he says is found to be forcefully autobiographical.

In addition to those already mentioned, his subjects and methods include allegory and fictional narratives; literary criticism including essays on the new rage for fiction and a revolutionary one on biography (number 60) which is constantly anthologised; and social reform concerning prisons, orphanages, prostitution, slavery and capital punishment. Among the many moral topics, often constituting thematic clusters, are family tyranny, private and public abuse of authority, women and marriage, envy, happiness, endless incarnations of tormenting self-delusion, tragic waste of time, absurd preoccupation with the future, idleness and procrastination, vanity, grief, melancholia, biography, death, authorship, and the proper responsibilities of the worlds of learning and authorship. An overarching principle embracing Johnson's complex morality in all these essays is that it is no good trying to be virtuous in the abstract, or judging others from 'speculative reason': 'It is not but by experience, that we are taught the possibility of retaining some virtues, and rejecting others, or of being good or bad to a particular degree' (number 7). Complicated human behaviour cannot be reduced to easy choices. Nobody can attain perfection, so to judge others is a dangerous and misguided business.[22]

There is a restless, persistent probing in the typical *Rambler* moral essay, as he took up an idea, explored it from various angles, qualified and amplified it. Very little of the argumentative process is sustained with ref-

erence to Christianity. He kept pushing for human connections and revelations, telling readers about themselves, insisting on honesty (his own
and ours), realism, and truth to experience. Just when the reader thinks
Johnson has dealt with some aspect of an idea and is about to drop it, he
is on his way again, casting yet more light on the dark corners of the mind,
appealing to the uncompromising demands of common sense. He was a
rebel-moralist, overturning and reconstructing. It was all given an inimitable strength by his balanced elegance of style, which is inseparable from
the force and energy of his argument – 'truth is recommended by elegance, and elegance sustained by the truth'. And in spite of frequent complaints about his 'hard' words, it is all kept down to earth by the insistent concreteness of his imagery that matches his practical morality. It is
a humane journey of scepticism and reassuring, if sometimes painful,
moral clarity.

CHAPTER 18

Darkness Falls

I

JOHNSON WROTE ABOUT 170 of the 208 *Rambler* essays while he did nothing on the *Dictionary*. He knew the proprietors were waiting impatiently for him to finish it, but in his anxiety over the huge amount left to be done and what appears to have been a taste of writer's block, he did not return to it until late November 1751, by which time the *Rambler* had only three and a half months left to run. Several of the *Rambler* essays contain clues to his fear, timidity, and deepening angst, to what felt like idleness and was exposing him to melancholia again. In number 134 (29 June 1751), he wrote bleakly: 'Life is languished away in the gloom of anxiety, and consumed in collecting resolution which the next morning dissipates; in forming purposes which we scarcely hope to keep, and reconciling ourselves to our own cowardice by excuses, which, while we admit them, we know to be absurd . . . every submission to our fear enlarges its dominion.' Indecision about how to proceed was paralysing him. If he was going to return to the work, not 'freeze in idleness', clearly it would take a huge display of self-discipline and courage.[1]

A stiff word or two from Strahan on behalf of the other disgruntled proprietors, threatening to cut off money and supplies if he did not get back to work and start sending copy again to the printer, jolted him. After five years of work only 'A', 'B' and a little of 'C' had been printed, and they had been completed several months back. They demanded to meet with him for the purpose of exerting more pressure. Not surprisingly, he did not like their complaints and took his anger out on Strahan in November

1751 with a stinging reply. He would not write if he did not want to – 'I shall *not* write' – nor would he meet with any of them until it suited him: 'my resolution has long been, and is *not* now altered, and is now *less* likely to be altered, that I shall *not* see the Gentlemen Partners till the first volume is in the press', which they may support or not as they liked. And he issued this threat: 'Be pleased to lay this my determination before them this morning, for I shall think of taking my measures accordingly tomorrow morning, only this that I mean no harm, but that my citadel shall not be taken by storm while I can defend it, and that if a blockade is intended, the country is under the command of my batteries.'[2]

2

In the meantime, a new woman came into his life, the novelist and dramatist Charlotte Lennox (1729–1804), who became another in his string of female protégées. Lennox was something of an enigma, definitely an outsider. Though well known for her novels, not much is known of her life. Born probably in Gibraltar, she moved to New York in 1739. Her father was a lieutenant in the British army. When he died in 1743, she emigrated to London where she briefly came under the patronage of Lady Isabella Finch. She had no money there and was in the process of preparing herself for a position at court when, at the age of eighteen, she unwisely married the impoverished and useless Scot Alexander Lennox who worked for Johnson's printer Strahan. He provided no relief from her relative poverty, so she was reduced to trying to make her way as a writer and actress. In 1747 she published *Poems on Several Occasions* which won her some literary attention – Horace Walpole described her as 'a poetess and deplorable actress'; and then in 1750 she came out with her first novel *The Life of Harriot Stuart*, among other things an indictment of the system of patronage.

Johnson had liked her when they met through her husband's connection with Strahan, but when her novel came out he was so taken with it he decided to organise a big dinner party in her honour, 'a whole night spent in festivity', at a meeting of the Ivy Lane Club at the Devil Tavern near

Temple Bar. At eight o'clock Lennox, her shiftless husband, and eighteen others assembled. Hawkins, who was there but did not want to be, described the event: 'Our supper was elegant, and Johnson had directed that a magnificent hot apple pie should make a part of it, and this he would have stuck with bay leaves, because, forsooth, Mrs Lennox was an authoress, and had written verses; and further, he had prepared for her a crown of laurel, with which, but not till he had invoked the muses by some ceremonies of his own invention, he encircled her brows.' The night passed in 'pleasant conversation' and 'harmless mirth'. At five in the morning Johnson was in full stride, his face shining 'with meridian splendour, though his drink had been only lemonade; but the far greater part of us had deserted the colours of Bacchus, and were with difficulty rallied to partake of a second refreshment of coffee, which was scarcely ended when the day began to dawn'. The waiters were all asleep, so nobody could get the reckoning for hours and it was eight before 'the creaking of the street door gave the signal for our departure'. The only sour note was provided by Hawkins himself who wrote that as he walked out the door a 'sensation of shame' overwhelmed him because of the evening's resemblance to 'a debauch'. Hawkins thought Johnson depended on nights like this to drive away melancholia, 'which the public now too well knows was the disease of his mind'. The longer he stayed up, the longer he could delay stepping back into his loneliness at home. Hawkins even maintained that he may have had to stop writing the *Rambler* because its intensity threatened 'the relaxation of his mind'.[3]

Bright young spirits like Charlotte Lennox were good medicine for Johnson. Boswell recorded his comment a few months before his death that of all the young female authors he had known well, she was the one whom he thought was the ablest: 'I dined yesterday at Mrs Garrick's, with Mrs Carter, Miss Hannah More, and Miss Fanny Burney. Three such women are not to be found: I know not where I could find a fourth except Mrs Lennox, who is superior to them all.' It was not, however, a sentiment shared by his other female friends. She was quarrelsome, quick-tempered, and tempestuous, acquiring a reputation for ingratitude. Mrs Thrale once remarked that although Lennox's books were read, 'nobody likes her'. Regardless, Johnson admired her satirical audacity and energy, her independence and status as an outsider. He warmed to *Harriot Stuart* because it was a spoof on the exaggerated romantic expectations of women in heroic romance novels of the day, agreeing with her about the pernicious effects upon young, sensitive minds of such novels featuring heroines who expect 'nothing less than vows, alters, and sacrifices'. He took a detailed interest in her next ironical novel, *The Female Quixote* (1752), a highly successful imitation of Cervantes, spoofing again the young girl who gluts herself on romances and then sets out herself to live in a world of fantasy. He may have written all or part of the penultimate chapter for her, as well as the dedication, and helped her convince Richardson to publish it – 'our Charlotte's book', he called it. When she later bravely faulted Shakespeare in her three-volume *Shakespear Illustrated* (1753–4), a study of Shakespeare's sources, for which he wrote the dedication to the Earl of Orrery, Johnson and Garrick both joked that the book would have been more aptly titled *Shakespeare Exposed*. Johnson wrote to her wryly, with a Miltonic allusion, 'When Shakespeare is demolished your wings will be *full summed* and I will fly you at Milton; for you are a bird of prey, but the bird of Jupiter' – the god of tempests and thunderbolts. At times, however, even he became exasperated when she sprang at him for some imagined offence or insult: 'I wish you would for once resolve to use any method of transacting with your friends but that of letters. You will, in whatever part of the world you may be placed, find mankind extremely impatient of such letters as you are inclined to favour them with . . . I have no inclination to continue quarrels.'[4]

Johnson was the most important person in Lennox's literary life – unlike Elizabeth Carter who once remarked, 'I may make my fortune very prettily as Mrs [Elizabeth] Montagu's owl.' She remained part of, and very familiar with, his professional life for the rest of his days, although her publishing declined after the 1750s and she neither moved in his circles nor had anything to do with the Bluestocking circle of Mrs Montagu within which she might well have prospered. After he died she languished in distress for years with family problems, seeking charity and publishing a final novel in a desperate effort to earn income. She died in 1804. Very regrettably, she never kept a diary or wrote memoirs. If she had, we would surely have a valuable increment to our knowledge of Johnson as a friend and professional man of letters, especially in the 1750s.

3

The combined pressure of renewed penury, his remorse at not working on the *Dictionary* for about two years, together with the complaints of the proprietors, had swollen to such a pitch that by late 1751 Johnson finally had summoned up courage and forced himself to turn his attention to it again. In the next three or four months he appeared to make progress, completing and copying out for the printer words between *Carry* and *Dame* (some fifty sheets), and adding to material for *Dame* to *Kyd*. But it was difficult for him to concentrate and lead a normal life because Tetty's health was rapidly deteriorating. 'Poor Tetty Johnson's illness will not suffer me to think of going any whither, out of her call,' he wrote worriedly to Lennox on 12 March 1752. 'She is very ill, and I am very much dejected'. Then during the night of 17/18 March, only three days after the last *Rambler* and four days after he had presented her with the tender gift of his just-published four-volume edition of the essays, he received the news at Gough Square that her largely unhappy and lonely life since she married him had come to an end at her scruffy, rented lodging in Hampstead in which she had chosen to live the last months of her life.[5]

The effect Tetty's death had on him was profound. It was in many ways a pivotal moment in his life. Perhaps one has to experience the premature death of a spouse or extremely close loved one to appreciate properly the inconsolable grief that overwhelmed him. Immediately, the oppressiveness of loneliness was unbearable. In the anguish of the night he scribbled out a note to Taylor at his house in the Cloisters, Westminster, to come at once. At three in the morning Taylor flew over to Gough Square and found him weeping uncontrollably. The next morning Johnson implored him to come again, 'Let me have your company and your instruction. Do not live away from me. My distress is great.'[6]

Tetty was buried at Bromley in Kent, where John Hawkesworth lived and was able to organise her funeral, but he could not bring himself to attend it, and composed a sermon to be spoken by Taylor which was never delivered. According to Hawkins, who, unlike Boswell, did not hesitate to describe their marriage as largely a failure, he was dissuaded from 'so ostentatious a display of the virtues of a woman, who, though she was his wife, was but little known'. He could not summon up the courage to visit the grave for more than a year. When he got there on Easter Day 1753 he wrapped himself in a tissue of frantic prayers: 'I repeated mentally the commendation of her with utmost fervour . . . before the reception of each element at the altar. I repeated it again in the pew, in the garden before dinner, in the garden before departure, at home at night.' He did not get around to placing a memorial stone of black marble by her grave until shortly before he died, most likely because he could never bring himself to see or even think about the grave. His friend John Ryland, Hawkesworth's brother-in-law, saw to the stone for him. 'Shall I ever be able to bear the sight of this stone?' he asked him. He preferred to reflect on Tetty's continuing blessings on him and whether or not he was worthy of them. In Latin he wrote on the stone, here translated: 'Beautiful, polite, ingenious, pious . . . much loved and long lamented'.[7]

Four prayers crying for God's mercy that he composed between 24 April and 6 May go some way towards conveying his fear of grief and sense of desolation, combined as they were with remorse for not being a better, more patient husband and an abounding guilt over not having used his time better – time he felt should have made Tetty's life happier and more comfortable. He prayed repeatedly to be spared 'fruitless grief' and the pernicious onslaught of 'tumultous imagination' or wayward thoughts. 'Speak peace to my troubled soul,' he pleaded, that his thought might dwell on what made her life 'acceptable' and through the forgiveness of his sins enable him 'to begin and perfect that reformation which I promised her, and to preserve in that resolution, which she implored Thee to continue, in the purposes which I recorded in thy sight, when she lay dead before me'. He wrote these resolutions down and consulted them repeatedly over the next few years in an attempt to live more purely and consistently: 'to rise early', 'to lose no time', and 'to keep a journal'. He even asked God's approval for Tetty's spirit 'to have care of me . . . that I may enjoy the good effects of her attention and ministration, whether exercised by appearance, impulses, dreams'. This was no idle, sentimental prayer, for he did believe in the appearance of spirits, although he was concerned about the potential impiety of doing so.[8]

In his prayer for 6 May, in addition to a futile resolution to leave off grieving and 'return to the duties of my present state', he put his finger on a central problem of his mental health, calling upon 'our heavenly Father' to protect him from the idleness and perpetual 'negligence' that would 'lay me open to vain imaginations'. He became almost obsessive in his prayers against idleness. His verse paraphrase of *Proverbs* 6:6 just a few days after Tetty's death, entitled 'The Ant', pointed to another crisis of paralysis and a fresh chill of horror about lost time:

> How long shall sloth usurp thy useless hours,
> Year chases year, with unremitted flight,
> Till want, now following fraudulent and slow,
> Shall spring to seize thee like an ambush'd foe.

Very soon after Tetty's death he was also surprised to find himself indulging in sexual fantasies. He never referred to them in prayers before her death. These were insistent and would last for years. Lacking a woman in his house and life, even Tetty who had been unavailable to him sexually in the last few years, he prayed relentlessly to be spared these fantasies and the ensuing anguish over sensuality and sin. 'Habitual wickedness and idleness': he tended to lump them together in asking for protection against 'unchastity, idleness, and neglect of public worship', 'vain longings of affection', 'lust', 'sensuality in thought', 'pollutions', 'sinful habits', 'wickedness', 'thoughts clouded with sensuality'. There was, however, no way of beating down these devils. Tetty's death had opened up a sluice-gate for a stream, sometimes torrent, of private guilt and morbidity.[9]

His thoughts also ran to remarriage, which brought with them their unique baggage of guilt. On Easter Day thirteen months following her

death, after having attended the service in Bromley, he wrote: 'As I purpose to try on Monday to seek a new wife without any derogation from
dear Tetty's memory, I purpose at sacrament in the morning to take my
leave of Tetty in a solemn commendation of her soul to God.' On Easter
Monday he was relieved to be able to add, 'During the whole service I was
never once distracted by any thoughts of any other woman or with my design of a new wife which freedom of mind I remembered with gladness in
the garden.'[10]

His grief seemed to his friends all out of proportion with the nature
of the marriage. Hawkins said everyone was mystified that he was 'incapable of consolation' and 'could derive no comfort' from religion, especially
as 'their marriage was not one of those which . . . young people call love-
matches'. 'The melancholy, which seized Johnson,' he added, 'was not,
in degree, such as usually follows the deprivation of near relations and
friends: it was of the blackest and deepest kind.' The quarrelsome Italian
Giuseppe Baretti (1719–89), who knew and became friends with Johnson
perhaps as early as 1751, the year he came to live in England, told Mrs
Thrale that 'when this lady died, Dr Johnson was almost distracted with
his grief; and . . . the friends about him had much ado to calm the violence
of his emotion'. By the time he met Mrs Thrale in the 1760s, Johnson had
escaped the gnawing pain over his loss, but she remarked nonetheless that
'he never rightly recovered the loss of his wife'. In 1778 he said to the
cheerful Oliver Edwards, his old contemporary at Pembroke whom, as he
was walking down a London street with Boswell, he encountered for the
first time in fifty years, 'Sir, I have known what it was to have a wife, and
(in a solemn tender faltering tone) I have known what it was to *lose a wife*.
It had almost broke my heart.' Shaw's description of the effects of Tetty's
death on him was the most compelling: 'Johnson often said he never knew
how dear she was to him, till he lost her. Her death affected him so deeply,
that he grew almost insensible to the common concerns of life. He then
stayed little within, where her image was always recalled by whatever he
heard or saw. Study disgusted him, and the books of all kinds were
equally insipid. He carefully avoided his friends, and associated most with

such company as he never saw before.' He took to walking the streets at night, often with Baretti: 'This for many a lonesome night was his constant substitute for sleep.' For the rest of his life he kept the wedding ring he had given her in a little round wooden box, which after his death his servant Francis Barber offered to Lucy Porter. She declined it.[11]

CHAPTER 19

Once More unto the Breach: Back to the Dictionary

I

ALTHOUGH TETTY HAD SPENT LITTLE TIME at Gough Square in the last months of her life, Johnson now felt the house unbearably empty. Within two weeks of her death he took into his household as servant a Jamaican boy, formerly a slave (called 'Quashey' back home) brought to England by Colonel Richard Bathurst in 1750 and renamed Francis Barber, or 'Frank', as Johnson and everyone else called him. It was through the colonel's son, Johnson's dear friend Richard, that Frank (c. 1742–1801) came into Johnson's life. It appears to have occurred to Richard Bathurst that the boy was perfect for Johnson's hour of need.

Johnson quickly developed an affection for the boy, who was about ten, and in years to come 'whenever disputes arose in his household among the many odd inhabitants of which it consisted, he always sided with Francis against the others'. Mrs Thrale, who with Hawkins and other friends disapproved of Frank's volatility after Johnson died, felt that he 'was scarcely as much the object of Mr Johnson's personal kindness, as the representative of Dr Bathurst, for whose sake he would have loved any body, or any thing'. But Johnson's affection for Frank was beyond doubt, as was the strong bond that was forged between them for the rest of his life, not least on the basis of Johnson's hatred of slavery and his strong support for its abolition. Even more incredible was Mrs Thrale's contention that 'When he spoke of Negroes, he always appeared to think them of a race naturally inferior, and made few exceptions in favour of his own'. On the contrary, it delighted him that Richard Bathurst had inherited no slaves from the colonel and that in his will in April 1754 his father gave Frank his freedom and twelve pounds. This was highly unusual. In 1772 the black British population was about 15,000, most of whom were slaves. Moreover, there was from early in the century a deeply entrenched racism in British culture and politics. Johnson had no truck with this. On one occasion in Oxford in 1777 he expressed his fierce disapproval of slavery by proposing a toast in the company of 'some very grave men' to 'the next insurrection of the Negroes in the West Indies'. As Boswell put it, 'he had always been very zealous against slavery in every form.' 'No man is by nature the property of another,' Johnson wrote. As we shall see, in later years he directed his scorn on this subject at the hypocrisy of the Americans who kept slaves and yet issued the 'loudest yelps for liberty'.[1]

At home in Gough Square in 1752, this boy was a godsend. Frank told Boswell that when he came into Johnson's service he found his master in 'great affliction' from his wife's death. Aware of his desolation, the *Dictionary's* proprietors left him alone for a while. Though there is no doubt that he was completely thrown off his work by Tetty's death, in later years he tended to dismiss the notion that grief such as his could paralyse a writer, thinking it an affectation. George Steevens remembered that when Johnson once was informed of a certain critic's public announcement that he could not bring himself to attack Steevens's work any more because he had suddenly lost his wife, Johnson observed coldly, 'I believe that the loss of teeth may deprive the voice of a singer, and that lameness will impede the motions of a dancing master, but I have not yet been taught to regard the death of a wife as the grave of literary exertions. When my dear Mrs Johnson expired I sought relief in my studies, and strove to lose the recollection of her in the toils of literature'. This was, however, after months of mourning, and according to Steevens it was then only in his garret that he could do anything: 'After her death, though he had a whole house at command, he would study nowhere but in a garret. Being asked the reason why he chose a situation so incommodious, he answered, "because in that room only I never saw Mrs Johnson".'[2]

2

In November the wheels began to turn again. It may have been John Hawkesworth who got him moving by establishing a new twice-weekly periodical, *The Adventurer*, in November 1752. Johnson did not begin to contribute essays to it until the following March, but he helped Hawkesworth think through the scheme and agreed to contribute a Latin motto (with translation) for each of the numbers. Boswell stressed that Hawkesworth helped Johnson take his mind off his grief in this way as well as relieve the drudgery of the *Dictionary* once he started working on it again in earnest. Hawkesworth's idea was for a periodical containing essays about grave moral issues but also, in Johnson's words, lighter 'pieces of imagination, pictures of life', appealing to a wider readership. At first Hawkesworth and another anonymous contributor carried it, but his helper faltered and by the spring he needed Johnson to come to his rescue. Johnson agreed to contribute essays regularly. The paper paid two guineas per essay.[3]

The arrangement was that Hawkesworth would write forty-six, and Johnson and Joseph Warton (Thomas's elder brother) twenty-three each, though Johnson ended up writing twenty-nine and may have been tempted to write more except that the *Dictionary* beckoned and he was loath again to 'condemn himself to compose on a stated day'. The intervals between his essays vary between one and seven days, five being the most common. He also wanted Richardson and perhaps Elizabeth Carter to pitch in, but neither of them 'found the leisure' to contribute anything. The edition continued for 140 numbers and concluded in March 1754, with Johnson's last essay (number 138) appearing on 2 March.[4]

His friendship with the Wartons was not one of undiluted mutual admiration. Joseph Warton said that he and Johnson had 'contracted close friendship' in the autumn of 1752 and that he was 'quite intimate' with him. Johnson did at first reciprocate fully, 'I enter my name among those that love [you]', he wrote to him in March 1754. Warton was a clergyman and schoolmaster and would become Headmaster of Winchester College in 1766 for a long run of almost thirty years. Thomas became Oxford Professor of Poetry in 1757 and Poet Laureate in 1785. His greatest achievement was his *History of English Poetry* (1774–81), the first comprehensive assessment or 'ordering' of the subject ever written. Visited by Johnson often in Oxford over the years, he was a closer and more sympathetic friend to Johnson than his brother the headmaster, and was more of a kindred spirit. Johnson found neither of them communicative enough, however. 'A little, thick, squat, red-faced man', Thomas seemed to him cold: 'Johnson has been known to declare in terms of severity . . . that Tom Warton was the only man of genius, whom he knew, without a heart'. 'Your brother . . . is a better correspondent than you,' Johnson rebuked him. 'You might write to me now and then, if you were good for any thing. But . . . professors forget their friends'. As for Joseph, when he published the first volume of his important *Essay on the Writings and Genius of Pope* in April 1756, Johnson was put out that he had not mentioned anything of it to him in advance: 'When you and your brother were in town you did not think my humble habitation worth a visit . . . That way of publishing without acquainting your friends is a wicked trick.' He is once supposed to have said, 'I wonder that Joe Warton, a scholar by profession, should be such a fool.'[5]

Johnson needed the two guineas for each *Adventurer* paper but may have kept little or none of the money for himself. His friend Bathurst had fallen on hard times as a physician and apparently needed money even more than he did. Boswell recorded that, according to the blind poet Anna Williams who in 1754 appears to have taken up residence at Gough Square, Johnson dictated his essays to his friend who then could say he had written them and be paid for the effort: 'As he had *given* those essays to Dr Bathurst, who sold them at two guineas each, he never would own them; nay, he used to say he did not *write* them: but the fact was, that he *dictated* them, while Bathurst wrote.' Boswell said that when he read to Johnson what she had said, 'he smiled, and said nothing'. 'As his purse was ever open to almsgiving,' wrote Mrs Thrale, 'so was his heart tender to

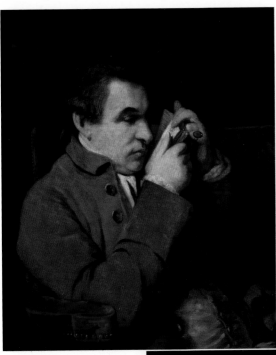

Giuseppe Baretti, after Joshua Reynolds. A quarrelsome and even violent man, the Italian Baretti was a linguist, translator, travel writer and member of the Club.

James Boswell at twenty-five, painted by George Willison in Italy while he was on his Grand Tour in 1765, during which he occasionally corresponded with his famous friend Johnson.

Mrs Hester Lynch Thrale and her daughter Queeney, by Joshua Reynolds, *c.*1779. With Mrs Thrale Johnson enjoyed a deeper if unsettled intimacy than with anyone else.

Streatham Place, the Thrales' home in Southwark which for almost twenty years served Johnson as a second home. It sometimes irritated Johnson's friends that they could not find him because he was at Streatham.

Samuel Johnson in the late 1760s, by Joshua Reynolds. He appears to be gesticulating awkwardly with his hands, in deep thought and in a manner described by Frances Reynolds 'as if he had been seized with cramp'.

Oliver Goldsmith,
Johnson's dear friend, by
Joshua Reynolds, *c.*1770.

James Boswell in middle age,
pencil sketch by Sir Thomas
Lawrence. His tour of the
Hebrides with Johnson in the
autumn of 1773 was one of the
great events of Johnson's life.

The Turk's Head tavern on Gerrard Street, Soho, where the famous Club first began to hold its meetings in 1764 with nine members. It met once a week at seven, later once a fortnight.

Samuel Johnson (centre), Oliver Goldsmith and Mrs Thrale at Streatham Place. Pen and ink drawing, early 1770s.

Anna Williams, Johnson's blind and quarrelsome housekeeper and member of his household on and off for more than thirty years, by Frances Reynolds. When she died, Johnson was devastated.

ABOVE: Charlotte Lennox, author and poet, whom Johnson once described as 'superior to them all'.

Detail from *Mr & Mrs Garrick Taking Tea Upon the Lawn of Their Villa at Hampton* by Zoffany, 1762. It may be Johnson who is seated on the left and who is said to have remarked, 'It is the leaving of such places that makes a death-bed terrible'.

FACING PAGE: *The Nine Living Muses of Great Britain* by Richard Samuel, 1778. The figures include Elizabeth Carter, Anna Laetitia Barbauld, Catherine Macaulay, Elizabeth Montagu and Hannah More.

The so-called 'Streatham' portrait of Johnson, by Reynolds, *c.*1773.

those who wanted relief. He gave away all he had, and all he had ever gotten, except the two thousand pounds he left behind.' And Murphy noted, 'It has been truly said that the lame, the blind, and the sorrowful, found in his house a sure retreat.' Bathurst lingered on in London, failing as a doctor, until January 1757 when he moved to Barbados. He died of a fever in Havana while serving as physician on the British naval expedition against Cuba during the Seven Years' War. For years Johnson continued to remember Bathurst in his prayers.[6]

Johnson initially did not reveal he was the author of any of these essays, identifying them merely with a 'T'. Warton, Hawkesworth and other contributors used other letters to conceal their authorship as well. Almost everyone was fooled, although Richardson was among several who noticed a resemblance of style between those written by 'T' and the *Rambler* essays. Catherine Talbot was on the right track in a letter to Elizabeth Carter in January 1753, 'I discern Mr Johnson through all the pages that are not marked A, as evidently as if I saw him through the keyhole with the pen in his hand.' When Hill Boothby, perceiving Johnson's hand in them, asked him outright about them, at first he was silent. After she persisted, he finally admitted writing them, to which she replied, 'I wonder not at your hesitating to impart a secret to a woman; but am the more obliged to you for communicating it as a secret, after so hesitating. Such a mark of your deliberate confidence shall be strictly regarded; and I shall seek for letter T, that I may read with *redoubled* pleasure.'[7]

3

The *Adventurer* with its multiple authorship proved to be a greater commercial success than the *Rambler*, partly because the *Rambler* had prepared the way for it and partly because its essays were lighter and more diverse. 'I like the *Adventurers*,' Talbot informed Carter, 'we all like them exceedingly; and I fancy they will soon become very fashionable . . . They do not abound in hard words, they are varied with a thousand amusing stories, they touch with humour on the daily follies and peculiarities of the times.' Realising after the *Rambler* that if he were ever to be involved in another periodical he would have to write essays easier to read, Johnson wrote this new batch with larger brush strokes for more casual readers. But he was no less indignant in exposing human flaws and vices. If anything, his language is even more strident. Several of them are also quite bleak.

His essays cover a few of the subjects and themes he had already written about in the *Rambler*, several of them under the general moral theme of vanity and its dangers: flattery, lying, learning, retirement, egocentricity, complacency, the 'contagion of desire', happiness, and the pride of 'singularity' or thinking of yourself as the exception to the rules that bind the rest of mankind. Writing with an autobiographical edge, he urged that life is a warfare and one must fight the good fight, although there is no assurance of victory either for the mind or soul: 'To strive with difficulties, and to conquer them, is the highest human felicity; the next, is to strive and deserve to conquer.'

Predictably, he devoted *Rambler* 39 to sleep and how life without enough of it is unendurable: 'A perpetual vigil [at night] will appear to be a state of wretchedness ... Sleep is necessary to the happy, to prevent satiety and to endear life by a short absence; and to the miserable, to relieve them by intervals of quiet.' He often complained of nights of fitful sleep, when his imagination would run rampant and like a mole burrow away at him, unearthing hidden fears. As a result he would sleep late. 'I do not remember that since I left Oxford I ever rose early by mere choice, but once or twice at Edial, and two or three times for the *Rambler*,' he entered in his diary in 1753.[8]

Authorship is a subject to which he turned with the scars of his own struggles on Grub Street. Is a life of writing of any real use and does it bring happiness to an author? The last two of his essays are about this (numbers 137 and 138), the first of which he launched with a motto from Pythagoras, 'What have I been doing?' How worthwhile can the *Adventurer*, or any other kind of writing for that matter, really be? 'Much of my time has sunk into nothing, and left no trace by which it can be distinguished, and of this I now only know, that it was once in my power and might once have been improved.' As for the *Adventurer*, he has had good intentions but wonders 'what has been the consequence of my labours', and whether the hours spent on them have been to 'good and laudatory purpose' or 'suffered to fume away in useless evaporations'. 'That the world has grown apparently better, since the publication of the *Adventurer*, I have not observed', he concluded, but perhaps some readers have caught some benefits from 'single sentiments'.[9]

His last essay on authors describes the personal suffering, isolation, self-deprivation and loneliness in a life of writing: 'Composition is, for the most part, an effort of slow diligence and steady perseverance, to which the mind is dragged by necessity or resolution, and from which the attention is every moment starting to more delightful amusements.' Moreover, just because a writer has worthwhile ideas does not mean he is going to find the words for them. Every writer at times finds himself 'deficient in the power of expression . . . obliged to ransack his memory for terms adequate to his conceptions, and at last unable to impress upon his reader the image existing in his own mind'.[10] The writer's lot is 'study and vexation', a private hell of incarceration within the four walls of his study or garret.

4

In November 1752 he knew he had to get back to the grind of the *Dictionary*. The proprietors could not tolerate any more delays. By then he had been working on it for six years and reached only as far as the word *dame*. The gravity of the moment was reflected in a prayer he composed at the start of the month titled, 'Before Any New Study', asking God to help him 'shun sloth and negligence' and keep him from lavishing away his time on 'useless trifles' and wasting his talents on 'searches after things which thou hast hidden from me'.[11]

By 3 April 1753 he had completed the first volume, leaving space in it for the preface and history of English grammar which he had not yet begun, and was moving into the second volume. At this point he began to work incredibly fast. Within the next eighteen months he completed the rest of the text, an astonishing eighty per cent of the whole book, with only Peyton and Alexander Macbean to assist him. Completing the text by late spring 1754, he was now able to devote himself almost entirely to proofreading and therefore dramatically increase the rate of printing the work.[12]

Such rapid progress was made possible by his new method. To begin with, he needed to decide what to do with the manuscript notebooks he had abandoned for letters A, B and the first part of C. Since the chaos of these manuscripts made them useless as printer's copy, he began by marking them up with revisions to be transcribed by Peyton and Macbean, shaping it in the way he wished it to appear in the book. In loose sheets, not in disastrously confining notebooks such as he had first used, they wrote down the entry-words, etymologies, definitions, illustrations, and anything else he had written in the old notebooks, leaving spaces for him to introduce additional information later. In the process Johnson also trimmed many of the illustrative quotations. He made these deletions on the manuscript itself, after which the amanuenses copied the cropped quotations directly on to the sheets. It all became more compact and clear. Many of the original entries, however, especially under A, tended to remain encyclopedic in content because he had too little time to keep working on them, or to tailor the quotations further.[13]

His progress became steady and more efficient with entries beginning with C, which were shorter, but the real retrenchment began with D. He abridged the illustrative quotations chosen for inclusion and shaped them to fit smoothly in entries after being transcribed from source texts. He continued to gather new ones to fill in gaps, but just about all of them for volume II had already been marked in books and transcribed by March 1753. This was crucial for rapid progress because he could now focus on preparing text and proofing copy. Similarly, Peyton and Macbean could now prepare copy for the printer more quickly because they no longer had to divide their time between that and transcribing quotes on to slips. He himself was humming along and, to the delight of Strahan and the proprietors, was for a change actually composing copy faster than it was being printed. He was also producing printer's copy that was manageable and easier to read, in spite of the sloppy copying that Peyton and Macbean often produced in an effort, as Johnson put it, 'to get to the end of a day's work'. 'One cannot always be on the watch,' he defended himself to Strahan. As for writing the text of the entries, he neared the end of that process by late spring 1754, when he was also revising the *Adventurer* and *Rambler* essays for new editions. He had been composing at the rapid rate of fifty-four to seventy pages per week. Probably by agreement with Strahan, he completed the whole of the manuscript for volume II before handing it over in May 1754. Typesetting and proofing then began and printing was completed in March 1755.[14]

Once he had handed over all the copy, Johnson was free (except for proofing) to prepare the collected edition of the *Rambler* in June and travel to Oxford in July to do extensive research in the Bodleian for his Preface, 'History of the English Language', and 'Grammar of the English Tongue'. His work 'now draws towards its end', he informed Thomas Warton on 16 July 1754, but he could not finish it 'without visiting the libraries of Oxford' in a couple of weeks: 'I know not how long I shall stay or where I shall lodge, but shall be sure to look for you at my arrival.' For his long five weeks there he lodged at Kettel Hall, near Trinity. The visit was more of an escape than a research trip, more social pleasure than drudgery. Warton told Boswell, 'he collected nothing in the libraries for his *Dictionary*'.[15]

He spent much of the time with Warton at Trinity and paying visits to other colleges. Their visit to Pembroke was a disappointment. Warton recalled that 'the master did not choose to talk on the subject [of the *Dictionary*], never asked Johnson to dine, nor even to visit him, while he stayed at Oxford. After we had left the lodgings, Johnson said to me, "*There* lives a man, who lives by the revenues of literature, and will not move a finger to support it. If I come to live at Oxford, I shall take up my abode at Trinity."' One day they walked out to the village of Elsfield, three miles out of town, to visit the Revd Francis Wise, the Radclivian librarian and Keeper of the Archives at Oxford, whose superb library of Northern literature, a 'nest of British and Saxon Antiquities', Johnson perhaps intended to, but appears not to, have used in researching the preliminary material for the *Dictionary*. In a different key, there was the pleasure of meeting Mary Jones, an 'ingenious poetess and . . . a most sensible, agreeable, and amiable woman' who 'was often of our parties'. Johnson took to calling her the 'Chantress' because she was the sister of the Chantor of Christ Church Cathedral at Oxford. A new world of friendships had opened up for him at Oxford, and he was loath to return to London to pick up the hard work of proofing copy.[16]

But return he did. Strahan's presses kept churning out the proofs rapidly and he had some catching up to do. More than just checking for printing errors, he was also altering quotations and definitions and rearranging text on a large scale. It was now he who was cracking the whip, and Strahan was not slow to respond. Everyone involved in the project was now bearing down hard. He composed most if not all of his Preface, 'History' and 'Grammar' in the autumn. The latter two he wrote carelessly and perfunctorily, impatient with them as hurdles over which he still needed to jump to conclude this massive work.[17]

The Preface was a different matter and revealed a great deal about him personally. What makes it such a powerful statement is that he invoked his own emotions and experience in explaining to the reader what he, as a mere mortal, has had to go through to produce this work.[18]

His strategy in the Preface was conventional in that it is an *apologia* for what he has done, a way of anticipating and deflecting criticism. But it is also a remarkably honest and moving personal revelation, although prefaces to dictionaries were often personal, even lugubrious – a tradition reaching back to the Renaissance. His own life, he confessed, especially in the nine years since he launched himself into treacherous lexicographical waters, had been an allegory of triumph and despair, hope and defeat in 'this gloom of solitude'. Art is long and life is short. He had discovered that lexicographers are 'unhappy mortals' who rather than 'aspire to praise' can 'only hope to escape reproach': 'When first I engaged in this work, I resolved to leave neither words nor things unexamined, and pleased myself with a prospect of the hours which I should revel away in feasts of literature ... and the triumph with which I should display my acquisitions to mankind ... But these were the dreams of a poet doomed at last to wake a lexicographer ... I saw ... that to pursue perfection, was, like the first inhabitants of Arcadia, to chase the sun, which, when they had reached the hill where he seemed to rest, was still beheld at the same distance from them . . . much of my life has been lost under the pressure of disease; much has been trifled away . . . a whole life cannot be spent upon syntax and etymology.' He had been on his own, 'with little assistance of the learned, and without any patronage of the great; not in the soft obscurities of retirement, or under the shelter of academic bowers, but amidst inconvenience and distraction, in sickness and in sorrow'. And it had taken so long that much of the pleasure from publication had perished with several of those dear to him: 'I have protracted my work till most of those whom I wished to please, have sunk into the grave, and success and miscarriage are empty sounds: I therefore dismiss it with frigid tranquillity, having little to fear from censure or from praise.' That last sentence was putting a brave face on it. He had much to fear.[19]

It was an enormous boost to his confidence that just before publication he was awarded what he had long coveted. He had no academic credentials, yet his credibility as the author of what he and the publishers hoped would be Britain's most celebrated *Dictionary*, as well as the book's saleability, must surely suffer without them. He very likely hinted something of this to Warton and Wise in Oxford, who talked about it and decided there was still time for a degree to be conferred on him before publication, 'that he may be able to write himself A. M. in the title page'. By 21 December the deal was virtually done. 'I will keep back the title page for such an insertion as you seem to promise me,' he informed Warton. 'I have mentioned it to none of my friends,' he wisely added, 'for fear of being laughed at for my disappointment.' There were frustrating and anxious delays but on 25 February 1755, he opened his front door at Gough Square and received Dr William King, Principal of St Mary Hall, who came bearing the gift of the diploma itself. In recommending the degree to the university, the Chancellor, the Earl of Arran, had praised him in terms that healed Oxford wounds long open: he had 'very eminently distinguished himself by the publication of a series of essays [*The Rambler*], excellently calculated to form the manners of the people, and in which the cause of religion and morality is every where maintained by the strongest powers of argument and language; and . . . shortly intends to publish a

Dictionary of the English Tongue, formed on a new plan, and executed with the greatest labour and judgement'. The public would now begin to know him as 'The Rambler' and 'Dictionary Johnson'. A few days after the news, the title page was run off with the letters 'A. M.' after his name.[20]

5

This was heady stuff, though it was soured by the unhappy news that Dodsley, his literary confidante, had suddenly lost his own wife. He felt his friend's pain far more than most, confiding in Warton, 'I hope he will not suffer so much as I yet suffer for the loss of mine', and adding a passage that revealed the depths of his own continuing grief, as if he were looking in at his own life through a window from the cold outside: 'I have ever since seemed to myself broken off from mankind a kind of solitary wanderer in the wild of life, without any certain direction, or fixed point of view. A gloomy gazer on a world to which I have little relation.'[21]

On the threshold of unimaginable fame, his heart also went out to two melancholic poets. William Collins (1721–50), whose lyrically intense poetry in the 1740s helped redefine English poetry in the second half of the century, had attended Winchester College where he met and shared poems with Joseph Warton, and then proceeded to Oxford where as a precocious student at Johnson's own college, Pembroke, he published his *Persian Eclogues*. Johnson met him in 1744 when Collins was trying to scrape together an existence in London; after that, he kept track of him through the Wartons. In around 1750, Collins began to suffer from depressive melancholia, a 'dreadful malady' for which he was shut up in a madhouse in Chelsea. 'I knew him a few years ago,' Johnson told Joseph Warton, 'full of hopes and full of projects, versed in many languages, high in fancy, and strong in retention.' Now his 'busy and forcible mind' had fallen into an abyss which, for much of his own adult life, Johnson feared might be his own fate. By 1754 'poor dear Collins' was living with his sister in Chichester. 'Would a letter give him any pleasure', Johnson asked Thomas Warton, 'I have a mind to write.' He did write but the letter has not survived; if it were found, it would surely provide further fascinating insight into the terrors of melancholia. Collins never replied, so far as we know, and Johnson was left to reflect on the vulnerability of the human mind in a letter to Joseph Warton: 'The moralists all talk of the uncertainty of fortune, and the transitoriness of beauty; but it is yet more dreadful to consider that the powers of the mind are equally liable to change, that understanding may make its appearance and depart, that it may blaze and expire'. 'Madmen are all sensual in the lower stages of the distemper,' he said to Boswell. 'They are eager for gratifications to sooth their minds'. 'I have often been near his state, and therefore have it in great commiseration.'[22]

After Collins died in 1759 at thirty-eight, Johnson sketched out a 'character' of his life for a collection of his verse in 1763, which he used later as the nucleus for his 'Life of William Collins'. He could be writing about himself as he touched on Collins's rough London days, 'A man, doubtful of his dinner, or trembling at a creditor, is not much disposed to abstracted meditation or remote enquiries . . . About this time I fell into his company . . . By degrees I gained his confidence; and one day was admitted to him when he was immured by a bailiff that was prowling in the street.' It was probably Johnson who helped Collins on that occasion escape prison by promptly persuading a publisher to pay him an advance for a promised literary work, much as he would do for his friend Oliver Goldsmith. But 'man is not born for happiness,' he wrote, and there was little more he could do. 'His disorder was not alienation of mind, but general laxity and feebleness, a deficiency rather of his vital than intellectual powers.' Boswell thought Johnson's account of 'the melancholy depression with which Collins was severely afflicted, and which brought him to his grave' was 'one of the most tender and interesting passages in the whole series of his writings'.[23]

The other mentally troubled poet was Christopher Smart (1722–71), who had recently hatched a plan to publish a periodical journal, *The Universal Visiter*, in collaboration with the miscellaneous writer Richard Rolt. Johnson met him through Arthur Murphy and had earlier written the 'Life of Cheyne' (1751), a Presbyterian who was President of St John's College, Oxford, for Smart's magazine, *The Student*. Smart's dilemma was that he was going mad at the time with a religious mania showing itself in an obsessive need for constant prayer. It was an affliction with which Johnson instinctively identified. When Smart for a short time was incarcerated in St Luke's Hospital, out of 'compassionate regard' Johnson stepped in to write at least three essays in the short lifespan (twelve issues) of Smart's new journal: 'I wrote for some months in "The Universal Visiter", for poor Smart, while he was mad,' he stated, 'not then knowing the terms on which he was engaged to write, and thinking I was doing him good. I hoped his wits would soon return to him. Mine returned to me, and I wrote in "The Universal Visiter" no longer.' Boswell tells of an exchange he heard between Burney and Johnson about Smart's insanity a few years later, by which time the poet had been locked up in a private madhouse in Bethnal Green for four years. When Burney asked for the latest about Smart, Johnson replied, 'It seems as if his mind had ceased to struggle with the disease; for he grows fat upon it . . . I did not think he ought to be shut up. His infirmities were not noxious to society. He insisted on people praying with him; and I'd as lief pray with Kit Smart as any one else.' He added as an afterthought, 'Another charge was, that he did not love clean linen; and I have no passion for it.' Smart was committed for debt to the King's Bench prison in 1770 and died there a year later, for the most part forgotten until the twentieth century in spite of having composed superb religious poetry like *A Song to David* while he was in the madhouse.[24]

6

Johnson was nervous as he awaited publication of the *Dictionary*. 'I now begin to see land, after having wandered . . . in this vast sea of words. What reception I shall meet with upon the shore I know not, whether the sound of bells and acclamations of the people . . . or a general murmur of dislike.' He was ready for criticism, though, and if it came at him like Polyphemus he would 'have at his eyes', he said, ignoring for the sake of the proverbial phrase the fact that Cyclops had only one eye. He knew himself and his combative spirit: 'I am a little afraid of myself, and would not willingly feel so much ill will in my bosom as literary quarrels are apt to excite'. This apprehensiveness was well founded. When his supposed 'patron' Lord Chesterfield, on hearing that the *Dictionary* was soon to be published, rushed into print with two puffs for it in the periodical *The World* (nos. 100 and 101), condescendingly praising Johnson, parading his own superficial and trivial knowledge of the language, and generally revealing a lack of understanding of Johnson's work, he struck at him with a frontal attack much as he promised he would fly at Polyphemus, in one of the most celebrated letters in English literary history. Chesterfield was too late and his casual return to the role of Johnson's patron was insufferable. Chesterfield had ignored both him and the project for nine years. Now on the eve of publication he was trying to move on to centre stage with Johnson. Johnson was furious. 'I have sailed a long and painful voyage round the world of the English language,' he said to Garrick, 'and does he now send out two cock-boats to tow me into harbour?' It was additionally galling that Dodsley, who was interested in sales, had plans to promote this intolerable fiction. He had to act immediately.[25]

Boswell went to considerable trouble to recover the letter from Johnson himself, who dictated it from memory in 1781 with 'an animated glow in his countenance' as he recalled his 'high-minded indignation'. In it he unloaded decades of bitter frustration and anger over his neglected genius and poured out his grudge that when Chesterfield had a chance to help him after Tetty died he did not. It is a letter professors love to introduce to their students as one of history's greatest and most public snubs:

> I have been lately informed by the proprietor of *The World* that two papers in which my Dictionary is recommended to the public were written by your lordship. To be so distinguished is an honour which, being very little accustomed to favours from the Great, I know not well how to receive, or in what terms to acknowledge.
>
> When upon some slight encouragement I first visited your lordship I was overpowered like the rest of mankind by the enchantment of your address, and could not forbear to wish that I might boast myself Le Vainqueur du Vainqueur de la Terre, that I

might obtain that regard for which I saw the world contending, but I found my attendance so little encouraged, that neither pride nor modesty would suffer me to continue it. When I had once addressed your lordship in public, I had exhausted all the art of pleasing which a retired and uncourtly scholar can possess. I had done all that I could, and no man is well pleased to have his all neglected, be it ever so little.

Seven years, my lord[,] have now past since I waited in your outward rooms or was repulsed from your door, during which time I have been pushing on my work through difficulties of which it is useless to complain, and have brought it at last to the verge of publication without one act of assistance, one word of encouragement, or one smile of favour. Such treatment I did not expect, for I never had a patron before.

. . . Is not a patron, my lord, one who looks with unconcern on a man struggling for life in the water and when he has reached ground encumbers him with help. The notice which you have been pleased to take of my labours, had it been early, had been kind; but it has been delayed till I am indifferent and cannot enjoy it, till I am solitary and cannot impart it, till I am known and do not want it.

I hope it is no very cynical asperity not to confess obligation where no benefit has been received, or to be unwilling that the public should consider me as owing that to a patron, which Providence has enabled me to do for myself.[26]

The letter was more than a mere personal rebuff. It has been said that when Boswell first published it the year before the *Life of Johnson* (in which it also appeared), it tolled the death of literary patronage in England. One critic has described it as 'the Magna Carta of the modern author, the public announcement that the days of courtly letters were at last ended'. It was an important skirmish in 'a dramatic power struggle for control of the language': the old polite world of letters pitted against 'living speech' of writers who wished chiefly to communicate and explore. In the almost ten years of work on the *Dictionary* Johnson had left well behind him both Chesterfield and the accepted notion that linguistic authority was invested in a privileged social class. He had none of the patience left that he mustered when, at Dodsley's request, he submitted to Chesterfield at the start. Other writers, too, were demonstrating in the hothouse of professional letters and the print revolution that the Chesterfields and their class were become irrelevant to language and letters: 'There is no absolute language, no ideal meanings for words, no set of eternal rules governing form and development of languages.' The 'King's English' had been democratised into the 'Authors' English'. Johnson's *Dictionary* was nothing if not revolutionary in this respect; his lexicographical vision was almost prophetic, neither conservative nor traditionalist. He and other good writers, not Chesterfield, were authorising the language. Who was Chesterfield anyway? As Johnson openly announced, he was not 'a Lord among wits; but only a wit among Lords'. His definition of 'patron' revealed the extent of his personal animus: 'Commonly a wretch who supports with insolence, and is paid with flattery'. In a revision of *The Vanity of Human Wishes* in 1755, he also changed the word 'garret' to 'patron' as one of the pernicious evils along with toil, envy, want and jail set to ambush the young scholar or writer.[27]

On a personal level, Johnson was indeed now known and did not need Chesterfield, but on 1 March in a pre-publication effort to promote sales, and now fully aware of Johnson's anger over Chesterfield's attempt to win credit as a good patron where no credit was due, Dodsley distributed free of charge 1,500 copies of Johnson's *Plan* with the address to Chesterfield now almost ten years old. That was what the general public saw. Chesterfield knew, though, that more privately a number of influential people were aware of, or actually had read, Johnson's stinging letter to him. So he may have tried to make the best of the situation and perhaps save face. The story got around, in fact, true or not, that he himself was so proud of being the target of such a consummate snub that he left a copy of the letter lying around in his house for visitors to read. His literary hauteur may not have let him acknowledge defeat. It is just as conceivable, of course, that Johnson, greatly incensed, saw to it that various people read his letter.

Johnson's boat finally made it safely to the shore when he sent his messenger to Andrew Millar with the last proofed sheet in April. Millar was not reticent in expressing himself when he received it: 'Thank God, I have done with him.' When the messenger later told Johnson what he said, he replied with a smile, 'I am glad that he thanks God for any thing.' The *Dictionary* was published on 15 April 1755, available in two folio volumes running to more than 2,500 pages in two columns at a price of £4. 10s. Strahan printed 2,000 copies. The volumes weighed twenty pounds, unwieldy for just about everyone, 'proud in its prodigious bulk', as he boasted to Thomas Warton. According to Hawkins, Johnson had received a total of at least £1,575, more than his contract stipulated, in fact, and although he may have hoped that the publishers would give him some more as some sort of bonus out of gratitude, he was disappointed when he learned that because of the work having stretched to nine years their own expenses had well exceeded their expectations and they were not about to give him any more.[28]

The reviews on the whole were extremely good. The *Public Advertiser* on 10 October even published a remark by the President of the Accademia della Crusca, the Marquis Nicolini, who had been presented with a copy by the Earl of Orrery, that the work would be 'a perpetual monument of fame to the author, an honour to his country in particular, and a general benefit to the republic of letters throughout all Europe'. Adam Smith recommended it in the *Edinburgh Review* (June 1755) as the best to be had, though he thought the definitions were somewhat chaotic and that there should be more from the author prescribing usage. Many reviews patriotically bore witness to the huge scale of Johnson's achievement for the glory of Britain. The poet Christopher Smart wrote nine months after publication that he looked on the *Dictionary* as he did St Paul's Cathedral: 'each the work of *one* man, each the work of an *Englishman*'. And Garrick composed a patriotically back-thumping poem on the occasion of the work's completion in which the last two lines read, 'And Johnson, well-arm'd like a hero of yore,/Has beat forty French, and will beat forty more'. The patriotic theme, repeated for decades in an increasingly jingoistic manner, was one that Johnson himself struck in his Preface: 'I have devoted this book, the labour of years, to the honour of my country, that we may no longer yield the palm of philology to the nations of the continent. The chief glory of every people arises from its authors.'[29]

He happily announced to Thomas Warton in June that the work 'sells well', but because of its price and unwieldy size it did not. Efforts to promote sales through publishing schemes did little better until a considerably condensed abridgement in a cheaper two-volume octavo third edition was published in January 1756 at ten shillings, one-ninth of the original price. All five thousand copies of that sold in the next four years; and other editions in 1760, 1766 and 1770 each sold a further five thousand. In 1773, Johnson came out with his extensively revised fourth edition in folio, for which he was handsomely paid £300 (about £30,000 today).

7

Much attention has been given to several of Johnson's humorous, idiosyncratic, overly wordy, personally charged, biased, self-deprecating definitions which have given the *Dictionary* a sensational and bizarre reputation and made it useful fodder for after-dinner talks and lively conversation. Many of them have gained currency in our language because they trip off the tongue easily and are perfectly shaped for one-liners and quick, witty effects. Johnson remarked that the definitions are 'that part of my work on which I expect malignity most frequently to fasten', partly because of mistakes, such as his definition of *pastern* as the 'knee of an horse' when it is in fact part of the foot. People seemed to make a sport of finding errors, though he was unflappable in the face of them. When a woman asked him how he came to get *pastern* wrong, Johnson (according to Boswell's embellishment) simply shrugged, 'Ignorance, Madam, pure ignorance.' He also expected criticism from 'critics of the coffee house', because many of the definitions are strongly opinionated, facetious, or malicious, such as: *Tory* ('one who adheres to the ancient constitution of the state, and the apostolical hierarchy of the church of England'), *Whig* ('the name

of a faction'), *party* ('a faction'), *pension* ('in England it is generally understood to mean pay given to a state hireling for treason to his country'),
freethinker ('a libertine'), *oats* ('a grain, which in England is generally given
to horses, but in Scotland supports the people'), *enthusiasm* ('a vain belief
of private revelation; a vain confidence of divine favour or communication'), *poetaster* ('a vile petty poet'), *stockjobber* (or stockbroker, 'a low
wretch who gets money by buying and selling shares in the funds'), *fox-
hunter* ('a man whose chief ambition is to show his bravery in hunting
foxes'), *excise* ('a hateful tax levied upon commodities, and adjudged not by
the common judges of property, but wretches hired by those to whom excise is paid'), and *dedication* ('a servile address to a patron'). There is
enough in that short list to have angered quite a cross-section of British
society. But, of course, they are an infinitesimal few among thousands.

He suspected that his tendency to wordy definitions, sometimes leaving the reader not much the wiser, would also subject him to ridicule. A
famous example is *network*: 'any thing reticulated, or decussated, at equal
distances, with interstices between the intersections'. Was a recent journalist inspired by this definition when explaining that the tennis professional Guillermo Vilas bore a thirty-year-old grudge against fellow-com-
petitor Ilie Nastase for defeating him with 'a spaghetti string racket that
imparted all manner of odd spins with its pattern of non-intersecting
strings on independent planes'? Another is *cough*: 'a convulsion of the
lungs, vellicated by some sharp serosity'.

He also knew he would be mocked for his huge selection of 'hard' or
out-of-the-way foreign and obsolete words. One waggish commentator
once remarked that Johnson wrote the *Rambler* to make the *Dictionary*
necessary and the *Dictionary* to explain the *Rambler*. A few examples from
the *Dictionary*: *dealbation, digladiation, dodecatemorion, enneatical, slubber-
degullion, immarcescible, impennous, repullulate, sciomachy, captation, tenti-
ginous, conterraneous, dapatical, fabaceous, furacious,* and *gemelliparous*. Johnson loved them. A popular pastime was to look up words to see if Johnson
included them, and if not, to roll one's head in disbelief. Catherine Talbot
wrote smugly to Elizabeth Carter, 'We have looked in Johnson for *athlete*,
no such word there, nor any thing of the kind by *athletic*, with explana-

tions everybody knows'. The *Dictionary* was fair game for all manner of scrutiny: it was national property.[30]

An enriching dimension to the *Dictionary* is its function as an encyclopedia. Johnson was candid about it in the Preface when he stated his intention 'to pierce deep into every science, to enquire the nature of every substance': 'When first I engaged in this work, I resolved to leave neither words nor things unexamined'. Even without the quotations the *Dictionary* would be more encyclopedic than any of its predecessors. One critic has divided the encyclopedic entries into three groups: complicated artefacts (*airpump, geneva, grenade, orrery*); natural objects and phenomena such as *vine* (which included a survey of no fewer than thirty-four species), *seahorse, crocodile, light, diamond,* and *epilepsy;* and human institutions and fields of learning (*jury, justice, architecture, astronomy, chemistry, logarithm*). Johnson borrowed most of these definitions from specialised reference works but reworked them carefully with his own readers in mind. These sources alone illustrate the breadth of his reading.[31]

The *Dictionary* was a supreme embodiment of eighteenth-century culture and ideas about language, an astonishing achievement. It made a huge impression on the nation, becoming a standard work against which past and future dictionaries were measured. It made Johnson famous overnight.

Part Five

Depression, Shakespeare, Travel and Anger

CHAPTER 20

Stalled

I

SUDDENLY JOHNSON WAS CELEBRATED but his letters suggest he was not happy. It is as if many of the problems, physical as well as mental, that he suppressed while he lost himself in the mighty concentration of the last three years rushed forward once his 'shackles' were broken. Writing at midnight on 30 December 1755 to Hill Boothby, whom he was now possibly hoping to marry, his mood was as dark as in the 'waste hour of darkness and vacuity': 'If I turn my thoughts upon myself what do I perceive but a poor helpless being reduced by a blast of wind to weakness and misery . . . Of the fallaciousness of hope, and the uncertainty of schemes every day gives some new proof . . . something rather felt than seen.' Publication of the *Dictionary* had brought him fame but no financial security. His confidence was 'depressed': 'No man can know how little his performance will conform to his promises, and designs are nothing in human eyes till they are realised by execution.' Each year after this he resolved to read the Bible through, until 1772 when he felt he had 'attained to know, even thus hastily, confusedly, and imperfectly what my Bible contains'. Except for the Bible, however, his resolutions evaporated.[1]

It deeply depressed him that he had squandered vast amounts of time on the *Dictionary* through blunders in the first years, blunders that had cost him the pleasure of presenting the finished work to Tetty before she died. He had not even had the pleasure of witnessing Cave's response to it as his former employer ('poor dear Cave, I owed him much') died on 10 January 1754. Arthur Murphy noted that 'it was a mortification to the author of that noble addition to our language, that his old friend did not live to see the triumph of his labours'. One of Cave's last acts was 'to press the hand that is now writing this little narrative,' Johnson wrote in a short life in *The Gentleman's Magazine*.[2]

It was his own knowledge of the *Dictionary*'s imperfections that weighed on him most. While he had now released the book to the public, it had not released him. He knew he had made lots of mistakes and felt he had not prevailed satisfyingly over the inexact science of lexicography. He also fretted that sooner or later he would have to return to the grind of revisions. About fifteen years later, when the Thrales put him in mind of 'four or five faults' and encouraged him to publish a revised edition, Johnson moaned, 'Alas . . . there are four or five hundred faults instead of four, but it would take me up [to] three months labour, and when the time was out, the work would not be done'. Young Charles Burney (1726–1814), then the organist of St Margaret's Church in King's Lynn in Norfolk who had taken a distant interest in the project ever since reading the *Plan* in 1747, wrote to him a few days before publication asking when he would be able to get a copy. Johnson replied, 'If you find faults, I shall endeavour to mend them; if you find none, I shall think you blinded by kind partiality.' Burney, incidentally, like Langton, had long ago become a disciple of the *Rambler* and was deeply frustrated he was stuck in Norfolk teaching music and unable to meet Johnson. He determined at least to forge a relationship by post: 'It is the fate of men of eminence to be persecuted by insignificant friends as well as enemies; and the simple cur who barks through fondness and affection, is no less troublesome than if stimulated by anger and aversion'. Johnson's heart was warmed, 'I have too much pleasure in pleasing men like you, not to feel very sensibly the distinction which you have bestowed upon me.' He hoped to receive 'another letter; and another yet, when you have looked into my Dictionary'. Burney's further praise two and a half years later – they still had not met – elicited a startling admission from Johnson, 'Your praise was welcome . . . because praise has been very scarce . . . among all my acquaintance there were only two who upon the publication of my book did not endeavour to depress me with threats of censure from the public, or with objections learned from those who had learned them from my own preface. Yours is the only letter of good will that I have yet received.'[3]

He was also sick from bronchitis for several weeks at the end of 1755, 'seized with a hoarseness which still continues'. From the 'convulsions' of a violent cough he once even fainted. His imagination was playing tricks on him and he feared the worst for his lungs. 'My physician bled me yesterday and the day before, first almost against his will, but the next day without any contest. I had been bled once before, so that I have lost in all 54 ounces.' It was the third time he was bled that winter. Like many of his contemporaries, he was already well into phlebotomy, the surgical opening or puncture of a vein to draw out blood, a lifelong madness that he inflicted on his ailing body with more assiduity than most. Rather than wait on a physician, he often impatiently bled himself with grisly deliberateness for all manner of ailments: coughs and colds, flatulence, an 'inflamed' eye, and especially breathing difficulties and shortness of breath. Fifty-four ounces is a great quantity of blood, though to the end of his life he believed that the practice was effective only if it were done in copious amounts. It was a horrible manifestation of his self-belief as an amateur medical practitioner. He wrote to his 'sweet angel' Hill Boothby, for example, who was alarmingly ill in December, 'Give me leave, who have thought much on medicine, to propose to you an easy and I think a very probable remedy for indigestion and lubricity of the bowels.' His remedy featured not phlebotomy but the use of dried orange peel, which he became known for scraping, cutting into pieces, and carrying in his pocket. He remained secretive about his use of the peel when Boswell questioned him closely about it in 1775, but in this instance he recommended that Hill Boothby either grind it into powder and drink it in a glass of port, or eat it first and then wash it down with heated port: 'This is a medicine not disgusting, not costly, easily tried, and if not found useful easily left off.' 'I love you and honour you, and am very unwilling to lose you,' he added.[4]

In his illness he also depended on Dr Thomas Lawrence (1711–83) whom he had met a couple of years earlier and who later was president of the Royal College of Physicians. Johnson would describe him as 'one of the best men whom I have known'. Lawrence recommended oil and sugar for his bronchitis, but he drank some Rhenish wine and water instead and promptly recovered his voice.[5]

These gloomy contours of body and mind deepened suddenly when Hill Boothby, 'his dear little miss', his 'dearest dear', died in January 1756, leaving him lonelier and emptier than ever. It was all his friends could do to 'calm the violence of his emotion'. He sought comfort in composing another prayer, 'Hill Boothby's Death', thanking God for her 'good example' and praying that he might learn from 'the knowledge of her life, and by the sense of her death'. In his prayer on the anniversary of Tetty's death on 28 March, he mentioned his life 'bereft of worldly comforts', an allusion not only to what now was his double grief over her and Hill Boothby but also to his dire finances. He was arrested on 16 March for a debt of £5 18s. While the bailiff waited impatiently, he shot off a letter to Richardson who rescued him from the sponging-house by promptly sending him six guineas. It was a near escape that induced him the following year to write two essays on the evils of imprisonment for debt. It was also a wake-up call that in his post-*Dictionary* doldrums he could not afford the luxury of feeling sorry for himself. He needed money and he needed it quickly. He had to think up new projects.[6]

2

Johnson did soon get down to earning some money. One of his sources of income was writing prefaces, introductions and dedications at the request of booksellers, friends and acquaintances. Although he did not generally like to be asked for them by friends who may sometimes have thought he would write them for nothing, he churned out more than thirty over the next dozen years. Moreover, he became an easy but unwilling target for people who simply wanted him to look over their manuscripts, especially friends like Lennox, Burney, Baretti and Reynolds. As for payment, he told Mrs Thrale he 'hated to give away literary performances, or even to sell them too cheaply: the next generation shall not accuse me of beating down the price of literature: one hates, besides, ever to give that which one has been accustomed to sell.' Boswell heard more or less the same thing: 'I am very unwilling to read the manuscripts of authors, and give them my opinion. If the authors who apply to me have money, I bid them boldly print without a name; if they have written in order to get money, I tell them to go to the booksellers, and make the best bargain they can.' If he agreed to write something on behalf of a work, often he would merely 'peep' into it before doing so. In February 1756, for example, he wrote a preface to Richard Rolt's *Dictionary of Trade and Commerce*: 'I never saw the man, and never read the book . . . I knew very well what such a Dictionary should be, and I wrote a Preface accordingly.' In November, he had produced a dedication to Lennox's edition of Sully's *Memoirs*, and in January he produced a dedication to William Payne's *The Game of Draughts*. And so it went. He could easily have eaten up most of his time writing these.[7]

He also got heavily into writing reviews of books on a wide range of subjects. His diary entry mentioning the 'infelicity'[8] of existing London review journals suggests he thought they were in a wretched state, especially ones that could review scholarly books and have an international focus. In *Rambler* 3 he had scolded overly critical reviewers who with 'elation of malignity' in that 'virulent generation' of mushrooming journalism 'either imagine it their duty, or make it their amusement, to hinder the reception of every work of learning or genius, who stand as sentinels in the avenues of fame, and value themselves upon giving ignorance and envy the first notice of a prey'. And in many reviews he did indeed act, as one critic has put it, as the author's defence attorney and client, pleading the case for the book and then leaving it to the readers to make up their own minds.[9]

To supply the need, he decided to edit a commercially promising new monthly review magazine for the 'general perusal' of a middlebrow readership entitled *The Literary Magazine*. He threw himself into it beginning with the first issue in May 1756 – in which, among other things, he again excoriated the slave trade by describing Jamaica as a 'dungeon of slaves'. This began a sustained period of intense creativity, his most important effort in the field of journalism. The magazine lasted for two years but his connection with it was only for about a year, in the course of which he wrote several editorial pieces and no fewer than forty reviews of books. In his prefatory essay, 'To the Public', for the first issue he wrote there was so much literary rubbish in the book trade that only a few books and pamphlets 'will deserve the distinction of criticism, and a few only will obtain it'.

He was an ideal reviewer because he could express informed judgements on a breathtaking variety of subjects, among them manufacturing processes, sciences (chemistry, zoology, biology, electricity, Newton's optics), medicine, geography, natural history, cartography, politics, international relations, public affairs, military science and what Boswell called 'the useful arts of life': beekeeping, tanning, bleaching, dairy products, china, meat, brewing, coinage, peat digging, kelp gathering, and many others. There was nothing highbrow about any of that. 'The meanest artisan or manufacturer', he wrote, 'contributes more to the accommodation of life, than the profound scholar and argumentative theorist . . . the public would suffer less present inconvenience from the banishment of philosophers than from the extinction of any common trade.'[10] He also reviewed books on moral philosophy, drama, poetry, travel, classical literature and journalism.

Having represented a good reviewer as one who kept himself pure from the 'elation of malignity', in his own reviews for *The Literary Magazine* he could turn quite hostile if he judged authors ignorantly egocentric and complacent or if certain political issues and topics inflamed him sufficiently. These hostile reviews are now more interesting for what they say about Johnson's personality and individuating, simmering anger than for his opinions of the books themselves. One book he attacked with the club of Hercules was Thomas Blackwell's *Memoirs of the Court of Augustus*. His review abounds with scornful words and phrases: he is 'disgusted' with Blackwell's 'vanity' and hubris; the author 'ought not to boast himself as a great benefactor to the studious world'; his language is loaded with 'gaudy or hyperbolic' epithets; he 'heated his imagination' and is 'bold in fighting shadows'.[11]

In a different key, Soame Jenyns's amateurish *A Free Inquiry into the Nature and Origin of Evil* provoked him to write a vitriolic, sardonic and sparkling review in three instalments from May to July 1757. Jenyns was a dilettantish poet, long-time member of Parliament and essayist. Some have claimed that this long review is the single most important statement of Johnson's philosophy. He was offended by Jenyns's incompetence as a philosopher – 'swelled in sound, and diffused in bulk' – as well as by his shallow optimism. No less repelling in his eyes was Jenyns's presumption that he had all the answers to perplexing moral and religious dilemmas. This violated his deep sympathy for suffering humanity in a complex world. The world he knew did not match Jenyns's rosy view: 'He decides too upon questions out of the reach of human determination, with too little consideration of mortal weakness, and with too much vivacity for the necessary caution.' The final straw was when Jenyns argued that there may be superior beings in the universe who treat us for diversion much in the way we treat animals. Johnson bristled with irony: 'Many a merry bout have these frolic beings at the vicissitudes of an ague, and good sport it is to see a man tumble with an epilepsy'. The one question he wished to put to Jenyns is, 'why he that has nothing to write, should desire to be a writer'.[12]

Inflammatory wording and political indignation in other reviews and editorial contributions were fired by the outbreak of the convulsive Seven Years' War in May 1756, which he opposed fiercely as warmongering and economic madness. The first issue of *The Literary Magazine* coincided with the declaration of war on France by Britain, so it was bound to focus on current affairs. The war was truly a global conflict, a clash with France (chiefly) for control of parts of Europe, the Mediterranean and Africa, the West Indies, North America and India. By the end of it, in 1763, Britain had succeeded beyond her wildest dreams, the Peace of Paris that year carving out the largest single accretion of the Empire in British history.

The early months of the war, however, with French gains on all fronts, were discouraging for Britain, bringing a sharp decline of national morale and confirming Johnson in his conviction that British foreign policy was benighted. It did not seem to him in this time of national gloom that much of anything was going right in the nation's politics, conduct of the war, foreign entanglements and exploitations or naval policy. He disliked William Pitt, the Elder (1708–78), Secretary of State in the new coalition government with the Duke of Newcastle, for his imperialist policies on the development of a standing army; nor did he think much of his speeches in the House of Commons, which he thought more histrionic than brilliant. He unloaded his frustration about the war and Pitt's determination to expand overseas in several extremely strident political essays in 1756–8 about military glory and imperial aggrandisement, notably in three editorial pieces of 'literary vituperation' for *The Literary Magazine* in 1756: *Remarks on the Militia Bill* (1756), *An Introduction to the Political State of Britain* (1756) and *Observations on the State of Affairs in 1756* – as well as in four other short 'Observations' in a new weekly paper in 1758, *The Universal Chronicle*. They amount to a self-portrait of a highly independent thinker stripping away the 'ideological clothing' with which Pitt had justified the war and exposing the plunder of other nations that he believed lay behind the war effort. They also point up Johnson's courage and combativeness in waging his own war against the reigning political establishment and its current cant and jingoism, for his views during this time of fevered 'patriotism' were highly unpopular.

His *Introduction to the Political State of Great Britain*, which began prominently on the first page of the first issue of the magazine, is a long historical survey of British foreign policy since Queen Elizabeth by way of a background to how Britain got into this sorry war to begin with. Its theme is the immorality of foreign exploitation. He concluded by remarking that British conduct towards the native Americans in the American colonies had been scandalous: 'Our factors and traders having no other purpose in view than immediate profit, use all the arts of an European counting-house, to defraud the simple hunter of his furs . . . we continue every day to show by new proofs, that no people can be great who have ceased to be virtuous.' In his *Observations on the Present State of Affairs*, which Boswell described as glowing 'with as animated a spirit of constitutional liberty as can be found anywhere', he was even more indignant towards the fraud and injustice of Britain's war with France over the boundaries of settlements in America which 'neither can occupy but by usurpation and the dispossession of the natural lords and original inhabitants'. He described the British Government as little more than 'a gang of bandits' trafficking in 'new modes of usurpation' and 'new instances of cruelty and treachery'.[13]

The proprietors of *The Literary Magazine*, however, were not pleased with the stridency of his tone and may even have forced him out since his extreme views on the evils of the Seven Years' War differed dramatically from theirs and had hurt sales of the magazine from the beginning. The magazine never did recover and it expired in July 1758. Even after the war had taken Britain to the threshold of glorious victory, Johnson's anger over government policy and its accompanying cant was undiminished – and at the time highly unusual. Indeed, the four sardonic anti-government 'Observations' that he wrote for the *Universal Chronicle*, in the spring of that year proved to be so upsetting to 'patriotic' readers that the publishers of that paper also slammed the door in his face, refusing to publish anything more from him on this theme.[14]

3

Johnson's household and personal life was in a state of flux. He had the boy Frank Barber living with him as a servant, but otherwise he was still lonely and rattling around in a large house. What he needed was immediate companionship and more people in his home; there were now plenty of bedrooms, especially now that after completing the *Dictionary* he had moved his library up to the garret. There was less natural light up there but the rest of the house had too many memories.

When little Frank, slight and delicate, first moved into Gough Square in 1752, Johnson did not really need him as a servant. From the start, he took pains to provide the boy with a good education. But Frank was volatile and in the autumn of 1756 'upon some difference', possibly having to do with schooling, he ran away to an apothecary in Cheapside and worked for him for two years as his assistant, 'during which he called sometimes on his Master and was well received' with the understanding that he would return to him. In December 1758, aged sixteen and restless, he ran away to sea. Somewhat stunned, Johnson later explained, 'Being disgusted in the house he ran away to sea, and was in the summer on board the ship stationed at Yarmouth to protect the fishery.' After two long years, 'in great distress' because Frank was 'of a delicate frame' and suffered from 'a malady in his throat', Johnson set in motion plans to recover him. He had a very low opinion of life at sea and could not imagine Frank was happy with it: 'No man', he once said, 'will be a sailor who has contrivance enough to get himself into a jail; for being in a ship is being in a jail, with the chance of being drowned.' He disliked the novelist Tobias Smollett but wrote to him anyway to see if, with his contacts in the navy, he could intervene to have Frank discharged. Smollett in turn called on John Wilkes, a political firebrand to whom Johnson would refer as 'a new retailer of sedition and obscenity' – Wilkes had mocked aspects of the *Dictionary* – to ask if he would write to the Admiralty on behalf of Johnson's 'lackey', in the process giving Johnson a tag by which he has been known ever since Smollett's letter became public in Wilkes's *Miscellanies* in the nineteenth century: 'I am again your petitioner, on behalf of that great CHAM of literature, Samuel Johnson. You know what manner of animosity the said Johnson has against you; and I dare say you desire no other opportunity of resenting it than that of laying him under an obligation. He was humble enough to desire my assistance on this occasion, though he and I were never cater-cousins.' Doubtless bemused, Wilkes wrote to Sir George Hay, one of the Lords of the Admiralty, and after a long delay Frank was discharged against his will in August 1760 and returned to Johnson who by then had moved out of Gough Square and was living less expensively in chambers at No. 1 Inner Temple Lane.[15]

The story of another boarder in Gough Square, Anna Williams (1706–83), is an unhappy one. Johnson's relationship to her was the result of a need for companionship, a desire to assist her and her father in their poverty, a mild respect for her poetry and other literary skills, and a curiosity regarding her interest in science. She developed a taste for science through her father Zachariah, who thought of himself as an inventor and whose great obsession was to win the £20,000 prize offered by the Government to anyone who could come up with a reliable method of measuring longitude at sea. In 1729, he became a pensioner of the Charterhouse, 'that asylum of age and poverty' founded in 1611 as a hospital for pensioners in buildings near Smithfield which had once housed a Carthusian monastery. His daughter, who had except for one brief period been blind since 1740, was unhappily prevented from living there with him, and in 1748 he himself was unceremoniously removed and reduced to living in poverty with her in unknown lodgings until he died seven years later.

Johnson took her in at Gough Square at intervals out of charity, originally while Tetty was still alive, for a brief spell around 1754, and finally more or less constantly shortly after her father died when she was penniless and alone. But he did more than this. To generate money and publicity for the indomitable but indigent Zachariah, who had not given up on the Longitude prize, he boned up on his invention and wrote a pamphlet under the inventor's name published as *An Account of an Attempt to Ascertain the Longitude at Sea* (1755). It failed to promote Williams's chances for the prize, and in any case Williams died that year. As for Anna, in 1752 he organised (with Hawkins's help) and paid for a painful cataract operation at Gough Square to restore her sight. It was unsuccessful and she remained blind for the rest of her life. To foster her literary ambitions, he also introduced her to Samuel Richardson by showing him a poem she had written in praise of the high moral tone of his recent novel *Sir Charles Grandison*. Later, when in desperate poverty, she tried to capitalise on Richardson's favour and influence by compiling a dictionary of scientific terms that he might promote, Johnson pressed him to help her: 'If you think her dictionary likely to shift for itself in this age of dictionaries, you will be pleased to encourage her.' Nothing came of the idea. Finally, one of her literary efforts did pay off because Johnson brought in Garrick who agreed to stage her play, *Merope*, in January 1756 for one benefit night. Johnson saw to the tickets being printed just the right way and talked up the play among his friends, with the result that she received £260, which for her was a fortune. By then she was running Johnson's home, even in blindness.[16]

It was a feature of Johnson's household that once he began to take in non-paying lodgers, 'whole nests of people', as Mrs Thrale put it, there was a good deal of quarrelling in it. What he gained in companionship, he lost in tranquility. 'Easily provoked to anger', Anna (known as Mrs Williams), was at the centre of his household's jarring lack of harmony and jealousy. For a start, she took a dislike to Frank. Hawkins praised her prudence and 'enlightened understanding', maintaining that she blessed Johnson with much good practical advice while he instructed her on 'religious and moral improvement', and Boswell especially enjoyed late-night cups of tea with her in the kitchen, but everyone agreed she was cranky. According to Hawkins, she was full of complaints about Frank's 'inattention to the interests of his master'. She would fly at Johnson about Frank, 'This is your scholar! Your philosopher! Upon whom you have spent so many hundred pounds!' Frank allegedly resented her 'for the authority she assumed over him, and [which she] exercised with an unwarrantable severity'. The churchman and antiquarian Thomas Percy remarked: 'So far from being a constant source of disquiet and vexation' to Johnson, 'although she was totally blind for the last thirty years of her life, her mind was so well cultivated, and her conversation so agreeable, that she very much enlivened and diverted his solitary hours'.[17]

Robert Levet, another argumentative and permanent addition to the household, was also presently lodging with Johnson intermittently. Mrs Thrale colourfully described him in 1777 as 'a superannuated surgeon' who had care of the whole *ship's company* in the house. He was never licensed as a physician but had gained good practical knowledge of the subject in France and Italy from experts in anatomy and pharmacy and was now prescribing medicines among the poor in London for 'whatever provisions his patients could afford him'. Sullen and something of a heavy drinker, he won Johnson's admiration for his good heart. 'Levet, Madam,' Johnson said to Mrs Thrale, 'is a brutal [awkward] fellow, but I have a good regard for him, for his brutality is in his manners, not his mind.' He was not a pretty sight in his mid-fifties when he moved into Gough Square, standing at five-feet five-inches tall, extremely thin, grey, and scarred by smallpox. Many of Johnson's friends found him grotesque, and his quarrels with Mrs Williams frequently descended to the vicious. He rarely spoke when company was present. Nevertheless, it was enough for Johnson that he was poor and miserable.[18]

One hanger-on, who did not join the 'nest' of lodgers, was the Frenchman and forger George Psalmanazar who further illustrated Johnson's charitable and instinctive attraction to the indigent, eccentric and even fraudulent fringes of society. 'I used to go and sit with him at an alehouse in the city,' Johnson remarked. Old Psalmanazar lived in Ironmonger Row off Old Street, where Johnson used to visit him, and it was at a 'club' or alehouse on Old Street that they used to pass the hours. Psalmanazar was a fraud and literary impostor, passing himself off in London during the early part of the century as a native of Formosa and concocting a new name and elaborate Formosan language and mythology to support his totally fraudulent book, *Historical and Geographical Description of Formosa* (1704). He enacted this pretence successfully until a religious conversion in the 1720s propelled him on a journey of penitence eventually bearing fruit in his *Memoirs* (1764), a published confession. From the 1720s until his death in 1763, he lived a religiously blameless life of poverty. In his novel *Humphry Clinker*, Tobias Smollett pauses to describe him as one 'who, after having drudged half a century in the literary mill, in all the simplicity and abstinence of an Asiatic, subsists upon the charity of a few booksellers, just sufficient to keep him from the parish'. Even children who passed him on the street would show 'the usual signs of respect'. Asked once whether he ever contradicted Psalmanazar, Johnson replied, 'I should as soon have thought of contradicting a bishop'. 'George Psalmanazar's piety, penitence, and virtue exceeded almost what we read as wonderful even in the lives of saints', he told Mrs Thrale with not a little exaggeration; he was the 'best' man he had ever known.[19]

Speaking of Grub Street and the 'regular' education Johnson nostalgically believed was to be had in that school of hard knocks, there was another man, a tailor, with whom he and Psalmanazar would retreat into the shadows of that club in Old Street and whom they dubbed the 'metaphysical tailor' because of the sage advice he dispensed. When the year before he died Johnson discovered to his surprise that his good friend John Hoole was this obscure tailor's nephew in Grub Street, that they had been 'brother authors' there in 'the mansions of our progenitors', he shouted, 'Let you and I, Sir, go together, and eat a beef-steak in Grub street.'[20]

4

There were other, more socially respectable, friends. The mercurial and exceptionally able Giuseppe Baretti was one, introduced to him by Charlotte Lennox. Baretti was too hot-tempered and opinionated to be friends with everyone, but Johnson and his circle were steady in their loyalty towards him and once teamed up to get him acquitted at a murder trial. Johnson had the highest regard for 'my Baretti', as he called him. Philosophical about his erratic behaviour, he admonished Mrs Thrale: 'Poor Baretti! Do not quarrel with him, to neglect him a little will be sufficient. He means only to be frank, and manly, and independent, and perhaps, as you say, a little wise. To be frank he thinks is to be cynical, and to be independent, is to be rude . . . his misbehaviour, I am afraid, he learned part of me.'[21] Johnson wrote prefaces to Baretti's *Introduction to the Italian Language* (1755) and *A Grammar of the Italian Language* (1760), among others, helped with his *Italian Library* (1757), and actually planned several of Baretti's other works for him.

A more tender friendship was with young Bennet Langton (1737–1801), who entered Trinity College, Oxford, in 1757 and studied under Thomas Warton. Tall and gangly at six feet six inches – Johnson nicknamed him 'Lanky', a 'very tall, meagre, long-visaged man, much resembling a stork standing on one leg' – Langton was quite thrown off balance by Johnson, whom he reverenced, when 'down from his bed-chamber, about noon, came, as newly risen, a huge uncouth figure, with a little dark wig which scarcely covered his head, and his clothes hanging loose about him.' But he was quickly seduced by his hero's conversation, and for his part Johnson, undoubtedly equally taken aback by Langton's prodigious height, took to the young man for his youthful zest, piety and 'exalted character', as well as for his old Lincolnshire family.[22]

While at Oxford, Langton met a young rake and fellow student, Topham Beauclerk (1739–80), the great-grandson of Charles II and Nell Gwyn and grandson of the 1st Duke of St Albans, who may be mentioned now although Langton did not introduce him to Johnson until the latter's next visit to Oxford in June and July 1759. Langton and Beauclerk cemented an affectionate friendship with each other at Oxford that never wavered. Apparently Johnson also took to Beauclerk immediately, whom he called 'Beau', although his friendship with this 'gay, dissipated' young man raised a few eyebrows. 'What a coalition!' said Garrick when he heard of it, with Falstaff in mind, 'I shall have my old friend to bail out of the Roundhouse.' 'Thy body is all vice, and thy mind all virtue,' Johnson once said to Beauclerk, who could take more liberties with his older friend, and get away with them, than anyone else. With Langton and Beauclerk Johnson had more sheer fun, often in youthful 'frisks', than with anyone else except, in different ways, later with Boswell. 'What, is it you, you dogs! I'll have a frisk with you', he announced to them 'with his little black wig on the top of his head, instead of a nightcap'. They had rapped at his door in Inner Temple Lane at three one morning in the early 1760s to commandeer him on a ramble into Covent Garden, 'where the green-grocers and fruiterers were beginning to arrange their hampers, just come in from the country'. After a few hours in a tavern drinking 'Bishop', a favourite drink of Johnson's made of a mixture of wine, oranges, and sugar, they boarded a boat and rowed down the Thames to Billingsgate. They were going to keep this up throughout the day but Langton abandoned them for breakfast with what Johnson teasingly described as 'a set of *un-idea'd* girls'. When Garrick caught wind of this escapade, he had to say, 'I heard of your frolic t'other night. You'll be in the Chronicle.'[23]

There is no doubt that his warmest and closest male friend was Joshua Reynolds (1723–92) who, since returning from Italy in 1752, had been on the fast track to becoming Britain's greatest and wealthiest portrait painter. To Cordelia Knight, a young woman growing up in London in the 1760s and 1770s, 'his features were coarse, and his outward appearance slovenly', and 'his pronunciation was tinctured with the Devonshire accent' that was a pleasant complement to Johnson's own Staffordshire accent. Nobody knew Johnson like Reynolds. 'If I should lose you, I should lose almost the only man whom I call a friend,' Johnson once said to him. He was his 'oldest and kindest friend'. He simply regarded Reynolds as a 'great man'. Reynolds maintained that Johnson 'formed my mind' and 'brushed off from it a deal of rubbish'. They appear to have met in 1756–7, the rough date given to their meeting by Reynolds's sister Frances, who had moved in with her brother in 1753 to keep house for him. In one of his memo-like pocket-books that listed such things as the sitters for portraits and sales he attended, he mentioned Johnson for the first time in January 1757 as sitting for a portrait, so it is likely they met not long before then.[24]

Frances Reynolds ('Renny', as Johnson called her), whose family thought she could have married Johnson if she had wanted to, remembered those early days fondly in her diary, especially 'the impression I felt in his favour, on his saying that as he returned to his lodgings about one or two o'clock in the morning, he often saw poor children asleep on thresholds and stalls, and that he used to put pennies into their hands to buy them a breakfast'. Even his 'best dress was, at that time, so very mean', she added, that at times he was mistaken for hired help and not introduced properly, which made him growl. A painter herself, she was somewhat highly strung. Charles Burney's daughter Fanny described her as 'in a habitual perplexity of mind and irresolution of conduct'.[25]

Renny is of particular interest because she painted a portrait of Johnson and also showed herself fascinated by his eccentric physical movements and appearance, especially the compulsive tics and gesticulations, the conspicuous movements and sounds. These included ritualised 'extraordinary gestures or antics with his hands and feet, particularly when passing over the threshold of a door, or rather before he would venture to pass through *any* doorway'. Boswell also commented on his counting his steps before passing through a doorway or carefully touching posts as he walked along a street. As for his foot movements, Renny added, they were 'scarcely credible': 'Sometimes he would make the back part of his heels to touch, sometimes the extremity of his toes, as if endeavouring to form a triangle, or some geometrical figure, and as for his gestures with his hands, they were equally as strange; sometimes he would hold them up . . . sometimes at his breast in motion like those of a jockey on full speed; and often would he lift them up as high as he could stretch over his head, for some minutes.' One day while walking in Twickenham meadows with him, she was distressed to see him suddenly launching into 'antics both with his feet and hands, with the latter as if he was holding the reins of a horse like a jockey on full speed'. This was so extraordinary that 'men, women, and children gathered round him, laughing. At last we sat down on some logs of wood by the river side, and they nearly dispersed.' The movement that she said astonished the most 'was his stretching out his arm with a full cup of tea in his hand, in every direction, often to the great annoyance of the person who sat next him, indeed to the imminent danger of their clothes . . . ; sometimes he would twist himself round with his face close to the back of his chair, and finish his cup of tea, breathing very hard, as if making a laborious effort to accomplish it.' It is now widely suspected that these movement disorders were symptoms of what has become known as the neurological disease that some now call Tourette's Syndrome, except without the extremes of profanity that often characterise it.[26]

By the time Boswell had met Johnson, it is possible that these jerks, gesticulations and other movement disorders had become even more severe and astonishing to onlookers. His description of them is even more complete and remarkable than Renny's:

> while talking or even musing as he sat in his chair, he commonly held his head to one side towards his right shoulder, and shook it in a tremulous manner, moving his body backwards and forwards, and rubbing his left knee in the same direction, with the palm of his hand. In the intervals of articulating he made various sounds with his mouth, sometimes as if ruminating, or what is called chewing the cud, sometimes giving a half whistle, sometimes making his tongue play backwards from the roof of his mouth, as if clucking like a hen, and sometimes protruding it against his upper gums in front, as if pronouncing quickly under his breath, *too, too, too*: all this accompanied sometimes with a thoughtful look, but more frequently with a smile. Generally when he had concluded a

period, in the course of a dispute, by which time he was a good
deal exhausted by violence and vociferation, he used to blow out
his breath like a whale . . .

In a character sketch of Johnson after he died, Joshua Reynolds disagreed with Boswell's assertion that Johnson lapsed into these movements
both when actively engaged with persons around him and when he was
alone or musing, lost in thought. He maintained that the movements were
not wildly involuntary and were noticeable only when Johnson withdrew
into himself: 'His mind appeared to be preying on itself; he fell into a reverie accompanied with strange antic gesticulations. But this was when his
mind was absent or deep in thought; he never did when his mind was engaged by the conversation.' Reynolds's opinion was that the movements
'proceeded from a habit which he had indulged himself in, of accompanying his thoughts with certain untoward actions'. Mrs Thrale never saw
him move like this in church, and Renny plausibly maintained that without the ability to control his body he could hardly have sat for portraits
that her brother and she painted of him. In any case, retrospective medicine is a risky business, and whether or not Johnson's well-publicised eccentric physical movements were due to Tourette's Syndrome exclusively
remains a complicated matter.[27]

5

What Johnson looked like the year after the publication of the *Dictionary*
brings us to the portrait of him by Reynolds in 1756–7. Reynolds's annual
income by the early 1760s was about £6000, in the region of £600,000 today, but it is unlikely that Johnson had anything in his pocketbook at all
to spare for this first portrait of himself. That so soon after meeting him
Reynolds should paint a full portrait of such an eccentric-looking writer –
a huge departure from his usual lucrative aristocratic subjects – is a measure of his fascination with the appearance of the now famous lexicographer and his desire to record an image from his post-*Dictionary* fame.
Indeed, the portrait is commonly referred to as 'Dictionary Johnson'

and now hangs in the National Portrait Gallery in London, attacked recently by a deranged knife-wielder. It shows Johnson sitting uncomfortably in a simple chequered-covered chair without arms, at a table covered with a plain green cloth. His face is open, clean, and relatively youthful with a smooth brow. There are no deep furrows and signs of worry. There is a coarseness about the face, though, with its fleshiness, large jaw, large nose and thick lips. He looks much as one may have expected Reynolds to represent a literary figure – without any social pretentiousness and looking, in his simple coat, like someone who may not have had too many other clothes to choose from in which to be painted.

Boswell said that when he first met Johnson he felt he was not looking at him for the first time because of this portrait: 'I found that I had a very perfect idea of Johnson's figure, from the portrait of him painted by Sir Joshua Reynolds soon after he had published his *Dictionary*, in the attitude of sitting in his easy chair in deep meditation which was the first picture his friend did for him, which Sir Joshua very kindly presented to me.' Boswell did not meet Reynolds until 1769, and since in his journal he never says he had seen the painting, he must be saying this for effect. As there is no look of 'deep meditation' in the original portrait, when Boswell set about having the painting engraved by James Heath, engraver for the Royal Academy, for the Frontispiece of his *Life* thirty-five years later, Reynolds (who had kept the portrait until he gave it to Boswell in 1789) thought the image 'was too young and not thoughtful enough' and advised Heath to make him look more like the now famous moralist and lexicographer, with another quill pen and inkpot and a copy of the *Dictionary* on the table, a face slimmed and frowning with more prominent eyebrows, his wig roughed up, and his clothes more respectable. It was a case of Johnson's reputation reaching back to the original portrait and altering it.[28]

Johnson would be painted by twelve painters during the rest of his life, and by Reynolds three or four more times. Only Pope was painted more often in the eighteenth century, but Pope was rich and had many aristocratic friends. Johnson was quite taken with the honour of Reynolds's portrait and the depth of understanding of his character, the 'colouring' of the mind, that he felt the painter had caught in it. Three years later he dearly hoped Reynolds would not squander his talents by painting 'historical pictures': 'I should grieve to see Reynolds transfer to heroes and to goddesses, to empty splendour and to airy fiction, that art which is now employed in diffusing friendship, in reviving tenderness, in quickening the affections of the absent, and continuing the presence of the dead.'[29]

CHAPTER 21

'Suffering Chimeras'

I

IF JOHNSON WERE NOT TO REMAIN stalled and poor, wasting hours in taverns, writing ephemera for magazines, and providing prefaces and dedications for friends and booksellers which did him personally little material good, he had to throw himself decisively into another major project. Hawkins wrote that in this hour of need it was again a consortium of booksellers led by Jacob Tonson who came to his rescue: they 'had their eyes upon Johnson' and were alarmed at the 'misapplication of his talents'. Tonson, we recall, claimed perpetual copyright in Shakespeare and defeated Cave's effort a decade earlier to have Johnson produce an edition of the Bard. Now on the strength of Garrick's stupendous popularisation of Shakespeare on the stage, Tonson himself decided there was an ideal market for a new complete edition of Shakespeare and that it was better to have Johnson, whom he realised was the ideal man to produce it, on his side. He and the others concluded correctly that Johnson's deep study of Shakespeare's language for the *Dictionary* and collection of thousands of quotations from the plays placed him in the best possible position to take on the edition.[1]

The contract dated 2 June 1756 specified that profits from a subscription to the first edition would be his, and the booksellers would keep the copyright. The edition would be 'elegantly printed' in eight volumes in octavo size. He would be supplied with 250 sets free of charge to sell to subscribers for two guineas each in loose sheets – the purchaser would have to see to his own binding. After that he would have to pay one guinea for subscriber sets. So Johnson would stand to make five hundred guineas if he could get that many subscribers. To round up as many as possible he turned to friends. He told Hector in October he was even bringing his aged mother into service: 'I have undertaken a new edition of Shakespeare, and that the profits of it are to arise from a subscription. I therefore solicit the interest of all my friends, and believe myself sure of yours without solicitation. The proposals and receipts may be had from my mother to whom I beg you send for as many as you can dispose of, and to remit to her money which you or your acquaintance shall collect.' Concerned for his mother's well-being, he added a month later, 'As you receive three or four guineas send them to my mother. She may want them.'[2]

On 8 June he published his *Proposals* for the edition, deploring the imperfections of early editions and the mangled state of the text in Shakespeare's lifetime and since, claiming a crucial need for yet more notes to shed the needed light: 'to correct what is corrupt, and to explain what is obscure'. He was hard on previous editors: Nicholas Rowe and Pope were 'very ignorant of English literature', William Warburton was 'detained by more important studies', and Lewis Theobald was content only with as much analysis as enabled him 'to embellish his page with the expected decorations'. None of them possessed the 'critical sagacity' which he would display in his own edition. Compounding the textual problems, he added, were obscurities of language and sources veiled by the mists of time: 'the figures vanish when the canvas has decayed'. 'With regard to obsolete or peculiar diction,' he declared, 'the editor may perhaps claim some degree of confidence, having had more motives to consider the whole extent of our language than any other man from its first formation'. He also needed to examine the literary context of each play and perform 'a careful collation of the oldest copies' for variant readings of the text, for which he made a desultory effort to round up books from public libraries and friends like Birch, Thomas Warton and Garrick.[3]

Potential lenders would have done well to think twice before lending him any, however, given his treatment of the books he borrowed for the *Dictionary*. As Boswell observed, 'considering the slovenly and careless manner in which books were treated by Johnson, it could not be expected that scarce and valuable editions should have been lent to him'. Garrick, however, did lend him volumes from his fine collection of old plays and Shakespeare quarto editions, one of the finest in the country, leaving a key to it with his servant and instructions to light a fire in the library so that Johnson could use it in comfort any time he wished. He was upset when he read this passage in the Preface to the edition, 'I collated such copies as I could procure, and wished for more, but have not found the collectors of these rarities very communicative.' Johnson's pride would not let him acknowledge the favour, especially since he regarded Shakespeare's text his own province, not Garrick's, and resented his crossing the line from stage to page through the power of his collection. When Boswell asked him why he did not mention Garrick in his Preface to the edition, he mocked his old pupil's alleged influence of the public's perception of Shakespeare: 'I would not disgrace my page with a player. Garrick has been liberally paid for mouthing Shakespeare. If I should praise him, I should much more praise the nation who paid him. He has not made Shakespeare better known. He cannot illustrate Shakespeare. He does not understand him'. Moreover, he denied that Frank Barber ever received any of Garrick's books. In his journal Boswell put this tempest in a teapot down to Johnson's jealousy, 'that *Davy* Garrick, who was his pupil and who came up to London at the same time with him . . . should be so very general a favourite and should have fourscore thousand pounds, an immense sum, when he had so little'. In an exasperated letter to Johnson in May 1765, Garrick said he could scarcely believe it when his brother asked him if he had subscribed to the edition: 'I told him yes, that I was one of the first, and as soon as I had heard of your intention; and that I gave you, at the same time, some other names, among which were the Duke of Devonshire.' Nonetheless, Johnson complained later that 'Garrick got me no subscriptions.'[4]

Johnson confidently agreed in the contract to finish by Christmas 1757. He knew his powers, but in retrospect eighteen months seemed to him and others totally unrealistic. Among other things, he underestimated the work involved in sifting through and dealing with previous editors on whose commentary and textual decisions he had to provide notes. Personal problems also lurked ahead to confound him. Still, he threw himself into the work and, remarkably, in December 1757, felt sanguine enough to be able to write to Burney, who had rounded up six subscribers among Johnson's Norfolk admirers, 'I shall publish about March.' He was hard at it but March came and still there was no edition. 'I am ashamed to tell you', he wrote to Burney that month, 'that my Shakespeare will not be out so soon as I promised my subscribers . . . It will however be published before summer . . . I have printed many of the plays and have hitherto left very few passages unexplained.' When he could not explain them, he added, he was confessing his ignorance, 'which is seldom done by commentators'. But if any subscribers needed reassurance that the edition would be out by then, he instructed Burney to let them read Arthur Murphy's 'splendid encomium' the previous April on his editorship: 'one of the best critics of this age . . . who has approved himself, in various branches of writing, an English classic of the first magnitude . . . possessed of a genius to which we may apply what was said of Caesar, "The Alps and the Pyreneans sink before him."'[5]

Burney still had not met him but in the winter of 1758 finally dropped in at Gough Square where 'he dined and drank tea with him, and was introduced to the acquaintance of Mrs Williams'. Johnson even took him up to his garret, where Burney could see for himself the sacred space where the *Dictionary* was created but which now was littered with Shakespeareana. There Johnson showed him the plays already printed as evidence that he was indeed getting on with the project. They spoke of literature and it was then that Johnson first conceived his respect for Burney's mind and enthusiasm, even if in his ambivalence about music he was less than enthusiastic that Burney was a musician. 'Music excites in my mind no ideas, and hinders me from contemplating my own,' he once remarked. The meeting was enough to push Burney's hero-worship of Johnson into the regions of idolatry. When he finally moved to London in 1760 with his wife and six children, he cultivated Johnson's company assiduously. He even perpetuated the reverence of his friend and fellow Norfolkian William Bewley by surreptitiously cutting off 'a few bristles of his hearth-broom' and posting them to Bewley as a type of relic. Learning of this, Johnson later called Bewley 'the Broom Gentleman'.[6]

By this time Johnson had attained the reputation as a superman among scholars. Shenstone wrote to Thomas Percy in January 1758, 'Do you hear that Mr Johnson's Shakespeare will be published this winter? I have a prejudice . . . in favour of all he undertakes; and wish the world may recompense him for a degree of industry very seldom connected with so much real genius.' Percy had met Johnson in the summer of 1756 at Gough Square and immediately promised to help collect subscriptions from his Northamptonshire and Shropshire friends, but he had his doubts when Johnson told him confidently he hoped to publish before Easter 1758. Indeed, Johnson's predictions of a publication date soon dried up. In spite of books lent him and notes which Warton, Percy and others sent his way, he encountered what Boswell called 'severe and remittent' obstacles, emotional and practical. Hawkins's overstated opinion was that the edition was not a labour of love and that this prevented him from really getting down to it. Johnson told him, 'I look upon this as I did upon the *Dictionary*: it is all work, and my inducement to it is not love or desire of fame, but the want of money, which is the only motive to writing that I know of.' Hawkins also claimed that Johnson not only failed to apply himself to systematic reading but also much of the time drifted about doing almost nothing: 'It was provoking to all his friends to see him waste his days, his weeks, and his months so long, that they feared a mental lethargy had seized him, out of which he would never recover.' Much to the confusion of subscribers and the general public, the edition did not appear in 1758 or the next year, or the year after that.[7]

One of the reasons for the delay may well have been complications arising from his methods.[8] He had already overshot his deadline by close to a year, and inasmuch as he had virtually finished what for him was the easiest part of the process, explication of themes and language in the plays, and was about to embark on the more troublesome textual work, it is likely he lost his drive to publish anywhere near his advertised deadline. The problem was that in the *Proposals* he had boasted he would undertake 'a careful collation' of 'all the copies that can be found'. It did not surprise him that when it came down to it he had no taste for combing the bibliographical landscape for early printed copies of the plays and exhaustively collating them.

Johnson had more accessible public libraries at his disposal than did preceding editors, so there was no excuse for his negligence in acquiring books he needed. The British Museum had been established in 1753 and formally opened its doors in January 1759 at the seventeenth-century mansion Montagu House in Bloomsbury, and even as he was working on his edition part of the Royal Library was transferred to it by George II in 1757. But rather than delight him, the dramatic increase in the availability of books made him sceptical. He saw darker meanings in the vast accumulations of printed volumes. While in *Adventurer* 85 he had derided those who believed libraries were filled only with 'useless lumber' from which 'men of parts' needed 'no assistance', he also was suspicious of them as 'bubbles of artificial fame' that could swallow up lives 'in vain endeavours'. For him a vast library, 'crowded on every side by mighty volumes', embodied 'the vanity of human hopes'. His approach instead was to balance research with the imaginative and pragmatic, to discover in literature not facts but a mirror to nature, the truth about human existence, 'appealing wholly to observation and experience'. A scholar who buries himself in manuscripts and wears out his days in 'perpetual research and solitary meditation', risks 'losing in his elocution what he adds to his wisdom'; he is in danger of approaching writing 'overloaded with his own notions, like a man armed with weapons which he cannot wield'. Squandering hours in the imaginatively deadening precincts of a library was the last thing he wanted to do. 'A ready man is made by conversation.'⁹

The real monster he feared was the textual work. He knew there were better Shakespeare editors out there who would censure him for slipshod work, and such a prospect troubled and somewhat paralysed him. It was not lost on him that critics had vigorously attacked Warburton's edition. So, in the Preface, he decided it might help to attack potential critics first by portraying them as maliciously irrelevant: 'The one stings like a fly, sucks a little blood, takes a gay flutter, and returns for more; the other bites like a viper, and would be glad to leave inflammations and gangrene behind him.' What he knew he really needed, though, was a textual collaborator who could have dealt with this meddlesome part of the labor – someone like George Steevens, one of the great Shakespeareans of the late eighteenth century who became his friend only in the later stages of the project, when it was too late. It was easy to write in the Preface that he wished for more early editions to collate, but he was loath to chase after them.[10]

As for notes from friends, even though he planned an appendix as a catch-all for any he received after the relevant plays were already printed, he found himself sticking in notes to the plays 'by means of asterisks and obelisks . . . interspersing them between the notes numbered numerically'. This practice was just not sustainable, for after a while it would involve drastic and expensive reconstituting of entire pages. It was all becoming a jumble, and the confusion postponed publication.[11]

2

The weight of anxiety about how the edition was going set in motion mutually reinforcing aggravations and worries. It was nourishing soil for the ever-lurking black dog and made him feel he *was* idle. 'Much of my time past has been lost in sloth,' he moaned in his Easter Day prayer on 26 March 1758, and then in his birthday prayer in September he implored God to 'enable me to improve the time which is yet before me', repenting 'days misspent in idleness and folly, that I may henceforward diligently attend to the business of my station in this world'.[12]

He was also worried about his mother, now just short of ninety and seriously ill in Lichfield. 'I will, if it be possible, come down to you,' he wrote in some panic on 20 January 1759 to Lucy, who was still living with her at home. 'God grant I may yet see my dear mother breathing and sensible. Do not tell, lest I disappoint her.' He did not go. Instead, her illness elicited from him a rare series of short letters to her, efforts partly to palliate or 'efface' his guilt over not having seen her for twenty years. 'The account which Miss gives me of your health, pierces my heart,' he wrote on 13 January. He suggested both spiritual and temporal remedies. Lucy could read to her from 'the Passion of our Saviour' and she should take 'a strong infusion of the bark'. 'Do, dear Mother, try it.' Then poignantly he added, 'forgive all that I have done amiss to you'. 'I know not how to bear the thought of losing you,' he wrote to his mother on 16 January. 'You have been the best mother, and I believe the best woman in the world. I thank you for your indulgence to me, and beg forgiveness of all that I have done ill.'[13]

He did not have money enough for an emergency flight to Lichfield, which he hoped to make before she died. Nor did he believe he could afford her funeral expenses when the sad event occurred. So he sat down and began to write a short philosophical tale or moral fable, to be titled *The Choice of Life or The History of ——— Prince of Abissinia*, eventually better known as *Rasselas*. He used the printer Strahan as his literary agent to settle on terms with Dodsley and another prominent bookseller William Johnston: £100 for the first edition and £25 for the second. Baretti thought he had sold it too cheaply: 'Any other person with the degree of reputation he then possessed would have got £400 for that work, but he never understood the art of making the most of his productions.'[14]

On the same day Johnson wrote to Strahan about this, Lucy wrote to say his mother had died. 'If she were to live again', he wrote to Lucy on the 23rd, 'surely I should behave better to her.' That was the day of her funeral. 'It is not of any use for me now to come down,' he wrote to her two days later, 'nor can I bear the place.' That same day he composed a prayer, asking forgiveness for unkindness towards her and committing to God 'the soul of my departed Mother'. Four days later he dashed out an essay on losing a loved one, with this telling passage: 'Every calamity comes suddenly upon us, and not only presses us as a burden, but crushes as a blow . . . The life which made my own life pleasant is at an end, and the gates of death are shut upon my prospects.' All that was left was a 'state of dreary desolation in which the mind looks abroad impatient of itself, and finds nothing but emptiness and horror'.[15]

Johnson felt a new kind of loneliness, which, with a dark look at himself, he expressed in *Rasselas* almost immediately: 'I have neither mother to be delighted with the reputation of her son, nor wife to partake the honours of her husband.' He reached out to Lucy like a drowning man: she was 'the only person now left in the world with whom I think myself connected . . . I have nobody but you . . . If you and Kitty will keep the house, I think I shall like it best'. Just the thought of them in it helped: 'Kitty may carry on the trade for herself, keeping her own stock apart, and laying aside any money that she receives for any of the goods which her dear good Mistress has left behind her . . . My mother's debts, dear mother! I suppose I may pay with little difficulty . . . I fancy Kitty can do nothing better, and I shall not want to put her out of a house where she has lived so long and with so much virtue . . . You must have what part of the house you please while you are inclined to stay in it, but I flatter myself with hopes that you and I shall sometime pass our days together.' All he asked was that she write to him once a week, 'for I am now very desolate, and am loath to be universally forgotten'. Perhaps taking in lodgers, she continued to live there until 1763.[16]

He was especially vulnerable to these new sensations of loneliness and dislocation because the previous September he had been forced to give up the lease on Gough Square, no longer able to afford it. 'I have left off housekeeping,' he informed Langton, with understatement that belied the upheaval he must have felt. It meant of course that his household of non-paying guests would have to disperse. Mrs Williams and Dr Levet suddenly had to move out and find other places. She was fortunate to be able to move to a boarding school in Bolt Court off Fleet Street, not far from Gough Square, where she continued to live for many years until she rejoined Johnson in a house large enough to take her and others in. He saw her every day, dropping in after midnight for his customary tea before going to bed.[17]

3

It would have been extraordinary if the awkwardness of having to move out of Gough Square had not interrupted his Shakespearean work. *Rasselas*, however, his 'little story book', he appears to have written almost on the run. He told Reynolds that in the urgency of raising money for his mother he 'composed it in the evenings of one week, sent it to the press in portions as it was written, and had never since read it over'. The book exploded from him. As Shaw wrote, it was 'an early conception, on which ideas were matured long before the completion of the work'. It was published anonymously – it was not long before he was discovered as the author – in two volumes on 20 April 1759 for five shillings, a bestseller if ever there was one in his life, translated several times over the next few years into Italian, French, German and Dutch, and eventually published in America in 1768. It reached fifty editions before the century was out.[18]

Johnson's most popular work, *Rasselas* was his only attempt at a lengthy piece of prose fiction. It is an extended moral parable in the style of the oriental or eastern tales he wrote for several of the *Rambler* essays. In it he expressed again his strong views about self-delusion and benighted efforts to find human happiness, about how mortal existence overflows with 'vanity and vexation of spirit'. 'Human life is everywhere a state in which much is to be endured, and little to be enjoyed,' says the philosopher and poet Imlac. The tale tells of a young and hopeful prince, Rasselas, and his sister Nekayah, who, although they have all their desires satisfied, feel bored, imprisoned and shut off from life's variety in 'the happy valley' surrounded by mountains that was the ancient residence of Abyssinian royalty. 'I have already enjoyed too much,' says the prince, 'give me something to desire . . . I shall long to see the miseries of the world since the sight of them is necessary to happiness.' He spends much of his time bemoaning his fate. Under the tutelage of Imlac, he and his sister finally escape from the valley through the mountains to find the 'choice of life' that will bring them happiness. They make their way to Cairo where they encounter spectacles, some of them ludicrous and pitiful, of misguided efforts to find happiness and fulfilment.[19]

The very first sentence of the book is strongly cautionary and leaves no doubt about the overarching theme to follow: 'Ye who listen with credulity to the whispers of fancy, and pursue with eagerness the phantoms of hope; who expect that age will perform the promises of youth, and that the deficiencies of the present day will be supplied by the morrow; attend to the history of Rasselas prince of Abissinia.' If Johnson needed any confirmation of this theme in his own life, he needed only to reflect on the failure of the *Dictionary* to bring him the happiness and comforts for which he longed, and on the confusion rocking him all over again with his Shakespeare edition. He voiced his own despondency with his description of the prince's: 'His imagination was now at a stand; he had no prospect of entering into the world; and, notwithstanding all his endeavours to support himself, discontent by degrees preyed upon him, and he began again to lose his thoughts in sadness.' Dominating all the major early biographies of Johnson by Boswell, Piozzi, Hawkins and Murphy was the theme that Johnson's despondency and melancholia were responsible for the bleakness of the tale.[20]

The tale consists mostly of moral reflections and philosophical scepticism through dialogue, with virtually no action to relieve it. After their long and sobering journey the travellers return to Abyssinia, wiser in the understanding that no single place or philosophy can shield men and women completely from the pain, suffering, disease, grief, disappointment and sadness of life. Throw away 'the encumbrance of precepts', Imlac demands. 'Be not too hasty to trust, or to admire, the teachers of morality: they discourse like angels, but they live like men.'[21]

One day in Cairo, Rasselas tells Imlac that he intends henceforth to devote all his days to 'literary solitude'. Imlac, who often may be taken as Johnson's own voice and has already warned Rasselas that there is nobody who does not dread 'the moment when solitude should deliver him to the tyranny of reflection', warns him immediately and firmly that before making this choice he 'ought to examine its hazards, and converse with some of those who are grown old in the company of themselves'. For Imlac too much isolated study in the vain hope of impressing the world leads to selfishness and the precincts of insanity. An astronomer they meet, who says he has always suspected himself of madness, chimes in bitterly with the same warning: 'I can only tell that I have chosen wrong . . . I have missed the endearing elegance of female friendship, and the happy commerce of domestic tenderness'. Whatever he has gained from retirement and isolated study has been costly in terms of 'fear, disquiet, and scrupulosity'; and with a crescendo of dismal finality he announces, 'I now see how fatally I betrayed my quiet, by suffering chimeras to prey upon me in secret; but melancholy shrinks from communication.'[22]

Imlac then launches into what we may read as one of Johnson's fullest analyses of insanity. A few passages will convey his sense of urgency and fear on the subject. 'All power of fancy over reason is a degree of insanity,' says Imlac; 'it is not pronounced madness but when it comes ungovernable, and apparently influences speech or action. To indulge the power of fiction, and send imagination out upon the wing is often the sport of those who delight too much in silent speculation. When we are alone we are not always busy . . . the mind dances from scene to scene . . . Then fictions begin to operate as realities.' Religious 'scruples' about 'futurity', vain speculations on the afterlife, also conspire against reason. And grief, too, can foster fear and propel one towards melancholia. It is a devilish congregation of mental scorpions. The astronomer later says to Imlac, 'I am like a man habitually afraid of spectres, who is set at ease by a lamp, and wonders at the dread which harassed him in the dark, yet, if his lamp is extinguished, feels again the terrors which he knows that when it is light he shall feel no more'. Imlac responds with the last word on this disease:

> No disease of the imagination is so difficult to cure as that which is complicated with the dread of guilt: fancy and conscience then act interchangeably upon us, and so often shift their places, that the illusions of one are not distinguished from the dictates of the other. If fancy presents images not moral or religious, the mind drives them away when they give it pain, but when melancholic notions take the form of duty, they lay hold on the faculties without opposition, because we are afraid to exclude or banish them. For this reason the superstitious are often melancholy, and the melancholy almost always superstitious.[23]

But as in the *Rambler* essays, the picture is far from totally bleak. Courage plays a great part. Johnson portrays the main characters with piety and compassion, hope and at times humour. Rasselas and Nekayah, in spite of their experiences and Imlac's counsel, return home with sustaining hope, but realising at the same time that they are not likely ever to obtain their desires. The final chapter is titled, 'The conclusion, in which nothing is concluded'. The important thing is to keep moving and aspiring. As Nekayah realises at the end, it is not the 'choice of life' but the 'choice of eternity' that is crucial to understand.

The critical reception of *Rasselas* was mixed. Shenstone thought the tale 'below Mr J'. The poet and essayist Hester Mulso (later Chapone), an intimate member of Richardson's literary coterie – his 'little spitfire' – and friend of Elizabeth Carter, was 'grievously disappointed' in 'the giant Johnson' because she thought the tale was too bleak, uninstructive (even harmful) therefore for young people, unnatural in its characterisation, ill-contrived, and inconclusive. 'I think the only maxim one can deduce from this story,' Mulso wrote to Carter in a gossipy vein, 'is that human life is a scene of unmixed wretchedness and that all states and conditions of it are equally miserable'. She admitted her anger that with his 'poisonous' inferences 'poor Mr Johnson . . . had considered the worst side of the character of human nature, and seems to be but little acquainted with the best and happiest of its affections'. The general complaints were also that *Rasselas* uses too many 'hard' (especially polysyllabic) words, its characters are indiscriminate cardboard figures who are merely mouthpieces for Johnson's ideas – the women come across as 'Johnson in petticoats' – and speak in an unrelieved high style, its narrative lacks emotional force, its tone is dictatorial, and its plot is anaemic. On the positive side it was praised for its sublimity, purity of diction, elegance and eloquence and moral insights on human affairs. It was also praised for its fine Eastern fable.[24]

4

After months in residential limbo, Johnson described his move on 23 March 1759 to Staples Inn as 'a change of outward things' which he hoped would be answered by 'a reformation of my thoughts, words, and practices'. Staples Inn is a well-preserved late sixteenth-century clutch of buildings around a courtyard with a half-timbered front that takes one by surprise today on a walk along noisy High Holborn. Then in an unattractive neighbourhood, the building was a lodging house for law students as well as others who came recommended. That summer he escaped to Oxford again for no fewer than seven weeks, staying at All Souls and Trinity colleges as a guest of Warton and Robert Vansittart, Regius Professor of Civil Law from 1767–89, whom he 'much esteemed'. He let himself go on this Oxford visit with boyish abandon, relieved to escape for a couple of months the gloom and impermanency of his life in London. He took to wearing his academic gown 'almost ostentatiously', which was 'at my first coming quite new and handsome'. 'I have swum thrice, which I had disused for many years. I have proposed to Vansittart climbing over the wall, but he has refused me.' And he joined in a procession in his gown to hear a lecture at the Sheldonian Theatre on the occasion of the installation of the seventh Earl of Westmorland as Chancellor of Oxford – 'I clapped my hands till they are sore', he wrote, after listening to the speech by Dr William King, Principal of St Mary Hall, who had personally brought Johnson's MA diploma to him in London in February 1755. Soon after he returned to London, he left Staples Inn for Gray's Inn until August 1760, when he moved yet again to chambers one flight of stairs up at 1 Inner Temple Lane. There he fixed himself until 1765.[25]

5

While he was working, or not working, on Shakespeare at the end of the decade, he felt the need again to get involved in writing he could do regularly without much effort and which would be read by the public immediately. In 1759, at the invitation of John Newbery, he wrote an Introduction to *The World Displayed*, a collection of short travel narratives published by Newbery between 1759 and 1761, in which he returned stridently to the theme of colonial and missionary exploitation of Africa, America and Asia by Europeans, chiefly the Spanish, Portuguese and Belgians, but also the British ('English barbarians'). His Introduction is loaded with outspoken anti-imperialism. It also attacks the start of the slave trade. Newbery also had him help choose the travel books for the collection and serve as one of its editors. In December that year he also wrote three letters to the *Daily Gazeteer* on behalf of the architect John Gwynn's entry in the competition for the erection of the new Blackfriars Bridge, in which he revealed a familiarity with engineering issues relating both to the bridge and architecture in general.[26]

Running steadily along every Saturday between 15 April 1758 and 5 April 1760 were Johnson's anonymous *Idler* essays, the third of his protracted periodical series. Newbery once more seems to have encouraged him to write them. Having decided to start his weekly eight-page newspaper, the *Universal Chronicle*, Newbery needed something original with which to launch the paper and lure readers.[27] Since the paper took almost all its copy from other periodicals, it was no surprise that readers turned to it mainly for the *Idler* essays published each week on the first page. Again, it did not take people long to discover Johnson was their author. Contending that Johnson accepted the commission to write them because of an 'aversion to a labour he had undertaken' – i.e. the Shakespeare edition – Hawkins maintained that the essays 'were extemporaneous compositions, and hardly ever underwent a revision before they were sent to the press'. 'Sir, you shall not do more than I have done myself,' he said when Langton asked to read one he was about to rush into the post. He wrote all but twelve of the 103 *Idler* essays.[28]

In order to attract more readers, he wrote them with 'less body and more spirit . . . more variety of real life'. As a result, readers turning to them for the accustomed depth of the *Rambler* often were, and still are, disappointed. Shorter and with briefer sentences and an easier style, many of their subjects are less consequential and more topical. Tired of writing periodical essays and impatient with weekly deadlines, Johnson did not appear to have his heart in them. Nonetheless, the essays were widely read and pirated by other journals and papers. The piracy grew so extensive, in fact, that he was driven in the 5 January 1759 issue of the *Universal Chronicle* to threaten retaliation by raiding other periodicals – he would 'degrade them . . . contract them into a narrow space, and sell them at a humble price'. The piracies so depressed the market that Newbery's first collected edition of them in 1761 sold only 1,500 copies over four years. With two-thirds of the profits, Johnson earned only about £85.[29]

There are a number of serious essays in the series, however. These include eighteen critical literary essays, as well as ones on history, slavery, the wisdom of self-denial, the frustrated expectations of pleasure, the frustrated expectations of achievement, the vanity of authorship, the oppression of native Americans by white invaders, the vacuity of much travelling and travel writing, weather as a psychological barometer, and the uncertainty of friendship. But of the greatest value to the biographer are essays for which Johnson once more turned the searchlight upon his own mental and physical state. At least sixteen essays are emotionally loaded biographically and autobiographically.

Returning to the subject of biography that he had eloquently considered in *Rambler* 60, he wrote urgently in *Idler* 84 about what he thought might be the most important moral imperative for any author: to write honestly about his private self. He never made a distinction between biography and autobiography – indeed, the word 'autobiography' did not then exist. Because biography is 'most easily applied to the purposes of life', the great issues of good and evil and vice and folly, in 'honest and impartial biography' we may be told 'not how any man became great, but how he was made happy; not how he lost the favour of his prince, but how he became discontented with himself'. The kind of biography that is most valuable, then, is that in which the writer includes 'his own story'. He has 'at least the qualification of an historian, the knowledge of the truth'. The problem, as always, was that although he admonished a number of people to write regularly about themselves in journals, he himself on the whole was failing to do so. And he recognised this, as he made clear in the penultimate essay (102) of the *Idler* series: 'the author, however conspicuous, or however important, either in the public eye or in his own', unfortunately all too often 'leaves his life to be related by his successors, for he cannot gratify his vanity but by sacrificing his ease'. And yet, scholars and authors, the 'sons of literature', capable of eloquent introspection and victims of the same distresses as everyone else, have more to impart than most.

The lives of writers are perpetual purgatory – and here he is writing under the burden of the Shakespeare edition he had yet to finish: 'They are entangled by contracts which they know not how to fulfil . . . Every publication is a new period of time from which some increase or declension of fame is to be reckoned. The gradations of a hero's life are from battle to battle, and of an author's from book to book.'[30]

Johnson saw in his own humanity a type of epitome of mankind. The most famous example of this is *Idler* 31 on idleness, about Sober, a fictitious figure Mrs Thrale insisted was a self-portrait. Sober is the portrait of an idle man who deceives himself. Idleness is pernicious and subtle because it is 'a silent and peaceful quality, that neither raises envy by ostentation, nor hatred by opposition'. It is often disguised by 'turbulence and hurry' and is the bedfellow of procrastination, the connoisseur of 'petty business'. Sober takes obsessive pleasure in conversation: 'there is no end of his talk or his attention; to speak or to hear is equally pleasing . . . and [he] is free for the time from his own reproaches'. He is fearful of solitude: 'there is a time when he must go home, that his friends may sleep' – 'these are the moments of which poor Sober trembles at the thought'. Sober has devised hobbies to suppress the misery of this fearful loneliness, momentarily at least, one of which is chemistry: 'He has a small furnace, which he employs in distillation, and which has long been the solace of his life. He draws oils and waters, and essences and spirits, which he knows to be of no use; sits and counts the drops as they come from his retort, and forgets that, while a drop is falling, a moment flies away'.[31]

Johnson repeats these themes in several other *Idler* essays. As in the last chapter of *Rasselas*, the only certain conclusion is that 'nothing is concluded'. The only real solution is to turn to God, of which the coincidence of the 1760 Easter season with the last *Idler* was an apt reminder. Easter is a time for 'the examination of conscience': 'the review of life, the extinction of earthly desires and the renovation of holy purposes'. This is when 'the imagination of the heart shall be brought to judgement, and an everlasting futurity shall be determined by the past'. In his birthday prayer that year, he resolved 'to reclaim imagination', to keep it from being overrun by chimeras.[32]

CHAPTER 22

'Vain and Corrupt Imaginations'

I

THE CRISIS OF JOHNSON'S MENTAL history beginning in the early 1760s was severe. It would last for most of the decade. Arthur Murphy, who was well tuned to Johnson's life at this time, composed a profile of his lassitude, debilitating self-doubt and fear of insanity in describing his worst sustained attack since immediately after quitting his studies at Oxford:

Indolence was the time of danger: it was then that his spirits, not employed abroad, turned with inward hostility against himself. His reflections on his own life and conduct were always severe; and, wishing to be immaculate, he destroyed his own peace by unnecessary scruples. He tells us, that when he surveyed his past life, he discovered nothing but a barren waste of time, very near to madness. His life, he says, from his earliest years, was wasted in a morning bed; and his reigning sin was a general sluggishness, to which he was always inclined, and, in part of his life, almost compelled, by a morbid melancholy, and weariness of mind . . . An apprehension of the worst calamity that can befall human nature hung over him all the rest of his life, like the sword of the tyrant suspended over his guest. In his sixtieth year he had a mind to write the history of his melancholy; but he desisted, not knowing whether it would not too much disturb him.

Several times he referred to his 'depression', but whether it was acute enough to have been regarded as madness by his own era's definitions – as he suspected it was – was something he would not discuss with anyone. He feared that if he spoke of it, what he hoped might be fictions of the imagination might 'begin to operate as realities, [and] false opinions fasten upon the mind'.[1]

His lodgings in Inner Temple Lane, where he lived in mild poverty between August 1760 to July 1765, did not do much to raise his spirits. The painter Ozias Humphry visited him there and remarked that the lodgings consisted of four filthy, dingy and worn-out rooms, one of which was like 'an old counting house' where the great man sat 'waving over his breakfast like a lunatic'. The furniture included 'a very large deal writing-desk, an old walnut-tree table, and five ragged chairs of four different sets'. According to Hawkins, Johnson also used the garret above his rooms as a chemistry laboratory where he carried on simple experiments to distil 'peppermint, and the dregs of strong beer, from the latter whereof he was able to extract a strong but very nauseous spirit, which all might smell, but few chose to taste'. Indeed, Humphry could not help thinking he was looking upon a madman: 'He is a very large man, and was dressed in a dirty brown coat and waistcoat, with breeches that were brown also (though they had been crimson), and an old black wig: his shirt collar and sleeves were unbuttoned; his stockings were down about his feet, which had on them, by way of slippers, an old pair of shoes.' It was one o'clock in the afternoon and Johnson had just got up from bed: 'He seldom goes to bed till near two in the morning; and Mr Reynolds tells me he generally drinks tea about an hour after he has supped.' Johnson's conversation was overbearing: 'every thing he says is as *correct* as a *second edition*: 'tis almost impossible to argue with him, he is so sententious and so knowing'. On another day, a Cambridge student and his friend who called on him there were amazed at what they saw. The student wrote that the wainscoted and dark entrance room led to the study, 'into which, a little before noon, came rolling, as if just roused from his cabin, the truly uncouth figure of our literary Colossus, in a strange black wig, too little for him by half, but which, before our next interview, was exchanged for that very respectable brown one in which his friend Sir Joshua so faithfully depicted him'. Thus he held court to those who could find him and were emboldened to look him up – which were many, according to the neighbour on the corner who told Hawkins that 'during the time he dwelt there, more inquiries were made at his shop for Mr Johnson, than for all the inhabitants put together of both the Inner and Middle Temple'.[2]

Visitors to Inner Temple Lane did not always come to see him. Hawkins reminisced that when he knocked on the door and Frank answered, 'a group of his African countrymen were sitting round a fire in the gloomy ante-room.' This is the first mention of Frank's use of Johnson's house as a meeting place for blacks, another sign of his master's sympathy for their plight as slaves in London.[3] Except for the mistake of thinking Frank an 'African', the image sounds credible enough, a glimpse of the informal, bohemian existence Johnson was leading. Frank's duties included waiting on the table when there were guests, running errands and answering the door. He and his master continued to live together until in the late 1760s Johnson sent him to a school in Hertfordshire for some serious schooling.

2

In 1760 he wrote little apart from drawing the *Idler* to a conclusion. In January he wrote in Baretti's name the Dedication to his *Dictionary of the English and Italian Languages*, an immensely successful book frequently reprinted for a century afterwards. In August he contributed the Introduction to the *Proceedings of the Committee for Cloathing French Prisoners*, a reminder of his generous commitment to humanitarian causes. Thomas Hollis, the political writer and republican friend of Benjamin Franklin, and benefactor of Harvard College whom Johnson described as a 'strenuous Whig' and defended as 'a dull poor creature as ever lived', asked him to write it for five guineas in an effort to ameliorate the condition of French prisoners during the Seven Years' War. In December at a meeting of the Society for Promoting Arts and Commerce, Hollis also suggested that the Society tempt Johnson with another five pounds to write a piece on the 'polite and liberal arts'. Johnson remembered in 1781 that Hollis 'pointed me out as the man who could do it best. This, you will observe, was kindness to me.' Kindness or not, he 'slipped away, and escaped it' with the spurious reason that he was 'not sufficiently informed' to do it.[4]

On 25 October 1760, between seven and eight in the morning, King George II died of a stroke in his water-closet at Kensington Palace and his grandson acceded to the throne as George III. At noon the next day he was proclaimed King outside Savile House in Leicester Fields. The bells of churches rang out and that night bonfires lit the night sky. Johnson had a low opinion of the first two Georges, but this one was different. 'We were so weary of our old King', he wrote in June 1761 to Baretti in Italy, 'that we are much pleased with his successor; of whom we are so much inclined to hope great things, that most of us begin already to believe them. The young man is hitherto blameless.' Horace Walpole immediately thought well of the new King when he kissed the King's hand three days later, remarking that there was none of that German insularity about him and that he enjoyed walking about and actually talking to people in good English. 'Farmer George', as he was called, was determined to please the people and, perhaps most important for Johnson, supported the arts, artists and writers. Anticipating the Coronation he 'lent his friendly assistance' to John Gwynn by writing the first four paragraphs of his *Thoughts on the Coronation* the preceding summer, urging in his best democratic spirit that the procession needed to be re-routed so that it could be seen by the public: 'Magnificence in obscurity is equally vain with *a Sun-dial in the Grave.*'[5]

Reynolds, for one, was sanguine about the prospect of royal patronage, though he appears to have offended the King right at the start by agreeing to do a sketch in oil of the Coronation procession to the Abbey a year later in September but for no less than one thousand pounds. The King, who doubtless thought he had honoured Reynolds sufficiently by asking him to do it in the first place, would have none of it and thereafter maintained a coldness towards him, disappointing his hopes of being appointed Painter to the King. When Johnson was asked if Reynolds minded being passed over, he replied that 'it has ever been more profitable to be popular among the people than favoured by the King: it is no reflection on Mr Reynolds not to be employed by them; but it will be a reflection on the Court not to have employed him'.[6]

Johnson was more discreet than Reynolds in dealing with the new monarch. In January 1761, he wrote an 'Address' to him on behalf of the 'Painters, Sculptors, and Architects' of the Society of Artists, patriotically championing British artists and praising the King's apparent appreciation and patronage of the arts: 'It is our happiness to live in the age, when our arts may hope for new advances towards perfection, assisted by the favour of a British King, of a monarch no less judicious to distinguish, than powerful to reward: who knows the usefulness and value of that skill, which delights the eye with beauty, but not corrupts the manners by unlawful passions.' This enthusiastic glorification of the arts seems to come from nowhere to many who believe Johnson had little interest in and appreciation of the arts. After all, had not Mrs Thrale (who met Johnson a few years later) stated plainly: 'Dr Johnson's utter scorn of painting was such, that I have heard him say, that he should sit very quietly in a room hung round with the works of the greatest masters, and never feel the slightest disposition to turn them if their backs were outermost, unless it might be for the sake of telling Sir Joshua that he *had* turned them.' He was 'too blind to discern the perfections of an art', she insisted, nor could he understand why Reynolds brushed his genius on such a perishable material as canvas. It was better to use copper. Sculpture came off even worse. Boswell heard him say, 'a fellow will hack half a year at a block of marble to make something in stone that hardly resembles a man. The value of statuary is owing to its difficulty. You would not value the finest head cut upon a carrot'.[7]

Johnson's activities, however, suggested he was far from indifferent to artists and their affairs. To begin with, he was the intimate friend of

Reynolds, the most popular painter of his day, from whom he absorbed a belief in the importance of painting. And it was largely through him that he became involved in the encouragement of painters and sculptors. In December 1756 he was elected to the Society of Arts, founded in 1754 as the Society of the Encouragement of Arts, Manufactures and Commerce to promote a partnership between the fine and practical arts. It was the first organisation ever set up in Britain to benefit both the arts and sciences. His name appeared on the first membership list along with other members of the famous Turk's Head Club, generally known simply as The Club: Reynolds, Burney, Goldsmith, Garrick and Gibbon. They were in good company, for the list also included a galaxy of the age's greatest painters, sculptors, writers, architects and musicians. In *Idler* 45, he urged that while 'genius is chiefly exerted in historical pictures' there was room in the nation for patronage of 'painting through all its diversities'. The next year he took the part of painters in the Society of Artists, a distinct group, by writing a letter for them to the Society of Arts asking for the use of its new Great Hall at Beaufort Buildings in the Strand to stage what would be the first ever public exhibition of art in England. In a 'Plan' he drafted to accompany the letter he justified the exhibition by declaring the need to prevent artists of ability from languishing in obscurity. The exhibition of 130 paintings by 69 artists, which took place in Sir William Chambers's innovative double-cube room eighty feet long and forty wide, was spectacularly successful, at least from the Society of Arts' point of view, with over twenty thousand people attending.[8]

But the exhibition turned into a mad scramble, almost a riot, which dramatised the differences in the approach to art between the artists and the Society. A portrait of Garrick as Richard III, for example, was so popular that the mob broke windows crowding in to see it. When a few months later the artists asked Johnson to draft a second letter to the Society of Arts for another exhibition, he obliged by urging the Society this time to charge an entrance fee of a shilling in order to deter multitudes of ignorant viewers, 'no proper judges of statuary or painting', from attending and turning the event into something of another commercial circus. As a result of its refusal, a philosophical and organisational schism between the two groups occurred and eminent artists like Reynolds, Hogarth and Gainsborough staged their own independent exhibition in Cock's auction rooms in Covent Garden. Eventually that schism led to the founding of the Royal Academy in 1769. An indication of his high profile as literary apologist for the art world at this time was the publication of a caricature, 'The Combat', featuring him as 'Toastmaster General' of the Society of Arts and author of what might be termed the Society of Artists manifestos.[9]

3

In the winter of 1761–2, for the first time in twenty years, Johnson travelled up to Lichfield. Both the town and Lucy were a disappointment to him. 'My daughter-in-law [stepdaughter], from whom I expected most,' he wrote to Baretti, 'and whom I met with sincere benevolence, has lost the beauty and gaiety of youth, without having gained much of the wisdom of age.' As for the town itself, the streets seemed shorter and narrower 'inhabited by a new race of people to whom I was very little known'. His old 'play-fellows' were now old and he felt himself 'no longer young'. He 'wandered about' for five days and then hurried back to London where 'if there is not much happiness, there is at least such a diversity of good and evil, that slight vexations do not fix upon the heart.'[10]

4

After 19 July 1762, Johnson had much more about which to write to his friends than merely the account of an uneventful 'journey of a wit to his own town' or local gossip. On that day, Alexander Wedderburn (Boswell's boyhood friend and later Lord Chancellor) informed him that the First Lord of the Treasury, Lord Bute, had approved and the King granted him an annual pension of £300 (about £30,000 today). More than anything else, it was a long-delayed expression of gratitude from a nation that thus far had deplorably neglected its lexicographical hero and great moralist. One moment he was desperate for money, moving dangerously close again to the fringes of Grub Street, the next he was lifted out of poverty and reflecting on the unfamiliar sensations of financial security. At first he hesitated to accept the award. People might think, in light of his past virulent attacks on government and especially his definition of *pension* as 'pay given to a state hireling for treason', that this was a payoff by the Government to keep him quiet in the future. But he canvassed his friends, especially Reynolds, for their opinions, and everyone agreed it was not a government bribe. When Johnson went to see him, Lord Bute told him, 'It is not given you for anything you are to do, but for what you have done.' Bute repeated this twice, to make sure Johnson understood. So he decided to accept it, though inevitably critics would continue to claim that he had been bribed, which made him wish the pension had been twice as much so that his critics might make 'twice as much noise'. To Bute he later wrote, 'You have conferred your favours on a man who has neither alliance nor interest, who has not merited them by services, nor courted them by officiousness; you have spared him the shame of solicitation, and the anxiety of suspense.' The money was slow in coming, however, and there was one little moment of awkwardness in November when he had to write to Bute to ask him to facilitate the payments.[11]

There was another financial windfall, less than a year later, but it only indirectly affected him. In the spring of 1763 Lucy's brother Jervis died, leaving her £10,000 (about £1,000,000 today). This changed Johnson's relationship with her significantly. She was no longer dependent on him and no longer needed to live in the family home with Kitty.

Johnson's friends now expected him to move out of Inner Temple Lane and begin to live in a manner more fitting the literary celebrity he had become. He did no such thing. His clothing remained shabby and he stayed in his 'decrepit' lodgings for three more years. 'Now that I have this pension,' he said to Boswell, 'I am the same man in every respect that I have ever been; I retain the same principles.' He could not help adding tongue-in-cheek, 'It is true, that I cannot now curse (smiling) the House of

Hanover; nor would it be decent for me to drink King James's health in the wine that King George gives me money to pay for. But, Sir, I think that the pleasure of cursing the House of Hanover, and drinking King James's health, are amply overbalanced by three hundred pounds a year.' Neither did the money have any perceptibly positive effect in lifting him out of his melancholic inertia, which may have been the reason he just stayed where he was.[12]

In August 1762 Reynolds decided that a trip with Johnson to Devon might just be the medicine he needed. Now a rich man earning approximately £5,000 a year (about half a million today), Reynolds had not been back to his native county for ten years. It turned out to be a great adventure, from which Johnson thought he had taken 'a great accession of new ideas'. He kept no known record of it, but Reynolds did.[13]

After spending two nights with Joseph Warton at Winchester College, they proceeded to Salisbury and visited the Earl of Pembroke's Wilton House about ten miles to the west of the cathedral town. Then it was on to Dorchester and nearby Corfe Castle. At Kingston Lacy there was a moment of embarrassment when Johnson became bored by the owner's explanations of the paintings in the house and (according to Frances Reynolds who heard of it from her brother) 'began to exhibit his antics, stretching out his legs alternately as far as he could possibly stretch; at the same time pressing his foot on the floor as heavily as he could possibly press, as if endeavouring to smooth the carpet, or rather perhaps to rumple it, and every now and then collecting all his force, apparently to effect a concussion of the floor'. 'Dr Johnson, I believe the floor is very firm,' the guide remarked, which made him stop. From Dorset they made their way to Exeter and Plymouth, stopping first at Torrington to see Reynolds's two other sisters Elizabeth and Mary – Renny was also there – where Johnson nonplussed everyone by swallowing no fewer than thirteen pancakes at a single sitting. They stayed three weeks in Plymouth at the home of Reynolds's boyhood friend the celebrated surgeon John Mudge, whose son William became Johnson's godson a few months later. He is supposed to have amazed his hostess there, too – who was counting assiduously – by drinking seventeen cups of tea in one sitting. When he asked for one more, she cried out, 'What! Another, Dr Johnson?', to which he replied, 'Madam, you are rude.'[14]

The splendour of the navy in Plymouth harbour and the industrial bustle of shipbuilding there fascinated him. When he was not prowling around the docks and sailing, he and Reynolds were entertained at a number of noble estates in the area, including Mount Edgcumbe with its glorious gardens. Perhaps it was on his birthday on 18 September that at one of these seats he exhibited the athleticism he had displayed as a youth. All someone needed to do to set him off was to mention having climbed this or that tree or wall in youth, or make an idle physical boast of athleticism. It was likely to be answered with Johnson's challenge to run a race, roll down a hill, leap over a wall, or jump into a pond for a swim. An anonymous writer in the *European Magazine* in 1798 remembered such feats as 'childish playfulness': 'It was no uncommon thing to see him hop, step, and jump.' Renny described a race at some country house near Plymouth where this time his competition was female: 'A young lady present boasted that she could outrun any person; on which Dr Johnson rose up and said, "Madam, you cannot outrun me"; and, going out on the lawn, they started. The lady at first had the advantage; but Dr Johnson, happening to have slippers on much too small for his feet, kicked them off up into the air, and ran a great length without them, leaving the lady far behind him, and having won the victory, he returned, leading her by the hand, with looks of high exultation and delight.' Bennet Langton had another example, recalling a rolling incident from the top of a hill at Langton, his Lincolnshire home. Looking down the hill, Johnson announced he had a mind 'to take a roll down'. Langton and others present attempted to stop him, but he persisted that 'he had not had a roll for a long time'. Emptying his pockets, he laid down 'parallel with the edge of the hill' and 'descended, turning himself over and over till he came to the bottom'. Stories abounded about his physical strength, including separating large fighting dogs, subduing thieves in London streets, threatening the actor Samuel Foote with an oak stick if he ever deployed his talent for mimicry in ridiculing him on stage, and throwing someone into the pit in a theatre, chair and all, who had taken his seat.[15]

5

They were back in London in late September, having been away for almost six weeks. The fresh air, exercise and change of scene had been a
tonic for Johnson. In October, however, he received a sobering jolt from
the poet Charles Churchill who mocked him in his poem *The Ghost* for
delaying the Shakespeare edition. A very witty and effective satirist, not
easy to ignore but ignore him Johnson did, Churchill took him to task in
The Ghost for deceiving his subscribers: 'He for subscribers baits his
hook,/And takes their cash – but where's the book?' (3:801–2). In December, Johnson took a second break by visiting Oxford again, this time staying at University College as the guest of young Robert Chambers. The
main reason he gave for the visit was to get rid of a 'violent' cough by escaping London air, but the visit had the look of still another flight from
Shakespeare. Little is known of this visit.[16]

His friendship with Chambers (1737–1803) was one of several with
young scholarly men that were blossoming around this time. There was a
strong element of mentorship in several of them. Chambers had been consulting with Johnson about an academic legal career ever since 1758 when
the Vinerian chair of law was established at Oxford and the distinguished
jurist Sir William Blackstone was elected to it, thus inaugurating the
academic study of law in Britain. They first met in the summer of 1754 at
Gough Square when seventeen-year-old Chambers began studying law
at the Middle Temple. And when he began his study that autumn at
Lincoln College, Oxford, Johnson began supervising his studies and coun-
selling him in general. 'Johnson, whose kind attractive Call/Led me at
Learning's Shrine to bend,' Chambers wrote in a poem of gratitude in
1766. Their friendship would expand into a three-year clandestine legal
collaboration after Chambers succeeded Sir William Blackstone as the
second Vinerian professor of English law. Chambers turned to Johnson
somewhat desperately for help with many of the sixty public legal lectures
he was required to give, a series amounting to a comprehensive review of
English law patterned after Blackstone's own lectures that were the nucleus of his famous *Commentaries on the Laws of England* (1765–9). They

reveal an extensive knowledge of English law that Johnson picked up over the years through reading and many friendships with lawyers like Walmesley, Taylor, Hawkins, Murphy, Burke and two later members of the Club, Sir William Jones and William Scott, first Baron Stowell, a famous jurist who once remarked that if Johnson had followed law instead of literature he 'might have been Lord Chancellor of Great Britain, and attained to the dignity of a peerage'.[17]

Beauclerk and especially Langton were two other young men with whom he was continuing to develop even closer ties. One piece of entertainment Beauclerk provided Johnson in 1763 was a visit to his shabby lodgings by the sparkling, beautiful and famous Madame de Boufflers, the mistress of the Prince of Conti, advisor to Louis XV. At her home in Paris she was well known as hostess to prominent writers, musicians, scientists, politicians and notables such as Mozart, Rousseau, David Hume and Jean D'Alembert. In London that summer she told Beauclerk she would like the novelty of meeting Johnson. Beauclerk sprang to it and took her around to see his famous friend. Years later he told Boswell that after 'she was entertained with his conversation for some time' they had just emerged from the house on to the street 'when all at once I heard a noise like thunder. This was occasioned by Johnson, who it seems upon a little recollection, had taken it into his head that he ought to have done the honours of his literary residence to a foreign lady of quality, and eager to show himself a man of gallantry, was hurrying down the staircase in violent agitation. He overtook us . . . and brushing in between me and Madame de Boufflers, seized her hand, and conducted her to her coach. His dress was a rusty brown morning suit, a pair of old shoes by way of slippers, a little shrivelled wig sticking on the top of his head, and the sleeves of his shirt and the knees of his breeches hanging loose. A crowd quickly gathered to watch all this and 'were not a little struck by this singular appearance'.[18]

Langton, who had recently returned from doing the Grand Tour in Italy with Beauclerk from March to August 1763, lugged home a copy of the French Academy's *Dictionnaire*, which he presented to Johnson as a present from the members of the Academy in token of their admiration for his *Dictionary*. After that he and Jonhson became good friends. It never seemed to matter to him that Langton did not fulfil his literary promise and scarcely ever published anything. 'The earth does not bear a worthier man than Bennet Langton,' he once announced. 'I know not who will go to heaven if Langton does not' – an allusion to what he called Langton's 'evangelical virtue'. But there was something of the ridiculous about him. Apart from mismanaging his affairs, living expensively in London, and lacking focus and a sense of direction, he was thought to be absurd as well as very odd-looking. Mrs Thrale was confused by him: 'Mr Langton seems to stand in a very odd light among us . . . he is acknowledged learned, pious, and elegant of manners – yet he is always a person unrespected and commonly ridiculous.' And yet he corresponded frequently with several members of the Club, among them Reynolds, Garrick and Burke, who liked and respected him. He married the Countess of Rothes in 1770 and had no fewer than ten children whom he indulged and who, on visits to the family, Johnson tended to find exceedingly wearing. He was more circumspect and equable than Beauclerk in his conversation with Johnson, more gentle and discreet. Even so, there was one courageous moment when Langton surprised Johnson by telling him that the one quality above all he should overcome in himself was his habit of being rough in conversation; and he occasionally urged Boswell not to encourage that in him by playing the fool.[19]

There was one other young admirer in the wings in 1763, a young Scot who in the last twenty years of Johnson's life would commit a large part of his life and soul to the 'Rambler' and, in the process, shape enormously the world's knowledge of him. For Johnson, who in this case was sought out and his friendship zealously cultivated by the young worshipper, the relationship was one of two new intimate friendships in the next two or three years that would help him through a deepening mental crisis.

CHAPTER 23

Boswell and Mrs Thrale

I

BY 1763, ROBERT LEVET had gone into hiding in Inner Temple Lane with Johnson and Frank. He joined them there after the prostitute he had disastrously married was arrested for street theft. From then on he lived with Johnson permanently until he died in 1782. There was no room for Anna Williams there but soon after receiving his pension Johnson began to give her an allowance. In addition to dropping in on her regularly at her lodgings, he made her life more interesting by occasionally taking her along with him on Sundays to dine with friends. She did not usually make a good impression: 'from her manner of eating, in consequence of her blindness, she could not but offend the delicacy of persons of nice sensations'.[1]

After taking Levet in, Johnson very likely discussed with him the complications and dangers of passion and marriage. He had strong views on the subject, which he had expressed frequently in his moral essays. On learning that in Italy Baretti had fallen hopelessly for the daughter of a friend in Milan, he was quick to point out dangers: 'There is indeed nothing that so much seduces reason from her vigilance, as the thought of passing life with an amiable woman; and if all would happen that a lover fancies, I know not what other terrestrial happiness would deserve pursuit. But love and marriage are different states.' John Taylor was also on the receiving end of his marital advice when his wife left him alleging he had had an affair with their household servant, which Taylor denied. For a clergyman and prominent owner of the manor of Ashbourne, the accusation was dynamite, true or not. 'Do not let this vexation take possession of your thoughts,' Johnson cautioned, 'or sink too deeply into your heart . . . The happiness of conjugal life cannot be ascertained or secured either by sense or by virtue, and therefore its miseries may be numbered among those evils which we cannot prevent and must only labour to endure with patience, and palliate with judgement.' His wife would return, Johnson reassured him, and 'mend her behaviour' when she ran out of money. 'Nature has given women so much power that the law has very wisely given them little.' Above all, Taylor must protect himself 'from melancholy and depression of mind, which is a greater evil than a disobedient wife. Do not give way to grief, nor nurse vexation in solitude'.[2]

Johnson had reached the stage in his life when he was ready and very willing to administer counsel. It veritably issued from him in a stream of moral and practical wisdom, especially for young people, whose company he particularly sought. 'I love the acquaintance of young people because, in the first place, I don't like to think myself growing old. In the next place, young acquaintances must last longest, if they do last; and then . . . young men have more virtue than old men . . . I love the young dogs of this age: they have more wit and humour and knowledge of life than we had' – though they were not such good scholars, he added. It was propitious, therefore, that when Johnson walked into Thomas Davies's bookshop near Covent Garden on 16 May 1763, and met a young Scot aged twenty-two who was taking tea with the bookseller, he discovered a person needing his mentorship and sage counsel, eager to drink it in more greedily than any other person he had ever met and would meet. Their meeting turned out to be one of the most important encounters in English literary history. From it and the friendship that ensued would come a great biography and a huge amount of what we know today about Johnson's life and thoughts. The Scotsman was, of course, James Boswell (1740–95).[3]

Boswell was in London to get away from Scotland and his dour and relentlessly pragmatic father, one of the fifteen judges on the High Court of the Judiciary of Scotland. His father was already convinced he was a fool, whose literary interests and fascination with English culture frivolously and irresponsibly distracted him from the central business of practising law in Edinburgh and preparing for the day he would take over as laird of Auchinleck, the family seat in Ayrshire. He was in love with the Edinburgh theatre to the immense annoyance of his father and had taken to keeping a journal. He had already shown signs of melancholia, experiencing at the age of seventeen a nervous breakdown. He also nourished a disgust for the provinciality of Scottish life and told his incredulous father he was little inclined to practise law. All this was a recipe for disaster for the father-son relationship, which, as the years passed, became more hostile on the father's side until he even contemplated disinheriting his son. The visit to London was the result of a temporary truce and agreement: James agreed to study law in Utrecht for one year, which seemed to him one of the dullest prospects on earth, in exchange for being allowed to spend a few months in London and (after the year in Utrecht) tour the loose federation of independent German principalities for several weeks. He promised his father that after this time abroad, which was not supposed to last much more than a year, he would finish his legal studies and knuckle down at home to the life of an advocate with a rich wife who could replenish the coffers of the depleted Boswell estates. To his father it seemed a tidy programme and a good bargain that would enable him to have his way in the end.

When Boswell met Johnson, he had already been in London six months, ecstatic over his new freedom and bridled only by the limited allowance his father sent him. He lived the life of a rake, doing his best to hobnob with aristocracy and meet famous political and literary personalities whom, back in Scotland, he could only dream of knowing. He was frequently at the theatre and gaming parties and in the beds of prostitutes. We know all of this in enormous detail from his now famous journal. His greatest ambition in London was to meet Johnson, for whom he confessed 'a kind of mysterious veneration' based chiefly on the *Rambler*. As Johnson frequently popped in to see Davies, Boswell repeatedly did the same, hoping he would appear one day while he was there. He finally did, Boswell wrote: 'a man of most dreadful appearance. He is a very big man, is troubled with sore eyes, the palsy [convulsive tics], and the king's evil. He is very slovenly in his dress and speaks with a most uncouth voice . . . He has great humour and is a worthy man. But his dogmatical roughness of manners is disagreeable.'

Boswell's account of the event is one of hundreds of beautifully crafted scenes in his journals and the *Life*:

> Mr Davies mentioned my name, and respectfully introduced me to him. I was much agitated; and recollecting his prejudice against the Scotch, of which I had heard much, I said to Davies, 'Don't tell where I come from.' – 'From Scotland,' cried Davies, roguishly. 'Mr Johnson, (said I) I do indeed come from Scotland, but I cannot help it.' . . . 'That, Sir, I find, is what a very great many of your countrymen cannot help.'[4]

Stunned and struggling to recover, Boswell then foolishly strayed into dangerous waters by ignorantly offering an opinion on Garrick. Johnson pounced on him: 'Sir, (said he, with a stern look), I have known David Garrick longer than you have done: and I know no right you have to talk to me on the subject.' Poor Boswell was down but not out: 'I now felt myself much mortified, and began to think that the hope which I had long indulged of obtaining his acquaintance was blasted.' But he 'remained upon the field' and heard some good conversation. Davies then left them alone for a while, just long enough for Boswell to discover 'there was no ill-nature in his disposition'. As Boswell walked out of the shop, he whispered to Davies he was afraid he had botched the meeting, but Davies reassured him, 'Don't be uneasy. I can see he likes you very well.' Johnson would take it as a compliment, he said, if he visited him at his chambers.[5]

Boswell spent the next few days madly doing the social rounds: meeting John Wilkes the political firebrand who had just founded his anti-government journal the *North Briton* and was anathema to Johnson; finding another future adversary of Johnson's, James Macpherson, whom he dubbed the 'Sublime Savage' and who read to him a few of the controversial Highland poems by the legendary Ossian he claimed to have discovered; and foolishly glutting himself on several prostitutes without 'armour [condoms]'. Surfacing for air 'from this chorus, which was rather too outrageous and profane', he finally decided to look in on his hero. He arrived at his 'slovenly' chambers to find there were people already there. When they got up to leave, he did, too: 'No, don't go away,' Johnson cried. 'Sir, I am afraid that I intrude upon you,' Boswell blurted out; 'It is benevolent to allow me to sit and hear you.' Johnson replied he was obliged to any man who visited him. They sat down to talk. Boswell, whose melancholia was fed partly by religious scepticism, was comforted by Johnson's argument in favour of Christian Revelation and resolved to read a few of the books he was then reading on the subject, including Zachary Pearce's *The Miracles of Jesus Defended* (1729). He got up to leave but Johnson still would not let him go and unexpectedly found himself confiding in this raw youth: 'He said he went out at four in the afternoon and did not come home, for most part, till two in the morning.' Boswell's reply illustrated the audacity for which he would become well known, 'I asked him if he did not think it wrong to live so and not make use of his talent.' Johnson could only nod, 'He said it was a bad habit.' Three weeks later he pleased Johnson by calling on him again: 'He shook me by the hand at parting, and asked me why I did not call oftener. I said I was afraid of being troublesome. He said I was not; and he was very glad to see me. Can I help being vain of this?'[6]

Two weeks later they had a meal together at the Mitre Tavern, a popular haunt to dine and meet in Fleet Street. 'I was quite proud to think on whom I was with,' Boswell purred, though Johnson's ravenous way of eating amazed him: 'When at table, he was totally absorbed in the business of the moment; his looks seemed riveted to his plate; nor would he, unless when in very high company, say one word, or even pay the least attention to what was said by others, till he had satisfied his appetite, which was so fierce, and indulged with such intenseness, that while in the act of eating, the veins of his forehead swelled, and generally a strong perspiration was visible.' He had been longing to confide in Johnson about his life and fortunes, to lean on him as a substitute father-figure. On mentioning he was a strict Christian but had strayed into 'infidelity' and finally recovered his faith, Johnson declared, 'Give me your hand, I have taken a liking to you.' Encouraged, Boswell told him of troubles with his father. 'A father and a son should part at a certain time of life,' Johnson consoled him. 'I never believed what my father said. I always thought that he spoke *ex officio*, as a priest does.' He then offered to put the young man on a reading programme to increase his general knowledge. Boswell could scarcely believe his luck: 'I put out my hand. "Will you really take a charge of me?" . . . "Sir, I am glad we have met. I hope we shall pass many evenings and mornings too together."' They stayed at the Mitre talking until the early hours of the morning, finishing off a couple of bottles of port before Johnson pulled himself away reluctantly to return to his solitude at home.[7]

In the ensuing days, their conversation eventually got around to the Irishman Oliver Goldsmith (*c*.1728–74) whom Johnson described as 'one of the first men we now have as an author, and he is a very worthy man too'. It is his earliest known reference to Goldsmith, though they had already met through Percy about four years earlier. A proof-reader for Richardson and hack writer, Goldsmith was not yet well known but would soon become 'one of the brightest ornaments of the Johnsonian school'. Johnson recognised him as an extraordinarily versatile literary genius and loved his good nature and generosity. As Boswell's *Life* frequently illustrates, however, Johnson made a habit of poking fun at him. Aware that others called him an 'idiot inspired', he regarded him as a jealous and at times ridiculous man, as well as affected and a bit of a fool in conversation. Garrick threw up a couplet once by way of an epitaph on him: 'Here lies Nolly Goldsmith, for shortness call'd Noll,/Who wrote like an Angel, but talked like poor Poll'. When it came to defending and helping him, however, Johnson was unhesitating, as in the case of Goldsmith's novel *The Vicar of Wakefield*. According to Boswell's account,[8] on the verge of being thrown out of his lodging in October 1762 by an irate landlady demanding he pay his overdue rent, in a panic Goldsmith scribbled a message to Johnson imploring him to come quickly. Sending off a pound ahead of him, Johnson hurried over to discover that the landlady had Goldsmith under arrest and was about to have him removed. Spotting the manuscript of Goldsmith's incomplete novel on a table, he glanced over it and decided instantly to sell it to a publisher to obtain the rent money. As he was stepping out of the room with it he told the land-lady firmly he would return promptly. He found the bookseller John Newbery, sold the manuscript to him for sixty guineas, and then flew back with the money to pay the landlady. The novel was published to popular acclaim.[9]

Now totally at ease as Johnson's companion, Boswell knew he had been truly allowed into the inner sanctum of Johnson's confidence when Levet took him up secretly to see his chaotic library located in the two garrets above his chambers. Manuscripts in Johnson's handwriting lay scattered everywhere and he half expected to see those of *Rasselas* and the *Rambler* lying about like gold dust. His departure for Utrecht was approaching and at the Turk's Head tavern in Gerrard Street, Soho, one day the talk turned to travel. Johnson recalled that when he was a boy his father had put into his hands a copy of Martin Martin's *Description of the Western Islands of Scotland* (1703), which made a deep impression. 'He said he would go to the Hebrides with me, when I returned from my travels, unless some very good companion should offer when I was absent, which he did not think probable; adding, "There are few people to whom I take so much to as you . . . my dear Boswell, I should be very unhappy at parting, did I think we were not to meet again."' Whether or not Johnson was serious about the 'romantic fantasy' of a Hebridean expedition, the idea stuck in Boswell's mind.[10]

Three days later, again at the Turk's Head, Boswell asked for his advice on a method of study at Utrecht, upon which Johnson shouted out, 'Come, let us make a day of it. Let us go down to Greenwich and dine, and talk of it there.' Arm-in-arm they walked down the Strand back to Inner Temple Lane. The following Saturday they hired a sculler at nearby Temple Stairs and off they sailed down the Thames. They disembarked above London Bridge and, to avoid the rapid water, walked to Billingsgate where they 'took oars and moved smoothly along the silver Thames' on a lovely day. Walking in Greenwich Park, Boswell surprised Johnson by plucking out of his pocket a copy of *London: A Poem* and reading aloud the lines on the village. 'Is not this very fine?', Johnson asked. 'Yes, Sir; but not equal to Fleet-street.' 'You are right, Sir.' They ended the day back at the

Turk's Head where Boswell regaled Johnson with accounts of his seat at Auchinleck. 'I must be there, Sir,' Johnson exclaimed, indulging in another fantasy, 'and we will live in the old castle; and if there is not a room in it remaining, we will build one.' That also stuck in Boswell's mind.[11]

Suddenly, these magical weeks with Johnson were at an end and Boswell had to move on to Utrecht. Reluctant to part, Johnson decided to go with him to Harwich, his port of embarkation: 'I must see thee out of England.' Johnson's humour, to which Boswell responded as fully than anyone who ever knew him, broke out en route as he entertained a woman at an inn about his travelling companion: 'that gentleman there (pointing to me) has been idle. He was idle at Edinburgh. His father sent him to Glasgow, where he continued to be idle. He then came to London, where he has been very idle; and now he is going to Utrecht, where he will be as idle as ever.' In the church at Harwich, Johnson made Boswell kneel: 'Now that you are going to leave your native country, recommend yourself to the protection of your CREATOR and REDEEMER.' Then they walked down to the beach together and embraced. As Boswell stood on deck watching the receding shore, he kept his eyes focused on Johnson's lonely figure: 'As the vessel put out to sea, I kept my eyes upon him for a considerable time, while he remained rolling his majestic frame in his usual manner: and at last I perceived him walk back into the town, and he disappeared.'[12]

2

Johnson advised Taylor to dissipate his 'vexation' of mind with short journeys and a 'variety of scenes', but he does not appear to have taken his own advice except for a few days in January 1764 with Langton and his parents at their family home in Lincolnshire. In February his depression set in. He had little desire to see anyone – 'the most fatal symptom of that malady', especially for him who (as Reynolds put it) thought 'any company . . . better than none'. Dr Adams, his Oxford tutor, came to visit and as an old friend was 'admitted'. He found him 'in a deplorable state, sighing, groaning, talking to himself, and restlessly walking from room to room'. At one point Johnson cried out, 'I would consent to have a limb amputated to recover my spirits.'[13]

Alert to his despondency and loneliness, in February 1764 Reynolds proposed to him they form a new club of like-minded individuals with strong literary interests and good backgrounds in the classics. Johnson was at first reluctant but came around to the idea. It would be an intellectual and social dining club meeting at the Turk's Head one evening per week at seven, until late at night if anyone wished. It would be called the Turk's Head Club, or simply the Club. Politics and religion would be forbidden topics, and a minimal requirement of all members was 'clubbability'. The nine founding members were Johnson, Reynolds, Goldsmith, Langton, Beauclerk, Hawkins, Burke, Christopher Nugent (Burke's father-in-law) and Anthony Chamier (a politician with links to Burke). It became the most famous club in the eighteenth century, a period generally famous for its London clubs.[14]

After Johnson, Burke (1729–97) was the Club's most imposing member. They had met on Christmas Day in 1758 but curiously there is little evidence of their friendship until the Club was formed. Beyond sharing a high regard for trust, honesty and consideration for others, and personal charity towards the unfortunate, they had the highest admiration for each other's intellects. Burke had one of the greatest minds in the eighteenth century and was widely celebrated for his conversation and parliamentary speeches. Just a few months before he died, Johnson said of Burke, 'if a man were to go by chance at the same time with Burke under a shed, to shun a shower, he would say, "this is an extraordinary man"'. There was a magnetism and force about him that became almost legendary in his lifetime, even if many disagreed strongly with his views. By 1764 he was an intimate friend of Reynolds's as well, which is one of the reasons he was included as a founding member of the Club. Fanny Burney summed up Burke and Johnson by calling Burke 'the second man in this Kingdom' and Johnson 'the first of *every* kingdom'.[15]

One founding member who became distinctly unpopular was Hawkins, especially after rudely attacking Burke one night. Johnson called him 'a most unclubbable man'. He was more or less pushed out,

though he put it about that he 'seceded' because the meetings were inter-
fering with his family life. It is surprising that Hawkins was included
in the original nine and not Garrick. Soon after the Club was formed
Reynolds mentioned it to Garrick who piped up, 'I like it much, I think I
shall be of you.' Reynolds reported this to Johnson whose classic comment
was, '*He'll be of us*, how does he know we will *permit* him? The first Duke
in England has no right to hold such language.' Perhaps Johnson was
afraid that Garrick's 'buffoonery', as he put it, would devalue the conversation. Mrs Thrale reported Johnson as saying, 'If Garrick *does* apply, I'll
black-ball him. Surely, one ought to sit in a society like ours, "unelbow'd
by a gamester, pimp, or player"', although Boswell accused her of misrepresenting Johnson with the remark. All it took was one black ball to doom
an application. Garrick was not admitted until 1773. Johnson was against
the rapid growth of the Club in any case: 'He said it was intended the
Club should consist of such men, as that if only two of them chanced to
meet, they should be able to entertain each other, without wanting the addition of more company to pass the evening agreeably.' In 1768 the number was expanded to twelve, and by 1776 Johnson felt the Club 'was now
quite spoiled by the introduction of too many members, and that without
attention to their being agreeable to all the rest'. He seldom attended in
the final years of his life. When he died there were thirty-five members,
none of whom ever was a woman because the Club was conceived as a
gentlemen's private club for dining and drinking.[16]

Even with the Club to sustain him, Johnson fought an uphill battle
against his advancing despair. Physical ailments did not help. He was going to bed at two or three in the morning, often rising at two in the afternoon, sleeping badly, experiencing flatulence, defecating with difficulty –
he used the symbol 'M' to keep track of his bowel movements[17] – and experiencing unfamiliar physical pains in his face while he tried to sleep. 'My
memory grows confused, and I know not how the days pass over me,' he
complained. When he was out in society, he was also struggling to give up
wine – he 'resolved or hoped to combat sin and to reform life, but at night
drank wine,' he wrote on 17 January. Late-night tea vigils with Mrs Wil-

liams were a comfort, but sometimes he would not return home from her until four in the morning.[18]

There was a pressing need for him to be able to work because he had wound himself up again to make a final push on his Shakespeare edition. The only way to write was to sit down and write, he once said, but in late June 1764 he succumbed instead to another diversion. To raise his spirits with more 'variety of scenes' he took time off to travel to the village of Easton Maudit in Northamptonshire with Frank and Mrs Williams for a long-delayed visit to Percy and his wife Anne. Percy had been dreaming of this visit for five years and later remarked he had never found Johnson more 'cheerful or conversible' than during those weeks. There were rural pursuits that helped take him out of himself, among other things helping Anne Percy feed her ducks, making excursions in the district, and reading proof sheets of *Othello* which arrived regularly for his corrections. Back in London in mid-August, he soon became restless again and had to spend a few days in October with Chambers in University College. While he was there he received a bizarre invitation from Renny to accompany her and others on a cruise to the Mediterranean courtesy of a Captain George Collier. 'I cannot go now. I must finish my book [his edition of Shakespeare]', Johnson replied, adding that he did not think 'the grossness of a ship' suitable for a lady.[19]

3

There was another woman who, in January 1765, threw him a lifeline. On the 9th he scribbled into his diary cryptically, 'At Mr Trails'. This was Henry Thrale, husband to Hester Thrale (1741–1821). In her *Thraliana* for September 1777, she remembered this was the first time she ever laid eyes on Johnson: 'Murphy[,] whose intimacy with Mr Thrale had been of many years standing, was one day dining with us at our house in Southwark; and was zealous that we should be acquainted with Johnson, of whose moral and literary character he spoke in the most exalted terms; and so whetted our desire of seeing him soon, that we were only disputing *how* he should be invited, *when* he should be invited, and what should be the pretence.' Aware of Johnson's compassion and empathy for the poor, they and Murphy came up with a plan of inviting to dinner a shoemaker-poet called [James] Woodhouse, who was then being talked about as something of a literary oddity, and using him as 'a temptation to Mr Johnson to meet him'. Johnson came. Woodhouse knew what was going on and thought Johnson regarded him as some kind of 'wild beast from the country', but he played along. The truth was that Johnson scoffed at the supposed novelty of a poet-cobbler and was not at all curious about Woodhouse: 'They had better furnish the man with good implements for his trade, than raise subscriptions for his poems. He may make an excellent shoemaker, but can never make a good poet.' Murphy had given the Thrales fair warning of Johnson's figure, dress or behaviour, including his mannerisms and noises. They hit it off so well with him that they met again the following week, this time without the shoemaker. After that he dined with them 'every Thursday through the winter', Mrs Thrale wrote, and 'has remained till this day, our constant acquaintance, visitor, companion and friend'.[20]

Mrs Thrale was the daughter of a wealthy Welsh landowner. Against her will she found herself in 1765 at twenty-four in a loveless marriage to a dull, prosperous, gentleman-like London brewer in Southwark with little hope of ever feeling any passion for him. Nor did he have much of a taste for culture. She once reminded Johnson that in the first six years of her marriage 'I never set my foot in any theatre or palace of entertainment at all.'[21] It did not help that he kept a mistress. Nevertheless, she successfully promoted his efforts (with Johnson's help) to become a member of Parliament for Southwark from 1765 to 1780. Her greatest joy and solace were her children – there were twelve births over a period of fifteen years, only four of whom (all girls) survived into adulthood. She also had considerable literary interests and was a highly successful hostess at her 'charming villa' in Streatham, ten miles south of central London. A small woman, she was not a beauty, but her lively intelligence, wit and wide reading pleased Johnson. From that first meeting, the Thrales (especially Hester) held centre stage in his life, so much so that his closest London friends from time to time complained they could not find him at home because of the frequency and length of his visits to Southwark and Streatham.

Boswell, who still was not back from his travels, later became jealous of Johnson's dependence on her and was of the opinion that she took him in chiefly because he was a literary ornament to her social life, a prize she liked to show off. But this was unfair, even if it was true that once Johnson became a regular feature at her Streatham dinners her social standing as a hostess of poets and artists soared. He soon fell into a regular pattern of sleeping several nights a week there which continued for almost the rest of his life. Indeed, he came to think of the place as a second home. In the autumn, he 'followed' the Thrales to the small fishing village then called Brighthelmstone (Brighton): 'When business is done what remains but pleasure? And where should pleasure be sought but under Mrs Thrale's influence?' The village had recently become known as a good place for sea-bathing. The Thrales were among the first to make holidaying there fashionable and shortly after meeting Johnson bought a house on West Street, about fifty metres from the sea. Johnson never liked Brighton but would spend several holidays there with them. The first one did not get off to a good start, however. Arriving on their doorstep, he was annoyed to discover they had left because of Mrs Thrale's advanced pregnancy. So he went swimming on his own. The man whose job it was to dip people into the sea was impressed: 'Why Sir (says the dipper), you must have been a stout-hearted gentleman forty years ago.' There were painfully poignant moments for him there as well. In a meditation fifteen years later, he recalled gazing out at the sea on this visit, overcome with renewed grief for Tetty: 'When I recollect the time in which we lived together, my grief for her departure is not abated, and I have less pleasure in any good that befalls me, because she does not partake it. On many occasions I think what she would have said or done. When I saw the sea at Brighthelmstone I wished for her to have seen it with me.' At least now he could tell himself he had in Mrs Thrale a new friendship that promised him comfort and healing.[22]

Free now from the onerous drudgery of heavy Shakespearean editing, on his return from Brighton he threw himself into some electioneering in

Henry Thrale's campaign for a parliamentary seat. It was good therapy, a rough-and-tumble change of pace. Thrale had lost two previous elections elsewhere, but this time the signs were good because of his family's reputation in Southwark. Johnson wrote at least one 'advertisement' for him to the electors, though his main value seems to have been in interacting with the populace, at which Mrs Thrale wrote he excelled because of his empathy for 'the lower ranks of humanity' dating from those earlier days when 'he and they shared pain and pleasure in common'. The election illustrated 'his toleration of boisterous mirth, and his content in the company of people whom one would have thought at first sight little calculated for his society'. He could throw his hat 'up in the air and huzza' with the best of them when Thrale won.[23]

With his pension, a new confidante in Mrs Thrale, the unfamiliar comforts of Streatham at his disposal, and his edition about to be published, it seemed that at last everything had begun to come right for him in his external life. Topping it off, in July he was awarded the 'spontaneous compliment' of an LL.D. (*Legum Doctor*) by Trinity College, Dublin, making an Irish university the first to create the title 'Dr Johnson' by which he became known in his lifetime and to posterity. It was another sweet reward for decades of labour in his now vanished wilderness of literary and social neglect. In March he had also managed his first triumphant visit to Cambridge with Beauclerk where he was a star attraction. One of the fellows, Dr John Sharp, recalled the visit in a letter published in 1785: 'He drank his large potations of tea with me, interrupted by many an indignant contradiction, and many a noble sentiment. He had on a better wig than usual. Several persons got into his company the last evening at Trinity, where [at] about twelve, he began to be very great; [metaphorically] stripped poor Mrs [Catherine] Macaulay to the very skin' – she was the historian whose republican views impelled him to make crude jokes about her – 'then gave her for his toast, and drank her in two bumpers'. Sharp referred to him as 'Caliban' who 'was not roused from his lair' before noon on Sunday, the day after he arrived in town, surmising that 'his breakfast probably kept him till night'. Nobody saw anything of him until Monday afternoon. He also dropped in at Emmanuel College to look in on Richard Farmer who the following year would publish his own celebrated piece of Shakespeareana, *An Essay on the Learning of Shakespeare*. Farmer promised him 'an habitation in Emmanuel College' whenever he chose to come again. The judgement of another Fellow was less happy, 'I don't believe Dr Johnson belongs to us: I only wish he did. But we do not deserve him.'[24]

In August he finally roused himself to move from the shabby lodgings in Inner Temple Lane to a spacious and more comfortable house where he lived for the next twelve years. Number 7 Johnson's Court, off Fleet Street, was named after a tailor who had lived in the square for many years. And perhaps that same summer the 'Mr Johnson' Reynolds entered in his Sitters Books was him, posing for a portrait then and several times more in 1766–7 that undoubtedly became the one dated 1769 in which Reynolds said his mind was 'preying on itself in a reverie, accompanied with strange antic gesticulation'.[25]

CHAPTER 24

Shakespeare and the
Living World

I

AFTER YEARS OF DELAY and intermittent work, Johnson completed the final two volumes of his Shakespeare edition, completed the notes in the Appendix, and wrote the Preface in the summer of 1765. At last, he breathed the deepest sigh of relief when *The Plays of William Shakespeare* appeared in eight volumes on 10 October. Now after all those years, as with the *Dictionary*, he felt anticlimax. 'To tell the truth,' he confided in Joseph Warton the day before, 'I felt no solicitude about this work, I receive no great comfort from its conclusion; but yet am well enough pleased that the public has no farther claim upon me.' More than twenty years of literary drudgery were behind him, and with his pension he no longer needed to play hostage to the public in an unceasing effort to make a living by his pen. Moreover, he wanted nothing to do with distributing the edition to friends who had gathered subscriptions for him. Selling briskly, the first impression of one thousand copies was gone in one month.[1]

The edition was maligned in the nineteenth century for slovenliness and careless scholarship and had to wait until the twentieth century for a recovery of its reputation, but when it appeared it was well received as a noble critical effort that urged on readers the emotional truth of their national poet. Among its best qualities is that it is enjoyable to read. This is because of the illuminating common sense Johnson applied to explaining passages in the plays, for which he was linguistically more qualified than any previous critic. More intensely than ever before, he insisted that if literature was to be worth reading it had 'to enable the reader better to enjoy life, or better to endure it'. 'The end of writing is to instruct; the end of poetry is to instruct by pleasing.' What we are struck with in his edition is his imaginative and moral identification with Shakespeare. His power as a critic was forged not in academe but in the labyrinths of his own human career. He was above all an experiential critic, subjective, impatient with abstract critical principles. He understood the poet's greatness as located in what Harold Bloom has called 'a diversity of persons':

> For Johnson, the essence of poetry was *invention*, and only Homer could be Shakespeare's rival in originality. Invention, in Johnson's sense as in ours, is a process of finding, or of finding out. We owe Shakespeare everything, Johnson says, and means that Shakespeare has taught us to understand human nature . . . One way of defining Johnson's vitality as a critic is to note the consistent power of his inferences: he is always sufficiently *inside* Shakespeare's plays to judge them as he judges human life, without ever forgetting that Shakespeare's function is to bring life to mind, to make us aware of what we could not find without Shakespeare.

To paraphrase Pope, Johnson found that nature and Shakespeare were the same.[2]

There is little pedantry in his edition, little accumulation of commentary and textual notes merely to display his learning and superiority to previous editions, or with which to prop himself up, although he felt bound to include many of the notes of previous editors and friends: 'I do not always concur with my friends in their opinion, but their abilities are such as make me less confident when I find myself differing from them, and the public might justly complain if I suppressed their sentiments either by pride or timidity.' This modesty was a protection against being thought an authoritative critic arrogantly donning the mantle of a legislator or literary dictator, for the proper role of criticism was not, in his view, a matter of dictatorial and fashionable pronouncements. In this sense he was a disinterested critic, against what in *Rambler* 93 he called the critic's 'interest and passion' that disturb the innocency of a reader's response: 'Critics, like all the rest of mankind, are very frequently misled by interest . . . kindness or malevolence, veneration or contempt'. In his *Proposals*, he had written, 'The editor, though he may less delight his own vanity, will probably please his reader more, by supposing him equally able with himself to judge of beauties and faults.' Furthermore, he was not going to indulge in 'cruelty to crush an insect who had provoked me only by buzzing in my ear'. It was from the poetry, not the joint authority of critics cited in the notes of a Shakespeare edition, that he would draw whatever authority he could claim.[3]

Still, 'he that writes may be considered as a kind of general challenger, whom every one has right to attack . . . To commence author is to claim praise, and no man can justly aspire to honour, but at the hazard of disgrace.' His own glosses on about two thousand words and phrases number among the most insightful and helpful ever provided. The components of his edition equipped it also with all that it needed for him and the booksellers to claim that this was now the complete up-to-date Shakespeare, the defining edition beyond which the public need not look any further. He included a variety of elements or critical 'apparatus' that turned the edition into what is generally called a variorum edition. Shakespeare had become such a commodity and so many were getting into the act as commentators, jostling for advantage, that this kind of institutional authority was deemed crucial as well.[4]

As for collating and textual work, he did a good amount but nowhere near so much as a few of his predecessors and many of his immediate successors. He adopted William Warburton's 1747 edition as a copy-text, augmented by Lewis Theobald's text when a new edition of his work came out. To a great extent it could be said Johnson was stuck with these. He was far from systematic in gathering variant readings from earlier editions. The troublemaking, spiteful critic Joseph Ritson may have had a greater portion of character defects than most Shakespeareans, but he was a superb textual editor and he called it as he saw it, declaring that Johnson 'never collated any of the folios' – not entirely true – and left the text in the 'same state of corruption as was in the time of Rome'. Thomas Babington Macaulay continued this line of attack a few decades later by sneering that 'it would be difficult to name a more slovenly, a more worthless edition of any great classic'.[5]

Johnson's edition was soon superseded by others, but the Preface remained a triumph in his lifetime, acclaimed as another example of his sturdy common sense and brilliant humanly anchored moral insight. It was too progressive for Voltaire, who criticised Johnson for his defence of Shakespeare's violation of the classical unities of time, place and action. Johnson retaliated by comparing Voltaire's brand of remarks to the 'petty cavils of petty minds'. The Romantics, who thought the edition was too institutionalised, not sufficiently imaginative, manhandled it in the next century – Samuel Taylor Coleridge, for instance, accusing Johnson of not understanding the character of Hamlet. They particularly disliked Johnson as a Shakespeare critic because they concluded he was defending classical literary 'rules' in enumerating the poet's literary shortcomings. They tended to dump him indiscriminately into the outmoded neoclassical bucket without valuing sufficiently what he was writing throughout the Preface about Shakespeare's sublime imagination and his judgement of the poet's genius in representing the infinitely 'mingled drama' of life on earth – what Johnson called 'the real state of sublunary nature'. The Romantics therefore accused him of defending neo-classicism while Voltaire and other neo-classical critics accused him of violating it.

The eminent Shakespearean critic David Nichol Smith wrote at the start of the twentieth century that by then those nineteenth-century critical opinions had not changed: 'Johnson's *Preface* in particular was remembered only to be despised. It is not rash to say that at the present time the majority of those who chance to speak of it pronounce it a discreditable performance . . . [it] has received scant justice'. He added, 'Not only was Johnson's edition the best which had yet appeared; it is still one of the few editions which are indispensable'. By 1910, Walter Raleigh in his *Six Essays on Shakespeare*, a landmark in the turn towards Johnson's work, felt that 'the Romantic attitude begins to be fatiguing'. Johnson was able 'to go straight to Shakespeare's meaning, while the philological and antiquarian commentators kill one another in the dark'. By 1928, Smith was writing of the Preface that 'by common consent nowadays it is one of the greatest essays on Shakespeare that has ever been written'.[6]

Johnson's Preface is his earliest detailed analysis of any writer. It speaks of his gratitude to Shakespeare's genius for striking a chord with his own inner moral convictions and psyche, for projecting the realities of human nature with 'common conversation and common occurrences'. His characters 'are the genuine progeny of common humanity, such as the world will always supply, and observation will always find. His persons act and speak by the influence of those general passions and principles by which all minds are agitated, and the whole system of life is continued in motion.' While he wrote that Shakespeare's 'first defect' was not going far enough in projecting what mankind should be, and thus not rising to 'a writer's duty to make the world better', he nonetheless believed that Shakespeare's portrait of a vast panorama of human behaviour and thought conveyed (without being didactic) what mankind ought to be like. 'This therefore is the praise of Shakespeare,' he wrote, 'that his drama is the mirrour of life; that he who has mazed his imagination, in following the phantoms which other writers raise up before him, may here be cured of his delirious extasies, by reading human sentiments in human language, by scenes from which a hermit may estimate the transactions of the world, and a confessor predict the progress of the passions.'[7]

As for the classical unities, he observed that 'a play read, affects the mind like a play acted. It is therefore evident, that the action is not supposed to be real, and . . . that no more account of space or duration is to be taken by the auditor of a drama, than by the reader of a narrative, before whom may pass in an hour the life of a hero, or the revolutions of an empire.' In invoking the authority of Shakespeare to demolish the critical tyranny of the unities, he knew he was in dangerous territory: 'I am almost frighted by my own temerity; and when I estimate the fame and the strength of those that maintain the contrary opinion, am ready to sink down in reverential silence.' To sink into silence was not something he was about to do, however.[8]

Although he called explanatory and textual notes 'necessary evils' by which the text is 'refrigerated', his own are, next to the Preface, where the chief value of his edition lies. They amount to a sustained commentary on the individual plays and rank as the finest literary criticism he ever wrote. Several of them like the sketch of Polonius in *Hamlet* or Falstaff in *Henry IV* are among the best ever written about these characters, impregnated with a humane largeness of mind and a refusal to descend to myopic, sanctimonious, moral censure. They are like character sketches in his moral essays. The redeeming quality he singles out in Falstaff, for instance, 'thy compound of sense and vice; of sense which may be admired but not esteemed, of vice which may be despised, but hardly detested', is one he especially valued when he encountered it in his own life: 'the most pleasing of all qualities, perpetual gaiety . . . an unfailing power of exciting laughter . . . easy escapes and sallies of levity, which make sport but raise no envy'.[9]

His 'General Observations' at the end of each play often contain an assortment of short, critical comments on, among other subjects, the sources of the play, Elizabethan versus modern taste, the propriety or not of the language, and the believability or not of character and action. Many of them are highly personal and to a degree as unpredictable as his critical judgements could be in his conversation. About *As You Like It*, he remarks, 'I know not how the ladies will approve the facility with which both Rosalind and Celia give away their hearts. To Celia much may be forgiven for the heroism of her friendship.' He properly castigates Bertram in *All's Well That Ends Well*: 'I cannot reconcile my heart to Bertram; a man noble without generosity, and young without truth; who marries Helen as a coward, and leaves her as a profligate: when she is dead by his unkindness, sneaks home to a second marriage, is accused by a woman whom he has wronged, defends himself by falsehood, and is dismissed to happiness.' Of Edmund's evil art in *King Lear* he takes note of the 'important moral, that villainy is never at a stop, that crimes lead to crimes, and at last terminate in ruin'. But he is unhappy with Cordelia's tragic death because of the moral failure of the play in allowing the wicked to prosper: 'Since all reasonable beings naturally love justice, I cannot easily be persuaded, that the observation of justice makes a play worse; or, that if other excellencies are equal, the audience will not always rise better pleased from the final triumph of persecuted virtue.' He actually preferred the happy ending of Nahum Tate's 1681 adaptation in which Cordelia survives. He was emotionally shocked by Shakespeare's conclusion, just as he was terrified as a boy by Hamlet's ghost: 'if my sensations could add any thing to the general suffrage, I might relate, that I was many years ago so shocked by Cordelia's death, that I know not whether I ever endured to read again the last scenes of the play till I undertook to revise them as an editor.' Equally, of Desdemona's murder in *Othello* he confesses, 'I am glad that I have ended my revisal of this dreadful scene. It is not to be endured.' He is in no doubt that the fall of Macbeth is correct emotionally, ethically, and morally: 'The passions are directed to their true end. Lady Macbeth is merely detested; and though the courage of Macbeth preserves some esteem, yet every reader rejoices at his fall.'[10]

Johnson believed that the best way to learn about a Shakespeare play was to read it as a type of ethical poem, not to see it on the stage. He appears even to have felt that seeing one of the plays on stage could be an impediment to a proper understanding of it. He was once supposed to have said, 'It would afford him more entertainment to sit up to the chin in water for an hour than be obliged to listen to the whining, daggle-tailed [Mrs] Cibber, during the tedious representation of a fulsome tragedy without the possibility of receiving from it either pleasure or instruction.' Goldsmith confronted him over his alleged indifference to the theatre in February 1766: 'I think, Mr Johnson, you don't go near the theatres now. You give yourself no more concern about a new play, than if you had never had any thing to do with the stage.' According to Boswell, Johnson agreed at that moment, 'our tastes greatly alter. The lad does not care for the child's rattle, and the old man does not care for the young man's whore'. Whores and rattles aside, years after seeing Goldsmith's *She Stoops to Conquer* in 1773, he 'could scarce recollect having seen the inside of a playhouse . . . To speak the truth, there is small encouragement there for a man whose sight and hearing are become so imperfect as mine.'[11]

Nonetheless, he continued to attend the theatre over the years, especially to see Shakespeare, and the year before he died he delighted in a visit from Sarah Siddons, the great tragic actress of the day and some said a rival of Garrick's in tragedy. She came with her brother, the popular actor John Philip Kemble. When she told him that her favourite tragic role was Catherine in *Henry VIII*, he replied that if she were ever to act the part again he would 'once more hobble out to the theatre' to see her. She then promised she would 'do herself the honour of acting his favourite part for him'. He then demonstrated a close knowledge of the contemporary stage by running through what he thought were the strengths of the leading actors and actresses in his lifetime, especially Garrick whose praises he sang for both comedy and tragedy. He had seen him in probably all his Shakespearean roles, particularly in *Richard III*, *Hamlet*, *King Lear* and *Macbeth* as well as in his comic hit as Benedick in *Much Ado About Nothing*. 'Garrick, Madam, was no declaimer,' he told Mrs Siddons, 'a true conception of character, and natural expression of it, were his distinguishing excellencies.'[12]

2

The Thrales were now a regular and comforting feature of his existence, but he wanted Boswell back, who was in Paris on his way home when he wrote to him there in January 1766. Johnson's esteem for him had steadily increased as the young man coursed through Germany, Switzerland, Italy, and finally Corsica, cultivating relationships with Rousseau, Voltaire, Paoli, and a multitude of other eminent persons: 'I long to see you and to hear from you, and hope that we shall not be so long separated again. Come home and expect such a welcome as is due to him whom a wise and noble curiosity has led where perhaps no native of this country ever was before.' He was referring to Boswell's hazardous journey across Corsica by foot to find Paoli.[13]

Boswell arrived in London on 12 February 1766 and the next day dropped in on Johnson at his new 'good house' in Johnson's Court. He found Mrs Williams was occupying an apartment on the ground floor and Levet had taken over a room in the garret. Their separation by two floors was calculated to reduce strife in the house. This was the beginning of the long final period of Johnson's life when he had these two, and several years later also Elizabeth Desmoulins and Poll Carmichael, living with him constantly, not to mention others who would come and go for short periods.

Boswell walked in, fell on his knees before Johnson, and immediately asked for his blessing. Johnson hugged him 'like a sack' and grumbled, 'I hope we shall pass many years of regard.' Later they dined alone at the Mitre and talked of Boswell's travels and their mutual friends. For Boswell, their reunion climaxed when Johnson enthusiastically endorsed his idea of writing an account of Corsica – 'Give us as many anecdotes as you can,' he urged him – although by late summer, months after Boswell had returned to Scotland, he had changed his tune: 'You have, somehow or other, warmed your imagination. I wish there were some cure, like the lover's leap, for all heads of which some single idea has obtained an unreasonable and irregular possession. Mind your own affairs, and leave the Corsicans to theirs.' A couple of days later they were together again at the Mitre, talking of Boswell's having struck up friendships with Rousseau and Wilkes, not exactly two of Johnson's favourite characters. Johnson was incensed. Rousseau had recently retreated from Switzerland to England to escape the abuse he was receiving there for his progressive and scandalous writings on society and education. Johnson glared at Boswell: 'If you mean to be serious, I think him one of the worst of men; a rascal, who ought to be hunted out of society as he has been. Three or four nations have expelled him.' Boswell simply thought to himself that Johnson misread Rousseau's 'heart', but the resentment ran deeper than that, for Johnson regarded Rousseau a seductive threat to society as he knew it, an enemy of the Judeo-Christian tradition of learning and rational philosophy.[14]

The following day they spoke of another infidel, David Hume, whose religious scepticism Johnson deplored, and of hierarchy and subordination within society. Even this early, with the somewhat affected habits he had picked up on the Continent of pressing people in conversation, Boswell began to irritate Johnson. 'My dear Bozzy,' Johnson broke in when he thought Boswell was going to oppose him again, 'let us have no more of this. It is extremely disagreeable to me. You are making nothing of this argument. I had rather you'd whistle me a Scotch tune.' When Boswell persisted with pesky questions, Johnson had had enough: 'This now is just such stuff as I used to talk to my mother when I first began to think myself a clever fellow, and she ought to have whipped me for it.' Boswell, however, was resilient – 'You ought then to whip me' – but he was surprised by Johnson's 'roughness', that he 'tossed and gored' people in conversation, which seemed 'more striking to me now, from my having been accustomed to the studied smooth complying habits of the Continent'. Goldsmith had noticed Johnson's greater impatience and irritation, too. 'Don't you think that head's failed?' he asked Boswell ten days later. 'No, Sir, I think he is rather more impatient of contradiction than he was'. Goldsmith agreed. 'No man is proof against continual adulation.'[15]

The impulse came upon him in the spring to write a short fairy tale, *The Fountains*, to be included in a volume of Mrs Williams's poems, *Miscellanies in Prose & Verse*, for which as far back as 1750 he had written proposals but had done nothing since to promote. The obstacle to publication still was that Mrs Williams had not written enough pieces to fill a volume, so he asked Mrs Thrale and a few others if they had written or could write anything they would be willing to have appear in the volume and charitably pass off as Mrs Williams's. Mrs Thrale promptly came up with something, upon which Johnson himself (in her words) rose to the occasion: 'He said come Mistress, now *I'll* write a tale and your character shall be in it; so he composed The Fountains in the same book.' He wrote it swiftly, either in Southwark or Streatham, basing the main character of a clever and witty young woman Floretta on Mrs Thrale and setting the story appropriately at the renowned and magical Mount Plinlimmon in Wales, her homeland. The story is framed by the so-called 'choice of life' theme central to both *The Vision of Theodore* and *Rasselas*. The point is that Floretta, like Mrs Thrale, unwisely made choices based on earthly happiness. In addition to this fairy tale, Johnson wrote or revised seven of his own poems for the *Miscellanies*, including 'The Ant', 'The Happy Life', and 'An Ode on Friendship'. Percy, Mrs Thrale and Renny (who painted Mrs Williams's portrait for the volume) contributed poems as well. The volume was published by Thomas Davies in April and enjoyed modest

praise. Catherine Talbot thought *The Fountains* was 'enchantingly beautiful' but too depressing and melancholy in having Floretta ultimately sink
under the weight of human folly.[16]

All these were good signs, but a mental crisis was fast approaching. He
was already in its early stages.

3

For several months, perhaps as long as a year, Johnson had been physically
ill, and early in 1766 his condition worsened. He scarcely ever attended the
Club. On the day before Easter, worries haunted him about his religious
frame of mind, 'I do not feel myself today so much impressed with awe of
the approaching Mystery.' He prayed that he might be neither 'harassed
with vain terrors' nor 'linger in perplexity, nor waste in idleness that life
which thou hast given and preserved'.[17]

Then all of a sudden he succumbed to a severe mental breakdown.
While Boswell wrote nothing of this, Mrs Thrale highlighted it in her *Anecdotes.* She and her husband had been keeping a close eye on him and
feared that something like this was coming. She wrote that for weeks 'he
could not stir out of his room in the court he inhabited'. He 'often lamented to us the horrible condition of his mind, which he said was nearly
distracted'. One day near the end of June they found him imploring a
guest to pray for him 'in the most pathetic terms'. Shocked, Thrale 'invol-
untarily lifted up one hand to shut his mouth'. Then and there, Mrs
Thrale decided to take over, removing him from his 'close habitation in the
court' and whisking him off to Streatham Park where for three months
she nursed him until his physical (if not mental) health returned.[18]

Those three months were a turning point in his life. For the next sixteen years he spent much of his time with Mrs Thrale and her husband at
Streatham and Southwark, virtually as a member of the family. His relationship with her became, apart from his marriage to Tetty, the most important one in his life. She became his 'Mistress' and Thrale his 'Master'.
The 'Master' did his part, prevailing on him 'to change his shirt, his coat,
or his plate, almost before it became indispensably necessary to the com-

fortable feelings of his friends'. After the death of their infant daughter (they already had one daughter, Queeney) the previous October, Johnson was another focus for Mrs Thrale's maternal instincts. In him she now also had an intellectual companion for lively talk and banter, as well as someone with whom to compose poetry and discuss literature. An invitation to her house often meant a chance to meet and talk with the famous Samuel Johnson. He drew there the likes of Reynolds, Goldsmith, Burke, the Burneys and other geniuses. The one irritant for her was her aged mother, Mrs Salusbury, who lived with her much of the time and disliked Johnson, a feeling he reciprocated because of her constant gabble about what she read in the papers. They disliked each other also because each thought the other had too much influence over Mrs Thrale. He could not really complain, however, for he had never known anything like the domestic pleasures in his elegant new 'home' that now dropped plentifully into his lap: the finest and most nutritious food, a lovely garden, wonderful country walks, and the constant stream of distinguished visitors from the literary, artistic, religious, political and highest social ranks of English society. They also set him up with an apartment 'over the counting house [of the brewery in Southwark] two pairs of stairs high – and called it the Round Tower'.[19]

Johnson and Mrs Thrale quickly fell into the habit of sharing secrets. He believed she was little more than a kept mistress, 'shut from the world, its pleasures, or its cares'. She complained frequently to him about her life, complaints to which her husband turned a deaf ear, although she was ever loyal to him, a talented and shrewd support in his political and business affairs as a successful brewer, and a dutiful and worried mother. On the other hand, she wrote that having Johnson as a frequent and prolonged guest soon enough became a cross she had to bear. When after his death she wrote her Anecdotes about him, based on her journal and commonplace book, Thraliana, many people – especially those in his circle – called her ungrateful, 'a little artful impudent malignant devil'. They felt that when she described her long relationship to him as 'a bondage, which she had endured to please Mr Thrale, but when he was dead . . . became insupportable', she revealed her true colours.[20]

What were her complaints? For one thing, he wanted her to exercise her intellect and not be such a slave to her family, but he never challenged Thrale's authority in the house and in squabbles between man and wife almost always defended him. 'I know no man', Johnson once said, 'who is more master of his wife and family than Thrale. If he but holds up a finger he is obeyed.' His conversation was brilliant but also trying if people had places to go, such as retiring to bed. After he had lectured the assembled company at length one day and was about to embark on a new subject, Thrale interrupted, 'There, there, now we have had enough for one lecture . . . we will not be upon education any more till after dinner, if you please.' Mrs Thrale wrote that his social habits were so sprawling that he upset family routines. His insomnia and fears of loneliness often forced her to stay up with him into the early morning hours. 'Mr Johnson loved late hours extremely, or more properly hated early ones. Nothing was more terrifying to him than the idea of retiring to bed, which he never would call going to rest, or suffer another to call so. "I lie down (said he) that my acquaintance may sleep; but I lie down to endure oppressive misery, and soon rise again to pass the night in anxiety and pain."' As a result, she claimed, 'I hurt my own health not a little by sitting up with him when I was myself far from well'; she was 'forced' by 'his vehement lamentations and piercing reproofs, not to quit the room, but to sit quietly and make tea for him, as I often did in London till four o'clock in the morning'. At Streatham she said she fared better because often there was some guest there who could take her place sitting with him late into the night.[21]

Her recitation of his personal habits was so stinging that one suspects it is exaggerated and overcharged, the result of accumulated vexations: he 'would not rise in the morning till twelve o'clock perhaps, and oblige me to make breakfast for him till the bell rung for dinner, though much displeased if the toilet was neglected, and though much of the time we passed together was spent in blaming or deriding, very justly, my neglect of economy, and waste of that money which might make many families happy'. She maintained he was frequently 'on the verge of a quarrel'. 'Have a care,' she said she heard him saying to a guest one day just as she walked into the drawing room, 'the Old Lion will not bear to be tickled.'

She protested that helpful as he was with Queeney and later the other children, he was insufferably opinionated in advising her how to bring them up. She also disliked what she felt were his overbearing opinions of women's clothes he did not like, which at times caused distress to the women concerned. At first, she felt it was all worth it because she and her husband saw themselves as saving him; later, she chafed under a 'perpetual confinement' that was 'terrifying in the first years of our friendship, and irksome in the last'. She insisted that after her husband's death in 1782, she could scarcely bear his capriciousness and roughness in the house. She felt the world owed her a debt of gratitude because 'the shelter our house afforded to his uneasy fancies' and 'the pains we took to sooth or repress them' enabled him to continue to write.[22]

There was something even more disturbing in his relationship with Mrs Thrale, a darkness that went deeper than her irritation with him, reached to his melancholia and terrifying fear of madness, and placed her in compromising, even unsavoury situations.

In May 1779 she entered a passage in her *Thraliana* that is as mysterious as it is intriguing. She noted that in 1767 or 1768 'our stern philosopher Johnson trusted me . . . with a secret far dearer to him than his life', one that placed him 'in her power' as his nurse or warden. This passage, hotly contested by critics and biographers, has remained an enigma. Some have supposed the secret was his past enslavement to another woman. Indeed, Mrs Thrale recorded his comment once that 'a woman has *such* power between the ages of twenty five and forty five, that she may tie a man to a post and whip him if she will'. 'How many times', wrote Mrs Thrale, 'has this great, this formidable Doctor Johnson kissed my hand, ay & my foot too upon his knees!' She acknowledged that she herself would not have such 'power' over him were she not a woman, for he never would have trusted any man with 'such secrets' 'entrusted to me'. But more psychologically complex explanations than mere sexual passion have been offered for the meaning of this 'secret'.[23]

The editor of Mrs Thrale's journal long ago made a connection between the secret and another reference of hers to 'the fetters & padlocks [probably just one] [that] will tell posterity the truth'. The padlock and mysterious fetters undoubtedly were the same ones that turned up among her effects sold at auction in 1823, which she identified as 'Johnson's padlock, committed to my care in the year 1768'. What were the fetters and padlock for? The likelihood is that he asked her to chain him with them, fearing perhaps sleepwalking and the insanity that he thought was a present possibility and could do him physical harm. In 1767–8 his desperate thoughts ran to such extremes. And there is evidence that his self-delusory thoughts of insanity continued, perhaps not so violently, throughout the next few years. On 24 March 1771, for example, he wrote in his pocket-diary (in Latin), 'Insane thoughts on fetters and hand-cuffs'. Perhaps he even enjoyed the idea of being confined in this way by his nurse and warden, the feeling of being secure in her control.[24]

Katherine Balderston's suggestion that Johnson may have taken a perverse sexual pleasure in such confinement has been discredited. It is based on a letter he wrote in French to Mrs Thale in early June 1773 while he was in the house staying with her. Balderston called it a 'pathological document' exhibiting 'erotic maladjustment' and 'masochistic fantasies'. Johnson was there in the house at an awkward time for her because her mother was dying and he was left largely on his own, in 'profound solitude', while she attended to her. In this letter he was either merely sulking at being left alone so much or genuinely worried that given his mental state he could not vouch for his behaviour during such unrelieved solitude. The letter pleads for help, 'Tell me whether you wish me to wander abandoned or to confine myself within certain prescribed limits.' If this was merely about staying out of the way at a time when Mrs Thrale was preoccupied with nursing her dying mother, a plea for order in a disordered house where children were also sick and builders were being disruptive, not about strict confinement, one wonders what the padlocks and chain were for. He added, 'if it seems best to you that I should remain in a certain place, I beg of you to spare me the necessity of constraining myself by taking away from me the power to leave the place where you want me to be. Which will not cost you more than the trouble to turn the key in the door twice a day . . . your judgement and vigilance may come to the rescue of my weakness . . . I desire, my patroness, that your authority should always be palpable to me, and that you should hold me in the slavery that you are well able to render happy'.[25]

Mrs Thrale's in-house letter to him, apparently in immediate response to his, has been read by some as simply a recognition that his letter was a plea for loving attention. But there was more going on here than that, even if we do not accept the wild theory that Johnson was a flagellant demanding to be scourged and manacled. The leading medical historian among Johnson scholars has reasoned that in the late 1760s the Thrales had turned Streatham into a retreat, a centre for therapy, with her as the therapist. Johnson was in the grips of a severe mental crisis of melancholy, when the black dog was 'upon his back' – a phrase in current use at Streatham to describe both Johnson and Henry Thrale's melancholia. They would use the phrase, wrote Mrs Thrale, as 'a sort of *byword* or *hack joke* here at Streatham, and in the letters I published between Dr Johnson & myself, it is almost perpetually recurring'. He desperately needed and wanted some loving confinement, whether enforced by a padlock or his own self-discipline. Her letter alludes to this need in kindly urging him, after six or seven years, to use self-discipline instead of making her resort to an 'irksome and dangerous idea' – namely, having recourse to strict confinement. She was gentle and tactful but did not want anything more to do with 'fetters to the body': 'If it be possible shake off these uneasy weights, heavier to the mind by far than fetters to the body. Let not your fancy dwell thus upon confinement and severity. I am sorry you are obliged to be so much alone.' She had become 'an unwilling performer in Johnson's psychopathological drama'. She also recognised that Boswell could teach him a thing or two about how to sweep his mind clean of melancholic rubbish.[26]

Apparently an agreement was reached that determined the pattern of his life with the Thrales for almost the rest of his days: he would normally have the run of the house, interacting fully with the family, but when his melancholia was severe and he felt the need to confine himself, he would shut himself up in his room for lengthy periods. There he would be without distractions and provocations, could occupy himself with complicated mathematical computations that he commonly used to combat the phantoms of madness, and read. Mrs Thrale thus patiently combined confinement with kindness as a recipe to 'sooth' Johnson and attempt to shake off the black dog. It is cruelly ironic that soon after his death she registered in her diary her fear that the phalanx of biographers lining up to write his life 'will leave *nothing untold* that I laboured so long to keep secret; & I was so very delicate in trying to conceal his fancied insanity, that I retained no proofs of it – or hardly any.' It was she of all the eventual biographers who wrote most of his phobia about madness and whom Boswell chiefly had in mind when he mentioned disdainfully those who wishing 'to depreciate him, should, since his death, have laid hold of this circumstance, and insisted upon it with very unfair aggravation'.[27]

4

By December, Robert Chambers, the new Vinerian Professor of Law, still had not come up with any of the lectures expected of him. It was time for concerted action, Johnson wrote: 'Come up to town, and lock yourself up from all but me, and I doubt not but lectures will be produced. You must not miss another term . . . Come up and work, and I will try to help you.' Chambers came and they began a secret collaboration which lasted three years. In January 1767, Johnson was urging Chambers to come again 'to sit very close, and then there will be no danger, and needs to be no fear'. A week after returning home from three months in Streatham, he departed hurriedly to Oxford for a month. University College again gave him a room. Chambers would draw him to Oxford no fewer than eight or nine times during the next three years for work on the lectures.[28]

Chambers's *Course of Lectures on the English Law* was the fruit of the largest intellectual collaboration in Johnson's life. Because the lectures were not published until 1985, his work on them has not until recently been studied and appreciated. They posed problems for Chambers because after Blackstone's *Commentaries on the Laws of England* he ran the risk of treading over the same ground. His and Johnson's solution was to simplify Blackstone's lengthy legal explanations by stressing the need for law and order. Such a theme reflected Johnson's characteristic humanitarian insistence that the British Constitution must respond to human institutions and needs in order to be properly used and understood. He supervised the writing and Chambers may have used paragraphs and entire lectures written by Johnson, but their collaboration was balanced, a joint authorship.[29]

5

In February 1767, Lucy urged Johnson to pay a visit to Lichfield, but he saw no point in it except to see Kitty who was seriously ill and dying. Lucy herself seemed to be cold towards him these days. It was a good thing he did not go. That month he was distinguished with 'one of the most remarkable incidents' of his life, an interview with the King that raised his spirits considerably. He jotted down the conversation (the so-called 'Caldwell Minute') immediately afterwards for a friend, Sir James Caldwell, from whom Boswell obtained it. Reynolds, Goldsmith, and a few others afterwards heard him talk with undisguised pride and earnestness about it. The scene of the interview was the King's Library in the royal residence known as the Queen's House, formerly Buckingham House, on the site where Buckingham Palace now sits. This great library was built from 1762–6 by Sir William Chambers to accommodate the great collection of books and manuscripts George III had amassed. The royal encounter came about because when the King was informed that Johnson, the most distinguished man of letters in England, occasionally came to the royal library to study, he made it known that he would like to meet him on his next visit. Seeing Johnson enter and settle down with a book by the fire in the library, the King's godson and future Librarian, Sir Frederick Barnard, promptly informed the King and led him briskly by candlelight along some dark passages and through a private door into the library. When Barnard whispered into his ear, 'Here is the King', Johnson 'started up' and stood motionless facing the sovereign. The King walked over to him and they began to talk.[30]

This encounter has been represented, particularly as rendered by Boswell, as a cordial confrontation between the old courtly, aristocratic world of letters and patronage and the new professional, Johnsonian world of print culture where the market did the bidding, not kings. Boswell dramatised his source, the 'Caldwell Minute', making Johnson and the relatively new print culture the heroes of his beautifully orchestrated scene. The King is cast as the supreme patron pressing the Aeneas of British literature and culture to perform again for the good of the country. Perhaps he wondered whether the pension he had granted him had in fact been good for him if it had silenced his pen. He questioned him about his writing four separate times. First the King asked if he 'was then writing anything', to which Johnson replied, 'he was not, for he had pretty well told the world what he knew' and had to do more reading. A few minutes later, the King tried again, urging him 'to continue his labours'. This time Johnson told him what in exasperation, bordering on anger, he had told others who prodded him to write more, that he thought he 'had already done his part as a writer'. Cordially, the King remarked he would agree with him if he had not written so well. At this Johnson remained silent, struck deeply by the compliment. Finally, with one more effort the King recommended he write 'a literary biography of this country', for nobody else could do it. This time Johnson gave way and 'signified his readiness to comply with his Majesty's wishes'.[31]

Boswell wrote that throughout this interview Johnson conducted himself in the 'firm manly manner' befitting a respectable professional man of letters, not in the obsequious mode of a suppliant. When later at Sir Joshua's house Johnson regaled his host, Goldsmith, and others with an account of the exchange, they all hung on his words as a kind of returning hero who for a few minutes before the sovereign – 'the finest gentleman I have ever seen' – had enacted the new era of independence of artists and writers in the public face of patronage. Often jealous of Johnson's ability to dominate and take command of conversations, Goldsmith at first sulked on a sofa, but he finally came forward with a telling compliment to the man of the hour: 'Well, you acquitted yourself in this conversation better than I should have done; for I should have bowed and stammered through the whole of it.'[32]

CHAPTER 25

Coliseum of Beasts

I

IN THE SUMMER OF 1767, shortness of breath, especially in bed, made Johnson's mind race with fears of worse things. He also began to experience spasms in his stomach, throat and neck. Flatulence (possibly caused by a gall stone) and rheumatic pains, which had been a problem for years, rounded out the dreary procession of ailments. All his would go on for years. In April 1770 he complained in his diary of 'lumbago, or rheumatism in the loins, which often passes to the muscles of the belly, where it causes equal, if not greater, pain'. He wrapped himself up in flannel at night with 'a very great fire near my bed', but lying down only increased his pain and he could stay in bed only for a couple of hours at a time. He was also resorting to blisters on his back and opium.[1]

His inability to breathe properly increasingly made him feel incapable of rising to occasions, to settle to work and get on with life. His references to uneasiness, disturbed and unsettled nights and 'freedom of mind' were coded references to depression. While he was in Oxford in early 1768 helping Chambers again with his lectures, he suffered another severe attack of physical illness and melancholia, which forced him to extend his stay in New Inn Hall to two entire months. He remembered this attack vividly fifteen years later in a letter to Chambers, who was then in Calcutta: 'That dreadful illness which seized me at New Inn Hall left consequences which have I think always hung upon me. I have never since cared much to walk. My mental abilities I do not perceive it impaired.' Over the years since, he added:

my constitutional maladies pursued me. My thoughts were disturbed, my nights were insufferably restless, and by spasms in the breast I was condemned to the torture of sleepiness without the power to sleep. Those spasms after enduring them more than twenty years I eased by three powerful remedies, abstinence, opium, and mercury, but after a short time they were succeeded by a strange oppression of another kind which when I lay down disturbed me with a sensation like flatulence or intumescence which I cannot describe.

'I have been really very bad', he wrote in April to Mrs Thrale who had recently given birth to another daughter, 'and am glad that I was not at Streatham, where I should have been troublesome to you'; and again later that month, 'I am better, having scarce eaten for seven days.' These were 'disorders of the body, and disturbances of the mind very near to madness' which now made up so much of his life that he could not bear to think of them. 'I have now begun the sixtieth year of my life,' he wrote in his birthday prayer: 'How the last year has past I am unwilling to terrify myself with thinking. This day has been passed in great perturbation.'[2]

Instead of returning to London from Oxford in May, he rushed to Lichfield because Kitty Chambers was on her deathbed. It was a measure of his deep affection for his family's servant of over more than forty years. After seeing how very ill she was, he wrote desperately to his physician Thomas Lawrence in London with detailed accounts of her symptoms to determine if she could be cured. The letters are extraordinarily clinical, anticipating his letters about his own sicknesses in following years. 'Kitty is, I think, going to heaven,' he wrote. She hung on for two more months, forcing him to stay in town depressingly longer than he had anticipated. Waiting for her to die became a kind of enforced idleness. 'My old melancholy has laid hold upon me to a degree sometimes not easily supportable,' he wrote to Robert Chambers in Oxford. He pined for the comforts of Streatham Park, complaining to Mrs Thrale about 'the shackles of destiny' he felt in Lichfield – 'there has not been one day of pleasure, and yet I cannot get away'. 'I hope soon to return from exile.' Finally, unable to wait any longer, he took his leave of 58-year-old Kitty in mid-October, recording the moments of parting in a touching passage: 'I desired all to withdraw, then told her that we were to part for ever, that as Christians we should part with prayer, and that I would, if she was willing, say a short prayer beside her. She expressed great desire to hear me, and held up her poor hands, as she lay in bed, with great fervour, while I prayed, kneeling by her ... I then kissed her. She told me that to part was the greatest pain that she had ever felt, and that she hoped we would meet again in a better place. I expressed with swelled eyes and great emotion of tenderness the same hopes. We kissed and parted.' The person he was most sorry to leave, apart from Kitty, was Elizabeth Aston, for whose sister Molly he had nourished such a strong, even amorous, affection. Elizabeth had never married and lived alone up at Stowe Hill, the house she had built just outside Lichfield. She would be his most intimate friend in Lichfield on future visits, a warm and vital compensation for the otherwise dreary and barren months he would spend there.

He rushed back to Oxford, regretting he could not bring himself to stop for a few hours with Hector in Birmingham: 'A few serious and a few jocund hours would have brought back a little of our former lives. Surely we shall meet some time again.' With his health and spirits as they were, it may have occurred to him this would never happen.[3]

2

There was not much to occupy him in London in the next several months. He did a little reading of Pascal's *Pensées*, continued helping Robert Chambers, and wrote the Dedication for William Payne's *Introduction to Geometry*. He thought of geometry as 'the primary and fundamental art of life', extending throughout all 'operations of human skill'. Mrs Thrale was particularly struck by the psychological use to which he could put his delight in mathematical computations, even to the point of timing how long it would take a fingernail to grow. She wrote that he had 'a singular power of withdrawing his attention from the prattle he heard round him, and would often sit amusing himself with calculating sums while there was a noise in the room enough to perplex any common mortal. He used indeed to be always tormenting one with showing how much time might be lost by squandering two hours a day, how much money might be saved by laying up five shillings a day, how many lines might be written by putting down only ten every day with a hundred such like propositions.' Once he got over an attack of stomach spasms by calculating the national debt, which he said if converted to silver would 'make a meridian of that metal' around the circumference of the earth, which could be called 'the *Meridian of London*'.[4]

When Parliament was dissolved early in 1768, Johnson assisted Thrale again in another campaign for re-election. This national election turned out to be especially violent because the hard-hitting John Wilkes was back in London stirring up public discontent. He had fled to France four years earlier when both houses of Parliament sought to prosecute him for seditious libel in attacking the King and his Ministers in his periodical *The North Briton* (no. 45), and for his pornographic *Essay on Woman*. He was now campaigning to re-enter Parliament as Member for Middlesex, flying in the face of the political establishment, the King and the Prime Minister by whipping up a frenzy of public support for his radical reforms in favour of popular rule, including enfranchisement for the poor. A rallying point for the 'patriot' Opposition, he was suddenly the people's hero and cries of 'Wilkes and Liberty!' echoed in the streets as rioting broke out. Benjamin Franklin, then living in London, described how the mob required 'gentlemen and ladies of all ranks, as they passed in their carriages, to shout for Wilkes and liberty, marking the same words on all their coaches with chalk, and No. 45 on every door'. On the road to Oxford from London, Boswell was fascinated by people 'roaring with "Wilkes and Liberty", which, with "No. 45", was chalked on every coach and chaise'. Although Wilkes was a magnetic and likeable personality, he was suspected of being less interested in the people's rights than in restoring his own personal fortunes because a Member of Parliament could not be arrested for debt. He won the March election but the following month was arrested on the old charges, fined £1,000, and promptly thrown in jail for twenty-two months. That the new MP for Middlesex should be stewing in prison only incited further mob violence. Then he was unwisely deprived of his office, an act that raised constitutional issues later taken up by Johnson in his political pamphlet, *The Patriot*, in 1770. As for Thrale, who opposed Wilkes strongly, he narrowly won his seat for Southwark in March thanks in no small part to his wife's untiring campaigning efforts while carrying another baby due in April.[5]

In the spring of 1768 Boswell, who (so far as we know) had not had a letter from Johnson since August 1766, re-entered his life. He had been busy in Edinburgh earning his living as a new advocate and looking for a rich wife, but he expended most of his creative impulses in authorship. Drawing on his colourful journal record of his intrepid visit to Corsica, in February 1768 he published his *Account of Corsica*. The book sold so well that for a time he became famous as 'Corsica Boswell'. With the delicious glow of fame lighting his way, he was eager to get to London on his new footing of literary success, although he was also nervous about seeing Johnson because without his permission he had included in his book a passage from one of his letters to him in Paris in January 1766. Someone had told him Johnson was 'offended'. 'In short, I was quite in the dark concerning him,' Boswell scribbled in his journal. It was just as well he had left Edinburgh before reading Johnson's letter: 'I could now tell why I should not write, for who would write to men who publish the letters to their friends without their leave?' He added that while he would be glad to see him, 'I wish you would empty your head of Corsica, which I think has filled it rather too long.' When he got around to reading *Corsica*, Johnson liked the personal part of the book because it was full of images 'which operated strongly upon yourself', but as for the history of the island he thought it was borrowed and dull.[6]

Finding Johnson was in Oxford, Boswell followed him there. He checked in at the Angel and quickly made his way to New Inn Hall, where Chambers received him graciously and gave him tea. A little while later Johnson came in and promptly quieted all his anxieties: 'He took me all in his arms and kissed me on both sides of the head, and was as cordial as ever I saw him.' He was flattered his young friend had come all the way to Oxford just to see him and delighted to hear he was now earning £200 per year as an advocate: 'What, Bozzy? Two hundred pounds! A great deal.' Immediately, Boswell took in the Johnsonian ether and began to record their conversations. They spoke also of the legal profession and literature, especially of Goldsmith, and Johnson renewed his promise to visit the Hebrides with him. Chambers invited Boswell to spend the night with them and the next evening they supped together at the Angel.[7]

The conversation flowed at the Angel, running in and out of subjects with ease and jollity. At one point, Johnson's sense of humour got the better of Boswell's bizarre ideas about reincarnation. 'Why not allow a dog to be immortal', Boswell blurted out. When he remarked that whenever he saw a very intelligent dog he did not know what to make of him, Johnson 'growling with joy', replied, 'No, Sir, and when we see a very foolish fellow, we don't know what to make of him.' He then suddenly rose from his chair, 'bounced along, and stood by the fire, laughing and exulting over me'. Boswell was struck again by Johnson's determination to talk for victory: 'When Mr Chambers was getting the better of him in an argument, he said to him as to a boy, "My dear Chambers, take it to you, take it to you, since you will have it so", as if he made a concession to please him, when in reality he did not know how to answer him.' They spoke of how they felt a woman's adultery is so much more to blame than a man's because her 'crime' breaks the peace of families and introduces the 'confusion of progeny' whereas the man's, though 'criminal in the sight of God', injures only her. As for chastity, Boswell asked Johnson whether it was fair that a woman's 'deviation' from it should absolutely ruin her. Johnson replied: 'The great principle which every woman is taught is to keep her legs together. When she has given up that principle, she has given up every notion of female honour and virtue, which are all included in chastity.' Completely out of touch with Johnson's mental and physical ordeals in Oxford, Boswell noted only his energy, laughter and cheerfulness: 'His mixing more in society had dissipated much of that gloom which hung upon his mind when he lived much alone, when he brooded in the Temple.'[8]

Johnson returned to London at the end of April to find that Boswell, feeling 'really the *Great Man* now', was still there though recovering in his

room in Half-Moon street from one of the seventeen attacks of gonor-
rhoea he endured during his lifetime. He called to see him one morning.
Already thinking of cashing in on his friendship with Johnson, Boswell
asked him if he would object to his publishing his letters after his death.
'Nay, Sir,' Johnson answered, 'when I am dead, you may do as you will'.[9]

Johnson continued to take an interest in the development of the Royal
Library, writing in May 1768 an uncharacteristically long letter to the
King's Librarian, Frederick Barnard, containing detailed advice on what
rare books to buy by 'ransacking other countries': 'every country has literature of its own which may be best gathered on its native soil . . . you must
catch up single volumes where you can find them. Try every place, things
often occur where they are least expected.' Reflecting his own interest in
geography, topography and the history of printing, he strongly recommended acquiring maps and first editions of early printed works as 'great
ornaments' for the library.[10]

On 7 June Boswell arranged a dinner for Johnson at the Crown and
Anchor in the Strand which included Percy, Langton and Davies, as well
as two distinguished members of the Edinburgh literati who wished to see
him, Dr William Robertson the historian who became principal of Edinburgh University in 1762, and Dr Hugh Blair the divine and critic who
since 1762 had been Regius Professor of rhetoric and belles-lettres at the
university. Blair, who once criticised Johnson's style in the *Rambler* for being 'too pompous', had met him in 1763 and remembered the rough treatment he received then from 'the Giant in his den'. Defending the authenticity of the Ossianic poems, he now came in for a bit more. He asked
Johnson if he still thought 'any man of a modern age could have written
such poems?' Johnson turned on him, 'Yes, Sir, many men, many women,
and many children.' After that the dinner proved disappointing for Johnson because, according to Boswell, Robertson and Blair were so cowed by
him that 'they hardly opened their lips, and that only to say something
which they were certain would not expose them to the sword of Goliath;
such was their anxiety for their fame when in the presence of Johnson.'
And on that night it was a good thing they did not confront him. Davies
took some direct hits, as did Percy who characteristically got up and left

in a huff. In the morning, before leaving for home, Boswell found Johnson pleased with his 'colloquial prowess'. 'Yes, Sir,' Boswell observed, 'you tossed and gored several persons.'[11]

By then Johnson's reputation for conversational roughness, even rudeness, was widely known. Horace Walpole, who went out of his way to avoid meeting Johnson and therefore remained largely dependent on rumour, did not mince his words, describing him in 1775 as 'an odious and mean character' whose 'gross brutality' made him want 'to fling a glass of wine in his face'. 'I have no patience,' he added, 'with an unfortunate monster trusting to his helpless deformity for indemnity for any impertinence that his arrogance suggests, and who thinks that what he has read is an excuse for everything he says.' The epithet circulating was that he was a 'bear'. Baretti thought that with more polish he might have been 'a dancing bear'. Boswell heard Goldsmith say in his defence, 'Johnson, to be sure, has a roughness in his manner; but no man alive has a more tender heart. *He has nothing of the bear but his skin.*'[12]

Sometime in 1768, or perhaps earlier, Johnson sent Frank off to Bishop's Stortford Grammar School in Hertfordshire to be educated properly. Hawkins disapprovingly remarked that Frank stayed at the school for five years and (according to Mrs Williams) cost Johnson no less than £300 (some £30,000 today) over that period. He thought it was money down the drain. But Johnson never wavered in his determination to raise the boy with the advantages of a good education, writing more than two years later, 'I am very well satisfied with your progress . . . Let me know what English books you read for your entertainment. You can never be wise unless you love reading.' He was even ordering clothes for him and promised he would never forget or forsake him.[13]

He visited Oxford three times in 1769 to see his friends and continue helping Chambers, including six weeks in the spring and summer soaking up the attention and comforts he received there. In September the Thrales took him on a short excursion into Kent, hoping that a change of scene would benefit his health, and there were plans that autumn also for some time in Brighton with them which did not materialize. When their baby girl Lucy Elizabeth was born on 22 June, he was 'honoured' to be asked to be her godfather. He 'insisted' on her being called Elizabeth in memory of Tetty. 'I always wished it might be a Miss,' he wrote. 'Surely I shall be very fond of her. In a year and half she will run and talk.' Ominously, he slipped in the comment, 'how much ill may happen in a year and a half'. It took longer than that, but his goddaughter, Mrs Thrale's favourite, died four years later.[14]

His prayer on his sixtieth birthday in September recorded his horror once again that he was not achieving anything and that his physical recovery was slow: 'My days are easier, but the perturbation of my nights is very distressful. I think to try a lower diet. I have grown fat too fast. My lungs seem encumbered, and my breath fails me, if my strength [is] in any unusual degree exerted, or my motion accelerated.' Such worries bred fears of an unprepared death that cropped up frequently in his letters: 'though I feel all these decays of body, I have made no preparation for the grave. What shall I do to be saved?' Boswell's compelling passage on 26 October describing Johnson's mind in combat with itself, elicited by Garrick's remark that he believed Johnson 'to be harassed with doubts', is the most vividly terrifying ever written by someone who had the chance to study him closely:

> His mind resembled the vast amphitheatre, the Coliseum at Rome. In the centre stood his judgement, which, like a mighty gladiator, combated those apprehensions that, like the wild beasts of the *Arena*, were all around in cells, ready to be let out upon him. After a conflict, he drove them back into their dens; but not killing them, they were still assailing him. To my question, whether we might not fortify our minds for the approach of death, he answered, in a passion, 'No, Sir, let it alone. It matters not how a man dies, but how he lives ... It will do him no good to whine.'

Brave but desperate words. Boswell was in forbidden territory but foolishly persisted talking about death: 'He was so provoked, that he said, "Give us no more of this"; and was thrown into such a state of agitation, that he expressed himself in a way that alarmed and distressed me;

showed an impatience that I should leave him, and when I was going away, called to me, sternly, "Don't let us meet to-morrow." Licking his wounds, the next day Boswell bravely called to apologise and managed to soften his 'ferocity' so successfully that as he was leaving Johnson stopped him 'and smiling said, "Get you gone – *in*"; a curious mode of inviting me to stay, which I accordingly did for some time longer'.[15]

3

'My friends at Lichfield must not think that I forget them', he had told Lucy in June 1768, 'neither Mrs Cobb, nor Mrs Adey, nor Miss Adey, nor Miss [Anna] Seward, nor Miss Vise'. Elizabeth Aston also was waiting for him up at Stowe Hill. With the prospect of a warmer Lucy, 'my dear darling', there to welcome him, in August 1769 he ventured another Lichfield visit. Lucy's well-being had been especially on his mind and there was a string of other women he wished to see. He set out on 10 August with Frank, who was spending the holidays at home. Lucy received them warmly – she saved 'her best gooseberries upon the tree for me', he exulted, though they were no match for the pineapples and strawberries and cream which he identified with the plentitude of Streatham Park. 'Not yet well', he 'rambled' out into the countryside, pleased (in Horace's words) with 'the familiar streams and sacred springs' and courting the 'cooling shades'. On the other hand, the town council's (those 'wicked men' and 'audacious aldermen') had 'violated' 'ill-fated' George Lane in town by denuding it of its lovely trees. This time there was less chance to get bored with the town, as he also squeezed in a visit to Taylor at Ashbourne.[16]

He fretted he might not be able to get back to London in time to accompany the Thrales to Brighton. As it happened, he had to make his way there on his own in mid-August, where the days passed pleasingly enough. Not with enormous pleasure, one imagines, he hunted on the Downs with Thrale; more pleasurably, he swam in the sea with Mrs Thrale and little Queeney. While he was there he received a letter from Boswell who had arrived in London at the beginning of September and, dressed flourishingly as a Corsican patriot, was on his way to Stratford to participate in Garrick's famous extravaganza known as the 'Shakespeare Jubilee' – a few days of festivities in honour of the Bard which were washed out in torrential rains. Boswell thought it was shameful that Johnson, the great modern editor of Shakespeare, was in Brighton and not in Stratford, getting wet with the rest of them: 'almost every man of eminence in the literary world was happy to partake in this festival of genius, [and] the absence of Johnson could not but be wondered at and regretted'.[17]

When he returned to London in late September, Boswell could not devote himself to him as completely as on previous visits. The reason was that Paoli, who had failed in his valiant struggle for Corsican independence from the French, had fled the island in the summer and was forced into exile in London. Boswell saw it as his 'duty, as well as my pleasure, to attend much upon him', which included the thrill of introducing the famous Corsican and the greatest literary personality of the age to each other: 'They met with a manly ease, mutually conscious of their own abilities and of the abilities one of each other.' Immediately, Johnson conceived a lasting respect for the noble ideals and dignity of the Corsican patriot, telling Boswell later at his lodgings in Old Bond Street, while they drank tea late into the night, that Paoli 'had the loftiest port' he had ever met in a man. Even so, Johnson was still fed up with all of Boswell's chatter about Corsica. At Streatham, to which at Johnson's request Boswell was invited for dinner one October evening, Johnson was in a mocking, hilarious mood at the expense of both Scotland and Corsica. This was not the first or last time that in the company of Mrs Thrale he felt the impulse to be especially hard on Boswell, in this instance shocking him with his violent declamation against Corsican failure to take one single fortified town from the Genovese in twenty years: 'They might have battered down the walls and reduced them to powder in twenty years. They might have pulled the walls in pieces, and cracked the stones with their teeth in twenty years.' There was no opposing him that night. As Goldsmith once remarked about Johnson's 'talking for victory', adopting the words of a character in one of Colley Cibber's plays, 'There is no arguing with Johnson, for "when his pistol misses fire, he knocks you down with the butt end of it."'[18]

The last intimate moment with Johnson that Boswell recorded on this London visit was of his returning to Johnson's Court with Johnson on 26 October to have tea with Anna Williams. The scene provides a snapshot of her in Johnson's home and Johnson's silent forbearance of her. She made the tea with 'sufficient dexterity notwithstanding her blindness, though her manner of satisfying herself that the cups were full enough was a little awkward. She put her finger down a certain way till she felt the tea touch it'. They quietly sipped and talked. Boswell could have hugged himself with the 'elation at being allowed the privilege of attending Dr Johnson at his late visits to this lady': 'I willingly drank cup after cup, as it had been the Heliconian spring.'[19]

4

After Boswell left London on 10 November, the 'tedious and painful rheumatism' that flared up in the spring of the new year brought Johnson another layer of considerable suffering. Drawing to a close his collaboration with Chambers, who by the end of the academic year in July had given all his required Vinerian lectures and been paid for them, he was in Oxford for four days in January and then again a week in April, but during the latter visit he was in great pain. He tried blistering and took opium when he got back to London, only imagining he felt some relief from the former. After briefly taking refuge again at Streatham, he returned home on Good Friday because of his rheumatic discomfort, to treat himself and fast 'unobserved'. 'I came home late, and was unwilling to carry my rheumatism to the cold church in the morning, unless that were rather an excuse made to myself.' He tried to be philosophical: 'The pain harasses me much, yet many have the disease perhaps in a much higher degree with want of food, fire, and covering, which I find thus grievous with all the succours that riches and kindness can buy and give.' On Saturday he sat up to compose a lengthy Easter prayer, and 'having ordered the maid to make the fire in my chamber at eight went to rest, and had a tolerable night'. He resolved again to read the Scriptures every Sunday, which he was failing to do: six hundred verses in the Old Testament 'in any language' and two hundred in the New Testament in Greek every week, from which sometimes he would read a little 'with a solemn hum, and sometimes talk to himself, either as meditating or as praying'. To help him adhere to this plan he even kept tables of how much of the Bible he was reading.[20]

He greeted the new decade with shame and guilt that the black dog was still his regular companion and he could rouse himself neither to work nor take command of his thoughts and days. 'For the last year I have been slowly recovering both from the violence of my last illness, and, I think, from the general disease of my life.'[21]

CHAPTER 26

Back to Shakespeare and
the Dictionary

I

JOHNSON SAT DOWN ONE NIGHT in January 1770 at the Thrales' South-wark house and began writing his first political pamphlet, *The False Alarm,* since being granted a pension in 1762. He thus embarked on a period of political writing in the early 1770s in which he produced four pamphlets in the persona of an *enfant terrible,* a role he relished. They brought him widespread criticism partly because he was thought by many to have accepted his pension on condition he would not stray again into politics. There were accusations of ingratitude. It took him about a day to write the twenty-five pages. Mrs Thrale wrote she would never forget the pleasure it gave him to write it. Just the sensation of letting his pen flow again freely must have been exhilarating. Strahan rushed the pamphlet into print, publishing five hundred copies on 16 January, followed by three more impressions of five hundred copies each in February and March. It was published anonymously but as usual in a very short time everyone knew he was the author.[1]

Johnson saw the pamphlet as a way to get back at Wilkes (that 'abusive scoundrel') for ridiculing in *The North Briton* (nos. 11 and 12) several of his definitions in the *Dictionary* when it first came out. But there were more important reasons for writing it. One was a letter to the *Public Advertiser* by Junius, whose identity remains unclear even today, defending Wilkes's right to take his seat in the House. Junius had also taken delight in repeatedly attacking the King, for whom at this point Johnson had a very high regard, so this was his small way of evening the score on behalf of the monarch, too. Of Wilkes, he said he wished to say little except that 'lampoon itself would disdain to speak ill of him of whom no man speaks well. It is sufficient that he is expelled from the House of Commons, and confined in jail as being legally convicted of sedition and impiety . . . We are now disputing . . . whether Middlesex shall be represented or not by a criminal from a jail'. Beyond this, there was a constitutional issue raised by Wilkes having been denied his seat by the Commons. Johnson's main argument was that this so-called 'alarming crisis' (a favourite expression of the Wilkites) was a manufactured spin, a false alarm, and that the Commons was perfectly within its constitutional right to allow another man, who obtained far fewer votes, to take up the seat instead. His position is another complicating factor in the misdirected effort to fix on him the label of either Tory or Whig.[2]

As a monarchist and defender of the established Church, as one who had a revulsion for republicanism and dissenting attitudes towards religion, Johnson was understood to be a Tory by his contemporaries. Both monarchy and the Church of England, in his view, protected the nation from constitutional, religious and moral instability. But when it got down to social and economic realities, to the individual welfare and condition of human beings, he appeared much more like the 'liberal' of today. It has also been argued that because Johnson defended Parliament's right to control its own membership, in spite of what the electors decided, he was behaving like a strong Tory. Another view, however, is that the latter was in fact a 'Whig' position, that Johnson – even as he encouraged political awareness and concern by the average citizen – regarded inflammatory politicking by firebrands like Wilkes, the chaotic cant of mobs that could rouse the populace to rioting, and vague talk about 'rights' without an understanding of political realities, as dangerous to the fabric of effective government, harmony of society and happiness of the individual. 'The perpetual subject of political disquisition is not absolute, but comparative good.' Anarchy was itself a kind of tyranny.[3]

His language grows angry and abusive in the pamphlet over what he saw as irresponsible electoral agitators who have whipped up 'this tempest of outrage'. Boswell described it as 'extreme coarseness of contemptuous abuse' from one accustomed to wielding such language against the establishment but now aiming it against the 'declaimers or the plotters of a city-tavern'. His fury was stoked by the spectacle of the ignorant, uneducated masses, even mobs, presuming to dictate to Parliament how to govern. The 'weeping patriots' were 'puny controvertists': 'If infatuation be, as the proverb tells us, the forerunner of destruction, how near must be the ruin of a nation that can be incited against its governors, by sophistry like this.' His temperature rose as he sarcastically exposed the bathos of 'fever of epidemic patriotism'. Every moment brings a new crisis, 'quiet and security are now at an end', 'we hear the thunder while the sky is clear': 'the tailor slips his thimble, the drapier drops his yard, and the blacksmith lays down his hammer; they meet at an honest alehouse, consider the state of the nation, read or hear the last petition, lament the miseries of the time, are alarmed at the dreadful crisis, and subscribe to the support of the Bill of Rights.' The entire conduct of this 'despicable faction' could be summed up as 'plebeian grossness, and savage indecency', fired by 'the insolence of invective'. These 'low-born railers' have insulted the King with rudeness when they should rather have been grateful that he is the first monarch in a century who has desired and tried to deserve their affections and be 'the common father of all his people'. The Tories, moreover, have been shameful with their 'frigid neutrality' towards the 'fomenters of sedition, and confederates of the rabble', their chronic suspiciousness of whatever administration was in power in Westminster.[4]

As a historical postscript to this pamphlet, Wilkes was elected for Middlesex again in the general election of 1774 and allowed this time to retain his seat. With the financial assistance of powerful backers from both politics and trade who enabled him to recover financially, he later became Mayor of London. Two years after his election he would meet Johnson, with unexpected results.

2

Johnson may or may not have attributed to his fervent prayers for a return of literary activity an intense period of revision of both the Shakespeare edition and the *Dictionary* in the early 1770s. By January 1770 he had begun revising his edition, for which he called on the scholarly help of Steevens, whom one critic has called the nastiest person in Johnson's circle. This was because of his sly and treacherous relish for tricking people into arguments with each other. He was fond of writing embarrassing pieces for the newspapers and attributing them to others, inventing information to decoy and trap rival scholars, and attacking his friends in anonymous articles for newspapers. When once at Langton's house for dinner in 1778, Johnson remarked he would 'be sorry if any of our Club were hanged', though 'I will not say but some of them deserve it', Beauclerk piped in, 'You, Sir, have a friend [Steevens] who deserves to be hanged; for he speaks behind their backs against those with whom he lives on the best terms, and attacks them in the newspapers. *He* certainly ought to be *kicked . . .* He is very malignant'. Johnson did not entirely agree, 'No, Sir; he is not malignant. He is mischievous, if you will. He would do no man an essential injury; he may, indeed, love to make sport of people by vexing their vanity.' 'If he is a man of principles,' Beauclerk insisted, 'he does not wear them out in practice.' As a Shakespearean and Renaissance scholar, however, Steevens definitely knew his way around and was extremely well read in Elizabethan literature. He appears to have been among those with whom Johnson supped in the Temple on the night before publication of the 1765 edition, and who kept him up until after five in the morning. According to Steevens, when Johnson looked at his watch, he exclaimed, 'This is sport to you, gentlemen; but you do not consider there are at most only four hours between me and criticism.'[5]

Without Steevens, he could not have completed the Shakespeare revision, which became known as the Johnson-Steevens edition, published in 1773. The edition contained eighty-four new notes signed by Johnson to which possibly Steevens added without telling him. Steevens also was the chief contributor of supplementary notes for the three appendices that conclude the tenth and final volume. And he took the textual editing far beyond anything Johnson attempted for the original edition, although the crotchety critic and giant-killer Joseph Ritson complained that in this, and the next edition in 1778, Steevens and Johnson had 'never collated any of the folios'. Even Johnson's friend, the scholarly Irishman Edmond Malone, who will soon come into his life (although they had met briefly in 1765 when Johnson was living in Inner Temple Lane), had a low regard for the textual editing and felt that Shakespeare's text after the Johnson-Steevens edition was in such a sorry state that he needed to do a whole new edition of his own, which was eventually published in 1790.

3

Johnson spent a couple of weeks in July 1770 with Lucy in Lichfield, where it was wet and miserable, he ached with rheumatism, and failed to see his favourite Miss Aston because she was away. He then dallied with rural novelties at Ashbourne for a couple more, feeding the fawns from his hand upon the lawn, measuring Taylor's 'great bull', and haymaking. Mrs Thrale missed him sorely, 'I hope we shall all spend our Christmas comfortably together.' He was home in the first week of August where he did not find much to do for five months except help Goldsmith with what became one of the most famous of eighteenth-century poems, *The Deserted Village*.[6]

In December, Spain provoked an international crisis that banished thoughts of measuring bulls and haymaking from his mind and concentrated it instead on writing another political pamphlet. With a sudden show of naval force Spain invaded the Malvinas or Falkland Islands and succeeded in removing the miniscule English garrison there. When news of the invasion got back to London, Lord North's ministry rapidly prepared a naval force to sail back and reclaim the islands. But William Pitt (the Elder) and others in opposition contrived to trip up Lord North. They urged a war against Spain that they were sure England would lose because of the enemy's probable alliance with France, talking up the ugly face of the impending war in order to induce North to lose courage and accept a humiliating defeat. This, they hoped, would force him to resign as Prime Minister, whose ministry Johnson supported.

Perhaps at Strahan's request and with information he was given by the Government, in late February or early March 1771, Johnson wrote *Thoughts on the Late Transactions Respecting Falkland's Islands*, which was out on the streets by 16 March. Although it was not as controversial as *False Alarm* and to his mind lacked its 'subtlety of disquisition', it had 'fire'. It attacked 'the howl of plebeian patriotism' broadcast by the likes of Wilkes and Junius, the exploitative greed of the trading interests of the City, and Pitt, Lord Grenville, and the Opposition in general. 'Like vultures waiting for a day of carnage', Pitt and his cohorts played the game of 'domestic sedition', Johnson wrote. Neither of these scenarios came to pass and England on the contrary humiliated Spain into backing down and getting out of the Falklands without a single shot being fired – all this in spite of what Johnson called 'the machinations of these pygmy rebels', 'the noisy faction which has too long filled the kingdom, sometimes with the roar of empty menace, and sometimes with the yell of hypocritical lamentation.'[7]

Johnson took aim at the warmongers who stood to get rich by war, and the patriotic cant of the rabble whipped up by the power brokers in order to realise their own personal ambitions. His indictment of war is an eloquent, incensed plea against the 'diseases of animal nature' that send young men to their deaths marching to slogans, doomed by political ideology: 'It is wonderful with what coolness and indifference the greater part of mankind see war commenced. Those that hear of it at a distance, or read of it in books, but have never presented its evils to their minds, consider it as little more than a splendid game; a proclamation, an army, a battle, and a triumph.' He also struck again at Junius's 'blaze of impudence' and 'thirst of blood': 'He cries *havoc* without reserve, and endeavours to let slip the dogs of foreign or of civil war, ignorant whither they are going, and careless what may be their prey.' Junius 'drew the rabble after him as a monster makes a show'. As Boswell said, we find Johnson in this pamphlet 'lashing the party in opposition with unbounded severity, and making the fullest use of what he ever reckoned a most effectual argumentative instrument – contempt'.[8]

Strahan, a Member for Parliament as well as successful printer, was so impressed by Johnson's two recent political pamphlets, by his relish for entering into the fray, that he got it into his mind that Johnson should himself become a Member of Parliament and be able to influence current affairs more directly. Presumably with Johnson's approval, he wrote to the House of Commons in March 1771 proposing he would make 'an excellent figure' there and asking that the idea be presented to Lord North. Johnson had all the necessary credentials, he urged, eloquence, sharp analytical powers, 'extraordinary sense and unimpeached virtue', an amazing capacity for work, and strong support for the ministry. Friends of the King would 'find him a lamb', his enemies 'a lion'. But Johnson now was widely regarded as too politically independent. Back in 1762, when recommendations were sought for his pension, Richard Farmer wrote to Lord Bute: 'I am told that his political principles make him incapable of being in any place of trust, by incapacitating him from qualifying himself for any such office – but a pension My Lord requires no such performances.' As for Johnson's willingness to be a Member, 'Yes, yes, he would have *approved* it,' Mrs Thrale noted regarding Strahan's idea. However, the matter raises the question whether or not Johnson would have been any good as a speaker in the House since the long, sustained speeches required there were not in his mode of 'sententious brevity'. Boswell thought he would have been a sensation; others disagreed. There is almost no knowledge of Johnson delivering speeches to large assemblies, except several times at the Society of Arts and Sciences when the reception was mixed. On one of those occasions, he himself admitted, 'all my flowers of oratory forsook me'.[9]

4

For a year and a half after his marriage to his cousin Margaret Montgomerie – who did not bring him the wealth he had hoped for through marriage but who turned out to be the perfect wife for him – Boswell had turned his mind away from Johnson, London, and the attractions of gambling and whoring that had patterned his existence since returning from the Continent. He broke his silence in April 1771 by inviting his friend to Scotland for the tour of the Highlands and Hebrides they had kept alive in imagination for years. 'Whether we climb the Highlands, or are tossed among the Hebrides,' Johnson replied two months later, 'I hope the time will come when we may try our powers both with cliffs and water.' The next day he was off again with Frank on another 'furlough' (as Mrs Thrale put it) to Lichfield and Ashbourne. He wanted to be well away at the end of another of her difficult pregnancies. He could leave with the pleasing sensation of improved relations with her mother, for whose breast cancer he was constantly trying to find remedies and seek medical advice. For her part, Mrs Salusbury had decided after all that following her death Johnson would remain a good, protective influence for her daughter as friend and counsellor.[10]

As usual he found little in Lichfield 'to please me' because Elizabeth Aston was not well, another of his schoolfellows had died, and there were 'no temptations to prolong my stay'. His vanity was aroused, however, by hearing from Lucy that the portrait of him Reynolds finished in 1769, of which a copy had been painted for her, was 'much visited and much admired'. 'Every man has a lurking wish to appear considerable in his native place.' His thoughts were often on the Thrales and what by now he thought would be the new 'pretty little stranger in the cradle'. As it turned out, the baby was a month overdue, causing considerable pain and anxiety to the mother. He imagined that at this rate the baby would be 'a giant' like Richard III, not an especially pleasing thought. In late June he made his way to Ashbourne, where there was nothing new to entertain him. Trying to take his mind off the rheumatism that he again experienced in his face and mouth by looking forward to seeing the 'furnace' or chemical laboratory the Thrales were building at his urging in the kitchen garden at Streatham, he promised to bring back some iron, copper and lead ore so the children could see lead smelted in it. He also bought Queeney a cabinet in which to keep such curiosities as shells and minerals as he managed to obtain on his travels.[11]

5

On his return to London, there was a large task awaiting him, a revision of the *Dictionary*. As Mrs Thrale also declared, the initiative for revision came from the proprietors: 'the booksellers suggested the project' and 'paid Johnson well' – some £300, the same amount as his annual pension.[12]

Because existing common law in practice gave London booksellers (i.e. publishers) copyright ownership of a book in perpetuity, in spite of the Copyright Act of 1709 giving authors, not booksellers, proprietary owner-ship of their own works and the option to assign to booksellers the rights to publish for only two fourteen-year periods before a work entered the public domain, Johnson, like all authors, had to do their bidding and could not decide on his own to have any of his works republished. Having been asked by Strahan and the other publishers twice in the space of a year to revise his two major publications, Johnson found himself thinking freshly about literary property. Also, in July 1773, Boswell won a highly important 'cause' (the Scottish term for a legal case) in the Edinburgh Court of Session regarding literary property on behalf of the Edinburgh bookseller Alexander Donaldson's fight against the London booksellers. Johnson read his notes on the cause and offered his viewpoints on them before they were published separately as a pamphlet early in 1774. On be-ing asked by Strahan in March to state his ideas on copyright as part of the London publishers' efforts to appeal the Edinburgh ruling to the House of Lords, he clearly laid out his ideas on the subject in a balanced and impartial way that could not have entirely pleased Strahan: 'The au-thor has a natural and peculiar right to the profits of his own work . . . It is inconvenient to society that a useful book should become perpetual and exclusive property . . . an author should retain during his life the sole right of printing and selling his work'. Still, authors had to live in the real world: 'the author must recede from so much of his claim, as shall be deemed injurious or inconvenient to society'; and an author's claim would indeed prove to be harmful if fifty years down the line a revision were badly needed and could not be done because the text was not in the public domain. Therefore, by his scheme a book 'may continue the property of the author or of those who claim from him about fifty years, a term sufficient to reward the writer without any loss to the public'. In effect, Johnson offered Strahan a commonsense compromise between what he saw as the author's rights as creator of an original work and the realities of the book trade and how it might protect him from piracy and earn him a profit.[13]

He went at the revision meticulously, using notes he had kept over the years of changes and additions he wanted to make if he ever got around to it; resurrecting the manuscript notebooks crammed with text and recyclable quotations that the desperate crisis in his original method had forced him to reject; eliminating many illustrative quotations and adding thousands of new ones; and correcting, deleting and adding to the definitions and notes on etymologies and usage. He also made some minor changes in the prefatory essays. He never revised any other of his other works so extensively.

Working with two of his old assistants, Peyton and Alexander Macbean, in an effective division of labour over which he maintained strict control, his efficiency was exemplary. From the outset his successful strategy was more or less simultaneously to complete large portions of the text across the alphabet so that Strahan's men could print several sections of the work at the same time. Except for one delay caused by the loss of the interleaved first edition sheets, he never delayed the printing process, varying his working methods as required and marking the changes directly on printed sheets of the first edition. In a review of 1772–73 in his diary he noted, 'I was able in those seasons to examine and improve my dictionary, and was seldom withheld from the work, but by my own unwillingness.' He was spared any illness until a few days after the fourth edition was published when he succumbed to a cold which grew violent for some ten weeks.[14]

Of all the changes he made in the *Dictionary*, by far his most substantial consisted of the illustrative quotations he deleted and added. There were largely three categories of additions: the Bible (drawn almost entirely from Alexander Cruden's *Concordance*), reflecting his systematic reading of the scriptures; poetry from the sixteenth, seventeenth and eighteenth centuries, mainly by Milton and Edward Young (whose death in 1765 freed Johnson to use him heavily); and religious prose by orthodox Anglican apologists and controversialists. The poetry quotations were dominated by Milton, whom he cited even more than Shakespeare. 'I think more highly of him now than I did at twenty,' he told Boswell a month after the edition was published, signifying that Milton's poetry, heavily inspired as it is by the Bible, was now a greater spiritual experience for him than ever before. What is interesting about all these additions and adjustments are the religious shifts in emphasis they introduce. His intention was to increase the religious and meditative associations of some words, making the entries sometimes feel like mini-prayers on the need for a stronger faith.[15]

There is another theme governing the illustrative quotations Johnson added that concerns Christianity in a political and doctrinal rather than inspirational way. He drew on a wide variety of writers, not always especially good ones, for hundreds of passages of theological prose to shore up his defences against aggressive pressure from many quarters for reform of Church of England doctrine. The passages, described by one critic as a 'stream of reminders', amount (in such a large work) to a necessarily diffused polemic against dissident writers and thinkers, potential parliamentary legislation affecting doctrine, and what he described as the irresponsible 'yelps' against the King and Lord North's ministry, particularly in the early 1770s. More personally, he felt that the chipping away at the Anglican liturgy, the Thirty-Nine Articles of the Church, the *Book of Common Prayer*, and the role of the clergy was endangering Christian faith in general and his own in particular. 'I think that permitting men to preach any opinion contrary to the doctrine of the Established Church tends, in a certain degree, to lessen the authority of the church,' he insisted to Langton, 'and consequently, to lessen the influence of religion.' He was hostile towards any challenge to the Church in the guise of Whig liberalisation.[16]

Reform of Church doctrine, in fact, was one of those subjects, along with death, Wilkes, America, monarchy, and a few others, that could make him erupt angrily in conversation if he were resisted. Although he was on

Samuel Johnson. Generally accepted as the 1775 'blinking Sam' portrait by Reynolds. It shows Johnson poring over a book, obviously near-sighted and struggling to make out the words.

Unfinished portrait of Johnson by James Barry, *c.*1777–80.

A Young Black by Reynolds, *c.*1770. It is now generally accepted that this is Francis Barber, Johnson's servant, who at the age of ten in 1752 was placed in his care.

blessing of God, is to contend with
them, and, if I can, to conquer them.

My Resolutions are
~ To conquer Scruples. Dij.
~ To read the Bible this year.
To try to rise more early.
To Study Divinity.
~ To live methodically.
~ To oppose Idleness.
To frequent Divine Worship.

Almighty and most mer-
ciful Father, before whom I now appear gone loaden with the sins of
another year, Suffer me ~~once~~ ~~more~~ yet again
to call upon thee for pardon and
peace. O God, grant me repentance,

A page from his diary in which Johnson lists resolutions 'to conquer scruples. To read the Bible this year. To try to rise more early. To Study Divinity. To live methodically. To oppose idleness. To frequent Divine Worship.'

Frances ('Fanny') Burney, author of the bestseller *Evelina* (1778). She was a personal favourite of Johnson's, a young friend and admirer.

Hannah More, philanthropist and religious writer, by Frances Reynolds, c.1780. She was befriended by Johnson and was a great success in his and Elizabeth Montagu's circles.

Frances Reynolds, painter and sister of Joshua Reynolds. Members of her family thought she might have married Johnson if she had wished to.

Edmund Burke in the 1780s. Burke was a member of the Club and one of Johnson's closest and most respected friends.

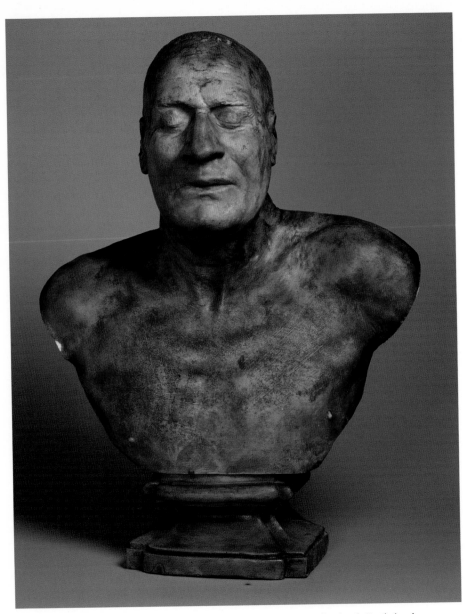

A plaster cast of the 1784 bust of Johnson by William Cumberland Cruikshank and James Hoskins, incorporating the death-mask.

the whole lax about attending church and taking Communion, except in the Easter period, such talk cut to his deepest fears about faith and salvation. On one occasion, when Boswell strayed into the always dangerous territory of Church doctrine, he witnessed Johnson's 'explosion of high-church zeal' – 'he had come close to my chair, and his eyes flashed with indignation'. Boswell 'bowed to the storm' and this time sensibly changed course.[17]

Johnson was finished with his *Dictionary* work in early October 1772 (except for reading of proofs) and the revised fourth edition came out in March 1773. It did not make much of a splash, receiving scarcely any critical attention in the press beyond what was written when the first edition came out almost two decades earlier. A couple of months after publication, he considered, 'Whether I shall ever revise it more, I know not.' He did not.[18]

6

Frank Barber, who was now living with Johnson again after five years at school, showed Boswell to the upstairs study in Johnson's Court when he arrived for his spring visit in mid-March 1772. 'Frank and I were pleased to renew our acquaintance', Boswell noted. 'I waited a little and then heard the great man coming upstairs. The sound of his feet upon the timber steps was weighty and well announced his approach. He had on an old purple cloth suit and a large whitish wig'. Delighted to have Boswell's 'noisy benevolence' with him again, Johnson embraced him, 'I am glad to see thee, I am glad to see thee. Come sit you down.' As he was leaving late at night after tea with Mrs Williams, Johnson burst out, 'I do love thee. I do love thee . . . Good night, dear Sir. I am glad to see you again, very glad to see you again.' Thus began another of Boswell's annual recharges in Johnson's company.[19]

It was on this London visit, after dinner with him at General Paoli's on 31 March, that he first confided in his journal his momentous decision to write Johnson's biography: 'I have a constant plan to write the life of Mr Johnson. I have not told him of it yet, nor do I know if I should tell him. I said that if it was not troublesome and presuming too much, I would beg of him to tell me all the little circumstances of his life, what schools he attended, when he came to Oxford, when he came to London, etc., etc. He did not disapprove of my curiosity as to these particulars, but said, "They'll come out by degrees". Johnson had just remarked that 'nobody could furnish the life of a man but those who had eat and drank and lived in social intercourse with him', so Boswell felt pretty good about his chances. There is no evidence that Johnson had given much serious thought to who was best qualified to be his biographer, but with two intimate friends keeping journals, both of whom he encouraged to do so, the matter must occasionally have crossed his mind. At Johnson's Court late that night, he and Boswell spoke of their mutual friends and of writing biographies. 'I hope you'll write all their lives,' Johnson threw out.[20]

For the present, Mrs Thrale was too wrapped up in her family problems even to contemplate such a fanciful idea as writing the *Life* of her great friend, although she had far more opportunity throughout the year to hear him talk and observe his behaviour than Boswell did. Johnson involved himself in the welfare of the children and Mrs Salusbury ever more deeply and relished the chemical experiments he was able to conduct in the new laboratory Thrale had set up for him, 'drawing essences and colouring liquors'. Regrettably for him, his mad scientist behaviour one day spelled the abrupt end to the laboratory when, with the children and servants watching, he almost set himself on fire, or at least according to Mrs Thrale her husband thought so: 'the master of the house [was] persuaded, that his short sight would have been his destruction in a moment, by bringing him close to a fierce and violent flame. Indeed it was a perpetual miracle that he did not set himself on fire reading a-bed, as it was his constant custom, when exceedingly unable even to keep clear of mischief with our best help; and accordingly the fore-tops of all his wigs were burned by the candle down to the very net-work.' Thrale closed down the laboratory immediately. There were more serious problems at Streatham than that. Three of the little girls were ill with either rickets, scurvy, boils, hernias or ear infections. At least five-year-old Harry was 'strong and lively', and exceedingly bright, though not (in his mother's eyes) very attractive.[21]

In June calamity struck. After a run of foolish speculation and investments in his brewery business through which he hoped to outflank the rival brewer Samuel Whitbread, Thrale found himself facing bankruptcy. Neither Mrs Thrale nor Johnson had ever taken much of an interest in the business, but now they sprang to his aid with the help of the chief clerk John Perkins, taking over the management of the brewery from the dazed Thrale. Mrs Thrale obtained several loans which, along with the pacification of the restive employees and reforms of business practices, enabled them to keep things going in the face of mounting debts. It would take nine years to pay them off. The crisis had a lasting effect on Thrale as he succumbed to the black dog, a 'horrible stupor which at last quenched entirely the spark of life'. To add to the misery, an eighth child was born in September and died ten hours later. 'One cannot grieve after her much,' Mrs Thrale wrote stoically, 'and I have just now other things to think of – this has been a sad lying in: my mother dying – & everything going wrong.'[22]

Johnson's role at this point was to steady Thrale who in his extremity and relative helplessness now resented the business being run by Perkins so effectively, and to assist his wife by encouraging her and the children. Mrs Salusbury too, very ill, relied on him in her last days and in gratitude gave him the present of a chair that her daughter had covered in needlepoint as 'a good little girl'. They all needed him, so it was a huge loss to them when he left again for Staffordshire. 'I am about to set out at nine tonight,' he wrote to Mrs Thrale on 15 October, comforting her as best he could: 'Do not be dejected, send for me, if I can do you either service or pleasure.'[23]

CHAPTER 27

The Road to the Hebrides

I

THE ONLY THING that seemed to occupy his attention in Lichfield was the state of affairs at Streatham. 'The brewhouse must be the scene of action,' he reminded Mrs Thrale. Unless the beer could be produced more economically, 'nothing can help us', but the problem was the fluctuating price of malt. The big news from her was that in her self-appointed role as 'skinflint' she had decided for the time being to move the family in November from Streatham to the Southwark house she hated. The role that Johnson took on in helping with the family finances appealed to his mathematical logic: 'Suppose that our former mode of life kept us on the level, we shall by the present contraction of expense, gain upon fortune a thousand a year, even though no improvements can be made in the conduct of the trade. Every two thousand pounds saves an hundred pound interest, and therefore as we gain more we pay less. We have a rational hope of success . . . Let us therefore not be dejected'. 'If I make haste' to return, he asked, 'will you promise not to spoil me?' After spending November with Taylor watching the grass grow and admiring the bulls again, 'sometimes reading, and sometimes talking, not sleeping much', he was home by mid-December, bearing a gift of shells for Queeney from Miss Aston.[1]

Unfortunately, he could not resume his life with the Thrales because he suffered his first attack of gout and another onslaught of violent coughs – 'a vexatious catarrh' – that kept him housebound and feeling sorry for himself until the end of February 1773 as he waited for the revised *Dictio-*

nary to be published. 'Here am I, sitting by myself, uncertain whether I shall dine on veal or mutton,' he grumbled to Mrs Thrale. 'I have been sometimes near fainting'. For more than ten weeks Frank and Mrs Williams allowed no one in to see him except Mrs Thrale for breakfast a few times when she came into town on business. His house was fuller than ever because Frank had recently married a white woman, Elizabeth Ball (Betsy) who was now also living there. 'Frank has carried the empire of Cupid farther than many men,' Johnson told Mrs Thrale. It was not a happy marriage.[2]

In March his health improved somewhat and by April he was getting about town again. There was cheerful news about Goldsmith. His new comedy, *She Stoops to Conquer*, was produced by George Colman on 15 March at Covent Garden and was proving to be a smash hit. Johnson had to use 'a kind of force' to get Colman to stage it. Goldsmith's comment to Boswell was that 'stage earning is the dirtiest money that ever a poor poet put in his pocket, and if my mind does not very much alter, I have done with the stage'. Johnson loved the play, 'I know of no comedy for many years that has so much exhilarated an audience, that has answered so much the great end of comedy – making an audience merry.' But his relationship with Goldsmith remained a work in progress. Beauclerk told Boswell when he arrived in town in early April for six weeks that they remained as testy as ever with each other. The problem Johnson recognised in Goldsmith was that 'he should not attempt [to talk] as he does, for he has not the temper for it. He's so much hurt if he fails'. For all that, after an evening's wrangling with Johnson, Goldsmith was seldom reluctant to walk home with him, who was never slow to praise Goldsmith to the skies as a literary genius – 'he stands in the first class'. Johnson even felt that Goldsmith could be his 'best' biographer except that he distrusted him: 'his particular malice towards me, and general disregard for truth, would make the book useless to all'.[3]

To Boswell's astonishment Johnson asked him to dine with him on Easter Sunday – 'Sir, I generally have a pie on Sunday'. Boswell had never heard of any of his friends ever having dined at his house 'in the dusky recess of a court in Fleet Street'. He imagined they would be eating the anticipated pie without the use of knives and forks, but what he was served was a feast of soup, boiled leg of lamb and spinach, a veal pie, rice pudding, pickled walnuts and onions, and wine. By then Johnson knew his Scottish friend seriously intended to write his *Life*, 'I hope you shall know a great deal more of me before you write my Life', and he proceeded to shower him with details of his boyhood in Lichfield.[4]

The climax of this London visit for Boswell was when Johnson asked Goldsmith to propose him on his behalf for membership in the club. He would have done it himself except he was on his way to Oxford. Johnson later revealed to Boswell that 'several of the members wished to keep you out . . . [but] knew, that if they refused you, they'd probably never have got in another. I'd have kept them all out.' When he heard he had been elected, Boswell rushed over to the Turk's Head and 'was introduced to such a society as can seldom be found. Mr Edmund Burke, whom I then saw for the first time . . . Mr Garrick [elected that same spring], Dr Goldsmith . . . Upon my entrance, Johnson placed himself behind a chair, on which he leaned as on a desk or pulpit, and with humorous formality gave me a *Charge*, pointing out the conduct expected from me as a good member of this Club'.[5]

2

Before leaving for Scotland, Boswell firmed up with Johnson their plan that in August he would travel up to Edinburgh for their tour of the Highlands and Hebrides. All the signs were now positive, though Goldsmith seemed sour about the tour and talked it down to Boswell, saying 'he would be a dead weight for me to carry, and that I should never be able to lug him along through the Highlands and Hebrides'. Only time would tell if Boswell would be able to pull it off.[6]

Throughout the summer everyone was uncertain if Johnson would actually embark on this great adventure. He suffered from fevers, a severe eye inflammation, numerous purges, and dreadful nights. 'It is not a very happy state,' he wrote to Mrs Thrale, 'when the mere preservation of life becomes its chief business.' Neither was he happy about abandoning Mrs Thrale when her family problems were increasing. Her mother was on her deathbed, his goddaughter Lucy Elizabeth was very ill, and Mr Thrale was turning his back on them all. She did not want him around and told him so, though he insisted that he live at Streatham part of the summer, adding another gloomy layer to her life just then. The Hebridean tour seemed to her what Johnson needed. She would be spared having to care for him in addition to everyone else, and for a while he would be able to get out of himself: 'Dissipation is to you a glorious medicine,' she told him, 'and I believe Mr Boswell will be at last your best physician'.[7]

The time of his departure was determined by the end of the summer term of the Court of Session in Edinburgh, which required Boswell's attendance, and also by the plans of Robert Chambers who, within the year, would leave for Bengal to take up his post there in the Supreme Court and who wished to bid farewell to his relations in Newcastle. The plan was for him to accompany Johnson this far. 'What an intellectual feast is before me!' Boswell wrote excitedly to Langton on 14 August, 'I shall never murmur though he should at times treat me with more roughness than ever.' With no small amount of encouragement and coaxing, much of it rigged by Boswell, Johnson launched himself from the metropolis on 6 August 1773.[8]

On the way up Johnson did his best to slide into the tourist mode in preparation for months of travel with Boswell. He and Chambers stopped at York, Durham and Alnwick Castle, the seat of Percy's patron the Duke of Northumberland who welcomed them for a few hours and showed them around the estate. Arriving in Newcastle, they were entertained by Chambers's mother for a night. After a night in Newcastle, where he parted company with Chambers, Johnson made the last leg to Edinburgh by 14 August. He sent word to Boswell from Boyd's Inn off the Head of Canongate that he had arrived. Boswell rushed down the High Street to meet him and arm-in-arm they marched back up it. On the way, with the evening effluvia wafting pungent all around them, Johnson leaned towards his host and said teasingly, 'I smell you in the dark!'[9]

Johnson had had no experience of travel, not having money for it until his pension and then finding himself constitutionally indisposed to do it except for short trips to Devon, Brighton and Staffordshire. If his pension had come his way twenty years earlier, he commented, he 'should have gone to Constantinople to learn Arabic', but now it was almost too late. He spoke from time to time of visiting Cairo, the Red Sea and the Great Wall of China, among other places – and the act of moving, getting somewhere, appealed to him greatly. The Hebridean journey had been initially his idea, a fulfilment of his fascination with the Hebrides ever since his father introduced him to Martin Martin's *Description of the Western Islands*. One of the (as yet) untapped resources he had in abundance as a potential traveller, as Boswell soon discovered, was his great physical strength and lack of squeamishness. Most of his friends were not up to such a journey. When Boswell mentioned to Voltaire in Ferney in 1764 that he and Johnson had spoken of such an adventure, Voltaire looked at him as if he had mentioned the North Pole: 'You do not insist on my accompanying you?' 'No, Sir'. 'Then I am very willing you should go.' Adventure and the prospect of observing the lives, culture and manners of distant peoples in sublime and obscure regions at the edges of the planet – wild, primitive, or savage life – were what ultimately persuaded Johnson in this instance to overcome his resistance to translating his dreams into reality. His good fortune was to have in Boswell an ideal travelling companion – full of 'good humour and perpetual cheerfulness'.[10]

Boswell did not anticipate the extent to which Johnson, even in the remote Hebridean islands, would keep thinking about Mrs Thrale. Her 'enchantment over him seldom failed,' he wrote.[11] Johnson seemed constantly to be writing to her, letters he later used as the basis of his account of the trip in *Journey to the Western Islands of Scotland* (1775). It would have depressed Boswell to know that his companion, now in the spirit of travel, was already planning a trip to Wales with the Thrales.

Johnson stayed with Boswell and his wife Margaret for three days in their house in St James's Court. For most of that time the 'great, the learned, and the elegant' filed through the house at all hours of the day to

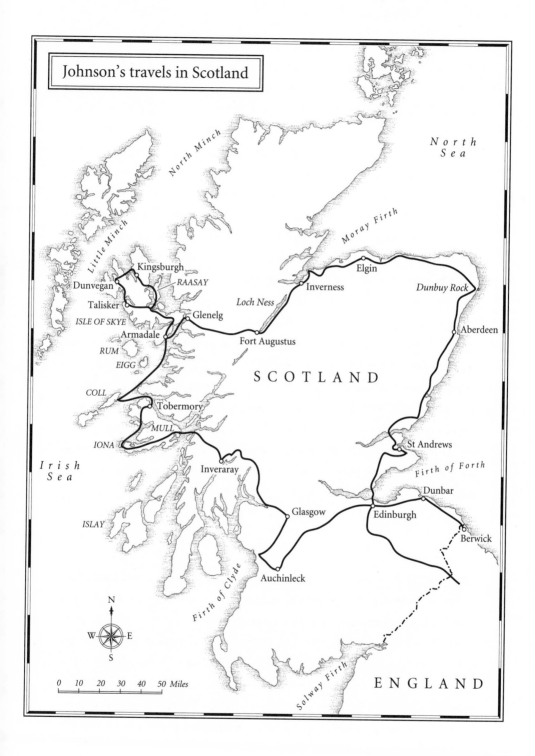

Johnson's travels in Scotland

North Sea

North Minch

Moray Firth

Little Minch

Kingsburgh
RAASAY
Dunvegan
Elgin
Dunbuy Rock
Talisker
Inverness
Loch Ness
Glenelg
Aberdeen
ISLE OF SKYE
Armadale
Fort Augustus
RUM
EIGG
S C O T L A N D
COLL
Tobermory
MULL
St Andrews
IONA
Firth of Forth
Irish Sea
Inveraray
Dunbar
ISLAY
Glasgow
Edinburgh
Berwick
Auchinleck
Firth of Clyde
N
W E
S
Solway Firth
E N G L A N D

0   10   20   30   40   50 Miles

meet him – for breakfast, dinner, teas and supper. Margaret agreed to pour tea for him and guests anytime it was needed, and according to her husband she insisted in giving up her own bedchamber to him. But all was not well with her. 'The truth is,' Boswell wrote in the *Life*, 'his irregular hours and uncouth habits . . . could not but be disagreeable to a lady'. As a result, Johnson incurred her displeasure which it took him years of patient cajoling to overcome. This was, after all, the man who was pulling her husband away from her to London almost annually and who she thought had altogether too much influence over him. On the very first night he and Boswell sat up until two, long after Margaret had gone to bed. He also felt 'poorly' and probably needed some special attention from her. On top of that, his frightening appearance threw her off balance. Boswell described him: 'He was now in his sixty-fourth year, and was become a little dull of hearing. His sight had always been somewhat weak . . . His head and sometimes also his body shook with a kind of motion like the effect of a palsy; he appeared to be frequently disturbed by cramps or convulsive contractions, of the nature of that distemper called St Vitus's dance.' As for Edinburgh, it did not impress him, reminding him of 'the old part of Birmingham'. All in all, it was a nervous beginning. With a sigh of relief, Boswell finally got him into a post-chaise on 18 August with his servant and off they went towards St Andrews on a journey that would last more than three months.[12]

3

The first leg of Boswell's itinerary took them up the east coast via St Andrews to Aberdeen. In both places Johnson was received with wonder and plaudits from all manner of people, especially university faculty who were eager to meet him. He seemed less interested in the professors at St Andrews, however, than in an old woman who lived in the ruins of the cathedral vault with her cat and 'claimed a hereditary residence in it'. What interested him about her was what would chiefly interest him throughout the trip as a 'moral explorer' and amateur anthropologist – the way people lived their lives: 'Her habitation contained all that she had, her turf for fire was laid in one place, and her balls of coal dust in another, but her bed seemed to be clean.' Although he was given the freedom of the city in Aberdeen, Boswell became annoyed that the professors at Marischal College were afraid to speak to him.[13]

Towns were not, in any case, what Johnson had come to Scotland for. 'He always said', wrote Boswell, 'that he was not come to Scotland to see fine places, of which there were enough in England, but wild objects — mountains, waterfalls, peculiar manners'. He hoped to throw himself into the wilderness of the Highlands and Hebrides and participate in the primitive culture he found there. 'I have now the pleasure', he would write from the Isle of Skye, 'of going where nobody goes, and seeing what nobody sees.' Continuing north from Aberdeen, his spirits rose as they passed through rugged, wild, romantic beauty. His energy level soared. They came to Dunbuy Rock — 'just an island covered with seafowl' — and Bullers of Buchan, a large and dangerous basin surrounded by 'tremendous rocks' through one of which the sea boiled in furiously. They walked around this 'monstrous cauldron' on very narrow rocky edges 'so that it is somewhat horrid to move along'. Johnson warmed to the adventure and took off over the rocks with alacrity and courage. Boswell was alarmed to see him 'poking his way'. They clambered into a little boat and launched themselves into the thrashing waters, a foretaste of what lay ahead in tempestuous Hebridean waters: 'He was stout and wonderfully alert.'[14]

Travelling along the north-east coast, they then headed for Inverness, passing on the way 'the bleak and blasted heath' where Macbeth met the witches. 'I have had great romantic satisfaction in seeing Johnson upon the classical scenes of Shakespeare,' Boswell wrote to Garrick. Johnson did admit to their imaginations being 'heated' but was not otherwise solemn, as Boswell was, on seeing the heath. Instead, he managed to spook Boswell that night with warnings that 'the witches would come and dance' at the foot of his bed. Boswell became so jittery he had to sleep with the door of his room open to Johnson's: 'This gave me security, and I soon fell asleep.'[15]

4

Their comfort level dropped suddenly after they turned south from Inverness. There they had to mount horses and with guides to lead the way ride along Loch Ness to Fort Augustus and then west to Glenelg, a little outpost next to the narrow channel they had to cross over to Skye. At Inverness, wrote Johnson, 'the appearance of life began to alter' as Highland manners became more evident. 'We were now to bid farewell to the luxury of travelling, and to enter a country upon which perhaps no wheel has ever rolled.' As they trekked down Loch Ness, Johnson's curiosity about the modes of life in this savage country came into full play, and even the sublime landscape somewhat stirred him: 'On the right the limpid waters of *Lough Ness* were beating their bank, and waving their surface by a gentle agitation. Beyond them were rocks sometimes covered with verdure, and sometimes towering in horrid nakedness.' Even so, it was not the wild beauty as much as the topography, geology, climate, movement of water and animal life that he found absorbing. Sitting down on a bank, 'such as a writer of Romance might have delighted to feign', with trees whispering over his head and 'a clear rivulet' streaming at his feet, he felt the calm soft air and that 'all was rudeness, silence, and solitude'. 'Whether I spent the hour well I know not,' he noted, referring mock-modestly to the fact that it was there he got the idea for his *Journey to the Western Islands of Scotland*.[16]

When they spotted a Highland hut on the banks of the loch – Boswell called it a 'wretched little hovel' – on an impulse they turned their horses towards it since 'our business was with life and manners'. In his *Journey* Johnson describes carefully how the hut was built and how the old woman they found within lived. The only light inside came through the front door and a hole in the thatch and, on entering, they could just make out the woman boiling goat's flesh in a kettle. Johnson questioned her about her family (five children and an eighty-year-old husband), their diet and 'whole system of economy', and religion. It is amazing he was able to understand her. Outside she had some poultry, a potato garden, goats, and some barley: 'She has all this from the labour of their own hands, and for what is necessary to be bought, her kids and her chickens are sent to market.' He was struck that such primitiveness could still exist in modern, industrial Britain: 'Such is the general structure of the houses in which one of the nations of this opulent and powerful island has been hitherto content to live.' The woman 'with true hospitality' then asked them 'to sit down and drink whisky', asking if they had any snuff to spare. The visit turned out to be richly comic when she said she was afraid they wanted to go to bed with her. Later they made merry over it, Boswell insisting it was Johnson 'who alarmed the poor woman's virtue. "No, sir," said he. "She'll say, there came a wicked young fellow, a wild young dog, who I believe would have ravished me had there not been with him a grave old gentleman who repressed him. But when he gets out of the sight of his tutor, I'll warrant you he'll spare no woman he meets, young or old." "No," said I. "She'll say, there was a terrible ruffian who would have forced me, had it not been for a gentle, mild-looking youth, who, I take it, was an angel!"'.[17]

Boswell spotted further comedy and incongruity in the spectacle of Johnson on a horse. A few days earlier, the tediousness of travel beginning to get to him, Johnson had complained about the prospect at some point of having to mount one. 'If we must *ride* much, we shall not go and there's an end on't'. 'You're a delicate Londoner,' Boswell teased him, 'you can't ride!' Johnson would have none of it, 'Sir, I shall ride better than you. I was only afraid I should not find a horse able to carry me.' Boswell had been spellbound by the sight of Johnson on a horse as they rode out of Inverness, 'As I saw him now for the first time ride along . . . I thought of *London, A Poem*, or the *Rambler, The False Alarm*; and I cannot express the ideas which went across my imagination.' He later found other words to describe him on a horse as they approached Glenelg down a steep hill when both Johnson and the horse, which 'staggered' under his weight, were fatigued after having climbed in 'the dreariness of solitude' over one thousand feet in three miles. The scene blends rich humour with an outbreak of Johnson's anger: 'As Mr Johnson was a great weight . . . it did not go well, and he grumbled'. Boswell was entertained by the sight of the guides trying to distract him from the dangers by whistling at the goats and then saying to him, 'See such pretty goats', as they ran off: 'Here was now, a common ignorant horse-hirer imagining that he could divert, as one does a child, *Mr Samuel Johnson!* . . . I laughed immoderately, and must laugh as often as I recollect it'. Johnson did not see anything funny in it, 'the only moment of my journey, in which I thought myself endangered'. As darkness came, Johnson became furious when Boswell suddenly rode off ahead to enquire about the inn at Glenelg: 'Mr Johnson called me back with a tremendous shout, and was really in a passion with me for leaving him.' They quarrelled and later Johnson told him, 'had you gone on, I was thinking that I should have returned with you to Edinburgh and then parted, and never spoke to you more.' Later at the inn Johnson admitted he had spoken in a 'passion' and that storming back to Edinburgh would have been ten times worse than Boswell's 'incivility'.[18]

On top of their fatigue and hunger, it was a bleak arrival at the watery threshold of the Hebrides because, as Johnson explained to Mrs Thrale, they found that the innkeepers were ill-prepared, with 'neither wine, bread, eggs, nor anything that we could eat or drink. When we were taken upstairs, a dirty fellow – "black as a Cyclops from the forge" – bounced out of the bed in which one of us was to lie.' The landlord produced some chops they could not eat and killed a couple of hens, 'of which Boswell made his servant broil a limb, with what effect I know not. We had a lemon, and a piece of bread, which supplied me with my supper'. 'Mr Johnson was calm,' Boswell wrote; 'I said he was so from vanity. "No," said he, "'tis from philosophy."' They then bedded down for the night on hay. Margaret Boswell had slipped sheets into their baggage, lest they 'catch' something along the way, but Johnson had his doubts: 'I thought sheets a slender defence, against the confederacy with which we were threatened, and by this time our Highlanders had found a place where they could get some hay; I ordered hay to be laid thick upon the bed, and slept upon it in my great coat. Boswell laid sheets upon his hay and reposed in linen like a gentleman.'[19]

They rose in the morning 'rustling from the hay' and crossed over to Skye, making their way to Armadale, the home of Sir Alexander Macdonald and his wife. There they found miserly and boorish hospitality, Boswell's portrayal of which in the *Tour* more than a decade later infuriated Macdonald so much that he challenged Boswell to a duel. There was some compensation for them in Johnson's mimicry of the beautiful Lady Macdonald, whose apparent stupidity was beyond belief to them. 'This woman would sink a ninety-gun ship,' Johnson complained. 'She is so dull – so heavy.' He kept mimicking her throughout the trip, adding later, 'the difference between that woman when alive, and when she shall be dead, is only this. When alive she calls for beer. When dead she'll call for beer no longer.' And Skye did not at first impress Johnson: 'A walk upon ploughed ground in England is a dance upon carpets, compared to the toilsome drudgery, of wandering in Skye.' Neither did he find, 'as zoologist', anything besides a huge otter to interest him. He reminded Mrs Thrale that he was not journeying through paradise: 'The use of travelling is to regulate imagination by reality, and instead of thinking how things may be, to see them as they are.' Everything at this point looked wildly bleak to him and the landscape bored him, 'a naked desert' with scarcely a village to be found. Philosophers like Rousseau who try to argue that life in such a place is happy, he wrote to Mrs Thrale, are deluding themselves.[20]

Matters improved when they were rowed in an open boat out of Broadford Bay ten miles out to the lovely island of Raasay for a few days at the invitation of the Macleod clan. Johnson sat 'high on the stern like a magnificent Triton', the wind whipping up the seas all around them. Boswell began to get sick but Johnson exulted, 'This now is the Atlantic. If I should tell at a tea-table in London that I have crossed the Atlantic in an open boat, how they'd shudder and what a fool they'd think me.' At Raasay they found hospitality, charm, grace, excellent food, dancing and intelligent conversation, 'all the marks of improved life'. It seemed as if people were coming out of the woodwork to see them.[21]

5

Returning to Skye they mounted horses again for Kingsburgh, where they met the famous Flora Macdonald who had helped the Young Pretender Prince Charles Edward, more popularly known as Bonnie Prince Charlie, escape after the Battle of Culloden, smuggling him dressed as her maid from Lewis to Portree, from where the Macleods took him to Raasay. Johnson slept 'in the bed in which the Prince reposed in his distresses', remarking facetiously, 'I have had no ambitious thoughts in it.' He told Boswell he would have given anything not to have slept in the bed, but at least he was not sleeping in the Prince's sacred sheets, 'which were never put to any meaner offices, but were wrapped up by the lady of the house, and at last, according to her desire, were laid round her in her grave'. It is not certain whether any Jacobite sentiment stirred in him as he lay there, but Boswell summed up his feelings about the Stuarts: 'Mr Johnson is not properly a *Jacobite*. He does not hold the *jus divinum* of kings . . . He said to me once that he did not know but it was become necessary to remove the King at the time of the Revolution; and after the present family have had so long a possession, it appears to him that their right becomes the same that the Stuarts had . . . I have heard him say he was so dubious that if holding up his right hand would have gained the victory to the Highland army in 1745, he does not know if he would have done it.'[22]

On the way to Flora Macdonald's beautiful home, Dunvegan Castle, built upon a rock overlooking the sea, Johnson fell off his horse, the only time this happened on the entire journey. It was so comfortable at Dunvegan that the foul weather making them extend their stay did not disturb him unduly. The gentle and soft-featured mistress of the house charmed him. But there was a sad awareness that financial plight would soon force her and her husband to emigrate temporarily to North Carolina, which they did the following year.[23]

After eight days the storms eased and they moved on to other Macleod homes at Ullinish and Talisker. The latter, like Raasay, turned out to be a model of grace and hospitality: 'You find that all the islanders even in these recesses of life are not barbarians'. A visitor while they were there, Donald Maclean or 'young Coll', who pleased Johnson with schemes of improving the family estates 'without hurting the people or losing the ancient Highland fashions', offered to take them on a tour of the smaller islands of Eigg, Muck, Coll and Tyree on the way to Mull, but there was unnerving news while they were there of shipwrecks along the coast in wild weather. Added to this, Johnson was becoming impatient with the weather and restless to return to Edinburgh: 'we grow afraid of deviating from our way home lest we should be shut up for months upon some little protuberance of earth, that just appears above the sea, and perhaps is scarcely marked upon a map.' He had had enough of the primitive.[24]

'I cannot but laugh to think of myself roving among the Hebrides at sixty,' Johnson observed while they waited to launch themselves on the next watery stage of their trip, 'I wonder where I shall rove at fourscore.' Upon the sea at last on 3 October in a twelve-ton vessel that had a little 'den' in the forecastle with two beds and a fire in it, this time it was Johnson who began to turn green. 'I exulted in being a stout seaman,' Boswell wrote, 'while Mr Johnson was quite in a state of annihilation', but soon he also became 'woefully sick'. They made for Iona, known also as Icolmkill. It was a furious and dangerous voyage and in an emergency, with night falling, they had to change course for the harbour at Coll with no guarantee that even if they could get there the waves would allow them to enter it. A man with one eye steered. After hours of dramatic plunging into the sea, well after midnight, they made it. Kept in some ignorance below, Johnson 'had all this time been quiet and unconcerned. He had lain down on one of the beds, and having got free of sickness, was quite satisfied ... He was lying in philosophic tranquility, with a greyhound of Coll's at his back keeping him warm'. They spent the night in the boat cold and wet.[25]

The greater trial for Johnson was the tedium of being marooned for ten days on Coll, a 'barren island' where there was almost nothing to do while the storm blew and it rained incessantly. Coll had an unused elegant house there in which they waited. Johnson grew peevish. 'I want to be on the mainland, and go on with my existence,' he protested. 'My eye is ... not fully recovered, my ears are not mended, my nerves seem to grow weaker, and I have been otherwise not as well as I sometimes am ... This climate is perhaps not within my degrees of healthy latitude.' They were reduced to arguing over whose bed had the best linen and bed posts. 'If you have the best posts,' Johnson declared, 'we'll have you tied to 'em and whipped.' Finally, they found a sloop carrying kelp and convinced its master to take them to Tobermory in Mull from where Johnson hoped they could easily return to the mainland, perhaps without seeing Iona.[26]

When Boswell bragged that Mull was now the fourth Hebridean island they had set foot on, Johnson was not impressed: 'Nay, we cannot boast of the number we have seen. We thought we should see many more. We thought of sailing about easily from island to island; and so we should, had we come at a better season.' Still, he admitted they had seen enough for a good idea of 'the system of insular life'. Boswell was determined that they would not miss Iona, so after a couple of days of confining rain, they mounted little Mull horses for a seriously rugged, exhausting ride 'over rocks naked and valleys untracked' towards the western side of the island where they could cross to the beautiful tiny island of Inchkenneth, leased by Sir Allan Maclean. At one point they had to plunge into deep water to cross a rivulet. Johnson was cranky and totally disinclined to hear the history of the Maclean clan. 'I'd rather hear the history of the Thrales,' he muttered. Arriving at the western coast of Mull in the dark 'weary and dejected', without any place to sleep, they were rescued luckily by an Irish boat on which they crossed to Ulva, a small island just off the coast, where they spent the night. The following day they crossed to Inchkenneth, an island a mile long and half a mile wide to stay with the Macleans in their humble cottage. They were the only family on the island.[27]

Leaving Inchkenneth behind as they rowed off with Maclean towards Iona some forty miles down the coast, Johnson showed his mettle again when by candlelight they penetrated five hundred feet into Mackinnon's Cave, accessible only in low tide. Emerging well before the tide could trap them, they continued down the coast while the rowers sang Erse songs, took a quick meal on some black rocks, and found themselves again in the dark at sea as they approached Iona. To their right they had been able to make out the island of Staffa, described by Sir Joseph Banks the previous year as one of the world's greatest natural curiosities, but it was late and the sea was too rough to contemplate landing on it in order to see the famed Fingal's Cave, immortalised in 1830 by Mendelssohn in his *Hebrides Overture*. 'This is roving among the Hebrides, or nothing is,' Johnson shouted out. They ploughed through rough water by moonlight. The lights of the little village on Iona then came into view and soon they were safely ashore at 'the venerable seat of ancient sanctity, where secret piety reposed.' Boswell and Maclean were carried ashore by the rowers, but Johnson 'sprang into the sea and waded vigorously out'. They slept that night in a barn 'well stocked with hay'.[28]

Taking in all the religious sites the next morning, which Johnson described at length in his *Journey*, they returned to Mull the same day and, taking leave of Maclean, were back on the mainland on 22 October. 'The difficulties of peregrination' (as Johnson put it) now at an end, they immediately struck out by horseback for the Duke of Argyll's seat at Inveraray where Boswell had an invitation for them to stay for two days, awkward ones for him as it turned out, since the duchess disliked him. From there they made their way down through 'a black and dreary region', the hills 'streaming with waterfalls' filled with almost constant rain, to the banks of Loch Lomond, then to Glasgow, and finally further south to meet up with Boswell's father at the family estate at Auchinleck just east of Ayr. Johnson did not mention it in his letters to Mrs Thrale, but in spite of Boswell's warning he fell into a violent argument with Lord Auchinleck in the upstairs library over Whiggism, Presbyteriansim, Toryism and Episcopacy. Boswell was desperately unhappy over the anger that ignited between these two 'intellectual gladiators', and was helplessly caught between them. On 9 November the two travellers returned to Edinburgh, eighty-three days after leaving it. Again people streamed into Boswell's house to see the famous scholar and moralist fresh from his remarkable expedition, and again Margaret found herself devoting 'the greater part of the morning to the endless task of pouring out tea for my friend and his visitors'.[29]

None too soon for her, on 19 November, Johnson left the city in a post-chaise and, stopping at various places on the way, arrived home on the 26th. 'I know Mrs Boswell wished me well to go; her wishes have not been disappointed,' he wrote to Boswell the day after. 'She is a sweet lady,' he added the following March, 'only she was so glad to see me go, that I have almost a mind to come again, that she may again have the same pleasure.' Now there were other things to think about. The epic Hebridean odyssey had whet his appetite for another lengthy expedition and he was already setting his sights on one to Wales with the Thrales. She had written to him in October: 'When you sigh for an island of your own remember that Rasselas could never settle the limits of his imaginary dominion, but a sight of Wales in the meantime may not be amiss. 'Tis long since I saw my own country, but there are untrodden paths in it which may perhaps be as curious as any in Scotland; barefooted girls too in plenty as I remember.' 'I am grown very superior to wind and rain,' he wrote from Auchinleck, 'and am too well acquainted both with mire and with rocks, to be afraid of a Welsh journey.' For three months Boswell had him all to himself. Now it was the Thrales' turn.[30]

CHAPTER 28

Politics and Travel

I

HE SET TO WORK IMMEDIATELY gathering materials for his *Journey to the Western Islands of Scotland*, through the winter and into the spring badgering Boswell to provide him with what he needed. In addition to what Boswell and a few others sent him, he had a few notes of his own to draw on – more like a haphazard notebook than a journal – which have, unfortunately, been lost, and his letters to Mrs Thrale which as always she was careful to keep. Boswell's journal was a goldmine of information but he did not bring it with him to London until his next visit in March 1775, too late to be of any help.[1]

Once he got down to composing his *Journey* in the spring, he wrote it rapidly. He delivered almost the entire manuscript to Strahan on 20 June. By mid-October 240 pages had been printed and he anticipated that the book would be out in a month or so, 'a pretty book, I hope, it will be.' The printing, however, was not finished until about mid-December and two thousand copies of the book not published until 18 January 1775 at a price of five shillings. Strahan thought the book would sell well, so while it was printing he decided on another two thousand copies for a second edition. Johnson received 200 guineas for the book.[2]

It was favourably reviewed in London and sold briskly, and in Dublin three pirated reprints appeared within a few months. It was the talk of the town. He sent a copy in December to the King who 'fell to reading the book as soon as he got it, [and] when anything struck him, he read aloud to the Queen'; the Queen, however, 'would not stay to get the King's book' and borrowed her own copy. When Boswell came to London in the spring, Lord Mansfield greeted him with, 'We have all been reading your travels, Mr Boswell.' Concerned that Johnson would say things in the book that would embarrass him at home, Boswell had asked him if he could read the book in manuscript. Johnson reassured him it was all right because he was dealing 'more in notions than facts'. He also ignored his fellow traveller's offer to correct errors in the first edition. What was more difficult to ignore was the hue and cry raised by many in Scotland.[3]

Just before publication Strahan showed James Macpherson some passages ridiculing his claim that he used authentic Gaelic manuscripts for his *Ossian*. In the book Johnson called Macpherson a fraud and demanded the only proof that would satisfy him: the manuscripts. Macpherson was by then accustomed to his fame as the man who had brought Ossian to the attention of European writers, artists and composers. Proud and incensed at Johnson's challenge, he wrote to him rudely, demanding a retraction. We do not have this letter, but we have Johnson's celebrated response on 20 January 1775, which is about as famous as his snub of Lord Chesterfield: 'I received your foolish and impudent note. Whatever insult is offered me I will do my best to repel, and what I cannot do for myself the law will do for me. I will not desist from detecting what I think a cheat, from any fear of the menaces of a ruffian . . . I thought your book an imposture from the beginning . . . You may print this if you will.' Macpherson 'little knew the character of Dr Johnson,' Boswell wrote, 'if he supposed that he could be easily intimidated.' The controversy continued for years, however, and Johnson even became cross with Boswell for his mild prevarication on the matter: 'You then are going wild about Ossian? . . . If there are manuscripts, let them be shown, with some proof that they are not forged for the occasion.' Beyond Macpherson, as Johnson told Hector, 'the Scotch are angry'. His prejudice against the Scots and alleged Jacobitism were revived in Scottish reviews as he was comprehensively accused of rudeness and downright obtuseness by insisting, for example, that Scotland had virtually no trees. Boswell felt this was grossly unjust: 'Johnson treated Scotland no worse than he did even his best friends, whose characters he used to give as they appeared to him, both in light and shade.'[4]

Far less personal and autobiographical than Boswell's *Tour to the Hebrides* (1785), the *Journey* is a sweeping and far deeper assessment of life in the Highlands and Hebrides, including the clan system, the nature of an oral society, mountain isolation, Gaelic culture, the unexpected appearance of civilised culture in the middle of the primitive, Catholicism unaffected by the Protestant Reformation, and the poverty and customs of crofting life that made him reflect on the benefits of civilisation and culture. One important effect of the book was an increased awareness of the economic plight of the Highlanders and what was driving them to emigrate to America. It also accelerated interest in travel to the Highlands and more generally the north of Britain, which became popular tourist destinations in the late eighteenth century, the subject of popular travel accounts in the nineteenth century, and the setting for musical compositions, novels and poetry.[5]

2

Chambers's departure for Bengal (now Bangladesh), newly married, in the spring of 1774 genuinely saddened Johnson. They would never see each other again although Johnson's imagination travelled with him. His deep affection for the young judge never dimmed and he continued to write to him, maintaining his considerable interest in the culture and traditions of India. His oriental tales in the *Rambler* were all set in the country. In a letter to his acquaintance Warren Hastings, Governor-General of India, which Chambers personally delivered, he declared his desire for information about India and the 'traditions and histories of the East' and urged Hastings to explore the 'remains of its ancient edifices, and trace the vestiges of ruined cities' so that on his return to England 'we shall know the arts and opinions of a race of men from whom very little has been hitherto derived'. He himself had cherished dreams of emigrating to India ever since the early 1750s when he almost accompanied his friend Joseph

Fowke who was returning there to make a fortune with the East India Company. 'Had I thought then, as I do now,' he remarked in 1776, 'I should have gone.'[6]

He suffered the greatest shock, however, in early April 1774. 'Chambers . . . is gone far,' he wrote to Langton, 'and poor Goldsmith is gone much further.' Goldsmith had suddenly and tragically died of a fever, just a few months following the stage triumph of his *She Stoops to Conquer*. It was widely suspected that his death was hastened by the use of Dr Robert James's fever powder. He was forty-four. The members of the club took this 'catastrophe' badly, although none attended his burial on 9 April 1774 in the Temple Church burial ground. Boswell wrote to Garrick, 'I have not been so much affected with any event that has happened of a long time.' Johnson was quiet in his letters about the tragedy except for this qualified eulogy to Langton: 'He died of a fever exasperated, as I believe, by the fear of distress. He had raised money and squandered it, by every artifice of acquisition and folly of expense. But let not his frailties be re-membered. He was a very great man.' Reynolds later organised a monu-ment for him in Westminster Abbey, paid for by the Club, for which Johnson wrote a Latin inscription; and in 1776 Johnson took over from Percy the task of writing his biography, which he never accomplished. There would now be no more quarrels with 'Goldie' at the Club.[7]

Happier days were ahead. The Thrales were planning a tour through Italy with Baretti as their guide. Now in the travelling mode, Johnson had his heart set on it far more than he had on the Hebridean tour. For a long time he had been thrilled with the expectation of a visit to the 'clas-sic ground' of Italy as a fulfilment of his studies as a classical scholar. But Mrs Thrale was preoccupied with her inheritance on her mother's death of some Salusbury family property at Bach-y-Graig in Flintshire of which she was eager to take possession. So after much indecision the Italian tour was shelved and replaced by the less promising scheme of a trip to Wales to see to the family home, visit friends along the way, and have a look at the northern part of the country. Leaving Baretti behind in charge of Streatham, on 5 July 1774 the Thrales, Queeney and Johnson, rather grandly in Thrale's coach with four post-horses, left for Wales via

Lichfield and Ashbourne. They did not plan on the trip consuming as many as ten weeks.

The Thrale expedition made its way first to Lichfield where they stayed three days. Johnson kept the Thrales busy there, taking them to Richard Greene's museum, his home which filled Mrs Thrale 'with emotion', and the cathedral. They also visited Erasmus Darwin – never one of Johnson's favourites – at his house in the Close, Lucy at her large house who showed them Reynolds's portrait of Johnson and one of her mother, and Elizabeth Aston at Stowe Hill, whom Mrs Thrale described as something of an 'oddity' but 'a high-bred woman, quite the remains of an old beauty'. At Ashbourne, Mrs Thrale was astonished by the 'magnificence' of Taylor's seat – no wonder, she must have thought, Johnson came to visit him so often. From there they made an excursion to Chatsworth which did not please her in any way, and Kedleston Hall which did not please Johnson – 'more cost than judgement'. They stayed ten days with Taylor, 'one of the happiest of the human race', as Mrs Thrale oddly described him.[8]

So much for the part of the journey Johnson planned. The rest was up to the Thrales as they passed into northern Wales at the end of July, keeping close to the north coast. When they reached Bach-y-Graig they were all disappointed. The house was small, the woods were sparse, and there was no garden, though Mrs Thrale felt the place had potential. Johnson's diary reveals he was not slow to belittle what struck him as the ordinariness of certain Welsh scenes like the River Clwyd, which he called 'a brook'. 'Let us', he proposed to Mrs Thrale, 'jump over it directly, and show them how an *Englishman* should treat a *Welch* river.' He appeared to be little interested in buildings, especially ruins, although Boswell noted he agreed that Wales abounded with magnificent castles: 'One of the castles in Wales could contain all of the castles he had seen in Scotland'. What aroused his enthusiasm most were signs of modern industry. At Holywell, it was not the history and beauty of St Winifred's Well, one of the so-called Seven Wonders of Wales, that spurred him to write in his diary at length but the brass, copper and iron works nearby where the river turned nineteen mills in the space of two miles. 'I have enlarged my notions', he wrote. The busy spectacle of such 'multiplied operations' of manufacturing processes lifted his spirits and temporarily made him for-get his ailments.[9]

After reaching as far as Carnarvon and the foot of Mt Snowdon, they began their faster return journey. Crossing into England, they rode south in a downpour into the landscape of Johnson's youth, very near Stourbridge and Pedmore and full of memories for him of Cornelius Ford and his old grammar school. Hagley Park was next, the seat of the Lytteltons, where 'respect and kindness' were wanting, reviving for Johnson not entirely pleasant memories of his visit there as a boy with Cornelius. 'We made haste from a place where all were offended,' he wrote.[10]

They spent a night with Hector and his sister in Birmingham and saw more manufacturing wonders, including the factory of Matthew Boulton, who in partnership with James Watt, invented the steam engine. The fac-tory turned out Sheffield plate, buttons, spoons and other items. It frus-trated him that his eyesight did not allow him to see the 'enginery' dis-tinctly. The next stop was Blenheim, which made little impression on Johnson, and after that Oxford, which greatly impressed Mrs Thrale. They spent the next few days there, visiting the Bodleian and several col-leges and dining splendidly with their host John Coulson in the Hall at University College and with Johnson's good friend the melancholic Robert Vansittart, Regius Professor of Civil Law, who cornered Johnson to talk to him about melancholia.[11]

The last stop before returning to London was Burke's seat Gregories near Beaconsfield in Buckinghamshire, where they spent the night. They were received with 'open arms', though Burke had to be away the next day and returned late, said Mrs Thrale, 'much flustered with liquor'. They awoke to the news that Parliament had been dissolved and there was to be a new general election, distressing news for Mrs Thrale who realised im-mediately they would now have to return to dreary Southwark to cam-paign for her husband's seat instead of easing into the bucolic peace of Streatham with the family after almost three months on the road.[12]

While Johnson found the country 'beautiful and rich', he assured Boswell in October that Wales 'is so little different from England, that it offers nothing to the speculation of the traveller'. 'I am glad that I have seen it,' he told Taylor, 'though I have seen nothing, because I now know that there is nothing to be seen.' When Boswell became restless in the autumn of 1777 for another journey with Johnson and spoke of travelling to Wales, Johnson was nonplussed: 'Except the woods of Bachycraigh,' he wrote to him, 'what is there in Wales? What that can fill the hunger of ignorance, or quench the thirst of curiosity?' 'Shall we go to Ireland,' Boswell suggested, 'of which I have seen but little?' Johnson's mind was turning on something much more exotic and adventurous, a trek to the Baltic and perhaps some 'more northern regions' that Boswell had half seriously suggested when they were on Skye but now was 'shrinking' from.[13]

The trip to Wales had not been a huge success. Queeney had been ill much of the time, Thrale uncommunicative, and Johnson on the whole unimpressed and unimpressive, at least to Mrs Thrale. Indeed, she wrote in her journal, 'Travelling with Mr Johnson I cannot bear'.[14] She, too, was ill for much of the second half of the journey. She hated the rough roads, and was, moreover, pregnant again. She knew Johnson would never produce a book about their travels to match the one he was about to publish about the Hebrides. He knew it, too.

3

It was timely that Johnson should hear of the new election while staying at Gregories since Burke would play such a large part in it. His admiration for Burke's intellect was greater than ever, but there was a persistent political tension between them. When he first met Burke at Garrick's house in 1758, and Burke firmly disagreed with him on the subject of Bengal and the Government's efforts to control the East India Company's activities there, Johnson suddenly conceived a liking for the man. He said to Arthur Murphy later, 'If this be the kind of man he is, would that he were ours' – that is, he would be better politically employed in what in some respects might have passed for Tory circles. In 1765, when the Whig Marquess of Rockingham became prime minister, Burke became his private secretary, and after he was elected member for Parliament in 1766 joined the so-called Rockingham Whigs. 'Burke is a great man by Nature, and is expected soon to attain civil greatness,' Johnson said – but his controversial views and fiery obsessiveness kept him down. He is 'unequal', Johnson said, 'he is a lion, who lashes himself into a fury with his own tail'. He tended to divide the world into friends and enemies, which Johnson thought was his worst enemy.[15]

They also differed in that Burke was idealistic and Johnson sceptical and rational. Burke was drawn to abstract ideals whereas Johnson tended to reason from the more complicated 'moral' standpoint of individual human beings. The two men did not discuss politics seriously in the presence of each other, but what Johnson objected to was Burke's narrow party adherence, 'right or wrong', in the belief that in order to rise to power his best option was to stick with the Rockingham Opposition. This smacked of dishonesty to Johnson: 'I do not say that he is *not* honest; but we have no reason to conclude from his political conduct that he *is* honest.' For his part, Burke's judgement of Johnson's politics was equally harsh, asserting, even after Johnson's death, that in his pamphlet on the Falklands he knew he was wrong in charging that the Opposition were 'endeavouring to involve the nation in a war on account of the Falkand Islands'. Boswell thought Burke was even abusive on the subject.[16]

Johnson's part in what Mrs Thrale called 'this filthy election' was to help her husband by writing three brief political addresses to the electors of Southwark. 'We lead a wild life', Mrs Thrale wrote to him on 4 October 1774 at Johnson's Court, but it would be all over in a week. She felt Thrale would win but not by much. 'The patriots have the mob of course,' she added. It was at these 'patriots' of the opposition Johnson took aim in his third major political pamphlet of the 1770s, The Patriot, published anonymously on 12 October. Boswell worried when he heard about his pamphlet that it had taken time away from his work on the Journey, but Johnson reassured him he wrote it in one day and had 'heard little of it' since.[17]

The pamphlet was an excuse to take another swipe at Wilkes by attacking the popular cant about 'patriotism'. It was obviously not that Johnson failed to support liberal ideas of personal, social and religious freedom central to the Enlightenment. Far from it. Since the 1730s he had argued for them in all sorts of ways. Rather, his anger was over the appropriation of these ideas by the loud malcontents who indiscriminately slung around the term 'patriot' on behalf of political expediency, to rouse up the masses for selfish personal ends, especially in opposition to the King and even to the point of rejoicing in the successes of Britain's foreign enemies: 'A man may have the external appearance of a Patriot, without the constituent qualities; as false coins have often lustre, tho' they want weight.' These are fraudulent patriots 'who rave and rail' yet do not care for the public, hoping 'to force their way to riches by virulence and invective, and are vehement and clamorous, only that they may be sooner hired to be silent'. And looking across the Atlantic to the growling turbulence in America, he anticipated his next explosive pamphlet: 'That man therefore is no Patriot, who justifies the ridiculous claims of American usurpation; who endeavours to deprive the nation of its natural and lawful authority over its own colonies: those colonies, which were settled under English protection; were constituted by an English charter; and have been defended by English arms'.[18]

The pamphlet had no influence on the election because it was published after it was over. Thrale won anyway with a reduced majority over candidates who were Wilkes supporters and had provoked a good deal of rioting in the borough. 'Mr Thrale has had a very violent and formidable opposition which he has very triumphantly overcome,' Johnson announced to Taylor on 20 October 1774. While Mrs Thrale, her family and Johnson rejoiced that the 'cruel fatigues' of the election were behind them, Johnson was primed to write something else about 'patriots', the American problem and the political state of Britain in general.[19]

After obliging Charlotte Lennox first thing in January by writing 'Proposals' for her Works, he was ready to turn his attention to America. 'I am going to write about the Americans,' he informed Boswell on 21 January 1775 – 'But mum, it is a secret'. The reason it was secret was that Lord North's ministry had asked him to write a reply to a so-called 'Bill of Rights' that the American Continental Congress – which Johnson in the third edition of the pamphlet in 1775 called 'a seditious meeting punishable by law' – had drawn up during its first ever session held between 5

September and 26 October. That document insisted on colonial autonomy regarding fiscal legislation and rehearsed the grievances and justification of the Colonies in the face of what it described as British oppression. By the end of February, Johnson had completed his *Taxation No Tyranny* and Strahan had printed it.[20]

The Americans were complaining that British taxation of them was unconstitutional because as subjects of a sovereign state they could be taxed only by their consent through representation in Parliament, and such representation did not exist. They protested they were too far away to be directly represented. Johnson devoted the first part of his pamphlet to disproving both these contentions. 'In sovereignty there are no gradations', and Americans could not expect any special treatment among the many British colonies. 'A colony is to the mother-country as a member to the body . . . the body may subsist, though less commodiously, without a limb, but the limb must perish if it be parted from the body'. Perhaps, he continued, 'Our colonies . . . however distant, have been hitherto treated as constituent parts of the British Empire', and as such they have their privileges and obligations. The American colonies 'as subordinate communities are liable to taxation, because they all share the benefits of government'. It is incumbent on them to prove 'that the Parliament ever ceded to them a dispensation from that obedience, which they owe as natural-born subjects'. By seditiously raising armies and forming alliances with rival countries, they run the risk of forfeiting their colonial charters and having to be subdued by 'stricter laws and stronger obligations'. In the second part, Johnson accuses them of ingratitude and being hoodwinked by 'patriots' and self-seeking anarchists. In response to the efforts of American 'croakers of calamity' and 'dictators of sedition' to spread terror in British hearts by suggesting that if the British Government could make slaves of them in North America, it could just as easily make slaves of its subjects at home, his anger swelled: 'I should gladly see America return half of what England has expended in her defence . . . But probably in America, as in other places, the chiefs are incendiaries, that hope to rob in the tumults of a conflagration, and toss brands among a rabble passively combustible'. Agitators like the 'master of mischief ' Benjamin Franklin, he protested, are in the business of putting 'in motion the engine of political electricity' – an allusion to Franklin's electrical experiments that, in fact, he much admired. It is all absurd cant, just as it is in Britain in the mouths of Whigs like Wilkes. 'If slavery be . . . fatally contagious,' he asks, 'how is it that we hear the loudest yelps for liberty among the drivers of Negroes?' The hypocrisy of the American position, he gasped, was breathtaking.[21]

There is more than just a hint of Johnson's repulsion over the American thirst for independence in the diary of the Revd Thomas Campbell, an Irish clergyman who came to London in the spring of 1775 specifically to meet Johnson and a few other luminaries. Befriended by the Thrales, he was invited by them several times to dinner where he met Johnson, Boswell, Langton, Murphy, Baretti and Dr Nathan Wetherell, the new Master of University College, Oxford. Johnson called him 'a fine showy talking man'. The diary provides a rare glimpse – apart from Boswell – of the Johnsonians relaxing with each other over good food and unguarded conversation. He recorded Johnson saying that one of the measures he advocated to humble the Americans, which 'the Ministry expunged', was 'to quarter the army in the cities, and if any refused free quarters, he would pull down that person's house, if it was joined to other houses, but would burn it if it stood alone'. When Campbell 'coolly' suggested that the Government had not 'succeeded so well in burning the cities, and roasting the inhabitants of America', Johnson agreed that Britain had erred on the side of too much diplomacy: 'had we treated the Americans as we ought, and as they deserved, we should have at once razed all their towns – and let them enjoy their forests'. This was no exaggeration of his violent attitudes regarding the Americans. Three years later at Charles Dilly's house one evening in the company of the Quaker Mrs Mary Knowles, he was still fuming over them: 'I am willing to love all mankind, *except an American.*' Boswell was surprised by the ferocity of his remarks, that he 'breathed out threatenings and slaughter', called the Americans 'rascals – robbers – pirates', and exclaimed that he would 'burn and destroy them'. When checked by someone, he 'roared out another tremendous volley, which one might fancy could be heard across the Atlantic'.[22]

The pamphlet went into four editions in 1775, and was reprinted with the other three political tracts of the 1770s in *Political Tracts* the following year under his name. It was greeted with a howl of criticism in a stream of hostile pamphlets, newspapers, and reviews. 'The patriots pelt me with answers,' he noted. Fretting somewhat that the pamphlet had not sold enough, he said to Boswell, 'I think I have not been attacked enough for it. Attack is the re-action; I never think I have hit hard, unless it rebounds'. The response in America was of course predictably hostile. When some-one said his works would no longer be admired there, Boswell piped up, 'No, we shall soon hear of his being hung in effigy'. 'I should be glad of that,' Johnson replied, 'that would be a new source of fame'. Nonetheless, the Government was grateful and three weeks later he received an honor-ary D.C.L. from Oxford. 'They have sent me a degree of Doctor of Laws,' he wrote to Mrs Thrale from Oxford on 1 April, 'with such praises in the diploma, as, perhaps ought to make me ashamed; they are very like your praises. I wonder whether I shall ever show them to you.' With the ap-proval of Lord North, the degree had been organised by his new friend Nathan Wetherell of University College, who anticipated and met with some opposition to awarding the degree. When he and Johnson visited Oxford together the following March, Boswell got the impression from Wetherell that 'there were at Oxford some who did not admire and rever-ence Mr Johnson as some of us do'.[23]

4

Johnson's political pamphlets, especially *Taxation No Tyranny*, landed him in political skirmishes within a highly vexed political environment. These fed the adrenalin in his naturally combative temper, but they brought him notoriety more than literary praise as England's most esteemed author. Some were even saying they could no longer read his moral essays with undiluted satisfaction knowing now that he had 'prostituted' his talents 'under the character of a political writer'.[24] When it came down to it, he himself felt he had written them only for the moment and that they had left him with an empty feeling. He did after all tell Boswell, 'politics are now nothing more than means of success in life', devoid of principles, although the subject continued to fascinate him.[25]

On his spring visit in 1775, Boswell noticed that Johnson seemed to have become more extreme than ever in many of his opinions, something of a caricature of himself. His views on America were especially exaggerated. 'Such extravagance is really ludicrous,' Boswell noted. Dr Campbell was not at all pleased when he first met Johnson at this time: 'he has the aspect of an idiot, without the faintest ray of sense gleaming from any one feature – with the most awkward garb, and unpowdered grey wig, on one side only of his head – he is forever dancing the devil's jig, and sometimes he makes the most drivelling effort to whistle some thought in his absent paroxysms.' He 'flew in[to] a passion' rather too much. His remarks on people were inordinately critical. About Thomas Gray, whose poetry he did not on the whole admire, he was contemptuous: 'he was dull in company, dull in his closet, dull everywhere. He was dull in a new way; and this made many people think him great.' 'You are not a lukewarm man,' Campbell had the temerity to say to him. At Oglethorpe's for dinner, Johnson could not bear Boswell's questioning any longer and simply got up and abruptly left. On the way home in Langton's coach, he complained, 'Boswell's conversation consists entirely in asking questions, and it is extremely offensive.'[26]

None of this alienated Boswell, who was as bold as ever asking frank questions. He understood that 'Johnson's roughness was only external, and had no participation with his heart,' and also that he often seemed unaware of the bludgeoning he often gave people. On a coach ride to Twickenham to dine with the minor poet Owen Cambridge at his beautiful seat on the Thames, Johnson stretched himself out and amazed Boswell with, 'I look upon *myself* as a good-humoured fellow.' Boswell came back at him, 'No, no, Sir; that will *not* do. You are good-natured, but not good-humoured. You are irascible. You have not patience with folly and absurdity.'[27]

Boswell saw Johnson everywhere, at the Thrales', Reynolds's, Strahan's, Dilly's, Davies's, Beauclerk's, the Club, and the Mitre, but it was their private meetings he valued the most. He sought his advice about moving to London permanently. 'If you come to settle here,' Johnson answered, 'we will have one day in the week on which we will meet by ourselves. That is the happiest conversation where there is no competition, no vanity, but a calm quiet interchange of sentiments.' They took their ritual teas with Mrs Williams deep into the night. On Good Friday, as Boswell tells it, 'after we had drank tea with Mrs Williams, he asked me to go upstairs with him, and we sat a long time in a sort of languid, grave state, like men watching a corpse; or nearly like that'. They spoke only when Johnson started a subject. Boswell was thrilled when Johnson offered him a room, 'where I might sleep occasionally, when I happened to sit with him, to a late hour. I took possession of it this night'. Attended by Frank, he was surprised to find everything 'in excellent order'. Breakfast in the morning was quite an affair: 'His tea and rolls and butter, and whole breakfast apparatus were all in such decorum, and his behaviour was so courteous' that another guest present was 'quite surprised . . . having heard so much said of Johnson's slovenliness and roughness'. The last impression Boswell leaves us as he departs in late May 1775 is of Johnson's laughter: 'I never knew a man laugh more heartily . . . Johnson's laugh was as remarkable as any circumstance in his manner. It was a kind of good humoured growl. Tom Davies described it drolly enough: "He laughs like a rhinoceros."'[28]

5

Johnson had delayed his next Staffordshire visit to accommodate Boswell: 'I had no great reason for haste, and therefore might as well gratify a friend . . . Boswell would have thought my absence a loss, and I knew not who else would have considered my presence as profit'. He was also delayed by Thrale's insistence that a suit of his 'be made like other peoples, and they are gone to the tailor'. After ten days in Oxford, he and Frank 'thundered' away on 8 June for Lichfield, where he stayed until the end of the month in the lap of all his lady friends, Elizabeth Aston and her sister Jane Gastrell at Stowe Hill, who gave him 'good words, and cherries, and strawberries', and Mary Cobb and Mary Adey to whom he behaved 'with a kindness and easy pleasantry, such as we see between old and intimate acquaintance'. Restless afterwards at Ashbourne watching Taylor garden, he dreamed of seeing 'other forms of existence' by going to Cairo 'and down the Red Sea to Bengal' and taking 'a ramble in India', which would give more 'variety to the eye, and amplitude to the mind' than building and planting. While he was there he heard from Mrs Thrale that little Ralph Thrale, sick for some time, had died from brain damage. He was home by mid-August.[29]

6

The Thrales again delayed plans for an Italian excursion, but there was now a window of opportunity for a shorter trip to France since Mrs Thrale was not, for a change, pregnant. The trip would be a trial run for Italy the following year and Baretti, whose published guides for the European traveller made him an ideal guide and who would be expected to continue giving Queeney her Italian lessons, would come, too. Mrs Thrale would keep a journal again, and this time Johnson promised he would keep one, too. Unfortunately, only one of three journal notebooks he kept during the tour has survived. 'Shall we have *A Journey to Paris* from you in the winter?' Boswell asked him. This would be his first visit to the Continent. They left Streatham on 15 September and met Baretti at Dover for the smooth crossing on a sloop to Calais.[30]

If Johnson thought this two-month journey would enrich him with a new assortment of imagery and an excitement about unfamiliar manners and modes of existence, stimulating him to write another travel book, he would soon be disillusioned. The way Baretti, mostly, and Mrs Thrale organised the route to Paris, comfort and convenience were absolute requirements. Johnson wrote to Boswell from Calais on his birthday that their 'regular recommendations' along the way would keep them from being mistaken for 'vagabonds'. With Mrs Thrale and eleven-year-old Queeney in the group, they could hardly have travelled any other way – the hardships they had encountered in Wales had been occasions for much moaning, though not by Johnson. If they had travelled in France more as vagabonds, more as he and Boswell did through the Highlands and Hebrides, Johnson surely would have been more animated and less detached. As it was, they made a 'prodigious fine journey' of it, taking in the main tourist sites, travelling in two coaches, staying in good accommodation, and spending a huge amount of money. The fifty-nine days cost Thrale more than £800 (some £80,000 today), which he could not really afford.[31]

From Paris, he wrote to Boswell, 'Paris is, indeed, a place very different from the Hebrides, but it is to a hasty traveller not so fertile of novelty, nor affords so many opportunities of remark.' 'I have seen nothing that much delighted or surprised me,' he told Hector when he got home. Paris 'in general makes a very mean appearance'. He could not really say, as he had after the Hebrides, that he had seen 'a new region'. Most important, he confided in Taylor that the trip had not made any impression on his feelings about himself and sense of direction: 'Is not mine a kind of life turned upside down. Fixed to a spot when I was young, and roving the world when others are contriving to sit still, I am wholly unsettled. I am a kind of ship with a wide sail, and without an anchor.' The main benefit of the trip was that 'the French have a clear air and a fruitful soil' that improved his health. At Versailles he felt so good that 'I ran a race in the rain this day, and beat Baretti.'[32]

Mrs Thrale's journal is conspicuous for seldom mentioning Johnson's conversation and actions. When she did mention him, it was often with impatience and irritation or to find fault with him. One reason for this is simply that he did not command the attention on the journey that normally he was accustomed to in a gathering at Southwark or Streatham. There were other things to think about, and his interaction with the French was limited by his reluctance to speak French, which he could not do as well as read or write it. She allowed a few glimpses of him, however, such as when a Parisian wig he had acquired almost proved to be too much for some Frenchman who 'refrained from laughing out with the greatest difficulty'; or when one evening in Paris she sat at home with him while others went out: 'we criticised & talked & were happy in one another – he in hugging me, & I in being hugged'; or when an Irishman living cheaply in Paris 'found the way to Dr Johnson's heart by abusing the French'. Such French bashing extremely annoyed Baretti who was extolling French virtues right and left throughout the trip, but it had long been typical of English tourists. Johnson certainly indulged in his share of stereotyping the French with an assortment of stock prejudices against them: 'Their meals are gross', 'the French have no laws for the maintenance of their poor', 'in France there is no middle rank', and 'nobody but mean people walk in Paris'. He remained firm in these views of Paris, for at Reynolds's house for dinner three years later he declared, 'I question if at Paris such a company as is round this table could be got together in less than half a year.' Boswell heard Johnson say that the meat markets in Paris were 'such as would be sent to a gaol in England'.[33]

Johnson's own journal – what we have of it – is on the whole predictably impersonal, though he made an effort to be descriptive of some of the palaces, libraries and churches he saw. Libraries appealed to him most, especially the King's Library, where he had the thrill of handling the Gutenberg Bible, and the libraries at the Sorbonne and St Germain des Prés. He was 'well used' by the English Benedictine friars, and while Mrs Thrale went off yet again to see the pictures at the Palais Royale he spent the last day in Paris entirely with them, speaking Latin and exploring their library: 'I lived at the Benedictines, meagre day. Soup meagre, herrings, eels, both with sauce. Fried fish. Lentils, tasteless in themselves . . . I parted very tenderly from the Prior.' The Prior, Father Cowley, who offered him the use of a cell anytime he wished it, would remain a friend and visit him in London in 1777. 'I dined in their refectory, and studied in their library, and had the favour of their company to other places, as curiosity led me.' He was not as pleased with the lives of the English Austin nuns at Nôtre Dame de Sion where he came to fetch Mrs Thrale one afternoon at tea time. He disapproved of the religious austerity there and said to the Lady Abbess, 'Madam, you are here, not for the love of virtue, but the fear of vice.' She replied she 'would remember this as long as she lived'. His lengthiest description was of an entirely different realm of French life, the process of manufacturing at a mirror factory in Paris, having the day before seen the mirrors in the great gallery at Versailles.[34]

The trip was a pleasure and success for the Thrales but not for Johnson. He was virtually ignored by the eminent French authors, philosophers and scientists, who either seemed unaware that he was there or were uninterested in seeing him. Like the Welsh trip, this excursion to Paris was for the Thrales mostly about sightseeing. He met fewer scholars than even Boswell did when he was there in his early twenties. What Johnson did take back with him above all else was a distaste for the wastefulness and 'luxuriousness' of the French aristocracy, ripe for destruction in the French Revolution, as well as with the corrupt social system and dismal poverty it created. 'The French are a gross, ill-bred, untaught people,' he said a few years later. 'What I gained by being in France was, learning to be better satisfied with my own country.'[35]

Part Six

BIOGRAPHY AND
'THE RACE WITH DEATH'

CHAPTER 29

'A Very Poor Creeper
upon the Earth'

I

EVEN BEFORE RETURNING HOME in mid-November 1775, they all began making plans for an expedition to Italy in the spring. Queeney would be included and Baretti was to be in charge again of making all the arrangements and acting as their courier. He had in mind no short excursion this time but a Grand Tour over a whole year, the chief part to be spent in Tuscany for the winter. Johnson was amenable to a year, as was Thrale, but Mrs Thrale insisted on only six months from April to October because she wished to be back when young Harry entered Westminster School.

The expensive plan was to leave on 8 or 9 April in three post-chaises with a maid and two manservants, hiring additional servants in cities where they would be staying for some time. 'With money one can do everything,' wrote Mrs Thrale tentatively. They would head for Lyons via Paris, cross the Alps to Turin, proceed to Genoa and Milan, and then turn south to Rome. Baretti was all for making short stops in small towns so that his relatives could meet Johnson, whom he described to an Italian friend as 'my British sack of learning, my Samuel Johnson'. Wishing to prepare a relative for meeting this remarkable and unusual man, Baretti also cautioned that he was 'a nasty old man, a giant both in body and mind, always absent-minded, fierce, touchy, dirty, full of unpleasant habits, always shifting his body when he is seated, and always moving his jaw like

an ox chewing the cud; but as he is rightly believed to possess more learning than any other man in this kingdom, he is feared and respected by all,
perhaps more than he is loved.' Baretti proposed an excursion even to Sic-
ily before returning north to winter in Tuscany, but Johnson was concerned that with such an itinerary they might not properly see the major
cities: 'We must, to be sure, see Rome, Naples, Florence, and Venice, and
as much more as we can.' He insisted on changes. Baretti could not actually take them to Venice because if he did so he risked being arrested
there for some politically daring writings. Johnson began brushing up on
his Italian and wondered if he might write a book about his travels there.
'I do not see that I could make a book upon Italy,' he remarked to Boswell,
'yet I should be glad to get two hundred pounds, or five hundred pounds,
by such a work.' Thinking this 'a proof that he supposed he *might* compose
a valuable journal', Boswell and others were thrilled at the prospect that
some day Johnson might well be offering the public his insights on Italy
'through his noble intellectual glass'.[1]

In the spring Boswell was preparing for his annual dose of the Johnsonian ether, but Johnson was concerned that he was coming chiefly to
cling to him in the hope of shaking off months of melancholia that were
ruining his life: 'I am very sorry that your melancholy should return and
should be sorry likewise if it could have no relief but from my company
. . . if you will come to me, you must come very quickly' before they left for
Italy. If he hurried, they might even be able to squeeze in a trip to Oxford,
Lichfield and Ashbourne.[2]

Johnson had his own problems. There was the alarming example of
Charles Congreve, a classmate of Taylor, Hector and his whom he had recently discovered languishing in a stupor in a London room ten-foot
square, 'willing, I am afraid, to forget the world, and content to be forgiven
by it, to repose in that sullen sensuality, into which men naturally sink,
who think a disease a justification of indulgence.' Johnson feared that very
sullenness and despondency in himself. He could see Congreve had allowed himself to descend into a form of madness. His Easter Day diary
entry sounds as worried as any he ever wrote: 'My reigning sin, to which
perhaps many others are appendant, is waste of time, and general slug-

gishness, to which I was always inclined and in part of my life have been almost compelled by morbid melancholy and disturbance of mind. Melancholy has had in me its paroxisms and remissions, but I have not improved the intervals, nor sufficiently resisted my natural inclination, or sickly habits.' If only he could rise at eight and feel more regularly the 'radiations of comfort' obtainable by turning to the 'Holy Spirit', the rest of the day might properly fall into place.[3]

One method of getting out of himself was to help others. In January he had tea with the gentle moral reformer and educator Hannah More (1745–1833) and read her freshly published poem *Sir Eldred*. 'We fell upon *Sir Eldred*,' she wrote, for which he suggested 'some little alterations' and composed a new stanza. She had recently arrived in London from Bristol, where she kept a boarding school with her sisters. When they first met at Reynolds's house in June 1774, she was astonished to discover he knew something of her writings. He met her 'with good humour in his countenance, and continued in the same pleasant humour the whole of the evening'. They took to each other immediately, although it may have been this same evening that he not so mildly rebuked her, as he often did Mrs Thrale, for constantly flattering him: 'Dearest lady, consider with yourself what your flattery is worth, before you bestow it so freely.' They next met a few days later when Renny took it upon herself to take her and her sister to 'Dr Johnson's *very own house*'. On the way, with their hearts palpitating, the three ladies broke into raptures over him, 'Abyssinia's Johnson! Dictionary Johnson! Rambler's, Idler's and Irene's Johnson!' When they got there Hannah seated herself in Johnson's great chair in the parlour, 'hoping to catch a little ray of his genius'. He laughed when he heard of it, but informed her he never sat in that chair. Renny told Johnson of their 'rapturous exclamations' on the way, on which he looked at Hannah and said, 'She was a *silly thing*'. 'Why should she flatter *me*?' he asked. 'I can do nothing for her. Let her carry her praise to a better market'.[4]

Hannah became a great favourite of his. For tea at Reynolds's house one day the following year, she 'was placed next him, and they had the entire conversation to themselves . . . The old genius was extremely jocular, and the young one very pleasant'. At Elizabeth Montagu's splendid house in Portman Square, the 'Queen of the Blues' and 'female Maecenas' (as she was called) about whose writings and friendships with Horace Walpole and Thomas Gray Johnson had mixed feelings, she sorted her way through 'half the wits of the age' assembled there and finally sat down next to him for the rest of the evening. She then accompanied him home, 'although Mrs Montagu publicly declared she did not think it prudent to trust us together, with such a declared affection on both sides'. He invited himself to tea with her and her sister the following day 'that we may read Sir Eldred together . . . He repeats all the best stanzas by heart, with the energy, though not the grace of a Garrick'. This great Dr Johnson had found his way into her heart: 'To enjoy Dr Johnson perfectly, one must have him to oneself, as he seldom cares to speak in mixed parties.' For her part, in addition to her exemplary and modest moral nature, she provided him the uncluttered female grace and wit he craved to keep up his spirits. Hannah's sister even joked a wedding might be in the offing between the 'mother of Sir Eldred, and the father of my much-loved Irene'. Mrs Montagu chimed in that this was not that improbable since Johnson could be overheard calling her 'child', 'little fool', 'love', and 'dearest' through the din of conversation. She once playfully called him her 'beau' and 'gay libertine'. 'I love you both,' he declared to her and her sister – 'inamorato', as Hannah related it. He promised to visit her and her school in Bristol, which he did with Boswell in the spring.[5]

Garrick also frequented these parties – laughing boisterously with Johnson about their Lichfield youth, as did Dr Burney. Johnson wrote the Dedication to the Queen for Burney's monumental four-volume *General History of Music*, the first volume of which was published in January; he also added to it his translation of a passage from Euripides on 'the joys of music' and read proofs. Such involvement could be taken as evidence that he was more appreciative and understanding of music than most of his friends believed. He remarked about Burney's book that it 'evidently proved that the author of it understood the philosophy of music better than any man who had ever written on that subject', a comment prompting Renny to write, 'it must be supposed that he had felt its power, and that he had a taste for music'. On the other hand, his writings and other sources are sprinkled with his comments that he took little pleasure from music, and not entirely because he was hard of hearing. He could be quite scornful and dismissive of both music and musicians: 'no man of talent, or whose mind was capable of better things, ever would or could devote his time and attention to so idle and frivolous a pursuit'. On being asked at Burney's house a question about Bach, he replied mischievously, 'And pray, Sir, *who is Bach?* Is he a piper?' 'Music excites in my mind no ideas, and hinders me from contemplating my own,' he is supposed to have said – at least according to the biased Hawkins whose own *History of Music*, also published in 1776, was mocked by Johnson and club friends. Although with such comments Johnson was knowingly acting out the popular notion that he had little use for music, Dr Burney himself is our most reliable witness when he asserted that he was 'wholly deaf & insensible to it'.[6]

Boswell arrived in London in mid-March, eager to have at least two or three weeks with him before he left for Italy. He discovered on his arrival at Johnson's doorstep that he had recently moved to a house in a narrow alley at No. 8, Bolt Court, very close to his previous residences just off Fleet Street – a 'much better one' with 'good rooms and a pretty little spot of background'. Johnson was at the Thrales' so Boswell 'sailed to Southwark' from Blackfriars Bridge where he found his hero in 'the full glow of conversation'. Johnson confirmed that before leaving for Italy he would indeed take a 'jaunt' to Oxford, Birmingham and Lichfield. 'I shall go in a few days,' he announced, 'and you, Boswell, shall go with me'. This would be Boswell's first opportunity to walk in the footsteps of his hero's early years and interview Hector and others about them. Three days later they were on their way.[7]

They were well into their stay at Lichfield when a letter from Mrs Thrale brought an end to it. Reading it during breakfast at Lucy's, Johnson solemnly announced, 'One of the most dreadful things that has happened in my time . . . Mr Thrale has lost his only son'. This meant they had to cut short their time in Lichfield and after a short stay at Ashbourne rush back to London so Johnson could comfort the Thrales. For the time being, in any case, he had run out of patience with Boswell's biographical mission and endless questions and note-taking. Boswell complained that the 'rattling' of the wheels of the chaise as they thundered their way south drowned out Johnson's answers to questions, whereupon Johnson shouted at him, 'Then you may go hang yourself.' A few days and many questions later, he was equally forceful, 'You have but two topics, yourself and me, and I'm sick of both.'[8]

Mrs Thrale, Baretti and Queeney were just leaving for Bath when Johnson arrived at Streatham. He declined to go with them, preferring to stay and comfort Henry Thrale in his grief. Inconsolable, Thrale sent him away. That same day Johnson sat down and wrote a perceptive letter to Mrs Thrale on grieving: 'I know that such a loss is a laceration of the mind. I know that a whole system of hopes, and designs, and expectations is swept away at once, and nothing [is] left but bottomless vacuity. What you feel, I have felt.' He wrote to her almost every other day until in mid-April he joined her in Bath. By then he had met with a huge disappointment. The Thrales yet again had cancelled the Italian tour. Only he and Baretti still had any heart for it. He pretended to Mrs Thrale he was not that disappointed. She wrote to him, 'Baretti said you would be very angry . . . but I knew you better . . . Mr Thrale says he shall not die in peace without seeing Rome, and I am sure he will go nowhere that he can help without you.' That was small consolation. Without seeing Italy, he felt incomplete, as he told Boswell at Paoli's house before hearing the bad news: 'A man who has not been in Italy is always conscious of an inferiority . . . the grand object of travelling is to see the shores of the Mediterranean. On these shores were the four great empires of the world: the Assyrian, the Persian, the Grecian, and the Roman. All our religion, almost all our law, almost all our arts, almost all that sets us above savages, has come to us from the shores of the Mediterranean.'[9]

From Bath he summoned Boswell, 'Come . . . as soon as you can'. In a matter of a few days Boswell was there. The most memorable event in their time there together was an excursion to Bristol to look into the authenticity of manuscript poems at St Mary Redcliffe Church allegedly written by Thomas Rowley, a fifteenth-century priest. Just as Johnson had demanded of Macpherson proof of the authenticity of Ossian's poetry in the form of authentic Gaelic manuscripts, he now wanted to satisfy himself regarding another controversial forgery of the day. Thomas Chatterton, 'the marvellous boy', as he was called for his poetic genius, had published these manuscript poems which he claimed he found in the church archives. The fact was he had written the beautiful verses himself, and soon after publishing them had moved to London where in 1770, in a lonely garret, without any money, he appears to have poisoned himself at the age of eighteen – an act memorialised magnificently by Henry Wallis's painting, *Chatterton*, one of the minor masterpieces of the Pre-Raphaelite movement. But for years the controversy about their authenticity continued, with names of believers and disbelievers published occasionally in the newspapers. Johnson pronounced the alleged 'originals' impostures the moment he saw them. Indeed, he found 'this wild adherence to Chatterton more unaccountable than the obstinate defence of Ossian' even as he and many others wondered at Chatterton's poetic skills: 'This is the most extraordinary young man that has encountered my knowledge. It is wonderful how the whelp has written such things.'[10]

On his return to London, he was greeted with the just-published octavo edition of his *Political Tracts* containing *Taxation No Tyranny* and the three other pamphlets; somewhat ironically, in light of the signing of the American *Declaration of Independence* in July and General George Washington's major success in driving the British from Boston and New York that year. More satisfactory to him politically than what was happening in America was Parliament's rejection of Wilkes's Bill for Parliamentary reform. The timing could not have been better, therefore, for one of Boswell's greatest coups on 15 May when he brought together Johnson and Wilkes for dinner at Charles Dilly's home in the Poultry, where Johnson said he always found a good dinner. It was the prospect of such a dinner that Boswell, who was staying in the room set aside for him in Johnson's house, used as a lure to get him to Dilly's house that night. Johnson of course knew nothing of the plan, which Boswell hatched with Dilly's collusion, to have Wilkes there as well. Boswell was playing with fire. It was just the sort of awkward situation he longed to put Johnson into in order to see how he would behave. When he suggested a meeting between him and Mrs Macaulay, for instance, Johnson scolded him, 'No, Sir, you would not see us quarrel, to make you sport.' When the evening at Dilly's arrived the plan nearly unravelled because Johnson had forgotten about the dinner and ordered a quiet meal instead at home with Mrs Williams and Boswell. Mrs Williams came to the rescue, however, after some persuasion from Boswell, and in a few minutes Johnson was calling out, 'Frank, a clean shirt'. Soon they were in a hackney coach on their way to the Poultry.[11]

When they got to Dilly's, almost immediately Johnson wanted to know who a man in lace across the room was. 'Mr Wilkes, Sir,' was the simple answer, whereupon he grabbed a book sulkily and sat down to compose himself. Dinner was then called. Wilkes, who had little problem with Johnson being there even though, alluding to his pension, he regarded him 'a slave of the state', sat down boldly next to him and was so attentive and cordial, seeing to it that Johnson was served with all that he wished, that Johnson gradually began to melt. '"Sir, Sir, I am obliged to you, Sir"', Johnson grumbled, 'bowing, and turning his head to him with a look for some time of "surly virtue".' Before long he had relaxed and was enjoying sparkling conversation with the man whom he had described as 'a criminal from a gaol'. Boswell sat back hugging himself, not minding at all their ganging up on him as Johnson began 'breaking jokes with Jack Wilkes upon the Scots'. At Bolt Court later, Johnson was all praise for his arch-enemy and the evening. Burke learned of this encounter later – 'there was nothing to equal it in the whole history of the *Corps Diplomatique*,' he told Boswell. With the glow from his triumphant stage-managing warming him, Boswell left London the next day. 'Pray take care of him, and tame him,' Johnson wrote to his wife. 'The only thing in which I have the honour to agree with you is, in loving him; and while we are so much of a mind in a matter of so much importance, our other quarrels will, I hope, produce no great bitterness.'[12]

That summer Johnson suffered a strong attack of gout: 'I enjoy all the dignity of lameness . . . I am a very poor creeper upon the earth, catching at anything with my hands to spare my feet.' 'It is of my own acquisition, as neither my father had it nor my mother.' For mental and physical relief he trudged off to Brighton again with the Thrales in the last week of September and stayed until the end of October. He even tried swimming, 'though I know not that it does me any good'. He still disliked the town, he wrote to Boswell: 'The place was very dull, and I was not well; the expedition to the Hebrides was the most pleasant journey that I ever made. Such an effort annually would give the world a little diversification. Every year, however, we cannot wander.' Mrs Williams was seriously ill, too, in November, 'in a feeble and languishing state, with little hope of growing better', though Dr Levet remained 'sound, wind and limb'. There was also trouble at Streatham when (in Johnson's words) after one too many quarrels with Mrs Thrale 'in some whimsical fit of disgust, or ill-nature' Baretti put down his teacup at breakfast one morning in July and walked out of the house without saying a word, resolving never to see her again. The timing of this was not wonderful since she was pregnant again.[13]

His health continued poor into the spring. Desperate to sleep one night, he took ten ounces of his own blood so inexpertly that Frank and Levet had to help him 'stop the stream'. Thrale was furious when he heard he had put his life in danger like this. Lawrence bled him again later, making it thirty-six ounces in two or three days. He spent much of every night sitting up in bed. Good sleep was hard to come by. Also common was the claustrophobic feeling of helplessness: 'Days and months pass in a dream, and I am afraid that my memory grows less tenacious, and my observation less attentive. If I am decaying it is time to make haste. My nights are restless and tedious, and my days drowsy. The flatulence which torments me, has sometimes so obstructed my breath, that the act of respiration became not only voluntary but laborious in a decumbent posture.' Neither was he attending church, having missed almost every Sunday of the year thus far. He looked to Reynolds, Burney and Mrs Thrale for moral support and comfort, as well as to Boswell from afar – 'your kindness is one of the pleasures of my life' – and he was cheered that his 'old enemy' Margaret Boswell had shown him some affection by sending him a jar of her marmalade – 'she is after all a dear, dear lady'. 'We must all help one another,' he wrote to her.[14]

One of the new and brightest lights on his horizon that spring was Dr Burney's twenty-five-year-old daughter Fanny, whom he met for the first time at a morning party at the Burney house. In a few months she would secretly publish her classic bestseller, *Evelina*, keeping her authorship unknown for months, even from her publisher, because of her shyness and the terror of the stigma of female authorship. She was an undiluted joy for Johnson, young, shy, charming and intelligent, and she reciprocated his regard with a deep affection for him for the rest of his life. Her journal was all that Mrs Thrale's, with her family troubles and constraints, could never be: full and rich with the novelist's wit and vibrantly recorded scenes that make it, along with Pepys's and Boswell's, among the most engaging in British literary history.

Fanny Burney was taken aback when she first saw Johnson: 'He is, indeed, very ill-favoured; is tall and stout; but stoops terribly; he is almost bent double. His mouth is almost continually opening and shutting, as if he was chewing. He has a strange method of frequently twirling his fingers, and twisting his hands. His body is in continual agitation, *see-sawing* up and down; his feet are never a moment quiet; and, in short, his whole person is in *perpetual motion.*' As for his dress, it was 'as much out of the common road as his figure' with 'large wig, snuff-colour coat, and gold buttons, but no ruffles to his shirt . . . and black worsted stockings'. She said his near-sightedness was so bad that not until someone held out a hand to him did he know who it was. Inspecting the library shelves, which he did within five minutes of being announced, he almost touched the backs of the books with his eyelashes. He plucked a book off the shelf and fell solitarily to reading it, much to the dismay of others in the room who longed to hear him talk. Fanny quickly caught on that if Johnson was to talk he first had to be 'drawn out'. She was a fine acquisition for him, another young female admirer of delicacy and taste, with a fine satiric impulse, who had little patience with affectation, buffoonery, and hypocrisy – one on whom he doted extravagantly, at times somewhat to her embarrassment, as when in front of a roomful of people he drew her 'very unexpectedly towards him, and he actually kissed me!'.[15]

2

Two major events occurred in the early months of 1777, one criminal, the other literary. The literary development was that on 29 March he was approached by a consortium of no fewer than forty-two booksellers and six printers to write brief biographical vignettes or *Prefaces* for each of the poets in their projected collection of British poetry. 'I am engaged to write little Lives, and little Prefaces, to a little edition of the English poets,' he announced lightly to Boswell four days later. His old friends Davies, Strahan and Thomas Cadell came to him to propose the project on behalf of the other booksellers. The idea was their immediate retaliation to an offensive by the Scottish bookseller John Bell, who announced he would publish over one hundred volumes of English poets that threatened commercially to bury once and for all any claim London booksellers still had to English authors as their exclusive literary property. 'Johnson' was the name they wanted at the head of the publishing venture in order to endow it with the merchandising clout and literary prestige it needed.[16]

Johnson almost certainly had advance notice of the project, perhaps from Steevens who appears to have recommended him for it. He was pleased and accepted 'very politely'. Their project had a patriotic twist to it since he felt 'the chief glory of every people arises from its authors' and England, facing the revolution in the American colonies, the financial and political pressures it created, and threats of French and Spanish invasion, needed to be reminded of its greatness. He profoundly believed that no other country on the Continent could come close to rivalling it as 'the capital of literature'. The downside of the commission was that at an advanced age, and amid growing health worries, it saddled him with a literary project requiring several years of hard work, painful self-sacrifice and confinement to his study. Left to decide how much he would be paid, he modestly (and foolishly) agreed to do the Prefaces for 200 guineas, later revised to £300, feeling this was a respectable sum given the original agreement that he would provide only 'a concise account' for each poet. He felt he could supply the booksellers easily and quickly with what they wanted

– and they wanted it quickly in order to compete with Bell's edition. Later, he defended the contract price: 'The fact is, not that they have paid me too little, but that I have written too much.' He ended up writing over fifty lives, several of them very long. It would be his greatest biographical effort.[17]

The criminal event had a more immediate personal and emotional effect on him.[18] The Revd William Dodd, 'the macaroni parson', as he was called because of his recklessly extravagant social climbing, was a high-spending clergyman and somewhat successful author who through luck and industry had managed to gain some prominence in high society. He was chaplain to the King, Bishop of St David's and (ironically as it turned out) tutor to Philip Stanhope, godson of Johnson's would-be patron for the *Dictionary*, the fourth Earl of Chesterfield. By the time of the crime the godson had succeeded to the earldom. A hopeless spendthrift, Dodd was so desperate for money that he forged the signature of the fifth Earl to a bond valued at £4,200. In less than a week he was exposed and arrested, charged for the capital offence of forgery. He came to trial at the Old Bailey on 22 February, at which he made a melodramatic speech defending himself. It did no good. He was found guilty and on 16 May sentenced to hang, by which time the press had reported the trial so sensationally that the public wept to hear the man's fate. After fainting, Dodd was carted off to Newgate to await execution.

In his extremity he apparently recollected Johnson's *Rambler* essays (especially no. 114) on modern justice and the legal system and asked for his help through the Countess of Harrington and his friend, the printer Edmund Allen, Johnson's landlord and neighbour in Bolt Court. Johnson read Lady Harrington's letter to him 'walking up and down his chamber ... much agitated, after which he said, "I will do what I can."' 'Poor Dodd was sentenced last week,' Johnson informed Taylor on 19 May. 'It is a thing almost without example for a clergyman of his rank to stand at the bar for a capital breach of morality. I am afraid he will suffer ... How little he thought six months ago of being what he now is'. He kept up the fight over the next four months. He wrote 'The Convict's Address to his unhappy Brethren', a sermon that Dodd delivered to fellow prisoners at

Newgate on 6 June, two letters to the Lord Chancellor, one to Lord Mansfield, the Lord Chief Justice of the King's Bench, 'A Petition from Dr Dodd to the King', 'A Petition from Mrs Dodd to the Queen', several pieces for the newspapers, and 'Dr Dodd's last solemn Declaration'. He implored Dodd not to let it be known that he wrote the letter to the King: 'I hope I need not tell you, that I wish it success. But do not indulge hope. Tell Nobody.' Dodd and he exchanged several letters, carried back and forth by Allen, who was a friend of the Keeper of Newgate, but Johnson never visited him in Newgate, feeling 'it would have done *him* more harm, than good'.[19]

Johnson's plea to the Under-Secretary of State came back with a 'dreadful answer'. He knew the die was cast and wrote immediately to Allen on 17 June, urging him to tell Dodd to write 'the history of his own depravation' for the moral benefit of the public. And he was definite on one particular point: 'Let him . . . shut his doors against all hope, all trifles, and all sensuality' and turn to God for mercy and salvation. But still he did not give up, imploring Lady Harrington on 25 June to make a direct appeal to the King and pressing Allen to send the Newgate sermon to anyone who might be able to help, even to the King and the highest ministers in the land. There was an element of panic in his last efforts. To Dodd, finally, he wrote on the 26th, telling him to prepare for death: 'Be comforted: your crime, morally or religiously considered, has no very deep dye of turpitude. It corrupted no man's principles; it attacked no man's life'. Hawkins, who chaired the Grand Jury that brought Dodd to trial, differed from Boswell in maintaining that Johnson privately did not think Dodd worthy of his efforts to save him, judging that the effort was another example of Johnson's misplaced 'indiscriminate humanity'. Dodd was finally executed on 27 June. 'Poor Dodd was put to death yesterday,' Johnson told Boswell angrily, 'in opposition to the recommendation of the jury – the petition of the city of London – and a subsequent petition signed by three-and-twenty thousand hands. Surely the voice of the public, when it calls so loudly, and calls only for mercy, ought to be heard . . . He applied to me often. He was, I am afraid, long flattered with hopes of life; but I had no part in the dreadful delusion.'[20]

3

The sermon Johnson wrote for Dodd was one of more than forty he wrote in his lifetime. Their bulk comprises one of his most impressive literary and spiritual achievements – especially impressive, in personal terms, because he wrote them secretly for 'sundry beneficed clergymen' at their request – twenty-five were for Taylor alone – with the demand that they must never reveal his authorship. That it was not an uncommon practice for clergymen to have sermons written for them, and that he charged two guineas each for them and felt, therefore, he had no further right to be identified as their author, does not diminish the selflessness and charity of the act in a lifetime of writing anonymously for others in a multitude of ways. When someone told him he doubted Dodd wrote the sermon to the Newgate convicts because he lacked 'the force of mind' needed, he coyly kept up the deception: 'Depend upon it, Sir, when a man knows he is to be hanged in a fortnight, it concentrates his mind wonderfully.' Hawkins was one of the few who suspected he wrote many of Taylor's sermons. He claimed later that he recognised Johnson's 'sentiments, style, and method' in them when he heard Taylor ineffectively deliver several at the Church of St Margaret in Westminster.[21]

He wrote the sermons rapidly. 'The composition of sermons is not very difficult,' he wrote in 1780 to Thomas Lawrence's son who had recently been ordained deacon. 'Invent first and then embellish . . . Set down diligently your thoughts as they rise in the first words that occur'. 'I have begun a sermon after dinner, and sent it off by the post that night'. On 20 April 1778, he noted in his diary that he had written a 'little' of the *Lives* and composed more sermons 'as readily as formerly' in spite of 'a vacillation and vagrancy of mind' owing to his 'unsettled' life, the feeling that for the last year his life had been 'very melancholy and [a] shameful blank', and 'painful and fatiguing' nights affected by breathing difficulties so severe that 'asthma was suspected'. Modern medicine has tended to agree it was emphysema more than asthma. The concentration on deeply religious thought in his sermons during the late 1770s occurred to him as not unrelated to a sudden remission of these terrifying 'convulsions' in his breast and breathing difficulties on 18 June 1779. A year later he was so grateful still to be free from them that he composed a prayer of 'Thanksgiving' for 'that recovery and continuance of health which thou hast granted me'.[22]

'Manly sense, deep penetration, and ardent love of virtue': such words have often been used to describe Johnson's sermons. Steeped in the English homiletic tradition of the sixteenth and seventeenth centuries, especially the sermons of Richard Hooker, John Tillotson and Jeremy Taylor, the sermons are much more than standard variations on Anglican theological themes of communion, vanity, repentance and charity, among others. With their strong moral reflections, they make one think immediately of the *Rambler* essays and their insight into the recesses of the human mind. They are all about making one's way as best as one can in this mortal existence with realism, dignity and spiritual sensitivity and devoutness. The themes Johnson wrote about include marriage, the vanity of human wishes and self-deception, arrogance and intellectual pride, envy, war, death, law and morals, capital punishment, idleness, charity and the 'compassionate heart', friendship and God. It has been well understood that Taylor's hot-tempered character, ambition and avarice – he was called 'Midas' by his Ashbourne neighbours – all made him an unlikely deliverer of these sermons, quite apart from his intellectual inability to write them and his apparently poor performance in the pulpit. But we can forgive all this because if he had not asked Johnson to write them on visits to Ashbourne, they simply would not exist.[23]

4

In 1777 Johnson took on another lodger, Tetty's old friend Mrs Desmoulins, who for many years had been living in Chelsea in poverty. Although he did not much like her, he felt a lingering obligation to her not only on account of Tetty but also because she was the daughter of his godfather, after whom he had been named and who had helped him get to Oxford with some small financial assistance. He gave her an allowance of half a guinea per week and allowed her (with her daughter) to move into the same room with a 'Scotch wench', Poll Carmichael, whom Johnson may have taken in as early as 1773, if she was one and the same as the prostitute he found nearly lifeless in the street one day and carried home on his back. He took care of Poll tenderly for years and had long been assisting her to recover a small patrimony she said she had been unjustly denied. She did not work out in the house as well as he had hoped: 'we could spare her very well from us; Poll is a stupid slut', he remarked to Mrs Thrale in 1778.[24]

Desmoulins and her daughter brought to seven the total number of dependants living at Bolt Court in the summer of 1777. She completed the recipe for domestic chaos in the house, for she and Mrs Williams despised each other and the normal bickering in the house increased exponentially. Mrs Thrale was both amused and horrified that Johnson's house was 'overrun with *all* sort of strange creatures, whom he admits for mere charity', 'but as they can both be occasionally of service to each other, and as neither of them have any other place to go to, their animosity does not force them to separate'. None of the inhabitants, in fact, liked Mrs Desmoulins. 'Mr Levet who thinks his ancient rights invaded, stands at bay, *fierce as ten* furies', Johnson grumbled to Mrs Thrale; 'Mrs Williams growls and scolds, but Poll does not much flinch.' After a year with all of them, Johnson summed up the turmoil in the house: 'We have tolerable concord at home, but no love. Williams hates everybody. Levet hates Desmoulins and does not love Williams. Desmoulins hates them both. Poll loves none of them.' Mrs Williams was so ill during the summer that in July, Johnson sent her out into the countryside for her recovery, but he feared the worst. Levet, in spite of feeling besieged by all those women, and Frank were the only stable ones among them. The seventy-two-year-old Levet was good company for Johnson, breakfasting with him and costing little because of his medical attentions to the poor and indigent living in the neighbourhoods of Marylebone for which they were able to pay him one way or another. Johnson's deep affection for Levet and his charitable work never wavered. However, lengthy visits to Staffordshire became more than ever a way to escape the cacophony of argument at home. This pattern of existence would last to the end of his life.[25]

CHAPTER 30

Biographical Straitjacket

I

INSTEAD OF SEEING BOSWELL in London in the spring of 1777, Johnson proposed they meet up at Taylor's in September: 'If you live awhile with me at his house, we shall have much time to ourselves, and our stay will be no expense to us or to him . . . Our ramble in the islands hangs upon my imagination, I can hardly help imagining that we shall go again . . . When we travel again let us look better about us'. He stopped in Oxford for a week on the way north in late July and this time stayed with his friend William Scott, Professor of Ancient History, during which he made a cursory inspection of biographical materials for the *Lives* – 'and a little I have got'. In Lichfield he lived with Lucy for a month, 'barren of entertainment', looking in occasionally on Elizabeth Aston who was recuperating from a stroke and 'in great danger'. Stowe Hill was 'a collection of misery' with everyone there ill in some way. His own health was uncertain: 'When I came hither, I could hardly walk, but I have got better breath and more agility . . . But I have miserable, distressful, tedious nights'. 'I could not walk but with great difficulty from Stowhill to Greenhill.' By the end of August he was in Ashbourne where the tedium did not surprise him much: 'if you were to lay a pebble' on Taylor's mantelpiece, 'you would find it there next year'. There was little to do but get on with the lives of Cowley and Denham, write to Mrs Thrale, and wait for Boswell's delayed arrival. Shocked by his efforts to medicate himself there, Mrs Thrale implored him not 'to torture that iron constitution of yours quite to ruin, because you have nothing else to do. It were better to bind books again as you did one year in our thatch'd summer house,' she wrote, than inflict on himself 'doses of Mercury and Opium which are not wanted, and then complain that you are *hermetically seal'd* . . . Oh dear Sir, do pray try to govern your own [health], and do not take physic for fun.' 'Mr Boswell will make Ashbourne alive better than three hautboys and the harpsichord', she hoped.[1]

Johnson was not eager to talk to Boswell about the *Lives of the Poets*, which he now worried was a very large project for a man his age, but one evening they spoke of death: 'He lied,' Johnson exclaimed, when Boswell told him that David Hume, who had died several months earlier, had been 'easy at the thought of annihilation . . . Dr Dodd would have given both his hands and legs to have lived'. Impatient of the morbid subject, he preferred to think of other things: 'If I had no duties and no reference to futurity [life after death], I would spend my life driving briskly in a post-chaise with a pretty woman, one who could understand me, and would add something to the conversation'.[2]

One evening after supper Johnson dictated an argument to help him plead a cause in the Court of Session in Edinburgh on behalf of Joseph Knight, an African slave brought to Scotland who was petitioning for liberty. Johnson's argument was totally consistent with his lifelong hostility towards slavery. Only the previous July, he had written to Boswell in support of the decision in 1772 by Lord Chief Justice William Murray, the first Earl of Mansfield, that a slave by law was free the moment he set foot on British soil; and in *Taxation No Tyranny* he endorsed a proposal to set free all the slaves in America, for which an enraged Benjamin Franklin denounced him for inciting slaves to rise up against whites. The argument he dictated to Boswell was a strong anti-slavery statement, especially castigating racism and violence as its basis: 'His colour is considered as a sufficient testimony against him. It is to be lamented that moral right should ever give way to political convenience.' Boswell used the argument successfully in obtaining Knight's freedom, but in the *Life* he asserted that Johnson's zeal was 'owing to prejudice, and imperfect or false information'. The abolition of slavery, he argued, would be 'wild and dangerous' and would interfere with commercial interests.[3]

The most unpleasant moment occurred when they fell into a furious quarrel about the Americans, the only subject, Johnson maintained, of 'great importance' that Parliament had ever debated in his lifetime. Sympathetic to the American revolutionary cause, Boswell refused to submit, making Johnson explode in anger: 'the violent agitation into which he was thrown, while answering, or rather reprimanding me, alarmed me so, that I heartily repented of my having unthinkingly introduced the subject'. They both returned to their rooms, Johnson steaming and Boswell badly bruised. True to form, the next morning Johnson had cooled off and was in a conciliatory mood as Boswell sat on his bed and they talked. Boswell left the next morning, content with having 'derived a considerable accession to my Johnsonian store'.[4]

2

Johnson lingered at Ashbourne, 'awkward at departing', on 6 November finally rejoining his feuding household in Bolt Court after a three-month ramble of 'very little pleasure'. At Ashbourne he had acknowledged one of the reasons for dallying there: 'You know, I have some work to do. I did not set to it very soon, and if I should go up to London with nothing done, what would be said, but that I was – who can tell what? I therefore stay till I can bring up something to stop their mouths.' Six months had disappeared since he agreed to write the *Prefaces*. 'Little lives and little criticism may serve,' he tried to tell himself unconvincingly. Soon after his return, he began to write the *Life of Edmund Waller*, receiving proofs of it by mid-April, but by then he still did not have the momentum he and the booksellers expected, although by December the *Life of Cowley* was being printed, complete with his long, innovative, critical discussion of what he called the 'metaphysical' poets of the seventeenth century. He indulged in another small procrastination in January when he accompanied Burney and his son to Winchester College to make sure, through his friendship with Joseph Warton, that the boy was 'well received'. On Easter Monday in 1778, he looked back over the year with the stark realisation, 'so little has been done that days and months are without any trace'. It was imperative that he pick up the pace. If only he could keep at bay 'the hand of time, or of disease . . . very heavy upon me'.[5]

After Easter he shot ahead on a new trajectory, no longer comforting himself with notions of 'little' Prefaces that never seemed to ignite his enthusiasm and resolving to write long, substantial ones, solid with literary criticism and reflections on literature. *The Life of Dryden*, which he began in the spring, was a dramatic turning point. It turned out to be one of the longest and most complex. 'You have now all *Cowley*,' he wrote in late July to John Nichols (1745–1826), the printer, editor and author. 'I have been drawn to a great length, but *Cowley* or *Waller* never had any critical examination before. I am very far advanced in *Dryden*, who will be long too. The next great life I purpose to be *Milton's*.' Familiar with the publishing world inside out and later editor of *The Gentleman's Magazine*, Nichols now moved to centre-stage in helping Johnson get his Prefaces edited, revised and printed. He was only thirty-three, but with his voracious appetite for literature and tracking down anecdotes and fugitive poems which he knew Johnson would never find without him, he was a goldmine of biographical and other kinds of literary information. Years later, Nichols wrote of Johnson: 'In the progress of his "Lives of the Poets", I had the good fortune to conciliate his esteem, by several small services; though, at the same time, I was perpetually goading him to furnish the press with copy'. 'You now have the life of Dryden, and you see it is very long,' he wrote again to Nichols in mid-August. These 'big' lives at last satisfied the booksellers that he was sailing.[6]

A distinctive feature of his labours on the Prefaces was that they were to some extent the result of teamwork. Nichols (especially), Steevens, Isaac Reed (another great Shakespearean), Thomas and Joseph Warton, Percy and other scholars and librarians sent him facts and books in response to his requests. He even asked Boswell in Scotland to gather up what he could on the Scottish poet James Thomson. When a biography was freshly printed, he would take the proof sheets to Streatham and let Mrs Thrale, Fanny Burney and others read them aloud over breakfast or tea. 'Dr Johnson was very communicative concerning his present work of the Lives of the Poets,' Fanny observed. She recounted the playfulness with which he floated the biographies among them: 'I was then looking over the Life of Cowley, which he had himself given me to read, at the same time that he gave to Mrs Thrale that of Waller. They are now printed, though they will not be published for some time. But he bid me put it away . . . "Do,["] cried he, ["]put away that now, & prattle with us . . . I can't make this little Burney prattle . . . and I am sure she prattles well[."]' 'I could not help remarking how very like Dr Johnson is to his writing,' she added, 'and how much the same thing it was to hear, or to read him . . . but that nobody could tell that, without coming to Streat-ham, for his language was generally imagined to be laboured & studied, instead of the nice common flow of his thoughts.'[7]

3

Boswell was in London in the spring of 1778, recording more than 150 pages of Johnson's conversation. One of the most famous scenes in the *Life* he captured on this visit was Johnson's ill-tempered quarrel with the priggish Percy over the literary merits of Thomas Pennant's *Tour in Scotland* (1771). Johnson praised the book but Percy 'opposed Johnson eagerly' because Pennant did not like his precious patron the Duke of Northumberland's estate at Alnwick. To Johnson this was nonsense and self-interest. They fell to arguing about whether or not Pennant was correct in describing Northumberland's gardens as excessively 'trim', a criticism that could sting anyone who wished to be thought of as at the forefront of the new natural style of landscaping. Percy was so fired with indignation he foolishly said to Johnson he was in no position to judge anyway because he was short-sighted. Johnson retaliated by accusing Percy of 'the resentment of a narrow mind'. The temperature rose when Percy blurted out, 'Sir, you may be as rude as you please'. Johnson shouted back, 'Hold, Sir! Don't talk of rudeness; remember, Sir, you told me (puffing hard with passion struggling for a vent) I was short-sighted. We have done with civility. We are to be as rude as we please'. A few minutes later Percy, realising his horrible blunder, rushed across the room to apologise and they were immediately reconciled. 'I am willing you shall hang

Pennant,' Johnson then announced. 'Hang him up, hang him up.' As he confessed to Mrs Thrale, 'I am always sorry when I make bitter speeches, & I never do it, but when I am insufferably vexed.' 'But you do suffer things to vex you, that nobody else would vex at. I am sure I have had my share of scolding from you!'[8]

Another memorable exchange was at Dilly's between Johnson and the 'ingenious Quaker lady' Mary Knowles. Except for their belief in an 'inward light' that ruled out any need for the clergy, Johnson maintained a respect for the piety of Quakers: 'I have always loved the simplicity of manners, and the spiritual-mindedness of the Quakers . . . the essential part of religion [is] piety . . . and many a man [is] a Quaker without knowing it'. But he bolted at the progressive Quaker position on the social roles of women. When she complained that men had much more liberty than women, his reply was intensely conservative, 'Madam, women have all the liberty they should wish to have'; he argued that men have all the dangers and that all they do is for women: 'If we require more perfection from women than from ourselves, 'tis doing them honour. And women have not the same temptations we have. They may always live in good company. Men must mix indiscriminately.' She resisted, ending with, 'Well, I hope that in another world the sexes will be equal.' He had the last word: 'You are too ambitious. We may as well desire to be angels.' Such views of his on women were only part of the picture. In coaxing Boswell to abandon his unreasonable plan to entail his estate so as to exclude the female line, he took a position he had long argued: 'Women have natural and equitable claims as well as men, and these claims are not to be capriciously or lightly superseded or infringed.' On the subject of death, Mrs Knowles's remark that it was the 'gate of life' had a different effect on him, drawing a curtain momentarily on his cheerfulness as he stood 'with his face to the chimney and [with] a serious, solemn and somewhat gloomy air, said that no rational man would die without apprehension'.[9]

There was no time for his annual summer-autumn visit to Staffordshire in 1778. Instead, he paid Langton a five-day visit in September at Warley Camp in Essex. In spite of an injured knee and other ailments,

Langton recalled, 'he sat, with a patient degree of attention, to observe the proceedings of a regimental court martial', did the rounds of the camp at eleven one night, and entered with informed interest into conversation on military subjects, especially gunpowder. It was damp and cold, and he worried over his own and Langton's health.[10]

In London there was plenty of elegant socialising to keep him busy, especially at Streatham and with the Burneys and the grand Elizabeth Montagu. When he had to miss one dinner with Mrs Montagu because of a cold and cough, he had to reassure her he was not making up excuses. He himself felt slighted when she neglected to give him a print of herself after a portrait by Reynolds: 'I shall think myself ill rewarded for my love and admiration if she does not give me one . . . But I never could get anything from her but by pushing a face'. When she heard of his disappointment, she quickly sent him one.[11]

4

During these years and to the end of his life Johnson was especially amenable to having his likeness cut in stone or painted, and artists were clamouring to be allowed to 'perpetuate his image'. In 1777 his friend the prominent sculptor Joseph Nollekens, who had sculpted a monument for Goldsmith in Westminster Abbey which Johnson supplied with an epitaph, carved his bust and exhibited it at the Royal Academy. Johnson was not unaware of the honour done him by this, sending a cast of it to Lucy in Lichfield who, along with Mrs Thrale, Renny, Sir Joshua and Garrick's wife, did not like it. 'I think my friend Joe Nollekens can chop out a head with any of them,' he once remarked, but the head did not much please him because he thought it deprived him of his individuality by showing him with too much hair – 'the flowing locks of a sturdy Irish beggar' – and making him look like just another ancient poet in an art gallery. He seemed to be covering his embarrassment by dismissing the bust as not his idea: 'These things [like paintings of him] have never cost me anything, so that I do not much know the price.' The bust was made for the exhibition at the Royal Academy in 1777, he added, 'and shown for the honour of the artist, who is a man of reputation above any of the other sculptors'. He sat for this third portrait by Reynolds in 1774 or 1775 and in October 1778 sat for him twice for his fourth.[12]

The third, possibly the one commonly called the 'Blinking Sam' portrait, shows Johnson poring over a book, obviously near-sighted and struggling to make out the words. He was unhappy with it, too, according to Mrs Thrale, remarking that he 'would not be known by posterity for his defects only, let Sir Joshua do his worst'. Reynolds apparently had no such vanity since his self-portrait then hanging in the Library at Streatham, said Mrs Thrale, depicts his difficulty in hearing. Johnson was unimpressed. 'He may paint himself as deaf if he chooses', Johnson insisted, 'but I will not be blinking Sam.' There are problems in connecting with any certainty the account by Mrs Thrale to this painting, but the portrait itself is a penetrating study of Johnson at the age of sixty-six, not long after the Hebridean tour, as if in the act of reading some political pamphlet which he was about to attack with relish. The 1778 portrait pleased him and others more. Known as the Streatham portrait (now at Tate Britain) because it was painted as one of a series of eminent friends of the Thrales to hang in the new library there, it shows him in a white wig with something of a pained look on his face, as if struggling for breath. Hawkins had a different take on it: 'There is in it that appearance of a labouring, working mind, of an indolent reposing body, which he had to a very great degree.' Johnson was concerned most with how it would please Mrs Thrale: 'Sir Joshua has finished my picture, and it seems to please everybody, but I shall want to see how it pleases you.'[13]

5

By October 1778, the booksellers had finished printing almost all the the *English Poets*. Publication waited only on Johnson. Cadell tried to push him. 'I am exceedingly sorry for the delay', Johnson explained, 'but you see I have taken a course very different from what I originally thought on. I thought to have given four or five pages to an author . . . There are however but eight upon whom I can think of dilating, and of those when

Dryden is finished, four are done.' The booksellers had little option but to go ahead and publish all fifty-six volumes of the *English Poets* in the autumn and at the same time publish a separate volume of the Prefaces he had finished, including 'Milton' and several short ones which he could churn out quickly. The Prefaces would be available only to purchasers of the complete set, a strategy that backfired somewhat when people took to borrowing the volumes of Prefaces instead of acquiring them by buying the *English Poets*. Feeling the booksellers breathing down his neck, he completed 'Milton' by January and then went to work immediately on the short ones, several of which were relatively insubstantial and based almost entirely on *Biographia Britannica*. The following February he told Renny he had 'about a week's work to do'. By 1 March he had turned in twenty-two biographies of a total of fifty-two poets, making up four volumes that appeared that month as *Prefaces, Biographical and Critical, to the Works of the English Poets*. Fifteen hundred copies were printed, one of which he sent to the King, thus fulfilling a promise in that memorable interview in 1767 that he would someday publish 'a literary biography of this country'. 'If the King is a Whig, he will not like them,' he wrote to Mrs Thrale, 'but is any King a Whig?'[14]

Whigs, in fact, did not like the Prefaces, though most people admired Johnson's critical energy and insight in them. Edmond Malone gently pointed out that unfortunately his 'political principles break out' in them, especially in 'Waller' and 'Milton'; others were less gentle in lamenting his 'Tory' political prejudices. 'The hounds of Whiggism have opened in full cry', Boswell wrote. Malone also mentioned that while the 'critical parts' were 'amusing and instructive', the biographical sections were flawed by 'want of industry': 'He hates much trouble. A man of infinitely inferior parts (Horace Walpole, for instance) would have collected a great many anecdotes, and made a more entertaining work.' Johnson wrote in 'Dryden' that he did not know of any description of the poet's appearance, but Malone coolly observed, 'There are few English poets of whose external appearance more particulars have been recorded.' What did deeply impress Malone was the humanity and wisdom in the Prefaces that could never be matched by a mere accumulation of facts. Many reviewers and readers regretted Johnson had failed to turn up much new biographical information. Others were astounded that a man of seventy could write 'with so much fire'.[15]

6

The pleasure of publication was dampened considerably by the sudden death of Garrick on 20 January 1779. Swallowed up by his work, Johnson had been less alert to Garrick's illness than he would otherwise have been – 'a death, I believe, totally unexpected'. In his *Life of Smith*, he concluded with this famous comment on Garrick's death: 'What are the hopes of man! I am disappointed by that stroke of death, which has eclipsed the gaiety of nations, and impoverished the public stock of harmless pleasure.' Just over a year later, Beauclerk, too, would die suddenly on 11 March 1780 at the age of forty. 'Another will not often be found among mankind,' Johnson felt, although there was in his last days a dark side to Beauclerk's love for him. 'At his age he should be thinking of better things than to abuse people,' Beauclerk had grumbled. And Burke described a bitter quarrel between them at the Club as 'between Fury and Malevolence'. As usual, all was soon forgiven. In April 1781, as Johnson and Boswell were leaving Eva Garrick's house in the Adelphi Terrace after a happy and nostalgic evening with David's widow and friends including Hannah More, Elizabeth Carter, Reynolds and Burney, they paused by the rails and looked out over the Thames. Boswell reminded Johnson that they had recently lost two dear friends who lived in the Adelphi. 'Ay, Sir,' Johnson answered tenderly, 'and two such friends as cannot be supplied.'[16]

Johnson awoke on Good Friday, 1779, after a bad night and a 'disorder in my breast', went through the motions of fasting, and ended the day weighed down with post-publication melancholia. All he felt he had to show for the year was 'dismal vacuity', broken health, and the biographies, as well as a 'little charity' – which actually was quite a lot on behalf of Levet, Mrs Desmoulins, Mrs Williams, Tom Davies, Phoebe Herne, and a number of others including a few young people and pensioners. On Easter eve, his review of his life was 'comfortless': 'Little done . . . my mind has neither been improved nor enlarged. I have read little, almost nothing, and I am not conscious that I have gained any good, or quitted any evil habit.' He was under no illusions about the Prefaces, expecting to be attacked. 'The worst thing you can do to a man is to be silent. An assault of a town is a bad thing, but starving it is still worse,' he wrote, and 'It is very rarely that an author is hurt by his critics.'[17]

Fanny Burney failed to notice his melancholy. 'Dr Johnson has more fun, & comical humour, & laughable & . . . nonsense about him, than almost anybody I ever saw,' she wrote. 'I mean, though, when with those he likes; for otherwise, he can be as severe & bitter as report relates of him.' She herself thought twice before writing to him, as she said to him in a letter in November: 'How could I live so much at Streatham, & not perceive your cruelty to letter scribblers? Have I not again & again seen irony gathering in your eyes, & laughter trembling upon your lips as you have glanced over their unfortunate productions?' 'What pity that he will not curb the vehemence of his love of victory and superiority!', she observed a year later after he had savaged someone on the matter of Pope's wit, behaving, as usual, in a manner that made him 'dreaded by all, and by many abhorred'. According to Fanny, he was now 'constantly omitted' in invitations, 'either from too much respect or too much fear'. Mrs Thrale complained, too, which elicited this remarkable admission from him about his temperamental 'genius': 'have you not observed in all our conversations that my *genius* is always in extremes . . . I am very noisy, or very silent; very gloomy, or very merry; very sour or very kind? And would you have me cross my *genius* when it leads me sometimes to voracity and sometimes to abstinence? You know that the oracle said follow your *Genius*'.[18]

After a month away in Lichfield and Ashbourne in late spring 1779, where he said he had eaten more fruit than since he was twenty, his good spirits returned again. 'I grow light and airy,' he scribbled to Mrs Thrale in Brighton. 'A man that does not begin to grow light and airy at seventy, is certainly losing time, if he intends ever to be light and airy.' That autumn, however, the nation was feeling far from 'light and airy'. There was a good deal of political restlessness and concern: the American war was dragging on and there was economic recession from diminished trade and harsh taxation. There was also a lingering fear of invasion by the French and Spanish, who in June with a combined fleet of sixty-six ships and twelve frigates – sometimes referred to as 'the other Armada' – had sailed to within sight of Plymouth on their way to landing on the Isle of Wight and at Portsmouth. There were forty thousand troops at Le Havre and St Malo waiting to follow them. Confusion, perhaps an easterly wind, and illness among the French and Spanish sailors prevailed and the fleet was forced to sail back to Brest without having fired a cannon ball. The threat persisted, however. 'I suppose you are all frighted at Lichfield and indeed the terror has been very general,' Johnson wrote to Lucy on 24 August. 'Our ships are said to have greater guns, and to be better manned,' he tried to reassure her, adding that the battle promised to be 'of greater consequence than any battle in our time'. If they spilled ashore at Portsmouth, 'we . . . must fight for ourselves upon our own ground . . . If we are invaded the King is said to have resolved that he will head his own army'. It was also expected that Lord North's ministry would fall, but when Parliament reconvened in November, North saw off the challenge from the Opposition. 'Those are happiest who are out of the noise and tumult,' Johnson said on reflection.[19]

7

As winter drew on, he felt hemmed in by the large amount of work still to be done with the *Lives*. Boswell had tried to help him in May 1778. One day he stopped by the home of the Earl of Marchmont, once an intimate friend of Pope's who had much to tell about the poet. Marchmont modestly asked Boswell to tell Johnson he was willing to help him any way he could and that he would even call on him. Boswell agreed to arrange a meeting for the following day. Excited by the valuable and easy source of anecdotes he had secured for Johnson, that evening at Streatham he proudly announced the good news. 'I shall not be in town tomorrow. I don't care to know about Pope,' Johnson answered. Everyone was nonplussed except for Mrs Thrale, 'I suppose, Sir, Mr Boswell thought, that as you are to write Pope's Life, you would wish to know about him'. Johnson would have none of it: 'Wish! Why yes. If it rained knowledge I'd hold out my hand; but I would not give myself the trouble to go in quest of it.' It was a matter of pride, a protest against being drawn into 'a state of obligation' by Boswell's forward meddling. Still, he allowed that sometime or other he might draw on Marchmont. The meeting did not occur until an entire year later, when, after drinking chocolate at Paoli's, and dressed 'in his best suit and Parisian wig', he and Boswell called on the old statesman. Walking home after two hours, Johnson admitted, 'I would rather have given twenty pounds than not have come.' 'Pope' would be his last life and he would not earnestly begin work on it until six months later.[20]

Just when he needed it most a literary hoard fell in his lap, a fair copy of the manuscript of Joseph Spence's collection of anecdotes and observations on literature (chiefly Pope), later published as *Anecdotes* in 1820. Spence was a friend of Pope's in his later years and the important notes he kept of the poet's remarks and observations were a hugely valuable source that Johnson was the first ever to use extensively. He was given the chance to read Spence's notes by Sir Lucas Pepys, the Thrales' physician as well as his own in the last two years of his life, who arranged the loan with the owner of the manuscript, the Duke of Newcastle. Johnson disappointed a number of people by not properly acknowledging Newcastle as his benefactor in this instance. He did not use the manuscript much right away, but the possession of it spurred him on. By April 1780 he was not exactly in a gallop, rather more in a fast jog. He thought he would 'bolt upon' Mrs Thrale in Bath if he could finish 'Addison', 'Prior' and 'Rowe' before she returned to London, but he fell behind and she did not have a spare room for him anyway. He had about nineteen remaining, a total of 250 pages in the modern edition, of which those on Edward Young, Swift and (especially) Pope were going to be lengthy.[21]

Longing to be out of his biographical straitjacket, he envied Mrs Thrale who was among the living conquering hearts in 'places of high resort', while he was 'seeking for something to say about men of whom I know nothing but their verses, and sometimes very little of them'. He still had not finished 'Rowe' nine days later because of a stream of visitors. Neither did it help that he was dining out almost every night, 'I have had I am afraid, too many dinners of late', though for several months he had controlled his diet and brought his weight down considerably, and had made himself feel better than he had for twenty years. Colds and coughs continued to disturb his nights, for which he was being bled. 'My Lives creep on,' he declared, not knowing when he would 'smell hay, or suck clover flowers' again at Ashbourne. There was a brief, enjoyable change of pace at the Royal Academy exhibition in the newly opened Somerset House (designed by Sir William Chambers) on 1 May, where he was struck by the contrast of the 'contour' and 'grace' of the paintings to the dull monochrome of his existence. In June he began sitting for a portrait by Renny, which delighted him since it gave him the chance to relax with her. The summer of dejection wore on with no great results: 'I have sat at home in Bolt Court, all the summer, thinking to write the Lives, and a great part of the time only thinking . . . I still think to do the rest.' 'Pope', however, loomed on the horizon like Everest: 'I wish the work was over, and I was at liberty' – to do what, he was not sure in a life full of plans 'never brought into practice'. He pined to travel to Europe, Asia and Africa with Boswell. Particularly enticing was Henry Thrale's impulsive revival of an Italian tour, planned by Baretti, even if, like Mrs Thrale, he felt it was a foolish idea in light of the brewer's mental and physical health. Nevertheless, if the trip did happen he was determined not to be left behind'.[22]

8

In addition to the six remaining volumes of Prefaces that were published on 15 May 1779, the booksellers decided in March to print three thousand copies of a separate edition of all of them in four volumes, scheduled for publication also in May but delayed until June. The title for the first time identified the biographies as *The Lives of the Most Eminent English Poets; With Critical Observations on Their Works*. A purchaser of this set would get all the Prefaces and make it unnecessary for anyone to buy the complete set of the *English Poets* to acquire them. This decision was less a charitable act towards people who had not purchased the set in 1779 than a ploy to pre-empt Dublin booksellers trying to get in on the act. In August and September 1782 Johnson revised the *Lives* – chiefly with additions that Nichols, Boswell, Steevens and others had turned up, although he was fairly indifferent about the process – and in February 1783, three thousand copies of a new edition, 'considerably altered', was published, for which he was paid £100. Thus ended six long years of labour on the project.[23]

Johnson's achievement in the *Lives of the Poets* was uneven. While 'Milton', 'Dryden', 'Swift' and 'Pope' were book-length, and 'Cowley', 'Waller', 'Prior', 'Addison' and 'Young' were also lengthy, many were very short, perfunctory, ill-researched, borrowed, and merely adapted from existing biographies. The lengths were at times oddly disproportionate. Edmund Smith, Sir Richard Blackmore, Ambrose Philips and Nicholas Rowe, for example, not exactly giants in the English literary canon, commanded more pages than William Collins and Thomas Gray, whose poetry he disliked but who were among the most loved and influential poets of the late eighteenth century. Gray's odes are 'forced plants, raised in a hotbed', Johnson announced, 'and they are poor plants; they are but cucumbers after all', fit for hogs. 'I said to the Doctor he might have been kinder to Gray,' Boswell wrote in his journal. 'He very justly said he could not be kind . . . He was to tell what he thought; and if people differed from him, they were to tell him so.' Several poets were chosen simply because the booksellers decided to include them in their collection, not because Johnson saw them as promising or worthy subjects. Modern readers scratch their heads over the inclusion of poets like Broome, Duke, Halifax, Pitt, Smith, Somervile, Stepney and West most of whom are not even included in the *Oxford Companion to English Literature*, and are mystified that he left out of the *Lives* the following major poets: Richard Crashaw, Richard Lovelace, Robert Herrick, Andrew Marvell and Goldsmith. The omission of Goldsmith was not his fault but due to a bookseller who owned the copyright of one of his works and refused to allow him to be included.[24]

He divided the longer and middle-sized lives into three sections: the biographic, a character sketch, and literary criticism. As already mentioned, he was not resourceful in gathering biographical material, which he acknowledged somewhat disingenuously in his 'Advertisement': 'the succession of facts is not easily discovered . . . I must be supposed to have engaged in it with less provision of materials than might have been accumulated by longer premeditation. Of the later writers at least I might, by attention and enquiry, have gleaned many particulars, which would have diversified and enlivened my biography.' The character study was crucial because it mediated between literature and life, thus enabling him to demonstrate how a poet's life and works interacted with one another.[25]

What especially engaged his critical imagination and genius was the critical section. As in his Preface to his Shakespeare edition, in these biographies he took the reader into a more complex and discriminating critical study of literature than had ever before been attempted. This was not the work of an industrious commentator or editor but the fruit of a penetrating, enquiring, iconoclastic critic. It is putting it mildly to say that his readers did not always agree with his critical judgement, but he forced them to reason and to think about literature in ways that very few people were accustomed to doing with the existing English literary canon. In short, again, instead of literary fashion his endlessly flexible but pragmatic compass guided him to consider whether poetry conforms to 'truth' and the centrality of life. If he felt it did not, typically he was brisk and uncompromising in telling the reader forcibly why not, often exaggerating (as in conversation) to make his point. That led him to make many unconventional literary judgements which landed him in deep water. This drive to establish his critical principles and then apply them quickly to the experiences of life constituted his powerful voice and stability as a critic. 'To circumscribe poetry by a definition', he wrote in 'Pope', 'will only show the narrowness of the definer.' Literature was not for him a rarefied aspect of human expression but part of ordinary and endlessly complicated life itself; it was another of life's pleasures.[26]

His political bias, evident strongly in 'Milton', 'Waller' and 'Lyttelton', also outraged many. He called Milton 'an acrimonious and surly Republican'; and his contemptuous (and largely inexplicable) dismissal of the Staffordshire Whig George, Baron Lyttelton incurred the disapproval and even wrath of much of London polite society, friends as well as enemies, and notably Elizabeth Montagu and the bluestockings who struck him off their list. He told Mrs Thrale he had already begun 'to tremble for my admission' in Mrs Montagu's new house. 'I doubt I shall never see the inside of it.' Mrs Montagu's anticipated rejection prompted his priceless remark to Boswell: 'Now, Sir, there are people whom one should like very well to drop but would not wish to be dropped by.' His strong religious views also affected his critical judgement, openly in 'Milton', for example, and implicitly in the biographies of 'profane' authors like the Restoration dramatists Thomas Otway and William Congreve. His general view was that 'The ideas of Christian theology are too simple for eloquence, too sacred for fiction, and too majestic for ornament; to recommend them by tropes and figures is to magnify by a concave mirror the sidereal hemisphere.' He censured Milton's wonderful pastoral-Christian poem Lycidas for this reason.[27]

Above all, he did not get himself personally out of the way in many of the Prefaces, either critically, politically, socially or morally. As one commentator has put it, 'The individual, standing in the full shaft of light, is identical with the moving spirit of the whole vast impersonal enterprise.' One of his dominant autobiographical themes is the economic and social distress an author frequently endures. Money and indigence are often themes, as are the slipperiness of reputation and the monster of despair that spectrally haunts the imagination with the realisation that life is ebbing away. Writer's block and the notion that one can write only in a particular place or at a particular time are particular nonsense, he argues in 'Milton': 'The author that thinks himself weather-bound will find . . . that he is only idle or exhausted; but while this notion has possession of the head, it produces the inability which it supposes. Our powers owe much of their energy to our hopes . . . When success seems attainable, diligence is enforced; but when it is admitted that the faculties are suppressed by a cross wind, or a cloudy sky, the day is given up without resistance.'[28]

There were other hazards of authorship he understood intimately. Explaining why Pope took five years to translate the Iliad, he wrote feelingly about the rival claims of art and life and the folly of self-deluding deadlines to projects agreed to in the sunshine of early hope. He drew on his painful recollections of a career full of delays:

It is natural to suppose, that as much as has been done today may be done tomorrow; but on the morrow some difficulty emerges, or some external impediment obstructs. Indolence, interruption, business, and pleasure, all take their turns of retardation; and every long work is lengthened by a thousand causes that can, and ten thousand that cannot, be recounted . . . He that runs against time, has an antagonist not subject to casualties.

Pope was equal to such challenges. Addison sometimes was not and turned to the bottle. Johnson, who dedicated much of his life to avoiding wine and talking of its dangers, as well as to the use of conversation to resist loneliness and melancholia, wrote about Addison: 'From the coffee-house he went again to a tavern, where he often sat late, and drank too much wine. In the bottle, discontent seeks for comfort, cowardice for courage, and bashfulness for confidence . . . He that feels oppression from the presence of those to whom he knows himself superior, will desire to set loose his powers of conversation; and who, that ever asked succour from Bacchus, was able to preserve himself from being enslaved by his auxiliary?' Nor could Addison, any more than anyone else, control the vicissitudes of reputation: 'Time quickly puts an end to artificial and accidental fame . . . Every name which kindness or interest once raised too high is in danger lest the next age should by the vengeance of criticism sink it in the same proportion.' This turned out to be one of the major themes of the *Lives* – it was the old, persistent theme of the vanity of human wishes.[29]

9

The years 1778 to 1780 were difficult for the Thrales. Even as he continued to rely on them for support and comfort and threw himself into the *Lives of the Poets*, Johnson entered completely into their troubles. In spite of the help of friends and able assistants and managers, Thrale had been mismanaging his brewery business largely by brewing too much beer. He had also eaten up capital in 1777 on lavish improvements to Streatham instead of investing it in the business. Inevitably, in April 1778 there was a financial crisis. 'Here is a new agony,' Mrs Thrale bitterly complained to Johnson, 'my master dispirited and almost in despair about pecuniary matters . . . looks like death . . . and is likely to die himself instead of me'. She and others had to scramble to round up some money quickly to stave off bankruptcy. Thrale's melancholic moods were also vexing his wife as much as ever, making her feel ignored and unwanted. 'All sorrow that lasts longer than its cause is morbid, and should be shaken off as an attack of melancholy, as the forerunner of a greater evil than poverty or pain,' Johnson warned them. Not until November was Thrale better. This time the black dog had 'gnawed him to the bone', Johnson gloomily observed. The next time the dog was likely 'to pick my master's heart out'. Thrale's heart was indeed attacked but not by the dog. In June 1779, he had a severe stroke from which he recovered quickly but without ever regaining his strength completely. Johnson's advice to Mrs Thrale was to keep her husband 'cheerful' and herself 'airy' – 'be a funny little thing'. For months afterwards Johnson offered advice to Thrale on exercise, diet and mood to prevent another attack. Another cruel blow to Mrs Thrale was a miscarriage on 10 August 1779, 'in the utmost agony before they could get me into bed, after fainting five times'. Then the roof more or less fell in at the general election of September 1780, in the wake of a severe economic recession in 1779, when Thrale lost his Southwark seat in Parliament. 'Mr Thrale's loss of health has lost him the election,' Johnson reported to Boswell. From that moment, Thrale deteriorated rapidly.[30]

Then in June 1780, six days of violent civil unrest known as the Gordon riots did not help anyone's frame of mind, least of all the Thrales'. The Catholic Relief Act of 1778, freeing Catholics from restrictions on land ownership and inheritance, lay behind it. Lord George Gordon led a procession of fifty thousand people from Southwark to Westminster to call for a repeal, but inevitably the crowd turned hostile, attacking and burning the homes of prominent politicians and judges thought to be responsible for the Act, most sensationally Lord Mansfield's, even burning his possessions in the street. The mob targeted Catholic residences and businesses and opened all the major prisons and released prisoners, a chilling anticipation of the storming of the Bastille in Paris nine years later. They also set fire to the prisons, the flames of Newgate rising high into the sky. London had not seen fires like this since the Great Fire of 1666, as Johnson reported to the Thrales in Bath: 'At night they set fire to the Fleet [prison], and to the King's Bench [in Southwark], and I know not how many other places; you might see the glare of conflagration fill the sky from many parts. Some people were threatened, Mr Strahan moved what he could, and advised me to take care of myself. Such a time of terror you have been happy in not seeing.' The Thrales were terrified by his account and what they heard from their own sources because their brewery was in immediate danger. Had it not been for the courage of their manager John Perkins, who spoke to the rioters and offered them free beer, they probably would have burned it down as well. The episode marked a low point in the Thrales' roller coaster fortunes of recent years.[31]

Whatever elation Johnson may have felt on completing his *Prefaces* at the end of 1780 was checked suddenly in April 1781 by Henry Thrale's death at the age of fifty-two. Johnson was with him in his last hours: 'I felt almost the last flutter of his pulse, and looked for the last time upon the face that for fifteen years had never been turned upon me but with respect or benignity. Farewell.' Johnson urged Mrs Thrale to hold on to the brewery and manage it herself for a salary of a maximum of about £2,000 per year (about £200,000 today) – and he would help her. This did not seem like much to her. Before her husband's death, she had written on 29 January 1781, 'Mr Thrale *may* die, and not leave me sufficient to keep Streatham open as it has been kept, and I shall hate to live in it with more thought about expenses than I have done.' It was likely, she guessed, she would have to say 'farewell [to] pretty Streatham, where I have spent many a merry hour, and many a sad one'. On the strong advice of her husband's executors, however, within two months she had sold the brewery to Perkins and the Barclay family for £135,000 (about thirteen million today). Instead of income from the brewery, therefore, she would live on the interest from £30,000 (her portion of the sale proceeds), somewhat more than the projected brewery income; she also had both the Streatham and Southwark houses, and all the furniture in each. The rest of the sale proceeds would be held in trust for the children. Under Perkins, to whom she generously and out of gratitude gave the Southwark house and all the furniture in it, the brewery prospered, but in light of the manner in which she was accustomed to living her own finances were now cramped and she would have to take in her sails. Life now at Streatham would never be the same for Johnson.[32]

CHAPTER 31

Losing Ground

I

THRALE'S DEATH WAS A SEVERE BLOW to Johnson. He told Mrs Thrale that no death since Tetty's 'has ever oppressed me like this . . . I am afraid of thinking what I have lost'. 'I never had such a friend.' The loss signalled a changed world for him. 'With him were buried many of my hopes and pleasures,' he entered into his diary for Good Friday, 1781. 'I enjoyed his favour for almost a fourth part of my life.' The changes in store for him as a result of Thrale's death were far greater and less pleasing than he anticipated.[1]

Boswell's London visit that spring did not yield as large a crop of Johnson's conversations as did earlier visits, but it was notable for a bawdy *jeu d'esprit* he composed at Reynolds's house, *Ode by Dr Samuel Johnson to Mrs Thrale Upon Their Supposed Approaching Nuptials*. That he wrote it eight days after Thrale's death and only one after his funeral seems a supreme instance of bad taste. Since the song had Johnson saying to his 'dearest darling' that he was her 'slave', that Tetty 'no longer shall be prais'd', and that now Thrale was in his grave he was rescued from 'lonely gloom' in the 'Blissful Bower' by an 'aphrodisian spasm' with 'our limbs entwin'd/And lip in rapture glued to lip', it is not surprising that for months he was terrified lest either should learn of it. While Johnson never did, Mrs Thrale read it for the first time in the *Life*, never suspecting Boswell wrote it. For the sake of a bawdy song, Boswell was registering what he feared and enabling himself to laugh about it. Hawkins's daughter Letitia summed it up: 'On the death of Mr Thrale it was concluded by some that he would marry the widow; by others that he would entirely take up his residence in her house, which resembling the situation of many other learned men, would have been nothing extraordinary or censurable.' But on Hawkins's wife asking him if he was going to join Mrs Thrale at Bath, Johnson 'roared out', 'I know nothing of Mrs Thrale', and stormed out of their house. In Johnson's own house and well out of his hearing, his good friend William Scott (one of his executors) and Boswell 'agreed that it was possible Mrs Thrale might marry Dr Johnson, and we . . . wished it much' – a notion that anyone familiar enough with Mrs Thrale's heart and mind would have found ludicrous.[2]

2

After Thrale's death, the family at first picked up the pieces well enough to restore life at Streatham through the summer of 1781 with a pleasing routine and some semblance of happiness, with Johnson there almost constantly now that he had completed the *Lives*. He urged Mrs Thrale to put grief behind her, 'the world is all before us . . . I hope we shall never lose the kindness which has grown up between us'. He continued to instruct Queeney and occasionally Fanny (who spent most of the summer at Streatham) in Latin, and the children kept at their harpsichord lessons with Dr Burney. There was a relatively new figure present – another Italian besides Baretti – the singer and composer Gabriel Piozzi who taught the girls singing and encouraged them to translate Italian poetry. Liked by everyone including Johnson, Piozzi was a fixture there until early July when he left for a visit to Italy. Little did Johnson then suspect how Piozzi's presence ultimately would torment him and disrupt others' lives. Piozzi's cheerfulness and helpfulness enveloped Mrs Thrale with a feeling of warmth, consideration and affection that threw Johnson's demanding and critical presence into greater negative relief for her than ever before. She needed uncritical support. Suffering from nervousness, a rash that lasted for the month of September, and depression, she was losing weight and told Johnson, 'I fear I shall never be happy again in this world.' She did not let on to anyone, perhaps not even to herself, but the reason for her unhappiness was Piozzi's absence until late November. It is telling that Boswell's few visits to Streatham in the spring were enough to alert him to the especially warm relationship between her and Piozzi because in his *Ode* he joked that Johnson once saw Piozzi as a rival: 'Piozzi once alarm'd my fears/ . . . Indignant thought to English pride!/That any eye should ever see/Johnson one moment set aside/For Tweedledum and Tweedledee' – that is, for a musical performer.[3]

Having missed Lichfield the previous year, Johnson was determined to go in October 1781. He found Lucy deafer than ever and 'very inarticulate': 'I can scarcely make her understand me, and she can hardly make me understand her. So there are merry doings.' Her health was 'broken' and she ate and exercised little. He was relieved to find, for a change, that Elizabeth Aston's health had not deteriorated and that Mrs Gastrell was 'brisk and lively'. From his tired perspective, time seemed to stand oppressively still in Lichfield: 'All here is gloomy, a faint struggle with the tediousness of time, a doleful confession of present misery, and the approach seen and felt of what is most dreaded and most shunned.' He looked to Boswell and Mrs Thrale for rejuvenation. 'What enjoyment has a sick man visiting the sick?' he asked Boswell. 'Shall we ever have another frolic like our journey to the Hebrides?' And longing for Streatham, he sought to encourage Mrs Thrale with the thought that when he and Piozzi returned 'you will have two about you that love you'.[4]

'Dear Dr Johnson is at last returned,' Mrs Thrale entered in her journal on 17 December, but his appearance shocked her: 'My fear is lest he should grow paralytic, there are really some symptoms already discoverable I think, about the mouth particularly; he will drive the gout away . . . when it comes, and it must go *somewhere*.' More serious, immediately on his return the chronic bronchial infection from which he had suffered intermittently for twenty years became acute and developed into emphysema. Very concerned, over the next five months he wrote a series of letters to Dr Lawrence in Latin – Lawrence always insisted on discussing medical questions in Latin – reciting the symptoms and informing him what he had done and wished to do to alleviate his discomfort. With Lawrence's help, he began bleeding himself at an alarming rate, over fifty ounces in the next ten weeks, sometimes fairly certain it was doing him good, at other times not. His breathing was so difficult he often had to sleep, or try to sleep, sitting up in a chair. The opium he took only subjected him to the 'tyranny of vain imaginations'. It did not help that on 17 January Levet suddenly died at the age of seventy-seven. His 'faithful adherent for thirty years', Levet had been the healthiest person at Bolt Court and now he was gone.[5]

In March and April 1782 he composed an elegy, 'On the Death of Dr Robert Levet', which has been called 'one of the noblest short elegies in the language'.[6] It was published in the August 1783 issue of *The Gentleman's Magazine*. With its moving biographical realism it illustrates Johnson's habitual resistance to vague and conventional eulogy. Levet is no literary paragon of virtue but 'Officious, innocent, sincere/ . . . Obscurely wise, and coarsely kind;/ . . . His virtues walk'd their narrow round'/ . . . Unfelt, uncounted'. The poem celebrates Levet's particular and eccentric mode of charity amid real poverty, the 'power of art without the show', in the faceless London streets where 'hopeless anguish pour'd his groan,/And lonely want retir'd to die'. It is a feeling, soulful tribute to a sincere Christian who aspired to no material rewards. Death 'free'd his soul the nearest way' and his eternal destiny was in no doubt, even if 'letter'd arrogance' may have been inclined to scoff at his 'single talent well employ'd'.[7]

Levet's death did not interrupt Williams and Desmoulins's continued quarrelling, even when they were both ill. 'This little habitation is now but a melancholy place, clouded with the gloom of disease and death,' he moaned in early February. He helped Burney with the conclusion of his *General History of Music*, raved about Fanny Burney's new novel *Cecilia* in the summer, and wrote and edited for Shaw and Lawrence parts of works on which they were engaged; but otherwise there was little in the literary vein to occupy him. He prayed with and instructed Frank in religion and read the Bible regularly, scarcely stirring from home for months except to Mrs Thrale's where, as he recklessly told Malone (who had recently been elected to the Club), 'I can use all the freedom that sickness requires'.[8]

Even the political situation wearied him. The American war had been lost, and when Lord North resigned in March 1782, he prayed in gratitude with Frank. Lord Rockingham's succession elicited only his scorn: 'The men are got in whom I have endeavoured to keep out, but I hope they will do better than their predecessors; it will not be easy to do worse.' Then when Rockingham died in July and Lord Shelburne and Pitt took over, only to be thrown out in February 1783 by a Charles James Fox–Lord North coalition, he threw up his hands in disgust: 'We have now neither power nor peace, neither influence in other nations nor quiet amongst ourselves.' The state of the nation was deplorable: 'I cannot but suffer some pain when I compare the state of this kingdom with that in which we triumphed twenty years ago. I have at least endeavoured to preserve order and support monarchy.' The weakness of George III, however, and the 'tumultous' succession of weak and divided governments appalled him. He longed for the powerful prime ministers of the past. 'I'd as soon have a man break my bones as talk to me of public affairs, internal or external. I have lived to see things all as bad as they can be,' he complained bitterly to Boswell.[9]

Mrs Thrale felt stranded at Streatham as winter came on and decided at the start of the new year to take a house in Harley Street for three months even though she knew it would raise suspicion she was hunting for a husband. At least she was closer to Johnson there and could keep an eye on him. Back in Streatham by mid-April 1782, she had to rescue him from Bolt Court on 11 May, 'so very ill that I thought I should never get him home alive – such spasms on his breath; sure enough one would have believed on Thursday that he could not have lived till now: & old Lawrence his physician worse than he, dead [paralysed] on one side'. Johnson decided to try Oxford for a week or so in June for a 'change of air', but while there his thoughts were mostly on her: 'When I come back to retirement, it will be a great charity in you to let me come back to something else.'[10]

Something else other than what? He had felt her drifting away. Piozzi was to blame. She was restless and looking to the future. He represented the past while Piozzi could take her and her girls away from claustrophobic, gossiping London. She knew she and her family could not continue to live at Streatham on her smaller income, so in August she decided to act.

She would remove the family to Italy, with Piozzi as their courier, where she could live more cheaply and expose the girls to that wonderful culture. Piozzi was behaving 'like an angel' and would follow her anywhere and take care of her. By this time the girls and several friends knew she had fallen completely in love with him, and he with her, though she did not tell Queeney and Fanny Burney plainly until November. She did not tell Johnson even then. She would let Streatham for three years and rent a house in London for the winter. The tricky thing was how 'my monitor, my friend, my inmate, my dear Mr Johnson' would respond. She knew that at seventy-four and in his precarious health he could not come with them.[11]

He had been feeling somewhat better after a few days in Oxford, so one sunny August day at Streatham she decided to tell him about Piozzi, Italy – everything. He had seen this coming but the news was profoundly disturbing for him, especially since it meant he would once again be denied the sight of Italy. He put a brave face on it, however, so brave that she was thrown off balance and imagined herself slighted: 'See the importance of a person to himself! I fancied Mr Johnson could not have existed without me forsooth, as we have now lived together above 18 years, & I have so fondled and waited on him in sickness & in health. Not a bit on't! he feels nothing in parting with me, nothing in the least; but thinks it a prudent scheme, & goes to his book as usual.' It was only her husband he had loved, she thought.[12]

In September 1782, she let Streatham to no less a personage than Lord Shelburne, the Prime Minister, and by early October she was packing. Suffering from a cold and an injury to his leg incurred as he was stepping down from a coach, Johnson attended church at Streatham and bade it goodbye 'with a kiss'. Afterwards, they all met for a final supper in the dining room: 'I took my place in no joyful mood . . . When shall I see Streatham again?' On the evening of 6 October, he sat for the last time in the library, haunted by voices from the past, where portraits of 'Johnsonians' looked down on him. Alone in his room later, he prayed that he 'may with humble and sincere thankfulness remember the comforts and conveniences which I have enjoyed at this place and that I may resign them with holy submission, equally trusting in thy protection when Thou givest and when Thou takest away. Have mercy upon me, O Lord, have mercy upon me'. The next morning they set off early together for a stay in Brighton until 20 November, joined by Fanny Burney a few weeks later. It was a fairly disastrous six weeks. Johnson fell prey to a cold and he was cranky and wounded by Mrs Thrale's lack of attention. Fanny found him embarrassing when they went out – 'I dread him before strangers.' He was so noisy and rude, in fact, that people seldom included him in their invitations. 'I am sorry for it,' Fanny wrote, 'as he hates being alone'. This behaviour of his had been a problem for some time now, and although he was invited to large parties with Mrs Thrale and Fanny, his behaviour and the sting of his tongue, if he was displeased by something like a meal or a remark he disliked, could be offensive. A three-day excursion from Brighton on 8–10 November with Philip Metcalfe, a member of the Club, to Arundel (where 'my breath would not carry me to the old castle'), Chichester (whose cathedral charmed him with 'the final transition from the massive Norman to the lighter Gothic style') and Cowdray House in Midhurst, and then back via Petworth House ('furniture magnificent but chapel . . . gloomy'), Storrington, Steyning and Bramber in West Sussex, restored his spirits somewhat in early November.[13]

Johnson's 'sickly and melancholy year' of 1782 seeped into 1783. Short of breath and in pain from gout in his foot, Johnson began to sleep downstairs in January. By April he was feeling the delicious reprieve of 'a lucid interval': 'The cough goes and comes, but is not violent, I breathe with tolerable freedom, and the pain in my foot is gone. I may perhaps, with a little caution, have an easy summer'. Until she left for Bath, Mrs Thrale rented a house in Argyll Street that served him as a temporary sanctuary. For months London society and the newspapers had buzzed with gossip and indecent squibs about her scandalous love affair with Piozzi, a foreigner far beneath her socially. It was widely suspected that he was after her money. Fanny implored her to reconsider and Queeney (now age nineteen) was cruelly cold and calculating, threatening to set up house for herself and her sisters. The pressure on her was enormous, and finally before leaving for Bath where she could escape the furore, she surrendered, telling poor Piozzi in late January she could not marry him. 'Adieu to all that's dear, to all that's lovely. I am parted from my life, my soul! My Piozzi!' she cried into her journal. Suffering and undemanding, he continued to teach singing to her daughters for two months and finally parted from her 'courageously' on 6 April when the family, except for the two youngest girls (who remained behind to attend a boarding school in Streatham and one of whom died in a few days), left for Bath. The day before this, she also parted from Johnson who was full of compassion. 'I took leave of Mrs Thrale,' he entered into his diary on 5 April 1783, probably with a trembling hand; 'I was much moved. I had some expostulations with her. She said that she was likewise affected.' They never saw each other again.[14]

It was a crushing development aggravated in May when he began to 'languish' again in health, feeling forlorn and lonely. With Levet in his grave and two sick women in the house, he now had nobody to talk to in hours of solitude. When the two women did talk they quarrelled – at least until Mrs Desmoulins surrendered and in May left the house for a year, after which he had only Mrs Williams 'to fight or play with'. The death in June of Lawrence from a stroke, another old friend gone, only added to his loneliness.[15]

With an increased 'steadiness' from having become Laird of Auchinleck on his father's recent death, Boswell again came to his rescue for a couple of months in the spring – 'He is all that he was, and more,' Johnson wrote. Looking pale and breathing with perceptible difficulty, Johnson welcomed him with open arms, 'I am glad you are come. I am very ill . . . You must be as much with me as you can. You have done me good. You cannot think how much better I am since you came in.' They spent Good Friday and Easter Sunday together as usual. The day before leaving London at the end of May, Boswell invited him to make a return visit to Auchinleck, now that he was Laird. 'I cannot come this year,' Johnson answered. 'But when I grow better, as I hope I shall, I should gladly come. I should like to totter about your place, and live mostly on milk, and be taken care of by Mrs Boswell. We are good friends now, are we not?' Then came the supreme compliment that had never been possible while Mrs Thrale was in the ascendancy: 'If I were in distress, there is no man I would come to so soon as you. I should come to you and have a cottage in your park.' But Boswell was also nervous when they parted: 'I got up from him. He took me in his arms, and said with solemn fervour, "God bless you for Jesus Christ's sake" . . . I walked away . . . with agitation and a kind of fearful apprehension of what might happen before I returned'. He had a word with Mrs Williams before he left, who said Johnson had not yet made a will. Less than four months after Boswell's departure it was she who was to die.[16]

Johnson sat for a painting in June, perhaps an ongoing one by Renny which he thought made him look like 'a grimly ghost'. Now at Haverford College in Pennsylvania, it was assumed to be the fifth of him by her brother, finished perhaps in early 1783. It is an intimate portrait of a suffering, ill, asthmatic old man, looking tiredly at the painter, almost as if he is struggling not to fall out of his chair and with his open, pouting lips struggling for breath. It could have been painted only by someone he knew very well – someone for whom he had sat many times before and in his extremity was willing to sit for again. It may have been that the June sitting was for John Opie, a bold and exciting new Cornish genius who became Professor of Painting at the Royal Academy in 1805 and briefly carried on a courtship with Mary Wollstonecraft. He was certainly sitting on 3 September for Opie, whose known portrait shows him solemn and thoughtful but also haggard or ill, in a very bushy powdered wig, slightly stooping, looking out with eyes dim with age, and with lower lip rather pouting. Perhaps because it showed him so weary Johnson remarked it was 'not much admired'.[17]

3

Ever since April 1783 his legs and feet had begun to swell from an excess of watery fluid, an ailment known then as 'the dropsy' and today as oedema, which made it painful for him to walk. The night after sitting for this last portrait, at about three in the morning, he awakened suddenly with 'a confusion and indistinctness in my head which lasted, I suppose, about half a minute'. To test whether or not it was a stroke and had affected his mind, he immediately composed a prayer to God in Latin, discovering to his infinite relief that 'the lines were not very good, but I knew them not to be very good'. However, he also discovered he could not speak. Calmly, he drank 'two drams' of wine 'to rouse the vocal organs' and 'put myself into violent motion', but his speech would not come. He could say 'no' but not 'yes'. He then fell asleep. Thomas Davies felt great pity for him, writing to Mrs Thrale on 18 June: 'Yesterday morning early Dr Johnson was afflicted with a paralytic stroke . . . He is really much to be pitied. He has no female friend in his house that can do him any service on this occasion. Mrs Du Moulin [Desmoulins] has left the house for what cause, I do not know, and I would not ask.' But Johnson did not keep the crisis from Mrs Thrale in a letter that contains many writing errors and corrections, indicating a disorder known as 'dysgraphia' in which a person has difficulty expressing himself coherently in writing. He admitted to her, 'My hand, I knew not why, made wrong letters.' 'Dreadful event!' she wrote in her diary in Bath when she heard of the stroke, 'and I at a distance – poor fellow!'. A few days later he could repeat the Lord's Prayer, confident also that he had not lost any of his memory. Despite his doctors' hideous prescription of putting blisters on his back and throat (to draw noxious humours away), his voice improved steadily in the following weeks, though it was weaker and easily worn out with too much exertion. In July he was able to ride out to Hampstead and attend the Club. It was a narrow and remarkable escape, for which he wrote prayers of thanks.[18]

His diseases were becoming so complicated he decided to begin a regular, informal medical diary for Mrs Thrale, sending her close reports, diagnoses, and accounts of remedies. It makes for morbid reading, as he acknowledged to her, 'You will forgive the gross images which disease must necessarily present . . . The journal now like other journals grows very *dry*, as it is not diversified either by operations or events. Less and less is done . . . The first talk of the sick is commonly of themselves, but if they talk of nothing else, they cannot complain if they are soon left without an audience.' He thought of these letters as medical 'treatises', a sort of trial run for a more serious medical diary or 'Sick-Man's Journal' he was to keep in Latin later.[19]

Another effect of disease and its consequent solitariness was the intensification of his melancholia: 'The black dog I hope always to resist, and in time to drive [out] though I am deprived of almost all those that used to help me . . . When I rise my breakfast is solitary, the black dog waits to share it, from breakfast to dinner he continues barking . . . After dinner what remains but to count the clock, and hope for that sleep which I can scarce expect.' In the morning the whole cycle repeated itself. 'What shall exclude the black dog from a habitation like this? If I were a little richer I would perhaps take some cheerful female into the house.' It was not that he did not receive many callers, but that he could not frequently or easily get out of the house. If he could just feel well enough, he would try to 'change the air frequently this summer'.[20]

He got just that chance in mid-July, taking a two-week excursion to stay with Langton and his family in Rochester. Living with eight spoiled children in a small house does not seem like the perfect prescription for a sick and irritable man, but it turned out to be the best possible cure. The house was airy and full of light, overlooking the Medway and blessed with gentle sea breezes. After the fortnight there he felt better than he had for years. His good health continued through an extreme drought and heat wave and into September, when he accepted an invitation from William Bowles, a new friend from Wiltshire, to visit his estate, Heale House, not far from Salisbury, where Charles II had hidden in disguise for a week in October 1651. The gardens there impressed him perhaps more than any he had ever seen, like the scene of a romance, and he saw Stonehenge for the first time, immediately conceiving theories about its ancient history and function. Like everyone else's at the time, of course, they were incorrect. Salisbury Cathedral also thrilled him and he described the two places as 'the first essay and the last perfection in architecture'. Trying to keep Johnson diverted from his creeping melancholia, Bowles proposed that they take a short journey to Weymouth to see Mrs Thrale, who had gone there for the summer from Bath, but he discovered that Johnson 'had no

great mind to see Mrs Thrale,' undoubtedly because Piozzi had complicated their relationship.[21]

Before he had left for Wiltshire, Mrs Williams's condition had turned
critical, and while he was at Heale House she died on 6 September 1783.
He received the news by messenger on the same day. This was the final increment to his loneliness: 'when I come home I shall return to a desolate
habitation,' he moaned, for Frank and his wife had recently moved out of
Bolt Court. He arrived home on 18 September, 'not well enough to go
much out' and reduced 'to sit, and eat or fast alone' on his birthday. On
15 August he had composed a prayer for her preservation, 'Permit, O
Lord, thy unworthy creature to offer up this prayer for Anna Williams,
now languishing upon her bed, and about to recommend herself to thy
infinite mercy.' Now he wrote another of gratitude for her friendship over
more than thirty years, 'make me to remember, with due thankfulness, the
comforts which I have received from my friendship with Anna Williams.'
His immobility at that point was due to yet another acute physical problem. For some time he had experienced minor discomfort from testicular
swelling, which had grown worse after Rochester and extremely painful at
Heale House. A well-known Plymouth surgeon to whom he wrote about
it in detail recommended an immediate operation, but he waited until he
was home to consult with Dr William Heberden, a distinguished London
physician who had made a particular name for himself by identifying the
difference between chickenpox and smallpox, and two other surgeons,
William Cruikshank and Percival Pott, both of whom prevaricated about
'the fire and sword' of surgery. It turned out to be a 'sarocele' or tumour.
The only solution seemed to be surgery, which at his age, without an an-
aesthetic, was dangerous. A flare-up of his gout delayed the operation, so
in the meantime Cruikshank pierced the testicle to drain it, and gradually
it did drain with the result that its size and pain subsided and it healed
naturally. Johnson thus escaped yet another dangerous medical crisis.
'What a man am I!', he said to Hawkins, 'who have got the better of three
diseases, the palsy, the gout, and the asthma.' He was ready to fight these
illnesses wherever the cures may take him.[22]

Temporary relief in October 1783 enabled him to entertain theatrical celebrities Sarah Siddons and John Philip Kemble for tea, and to engage in a few minor distractions lifting him above the demoralising monotony of his sickness and immobility. One was a hot-air balloon craze that had begun in France in the summer and swept London in the autumn. Horace Walpole was amazed: 'All our views are directed to the air. Balloons occupy senators, philosophers, ladies, everybody.' With his quick scientific curiosity, Johnson considered the chemistry and physics of the invention, but most of all he was interested in its uses: 'If a case could be found at once light and strong a man might mount with his ball, and go whither the winds would carry him . . . The cases which have hitherto been used are apparently defective, for the balls come to the ground.' In spite of having written in *Rasselas* about the dark possibilities of flight, the idea of flying appealed to him psychologically, anchored heavily as he was to earth by his diseased body and destined to grope about with gout. It remained to be seen how soon someone would become airborne in a balloon and sustain a flight for some distance.[23]

Another more substantial diversion he took steps to provide for himself was clubbing. At first he and his old friend John Ryland, both original members of the Ivy Lane Club back in 1749, 'warmed ourselves into a wish' for a reunion and revival of the surviving members of that club. The old meeting-place had shut down and the neighbourhood was now unsavoury, so with Hawkins and the bookseller John Payne, the only other surviving members they could track down, they dined elsewhere in late November. 'One of us thought the other grown very old,' he commented ruefully, and their meeting was 'somewhat tender'. As Hawkins described the evening, 'when we were collected, the thought that we were so few, occasioned some melancholy reflections . . . We dined, and in the evening regaled with coffee'. They broke up early, however, at ten, 'much to the regret of Johnson, who proposed staying; but finding us inclined to separate, he left us with a sigh that seemed to come from his heart, lamenting that he was retiring to solitude and cheerless meditation'. Their idea was to meet once a month, but Johnson's health did not allow more than one further meeting in mid-April when they were 'as cheerful as in former times' except that he 'could not make quite so much noise' because of his weak voice.[24]

In any case, it was better to start a new club with a good membership, so with Brocklesby in December 1783 he founded the Essex Head Club as an alternative to the large, heterogeneous, commercially and professionally based Club with which he was now disaffected. This would be 'a little evening club' meeting three days a week in the Essex Head tavern kept by an old servant of Thrale's in Essex Street, close to home just off the Strand. Johnson specified rules that would ensure the orderly election and more or less regular attendance of its twenty-four members, including an obligatory payment of sixpence per person at each meeting and a fine of twopence for every meeting missed. Anyone who failed to attend for three months would be dropped. Among the members were Brocklesby, Nichols, Murphy, John Hoole, who wrote the most complete account there exists of Johnson's last three weeks and who was one of his most loyal friends in the last few years, the Virginian landowner John Paradise, and the athletic and eminent Whig politician William Windham who since 1778 had also been a member of the Turk's Head Club. Johnson invited Reynolds to join, but as his rival James Barry, who was Professor at the Royal Academy and also painted Johnson (c.1778–80), was also to be a member, he declined. The club was a good idea because Johnson could attend its meetings conveniently in his neighbourhood to escape 'the solitude of the long evenings' at home. The first one was on 8 December, but sadly after that he was 'hindered from attending . . . by want of breath'.[25]

Indeed, want of breath shut him down for four months. 'I am severely crushed by my old spasms,' he moaned near the end of December, which prevented him from getting any sleep at all at night. 'Spiritless, infirm, sleepless, and solitary, looking back with sorrow and forward with terror', he began to take opium copiously. Contrary to Hawkins's assertion that he had begun to take opium 'in large quantities' as early as 1764, he had taken his first opium in 1770 at Oxford for 'rheumatism in the loins'. But always wary of the drug and its dangers of addiction, he never took it heavily until his last months, as he explained to his friend John Ryland:

'When I first began to take opium, my usual dose was three grains, which I found was in the opinion of physicians a great quantity. I know not however that it ever did me harm, for I did not take it often; yet that the demands of my constitution might not increase, I tried to satisfy it with less, and the event is, that I have sometimes attained my purpose of appeasing spasms or abating chilness by half a grain . . . it is by frequent intermissions that so small a dose can preserve its efficacy.' The dropsy came on furiously in January. 'My legs and thighs are very much swollen with water, [with] which I should be content if I could keep there, but I am afraid that it will soon be higher . . . I am extremely afraid of dying.' He longed for a warmer climate like Italy, but with 'a diseased body', no companion, and even with his pension insufficient money for a long trip there was no chance of experiencing this.[26]

What was now beginning was a mighty battle, a warfare against accepting what sometimes seemed like the inevitable. Heberden told him he was all right, and that when the warm weather came he would perspire more and thus the 'watery disease' would at least drain partly away. But he knew Heberden was wrong: 'The sun has looked for five thousand years upon the world to little purpose, if he does not know that a sick man is almost as impatient as a lover.' He took matters into his own hands.[27]

Phrases like 'my physicians endeavour to make me believe' and 'the physicians pertinaciously told me that I was not very near death' indicate he had lost a good deal of faith in them. They tried to convince him, he told Boswell, that 'vernal breezes and summer suns' would help drain his 'half drowned body'. He wanted to believe in them, as he had in the past, but now the stakes were higher and he felt he knew as much or more about his condition than they did, and also how to treat it. On 13 February, for example, he asked Cruikshank to send him 'a large adhesive plaster' fourteen inches long as a 'defensative' (bandage) for his breast and specifying 'Pix Burgundica' (Burgundy pitch) as a healing ointment. On the 17th he commanded him to cut into his thigh 'to drain away the water'. There was something else he did, against the advice of his doctors, that was both dangerous and a potentially powerful remedy. On the 16th or thereabouts he took a very large dose of squill powder – he always believed in large doses of medicine, drastic bleedings, and extreme incisions in his body – a diuretic medicine that was used to regulate the heart and get rid of excessive fluids. After five days of misery when he thought he was going to die, the alarming result of the large unattenuated dosage, he rejoiced that he had 'emitted in about twenty hours, full twenty pints of urine, and the tumor of my body is very much lessened'. This was followed in a day or two by a remarkable recovery. Brocklesby wrote disapprovingly of Johnson's disobedience but also rejoiced in a letter to another doctor that 'every night and morning ever since his [dosage] excretions have surprisingly exceeded his liquids taken in and he is by this time entirely evacuated of all preternatural fluids in his legs and thighs as well as from his chest'.[28]

The dropsy had been vanquished, it seems. It was a divinely bestowed miracle, Johnson thought, following a day's intense prayer and preparation for death. Against Heberden's advice, he also dramatically reduced taking opiates, which were making him delirious. Not having left his house since 13 December, on Easter Day 1784 he took the Sacrament at home. His prayer that day thanked God for his intervention in 'my late deliverance from imminent death'.[29]

Finally on 21 April, after 129 days of being house-bound, he walked over to St Clement's Church to give thanks for his recovery; and on the 24th he showed himself to the public again at the annual exhibition of the Royal Academy where he 'admired nothing but myself' – his ability to walk up all the stairs 'without stopping to rest or to breathe'. He moved briskly with easier 'respiration' than he had known for two years. Brocklesby would not, however, go so far as to allow him to venture out into the chill night air to attend an Essex Head Club meeting. By May he had 'broken loose' into a number of friends' homes for dinners: 'I do not now drive the world about; the world drives or draws me.'[30]

4

Mrs Thrale's health in Bath had been wretched through the winter as a result of her heartbreak over Piozzi. In January the girls had been so concerned over her that they agreed – Queeney especially reluctantly – to call

Piozzi back from Italy. Released as from a spring in a box, she wrote to him frequently during the next few months, promising to marry him and agreeing to live in Italy although she knew it would mean a separation from her children. He agreed to return and marry her. Her health improved overnight and she waited impatiently for him. Johnson simply admonished her on 26 April, 'Settle your thoughts, and control your imagination, and think no more of Hesperian felicity' – a reference to her former desire to live in Italy which he thought had permanently been put to rest. It was he who was not controlling his imagination, however. He knew Piozzi would soon arrive in England but did not assume she would then necessarily marry him. She had been convinced to reject him once and could always send him away again.[31]

In town again in May, Boswell found him 'greatly recovered' and helped take his mind off her. They attended a meeting of the Essex Head Club in which Johnson was in 'fine spirits', and a few days later he was even willing to engage Boswell on whether or not he was rough in conversation. 'And who is the worse for that,' he objected. 'It hurts people of weak nerves,' Boswell replied. 'I know no such weak-nerved people,' Johnson shot back. Hearing Boswell describe this exchange later, Burke could only shake his head, 'It is well if when a man comes to die he has nothing heavier upon his conscience than having been a little rough in conversation.'[32]

Not having been in Oxford for two years, Johnson decided he must go in the first few days of June since he had in Boswell, 'my old fellow traveller', the perfect companion. It would prove to be an inspired decision because in the few days they were there Boswell was able to glean from Adams, with whom they stayed at Pembroke, many recollections of Johnson's early years. There were two particularly emotional discussions he recorded that speak volumes about Johnson's gloomy anxiety about dying soon. One arose when he mentioned his idea of compiling a book of prayers from other sources, adding his own, and prefixing the volume with a discourse on prayer. But he protested vigorously when Adams and Boswell pressed him to do it, 'Do not talk thus of what is so awful. I know not what time GOD will allow me in this world. There are many things which I wish to do.' When Adams persisted, Johnson shouted, 'Let me alone! Let me alone! I am overpowered!' He covered his face with his hands and lowered his head to the table. On another occasion he shocked the company 'with a look of horror, that he was much oppressed by the fear of death', adding dismally that he was convinced he was 'one of those who shall be damned'. Asked what he meant by damned, he replied, 'Sent to Hell, Sir, and punished everlastingly.' Boswell felt this was another instance of Johnson's melancholia surfacing in conversation. When the others present contradicted him, in 'gloomy agitation' he shouted them down, 'I'll have no more on't.' He maintained that life was definitely more miserable than happy: 'I would not lead my life over again though an archangel should request it'.[33]

At Oxford he began again to take squills and sleep poorly, once or twice in a chair because he was too hot and sleepless in bed. Back in London on 16 June, his breathing became difficult and his sleep fitful. The dropsy also was 'watching an opportunity to return'. Boswell proposed to him they travel north together as far as Ashbourne, and Johnson liked the idea – 'I love to travel with him,' he remarked – but Taylor was doing repairs to his house and could not have him. Hearing him more than once express a fear of the coming winter and wistfully express a wish to go to Italy to avoid it, unknown to him Boswell and a few others at Paoli's a few days later hatched a plan to try to get him there. They decided the ideal companion for him would be his Italian friend Francesco Sastres, the teacher and writer, who had settled in London in 1777 and was a member of the Essex Head Club. For such a trip, Johnson would need an increase in his pension, about which, after consulting Reynolds and just before leaving for Scotland on 2 July, Boswell wrote to Edward Thurlow the Lord Chancellor. On the strength of Thurlow's encouraging reply and promise to take the matter up with the King, Reynolds thought Boswell should now tell Johnson about the plan. Johnson's eyes filled with tears as he heard Boswell describe the scheme. 'God bless you all,' he exclaimed. Boswell, too, shed tears. After a few minutes of silence during which neither was able to speak, Johnson quickly left the room to recover his composure, returning a few minutes later. They agreed to dine quietly with Reynolds the next day and then Boswell promptly left Bolt Court, not knowing it was for the last time ever – 'I never was again under that roof which I had so long reverenced.'[34]

At their 'friendly confidential dinner' the next day, Johnson allowed himself to indulge in thoughts of additional money, either a doubling of his pension or a single payment that would enable him to live in 'splendour' before he died. Reynolds and Boswell tempted his imagination with scenes of happy and sunny Italy. 'Nay,' he said, 'I must not expect that. Were I going to Italy to see fine pictures, like Sir Joshua, or to run after women, like Boswell, I might to be sure have pleasure in Italy. But when a man goes to Italy merely to feel how he breathes the air, he can enjoy very little.' Afterwards, Reynolds's coach took him and Boswell to Bolt Court for what would prove to be their final parting. Boswell described the scene vividly in his journal: 'When we came to the entry of Bolt Court, he asked me if I would not go in with him. I declined it from an apprehension that my spirits would sink. We bade adieu to each other affectionately in the carriage. When he had got down upon the foot-pavement, he called out, "Fare you well!" and without looking back sprung away with a kind of pathetic briskness . . . which seemed to indicate a struggle to conceal uneasiness, and was to me a foreboding of our long, long separation.'[35]

Cruelly, Italy again was not to be. In September Johnson heard the King had decided against an increase of his pension. Thurlow instead offered a mortgage on the pension, but in a letter to him Johnson declined, adding somewhat bitterly that he had not expected to hear a refusal but that since he had not had time to 'brood hope' nor 'rioted in imaginary opulence, this cold reception has been scarce a disappointment'. It was, of course, a huge disappointment, the final nail in the coffin of a lifetime of Italian dreams.[36]

On 6 July 1784 he began his 'Sick-Man's Journal', which for four months recorded the return of his ailments. But a couple of days before Boswell left he suffered a more devastating blow to his peace of mind than anything asthma, dropsy and a multitude of other diseases could inflict on him. On 30 June Mrs Thrale had sent him and the children's other guardians an announcement that she was about to marry Piozzi, who was just then arriving in Bath to claim her. Queeney confirmed the news from

Brighton, to which she and her sisters had fled before Piozzi arrived. The Thrale family had in effect disintegrated. Before her marriage she wrote Johnson a note asking for 'pardon for concealing from you a connection which you must have heard of by many, but I suppose never believed', and declaring that all was 'irrevocably settled'. His reply was brutally stern, 'If I interpret your letter right you are ignominiously married, if it is yet undone, let us once talk together. If you have abandoned your children and your religion, God forgive your wickedness; if you have forfeited your fame, and your country, may your folly do no further mischief.' Regretting his harshness, six days later he 'breathe[d] out one sigh more of tenderness perhaps useless, but at least sincerely'. He was ready to contribute to her happiness in repayment 'for that kindness which soothed twenty years of a life radically wretched'. Thinking of the children, he implored her to persuade Piozzi to settle down with her in England, where she could live a more dignified and secure life: 'only some phantoms of imagination seduce you to Italy'. What she wanted almost as much as Piozzi himself, however, was to leave England. 'My heart rejoiced when I saw the shores of England receding from my view,' she wrote after they left the country in early September.[37]

There was bitter irony for him in the knowledge that she was departing for Italy's 'softer climate' with Piozzi while at least twice he had been denied the thrill of visiting the country with her and Thrale – an irony that deepened when the King closed the Italian door for him in September. 'The tears stand in my eyes,' he concluded, barely able to write more. London society did not shed tears; it was horrified by the marriage. Apart from the widespread hostile coverage of the marriage in the papers, Fanny Burney was numbed and Elizabeth Montagu said what many were thinking: 'I am, myself convinced that the poor woman is mad . . . I bring in my verdict [of] lunacy in this affair.' As for Johnson himself, he was done with her: 'If I meet with one of her letters, I burn it instantly. I have burnt all I can find. I never speak of her, and I desire never to hear of her more.' That was not entirely true, for he spared many of her letters from his bonfire.[38]

After seeing to it that his inscription would at long last be carved on Tetty's stone in Bromley, Johnson left for Staffordshire on 13 July 'in hope of air from the country' but mostly in pursuit of the comfort and peace to be gained from feeling secure at home with Lucy and friends in his native countryside. He was away over four months. From distant London he heard of the first successful balloon ascent in England by Vincenzo Lunardi which travelled twenty-four miles, and that Reynolds had been appointed Painter to the King, having against his inclination asked for the position. He also wrote the Dedication for Burney's *Commemoration of Handel*. The single, meagre recreation he enjoyed was a visit to Chatsworth again, this time meeting the beautiful, charming Georgiana, the Duchess of Devonshire, who told her mother 'he look'd ill, but, they say, is wonderfully recover'd. He was in great good humour and vastly entertaining tho' his first début was dry . . . the Duke took him under the lime trees'. Other than that, he was a sick man contriving desperately to do anything he could to get better, writing to numerous correspondents about little else than the progress of his health and his self-administered medication – among these were a series of nineteen dreary, morbid and dramatic letters to Brocklesby crammed with medical details. All of this was in addition to the medical journal he was keeping in Latin, recording minutely each day his sleep, bowel movements, urine discharge, and the fluids and drugs he gave himself. It was an obsessive warfare against his asthma and dropsy, what he knew might well be his final battle. He even used military metaphors to describe his medical arsenal: bottles of squill vinegar were among his 'weapons' and squill pills were his 'perfect bullets'. How 'perfect' remained to be seen.[39]

At first his breathing remained difficult and made motion painful, making him feel 'feeble, and very dejected' in spite of opiates, and under the influence of the squills his dropsy ebbed and flowed. 'I struggle hard for life . . . but who can run the race with death?' he told Burney. Then on 13 August he awoke to a wonderful remission of his asthma after giving himself a violent purge and a huge dose of squill, enabling him to move 'with more ease than I have enjoyed for many weeks'. As for the dropsy, it 'rises, though it does not rise very fast'. The remission lasted for weeks during which he seemed convinced that he was making progress, or at least that things were not getting worse. The dropsy completely disappeared. Then suddenly in October he began to complain of losing ground again, moaning to Brocklesby that for the past three weeks he had 'gone backwards'. Wretched nights followed. His dejection was now once more a mighty enemy. He fell prolifically to purges and taking drams of diacodium, numerous grains of opium and an abundance of squills. His breath was short and the water was beginning 'to threaten' again. He spent several nights sleeping in a chair. His strength evaporated – 'God have mercy,' he wrote desperately in the middle of the increasingly ghastly, farcical drama of drugs to which he was subjecting himself. He took so many opiates at one point that he described himself as 'comatose'. Just before leaving Lichfield, he informed Hawkins, 'I am relapsing into the dropsy very fast.' On 8 November 1784 he stopped writing his medical journal.[40]

On his way home he stopped for a last visit with Hector and his sister, and a few days with Adams in Oxford, feeling he was now 'in a right frame of mind' for writing his book on prayers.[41] While he was there his condition worsened dramatically, the dropsy rising aggressively and an increasing sense of helplessness beginning to overwhelm him.

CHAPTER 32

The Last Days

THAT WINTER WAS VERY COLD and severely snowy, just the sort of weather Johnson dreaded and had hoped to avoid by going to Italy. In the next weeks at home, full of pain, he was courageously busy. He carefully adjusted his will at Hawkins's insistence, beginning the enumeration of his legacies with what was for him the most important of all: 'I bequeath to GOD, a soul polluted with many sins, but I hope purified by JESUS CHRIST'. He tried to provide for his relations but was disappointed in being unable to discover enough about how and where they were. He left most money – a greater amount than he was generally thought to have – to Frank, some £1,500, including an annuity of £70 to be paid to him by Langton, which he frittered away in the next few years before moving to Lichfield with his wife where he opened a school in 1797. He died in 1810. Hawkins was irritated about this large bequest to Frank, grumbling something about 'a caveat against ostentatious bounty and favour to negroes'. Johnson also left to Langton £750, to the brewers Barclay and Perkins £300, and to Percy £150 – though nothing to Lucy, who was offended at being left out. He specified that the proceeds from the sale of the Lichfield house should be dispersed among people scarcely known to him, such as his godchildren and the children of the painter Mauritius Lowe. He also left £100 to his 'lunatic' cousin, Elizabeth Herne, for her maintenance at the madhouse in Bethnal Green where he had placed her. His large library was dispersed among his friends. He wrote an epitaph for his father, mother and brother which he asked Richard Greene to see to being engraved on a 'deep, massy and hard' stone to cover their graves. And he had Cadell send a package of his major publications to Adams for the Pembroke library. He gave George Strahan the manuscripts of his prayers for publication.[1]

As we know, in late November or early December, he did the almost unthinkable and burned a mass of his papers, having stated several times that the contemplation of his past filled him with misery, whereas there was hope in the future.

If Johnson's preparations and his seemingly endless talk about the progress of his illness and rapid deterioration comprised early scenes in the drama of his death, his final two weeks in his house and on his deathbed could be seen as a production in which he orchestrated the climactic final act. There was a steady stream of friends coming to Bolt Court to speak to him, including John Hoole, Langton, Reynolds, Burke, Taylor, Fanny and Charles Burney, Steevens, Malone, Sastres, Hawkins, Nichols, George Strahan (to whom he dictated his will on 8/9 December), Windham, John Ryland and John Perkins. To most of these he had memorable things to say, including advice on how to live the rest of their lives. He spoke much of his own life, fears and hopes. The doctors who were chiefly in attendance were Heberden, Brocklesby, Cruikshank and Richard Warren as supporting actors. Among those who saw him regularly as he was dying, Hoole and Hawkins wrote the most extensive accounts. Fanny also entered into her own diary what she saw and heard, as did Windham whose servant was in attendance much of the time and added firsthand observations. Boswell's account at the end of his *Life* is the most dramatic, well-rounded narrative, drawing not only on Hawkins and Hoole but also on a number of people like Sastres and Reynolds whom he asked for reports. The newspapers also carried daily reports of his progress. 'It may be said,' wrote Arthur Murphy, 'the death of Dr Johnson kept the public mind in agitation beyond all former example. No literary character ever excited so much attention; and, when the press has teemed with anecdotes, apothegms, essays, and publications of every kind, what occasion now for a new tract on the same threadbare subject?'

On Sunday, 28 November, Hawkins, who is a reliable witness of what happened in the closing days, wrote:

> I saw him about noon; he was dozing; but waking, he found himself in a circle of his friends. Upon opening his eyes, he said, that the prospect of his dissolution was very terrible to him, and addressed himself to us all, in nearly these words: 'You see the state in which I am; conflicting with bodily pain and mental distraction: while you are in health and strength, labour to do good, and avoid evil, if ever you hope to escape the distress that now oppresses me.' — A little while after, — 'I had, very early in my life, the seeds of goodness in me: I had a love of virtue, and a reverence for religion; and these, I trust, have brought forth in me fruits meet for repentance; and, if I have repented as I ought, I am forgiven. I have, at times, entertained a loathing of sin and of myself, particularly at the beginning of this year, when I had the prospect of death before me; and this has not abated when my fears of death have been less; and, at these times, I have had such rays of hope shot into my soul, as have almost persuaded me, that I am in a state of reconciliation with God.'

The following Sunday was even more dramatic as Johnson felt even more severely the inexorable end. Hawkins again tells what happened: 'I communicated with him and Mr Langton, and other of his friends, as many as nearly filled the room. Mr Strahan, who was constant in his attendance on him throughout his illness, performed the office. Previous to reading the exhortation, Johnson knelt, and with a degree of fervour that I had never been witness to before, uttered [a] most eloquent and energetic prayer.'

He was now suddenly grown so weak, unable even to kneel in prayer, Hawkins recalled, 'it was thought necessary that a man should watch with him all night; and one was found in the neighbourhood, who, for half a crown a night, undertook to sit up with, and assist him.' Nonetheless, he was not beyond thinking of where and how his stone would be placed:

'When the man had left the room, he, in the presence and hearing of Mr Strahan and Mr Langton, asked me, where I meant to bury him. I answered, doubtless, in Westminster Abbey: "If", said he, "my executors think it proper to mark the spot of my internment by a stone, let it be so placed as to protect my body from injury." I assured him it would be done. Before my departure, he desired Mr Langton to put into my hands, money to the amount of upwards £100, with a direction to keep it till called for.'

What several of the written accounts of these last days reveal is that the two dominant, opposing keynotes of his mental state during the last weeks of his life were desperation and calm acceptance of God's mercy. His desperation to try anything to survive gradually evolved into some measure of peace about what he realised was his imminent death, but it appears also that his desperation did not cease until very shortly before he died, and that a last frantic clutching at the possibility of life may indeed have hastened his end. He was not about to go gentle into that good night.

Most everyone in the room on that occasion understood that Johnson was repenting that it had taken him so long fully to accept God's grace and trust to his salvation. To do so was to be part of an inherited 'holy dying' tradition in which an eminent person's death could provide a religious example to others. Several witnesses, and in turn Boswell who cited a few of them, contended that several days before his death he had come to terms spiritually with the idea of dying and had resigned himself completely to the peaceful end of his mortal existence. Strahan, for example, from whom Johnson took communion a few days before his death in front of a number of people including Frank, said unequivocally that 'some time' before his death 'all his fears were calmed and absorbed by the prevalence of his faith'; and Boswell's brother David whom Boswell asked to interview Frank Barber, reported Frank's observation that Johnson appeared 'perfectly resigned' and 'seldom or never fretful or out of temper' once he knew his death was near. Boswell added that after Johnson asked Brocklesby to tell him plainly whether he thought he could recover and was told not without a miracle, he announced, 'Then . . . I will take no more physic, not even my opiates; for I have prayed that I may render up my soul to God unclouded.' It was also consistent with this view of his own death that in the middle of all the suffering he could still counsel Hoole regarding religion, repeatedly call his guests to his room for prayers by his bedside, bless a number of them, and admonish others regarding their future behaviour to remember 'that life is short, and that eternity never ends'. There is little reason to doubt that when the end finally came he was at peace, although the holy tradition these witnesses all hoped Johnson's manner of dying would illustrate may have prejudiced their comments somewhat.[2]

But it is unclear how soon before Johnson died he came to such a strong faith or 'conversion' that the afterlife would not, as he had feared all his life, hold any terrors for him. Whenever that was, it is at least clear that he defiantly and frantically, even violently, fought the battle against death. To begin with, he burned his papers, not the act of a man at peace with himself. Brocklesby reported that eight or ten days before he died, 'low and desponding', he cried out to him part of Macbeth's speech that begins with, 'Canst thou not minister to a mind diseas'd?' And when five days before his death John Ryland attempted to comfort him that there was great hope for everyone in the afterlife, Johnson replied quickly, 'Yes, we have hopes given us; but they are conditional, and I know not how far I have fulfilled those conditions.'[3]

What he most definitely did not want to hear were compliments on what a virtuous life he had led. Furthermore, the story Boswell told about his signing off medicine once Brocklesby told him only a miracle would save him, clearly misrepresents what happened since he took plenty of medicine afterwards and resorted to other physical means to recover. Nichols told Boswell that less than a week before his death Johnson had such little fear of the pain of a needed surgical puncture of the revived sarcocele that when Brocklesby began to take his pulse he grabbed his wrist and 'gave him a look of great contempt, and ridiculed the judging of his disorder by the pulse'. Instead, he asked 'if a puncture would not relieve him', and when Brocklesby advised that Cruikshank was the best judge, Johnson shouted, 'How many men in a year die through the timidity of those whom they consult for health! I want length of life, and you fear giving me pain, which I care not for.' Johnson tried to bully Cruikshank, too, when he appeared later, but the surgeon refused to pierce the sarcocele. Then he commanded him to make incisions in his legs to release the pressure of the hateful dropsy. The surgeon was again afraid a 'mortification' might set in from any deep penetration of the knife and was in the process of merely lancing the surface of the legs when Johnson cried out again, 'Deeper, deeper; I will abide the consequence: you are afraid of your reputation but that is nothing to me.' 'I would give one of these legs for a year more of life, I mean of comfortable life, not such as that which I now suffer,' he is supposed to have said.[4]

His truly terrifying and courageous act came on the morning of the last day of his life. From his servant's report, Windham recounted what happened:

> He had compelled Frank to give him a lancet, and had besides concealed in the bed a pair of scissors, and with one or the other of these had scarified himself in three places, two in the left leg, etc. On Mrs Desmoulins making a difficulty of giving him the lancet, he said, 'Don't you, if you have any scruples; but I will compel Frank . . .' He then made the three incisions above mentioned, of which one in the leg [was] not unskilfully made; but the other in the leg was a deep and ugly wound from which, with the others, they suppose him to have lost nearly eight ounces of blood.

Frank told Hawkins that he and the servant seized Johnson's hand when he tried to slip the lancet under the covers and implored him not to do anything rash. He said he would not but he had the lancet and seconds later they saw his arm move under the covers. They immediately pulled the covers off and saw 'a great effusion of blood, which soon stopped'. Soon after that, Johnson took scissors and 'plunged them deep in the calf of each leg'. He was so convinced dropsy was the root of most of his illness that he was determined to do anything in his power to get rid of it.

'He looked upon himself as a bloated carcass; and, to attain the power of easy respiration, would have undergone any degree of temporary pain,' Hawkins wrote. 'He dreaded neither punctures nor incisions.' If that butchering of his own body did not hasten his death, the experimental drug, digitalis, which he was given that last day in a major overdose, did.[5]

Boswell chose not to say anything about this self-mutilation, perhaps again because he did not trust Hawkins as a source or because he did not wish to conclude his biography on the note of Johnson's mental and physical turmoil at the end. Hawkins had no reservations: 'Many persons have appeared possessed of more serenity of mind in this awful scene . . . it may be deemed a discouragement from the severe practice of religion, that Dr Johnson, whose whole life was a preparation for his death, and a conflict with natural infirmity, was disturbed with terror at the prospect of the grave.'[6]

The final high drama of the death scene occurred on 13 December. Johnson slept for most of the day, taking some milk which he complained had not been given to him properly, and blessing a Miss Morris who had come in off the street totally unexpected to receive his benediction, but otherwise speaking to nobody. Nobody spoke to him because he seemed in a type of doze, breathing in short, regular breaths. Shortly after seven in the evening he took his last breath, awakening from his doze (according to Hawkins) just seconds before to say to Sastres, 'iam moriturus' ('now I am about to die').[7]

Hamilton said of Johnson what all the Johnsonians felt when it sank in that they no longer had with them the literary colossus who had touched and altered English life and the literary landscape so considerably in the last half of the century as well as their own lives in deeply personal ways: 'He has made a chasm, which not only nothing can fill up, but which nothing has a tendency to fill up. – Johnson is dead. – Let us go to the next best: – there is nobody; – no man can be said to put you in mind of Johnson.' Up in Scotland, Boswell heard of his death on the 17th and in his numbness could bring himself to write only the following in his journal: 'I was stunned and in a kind of amaze . . . I did not shed tears. I was not tenderly affected. My feeling was just one large expanse of stupour.'

'His death made a kind of era in literature,' remarked Hannah More. It was hard to believe that such a life had finally ended. John Hoole wrote of 'the most awful sight of Dr Johnson laid out on his bed, without life!'[8]

A sermon on his death was preached in St Mary's, Oxford, and there were numerous obituaries, the longest by Langton. Malone and Reynolds saw to it that a monument was raised in his honour beneath the dome of St Paul's Cathedral – unveiled in 1796. The critics had their innings, which made one observer remark, 'Ay, now that the old lion is dead, every ass thinks he may kick at him.' In 1786 Mrs Thrale published her *Anecdotes* that infuriated the Johnsonians, especially Boswell and Malone, and in 1788 she came out with an edition of her correspondence with Johnson. In 1787 the industrious Hawkins produced the first complete edition of Johnson's works, in which he included his *Life*, also the first complete biography to appear. Boswell was hard at work on his but would not be rushed. His *Tour to the Hebrides* appeared in 1785 and his monumental *Life* not until 1791, the year that Thomas Paine published *The Rights of Man*, William Wordsworth began his travels in revolutionary France, and William Wilberforce succeeded in having his motion for the abolition of the slave trade passed in the House of Commons. A new age was dawning as Boswell published his coda on one that was ending.

As for Johnson's funeral in Westminster Abbey on 20 December, it was a huge disappointment, even a scandal. As one of Johnson's executors, Hawkins saw to arranging it with the Abbey and chose the cheaper service without music because, as he put it, Johnson had little sensitivity to music anyway. The entire service proceeded without the sound of the organ or voices of the choristers. Moreover, the service was conducted by Taylor, a prebendary of Westminster, who delivered the sermon in a conspicuously lacklustre way, much as he had delivered the sermons Johnson had written for him, offending just about all of Johnson's friends. As Dr Burney wrote the day after the funeral, 'The executor, Sir John Hawkins, did not manage things well, for there was no anthem, or choir service performed – no lesson – but merely what is read over every old woman that is buried by the parish . . . Dr Taylor read the service – but so-so.' All the members of the Club who were in town attended, from whose ranks the pallbearers were drawn: Joseph Banks, Burke, Charles Bunbury, George Colman, Langton and Windham. They deposited the lead coffin in Poet's Corner, not far from Goldsmith's memorial slab and Garrick's grave at the foot of the famous Shakespeare monument. In his biographical memoir of Johnson published soon after his death, his friend Thomas Tyers wrote, 'Who should have thought that Garrick and Johnson would have their last sleep together.' An inscription was placed over the grave stating simply his name, degree, death date and age. When he was told days before his death that he was going to be buried in the Abbey, he replied simply, 'place a stone over my grave that my remains may not be disturbed'.[9]

NOTES

BIBLIOGRAPHY

ACKNOWLEDGEMENTS

INDEX

Notes

ABBREVIATIONS
Writings of Johnson

(1) Yale Works:

The Yale Edition of the Works of Samuel Johnson, 15 vols, 1958 onwards (not consecutive volumes because not all have been published)

Diaries	*Diaries, Prayers, and Annals*, ed. E.L. McAdam, Jr, with Donald and Mary Hyde, vol. I (1958)
Adventurer and Idler	*The Idler and The Adventurer* (ed. W.J. Bate, John M. Bullitt and L.F. Powell), in *Works*, vol. II (1963)
Rambler	*The Rambler* (ed. W.J. Bate and Albrecht B. Strauss), vols III–V (1969)
Poems	*Poems*, ed. E.L. McAdam, Jr, with George Milne, vol. VI (1964)
Johnson on Shakespeare	*Johnson on Shakespeare*, ed. Arthur Sherbo (with an introduction by Bertrand A. Bronson) vols VII and VIII (1968)
Journey	*A Journey to the Western Islands of Scotland*, ed. Mary Lascelles, vol. IX (1971)

Political Writings	*Political Writings*, ed. Donald Greene, vol. X (1977)
Sermons	*Sermons*, ed. Jean Hagstrum and James Gray, vol. XIV (1978)
Voyage to Abyssinia	*A Voyage to Abyssinia*, ed. Joel J. Gold, vol. XV (1985)
Rasselas and Other Tales	*Rasselas and Other Tales*, ed. Gwin J. Kolb, vol. XVI (1990)
Commentary on Pope	*A Commentary on Mr Pope's Principles of Morality, Or Essay on Man (A Translation from the French)*, ed. O.M. Brack, vol. XVII (2005)
Johnson on the English Language	*Johnson on the English Language*, ed. Gwin J. Kolb and Robert DeMaria, Jr, vol. XVIII (1990)

(2) Other Johnson editions:

Early Biographical Writings	David Fleeman, *The Early Biographical Writings of Samuel Johnson* (1973)
Journey	Samuel Johnson, *A Journey to the Western Islands of Scotland*, ed. J.D. Fleeman (1985)
Letters	*The Letters of Samuel Johnson*, ed. Bruce Redford (5 vols, 1994)
Lives of the Poets	*The Lives of the Most Eminent English Poets*, ed. Roger Lonsdale (4 vols, 2006)

Editions, Biographies and Critical Writings

AJ	*The Age of Johnson: A Scholarly Annual*, edited by Paul Korshin and Jack Lynch, 18 vols (1989–)

Boswell's Journals:

Applause: Boswell	*The Applause of the Jury 1782–17785*, ed. Irma S. Lustig and Frederick A. Pottle (1981)

Defense	*Boswell For the Defence 1769–1774*, ed. William K. Wimsatt, Jr, and Frederick A. Pottle (New York 1959, London 1960)
Extremes	*Boswell in Extremes 1776–1778*, ed. Charles McC. Weis and Frederick A. Pottle (1970)
Hebrides	*Boswell's Journal of a Tour to the Hebrides with Samuel Johnson, LL.D., 1773*, ed. Frederick A. Pottle and Charles H. Bennett (1963)
Laird: Boswell	*Laird of Auchinleck 1778–1782*, ed. Joseph W. Reed and Frederick A. Pottle (1977; rpt. Edinburgh University Press, 1993)
London Journal	*Boswell's London Journal 1762–1763*, ed. Frederick A. Pottle (New York, 1950; London 1951)
Ominous	*The Ominous Years 1774–1776*, ed. Charles Ryskamp and Frederick A. Pottle (1963)
Wife	*Boswell In Search of a Wife 1766–1769*, ed. Frank Brady and Frederick A. Pottle (1957)
Boswell's Notebook	R.B. Adam, *Facsimile of Boswell's Notebook* (1919)
BP	Boswell Papers, Beinecke Rare Book and Manuscript Library, Yale University
Burney's Diary	*The Early Diary of Frances Burney, 1768–1778*, ed. Annie Raine Ellis (2 vols, 1913)
Burney Early Journals and Letters	*The Early Journals and Letters of Fanny Burney (1788–94)* vol. III, ed. Lars E. Troide and Stewart J. Cooke (1994); vol. IV, ed. Betty Rizzo (2003)
CCSJ	*The Cambridge Companion to Samuel Johnson*, ed. Greg Clingham (1997)
Dictionary	David Crystal (ed.), *Dr Johnson's Dictionary* (2005)

Early Biographies	*The Early Biographies of Samuel Johnson*, ed. O.M. Brack, Jr, and Robert E. Kelley (1974)
Fifer	*The Correspondence of James Boswell with Certain Members of the Club*, ed. Charles N. Fifer (1976), Yale Research Editions: Correspondence, vol. III
Fleeman Bibliography	David Fleeman, *A Bibliography of the Works of Samuel Johnson* (2 vols, 2000)
Gleanings	Aleyn Lyell Reade, *Johnsonian Gleanings* (11 vols, 1909–52; reprinted 1968)
Greene Politics	Donald Greene, *The Politics of Samuel Johnson* (1960, 2nd edn 1990)
Hawkins's Life	Sir John Hawkins, *Life of Samuel Johnson, LL.D.* (1787), ed. Bertram H. Davis (1961)
JE	Pat Rogers, *The Samuel Johnson Encyclopedia* (1996)
JM	*Johnsonian Miscellanies*, ed. George Birkbeck Hill (2 vols, 1897)
JRL	Thrale letters, John Rylands Library, University of Manchester
Life	*Boswell's Life of Johnson*, ed. George Birkbeck Hill and L.F. Powell (5 vols, 1934; reprinted 1979)
Murphy's Essay	Arthur Murphy, *Essay on Johnson's Life and Genius* (in *JM*, vol. I)
New Light on Boswell	*New Light on Boswell: Critical and Historical Essays on the Occasion of the Bicentenary of The Life of Johnson*, ed. Greg Clingham (1991)
Nichols Literary Anecdotes	John Nichols, *Literary Anecdotes of the Eighteenth Century*, ed. Colin Chair (1967)

Piozzi Anecdotes	Hester Lynch Piozzi, *Anecdotes of the Late Samuel Johnson, LL.D. during the Last Twenty Years of His Life* (1786), Arthur Sherbo (1974)
Reddick	Allen Reddick, *The Making of Johnson's Dictionary 1746–1773* (1996)
Redford Life	*James Boswell's Life of Johnson: An Edition of the Original Manuscript*, ed. Bruce Redford (Boswell Yale Editions: Life of Johnson, vol. II, 1999)
Shaw's Memoirs	William Shaw, *Memoirs of the Life and Writings of the Late Dr Samuel Johnson* (1785), ed. Arthur Sherbo (1974)
Thraliana	*Thraliana: The Diary of Mrs Hester Lynch Thrale (Later Mrs Piozzi), 1776–1809* (2 vols, 1951)
Waingrow	Marshall Waingrow, *The Correspondence and Other Papers of James Boswell Relating to the Making of the Life of Johnson* (Boswell Yale Editions: Correspondence, vol. 2)
Waingrow Life	*James Boswell's Life of Johnson: An Edition of the Original Manuscript*, ed. Marshall Waingrow (Boswell Yale Editions: Life of Johnson, vol. I (1994), vol. II (1998)
Works	*The Works of Samuel Johnson*, ed. Arthur Murphy (1801), 12 vols

Preface

1. Bloom, *Shakespeare: The Invention of the Human*, p. 227.
2. Frances Reynolds, 'Recollections of Dr Johnson', *JM*, II: 274.
3. Ruskin, *Praeterita and Dilecta* (Everyman, 2005), pp. 198–200.
4. *Life*, IV: 275.

Chapter 1: Anecdotes of Beggary

1. *Letters*, I: 206; BP (C9801), box 20, f. 451.
2. Howard Clayton, *Coaching City: a Glimpse of Georgian Lichfield*, Chapter 1.

3. *Letters*, III: 49, 51, 166; I: 327; IV: 424; *Life*, I: 465; *Letters*, I: 345–6.

4. *Dictionary*, p. 300.

5. See Percy M. Lathwaite, *A History of St Chad's Church* (1938); Revd Thomas Harwood, *History and Antiquities of the Church of Lichfield* (1806); Mary Alden Hopkins, *Dr Johnson's Lichfield* (1952). The earliest history of Lichfield on which later historians have drawn is John Jackson, *History of the City and County of Lichfield* (1795).

6. *Boswell's Journal: Ominous Years*, p. 293; Defoe, *A Tour Thro' the Whole Island of Great Britain* (1724–26), as quoted in the edition by Pat Rogers (1992), p. 144.

7. *Thraliana*, 125.

8. *Diaries*, Piozzi Anecdotes, p. 148.

9. *Piozzi Anecdotes*, p. 163; *Diaries*, p. 66.

10. *Diaries*, p. 20; *Life*, Diaries, p. 6; *Piozzi Anecdotes*, p. 154.

11. *Gleanings*, X: 12–17. I have drawn on this monumental series, published painstakingly and lovingly across a span of more than forty years, for much of the detail about Johnson's early life, relatives, and early friendships in Lichfield, Birmingham and the nearby countryside.

12. *Diaries*, pp. 19–20; *Life*, V: 59–60.

13. *Piozzi Anecdotes*, p. 148; *Life*, I: 35, 37. Reade argues factually against this story in *Gleanings*, III: 14–17, although he documents certain family and other links between Michael Johnson and Elizabeth Blaney. The story first appeared in *The Gentleman's Magazine* (Feb. 1785, p. 100) and then in *Hawkins's Life*, p. 3, from which Boswell got it.

14. *Life*, II: 261; *Gleanings*, X: 2–3.

15. For an approximate idea of the value of contemporary currency, one needs to multiply it by one hundred.

16. *Diaries*, pp. 7–8.

17. The Ford family made the settlement more complicated through the provision of a Trust to be spent on property and any children's education, to which Michael himself was supposed to, but did not, contribute £100 within a year (*Gleanings*, X: 15–16).

18. *Gleanings*, X: 15–20.

19. Frances Reynolds, 'Recollections of Dr Johnson', *JM*, II: 257; *Life*, I: 35; *Piozzi Anecdotes*, p. 148.

Chapter 2: Stepping on the Duckling

1. *Diaries*, p. 3.

2. *Diaries*, pp. 4–5 and notes; *Life*, IV: 210; *Piozzi Anecdotes*, p. 63.

3. *Diaries*, pp. 5–6 and notes. See also *Gleanings*, X: 22. Much has been written about Johnson's poor health, but the reader will benefit from a recent short

summary by Graham Nicholls, "'The general disease of my life': Samuel Johnson and his Health,' in *The Tyranny of Treatment: Samuel Johnson, His Friends and Georgian Medicine*, ed. Natasha McEnroe and Robin Simon (2003). For a more lengthy analysis, see John Wiltshire, *Samuel Johnson in the Medical World* (1991), which deals also with Johnson's developed interest in medicine.

4. *Diaries*, pp. 6–7; *Gleanings*, X: 68–9.

5. *Diaries*, pp. 9–10. I and J were treated as the same letter in the eighteenth century.

6. *Nichols Literary Anecdotes*, p. 524; *Diaries*, pp. 8–9; Marc Bloch, *The Royal Touch: Sacred Monarchy and Scrofula in England and France* (1973).

7. *Diaries*, pp. 8–9; *Piozzi Anecdotes*, p. 63; Clayton, *Coaching City*, p. 19; *Life*, I: 43.

8. *Life*, I: 39. One problem with the story is that Sacheverell's only known visit was when Johnson was one year old. Also, he stopped preaching 1710–13.

9. *Diaries*, p. 10; *Piozzi Anecdotes*, p. 69.

10. *Diaries*, p. 10; F.A. Pottle, *James Boswell: The Earlier Years*, p. 2; *Life*, I: 67.

11. *Life*, I: 40; Charles E. Pierce, Jr., *The Religious Life of Samuel Johnson*, pp. 65–6.

12. *Piozzi Anecdotes*, pp. 63–4.

13. *Piozzi Anecdotes*, pp. 64–5; *Life*, I: 40; *Yale Works: Poems*, p. 54. Boswell's citation of the poem is his *Notebooks* version.

14. *Piozzi Anecdotes*, pp. 62–3; *Rasselas* (line 302), *Yale Works: Poems*, p. 105. Many pages of his *Annals* are missing, however, beginning about the time his brother was born.

15. *Piozzi Anecdotes*, pp. 65, 63; *Life*, IV: 8, n.3, I: 71n.1, II: 408; Johnson's *Observations on Macbeth* (1745), note xx; *Life*, I: 70.

16. *Piozzi Anecdotes*, pp. 66–7.

Chapter 3: Leaping over the Rail

1. *Lives of the Poets*, III: 1.

2. *Life*, I: 43, 39; *Boswell's Notebook*.

3. *The Weekly Journal or British Gazeteer*, 14 April 1716; *Life*, I: 43; *Gleanings*, III: 79–80; Thomas Harwood, *Lichfield*, p. 460; *Life*, I: 67–8.

4. *Life*, IV: 215; *Piozzi Anecdotes*, p. 66. See Pierce, *The Religious Life of Samuel Johnson*, pp. 25–7.

5. For a history of the school, see P. Laithwaite, *A Short History of Lichfield Grammar School* (1925).

6. *Diaries*, pp. 11–17.

7. Ibid.

8. *Diaries*, pp. 19–20.

9. *Life*, I: 44–5.

10. *Diaries*, pp. 17–19.

11. *Diaries*, pp. 22–3.

12. Davies, *Memoirs of the Life of David Garrick, Esq.* (4th edn, 1808), I: 4; *Life*, I: 44.

13. *Life* II: 146, I: 451, 46.

14. *Life*, I: 47; *Letters*, II: 163, 301–2, I:9, 115.

15. John Campbell, *The Lives of the Chief Justices of England. From the Norman Conquest till the Death of Lord Mansfield* (1849), II: 279; BP, Box 71, f. 1454 (C1524); *Life*, IV: 135; *Diaries*, p. 225; *Life*, I: 48.

16. *Hawkins's Life*, p. 4.

17. *Piozzi Anecdotes*, p. 70; *Letters*, II: 297, IV: 372; *Life*, I: 159.

18. *Life*, I: 48; 'On the stream flowing away from the Stowe Mill at Lichfield', trans. John Wain (*Johnson on Johnson*, 1975, p. 21).

19. *JM*, II: 395–6.

20. *Piozzi Anecdotes*, p. 119; *Letters*, IV: 182; *Life*, II: 339; BP, Box 24, f. 567 (C1523).

21. *Yale Works: Poems*, Introduction, pp. xi–xxiv, 3–4.

22. *Piozzi Anecdotes*, pp. 67, 68.

Chapter 4: Two Benefactors

1. *Piozzi Anecdotes*, p. 65.

2. *Letters*, II: 308; *Hawkins's Life*, pp. 268–9. In his Will, Johnson left £200 to 'the representatives of the late William Innys, bookseller'.

3. 'Life of Fenton', *Lives of the Poets*, III: 89; *Life*, III: 348.

4. *Thraliana*, I: 171; *Piozzi Anecdotes*, p. 65.

5. *Letters*, I: 369; *JM*, II: 208–9.

6. *Life*, I: 50.

7. *Poems*, pp. 4–27. Johnson told Mrs. Thrale that when he was sixteen he had made a start at translating Anacreon's verses on a dove, the first Greek verses that struck him when he was a boy. He completed the poem when he was sixty-eight (*Piozzi Anecdotes*, pp. 75–6).

8. BP, box 24, f. 567 (C1524); *Letters*, I: 146.

9. *Hawkins's Life*, p. 5.

10. *Life*, IV: 372–3; *JM*, II: 426–7.

11. *Life*, I: 56–8, 445; *Shaw's Memoirs*, p. 8.

12. *Life*, I: 445. The best analysis of Johnson's reading is by Robert DeMaria, *Samuel Johnson and the Life of Reading* (1997).

13. *Lives of the Poets*, II: 178–9.

14. Ibid.

15. *Greene Politics*, p. 43.

16. *Greene Politics*, pp. 43, 65–6.

17. Cited in M. Ashmun, *The Singing Swan: An Account of Anna Seward and Her Acquaintance with Dr Johnson, Boswell and Others of their Time* (1931).

18. *Life*, I: 82; *JM*, II: 326, 252.

CHAPTER 5: OXFORD: WIELDING A SCHOLAR'S WEAPON

1. *Life*, I: 43.

2. *Correspondence of Alexander Pope*, ed. George Sherburn (1956), I: 430.

3. *Life*, I: 59, 57.

4. *Life*, I: 59–60.

5. *Life*, I: 59–60, 272; *Piozzi Anecdotes*, p. 70; *Waingrow*, p. 162. On 12 July 1786 Adams denied Piozzi's assertion that Johnson ignored most of Jorden's lectures (*Waingrow*, p. 162).

6. See *Gleanings*, V: 33–6.

7. *Life*, I: 79, 61; *Piozzi Anecdotes*, p. 72; *Life*, I: 272.

8. Lawrence Stone, 'The Size and Composition of the Oxford Student Body, 1580–1910', in *The University in Society* (1975), p. 37; *Boswell's Journals: Ominous*, p. 281; *The Correspondence of Gray, Walpole, West & Ashton* (1915), I: 51. For background on Oxford, I have relied on Graham Midgley's *University Life in Eighteenth-Century Oxford* (1996).

9. Richard Graves, *Recollections of some particulars in the Life of the late William Shenstone Esq.* (1788), p. 30 (as quoted in Midgley, p. 66).

10. *Letters*, I: 245. See Lionel Salt, 'Samuel Johnson and His Pembroke College Contemporaries' (unpublished), Pembroke College 2005.

11. *A Plea Against an Order to Inhibit Wine-Cellars* (1734), Bodleian Library, G.A. Oxon. 4 6 (11); *Life*, III: 302–4.

12. Midgley, p. 91; *Life*, I: 273.

13. *Hawkins's Life*, p. 4.

14. *Life*, I: 73–4. See James L. Clifford, *Young Samuel Johnson*, p. 121 and 337 n.26; and *Waingrow*, p. 57, n.10.

15. *Life*, I: 73.

16. *Hawkins's Life*, p. 11; *Life*, II: 153; Goldsmith, *The Present State of Polite Learning*, chapter 13.

17. *Life*, II: 444, 529, and III: 23; *Gleanings*, V: 14–15, 129–35.

18. *Hawkins's Life*, pp. 6–7.

19. *Life*, I: 76–7. Boswell received most of his information about the shoe episode, Taylor's matriculation and the Bateman lectures from Taylor himself, recording them in 'Communications concerning Dr Johnson from the Revd Dr Taylor,' *BP*, box 32, f. 825 (C2641).

20. *Hawkins's Life*, p. 8; *Life*, I: 446.

21. *Life*, I: 446, 70, 57.

22. *Hawkins's Life*, p. 7; *Life*, I: 446, 272, 274 (Warton's testimony).

23. *Diaries*, p. 26; *BP*, box 24, f. 567 (C1524); *Life*, I: 74, 72.

24. See these articles: Donald Greene, 'A Secret Far Dearer to Him Than His Life': Johnson's "Vile Melancholy" Reconsidered', *AJ*, 4 (1991): 1–40; Barry Baldwin, 'The Mysterious Letter "M" in Johnson's Diaries', *AJ*, 6 (1994): 131–45; J.D. Fleeman, 'Johnson's Secret', *AJ*, 6 (1994): 147–9; and Aaron Stavisky, 'Johnson's "Vile Melancholy" Reconsidered Once More', *AJ*, 10 (1998): 1–24.

25. *Life*, I: 71; *Piozzi Anecdotes*, p. 70; *Life*, IV, 399.

26. *Life*, I: 60–62.

27. *BP*, box 24, f. 567 (C1524); George Steevens, *Anecdotes*, *JM*, II: 312–13. Two prose exercises and two poems of Johnson's, both in Latin, survive in the Pembroke College library.

28. *Life*, II: 187; *Hawkins's Life*, p. 1; Revd Luke Tyerman, *Life of Whitefield* (1876), I:19.

29. *Life*, I: 68, IV: 147–8, 215; *Thraliana*, I: 421.

30. *Life*, IV: 94.

31. *BP*, box 32, f. 825 (C2641); Waingrow, p. 185. Under December 1729 in his *Annales* Johnson wrote 'S.J. Oxonio rediit'. See *Gleanings*, V, chapter 4.

32. *Piozzi Anecdotes*, p. 72; *Life*, I: 74; *Letters*, I: 8.

33. *Memoirs of Hannah More*, ed. William Roberts (1834), I: 261–2.

Chapter 6: Horrible Imaginings

1. See Lawrence C. McHenry, Jr, 'Samuel Johnson's tics and gesticulations', *Journal of the History of Notes to Pages 000–000Medicine and Allied Sciences*, 22 (1967), pp. 152–68.

2. *Life*, I: 63–4, 66; *Life*, I: 64; *Hawkins's Life*, p. 273. Donald Greene expressed considerable doubt about the idea of a severely melancholic Johnson who in this period almost lapsed into insanity ('"A Secret Far Dearer to Him Than His Life": Johnson's "Vile Melancholy"', *The Age of Johnson*, IV [1991]: 28–34). Boswell, incidentally, confounded the date of Johnson's abandonment of Oxford, thinking that he returned to the University after the 1729 Christmas holidays and continued there until 1731.

3. MS. *Life*, *BP*; *Poems*, pp. 79–80. See *Life*, I: 92–9 and n.2; *Waingrow*, pp. 80–81, 439 and no. 2, 575–6. The poem was published in Robert Dodsley's *A Collection of Poems* in 1747, and later in the *Gentleman's Magazine* (1768), p. 439.

4. *The Diary of the Right Hon. William Windham* (1866); *Letters*, II: 199.

5. *Poems*, pp. 72–3. The poem was first printed in *The Gentleman's Magazine*, July 1743, p. 378.

6. *Yale Works: Rasselas and Other Tales*, XVI: 150–51.

7. *Hawkins's Life*, p. 9.

8. *Letters*, I: 3.

9. *Yale Works: Poems*, pp. 36, 38–40.

10. *Letters*, I: 3.

11. *Diaries*, pp. 28–30.

12. *Gleanings*, X: 91.

13. Hector to Boswell, 15 July 1786, *BP*, box 4, f. 117 (L637); *Life*, I: 84–5.

14. *Shaw's Memoirs*, p. 10; *Diaries*, p. 30 (translated from Latin); *Shaw's Memoirs*, p. 8.

15. *Life*, I: 148–9; *Yale Works: Poems*, pp. 68–9.

Chapter 7: Stirrings in Birmingham

1. Hector to Boswell, 28 March 1785, *Waingrow*, pp. 85–7 (*BP*, box 71, f. 1454 [C1524]).

2. Darwin cited from *The Age of Johnson*, ed. A.S. Turberville (1965), II: 245; *Boswell's Journal: The Ominous Years*, p. 292; *Life*, II: 464.

3. *Waingrow*, pp. 90–91; *Life*, I: 66.

4. *Letters*, I: 104–6, 107–8 (13 May 1755), 143 (7 October 1756). Roy Porter examined attitudes towards madness at this time in *Mind-Forg'd Manacles: A History of Madness in England from the Restoration to the Regency* (1987).

5. *Life*, I: 87.

6. *Waingrow*, pp. 87–8.

7. Thomas M. Curley, *Samuel Johnson and the Age of Travel* (1976), p. 1.

8. *Life*, I: 85–9. For a background introduction to Lobo and his travel accounts see *Yale Works: Abyssinia*, pp. xxxii–xxxix; *Life*, I: 86.

9. *Waingrow*, p. 88; *Life*, I: 87. See Paul Korshin, 'The Mythology of Johnson's Dictionary', *Anniversary Essays on Johnson's Dictionary*, ed. Jack Lynch and Anne McDermott (2005), pp. 10–23.

10. This background is much indebted to Thomas Curley's first chapter, 'Johnson's Lifetime 1709–1784: The Age of Travel', in *Samuel Johnson and the Age of Travel*, pp. 7–46.

11. *Idler*, no. 97 (23 February 1760), *Yale Works: Adventurer and Idler*, p. 298.

12. *Yale Works: Adventurer and Idler*, pp. 298–300; *Yale Works: Abyssinia*, pp. 3–4.

13. *Yale Works: Abyssinia*, pp. 4–5. See Curley, *Samuel Johnson and the Age of Travel*, p. 24.

14. *Waingrow*, p. 88; *Letters*, II: 310.

15. *Waingrow*, pp. 88–9; *Life*, I: 93–4. Waingrow says he found no evidence that either Johnson or James did not know Mrs Paul (*Waingrow*, p. 89 n.28); nor did he find evidence they did. See *Gleanings*, III: 124n, 164, 177 ff.

16. *Waingrow*, pp. 90–91; *Life*, I: 468.

17. *Diaries*, p. 32.

18. *Life*, I: 90 and n.2, 425; *JM*, II: 8.

19. *Diaries*, p. 33 (including the translation); *Waingrow*, p. 250. See H. W. Liebert, 'Dr Johnson's First Book', *Yale University Library Gazette*, XXV (1950), p. 28.

20. *Letters*, I: 6–7.

Chapter 8: Taking a Wife

1. *Waingrow*, p. 80; *Thraliana*, I: 178.

2. *Life*, I: 94–5 and note 4; *Piozzi Anecdotes*, pp. 157–8.

3. *Life*, I: 95; *Shaw's Memoirs*, p. 11; *Thraliana*, I: 178. I have benefited from Graham Nicholls's thoughts on Johnson and Mrs Porter's relationship as presented in his unpublished lecture about her and Sarah Johnson on 6 October 2004 to the Samuel Johnson Society of Lichfield.

4. *Life*, IV: 395–6; I: 94. See *Gleanings*, X: 108–13.

5. *Gleanings*, X: 111; *Boswell's Notebook*, p. 10.

6. *Life*, I: 98–9, 96. The artist and present whereabouts of the miniature are unknown. The earliest attention drawn to it was in the *Gentleman's Magazine*, LXXXVIII (March 1818), p. 194.

7. *Life*, I: 97; *Gleanings*, X: 104–5; *Letters*, I: 7–8, 10.

8. *Letters*, I: 11–12 and II: 156–7. A more complete version of the educational scheme he sent his cousin is in the *Life*, I: 99–100.

9. *Hawkins's Life*, p. 20; Ian McIntyre, *Garrick* (1999), pp. 22 ff.; Thomas Davies, *Memoirs of the Life of David Garrick, Esq.* (1780, 1808), I: 8; *Life*, II: 377.

10. *Hawkins's Life*, pp. 19–20; *Life*, I: 96, 531 (Appendix G); *Shaw's Memoirs*, p. 11. The letter to Walmesley is in the Pembroke College manuscripts.

11. *Thraliana*, I: 177–8.

12. *Piozzi Anecdotes*, pp. 110–11.

13. *Life*, I: 98–9; *Boswell's Journals: Applause*, p. 111; *Thraliana*, I: 178. See also *Life*, I: 531 and *Piozzi Anecdotes*, pp. 110–11. Edmond Malone thought Garrick's entertainment at Johnson's expense was mostly 'invention' (*Life*, I: 531).

14. *Life*, II: 464–5, I: 82.

15. *Piozzi Anecdotes*, p. 112–13; Anna Seward, *Correspondence*, p. 116; *Thraliana*, I: 538; *Piozzi Anecdotes*, p. 113; *Poems*, p. 43.

16. *Piozzi Anecdotes*, p. 113.
17. *Yale Works: Poems*, pp. 77–8, 82–4.
18. *Diaries*, p. 35; *Life*, II: 121, I: 97–8.
19. *Life*, IV: 407–8 and n.4; *GM* (3 January 1785), LV, i.
20. *Life*, IV: 199, I: 100; *Rambler*, no. 122 (18 May 1751), *Yale Works: Rambler*, pp. 290–91.
21. The MS of the first draft is in the King's Library (British Library). See Bertrand H. Bronson, *Johnson Agonistes and Other Essays* (1965), pp. 100–55. See also Marshall Waingrow, 'The Mighty Moral of *Irene*', *From Sensibility to Romanticism* (1965), ed. F.W. Hilles and Harold Bloom, pp. 79–82.
22. Act II, sc. vii, 55–8 (*Yale Works: Poems*, pp. 147, 148–9, 155).
23. *Life*, I: 101.

CHAPTER 9: STRANGER IN LONDON

1. *Life*, I: 102.
2. *Life*, I: 101, n.1; *BP*, box 31, f. 807 (C2543).
3. *Gleanings*, I: 1; *Life*, I: 229.
4. *Life*, I: 102 n.2.
5. *Life*, I: 105, 103.
6. Liza Picard, *Dr Johnson's London: Life in London 1740–1770* (2000), p. 199; *Johnson's England*, I: 180–81; *Life*, III: 305, 389, 381. *Life*, I: 103, n.3 reviews Johnson's drinking and on slender evidence maintains that Johnson never drank between 1736 to at least as late as 1757.
7. This famous remark about London has sometimes been denied Johnson on the grounds that it is not in Boswell's journal. Although in the *Life* Boswell quoted it for the year 1777, he often did draw on sources he knew from later in Johnson's life (and are therefore not in the daily journals) to illustrate earlier attitudes.
8. *Life*, III: 378–79, IV: 358, III: 178, 246.
9. Peter Ackroyd, *London: A Biography* (2000), 'Violent London' (chapter 52), pp. 477, 482; Boswell, *London Journal*, pp. 74 (11 December 1762), 86–7 (15 December 1762).
10. J.H. Plumb, *England in the Eighteenth Century* (1959), p. 33.
11. Ackroyd, *London: A Biography*, pp. 308–9; Roy Porter, *London: A Social History* (1994), pp. 125, 168ff.
12. Porter, *Enlightenment: Britain and the Creation of the Modern World* (2000), pp. 3, 6, xxiv, 11. See Pat Rogers, *Grub Street* (1972); also Roy Porter's *London: A Social History* (1994), chapters 5, 6, and 7 (pp. 93–184).
13. *Piozzi Anecdotes*, p. 112; *Life*, I: 106, V: 483–84, III: 194–6. On Johnson's sermon

on Charity for Hervey-Aston, no. 27, see *Yale Works: Rasselas and Other Tales*, pp. 287–99.

14. *Diaries*, p. 39; *Life*, I: 460–61.

15. *Letters*, I: 12–13.

CHAPTER 10: SONS OF MISERY:
FINDING RICHARD SAVAGE

1. *Life*, V: 230.

2. There is no firm evidence that Lucy moved in with Sarah Johnson then, but Seward (*Letters*, I: 116) says she 'boarded' with her and several letters in following years argue in favour of that (see *Life*, I: 110, n.3).

3. *Piozzi Anecdotes*, p. 110.

4. Castle Street is now called Eastcastle Street and his house stood partly on the site of what is now the Hotel York.

5. *Life*, I: 111; *Hawkins's Life*, pp. 27–8; letter to Thomas Birch, Birch MSS, BL Add. Ms. 4302; and *BP*, box 57, f. 1206; *Rambler*, no. 188, *Yale Works: Rambler*, p. 221.

6. *Life*, I: 112, III: 322; *Yale Boswell: Poems*, pp. 40–43. See Robert Folkenflik, *Samuel Johnson: Biographer* (1978), pp. 61–3.

7. *Letters*, I: 14–15.

8. *Letters*, I: 15; Jenny Uglow, *Dr Johnson, His Club, and Other Friends*, p. 24.

9. *Letters*, I: 15–16, 16–17; *Life*, I: 124. On this matter of the poem's anonymity, see *Early Career*, p. 20.

10. *Life*, I: 129; *Correspondence of Alexander Pope*, ed. George Sherburn (1956), IV: 194; *Life*, I: 534.

11. *Life*, I: 194; *Diaries*, pp. 37–8.

12. Letter to Birch, Birch MSS., BL Add. Ms. 4302; *BP*, box 57, f. 1206.

13. *Life*, V: 255, I: 159. The most readable source for Savage and his connection to Johnson, although it is not without its factual errors, is Richard Holmes' *Dr Johnson and Mr Savage* (1993), from which the translation of Johnson's epigram on Savage is cited (p. 177). See also *Early Career*, pp. 186–9; and Clarence Tracy, *The Artificial Bastard: A Biography of Richard Savage* (1953).

14. *Correspondence of Alexander Pope*, IV: 431.

15. *Lives of the Poets: Life of Savage*, III: 163. I cite here and below from Johnson's revised version in the *Lives of the Poets*.

16. *Life*, I: 161 n.3. I am indebted for this idea of 'Letter to a Noble Lord' genre to Robert Folkenflik.

17. *Lives of the Poets: Life of Savage*, III: 175, 177, 178; *Correspondence of Alexander Pope*, IV: 392.

18. *Hawkins's Life*, p. 29.

19. See Bertram A. Davis, *A Proof of Eminence: The Life of Sir John Hawkins* (1973) and Holmes, *Dr Johnson and Mr Savage*, chapter 3 ('Night'). The following account of *London* and *The Life of Richard Savage* is (with a few caveats) partly indebted to Holmes' reading of Johnson's anti-authority, satirical, psychologically intense, rebellious persona.

20. *Hawkins's Life*, pp. 29–30.

21. Kaminski, *Early Career*, p. 89.

22. *Yale Works: Poems*, pp. 47–61.

23. *Murphy's Essay*, p. 371. Thomas Kaminski argued against the identification of Thales and Savage in 'Was Savage "Thales"', *Bulletin of Research in the Humanities*, 85 (1982), pp. 322–35; for other views see *Waingrow*, p. 233 and n.6.

24. *Life*, I: 441; *Piozzi Anecdotes*, pp. 88–9, 95.

25. *Rambler*, no. 202, *Yale Works: Rambler*, pp. 287–8.

26. *Letters*, I: 32–3, 35–6.

27. *Letters*, I: 35–6; *Life*, V: 66–7. See J.D. Fleeman, 'The Making of Johnson's *Life of Savage, 1744*, *The Library* 22 (1967).

28. Holmes, *Dr Johnson and Mr Savage*, pp. 353, 351.

29. *Lives of the Poets: Life of Savage*, III: 165.

30. See Folkenflik, *Samuel Johnson: Biographer*, pp. 195–213.

31. *Lives of the Poets: Life of Savage*, III: 172.

32. *Lives of the Poets: Life of Savage*, III: 174.

33. *Lives of the Poets: Life of Savage*, III: 186, 188.

CHAPTER 11: 'SLOW RISES WORTH BY POVERTY DEPRESS'D'

1. *Hawkins's Life*, pp. 26–7; 'Life of Cave', GM (1754), pp. 55–58. There is no complete modern biography of Cave.

2. See John Brewer on eighteenth-century authors, publishers and literary culture in *The Pleasures of the Imagination: English Culture in the Eighteenth Century* (1997) especially section II, chapters 3–4.

3. Alvin Kernan, *Printing Technology, Letters & Samuel Johnson* (1987), pp. 13, 7–8, 16–18.

4. *Adventurer*, No. 115 (11 December 1753), *Yale Works: Adventurer and Idler*, p. 457.

5. Kaminski, *Early Career*, pp. 65–7.

6. *Yale Works: Rambler*, IV: 336.

7. *Letters*, I: 17; Kaminski, *Early Career*, p. 21–2.

8. *Life*, I: 135.

9. *Letters*, I: 126; Pennington, *Memoir*, I: 447; *Life*, I: 139; Pennington, *Memoir*,

p. 26; Kaminski, *Early Career*, pp. 34–40; *Life*, II: 319. See Norma Clarke, *Dr Johnson's Women* (2000), chapter 2.

10. Kaminski, *Early Career*, pp. 42–3.

11. John Nichols, GM (1785), p. 6; *Political Writings*, pp. 11, 16; Kaminski, *Early Career*, pp. 46–49.

12. *Letters*, I: 18–19.

13. William Cullen, *First Lines in the Practice of Physic* (1772), pp. xxxiii; John Wiltshire, *Samuel Johnson in the Medical World*, pp. 75–9; 'Life of Boerhaave', GM, 1739, pp. 37–8, 72–3, 114–16, 172–6.

14. Kaminski, *Early Career*, p. 54; *Life*, IV: 430. See Robert Folkenflik, *Samuel Johnson: Biographer*, pp. 58–62 (and his chapter, 'Johnson's Heroes').

15. *Letters*, I: 20; *A Commentary on Mr Pope's Principles of Morality, or Essay on Man* (1742), p. 123. See Kaminski, *Early Career*, pp. 77–8.

16. Kaminski, *Early Career*, pp. 54–9.

17. *Greene Politics*, pp. 236–42.

18. *Life*, I: 141.

19. *Correspondence of Alexander Pope*, IV: 194; *Hawkins's Life*, p. 41. See Greene, *Political Writings*, pp. 19–51; Kaminski, *Early Career*, pp. 100–1.

20. *Hawkins's Life*, p. 227; *Political Writings*, pp. 63, 72.

21. *Gleanings*, VI, chapter ix.

22. *Waingrow*, p. 58; *Life*, I: 133–4, 373.

23. *Gleanings*, X: 148; Kaminski, *Early Career*, pp. 73–6.

Chapter 12: Wandering in the Midlands

1. *Hawkins's Life*, p. 49; *Shaw's Memoirs*, p. 34; *Life*, IV: 395–6.

2. *Gleanings*, VI: 120; *Letters*, I: 22–4.

3. *Life*, III: 180–81.

4. *Gleanings*, VI: 125; *Life*, I: 82–3, III: 149; *Piozzi Anecdotes*, pp. 113–14.

5. *Letters*, I: 117–18; *Piozzi Anecdotes*, p. 114.

6. *Life*, I: 366, 547. See *Letters*, III: 169 and n.5, 371.

Chapter 13: London Revived: A Lion in Harness

1. *Yale Works: Poems*, p. 67.

2. *Life*, I: 102, n.2. See F.V. Bernard, 'The History of Nadir Shah: A New Attribution to Johnson', *British Museum Quarterly*, 34 (1970), pp. 92–104.

3. On the lives of Drake, Blake and Baratier, see Folkenflik, *Samuel Johnson: Biographer*, p. 99; Curley, *Samuel Johnson and the Age of Travel*, pp. 31–2, 61–4; Rob-

ert DeMaria, Jr, *The Life of Samuel Johnson* (1993), pp. 74–6; and Kaminski, *Early Career*, pp. 110–13.

4. Kaminski, *Early Career*, pp. 116–22.

5. 'Essay on Epitaphs', in *Samuel Johnson*, ed. Donald Greene (Oxford Authors, 1984), p. 101.

6. *Gentleman's Magazine*, XXIII (March 1753): 148; *Life*, IV: 408–9, I: 152.

7. *Murphy's Essay*, pp. 378–80.

8. *Life*, I: 314; *Hawkins's Life*, p. 56. For eloquent analyses of Johnson's method and achievement in the debates, see *Greene Politics*, pp. 112–40, and Kaminski, *Early Career*, chapter vii, on both of which I draw for my discussion.

9. Kaminski, *Early Career*, p. 131.

10. On the debates, see *Greene Politics*, pp. 122–9.

11. Kaminski, *Early Career*, pp. 166–70, 240 n.23, 148–53.

12. *Samuel Johnson*, ed. Greene, pp. 1 13–14; *GM* (1742), p. 634; Folkenflik, *Samuel Johnson: Biographer*, p. 64; Wiltshire, *Samuel Johnson in the Medical World*, pp. 101–2, 80; Kaminski, *Early Career*, pp. 158–61.

13. *GM* (1743), p. 550.

14. Kaminski, *Early Career*, p. 171.

15. *Piozzi Anecdotes*, p. 70.

16. *Letters*, I: 31.

17. *Life*, III: 405; *Letters*, I: 32.

18. *Thraliana*, I: 173; *Life*, I: 159.

19. *Early Biographical Writings*, p. 89; Wiltshire, *Samuel Johnson in the Medical World*, pp. 94, 99–100; *Lives of the Poets*, III: 415; *Life*, III: 355.

20. *Letters*, IV: 372; 'General Account of the Work' [James's *Medicinal Dictionary*] as cited by Wiltshire, *Samuel Johnson in the Medical World*, p. 74.

21. *Life*, I: 154; Kaminski, *Early Career*, pp. 174–84.

22. Osborne to Birch, BL Add. Ms. 4316, f. 98; 'Account of the Harleian Library', in *Samuel Johnson*, ed. Greene, pp. 117–19.

23. 'Account', pp. 117–19; *Hawkins's Life*, pp. 60–61, 63.

24. 'Introduction to the *Harleian Miscellany*', in *Samuel Johnson*, ed. Greene, pp. 123–4. The 'Introduction' is otherwise known as his 'Essay on the Origin and Importance of Small Tracts and Fugitive Pieces'.

25. *Letters*, I: 36, 37–9; *Life*, I: 163n.

26. *Diaries*, pp. 40–41. See *Early Career*, pp. 193–4.

27. *Johnson on Shakespeare*, p. 45.

28. *Johnson on Boswell*, p. xiv.

29. *Life*, I: 318, 134; *Hebrides*, p. 20; *Diaries*, pp. 9–10; *Life*, III: 195. Aleyn Reade contends that Adams's request dates very likely from this period, not in 1738 as Boswell claimed (*Gleanings*, VI: 116).

Chapter 14: A Lifeline: The Dictionary

1. *The Letters of David Garrick*, ed. D.M. Little and G.M. Kahrl, I.
2. *Life*, I: 177.
3. *Life*, I: 182–3; III: 405; *Letters*, I: 40–41.
4. The best comprehensive account of Johnson's work on the *Dictionary* is by Allen Reddick, *The Making of Johnson's Dictionary 1746–1773* (revised edn, 1996), to which I am heavily indebted. More recently, see Henry Hitchings's erudite and entertaining *Dr Johnson's Dictionary: The Extraordinary Story of the Book that Defined the World* (2005).
5. Thomas Carlyle, *Samuel Johnson* (1832, 1853), p. 75. 'It is a stout, old-fashioned, oak-balustrated house', wrote Carlyle.
6. *Piozzi Anecdotes*, p. 88.
7. *Diaries*, p. 134.
8. Jack Lynch has published an edition of selections from the *Dictionary*, with a useful Introduction: *Samuel Johnson's* Dictionary: *Selections from the 1755 Work that Defined the English Language* (2002, 2004). Because it is more widely available I cite from David Crystal's edition, *Dr Johnson's Dictionary* (2005).
9. Reddick, pp. 13–17; Lynch, *Samuel Johnson's Dictionary*, pp. 2–3; Hitchings, *Dr Johnson's Dictionary*, pp. 56–9.
10. Jonathon Green, *Chasing the Sun: Dictionary Makers and the Dictionaries They Made* (1996), p. 211.
11. *Life*, I: 186.
12. On the text of the *Plan*, see Gwin J. Kolb, 'Establishing the Text of Dr Johnson's Dictionary of the English Language', *Eighteenth-Century Studies in Honor of Donald F. Hyde*, ed. W.H. Bond (1970), pp. 81–7.
13. *Life*, I: 183. See Reddick, pp. 19–23; Paul Korshin, 'The Johnson–Chesterfield Relationship: A New Hypothesis', *Publications of the Modern Language Association*, 85 (March 1970); and Howard Weinbrot, 'Samuel Johnson's *Plan* and Preface to the *Dictionary*: The Growth of a Lexicographer's Mind', in *New Aspects of Lexicography*, pp. 73–94.
14. *Life*, I: 332–3.
15. *Dictionary*, pp. 1, 17–18.
16. *Dictionary*, pp. 16, 18.
17. For example, Hitchings, *Dr Johnson's Dictionary*, pp. 67–8. See also Green, *Chasing the Sun*, pp. 22–3, 234.
18. *Dictionary*, pp. 11, 16, 10.
19. Hitchings, *Dr Johnson's Dictionary*, p. 68; *Dictionary*, pp. 11, 15, 16; *Greene Politics*, p. 34; *Dictionary*, pp. 37–8, 29. Lynch agrees that Johnson 'was usually adamant that usage should be determined by consensus, not by fiat' (*Samuel Johnson's Dictionary*, p. 8); see also Robert DeMaria, *The Life of Samuel Johnson*,

p. 115. See also Robert Folkenflik's recent essay, 'The Politics of Johnson's *Dictionary* Revisited', *Age of Johnson*, 18 (2007), pp. 1–17, for a considered view of the controversy.

20. *Dictionary*, pp. 5–7, 16.

21. *Dictionary*, pp. 7–11.

22. *Dictionary*, pp. 12–18.

23. *The Orrery Papers*, ed. the Countess of Cork and Orrery, 2 vols. (1773), II: 43 (August 1747).

24. *Hawkins's Life*, p. 77. See also *Life*, I: 435–6, 328.

25. Hitchings, *Dr Johnson's Dictionary*, p. 60.

26. *Life*, I: 187, 536.

27. *Letters*, IV: 336. See J.D. Fleeman, *A Preliminary Handlist of Documents and Manuscripts of Samuel Johnson* (1967), p. 6, no. 35.

28. *Life*, I: 187, II: 379; *Letters*, II: 207–8; *Life*, III: 421; *Letters*, II: 315.

29. *Yale Works: Rambler*, IV: 286–7.

30. Hitchings, pp. 70–71.

31. *Dictionary*, pp. 32–3; *Life*, IV: 4.

32. Lynch, *Samuel Johnson's Dictionary*, p. 13. See also DeMaria, *Johnson's Dictionary and the Language of Learning* (1986), p. 37.

33. *Dictionary*, p. 32; *Thraliana*, I: 34; Thomas Tyers, *A Biographical Sketch of Dr Samuel Johnson* (1785), in *The Early Biographies of Samuel Johnson*, ed. O.M. Brack, Jr and Robert E. Kelley (1974), p. 82. See Robert Folkenflik, 'The Politics of Johnson's *Dictionary* Revisited', *Age of Johnson*, 18 (2007), pp. 1–17.

34. Green, *Chasing the Sun*, pp. 222–23; Rod Mengham, *The Descent of Language: Writing in Praise of Babel* (London, 1993), p. 113; Hitchings, *Dr Johnson's Dictionary*, p. 103; DeMaria, *The Life of Samuel Johnson*, pp. 122–27.

35. Reddick, pp. 37–41. See Folkenflik, 'The Politics of Johnson's *Dictionary* Revisited', *Age of Johnson*, 18 (2007), pp. 1–17.

36. Reddick, p. 54.

37. Reddick, pp. 42–51. Recently, the results of Reddick's careful reasoning were modified by Anne McDermott's own minutely researched conjectures presented in a lecture, 'How Johnson's *Dictionary* Was Made', at the Pembroke College, Oxford, conference on the *Dictionary* in August 2005. See also her essay, 'Johnson the Prescriptivist? The Case for the Defense', *Anniversary Essays on Johnson's Dictionary*, ed. Jack Lynch and Anne McDermott (2005), pp. 92–112.

CHAPTER 15: POETIC INTERLUDES

1. *Life*, I: 167, 168.

2. *Murphy's Essay*, p. 457.

3. *JM*, II: 318.

4. *JM*, II: 318, 314.

5. 'Prologue Spoken at the Opening of the Theatre in Drury Lane, 1747', *Yale Works: Poems*, pp. 87–90.

6. *Hawkins's Life*, p. 85; *Life*, I: 196.

7. *Life*, I: 200, 201, 196; *Waingrow*, pp. 146–7, 427; *JM*, II: 318. A racier version of Garrick's anecdote (omitted by Boswell) has Johnson referring to 'the white bubbies & the silk stockings' of the actresses that 'excite my genitals' (*Life*, I: 538–39).

8. *Life*, I: 197–8; Murphy's *Essay*, *JM*, I: 387; *Life*, I: 199 and n.2, II: 348–9. See *Waingrow*, pp. 106 and n.45, 22.

9. *Works*, ed. Murphy (1801), II: 236–8.

10. *Yale Works: Rasselas and Other Tales*, pp. 195–212.

11. *Diaries*, p. 41; *Yale Works*, XVI: 202–3, 212.

12. For Johnson's boast, see *Works* (1787), XI: 212; *Life*, II: 15.

13. *Yale Works: Poems*, pp. 90–109.

14. See Howard Weinbrot's insightful essay, 'Johnson's Poetry', in *CCSJ*, pp. 34–50.

15. *Life*, I: 193; Pat Rogers, *The Samuel Johnson Encyclopedia*, p. 410; *Life*, I: 194; Byron, *Works* (1835), V: 66; James Lockhart, *The Life of Sir Walter Scott* (1837–8), II: 307; Bate, *Samuel Johnson*, p. 278. *The Vanity of Human Wishes* appeared in a revised text in Robert Dodsley's *Collection of Poems* in 1755. The complete manuscript of the entire poem in an earlier version is in the Hyde collection at Harvard.

Chapter 16: Tetty and 'Amorous Propensities'

1. *Hawkins's Life*, pp. 105–6.

2. *Hawkins's Life*, pp. 110–11; *Life*, I: 28, n.1 .

3. *Letters*, I: 42.

4. *Diaries*, p. 53; *Life*, IV: 395–6. See Donald and Mary Hyde, 'Dr Johnson's Second Wife', in *New Light on Dr Johnson*, ed. F.W. Hilles (1959), pp. 133–51.

5. *Life*, I: 192 and n.4, 238.

6. *Boswell's Journals: Laird*, pp. 142–3; *Life*, IV: 200; letter from Boswell to Edmond Malone, 10 February 1791, *Waingrow*, p. 384.

7. *Life*, I: 238.

8. *Boswell's Journals: Applause*, pp. 110–13.

9. *Piozzi Anecdotes*, p. 110; *Life*, I: 99.

10. *Shaw's Memoirs*, p. 33; *Thraliana*, I: 178; *Hawkins's Life*, pp. 129–30.

11. *Life*, I: 349; *Dictionary*, p. 167; *Letters*, I: 43–4.

12. *Letters*, I: 43, 45–6.

CHAPTER 17: THE TRIUMPH OF THE MORALIST

1. *Yale Works: Rambler*, III: xxi, xxiii. See Lawrence Lipking, 'Johnson and the Meaning of Life', in *Johnson and His Age*, ed. James Engell (1984), p. 20.

2. *Yale Works: Rambler*, V: 312 (no. 207), 318 (no. 208).

3. *Yale Works: Rambler*, V: 316.

4. *Life*, I: 202; *Yale Works: Rambler*, IV: 204. On the publication and distribution of the essays, see Paul Tankard, 'A Petty Writer: Johnson and the *Rambler* pamphlets', *Age of Johnson*, X (1999), pp. 67–87. See also Introduction, *Yale Works: Rambler*, III: xxvi–xxvii.

5. *Yale Works: Rambler*, IV: 345–46; *Piozzi Anecdotes*, p. 76. Johnson was not as unprepared as he made out. Boswell tells that he had in his possession a commonplace book in which he wrote 'a variety of hints for essays on different subjects' (*Life*, I: 204–7).

6. *Diaries*, p. 43; *Yale Works: Rambler*, V: 320.

7. *Yale Works: Rambler*, III: 76.

8. On Johnson's style, see W.K. Wimsatt, Jr, *The Prose Style of Samuel Johnson* (1941) and *Philosophic Words: A Study of Style and Meaning in the* Rambler *and* Dictionary (1968); and Mark E. Wildermuth, 'Johnson's Prose Style: Blending Energy and Elegance in *The Rambler*', *The Age of Johnson*, VI (1994): 205–35.

9. *Correspondence of Samuel Richardson*, ed. Anna Letitia Barbauld (1804), I: 169, 164–5 – hereafter cited as *Richardson Correspondence*; *Yale Works: Rambler*, V: 317.

10. *Yale Works: Rambler*, V: 316.

11. *Yale Works: Rambler*, III: 132–3.

12. *Yale Works: Rambler*, III: xxviii.

13. *Yale Works: Rambler*, V: 198, 4; IV: 356, 197.

14. See W. Jackson Bate, 'Johnson and Satire Manqué', in *Eighteenth-Century Studies in Honor of Donald F. Hyde* (1970), pp. 145–60.

15. *Piozzi Anecdotes*, pp. 97, 150.

16. *Life*, I: 210.

17. *Life*, I: 213; *Richardson Correspondence*, I: 168; *Murphy's Essay*, p. 393.

18. *Yale Works: Rambler*, IV: 157, 159; *Richardson Correspondence*, V: 281–2; Norma Clarke, *Dr Johnson's Women*, p. 79; *Hebrides*, p. 386; *Thraliana*, I: 173; *Richardson Correspondence*, IV: 317; *Life*, V: 396, n.1; *Richardson Correspondence*, I: 164–6.

19. *A Series of Letters between Mrs Elizabeth Carter and Miss Catherine Talbot, from the year 1741 to 1770*, ed. Revd Montagu Pennington, I: 229–30.

20. Pennington, *A Series of Letters*, I: 235, 244, 295.

21. *Yale Works: Rambler*, III: 315; *Letters*, I: 57.

22. *Yale Works: Rambler*, IV: 5–6. Paul J. Korshin succinctly reviewed a few of the recurring moral themes in 'Johnson, the Essay, and the *Rambler*', *CCSJ*, pp. 51–66.

Chapter 18: Darkness Falls

1. *Yale Works: Rambler*, IV: 346–7.
2. *Letters*, I: 50–51. I am indebted for several details regarding the chronology of Johnson's work on the *Dictionary* to Anne McDermott's lecture, 'How Johnson's *Dictionary* was Made', at the Pembroke College conference on the *Dictionary* in August 2005.
3. *Hawkins's Life*, pp. 121–2, 123.
4. *Life*, IV: 275; Chauncey Tinker, *Dr Johnson and Fanny Burney* (1911), p. 205; *Letters*, I: 71, 56; V: 10–11. See Norma Clarke, *Dr Johnson's Women* (2000), pp. 221–5. On whether or not Johnson wrote the penultimate chapter of Lennox's novel, see Margaret Dalziel's edition (Oxford, 1970), pp. 414–15, and the Appendix to the edition by Duncan Isles, 'Johnson, Richardson, and *The Female Quixote*', pp. 418–27.
5. *Letters*, I: 59.
6. *Letters*, I: 61.
7. *Hawkins's Life*, p. 130; *Diaries*, pp. 52–3; *Letters*, IV: 430, 435. The poem was printed in Anna Williams's *Miscellanies in Prose and Verse* (1766), p. 1. He wrote 'The Ant' on a leaf dated 14 April 1752.
8. *Diaries*, pp. 44–7, 50.
9. *Yale Works: Poems*, p. 263; *Diaries*, p. 47 and *passim*.
10. *Diaries*, pp. 52–3. Johnson once almost asked his wife to promise that she would not marry again if he died before she did (*Life*, II: 77). Boswell did not like that, commenting that her marriage to him was a second marriage and that he overlooked that her first husband had a prior claim.
11. *Hawkins's Life*, pp. 130–31; *Piozzi Anecdotes*, p. 114; *Life*, III: 305; *Diaries*, p. 50; *Shaw's Memoirs*, p. 34.

Chapter 19: Once More unto the Breach: Back to the Dictionary

1. *Piozzi Anecdotes*, pp. 130–31; *Life*, III: 200; *Taxation No Tyranny*, in *Yale Works: Political Writings*, p. 454. James G. Basker delivered an overview of Johnson's strong abolitionist stance on slavery at the Johnson Society of London in July 2006, but it has not yet been published: 'Johnson, Boswell, and the Abolition of Slavery'. Aleyn Reade tells Francis Barber's complete story in *Gleanings*, II: 1–115.

2. *Life*, I: 241; *JM*, II: 316–17.

3. *Letters*, I: 63–4 (9 July 1752); *Yale Works: Adventurer and Idler*, II: 323–36; *Letters*, I: 67. See David Fairer, 'Authorship Problems in *The Adventurer*', *Review of English Studies*, 25 (1974), pp. 144, 148–9.

4. *Life*, I: 252.

5. *Life*, IV: 33, 300; *Letters*, I: 78; *Probationary Odes for the Laureateship* (1785), p. 116; *Letters*, I: 97, 133–4; *Life*, III: 84 n.2.

6. *Life*, I: 242 and n.1; *Diaries*, p. 79.

7. *Life*, I: 254; *Piozzi Anecdotes*, pp. 159, 95, 99; *Letters Between Mrs. Elizabeth Carter and Miss Catherine Talbot*, I: 320; *An Account of the Life of Dr Samuel Johnson, Written by Himself*, ed. Richard Wright (1805), pp. 47–8 – this edition is the first time Hill Boothby's letters to Johnson were printed; *Life* (3rd edn), I: 219n.

8. *Yale Works: Adventurer and Idler*, II: 346–7; *Diaries*, pp. 54, 55.

9. *Yale Works: Adventurer and Idler*, II: pp. 487–92.

10. *Yale Works: Adventurer and Idler*, II: 494–5.

11. *Diaries*, p. 48.

12. *Diaries*, p. 50.

13. *Reddick*, pp. 56–9, 70.

14. *Reddick*, pp. 70–71; *Letters*, I: 73. I am indebted to Anne McDermott's lecture at Pembroke College in 2005 for this probable schedule. See also *Reddick*, pp. 72–4.

15. *Letters*, I: 81–2; *Life*, I: 271; *Letters*, I: 94.

16. *Life*, I: 270 n.5; *Letters*, I: 88; *BP*, Box 35, f. 893 (C3075); *Life*, I: 271–2.

17. *Reddick*, pp. 75–7; *Letters*, I: 253. See Robert DeMaria, Jr, 'Johnson's Extempore History and Grammar of the English Language', *Anniversary Essays on Johnson's Dictionary*, pp. 77–92, based as he says on his and Gwin J. Kolb's edition, *Yale Works: Johnson on the English Language*, vol. XVIII.

18. *Dictionary*, p. 24.

19. *Dictionary*, pp. 21, 35, 40, 41. On the tradition of biographers' lugubrious characterizations of their tasks and lives, see *Yale Works: Johnson on the English Language*, Introduction, pp. xxii–xxv.

20. John Wooll, *Memoirs of Warton* (1806), p. 228; *Letters*, I: 88, 89–90, 98; *Life*, I: 280.

21. *Letters*, I: 90.

22. *Letters*, I: 77–8, 88, 89, 91; *Life*, III: 176.

23. *Lives of the Poets*, III: 335–40; *Life*, I: 383.

24. *Life*, II: 345, 397. Three essays for the *Universal Visiter* that it is known Johnson wrote were: 'Some Further Thoughts On Agriculture', 'An Essay on Epitaphs' (featuring Pope), and 'Reflections on the Present State of Literature' on self-deluded authors.

25. *Letters*, I: 92, 101; *Murphy's Essay*, p. 405.

26. *Life*, I: 260, IV: 128; *Dr Johnson's Dictionary*, p. 101; *Letters*, I: 94–7.

27. Alvin Kernan, *Printing Technology, Letters and Samuel Johnson*, pp. 199–203.

28. *Life*, I: 287, 304; Hitchings, *Dr Johnson's Dictionary*, pp. 192–3; *Letters*, I: 100, 105.

29. *Reddick*, pp. 83–8; *Life*, IV: 4; *The Universal Visiter*, January 1756, p. 4; *Dictionary*, p. 40. For a discussion of the encyclopedic nature of the *Dictionary*, see Jack Lynch, 'Johnson's Encyclopedia', *Anniversary Essays on Johnson's* Dictionary, pp. 129–46.

30. Woodman, *A Preface to Samuel Johnson*, p. 136; Hitchings, *Dr Johnson's Dictionary*, p. 134; *Letters Between Mrs Elizabeth Carter and Miss Catherine Talbot*, I: 390.

31. *Dictionary*, p. 35; Lynch, *Johnson's Encyclopedia*, in *Anniversary Essays on Johnson's Dictionary*, pp. 129–46.

CHAPTER 20: STALLED

1. *Letters*, I: 117; *Diaries*, pp. 56–8.

2. *Murphy's Essay*, pp. 403–4; *The Gentleman's Magazine*, February 1754.

3. *Thraliana*, I: 165; *Letters*, I: 103; Madame d'Arblay, *Memoirs of Dr Burney* (1832), I: 119–20; *Letters*, I: 157. See Roger Lonsdale, *Dr Charles Burney* (1965), pp. 45ff.

4. *Letters*, I: 116; Wiltshire, *Samuel Johnson in the Medical World*, p. 66; *Letters*, I: 120–21. For Johnson's evasiveness regarding orange peels, see *Life*, II: 330–31.

5. *Life*, IV: 143; *Letters*, I: 122.

6. *Piozzi Anecdotes*, p. 114; *Diaries*, pp. 59–60, 61; *Idler* nos. 22 and 38 (*Yale Works: Adventurer and Idler*, II: 69–71, 117–21).

7. *Piozzi Anecdotes*, p. 152; *Life*, II: 195, I: 359.

8. *Diaries*, p. 56.

9. *Yale Works: Rambler*, III: 15.

10. *Yale Works: Rambler*, V: 8.

11. *Literary Magazine*, II: 167, I: 239.

12. *Literary Magazine*, II: 299, 171; *Life*, I: 315.

13. *Yale Works: Political Writings*, pp. 147, 150, 186–8; *Life*, I: 310.

14. *Yale Works: Political Writings*, pp. 268–9.

15. *Waingrow*, pp. 164–9; *Reddick*, pp. 66–7; *Yale Works: Political Writings*, p. 333; *Letters*, I: 145, 188; *Life*, I: 348; *Gleanings*, II: 12. 'Cham' was 'the title of the Sovereign of Tartary . . . well applied to Johnson, the Monarch of Literature' (*Life*, I: 349 n.5). See Lyle Larsen, *Dr Johnson's Household*, chapter 3.

16. *Letters*, I: 79, 124, 126, 127.

17. *Thraliana*, I: 184.

18. *Thraliana*, I: 185; *Life*, I: 243.

19. *Life*, III: 314; *Hawkins's Life*, pp. 245–6; *Life*, III: 443–9 (Appendix A); *Piozzi Anecdotes*, p. 119.

20. *Life*, I: 296 n.2, IV: 187.

21. *Letters*, II: 248 (15 July 1775).

22. *Life*, I: 247.

23. *Life*, I: 249, 250–51.

24. Knight, *Autobiography*, ed. J.W. Kaye (1861), I: 9; *Letters*, I: 244 (August 1764); Reynolds, *Portraits*, p. 66; *JM*, II: 294; F.W. Hilles, *The Literary Career of Sir Joshua Reynolds* (1936; rep. 1967), p. 12 n.2; James Northcote, *The Life of Sir Joshua Reynolds* (2nd edn 1818), I: 79.

25. *JM*, II: 251, 259, 261; Frances D'Arblay, *Memoirs of Dr Burney*, I: 332.

26. *JM*, II: 273, 274, 297. See *Life*, I: 484. On Tourette's Syndrome, see Lawrence C. McHenry, Jr, 'Samuel Johnson's tics and gesticulations', *Journal of the History of Medicine and Allied Sciences*, 22 (1967), pp. 152–68, Wiltshire, *Samuel Johnson in the Medical World*, pp. 24–34, and T.J. Murray, 'Doctor Samuel Johnson's Movement Disorders', *British Medical Journal*, I (1979), pp. 1, 610–14.

27. *Life*, I: 485–6; Reynolds, *Portraits*, p. 70; *Life*, IV: 183 n.2, I: 144. See Wiltshire, *Samuel Johnson in the Medical World*, p. 29.

28. *Life*, I: 392; *The R.B. Adam Library* (1929), vol. II. Several of the alterations in Heath's engraving (which went through several stages) may well have been based on alterations Reynolds himself supervised over the years, as was his general practice, long before he gave Boswell the portrait in 1789. For a full history of this painting see Irma S. Lustig, 'Facts and Deductions: The Curious History of Reynolds's First Portrait of Johnson, 1756', *The Age of Johnson*, pp. 161–80; also Kai Kin Yung, *Samuel Johnson 1709–84* (1984), pp. 79–81.

29. *Yale Works: Idler*, II: 140.

CHAPTER 21: 'SUFFERING CHIMERAS'

1. *Hawkins's Life*, pp. 150–52.

2. *Life*, I: 545; *Letters* I: 142, 147, 153, III: 19 n.3.

3. *Johnson on Shakespeare*, VII: 51–6; *Letters*, I: 135.

4. *Boswell Journals: Defence*, pp. 123–4; *Life*, II: 192; *Letters of David Garrick*, ed. D.M. Little and G.M. Kahrl (1963), II: 460; *Hebrides*, p. 207.

5. *Letters*, I: 158, 159; *London Chronicle* (12–14 April 1757), pp. 358–9.

6. *Life*, II: 103, IV: 134. See Lonsdale, 'Johnson and Dr Burney', *Johnson, Boswell and Their Circle*, pp. 25–26.

7. *The Correspondence of Thomas Percy & William Shenstone*, ed. Cleanth Brooks, in *The Percy Letters* (1977), VII: 6; *Hawkins's Life*, pp. 151–2.

8. The bibliographical morass Johnson got himself into by working and printing

too fast off the starting blocks is outlined by Arthur Sherbo in *Johnson on Shakespeare*, VII: xvi–xxvi.

9. *Rambler*, IV: 200; Preface, *Johnson on Shakespeare*, VII: 59; *Yale Works: Adventurer and Idler*, II: 412–14. See Alvin Kernan, *Printing Technology, Letters, and Samuel Johnson*, pp. 243–5, 249.

10. *Johnson on Shakespeare*, VII: 100, 94.

11. *Letters*, I: 162.

12. *Diaries*, pp. 64–5.

13. *Letters*, I: 177, 174, 176.

14. James Prior, *Life of Edmond Malone* (1860), pp. 160–61.

15. *Letters*, I: 179, 180; *Diaries*, p. 67; *Idler* no. 41, *Yale Works: Adventurer and Idler*, II: 129, 131.

16. *Letters*, I: 182, 184.

17. *Waingrow*, p. 90; James Clifford, *Dictionary Johnson*, p. 201; *Letters*, I: 173. See Larsen, *Dr Johnson's Household*, pp. 38–9.

18. *Shaw's Memoirs*, p. 39.

19. *Yale Works: Rasselas and Other Tales*, XVI: 16, 18, 19.

20. *Yale Works: Rasselas and Other Tales*, XVI: 7; *Life*, I: 341–4.

21. *Yale Works: Rasselas and Other Tales*, XVI: 87, 74.

22. *Yale Works: Rasselas and Other Tales*, XVI: 66, 142.

23. *Yale Works: Rasselas and Other Tales*, XVI: 146–53, 162.

24. *Posthumous Works of Mrs Chapone* (1807), I: 108–10 (28 April 1759), I: 111–13 (15 July 1759), 118 (n.d.).

25. *Diaries*, p. 69; *Life*, I: 348; *Letters*, I: 186, 187.

26. Curley, *Samuel Johnson and the Age of Travel*, pp. 61–2; *Daily Advertiser*, 1, 8, and 15 December 1759; *Letters*, III: 46; *Hawkins's Life*, pp. 157–8; *Life*, I: 352. See Morris Brownell, *Samuel Johnson's Attitude to the Arts*, pp. 107–26 and (on Gwynn) 126–36.

27. Johnson wrote the two introductory essays to the journal that appeared in the first number on 8 April.

28. *Yale Works: Adventurer and Idler*, II: xv–xix; *Hawkins's Life*, p. 152; *Life*, I: 331.

29. *Life*, I: 330–31, 345 n.1; *Yale Works: Adventurer and Idler*, II: xx–xxiii.

30. *Yale Works: Adventurer and Idler*, II: 262–3, 312, 313–14. See Robert Folkenflik, *Samuel Johnson: Biographer* (1978), p. 27.

31. *Piozzi Anecdotes*, p. 76; *Yale Works: Adventurer and Idler*, II: 96, 97, 98.

32. *Yale Works: Adventurer and Idler*, II: 315, 316.

CHAPTER 22: 'VAIN AND CORRUPT IMAGINATIONS'

1. *JM*, I: 409; *Diaries*, p. 264 (Easter Day 1777); *Yale Works: Rasselas and Other Tales*, p. 152; Jackson, *Melancholia and Depression*, pp. 142–6.

2. *JM*, II: 400–1; *Hawkins's Life*, p. 178; John Nichols, *Literary Illustrations* (1817–1831), VI: 147–8; *Hawkins's Life*, p. 161.

3. John Nichols, *Literary Illustrations*, VI: 148.

4. *Life*, IV: 97–8, 197, 97; *Johnson's Prefaces and Dissertations*, ed. Allen T. Hazen, p. 193.

5. *Letters*, I: 198; Hazen, *Johnson's Prefaces and Dedications*, p. 42. See Ian McIntyre, *Joshua Reynolds* (2003), pp. 129–30.

6. *JM*, II: 401–2.

7. The 'Address' is cited by Morris Brownell, *Samuel Johnson's Attitude to the Arts*, p. 50; *Piozzi's Anecdotes*, p. 93; *Life*, II: 439. Robert DeMaria pointed out that in the *Dictionary* Johnson only sketchily covered the fine arts, the nomenclature of which he either omitted or poorly defined (*Johnson's Dictionary and the Language of Learning*, pp. 217–18).

8. *Yale Works: Adventurer and Idler*, II: 140.

9. Brownell, *Samuel Johnson's Attitude to the Arts*, pp. 46–55; Ronald Paulson, *Hogarth: His Life, Art and Times* (2 vols, 1971), II: 313–14; Hazen, *Johnson's Prefaces and Dedications*, pp. 204–5. See J.L. Abbott and D.G.C. Allen (eds.), *The Virtuoso Tribe of Arts and Sciences* (1992).

10. *Letters*, I: 206.

11. *Letters*, I: 207; *Life*, I: 374–5; *Letters*, I: 212.

12. *Life*, I: 429; *Letters*, I: 206.

13. Reynolds's engagement book is in the Royal Academy. See James Clifford, 'Johnson's Trip to Devon in 1762', *Eighteenth-Century Studies in Honor of D.F. Hyde* (1970), pp. 3–28.

14. *JM*, II: 275; *Life*, I: 145, 379.

15. *Life*, I: 377–79; *JM*, II: 278, 396; *Life*, II: 299, V: 329; *Life*, I: 477 n.1.

16. *Letters*, I: 216.

17. 'An Epistle from R.C. to Doctor Samuel Johnson on the Choice of Life, written about the Year 1766', ed. Herman W. Liebert, printed for the Annual Dinner of the Johnsonians, 19 September 1969; *Life*, III: 309–10. See Thomas M. Curley, 'Johnson, Chambers, and the Law', *Johnson After Two Hundred Years*, ed. Paul Korshin (1986), pp. 187–209; and Pat Rogers's convenient summary, *JE*, pp. 225–8.

18. *Life*, II: 405–6.

19. *Life*, III: 161, IV: 280; *Thraliana*, I: 106; *Life*, I: 249. See *Correspondence of James Boswell with Certain Members of the Club*, ed. C.N. Fifer (1976), pp. lii–lxxv.

CHAPTER 23: BOSWELL AND MRS THRALE

1. *Life*, III: 26.

2. *Letters*, I: 214, 225–7, 234, 228–9. See James G. Basker, 'Dancing Dogs, Women

Preachers and the Myth of Johnson's Misogyny', *The Age of Johnson*, III (1990), pp. 63–90.

3. *Life*, I: 445. There are several modern biographies of Boswell: F.A. Pottle, *James Boswell: The Earlier Years 1740–1769* (1966), Frank Brady, *James Boswell: The Later Years 1769–1795* (1984) and Peter Martin, *A Life of James Boswell* (1999).

4. *Life*, I: 383–4; *Boswell's Journals: London Journal*, p. 260; *Life*, I: 392.

5. *Life*, I: 392–5.

6. *Boswell's Journals: London Journal*, pp. 261–8, 279.

7. *Boswell's Journals: London Journal*, pp. 282–5; *Life*, I: 468.

8. Boswell said he had this story from Johnson's 'exact narration', but there is no record of it in his journals or *Life* papers (*Waingrow Life*, I: 287 n.7).

9. *Life*, I: 408, 417; *Boswell's Journals: London Journal*, p. 105; *Lives of the Poets*, II: 49; *Portraits by Sir Joshua Reynolds* (The Yale editions of the Private Papers of James Boswell, 1952), p. 41; *Life*, I: 416.

10. *Life*, I: 417, 421, 422, 425, 427, 433, 435–6, 445, 450.

11. *Life*, I: 457–62.

12. *Life*, I: 462, 465, 471, 472.

13. *Life*, I: 483; *Portraits by Sir Joshua Reynolds*, p. 68.

14. *BP*, 25, f. 606 (C1690); *Life*, I: 477–81. After Johnson's death the Club became better known as The Literary Club.

15. *Life*, IV: 275, II: 16–17.

16. *Life*, I: 479–81; Percy to Boswell, 29 Feb. 1788, *BP*, box 29, f. 733 (C2234) (*Waingrow*, p. 269); *Boswell's Journals: Ominous*, p. 200.

17. Donald Greene thought the 'M' could refer to masturbation, but this has not generally been accepted: see Greene, '"A Secret Far Dearer to Him than His Life": Johnson's "Vile Melancholy" Reconsidered', *The Age of Johnson*, 4 (1991), pp. 8–11; and Barry Baldwin, 'The Mysterious Letter "M" in Johnson's Diaries', *The Age of Johnson*, 6 (1994), pp. 131–45.

18. *Diaries*, pp. 84, 92, 89.

19. Robert Anderson, *The Life of Samuel Johnson, LL.D.* (1815), 3rd edn, p. 300n.; *Letters*, I: 247. See Bertram H. Davis, *Thomas Percy: A Scholar-Cleric in the Age of Johnson* (1989), pp. 120–25.

20. *Thraliana*, I: 158–9; *Life*, II: 127; *Piozzi Anecdotes*, pp. 101–2. For biographies of Mrs Thrale, see James L. Clifford, *Hester Lynch Piozzi (Mrs Thrale)* (rev. edn 1987); and W. McCarthy, *Hester Thrale Piozzi: Portrait of a Literary Woman* (1985).

21. 24 June 1775, JRL, Eng. Mss. 538, letter 12.

22. *Letters*, I: 250; *Piozzi Anecdotes*, pp. 98, 147; *Diaries*, p. 127.

23. *Piozzi Anecdotes*, pp. 131–2. On Johnson's electioneering, see David Fleeman, 'Dr Johnson and Henry Thrale, M.P.', in *Johnson, Boswell, and Their Circle*, p. 175.

24. *Life*, I: 487, 517.
25. *Diaries*, p. 103; *Portraits by Sir Joshua Reynolds*, p. 70. See Brownell, *Samuel Johnson's Attitude to the Arts*, pp. 87–8, and K.K. Yung, *Samuel Johnson*, p. 103. This is the so-called Type II Reynolds portrait. It was first displayed to the public in 1770.

CHAPTER 24: SHAKESPEARE AND THE LIVING WORLD

1. *Letters*, I: 255–6.
2. *Yale Works: Johnson on Shakespeare*, VII: 67; Harold Bloom, *Shakespeare: The Invention of the Human* (1998), pp. 1–2.
3. *Yale Works: Johnson on Shakespeare*, VIII (Appendix): 1049; *Yale Works: Rambler*, IV: 131–3; *Proposals* in *Yale Works: Johnson on Shakespeare*, VII: 57. I am indebted to Robert Folkenflik's paper, 'Samuel Johnson and the Authority of Shakespeare', delivered in June 2007 at the Pembroke College, Oxford, conference on Johnson and the theatre.
4. *Yale Works: Rambler*, IV: 133–4.
5. Ritson, *Remarks, Critical and Illustrative, on the Text and Notes of the Last Edition of Shakespeare* (1783). See Edward Tomarken, *A History of the Commentary on Selected Writings of Samuel Johnson* (1994), pp. 92–103.
6. *Yale Works: Johnson on Shakespeare*, VII: 71–4; Smith, *Eighteenth-Century Essays on Shakespeare* (1903), p. xxxi; Raleigh, 'Johnson on Shakespeare', *Six Essays on Johnson* (1910), pp. xviii, 84; Smith, *Shakespeare in the Eighteenth Century*, p. 68. See Steven Lynn, 'Johnson's Critical Reception', *CCSJ*, p. 245.
7. *Yale Works: Johnson on Shakespeare*, VII: 61–3, 65.
8. *Yale Works: Johnson on Shakespeare*, VII: 78–9, 80–81.
9. *Yale Works: Johnson on Shakespeare*, VII: 92–111, 523.
10. *Yale Works: Johnson on Shakespeare*, VII: 264, 404; VIII: 704, 1045, 795. Philip Smallwood writes of Johnson's sometimes dread of Shakespeare's force, in 'Shakespeare: Johnson's Poet of Nature', *CCSJ*, pp. 143–60.
11. The Cibber comment was recorded by Daniel Astle, a clergyman who met Johnson in a tavern in 1765 and was struck by his argumentative, satiric turn of mind (BP, Box 9, f. 258, C43); *Life*, II: 14; *JM*, II: 318.
12. *Life*, IV: 242–42; *Johnson on Shakespeare*, VII: xxxv–xxxvi. See James Gray, '"I'll come no more behind your scenes, David": A Fresh Look at Dr Johnson as Theatre-goer', *English Studies in Canada*, II (1976), pp. 27–60.
13. *Letters*, I: 261–2.
14. *Life*, II: 5–7; Macaulay, *Essays*, I: 390; *Life*, II: 7–8; *Letters*, I: 273.
15. *Boswell's Journals: GT* (ii), pp. 302–3, 312–13; *Life*, II: 66, 14–15.
16. Clifford, *Piozzi*, pp. 61–3; *Yale Works: Rasselas and Other Tales*, XVI: 215–29,

248; Allen Hazen, *Johnson's Prefaces and Dedications*, pp. 213–16; Pennington (ed.), *Letters between Mrs Elizabeth Carter and Miss Catherine Talbot*, III: 136.

17. *Diaries*, pp. 106–7.

18. *Piozzi Anecdotes*, p. 102.

19. *Piozzi Anecdotes*, p. 106; Clifford, *Piozzi*, pp. 66ff.

20. Edmond Malone, who has been called the midwife to Boswell's *Life*, a great champion of Johnson and determined to see Boswell's biography accepted as the only truly authoritative one, made most of these accusations. Peter S. Baker et al. (eds), *The Correspondence of James Boswell with David Garrick, Edmund Burke and Edmond Malone* (1986), in the *Yale Editions of the Private Papers of James Boswell: Correspondence*, IV: 314–17. See Peter Martin, *Edmond Malone* (1995), pp. 145–7.

21. *Piozzi Anecdotes*, pp. 155, 101, 156.

22. *Piozzi Anecdotes*, pp. 156, 155, 158, 154–5, 156, 158.

23. *Thraliana*, I: 384–5, 386, 415.

24. *Thraliana*, I: 415 and n.4.

25. *Letters*, I: 39 (cited in translation from Wiltshire, *Samuel Johnson in the Medical World*, pp. 44–5). Balderston elaborated on this idea in a psychological and sexual direction in her controversial essay, 'Johnson's Vile Melancholy', in *The Age of Johnson*, ed. F.W. Hilles and W.S. Lewis (1949), pp. 3–14. Her theory was attacked by James Gray, '*Arras! Hellas!*, A Fresh Look at Samuel Johnson's French', in *Johnson After Two Hundred Years*, ed. Paul Korshin (1986).

26. Wiltshire, *Samuel Johnson in the Medical World*, pp. 47–9; *Thraliana*, II: 785; JRL, Eng. Let. 539, letter 30.

27. *Thraliana*, II: 625.

28. *Letters*, I: 276–8. For the text of these Vinerian lectures and the help Johnson gave Chambers with them, see Thomas Curley (ed.), *A Course of Lectures on the English Law* (1986).

29. Curley, 'Johnson, Chambers and the Law', *Johnson After Two Hundred Years* (ed. Korshin), p. 195.

30. *Letters*, I: 274–5; *Life*, II: 34–42; *Letters*, II: 307–14.

31. Alvin Kernan has discussed this interview as such a confrontation in *Printing Technology, Letters and Samuel Johnson*, pp. 24–47.

32. *Life*, II: 42.

Chapter 25: Coliseum of Beasts

1. *Diaries*, p. 115.

2. *Diaries*, pp. 127–8; Wiltshire, *Samuel Johnson in the Medical World*, pp. 40–43; *Letters*, IV: 125, I: 302, 305; *Diaries*, p. 119.

3. *Letters*, I: 282–3, 284, 287, 286, 289; *Diaries*, pp. 116–17; *Letters*, I: 291.

4. Hazen, *Prefaces and Dedications*, p. 152; *Thraliana*, I: 190–91.
5. *Letters*, I: 294, 296; Franklin, *Writings*, V: 122 (16 April 1768); *Boswell's Journals: Wife*, p. 156; *Letters*, I: 296. On the Wilkes affair, see *Yale Works: Political Writings*, pp. 314–15.
6. *Boswell's Journals: Wife*, pp. 155–6; *Letters*, I: 298.
7. *Boswell's Journals: Wife*, pp. 156–8.
8. *Boswell's Journals: Wife*, pp. 164, 166–7.
9. *Life*, II: 60–61.
10. *Letters*, I: 307–14.
11. *Life*, I: 396, III: 172, 173, II: 62–6.
12. Walpole, *Letters*, IX: 313.
13. *Hawkins's Life*, pp. 138–9; *Letters*, I: 315, 350, 353.
14. *Letters*, I: 325, 326.
15. *Diaries*, p. 123; *Life*, II: 106–7.
16. *Letters*, I: 301, 317, 327 and n.3.
17. *Life*, II: 69; *Letters*, I: 329.
18. *Boswell's Journals: Wife*, pp. 333–4, 336; *Life*, II: 71; *Boswell's Journals: Wife*, p. 26.
19. *Boswell's Journals: Wife*, p. 347. In his recasting of this scene for the second edition of the *Life*, Boswell has Mrs Williams only touch the surface of the tea, not sink her finger into it (*Life*, II: 99; *Waingrow Life*, II: 51 n.7).
20. *Boswell's Journal: Defence*, p. 131; *Diaries*, pp. 128–9.
21. *Diaries*, p. 143.

Chapter 26: Back to Shakespeare and the Dictionary

1. *Piozzi Anecdotes*, p. 73; *Fleeman Bibliography*, II: 1172–4. The pamphlet was reprinted in Johnson's *Political Tracts* in 1776, slightly revised.
2. *Life*, I: 394; *Yale Works: Political Writing*, pp. 319, 343. The Wilkes controversy behind *The False Alarm* is discussed by Donald Greene in *Political Writings*, pp. 313–17 and *Greene Politics*, pp. 205–11. The 'Junius' letters were published in the *Public Advertiser* between January 1769 and January 1772.
3. *Life*, I: 394; *Yale Works: Political Writings*, pp. 318, 319, 327.
4. *Life*, II: 112; *Yale Works: Political Writings*, pp. 330, 335, 341, 342, 344.
5. *Life*, III: 281–2; *JM*, II: 320; *Letters*, I: 254.
6. *Letters*, I: 343, 344, 349; JRL, Eng. Let. 539, letter 6; *Life*, II: 77.
7. *Boswell Journals: Defence*. p. 43; *Yale Works: Political Writings*, pp. 361, 363, 379.
8. *Life*, II: 134; *Yale Works: Political Writings*, pp. 370, 376–7; *Life*, II: 134.
9. *Life*, II: 137–9 and n.1.
10. *The Correspondence of James Boswell with David Garrick, Edmund Burke and Edmond Malone*, IV: 42; *Life*, II: 139–40; *Letters*, I: 362–3.

11. *Letters*, I: 364 *passim*.

12. *Piozzi Anecdotes*, p. 78.

13. *Life*, I: 438; *Life*, II: 259; *Letters*, II: 130–31. On copyright, see Alvin Kernan, *Printing Technology, Letters and Samuel Johnson*, pp. 97–102.

14. *Diaries*, p. 154.

15. *Life*, II: 239. See Reddick, *The Making of Johnson's Dictionary*, chapters 6 and 7, especially pp. 122–30.

16. *Life*, II: 254; Robert DeMaria, *Johnson's Dictionary and the Language of Learning* (1986), p. 244. See Reddick, *The Making of Johnson's Dictionary*, chapter 7.

17. *Life*, II: 458, I: 464.

18. *Letters*, II: 30.

19. *Boswell Journals: Defence*, pp. 41, 54.

20. *Boswell Journals: Defence*, pp. 86–7.

21. *Piozzi Anecdotes*, p. 139.

22. *Thraliana*, II: 805; Hyde, *The Thrales of Streatham Park*, pp. 54–5.

23. *Chapman Letters*, I: 283; *Letters*, I: 396, 399, 398.

CHAPTER 27: THE ROAD TO THE HEBRIDES

1. *Letters*, I: 401, 404, 406, 404, 409.

2. *Letters*, II: 10; JRL, Eng. Let. 539, letter 19.

3. *Letters*, II: 26; *Boswell's Journals: Defence*, p. 160; *Life*, II: 233; *Boswell's Journals: Defence*, p. 191; *Piozzi Anecdotes*, p. 70.

4. *Boswell's Journals: Defence*, pp. 180, 183; *Life*, II: 215–16; *Diaries*, p. 156.

5. *Life*, II: 240 and n.1.

6. *Life*, II: 260; *Boswell's Journals: Defence*, pp. 45–6.

7. *Letters*, II: 40; JRL, Eng. Let. 539, letter 30.

8. JRL, Eng. Let. 539, letter 30; *Members*, p. 33.

9. *Letters*, II: 46–51.

10. *Hebrides*, pp. 3–4; *Letters*, II: 115.

11. *Hebrides*, p. 4.

12. *Life*, II: 269 n.1; *Hebrides*, p. 8; *Letters*, II: 51.

13. *Letters*, II: 55–6.

14. *Hebrides*, p. 81; Peter Levi (ed.), *Samuel Johnson and James Boswell* (1984), p. 12; *Letters*, II: 62; *Hebrides*, pp. 71–72.

15. *Yale Works: Journey*, pp. 18–19; *Hebrides*, p. 84.

16. *Yale Works: Journey*, pp. 21–24, 30–31.

17. *Yale Works: Journey*, p. 25; *Hebrides*, p. 100.

18. *Hebrides*, p. 58, 109–10, 112; *Journey*, p. 38.

19. *Letters*, II: 76–7; *Hebrides*, p. 112.

20. *Hebrides*, p. 304; *Letters*, II: 77–9; *Hebrides*, p. 117; *Letters*, II: 88.

21. *Hebrides*, pp. 127–8, 133, 152.

22. *Letters*, II: 90; *Hebrides*, p. 160.

23. *Hebrides*, p. 165; *Letters*, II: 92.

24. *Letters*, II: 93; *Hebrides*, pp. 212–13.

25. *Hebrides*, pp. 244, 247–51; *Yale Works: Journey*, p. 99.

26. *Hebrides*, pp. 271–2, 265; *Letters*, II: 98.

27. *Hebrides*, pp. 302–3.

28. *Yale Works: Journey*, p. 122; *Hebrides*, p. 328; *Letters*, II: 107.

29. *Yale Works: Journey*, p. 132; *Hebrides*, pp. 375–6, 386.

30. *Letters*, II: 120, 128; JRL, Eng. Mss. 538, letter 9; *Letters*, II: 114.

Chapter 28: Politics and Travel

1. *Letters*, II: 133.

2. *Letters*, II: 151.

3. *Letters*, II: 166; *Life*, II: 290 n.2; *Boswell's Journals: Ominous*, p. 98; *Letters*, II: 145. See Mary Lascelles, 'Notions and Facts: Johnson and Boswell on Their Travels', *Johnson, Boswell and Their Circle*, pp. 215–29.

4. *Letters*, II: 168–9, 174, 180; *Life*, II: 298, 306. See Fleeman's edition, pp. xxviii–xxxviii, for an account of the book's reception.

5. *JE*, pp. 214–15.

6. *Letters*, II: 136; *Life*, III: 20. See Thomas M. Curley, 'Samuel Johnson and India', *Re-Viewing Samuel Johnson*, ed. N. Jain (1991).

7. *Letters*, II: 147; *Correspondence of James Boswell with Garrick, Burke and Malone*, IV: 60. See *Life*, III: 81–5.

8. *Letters*, II: 149, 151; A.M. Broadley, *Dr Johnson and Mrs Thrale* (1910), pp. 160–75; *Diaries*, pp. 168, 170, 175.

9. *Life*, V: 441 n.4; *Life*, II: 285; *Diaries*, pp. 186–7.

10. *Diaries*, p. 211; Broadley, p. 206; *Letters*, III: 68; Broadley, p. 209; *Diaries*, pp. 217–18; Broadley, pp. 213–14.

11. *Diaries*, p. 220; *Boswell's Journals: Ominous*, p. 284.

12. Broadley, pp. 217, 219.

13. *Letters*, II: 149, 151 and III: 65–6; *Life*, III: 134. See Curley, *Samuel Johnson and the Age of Travel*, pp. 79–112.

14. *Thraliana*, I: 525 n.2.

15. *Life*, II: 450, IV: 19–20; *Boswelliana*, p. 299; *Life*, II: 138–9; *Murphy's Essay*, p. 421; *Life*, V: 575. On Johnson's friendship with Burke, see Elizabeth R. Lambert, 'Johnson on Friendship: The Example of Burke', *Johnson After Two Hundred Years* (ed. Korshin), pp. 111–23.

16. *Life*, II: 223, 348; 'Johnson on Friendship', p. 120. See *Greene Politics*, pp. 252–3.

17. JRL, Eng. Mss., vol. 539, Letter 33; *Life*, II: 288 n.2; *Letters*, II: 155.

18. *Greene Politics*, pp. 211–12 and *Yale Works: Political Writings*, pp. 387–9, 390–91.

19. *Letters*, II: 151.

20. *Letters*, II: 170, 173; *Yale Works: Political Writings*, pp. 401–2.

21. *Yale Works: Political Writings*, pp. 423, 425, 429, 442, 454.

22. Campbell, 'Anecdotes', *JM*, II: 53, 55, 56; *Life*, III: 290.

23. *Letters*, II: 198; *Life*, II: 335; Campbell, 'Anecdotes', *JM*, II: 51; *Letters*, II: 193–4; *Boswell's Journals: Ominous*, p. 144.

24. *Life*, II: 316.

25. *Boswell's Journals: Ominous*, p. 152.

26. *Boswell's Journals: Ominous*, pp. 87, 100; Campbell, 'Anecdotes', *JM*, II: 41, 48; *Boswell's Journals: Ominous*, pp. 126, 105.

27. *Boswell's Journals: Ominous*, p. 150.

28. *Life*, II: 359; *Diaries*, pp. 224–6; *Boswell's Journals: Ominous*, p. 145; *Life*, II: 375–6, 378; *Boswell's Journals: Ominous*, p. 274.

29. *Letters*, II: 205, 211, 217, 230, 235; JRL, Eng. Mss. 538, letter 13; *Letters*, II: 243.

30. *Letters*, II: 260.

31. *Letters*, II: 271; Moses Tyson and Henry Guppy (eds), *The French Journals of Mrs Thrale and Doctor Johnson* (1932), p. 143.

32. *Letters*, II: 274, 273, 276, 277, 274; *Diaries*, p. 249; *Letters*, II: 273.

33. *Letters*, II: 271; *French Journals*, pp. 163–4, 88–9, 143, 141, 142; *Diaries*, pp. 229, 231, 238, 239 and note; *Boswell's Journals: Extremes*, p. 254; *Life*, II: 402. See Curley, *Samuel Johnson and the Age of Travel*, pp. 108–12.

34. *Diaries*, pp. 233, 253; *Letters*, II: 338; *Life*, II: 435.

35. *Life*, III: 352.

CHAPTER 29: 'A VERY POOR CREEPER UPON THE EARTH'

1. *Life*, III: 19; Baretti cited in E.S. De Beer, 'Johnson's Italian Tour', *Johnson, Boswell and Their Circle*, pp. 159–62; *Boswell's Journals: Ominous*, p. 317; *The Correspondence of James Boswell and William Johnson Temple*, ed. Thomas Crawford (1997), I: 412.

2. *Letters*, II: 299.

3. *Letters*, II: 301; *Diaries*, p. 257.

4. W. Roberts, *Memoirs of Hannah More* (1834), I: 64; *JM*, II: 179; *Life*, IV: 341; *JM*, II: 180; *Life*, III: 293.

5. *JM*, II: 182–5, 187.

6. *Letters*, III: 196, 205; *JM*, II: 404, 286; *Dr Johnson and Fanny Burney*, ed. Tinker, p. 4; *Hawkins's Life*, p. 133. See Roger Lonsdale, *Dr Charles Burney* (1965), p. 252; and Brownell, *Samuel Johnson's Attitude to the Arts*, chapter 1.

7. *Boswell's Journals: Ominous*, pp. 255–6, 258; *Life*, II: 428.

8. *Boswell's Journals: Ominous*, pp. 295, 351.

9. *Letters*, II: 313; JRL, Eng. Mss. 538, letter 15; *Boswell's Journals: Ominous*, p. 329.

10. *Life*, III: 50–51; *Letters*, IV: 14.

11. *Life*, III: 185, 64–79.

12. *Life*, III: 77; *Letters*, II: 332; *Life*, III: 183, 330.

13. *Diaries*, p. 258; *Letters*, II: 339, 341, 347, 358, 360–61, 365.

14. *Letters*, III: 4, 11, 21, 9, 43; *Diaries*, p. 267.

15. Burney's *Early Journals and Letters*, III: 110.

16. *Letters*, III: 20.

17. *Life*, III: 110–11; John Nichols, *Literary Anecdotes*, VIII: 416–17 n.

18. See *JE*, pp. 121–3.

19. *Life*, III: 139–48; *Letters*, III: 25.

20. *Letters*, III: 27–8, 32–33; *Hawkins's Life*, p. 231; *Letters*, III: 33–4.

21. *Life*, III: 167; *Hawkins's Life*, pp. 167, 295. See *Yale Works: Sermons*, pp. xxi–xxix. The sermons for Taylor were first published in two volumes in 1788–9 by Revd Samuel Hayes. They were identified as 'left for publication by John Taylor, LL.D', but immediately many people were convinced that Johnson had written all of them.

22. *Life*, V: 67; *Letters*, III: 311–12; *Diaries*, pp. 276, 277, 279, 292, 300. See Wiltshire, *Samuel Johnson in the Medical World*, pp. 37–40.

23. *Monthly Review*, LXXIX (Dec. 1788), p. 529; *Yale Works: Sermons*, p. xxxi–xxxii.

24. *Burney's Early Journal and Letters*, III: 148, 146–7.

25. *Letters*, III: 140.

Chapter 30: Biographical Straitjacket

1. *Letters*, III: 41, 45, 51, 55; *Diaries*, p. 292; *Letters*, III: 81; *Boswell's Journals: Extremes*, p. 184; *Letters*, III: 61, 67–8, 81; JRL, Eng. Mss. 538, letter 16, Eng. Mss. 540, letter 71.

2. *Boswell's Journals: Extremes*, pp. 155, 162; *Letters*, III: 68, 83.

3. *Life*, III: 200–4.

4. *Life*, III: 206, 208.

5. *Life*, III: 189; *Letters*, III: 83; *Diaries*, pp. 291–2; Lonsdale, *Dr Charles Burney*, p. 242; *Letters*, III: 100. See *Lives of the Poets*, I: 1–103.

6. *Letters*, III: 122, 124; Nichols, *Literary Anecdotes*, II: 550 n; *GM*, 1785, p. 9.

7. *Lives of the Poets*, I: 28–9; *Burney Early Journals and Letters*, III: 105, 150, 153–4.

8. *Life*, III: 271–8; *Letters*, III: 113–14; *Burney's Early Journals and Letters*, III: 32.

9. *Life*, II: 457, III: 287; *Boswell's Journals: Extremes*, pp. 284–5, 290; *Life*, II: 416–23, III: 294.

10. *Fifer*, p. 316.

11. *Letters*, III: 110, 127.

12. *Letters*, III: 108–9.

13. *Piozzi Anecdotes*, p. 142; *Works of Samuel Johnson*, ed. Hawkins (1787), XI: 204; *Letters*, III: 134. See H.W. Liebert, 'Portraits of the Author: Lifetime Likenesses of Samuel Johnson', *English Portraits of the Seventeenth and Eighteenth Centuries* (1974), pp. 45–88; and *Life*, IV: 447–64.

14. *Lives of the Poets*, I: 30–31 (letter cited courtesy of the Hyde Collection, Harvard); *Waingrow*, p. 13; *Letters*, III: 151, 156.

15. *Reports of Historical Manuscripts Commission*, XII, 10: 344–5; *Life*, IV: 40, 206; *Boswell's Journals: Laird*, p. 80; Malone, *Prose Works of John Dryden* (1800), I: 430–37.

16. *Letters*, III: 152; *Lives of the Poets*, II: 179; *Boswell's Journals: Auchinleck*, pp. 83, 92; *Life*, IV: 99.

17. *Diaries*, p. 293–5; *Boswell's Journals: Laird*, p. 58.

18. *Burney's Early Journals and Letters*, III: 255–6, 436; *Dr Johnson and Fanny Burney*, ed. Chauncey Brewster Tinker (1911), pp. 151–2; *Letters*, III: 284.

19. *Letters*, III: 193, 202, 180–81, 197.

20. *Life*, III: 344–5, 392.

21. *Thraliana*, I: 424; *Letters*, III: 228, 233.

22. *Letters*, III: 237, 238, 248, 254, 264, 250, 273, 278, 303, 285.

23. *Lives of the Poets*, I: 47–52 (on Johnson's 'assistants' see pp. 52–80).

24. *Life*, IV: 13; *Boswell's Journals: Laird*, p. 295.

25. *Lives of the Poets*, I: 189.

26. *Lives of the Poets*, I: 189. See Clingham, 'Life and Literature', p. 164.

27. *Burney's Early Journals and Letters*, III: 151–2; *Life*, IV: 73; *Lives of the Poets*, II: 53–4.

28. John Wain, *Johnson on Johnson* (1976), p. xv; *Lives of the Poets*, I: 266–7.

29. *Lives of the Poets*, IV: 16, III: 21, 23.

30. Hyde, *Thrales of Streatham Park*, p. 201; *Letters*, III: 128, 139–40, 176 and n.6; *Thraliana*, I: 401; *Letters*, III: 318.

31. *Letters*, III: 268–9.

32. *Diaries*, p. 304; Hyde, *Thrales of Streatham*, pp. 227–32; *Thraliana*, I: 482, 491.

Chapter 31: Losing Ground

1. *Letters*, III: 330, 332, 334; *Diaries*, p. 304–5.

2. *Boswell's Journals: Laird*, pp. 319–21; *JM*, II: 140; *Boswell's Journals: Laird*, p. 324.

3. *Letters*, III: 342; JRL, Eng. Mss. 583, letter 24.

4. *Letters*, IV: 23; *Diaries*, p. 310; *Letters*, III: 361–79, IV: 4.

5. *Thraliana*, I: 521; Wiltshire, *Samuel Johnson in the Medical World*, pp. 39–40; *Letters*, IV: 9; *Diaries*, p. 312.

6. *JE*, p. 231.
7. *Yale Works: Poems*, pp. 314–15.
8. *Letters*, IV: 14.
9. *Letters*, IV: 29, 124; *Boswell's Journals: Applause*, p. 82.
10. *Thraliana*, I: 535; *Letters*, IV: 55–6.
11. *Thraliana*, I: 525.
12. *Thraliana*, I: 540–41.
13. *Diaries*, p. 338, 339, 346.
14. *Letters*, IV: 101, 133; *Thraliana*, I: 557; *Diaries*, pp. 358–9.
15. *Letters*, IV: 139.
16. *Letters*, IV: 126; *Boswell's Journals: Applause*, pp. 74, 152, 154.
17. *Boswell's Journals: Ominous*, p. 149; *Letters*, IV: 151, 193 and n.1.
18. *Letters*, IV: 151–3, 164; *JM*, II: 311.
19. *Letters*, IV: 154ff, 272. See Wiltshire, *Samuel Johnson in the Medical World*, pp. 51–3.
20. *Letters*, IV: 160.
21. *Letters*, IV: 168, 173–4, 222, 192; *Life*, IV: 523.
22. *Letters*, IV: 195, 199; Wiltshire, *Samuel Johnson in the Medical World*, pp. 53–4.
23. *Horace Walpole's Correspondence*, ed. Lewis et al. (1937–83), XXV: 449; *Letters*, IV: 204, 235, 272–3, 279, 281.
24. *Letters*, IV: 246–7, 259, 316; *Hawkins's Life*, p. 256.
25. *Letters*, IV: 256–7; *Hawkins's Life*, p. 259; *Life*, IV: 254 n.5; *Letters*, IV: 264.
26. *Letters*, IV: 260, 266, 285, 388–9. See Wiltshire, *Samuel Johnson in the Medical World*, pp. 67–8.
27. *Letters*, IV: 275.
28. *Letters*, IV: 300, 286–9; *BP*: C579. See Wiltshire, *Samuel Johnson in the Medical World*, pp. 54–60; and W.W. Fee, 'Samuel Johnson's "Wonderful Remission" of Dropsy,' *Harvard Library Bulletin*, 23 (1975), pp. 271–88.
29. *Letters*, IV: 297; *Diaries*, p. 368.
30. *Letters*, IV: 319, 321, 325.
31. *Letters*, IV: 321–2; *Boswell's Journals: Applause*, p. 213.
32. *Boswell's Journals: Applause*, p. 216.
33. *Boswell's Journals: Applause*, pp. 231, 234–5, 238; *Life*, IV: 299.
34. *Letters*, IV: 334, 335–6; *Life*, IV: 326–7, 337.
35. *Boswell's Journals: Applause*, pp. 254–5.
36. *Letters*, IV: 400.
37. *Letters*, IV: 338 and n.1; JRL, Eng. let. 583, letter 32; *Letters*, IV: 343–4.
38. *Letters*, IV: 344; Hyde, *The Thrales of Streatham Park*, p. 242 n.14, 241; *Diary and Letters of Madame D'Arblay*, ed. Austin Dobson (1904), II: 271.
39. *Letters*, IV: 398 n.5; Wiltshire, *Samuel Johnson in the Medical World*, p. 58. See *Diaries*, pp. 371–418.

40. *Letters*, IV: 353, 354, 368, 370, 422; *Diaries*, p. 403; *Letters*, IV: 436.
41. *Life*, IV: 376.

Chapter 32: The Last Days

1. The accounts of Johnson's final days are compared by Paul J. Korshin, 'Johnson's Last Days: Some Facts and Problems', *Johnson After Two Hundred Years*, pp. 55–76. For Johnson's will, see *Life*, IV: 405, n.2.
2. *Life*, IV: 416–18, 415. I an indebted to Graham Nicholl's '"The Race with Death": Samuel Johnson and Holy Dying', *The New Rambler* (2005–6), pp. 11–21.
3. *Life*, IV: 400; *JM*, II: 156.
4. *Life*, IV: 409.
5. *Life*, IV: 400; *Hawkins's Life*, pp. 272–73; *Life*, IV: 409; *JM*, II: 386; *Hawkins's Life*, p. 275; Wiltshire, *Samuel Johnson in the Medical World*, pp. 61–63.
6. *Hawkins's Life*, p. 275.
7. *JM*, II: 159.
8. *Life*, IV: 420–23.
9. *Life*, IV: 420–23; Johnstone, *Parr*, I: 533; *JM*, II: 378; *Boswell's Journals: Applause*, p. 271; *JM*, II: 378.

Bibliography

Primary Sources
Johnson's Works

The Yale Edition of the Works of Samuel Johnson, presently 15 vols, not consecutive (New Haven: Yale University Press, 1958 onwards):

    Diaries, Prayers, and Annals, ed. E.L. McAdam, Jr, with Donald and Mary Hyde, vol. I (1958)

    The Idler and The Adventurer (ed. W.J. Bate, John M. Bullitt and L.F. Powell), in *Works*, vol. II (1963)

    The Rambler, ed. W.J. Bate and Albrecht B. Strauss, vols III–V (1969)

    Poems, ed. E.L. McAdam, Jr, with George Milne, vol. VI (1964)

    Johnson on Shakespeare, ed. Arthur Sherbo (with an introduction by Bertrand A. Bronson), vols VII and VIII (1968)

    A Journey to the Western Islands of Scotland, ed. Mary Lascelles, vol. IX (1971)

    Political Writings, ed. Donald Greene, vol. X (1977)

    Sermons, ed. Jean Hagstrum and James Gray, vol. XIV (1978)

    Voyage to Abyssinia, ed. Joel J. Gold, vol. XV (1985)

    Rasselas and Other Tales, ed. Gwin J. Kolb, vol. XVI (1990)

    Johnson on the English Language, ed. Gwin J. Kolb and Robert DeMaria, Jr, vol. XVIII (1990)

    A Commentary on Mr Pope's Principles of Morality, or Essay on Man (a Translation from the French), ed. O.M. Brack, vol. XVII (2005)

The Works of Samuel Johnson, LL.D. (with life), ed. John Hawkins, (15 vols, 1787–89)

The Dictionary of the English Language (1st edn 1755)

The Dictionary of the English Language (4th edn 1773)

Lynch, Jack (ed.), *Samuel Johnson's Dictionary* (2002)

Crystal, David (ed.), *Dr Johnson's Dictionary* (2005)

Hazen, A.T. (ed.), *Samuel Johnson's Prefaces and Dedications* (1937)

Fleeman, J.D. (ed.), *The Complete English Poems* (1971)

Fleeman, J.D., (ed.), *Journey to the Western Islands of Scotland* (1985)

Chapman, R.W. (ed.), *The Letters of Samuel Johnson* (3 vols, 1952)

Redford, Bruce (ed.), *The Letters of Samuel Johnson* (5 vols, 1992–94)

BIOGRAPHIES, EDITIONS AND CRITICAL WORKS

This is a selective list of editions and writings that have most influenced this biography.

Abbott, J.L., *John Hawkesworth* (1982)

Adam, E.L., and L.F. Powell, *Dr Johnson and the English Law* (6 vols. 1934–50; vols. V and VI, 2d ed., 1964)

Adam, R. B., *Facsimile of Boswell's Notebook* (1919)

Baker, Peter et al. (eds), *The Correspondence of James Boswell with David Garrick, Edmund Burke, and Edmond Malone* (1986)

Balderston, K.C. (ed.), *Thraliana: The Diary of Mrs Hester Lynch Thrale* (2 vols, 1942)

Balderston, Katherine, 'Johnson's Vile Melancholy', in *The Age of Johnson*, ed. F.W. Hilles and W.S. Lewis (1949), pp. 3–14

Barbauld, Anna Laetitia (ed.) *Correspondence of Samuel Richardson* (6 vols, 1804)

Bate, Walter Jackson, *Samuel Johnson* (1977)

—— *The Achievement of, Samuel Johnson* (1955)

Bloch, Marc, *The Royal Touch: Sacred Monarchy and Scrofula in England and France* (1973)

Bloom, E.A. and L.D. Bloom (eds), *Piozzi Letters* (2 vols, 1989)

Bloom, E.A., *Samuel Johnson in Grub Street* (1957)

Bloom, Edward A. and Lillian D. Bloom (eds), *The Journals and Letters of Fanny Burney* (Madame D'Arblay) (12 vols, 1978)

Bloom, Harold, *Shakespeare: The Invention of the Human* (1998)

Bond, William H., *Eighteenth-Century Studies in Honor of Donald F. Hyde* (1970)

Boswell, James, *Journals: The Yale Editions of the Private Papers of James Boswell* (listed chronologically):

    Boswell's London Journal 1762–1765, ed. Frederick A. Pottle (1951)

    Boswell in Search of a Wife 1766–1769, ed. Frank Brady and Frederick A. Pottle (1956)

    Boswell for the Defence 1769–1774, ed. William K. Wimsatt, Jr. and Frederick A. Pottle (1960)

    Boswell's Journal of a Tour to the Hebrides with Samuel Johnson, LL.D., 1773, ed. Frederick A. Pottle and Charles H. Bennett (1961)

  Boswell: The Ominous Years 1774–1776, ed. Charles Ryskamp and Frederick A. Pottle (1963)

  Boswell in Extremes 1776–1778, ed. Charles McC. Weis and Frederick A. Pottle (1970)

  Boswell: Laird of Auchinleck 1778–1782, ed. Joseph W. Reed and Frederick A. Pottle (1977; rpt Edinburgh, 1993)

  Boswell: The Applause of the Jury 1782–1785, ed. Irma S. Lustig and Frederick A. Pottle (1981)

  —— *Notebook*, ed. R.B. Adam (1919)

Boswell Papers, Beinecke Rare Book and Manuscript Library, Yale University

Boswell's Life of Johnson, Together with Boswell's Journal of a Tour to the Hebrides and Johnson's Diary of a Journey into North Wales, ed. G.B. Hill, revd and enlarged by L.F. Powell (6 vols, 1934; rpt 1979)

Boulton, James T., *Johnson: The Critical Heritage* (1971)

Brack, O.M. and R.E. Kelley, *The Early Biographies of Samuel Johnson* (1974)

—— (eds), *The Shorter Prose Writings of Samuel Johnson* (1987)

Brady, Frank, *James Boswell: The Later Years 1769–1795* (1984)

Broadley, A.M., *Doctor Johnson and Mrs Thrale* (1910)

Bronson, Bertrand H., *Johnson Agonistes and Other Essays* (1965)

Brooke, John, 'The Library of King George III', *Yale University Library Gazette* 52 (1977)

Brooks, Cleanth (ed.), *Correspondence of Thomas Percy and William Shenstone* (1977)

Brownell, Morris, *Samuel Johnson's Attitude to the Arts* (1989)

Burney, Fanny, *The Early Diary of Fanny Burney*, ed. A.R. Ellis. (1889)

Burney, Frances, *The Early Journals and Letters of Fanny Burney* (vol III: part I, 1778–1770', ed. Lars E. Troide and Stewart J. Cooke (1994)

—— *The Early Journals and Letters of Fanny Burney* (vol. IV: part II, 1780–81), ed. Betty Rizzo (2003)

Chambers, Robert, *A Course of Lectures on the English Law*, ed. Thomas M. Curley (1986)

Chapin, C.F., *The Religious Thought of Samuel Johnson* (1968)

Chapman, R.W. (ed.), *The Letters of Samuel Johnson* (3 vols, 1952)

Clark, J.C.D., *Samuel Johnson: Literature, Religion and English Cultural Politics from the Restoration to Romanticism* (1994)

Clifford, James L., (ed.), *Dr [Thomas] Campbell's Diary* (1947)

—— 'Johnson's Trip to Devon in 1762', in *Eighteenth-Century Studies in Honor of Donald F. Hyde* (1970)

—— *Dictionary Johnson* (1979)

—— *Hester Lynch Piozzi* (1941, 1952)

—— *Young Sam Johnson* (1955)

Clingham, Greg (ed.), *The Cambridge Companion to Samuel Johnson* (1997)

Cochrane, J.A., *Dr Johnson's Printer: The Life of William Strahan* (1964)

Copeland, T.W. et al. (eds.), *The Correspondence of Edmund Burke* (1958–70)

Crystal, David, (ed.), *Dr Johnson's Dictionary* (2005)

Curley, Thomas M., *Samuel Johnson and the Age of Travel* (1976)

—— *Sir Robert Chambers: Law, Literature and Empire in the Age of Johnson*

—— (ed.), *A Course of Lectures on the English Law* (1986)

D'Arblay, Madame Frances, *Diary and Letters of Madame d'Arblay* (edited by her niece, 1842)

Davies, Thomas, *Memoirs of the Life of David Garrick* (1808)

—— *Miscellaneous and Fugitive Pieces* (1773)

Davis, Bertram H., 'Johnson's Visit to Percy', in *Johnson After Two Hundred Years*, ed. P.J. Korshin (1986)

—— *The Life of Samuel Johnson, LL.D. by Sir John Hawkins* (1961)

—— *Thomas Percy: A Scholar-Cleric in the Age of Johnson* (1989)

DeMaria, Robert, Jr, *The Life of Samuel Johnson* (1993)

—— *Samuel Johnson and the Life of Reading* (1997)

—— *Johnson's Dictionary and the Language of Learning* (1986)

Dobson, Austin, *The Diary and Letters of Madame D'Arblay* (1904)

Eaves, T.C.D., 'Dr Johnson's Letters to Richardson', *PMLA*, 75 (1960)

Eaves, T.C.D. and B.D. Kimpel, *Samuel Richardson* (1971)

Fairer, David, 'Oxford and the Literary World' in *The History of the University of Oxford*, vol. 5 (*The Eighteenth Century*), ed. L.S. Sutherland and L.G. Mitchell (1986)

—— 'Authorship Problems in *The Adventurer*', *Review of English Studies*, 25 (1974)

Fifer, C.N. (ed.), *The Correspondence of James Boswell with Certain Members of The Club* (1976)

Fleeman, J.D., *A Bibliography of the Works of Samuel Johnson* (2000)

—— *A Preliminary Handlist of Documents and Manuscripts of Samuel Johnson* (1967)

—— 'Some Notes on Johnson's Prayers and Meditations', *Review of English Studies*, n.s. 29 (May 1968), 172–9 [Corrections of Yale ed., vol. I]

—— (ed.), *Samuel Johnson: A Journey to the Western Islands of Scotland* (1985)

—— (ed.), *Early Biographical Writings of Samuel Johnson* (1973)

—— (ed.), *Samuel Johnson: The Complete English Poems* (1971)

Folkenflik, Robert, *Samuel Johnson: Biographer* (1978)

—— 'The Politics of Johnson's *Dictionary* Revisited', *Age of Johnson*, vol. 18 (2007), pp. 1–17

—— 'Johnson's Politics', in *The Cambridge Campanion to Samuel Johnson* (1977), pp. 102–13

Forbes, Margaret, *James Beattie and His Friends* (1904)

The Gentleman's Magazine (1731–1907)

Gray, James, 'Arras! Hellas!', A Fresh Look at Samuel Johnson's French', in *Johnson After Two Hundred Years*, ed. Paul Korshin (1986), pp. 85–6

Greene, Donald, *Samuel Johnson's Library* (1975)

—— 'Dr Johnson's "Late Conversion": A Reconsideration', *Johnsonian Studies*, ed. Magdi Wahba (1962)

—— *The Politics of Samuel Johnson* (1960, 2nd edn 1990)

Grundy, Isobel, *Samuel Johnson and the Scale of Greatness* (1986)

Guppy, H. and M. Tyson (eds), *The French Journals of Mrs Thrale and Doctor Johnson* (1932)

Hagstrum, Jean, *Samuel Johnson's Literary Criticism* (rev. edn 1967)

Hanley, Brian, *Samuel Johnson as Book Reviewer* (2001)

Harwood, Thomas, *History and Antiquities of Lichfield* (1806)

Hawkins, Sir John, *The Life of Samuel Johnson, LL.D.* (2nd edn 1787)

Hazen, Allen T., *Samuel Johnson's Prefaces and Dedications* (1937)

Hemlow, Joyce, *The History of Fanny Burney* (1958)

Hill, G. Birkbeck (ed.), *Johnsonian Miscellanies* (2 vols, 1897)

—— and L.F. Powell (eds), *Boswell's Life of Johnson* (5 vols, 1934; reprinted 1979)

Hilles, Frederick W. (ed.), *New Light on Dr Johnson* (1959)

Hitchings, Henry, *Dr Johnson's Dictionary: The Extraordinary Story of the Book That Defined the World* (2005)

Holmes, Richard, *Dr Johnson and Mr Savage* (1993)

Hopkins, M.A., *Dr Johnson's Lichfield* (1952)

Hyde, Mary, *The Impossible Friendship: Boswell and Mrs Thrale* (1972)

—— *The Thrales of Streatham Park* (1977)

—— 'The Library Portraits at Streatham Park', *The New Rambler*, (1979), pp. 10–24

Isles, Duncan, 'The Lennox Collection', *Harvard Library Bulletin* 19 (1971)

Jackson, John, *History of the City and Cathedral of Lichfield* (1805)

Jackson, Stanley W., *Melancholia and Depression: From Hippocratic Times to Modern Times* (1986)

Johnson, Boswell and Their Circle: 1965. Essays Presented to L. F. Powell (1965) by Mary M. Lascelles, James L. Clifford, J. D. Fleeman and John P. Hardy

Jonard, Norbert, *Giuseppe Baretti* (1963)

Kaminski, Thomas, *The Early Career of Samuel Johnson* (1987)

Kernan, Alvin, *Samuel Johnson and the Impact of Print* (1989)

Knight, Ellis Cordelia, *The Autobiography of Miss Knight*, ed. Roger Fulford (1960)

Kolb, G.J., 'Johnson's "Little Pompadour": A Textual Crux and a Hypothesis', in *Restoration and Eighteenth-Century Literature*, ed. Carroll Camden (1963)

Korshin, Paul J., 'Johnson and the Earl of Orrery', *Eighteenth-Century Studies in Honor of Donald F. Hyde* (1970)

—— (ed.), *Johnson After Two Hundred Years* (1986)

Larsen, Lyle, *Dr Johnson's Household* (1985)

Leslie, C.R. and Tom Taylor, *Life and Times of Sir Joshua Reynolds* (1865)

Lewis, W.S., *The Yale Edition of Horace Walpole's Correspondence*, ed. W.S. Lewis et al. (1937–83)

Liebert, H.W., 'Portraits of the Author: Lifetime Likenesses of Samuel Johnson', in *English Portraits of the Seventeenth and Eighteenth Centuries* (1974)

Lillywhite, Bryant, *London Coffee Houses* (1963)

Lipking, Lawrence, *Samuel Johnson: The Life of an Author* (1998)

Little, D.M. and G.M. Kahrl (eds), *The Letters of David Garrick* (3 vols, 1963)

Lonsdale, Roger (ed.), *Samuel Johnson: The Lives of the Poets* (4 vols, 2006)

—— *Dr Charles Burney* (1965)

Lustig, Irma S., 'The Myth of Johnson's Misogyny in the *Life of Johnson*: Another View', in *Boswell in Scotland and Beyond*, ed. Thomas Crawford (1997), pp. 71–88

—— '"My Dear Enemy": Margaret Montgomerie Boswell in the *Life of Johnson*', in *Boswell: Citizen of the World, Man of Letters*, ed. Irma S. Lustig (1995)

Lynch, Jack and Anne McDermott (eds), *Anniversary Essays on Johnson's Dictionary* (2005)

Lynch, Jack (ed.), *Samuel Johnson's Dictionary* (2002)

Lynn, Steven, 'Locke's Eye, Adam's Tongue and Johnson's Word: Language, Marriage and the Choice of Life', *Age of Johnson*, 3 (1990), 35–61

Martin, Peter, *A Life of James Boswell* (London, 1999; Yale, 2000)

—— *Edmond Malone, Shakespeare Scholar: A Literary Biography* (1995)

Mathias, Peter, *The Brewing Industry in England, 1700–1830* (1959)

Maxted, Ian, *The London Book Trades, 1775–1800* (1977)

McGuffie, H.L., *Samuel Johnson in the British Press, 1749–1784* (1971)

McHenry, Lawrence, 'Samuel Johnson's Tics and Gesticulations', *Journal of the History of Medicine and Allied Sciences*, 22 (1967), pp. 152–68

McIntyre, Ian, *Garrick* (1999)

Menninger, Roy W., "Johnson's Psychic Turmoil and the Women in His Life," *The Age of Johnson*, 5 (1992), pp. 179–200

Midgley, Graham, *University Life in Eighteenth-Century Oxford* (1996)

Morgan, Lee, *Dr Johnson's 'Own Dear Master': The Life of Henry Thrale* (1998)

Murphy, Arthur, *An Essay on the Life and Genius of Samuel Johnson* (1792) in *Johnsonian Miscellanies*, vol. I

Namier, Sir Lewis and John Brooke, *The House of Commons, 1754–1790* (3 vols, 1964)

Nicholls, Graham, '"The Race with Death": Samuel Johnson and Holy Dying', *The New Rambler* (2005–6), pp. 11–21

Nichols, John, *Literary Anecdotes of the Eighteenth Century* (9 vols, 1812–1815)

Northcote, James, *Life of Sir Joshua Reynolds* (1818)

Pennington, Revd Montagu (ed.), *A Series of Letters between Mrs Elizabeth Carter and Miss Catherine Talbot 1741–1770* (2 vols, 1809)

Percy, Thomas, 'Diary', BL Add. MS. 32, 332–6, 337 (begins 17 June 1753)

Piozzi, Hester Lynch, *Anecdotes of the Late Samuel Johnson, During the Last Twenty Years of his Life* (1786)

—— *Letters To and From the Late Samuel Johnson, LL.D.* (2 vols, 1788)

Porter, Roy, *Enlightenment: Britain and the Creation of the Modern World* (2000)

—— *London: A Social History* (1994)

—— *Mind-Forg'd Manacles: A History of Madness in England from the Restoration to the Regency* (1987)

Pottle, Frederick A., *James Boswell: The Earlier Years, 1740–1769* (1966)

—— *The Literary Career of James Boswell, Esq.* (1929)

Reade, A.L., *Johnsonian Gleanings* (11 vols, 1909–52; reprinted 1968)

Reddick, Allen, *The Making of Johnson's Dictionary, 1746–1773* (1990, 1996)

Redford, Bruce (ed.), *The Letters of Samuel Johnson.* (5 vols, 1992)

—— *James Boswell's Life of Johnson*, The Yale Editions of the Private Papers of James Boswell: Research Edition, vol. 2: 1766–1776 (1998)

Roberts, William (ed.), *Memoirs of the Life and Correspondence of Mrs Hannah More* (2 vols, 1834)

Rogers, Pat, *The Samuel Johnson Encyclopedia* (1996)

Rudé, George, *Wilkes and Liberty* (1962)

Sachs, Arieh, *Passionate Intelligence: Imagination and Reason in the Work of Samuel Johnson* (1967)

Schwartz, R.B, *Samuel Johnson and the New Science* (1971)

Seward, Anna, *The Swan of Lichfield: Correspondence of Anna Seward*, ed. Hesketh Pearson (1936)

Shaw, William, *Memoirs of the Life and Writings of the Late Dr Samuel Johnson* (1785)

Sherbo, Arthur (ed.), *Hester Lynch Piozzi: Anecdotes of the late Samuel Johnson, LL.D. during the Last Twenty Years of His Life* (1974)

—— (ed.), William Shaw, *Memoirs of the Life and Writings of the Late Dr Samuel Johnson* (1785, 1974)

—— *Samuel Johnson, Editor of Shakespeare* (1956)

Sledd, J.H. and G.J. Kolb, *Dr Johnson's Dictionary* (1955)

Small, M.R., *Charlotte Ramsay Lennox* (1935)

Smallwood, P.J., *Johnson's Preface to Shakespeare* (1985)

Thrale, Hester Lynch, *Thraliana: the Diary of Mrs Hester Lynch Thrale, 1776–1809*, ed. Katharine C. Balderston (2 vols, 2nd edn 1951)

Tomarken, Edward, *A History of the Commentary on Selected Writings of Samuel Johnson* (1994)

Tracy, Clarence, *The Artificial Bastard: A Biography of Richard Savage* (1953)

Twining, the Revd Thomas, *Recreations and Studies of a Country Clergyman of the Eighteenth Century* (1882)

Tyson, Moses and Henry Guppy (eds), *The French Journals of Mrs Thrale and Doctor Johnson* (1932)

Vance, John A., *Samuel Johnson and the Sense of History* (1984)

Wain, John, *Johnson on Johnson* (1976)

—— *Samuel Johnson: A Biography* (1974)

Waingrow, Marshall (ed.), *The Correspondence and Other Papers of James Boswell Relating to the Making of the 'Life of Johnson'* (1969), The Yale Edition of the Private Papers of James Boswell: Research Edition, Boswell's Correspondence, vol. 2

—— (ed.), *James Boswell's Life of Johnson*, The Yale Editions of the Private Papers of James Boswell: Research Edition, vol. 1: 1709–1765 (1994)

—— (ed.), *James Boswell's Life of Johnson*, The Yale Editions of the Private Papers of James Boswell: Research Edition, vol. 2: 1766–1776 (1998)

Weinbrot, Howard D., 'Johnson, Jacobitism and the Historiography of Nostalgia,' in *The Age of Johnson*, vol. 7 (1996), pp. 163 ff.

—— 'Johnson and Jacobitism Redux: Evidence, Interpretation and Intellectual History,' in *The Age of Johnson*, vol. 8 (1997), pp. 89–125

—— 'Meeting the Monarch: Johnson, Boswell and the Anatomy of a Genre,' in *The Age of Johnson*, vol. 18 (2007), pp. 131–50

Wendorf, Richard and Charles Ryskamp, 'A Bluestocking Friendship: The Letters of Elizabeth Montagu and Frances Reynolds in the Princeton Collection,' *Princeton University Chronicle*, 41 (1979–1980), pp. 173–207

Wendorf, Richard, *Sir Joshua Reynolds: The Painter in Society* (1996)

—— *The Elements of Life: Biography and Portrait-Painting in Stuart and Georgian England* (1990)

Wheatley, Henry B., *London Past and Present: Its History, Associations, and Tradition* (3 vols, 1891)

Wiltshire, John, *Samuel Johnson in the Medical World* (1991)

Wimsatt, William K., *The Prose Style of Samuel Johnson* (1941)

Windham, William, *The Diary of the Right Hon. William Windham 1784–1810*, ed. Mrs Henry Baring (1866)

Wooll, John, *Biographical Memoir of the Late Rev. Joseph Warton* (1806)

Woolman, Thomas, *A Preface to Samuel Johnson* (1993)

Wright, J.D., 'Unpublished Letters of Dr Johnson,' *Bulletin of the John Rylands Library* 16 (1932)

Yung, K.K., *Samuel Johnson, 1709–1784: A Bicentenary Exhibition* (1984)

Acknowledgements

I am grateful to the staffs of the following libraries for allowing and helping me to use their books and manuscripts, and permitting me to quote from their collections: the Beinecke Rare Book and Manuscript Library at Yale University; the Bodleian Library, Oxford University; the Cambridge University library; the Hyde Collection in Houghton Library, Harvard University; the British Library; Princeton University Library; the John Rylands Library, University of Manchester; the Lewis Walpole Library in Farmington, Connecticut; and the Pierpont Morgan Library in New York. For permission to quote from published material I am especially indebted to the Yale Edition of the Works of Samuel Johnson, the Yale Editions of the Private Papers of James Boswell (and their director Gordon Turnbull), Edinburgh University Press and Oxford University Press. For permission to publish illustrations I would like to thank the National Portrait Gallery; the British Museum; the Hyde Collection, Houghton Library, Harvard University; the Huntington Library in San Marino, California; Dr Johnson's House, Gough Square, London; the Johnson Birthplace Museum, Lichfield, Staffordshire; Lord Rees-Mogg; Tate Britain; the Beaverbrook Art Gallery, New Brunswick; the Scottish National Portrait Gallery; Museum of the Order of St John, St John's Gate, London; Dover City Museum; the Menil Collection, Houston, Texas; the Bridgeman Art Library; Pembroke College, Oxford University.

Note on quotations: For the sake of clarity, I have modernised spelling and capitalisation except in poetry and when the spelling reveals some idiosyncrasy of Johnson's.

Index